THE SELECTED LETTERS OF CHARLES SUMNER

THE SELECTED LETTERS OF Charles Sumner

EDITED BY

Beverly Wilson Palmer

Volume One

Northeastern University Press
Boston

Northeastern University Press

Some of the annotated letters have appeared in *Ohio History* (Summer–Autumn 1984; Winter–Spring 1990) and are used with permission.

Publication of this volume was assisted by a grant from the National Historic Publications and Records Commission.

Library of Congress Cataloging-in-Publication Data
Sumner, Charles, 1811–1874.
The selected letters of Charles Sumner / edited by Beverly Wilson Palmer.
p. cm.
Includes bibliographical references.
ISBN 1-55553-078-8 (alk. paper)
1. Sumner, Charles, 1811–1874—Correspondence. 2. Legislators—United States—Correspondence. 3. Abolitionists—United States—Correspondence. 4. Slavery—United States—Anti-slavery movements. 5. United States—Politics and government—1849–1877. I. Palmer, Beverly Wilson, 1936– . II. Title.
E415.9.S9A4 1990
973.7'092—dc20 90-6925
CIP

Designed by Virginia Evans

Composed in Garamond #3 by Graphic Composition, Inc., Athens, Georgia. Printed and bound by Edwards Brothers, Inc., Ann Arbor, Michigan. The paper is Glatfelter Offset, and acid-free sheet.

MANUFACTURED IN THE UNITED STATES OF AMERICA
96 95 94 93 92 91 90 5 4 3 2 1

CONTENTS

ILLUSTRATIONS

ACKNOWLEDGMENTS

The Selected Letters of Charles Sumner grows out of a previous project, the microfilm edition of Charles Sumner's correspondence. Thanks to those assisting with the background work for the present edition are listed in the *Guide and Index to the Papers of Charles Sumner*.

For providing financial and physical resources that have enabled me to complete these volumes, I wish to thank the National Historical Publications and Records Commission, especially Mary Giunta, acting director of publications, and the History Department at Pomona College. An additional travel grant from the National Endowment for the Humanities provided funds for checking some transcriptions against originals. I spent a profitable semester at the Perkins Library at Duke University, and I thank the university and the library staff for their help. I am grateful to the libraries, historical societies, and individuals for granting me permission, insofar as they are empowered to do so, to include letters from their collections. These repositories are listed, with their abbreviations, on pages xxii–xxv.

All editors of course benefit from the scholarly work that has preceded theirs. I have found invaluable David Donald's *Charles Sumner and the Coming of the Civil War* and *Charles Sumner and the Rights of Man*, Eric Foner's *Reconstruction*, and Andrew Hilen's *The Letters of Henry Wadsworth Longfellow*.

The editorial board, Eric Foner, John Y. Simon, Mary Lee Spence, and Hans Trefousse, carefully reviewed letters and offered important suggestions. Robert Hudspeth of the University of Redlands ably advised me in the early planning stages.

My colleagues John Niven and James McClure at the Salmon P. Chase Papers and Dorothy Twohig at the Papers of George Washington shared their expertise with me.

My editorial assistant, Gail Clark Stiffler, has contributed her sharp editor's eye, her competence, and her loyalty to all phases of this project. I am deeply appreciative.

My family—my husband, Hans C. Palmer, my mother, Harriet

Skinner Wilson, and my children, Margaret Palmer and David Palmer—have provided critical (in both senses of the word) assistance and support.

Timothy Connelly at NHPRC read through numerous nineteenth-century newspapers at the Library of Congress and helped me locate sometimes arcane references there and clear up many problems with Sumner's allusions. John Walsh, at Occidental College, checked references and read much of the Civil War and Reconstruction material.

At Pomona College I have been helped by my colleagues, who encouraged me, helped with selection of letters, read introductory essays, assisted with Latin and French translations, and advised me on the special subjects such as French history and international law generated by Sumner's many interests. These colleagues are Monica Augustin, Jamie Brandt, Elizabeth Brunazzi, Virginia Crosby, Leo Flynn, Richard Harrison, Vincent Learnihan, Thomas Pinney, Burdette Poland, Helen Young, and Helena Wall. The staff at Pomona's Seaver Computer Center has facilitated the production of the manuscript and index.

My editors at Northeastern University Press, Deborah Kops and Ann Twombly, have generously and thoughtfully assisted in the production of the volumes.

Finally, I wish to acknowledge the Pomona College students who worked resourcefully and energetically on this four-year project: Ruth Barber, Becky Bliege, Sean O'Brien, Suzanne Olivas, Jim Reed, and Julius Tsai. Above all I appreciate the expert assistance of Cheryl Anderson, Pomona College class of 1990. I also thank the many other friends and colleagues who offered encouragement and advice along the way.

Although these advisors and assistants have been crucial to the completion of this edition, whatever faults remain are entirely my own.

EDITING PRINCIPLES

CHARLES SUMNER would no doubt be surprised by the scholarly attention his letters receive in these volumes. "I write *currente celamo*," he wrote Hugh McCulloch at the beginning of Reconstruction. "I have no clerk, have no copy of any thing I write; for I write simply in the hope of inducing you to help produce a right-about-face in the present policy" (16 September 1865). In contrast, Sumner labored over both writing and revising his speeches and congressional reports (see letters to the duchess of Argyll, 31 July 1860, and to Samuel Gridley Howe, 18 September 1873). The collected edition of his speeches was, he said, "his life."

Sumner's letters have great significance today as the record of a leading antislavery legislator and intellectual, yet for him they were careless productions, written hastily, emended equally hastily. Although they often echoed points made in his speeches, Sumner gave little or no thought to his letters' composition.

This edition reflects Sumner's method as closely as possible, by transcribing letters with abbreviations, ampersands, and misspellings. When Sumner wrote "than," for example, and meant "that," his mistake has been preserved. In following principles of reasonably faithful transcription we adhere to Sumner's own: writing George Washington Greene about his biography of his grandfather, Sumner advised that Nathanael Greene's letters be presented as "literally exact, preserving even the errors" (14 May 1849, 68/581, PCS).

Editorial practices include:

Transcription

1. All misspellings and inconsistencies (for example, "correspondance" versus "correspondence," "shew" versus "show," "any thing" versus anything) are preserved. The thorn (or "ye") has been retained to reflect Sumner's use of it in the 1830s and 1840s. Punctuation has been supplied only to clarify meaning. A repeated word (for example, "that that") has been omitted. Sumner's end-of-line word divisions have not been reproduced, and new divisions have by necessity been formed.

2. Words that Sumner crossed out are omitted unless the cancellation shows some important element in his train of thought. Cancelled passages are indicated by angle brackets: for example, ⟨truth⟩.

3. Sumner's underlinings are reproduced as italics; his frequent double underlinings are reproduced in italics and underlined.

4. Words representing tentative readings are indicated with square brackets and a question mark, as [ripen?]. Italicized words in brackets designate editorial comments or identification, as [*inserted from margin*] or [*George N.*] Briggs.

5. Words written by Sumner above the line are silently incorporated into the line, as are abbreviations in which Sumner has written characters above the line, such as Pres^{dt}.

6. Sumner's paragraphing and spacing within the text of the letter are normally reproduced. Paragraphing has been added in Sumner's long letters from Europe in those places where he inserted long dashes between topics, no doubt to save space and postage.

Salutations, date placement, and the complimentary close have been regularized. All postscripts, whether designated "P.S." or not, have been placed at the end of the letter. The postscripts that Sumner often scattered around the margins or at the top of his letters are separated by line breaks to indicate separate postscripts.

When Sumner clearly marked in his letter that he meant to insert material, the text is inserted as he noted.

7. The few letters from printed sources are reproduced as they appear in the original text. Although Edward L. Pierce's transcriptions appearing in the *Memoir and Letters of Charles Sumner* were generally faithful to the content of Sumner's letters, he corrected spelling, regularized puncutation, and occasionally omitted personal or indiscreet references. Fortunately, holograph letters of the copies in the Pierce volumes exist (with the exception of Sumner's letters to John L. Motley and one to John Bright). Sumner's letters to Theodore Parker were apparently destroyed after Parker's wife, Lydia, copied them. All the Parker letters are transcribed exactly from the copies; obvious transcription errors are noted.

Annotation

1. Although it is often hard to determine who is well known, generally U.S. presidents, contemporary rulers, and authors such as Montesquieu and Shakespeare are not identified. Sources such as the *Dictionary of American Biography*, used for information that is readily available, are not cited.

2. Only rarely is a notation added for references that we have been unable to identify.

3. If enclosures have survived along with the letter, they are noted.

4. Since Sumner revised his speeches, often in great detail (see to Henry D. Gilpin, 5 June 1849), quotations are taken from the original pamphlet edition when available, or from the *Congressional Globe*. References to other speeches and writings are to the twenty-volume Statesman Edition of Sumner's works.

5. In order to keep the notes succinct and to give priority to the previously unprinted letters Sumner received (to be found in the comprehensive microfilm edition), we have avoided printing long passages from Sumner's speeches, already available in print.

CHRONOLOGY

1811	6 January. Born to Charles Pinckney and Relief Jacob Sumner in Boston.
1821–1826	Attends Boston Latin School.
1830	25 August. B.A., Harvard.
1831	September. Enters Harvard Law School.
1834	January. Completes studies at Harvard Law School (LL.B. awarded June 1834). Begins practice at office of Benjamin Rand, Boston. September. Admitted to bar and enters partnership with George Hillard at 4 Court Street, Boston. Writes for *American Jurist* and *North American Review.*
1835–1837	Lectures at Harvard Law School; edits *Sumner's Reports.*
1837–1840	European tour.
1839	24 April. Charles Pinckney Sumner dies.
1840	3 May. Returns to United States, resumes Boston law practice.
1845	4 July. Oration, "The True Grandeur of Nations," in Boston.
1846	5 November. Speech, "Slavery and the Mexican War," Tremont Temple, Boston.
1848	9–10 August. Attends Buffalo Free Soil Convention. 7 September. Named chairman of Free Soil State Central Committee. October. Runs unsuccessfully as Free Soil candidate for Congress.
1850	August. Runs unsuccessfully as Free Soil candidate for Congress. 6 November. Speech, "Our Immediate Antislavery Duties," Free Soil Meeting, Faneuil Hall, Boston.
1851	24 April. Massachusetts state legislature elects Sumner to U.S. Senate seat. 25 November. Moves to Washington.
1852	c. 27 June. Reunites with George Sumner after fifteen-year separation.

	26 August. Speech, "Freedom National," in U.S. Senate, denouncing Fugitive Slave Act.
1853	Fall. Campaigns unsuccessfully for Free Soil party platform and for Henry Wilson for Massachusetts governor.
1854	19 January. "Appeal of the Independent Democrats," protesting Kansas-Nebraska Bill, is issued, co-authored by Sumner. 21 February. Speech, "The Landmark of Freedom," in U.S. Senate. 7 September. Speech, "Duties of Massachusetts at the Present Crisis," at first convention of the Massachusetts Republican party, Worcester.
1855	30 May–6 September. Travels through Midwest and New England.
1856	19 and 20 May. Speech, "Crime Against Kansas," in U.S. Senate. 22 May. Assaulted in U.S. Senate by Preston Brooks.
1857	January. Reelected U.S. senator by Massachusetts legislature. 7 March–7 November. Travels in Europe. 7 December. Returns to Washington for 35th congressional session.
1858–1859	22 May. Sails from New York for France. 25 November 1858–6 March 1859. Recuperates in Montpellier, France. Spring and summer 1859. Travels in Italy, France, and England. 21 November. Returns to Boston.
1860	4 June. Speech, "Barbarism of Slavery," in U.S. Senate. 11 July. Speech, "The Republican Party: Its Origin, Necessity, and Permanence," Cooper Institute, New York. 6 November. Lincoln elected president. 20 December–1 February. Seven states of lower South secede from U.S.
1861	8 March. Becomes chairman of Senate Foreign Relations Committee. 12 April. Confederates fire on Fort Sumter. 17 April–20 May. Virginia, Arkansas, Tennessee, and North Carolina secede from U.S. 27 November. Speech, "The Rebellion: Its Origin and Mainspring," Cooper Institute, New York, and other northern cities.
1862	19 May. Speech, "Rights of Sovereignty and Rights of War: Two Sources of Power Against the Rebellion," in U.S. Senate. 22 September. Lincoln issues preliminary Emancipation Proclamation.
1863	1 January. Lincoln issues Emancipation Proclamation, freeing all slaves in states then in rebellion against U.S. January. Reelected U.S. senator by Massachusetts state legislature. 10 September. Speech, "Our Foreign Relations," Cooper Institute, New York.

1864 14 January. Named chairman of Select Committee on Slavery and Freedmen.

8 April. Speech, "No Property in Man: Universal Emancipation Without Compensation," in U.S. Senate, supporting Thirteenth Amendment.

19 April. Speech, "Final Repeal of All Fugitive Slave Acts," in U.S. Senate.

8 June. Speech, "Creation of the Freedmen's Bureau: A Bridge From Slavery to Freedom," in U.S. Senate.

8 November. Lincoln reelected president.

31 January. Congress approves Thirteenth Amendment, abolishing slavery.

1865 24–27 February. Speech, "No Reconstruction Without the Votes of the Blacks," in U.S. Senate.

5–9 April. Travels with Mary Todd Lincoln and others to meet Lincoln and tour City Point, Richmond, and Petersburg.

9 April. Lee surrenders at Appomattox.

15 April. At deathbed of Lincoln.

18 December. Thirteenth Amendment is ratified.

1866 5–6 February. Speech, "The Equal Rights of All," in U.S. Senate, protesting apportionment amendment.

19 February. President Andrew Johnson vetoes continuation of Freedmen's Bureau; on 22 February, denounces Republican Reconstruction policy.

7–9 March. Speeches, "Political Equality Without Distinction of Color. No Compromise of Human Rights," and "Opposite Sides on the Meaning of the Proposed Constitutional Amendment," in U.S. Senate, protesting apportionment amendment.

6 April. Congress overrides Johnson's veto of Civil Rights Bill.

13 June. Congress approves Fourteenth Amendment, granting citizenship to blacks and establishing new basis for congressional representation.

15 June. Relief Jacob Sumner dies.

17 October. Marries Alice Mason Hooper.

c. 27 November. Sumners set up housekeeping at 322 I Street, N.W., Washington.

1867 15, 17, and 18 January. Speeches, "Protection Against the President," in U.S. Senate, relating to the Tenure-of-Office Bill.

2 March. Congress passes Reconstruction Act of 1867.

9 April. Speech, "The Cession of Russian America to the United States," in U.S. Senate.

Mid-June. Alice Sumner leaves for Lenox, Massachusetts; thereafter Sumners are separated.

October. News of marriage breakup becomes public.

October. Family home, 20 Hancock Street, Boston, is sold.

c. 1 October–19 November. Speech, "Are We A Nation?," delivered in midwestern and eastern cities.

December. Moves to permanent home in Washington at H Street and Vermont Avenue, N.W.

1868

4 March–26 May. Impeachment trial of Andrew Johnson.

20–21 May. Republicans nominate U. S. Grant at Chicago convention.

28 July. Fourteenth Amendment is ratified.

c.19 August. Moves into Coolidge House as permanent Boston residence.

3 November. Grant is elected president.

1869

January. Reelected U.S. senator by Massachusetts legislature.

26 February. Fifteenth Amendment, granting all male citizens suffrage, passes Congress.

13 April. Speech, "Claims on England—Individual and National," in U.S. Senate Executive Session, advocating rejection of Johnson-Clarendon Convention.

22 September. Speech, "National Affairs at Home and Abroad," State Republican Convention, Worcester.

1870

15 March. Senate Foreign Relations Committee recommends rejection of treaty to annex Santo Domingo.

30 March. Fifteenth Amendment is ratified.

May. Volume I of *Charles Sumner, His Complete Works* is published; volumes II–IX, 1870–1874.

30 June. Senate rejects Santo Domingo treaty.

17 October–2 December. Addresses, "Lafayette" and "The Duel Between France and Germany," delivered on lecture tour in eastern and midwestern cities.

21 December. Speech, "Naboth's Vineyard," in U.S. Senate, opposing annexation of Santo Domingo to the United States.

1871

10 March. Senate approves Republican caucus's proposal removing Sumner from the Foreign Relations Committee.

27 March. Speech, "Violations of International Law, and Usurpations of War Powers," in U.S. Senate, denouncing Santo Domingo annexation.

24 May. U.S. Senate ratifies Treaty of Washington, establishing a commission to arbitrate *Alabama* claims.

1872

15, 17, 31 January, 5 February. Speeches, "Equality Before the Law Protected by National Statute," in U.S. Senate, supporting Supplemental Civil Rights Bill.

3 May. Liberal Republicans nominate Horace Greeley for U.S. president at Cincinnati convention.

25 May. Senate ratifies supplementary article to Treaty of Washington, withdrawing all indirect claims in the *Alabama* negotiations.

5 June. Republicans nominate Grant for president at Philadelphia convention.

29 July. Open letter to Colored Citizens of Washington, endorsing Greeley for president.

3 September–26 November. Travels in Europe.

	5 November. Grant reelected president.
	18 December. Massachusetts legislature censures Sumner for Battle Flags Resolution.
1873	10 May. Divorce from Alice Sumner is granted.
1874	27 January. Remarks, "The Supplementary Civil-Rights Bill: The Last Appeal," in U.S. Senate.
	11, 13 February. Massachusetts legislature rescinds censure of Sumner.
	11 March. Dies at 2:47 p.m.
1875	27 February. Congress passes modified Civil Rights Act.

ABBREVIATIONS

ALS	autograph letter signed
ANS	autograph note signed
C	contemporary copy
CS	Charles Sumner
Dft	draft
Enc	enclosure
LS	letter signed
PL	printed letter
TEL	telegram
TTR	typed transcription

Short Title List

British Documents	*British Documents on Foreign Affairs, Reports and Papers from the Foreign Office. Confidential Print. North America*, Part I, Series C, ed. Kenneth F. Bourne, 1986
CWL	*Collected Works of Abraham Lincoln*, ed. Roy P. Basler, 1953
DD,1	David Donald, *Charles Sumner and the Coming of the Civil War*, 1960
DD,2	David Donald, *Charles Sumner and the Rights of Man*, 1970
DW	*Papers of Daniel Webster: Correspondence*, ed. Charles Wiltse, Harold Moser, Michael J. Birkner, Wendy B. Tilghman, 1977–86
Executive Proceedings	*Journal of the Executive Proceedings of the U.S. Senate*
Foreign Relations	*Papers Relating to Foreign Affairs* (later called *Foreign Relations of the United States*)
Globe	*Congressional Globe*
HWL	*Letters of Henry Wadsworth Longfellow*, ed. Andrew Hilen, 1966–82
PCS	*Papers of Charles Sumner*, ed. Beverly Wilson Palmer, 1988 (microfilm reel and frame number follow each citation)
Prc	Edward L. Pierce, *Memoir and Letters of Charles Sumner*, 1877–93
"Recall of Minister Motley"	"Recall of Minister Motley," Senate Ex. Doc. no. 11, serial set 1440

Wilson	Henry Wilson, *Rise and Fall of the Slave Power in America*, 1874
Wks	*Charles Sumner: His Complete Works*, Statesman Edition, 1900

List of Cooperating Repositories

The following individuals and repositories, to the extent that they possess rights to the manuscript letters in their possession, have kindly granted permission for letters from Charles Sumner to be included in this edition. No part of any work published in this edition may be reproduced without written permission from those listed below.

CSfHS	Manuscript Collection, California Historical Society Library, San Francisco
CSmH	Huntington Library, by permission of the Huntington Library, San Marino, California, letters in Hiram Barney Collection (NB, Box 27); Huntington Manuscript Collection, HM23325, 22000, 22002, 21983, 21985, 21987, 10530, 25940–2, 25944, 25960–5, 25968–70, 25972, 25974–5, 25986, 51907–8, 51911–2, 51915, 51917, 51929, 51931, 51934–6, 51942, 51949, 51951, 51956–8, 51961–2, 51966–7, 25991, 51970, 21702, 4085, 20445, 2627, 23103; Lieber Collection (LI, Box 63)
CtHSD	Stowe-Day Foundation, Hartford, Connecticut
CtY	Manuscripts and Archives Department, Yale University, Charles Sumner letters from the Samuel Bowles and Woolsey Family Collections
CtYB	The Yale Collection of American Literature, Beinecke Rare Book and Manuscript Library, Yale University
DLC	Manuscript Division, Library of Congress
DNA	National Archives
FPsb	Bibliothèque Victor-Cousin, at the Sorbonne, Paris
GBCTC	Trinity College, Cambridge, Great Britain, by permission of the Master and Fellows of Trinity College, Cambridge
GBL	The British Library, John Bright Papers, Add 43390, ff. 123–286; Gladstone Papers, Add 44400, f. 204, Add 44402, f. 5; Iddesleigh Papers, Add 50038, f. 193; Ripon Papers, Add 43623, ff. 184, 204, by permission of the British Library
GBNU	Department of Manuscripts and Special Collections, Nottingham University Library
GBOAS	All Souls College, Oxford University, courtesy of The Warden and Fellows of All Souls College, Oxford

GBS	Director of Libraries and Information Services, Sheffield City Library and the Estate of the Earl of Wharncliffe, Sheffield, Great Britain
GBStR	Edward Charles Hatherton, eighth baron, for letters held in the Staffordshire Record Office, Stafford, Great Britain
GBUBi	University Library, The University of Birmingham, Birmingham, Great Britain
GBUCL	The Library, University College, London
GBWSR	Governors of Dunford House, Midhurst, Sussex, for letters from the Richard Cobden Collection; Trustees of Arundel Castle for letters from the Richard Pemell Lyons Collection; with acknowledgments to the West Sussex Record Office and the County Archivist
I	Illinois State Historical Library, Springfield, Charles Sumner Papers
ICbS	Morris Library, Southern Illinois University at Carbondale, Special Collections
ICHi	Chicago Historical Society
ICUJR	Department of Special Collections, University of Chicago Library, Miscellaneous Manuscript Collections
InND	Archives of the University of Notre Dame, Orestes Brownson Collection, previously published in the microfilm edition of the Orestes Brownson Papers
IU	Martin F. Tupper Collection, Rare Book Room, University of Illinois at Urbana-Champaign
KUS	University of Kansas Libraries, Lawrence, Branscomb Collection, Kansas Collection
LAMA	Archives of the American Missionary Association, Amistad Research Center, Tulane Univesity
MB	Boston Public Library, by courtesy of the Trustees of the Boston Public Library
MBApm	The Adams Papers, Massachusetts Historical Society, Boston
MBNEH	New England Historic Genealogical Society, Boston
MBU	Special Collections, Boston University Libraries
MCR	Schlesinger Library, Radcliffe College, J. G. Dodge Papers
MH-AH	Andover-Harvard Theological Library
MH-H	Houghton Library, Harvard University
MH-L	Harvard Law School Library, Simon Greenleaf Papers
MHa	Haverhill Public Library, courtesy of the trustees of Haverhill Public Library, Special Collections Dept.
MHi	Massachusetts Historical Society
MLNHS	Frances Appleton Longfellow Papers, Charles Sumner Papers, Longfellow National Historic Site, Cambridge, by permission of the National Park Service

MSaE	Whittier Collection, Bowditch Family Papers, Andrew Dunlap Papers, Essex Institute, Salem, Massachusetts
MWA	Charles Sumner Papers, American Antiquarian Society, Worcester, Massachusetts
MWelC	The English Poetry Collection, Wellesley College Library
MdHi	Reverdy Johnson Collection, MS. 1480, Manuscripts Division, Maryland Historical Society Library
MeHi	Maine Historical Society, Portland
MeU	Raymond H. Fogler Library, University of Maine at Orono, Hamlin Family Papers, Special Collections Department
MeWC	Special Collections, Colby College, Waterville, Maine
MiMp	Clarke Historical Library, Central Michigan University, Mt. Pleasant, Michigan
MiUc	William L. Clements Library, University of Michigan
MnHi	Minnesota Historical Society, St. Paul, Allyn Kellogg Ford Collection of Historical Manuscripts
N	Manuscripts and Special Collections, New York State Library, Albany
NBHi	Brooklyn Historical Society
NBu	Buffalo and Erie County Public Library
NIC	Department of Rare Books, Cornell University Library
NICO	Department of Manuscripts and University Archives, John B. Olin Library, Cornell University Libraries
NN	Bryant-Godwin Papers, James Hamilton Papers, Henry J. Raymond Papers, Rare Books and Manuscripts Division, The New York Public Library, Astor, Lenox and Tilden Foundations
NNBe	Henry W. and Albert A. Berg Collection, The New York Public Library, Astor, Lenox and Tilden Foundations
NNCB	Moncure D. Conway Papers, Charles S. Daveis Papers, Sydney Gay Papers, John Jay Papers, Charlemagne Tower Papers, Rare Book and Manuscript Library, Butler Library, Columbia University
NNHi	New-York Historical Society, courtesy of the New-York Historical Society, New York City
NRU	William Henry Seward Papers, Rush Rhees Library, the University of Rochester, Department of Rare Books and Special Collections
NSchU	Schaffer Library, Union College, Schenectady, New York
NSyU	George Arents Research Library for Special Collections at Syracuse University, Syracuse, New York
NcD	Manuscript Department, William R. Perkins Library, Duke University
NjMo	Lloyd W. Smith Collection, Morristown National Historical Park, Morristown, New Jersey

NjRD	Mabel Smith Douglass Library, Rutgers University, Theodore Stanton Collection
OCLWhi	Western Reserve Historical Society, Cleveland, courtesy of the Western Reserve Historical Society
OFH	William Claflin Papers, Mary Clemmer Ames Papers, Charles Sumner Papers, Rutherford B. Hayes Presidential Center, Fremont, Ohio
OHi	Ohio Historical Society, Columbus
OKtu	University Libraries, Kent State University
OO	J.D. Cox Papers, Oberlin College Archives
PCarlD	Dickinson College Library
PHi	The Historical Society of Pennsylvania, Philadelphia Museum and Library, Philadelphia
PU	Charles Patterson Van Pelt Library, University of Pennsylvania
RHi	Rhode Island Historical Society, Manuscript Collections, Channing Autograph Collection, Item 66
RPB	Brown University Library
SCUC	South Caroliniana Library, University of South Carolina, Columbia
TxU	Harry Ransom Humanities Research Center, The University of Texas at Austin
ViWWL	William W. Layton Collection, Millwood, Virginia
VtGEW	Gary E. Wait, Manuscript Collections, Brick Manse Library, West Newbury, Vermont
VtU	Special Collections, Bailey/Howe Library, University of Vermont, Burlington
WHi	State Historical Society of Wisconsin, Madison
WvCDH	West Virginia Department of Culture and History, Charleston, from the Boyd B. Stutler Collection, State Archives

LIST OF RECIPIENTS

I

EDUCATION AND EUROPEAN TRIP

September 1830 – November 1839

THE LETTERS OF Charles Sumner from his nineteenth to his twenty-ninth years yield few clues about the reformer and politician to come. To be sure, these letters show a young man with a good education, excellent powers of expression, and a wide-ranging curiosity. Yet Sumner differed little from countless Americans writing similarly perceptive and intelligent letters on either side of the Atlantic. Even by the time Sumner returned from Europe, he had little idea about what contribution, if any, he might make to society.

Some recurrent themes do appear. Sumner believed in the inherent worth of his fellow human beings, their "attainable excellence" (to Jonathan F. Stearns, 12 January 1833). Few were those, he wrote Samuel Gridley Howe around 1835, who "had not something of good" in them, and this goodness could be cultivated. Public opinion, as he later wrote Francis Lieber (26 October 1837), could be brought to bear on governments and bring about change. Although at times Sumner's beliefs bordered on naïveté, one can see here the signs of the later reformer.

The self-righteous, didactic Sumner also appears early in his correspondence. The eldest of nine children, he preached to his siblings, as his condescending and haughty letter of 6 September 1839 to George Sumner vividly illustrates. Sumner quickly developed a strong sense of both his moral rightness and his abilities: see his letter to Benjamin Stone on payment for his editing work and his presumptuous letter to Daniel Webster about the British diplomats Webster ought to meet in Britain.

Patriotic, vitally concerned about the United States' place in the world, Sumner recognized the narrowness of his own New England. He corresponded with the German scholar Karl Mittermaier about legal reforms, relished George Ticknor's description of the visit with Metternich, and saw a trip to Europe as the fulfillment of his dreams. Yet once in Europe, he emphatically praised his country and its achievements. Doubtless Sumner intended through his chauvinistic remarks to sponsors and elders like Joseph Story, Charles Daveis, and Simon Greenleaf to reassure them that he had not been carried away by the blandishments of Europe. Nevertheless, he was genuinely horrified at the depravity of Paris ("a perfect Sodom," he wrote George Hillard, 8 March 1838) and truly believed in America's "general intelligence and morality" (to Henry W. Longfellow, 24 January 1839). Sumner defended the United States' claims at the Maine border in his country's dispute with Great Britain. He promoted William Hickling Prescott's histories and Thomas Crawford's sculpture, and tried to get Joseph Story admitted to the Académie des Sciences Morales et Politiques. In November 1839 he wrote Longfellow that he was ready to return to the United States (of course, he was forced to, since his funds were depleted and he had no opportunities in Europe).

Despite Sumner's success as an American representative abroad, there was little evidence by 1840 that he would become anything more than a well-educated dilettante lawyer. His interest in politics fluctuated. Early on he complained to Harvard classmate Charlemagne Tower that political distraction interrupted his law studies (29 August 1831). Although caught up in the excitement of Washington during his first trip to the capital, Sumner declared, in typically extreme language, "Politics are my loathing," and vowed never to return (to Story, 20 March 1834). Still he was restless. While teaching temporarily at Harvard Law School, he wrote about a life "more stirring than the quiet scenes of the Academy" (to Greenleaf, 9 January 1837). Sumner was repeatedly attracted to national politics, as letters to Richard Peters and Story in 1836 and 1837 attest. Sumner criticized Supreme Court Chief Justice Taney's unprofessionalism and, sitting "on the Nation's sofa," deplored President Van Buren's ignorance (to Story, 3 December, 1837). Such irreverence, however, indicated only a passing interest in politics and none in the antislavery cause.

From Washington, in the middle of a rather pedestrian account of his reaction to the capital, Sumner described to his parents the first slaves he ever saw: "They appear to be nothing more than moving masses of flesh, unendowed with any thing of intelligence above ye brutes. I have now an idea of ye blight upon that part of our country in which they live" (24 February 1834, 62/036, PCS; Prc. 2:134). Nothing in this passage suggests that Sumner regarded slavery as much more than an embarrassment to a nation espousing freedom and equality. Nothing in any of these letters suggests that in fewer than twenty years

Sumner's national reputation would rest on his denunciations of that "blight." Instead, the early letters show that Sumner was well prepared for a number of careers, but among the least likely was that of an antislavery leader.

To Jonathan F. Stearns[1]

Boston Sept 28th 1830—

My Friend,

All hail to you—the flag-staff of Unitarianism—the Liberty-pole of Free Sentiment—How do you bear your colours? do they float proudly in the breeze & do all the admiring natives *strike to them?* Verily, with such a pole—(as tall as the mast of some great admiral) from which to wave, I should think they would attract most general attention.—I presume you are already firmly seated on your throne, crowned, anointed, & duly constituted the vice-gerent of ____ the Trustees; with your birchen rod, for a sceptre & your book for the ball of sovereignty—lord of all you survey—"both the *foul* & the *brute*" in your empire of 20 feet by 30— = 500 square feet. This sage mathematical calculation reminds me that I am now up to head & ears in Geometry—I am at present reading Milton ____ & Walker's Geometry & have more than half completed both. The fact is, all those things, which were the stumbling blocks to my Freshman Year–career, seem now as easy & intelligible as A.B.C.—They all vanish before my piercing gaze now, as do the morning dews before the sun—the bright leaves of summer before the Autumn frost—the drifting clouds of Heaven before the sweeping winds—a fine array of delicacies before hungry, commons-fed Colleges—or as any thing else vanishes before any thing else, you may choose to imagine. I began a week ago Monday & I have completed the first Section, on Lines, & shall in a day or two complete the second on Surfaces.—I have doomed myself for this year at least to hard labor—I intend to diet on study—go to bed late & get up early & leave none of my time unemployed. I have imposed upon myself the task of reading as follows—a course of Mathematics, not indeed so thorough as the Cambridge, but one which will give me all I want to know—(to be classically enthusiastic)—Juvenal & Tacitus (without ponies)—a course of Modern History, Hallam's Middle Ages & Constitutional History, Roscoe's Leo & Lorenzo, Robertson's Charles V &c,[2] with indefinite quantities of Shakespeare, British Poets &c—besides

writing an infinitude of long epistles. Is not there labor enough—however, I do not flinch —I shall not cry "Hold, enough"—until I have had a good great tug—I shall make labor my pleasure—, as some great lawyer has said—*labor ipse voluptas.*[3] And is not the gratification from labor the truest & most stedfast pleasure—unless that derived from indulgence, it is as lasting as the object which affords it.

What a gala-day was the 17th[4]—there was first the firemen & engines who made a long procession. And a glorious sight it was to see these Cup-bearers & Armor-bearers to Neptune "scour the plain"—with their chariots all bright & burnished, ready to send forth their water-javelins & water-darts—upon no fleshly enemy, but upon that subtlest servant of Vulcan —— Then came the grand procession of the day, the long-drawn pomp; & the innumerable hosts of spectators—boys & girls & "children of a larger growth,"

> Thick as Autumnal leaves that strew the brooks
> In Vallambrosa.

& but in addition to all this "goodly fellowship"—there was the "noble army" of militia, with plumes all-flaunting & coats "with colours dipt in Heaven, sky-tinctured grain."[5]—"hundreds & thousands trooping on"—to hear Josiah spout. There I was, in one of the aisles, plugged in between a lot of groundlings, who took a great pleasure in *kicking up a dust*—so that I often found myself circumvented by a complete halo. All this I endured & was richly paid. I was agreeably disappointed. I think the first part of Q's oration was rather ill-digested & I hope he will give it a revisal before he sends it to the press. It was then I thought all my forebodings would be realized. It was during this part, when they were clapping hugely, I heard a little child near me ask, with a most sincere simplicity—"what are they making that noise for"?—thought I—I can put the same interrogatory. Qy, however redeemed himself & I think held the attention of his large audience better the last hour than the first. D. Webster[6] said it was the best discourse he ever heard from *a pulpit* in his life. —— In the order Quincy gave me for my prize money,[7] there were no less than three downright grammatical errors.—

Your good chum has thrown up his Lowell school & joined Hubbard at Brookline for $800 & board[8]—that's no small affair—Browne is bloody hot at the law—Stuart,[9] poor fellow, is a wanderer upon the face of the earth. He has, as yet, no situation. Write me freely about your town, your folks, your school; but above all about that old Silenus—Tom Mason—how do you & he agree & what kind of creature is he?

bushels of good wishes to your from your Friend
Charles Sumner.—

Knapp[10] was hung to day—it is reported that he would have no priest to attend him on to the gallows—but running up the steps said—"well—cut away"—thus dying as he had lived—

ALS MH-H (62/007, PCS)

1. Jonathan French Stearns (d. 1889), Harvard A.B., 1830, later a clergyman, was then teaching in an academy in Northfield (Prc, 1:73). CS, living at home, was embarking on a year of individual study.

2. Henry Hallam (1777–1859), *The Constitutional History of England from the Accession of Henry VII to the Death of George II* (1827), and *A View of the State of Europe during the Middle Ages* (1818); William Roscoe (1753–1831), *The Life and Pontificate of Leo X* (1805) and *The Life of Lorenzo de' Medici* (1795); William Robertson (1721–93), *The History of the Reign of the Emperor Charles the Fifth* (1769).

3. "Labor itself is pleasure."

4. At Boston's bicentennial, Josiah Quincy (1772–1864; president of Harvard College, 1829–45) gave "An Address to the Citizens of Boston, on the XVIIth of September, MDCCCXXX, the Close of the Second Century from the First Settlement of the City."

5. Milton, *Paradise Lost*, 1.302 and 5.283, 285.

6. Daniel Webster (1782–1852), U.S. senator (Whig, Mass.), 1827–41, 1844–50, U.S. secretary of state, 1841–43, 1850–52.

7. CS received $30, a second-place prize in competition for Harvard College's Bowdoin Prize. His topic was "The Present Character of the Inhabitants of New England, as Resulting from the Civil, Literary, and Religious Institutions of the First Settlers" (Prc, 1:56).

8. Possibly Samuel McBurney (d. 1849), Harvard A.B., 1830, and a member (as was Stearns) of "The Nine," a private society formed in CS's senior year at Harvard (Prc, 1:55). Lucius Virgil Hubbard (d. 1849), Harvard A.B., 1824.

9. John W. Browne (d. 1860), Harvard A.B., 1830; member of "The Nine." Charles Stuart (d. 1880), Harvard A.B., 1830.

10. John Francis Knapp, accessory to the murder of Joseph White of Salem (DW, 3:82–83).

To Charlemagne Tower[1]

Boston 29th Aug 1831—Monday eve

My Dear Friend,

I am indebted to you for a letter from Albany & one from Waterville. The last tells me of your prospect for these months to come. I imagine your disappointment. I can fully sympathise in your feelings, arising from the severance from your studies. Yet I see in it much room for hope. Your mind will be brought at once into the hard conflict of the world—You will transact *business*; & get initiated in those perplexities which sooner or later all of the sons of Adam must meet. You will confirm yourself in a knowledge of the world & wear off the Academic rust with which exlusive students are covered. Time will allow you, I know (for I know you will lose no time) to prosecute your Law with profit; & you will find in your newly-assumed cares a grateful change perhaps from the abstract speculations in which Blackstone & Kent & Fearne[2] will engage you. And, more than all, you will have the consciousness that you are forwarding the wishes of your father & giving up your time, perhaps, that it may be added to his days. Your brother, I should think will be able to take from your back the greater part of the weight of business.

It is now two days before Court. I am stiff in the determination to commence the coming year in the study of Law at Cam; & if I, when there, keep one pint of the bushell-full of *resolves* that I have formed,—law & every study under the sun will be passed over. I intend to give myself to the law, so as to read satisfactorily the regular & paralell courses—to take hold of some of the Classics—Greek, if I can possibly gird up my mind to the work—to pursue Historical studies;—Say, & Stuart[3]—all mingled with those condiments to be found in Shakespeare & the British Poets. All empty company & association I shall eschew; & seek in the solitariness of my own mind the best (because the least seducing from my Studies) companion. Can I hold fast to these good determinations? I fear much the rebellious spirit of the *mortal*. However, "I *will* try."—I must endeavor to redress by future application my past remissness. The latter part of this year has been given up to unprofitableness. I have, indeed, studied, or passed my eyes over books; but much of my time & almost my whole mind has been usurped by newspapers & politics. I have reached in anxiety for the latest reports from Washington & watched the waters in their ebb & rise in different parts of the country. No more of this though. With Boston I shall leave all the little associations, which turned aside my mind from its true course.

In the way of Classics, I wish to read Tacitus, Lucretius, Virgil, Ovid, Sallust, Cicero, Horace—Homer, Thucydides & choice plays of the great Tragedians. Do you start? I only say I *wish* to do it; but I *mean* to do it, if impossibility is not written upon it. —I wish also to reacquaint myself with Political Economy & Intell. Philos. I find myself nonplussed daily in my own reflections, by my ignorance of these subjects. Jenks has been on here from the city of N.Y. He tells great stories of the probabilities before him. Simmons[4] will spend the coming year as an usher in a private school in N.Y. city. He thinks of embarking, though, in some collateral employment—as instruction in Elocution. His {part?} for Court is on "Radicalism" & is most unacademic in its character. It is a shot direct at all would be–reformers & demagogues whose cry is "change" & "reform" &c—Hopkinson[5] will reside this coming year in the study of his profession & the instruction of one boy at Groton—Stearns is too weak for employment, though he is cheerfull & contented, as I gather from a letter not long ago recd.—Browne will study Law at Cam—Frost will still keep school in Framingham—Coffin is worse in idiocy—Sawyer & Pitts[6] will start in Oct. for Missouri where they intend settling. The hardihood & self dependence shown in this determination affords a good augury.—McBurney is in good health & spirits.

I will send you the Order of Perf. or a newspaper containing them. J. Q. Adams has written a letter on masonry.[7] I will send it you, as soon as I can lay my hands upon it. Rumor says something on this may be expected soon from Webster. He is an Anti & in this I speak from more than report.

Your true friend, Charles Sumner

ALS NNCB (65/023, PCS)

1. Charlemagne Tower (c. 1810–89), Harvard A.B., 1830; later lawyer and railroad director.

2. William Blackstone (1723–80), British jurist. James Kent (1763–1847), American jurist. Charles Fearne (1742–94), British legal scholar.

3. Jean Baptiste Say (1767–1832), French economist. Dugald Stewart (1753–1828), Scottish philosopher.

4. Richard Pulling Jenks (d. 1872), Harvard A.B., 1830. William Hammatt Simmons (d. 1841), Harvard A.B., 1831.

5. Thomas Hopkinson (1804–56), Harvard A.B., 1830; later lawyer and president, Boston and Worcester Railroad.

6. Barzillai Frost (d. 1858), later Unitarian clergyman; Henry Rice Coffin (d. 1880); Franklin Sawyer (d. 1851), later superintendent of public instruction in Michigan and public schools in Louisiana; Samuel Pitts (d. 1868); all Harvard A.B., 1830.

7. In his letter of 22 August 1831 to "Dear Sir," John Quincy Adams stated that John Adams had never been a partisan of the Masons, as one Mr. Sheppard had charged (*Letters on Freemasonry* [1833], 3–5).

To Jonathan F. Stearns

Cambridge Jany. 12th 1833—

My Dear Friend,

I have recd & am grateful for your letter. The interest you manifest in my welfare calls for my warmest acknowledgments. I do not know how I can better show myself worthy of your kindness, than with all frankness & plainness to expose to you, in a few words, the state of my mind on the important subject upon wh you addressed me.

The last time I saw you, you urged upon me ye study of ye *Proofs of Xstianity*, with an earnestness that flowed, I was conscious, from a sincere confidence in them yourself & the consequent wish that all should believe, as in belief was sure salvation. I have had your last words & look often in my mind since. They have been not inconstant prompters to thought & speculation upon ye proposed subject. I attended Bishop Hopkins' Lectures[1] & gave to them a severe attention. I remained & still remain unconvinced that Christ was divinely commissioned to preach a revelation to men & that he was entrusted with the power of working miracles. But when I make this declaration, I do not mean to deny that such a being as Christ lived & went about doing good or that the body of precepts wh have come down to us as delivered by him, were so delivered. I believe that Christ lived, when & as ye Gospel says—that he was more than man [[viz above all men who had as yet lived]] & yet less than God—full of ye strongest sense & knowledge, & of a virtue superior to any wh we call Roman or Grecian or Stoic & wh we best denote when, borrowing his name, we call it *Christian*. I pray you not to believe that I am insensible to the goodness & greatness of his character. My idea of human nature is exalted when I think that such a being lived & went as a man, amongst men. And here, perhaps, the conscientious unbeliever may find good cause for glorifying his God—not because he sent his son into ye world to partake of its troubles & be ye Herald of glad tidings—but because he suffered a man to be born, in whom ye world shld see but one of themselves, endowed with qualities calculated to elevate ye standard of attainable excellence.

I do not know that I can say more without betraying you into a controversy, which I shld be loth to engage in & from wh I am convinced no good would result to either party.—I do not think that I have a basis for faith to build upon. I am without religious feeling. I seldom refer my happiness or acquisitions to ye Great Father from whose mercy they are derived. Of the 1st great commandment, then, upon wh so much hangs, I live in perpetual unconsciousness—I will not say disregard, for that, perhaps wld imply that it was present in my mind.—I believe, tho, that my love to my neighbor viz my anxiety that my fellow-creatures shld be happy & disposition to serve them in their honest endeavors, is pure & strong. Certainly I do feel an affection for every thing that God created & *this feeling is my religion*.

He prayeth well, who loveth well
Both man & bird & beast.
He prayeth best, who loveth best
All things both great & small;
For the dear God who loveth us,
He made & loveth all.

I ask you not to imagine that I am led into ye above sentiment by ye lines I have just quoted (the best of Coleridge's Rime of the Ancient Mariner), but rather that I seize ye lines to express & illustrate my *feeling*.

This communication is made in ye fullness of friendship & confidence. To your charity & continued interest in my welfare suffer me to commend myself, as

Your affectionate Friend Chas. Sumner

P.S—Browne has left Camb. & is for ye winter at Salem. Hopkinson has also left & is with H. H. Fuller[2] in Boston. McBrney has a charge in Boston wh keeps him happy & busy; ye former *par consequence* from ye latter.

I feel quite alone. My chief company is ye letters of my Friends.—

Write me. C. S.

ALS MH-H (62/025, PCS)

1. John Henry Hopkins (1792–1868), assistant minister, Trinity Church, Boston, 1831–32; Episcopal bishop of Vermont, 1832–65; presiding bishop, 1865–68.
2. Henry Holton Fuller (1790–1852), lawyer.

To Joseph Story[1]

Washington March 20th [*1834*]

My Dear Judge,

I trust you have recd my hasty epistle of yesterday—in which I gave a sketch of ye sene in ye Sup Ct on ye delivery of ye opinion in ye case Wheaton v Peters.[2] I have nothing to add to that description, except my sense of its weakness & imperfection, as giving an idea of what actually passed. The language, which I have tried to preserve, did not give ye idea. You must imagine Judge T. in a perfect boil, with Baldwin in a strong passion at his back—McLean, with mingled pride & feeling checked by the proprieties of ye place—[3] Ch. Justice M.[*arshall*] with a sobriety of manner that bespoke his regret that things were at such a pass, looking like ye good man whom Virgil has described as able to still the tumult of a crowd, by his very appearance—while Duval,[4] sitting in utter unconsciousness of ye strife around him added to ye grotesqueness of ye scene. Imagine also a large number of ye bar in front,—looking on in anxiety & grief, that such a scene should occur. The Ch. Justice regretted to Mr Peters, in ye afternoon, while on his way to ye Norfolk boat—that he had said any thing on this occasion, though what he did say appeared to my mind ye very words that were wanted. He did not wish Mr Peters to make any mention of the *differences* in his report of ye case.—I am told that report with [her?] hundred tongues, has magnified ye story beyond all imagination. Mr Choate[5] sought me particularly to day, that he might hear from me an unvarnished account of ye whole affair. I told it him, as I wrote you. He sd he was glad to hear—that it was nothing worse—he sd that *all Congress* had hold of it & had magnified it ten times over—though, he added, it was bad enough.

I have heard it more than hinted that Mr Wheaton was going to make an appeal to ye public. What will be ye nature of ye appeal I know not.

We have had today nothing but dust & dullness, the one sweeping in volumes up & down the Avenue & the other pervading ye Capitol, though in both houses able men have [been?] up. In ye Senate Wright replied, in his husky voice & measured sentences, to Webster's speech on his Bank Bill—was replied to very dryly by Webster—who was followed by Leigh, who did nothing, as I was told, (I did not hear him) but repeat in a different form what he had already given us in prior speeches—as a Jackson man observed to me—giving another turn to the kaleidescope of his mind.[6] The impression is quite current, that Leigh has but one set of ideas, which he is determined to bring out & use on every possible occasion. He has no fullness, fertility or variety.—In ye House Pinckney of S.C. has [bin?] ringing ye tones of nullification, to a listless audience, the only attentive member being Gov. Lincoln[7] who seems to give a studied attention to all things that pass, including, of course, all speeches delivered. He must have imposed *penance* upon himself, if he has determined to continue so faithful a Representative long. His speech last Monday, on presenting ye Worcester Memorial, though it reads well enough, is spoken quite slightly of by members present at its delivery. Mr Calhoun[8] has given notice that he shall speak tomorrow on Webster's Bank Bill. I shall hear him; & he probably will be ye last man I shall hear in Washington—*ever*. I shall never come here again. No inducement, I think,—at least none that my most flighty ambition can look forward to, will take me away from study & calm pursuit of my profession, wherever I shall determine to pitch my tent. Politics are my loathing.—My next & sole desire ahead is to visit Europe & my first professional gains shall be devoted to that purpose. This accomplished, I shall be ready for any circumstances of life—even what is called *settlement in life*. But why pester you with these whims & fancies of mine? Your kindness has given me too much freedom in addressing you—though, I do it ever with respect & affection.

Good evening & my love to you & yours—whom I hope you found happy & well— Chas. Sumner

---

ALS DLC (65/085, PCS)

1. Joseph Story (1779–1845), U.S. Supreme Court justice, 1811–45; professor of law, Harvard, 1829–45.

2. Henry Wheaton (1785–1848; former Supreme Court reporter, jurist, and U.S. minister to Prussia, 1835–46) claimed that the present reporter, Richard Peters (1780–1848), had violated Wheaton's copyright when Peters included Wheaton's volumes in Peters's *Condensed Reports*. See CS to Simon Greenleaf (1783–1853; Harvard law professor, 1833–48), 3 March 1834, 65/079, PCS.

3. Smith Thompson (1768–1843) served as Supreme Court justice from 1823–43; Henry Baldwin (1780–1844), 1830–44; John McLean (1785–1861), 1829–61.

4. Gabriel Duval (1752–1844), Supreme Court justice, 1811–35, was deaf.

5. Rufus Choate (1799–1859), U.S. congressman (Whig, Mass.), 1831–34; U.S. senator, 1841–45.

6. Silas Wright, Jr. (1795–1847), U.S. senator (N.Y.), 1833–44. Benjamin W. Leigh (1781–1849), U.S. senator (Whig, Va.), 1834–36. On 18 March 1834 Daniel Webster proposed that the charter of the U.S. Bank continue for another six years after its expiration on 3 March 1836 (*Gales and Seaton's Register of Debates of Congress*, 23rd Cong., 1st sess., 984–96, 1004). In debate on 20 March Wright protested the constitutionality of any U.S. Bank. Leigh stated that his main fear regarding a U.S. Bank was an increase of executive power (ibid., 1019–48).

7. Henry Laurens Pinckney (1794–1863; U.S. congressman [Dem., S.C.], 1833–37) criticized Andrew Jackson's use of executive power and stated it had only "confirmed the States Rights Party in South Carolina in their opinions" (ibid., 3082–115). Levi Lincoln (1782–1868; U.S. congressman [Whig, Mass.], 1834–41) on 17 March 1834 asked relief for Worcester through the restoration of public deposits in the U.S. Bank, and condemned specie currency (ibid., 3017–19).

8. John C. Calhoun (1782–1850), U.S. senator (Dem., S.C.), 1832–43, 1845–50; secretary of state, 1844–45.

To Joseph Story

Washington March 21st [*1834*]

My dear Judge,

Calhoun has spoken today[1] & made quite an impression. He had a large—very large audience—the House of Reps pouring in to hear his sayings. He had no flourish or rhetoric—was direct & succinct & pregnant. He shld vote for Mr Webster's Bill out of courtesy—though it did not meet his approbation. It was *uncertain* & *unfixed* in its character.—6 yrs were *too short* if it was intended as a recharter, *too long*, if it was intended merely to afford time to wind up.—He marched right up to the statement of his objections without parley or introduction. He discussed in a very close manner ye currency—the reasons of its grt sensibility—wanted ye question now before them to be treated as a *Currency question* & not as a *Bank question*. He thought—contrary to opinions expressed by different Senators—that many banks were as dangerous as one grt bank. He wld propose a bank for 12 yrs—to get ye benefit of ye experience of ye new British Bank, wh was for 10 yrs—with provisions agnst ye issue of notes smaller than $10, & agnst ye receipt by ye bank of ye notes of other banks, who issued notes under $10,. He wld endeavour to make gold more current—raise its value & lower that of silver—so that we shld have a light portable coin to take ye place of ye retiring paper. This last wld benefit Georgia, N. Carol. & Virginia who have gold mines.—He then addressed himself to the *States Rights men*, (so he called them)—asked if they cld join in ye carrying such a measure—he thought they could & he endeavoured to quiet their Constitutional scruples[2] —then addressed ye Administration-men.—The attention to him throughout was deep & we all felt, that we were listening to a man, who was more than an orator—who was an honest & able man, having earnestly at heart all that he was uttering, & indifferent to ye guise of his thoughts, so he cld make them understood.

Benton[3] followed Calhoun—praising very much ye manner in which Calhoun had treated ye subject. I & ye whole audience left upon the speech of the son of Missouri commencing.

—Saw Judge McLean today—who remarked much upon ye occurrence on ye bench—sd Thompson & Baldwin, neither of them, understood ye opinion of ye Ct—& further that they departed from ye established usage in animadverting upon ye opinion, instead of addressing [them]selves to ye subject. Judge Mc[*Lean*] sd he shld have you tried for desertion.

The Avenue has been horridly full of dust.

Tomorrow morning I bid *Good bye* to Washington—with Mr Peters.

I am as ever— Chas. Sumner

ALS DLC (65/089, PCS)

1. *Gales and Seaton's Register of Debates in Congress*, 23rd Cong., 1st sess., 1057–73.

2. "[*T*]he power under consideration, like other political powers, is a trust power, and . . . like all such powers, it must be so exercised as to effect the object of the trust. . . . [T]he object of the power was to secure to these States a safe, uniform, and stable currency. . . . If Congress has a right to receive any thing else than specie in its dues, they have a right to regulate its value; and have a right, of course, to adopt all necessary and proper means, in the language of the constitution, to effect the object" (ibid., 1069–70).

3. Thomas Hart Benton (1782–1858), U.S. senator (Dem., Mo.), 1821–51; U.S. congressman, 1853–55.

To William Channing Russel[1]

Boston Aug. 25th '35

My dear Russel,

I have recd yr various favors, straggling over a considerable space of time. Balestier's[2] came first—at an unlucky moment, when I was in the agony of a sick headache, (an affliction which was then trying me for the first & I trust the last time) which sent me to my bed, immediately after Balestier left my office, from which I did not rise for two days. Please present my regard to him & account for my neglect of him on any grounds but indifference to yr recommendation or his character. Bradford called upon me a day or two since, at so late a period of his stay as to leave me little opportunity of shewing him any civilities. He, however, walked with me to the Atheneum & the Lib. of Hist. Soc. I thank you also for the [dernier?] favor of the package from M. Foelix. (The direction "Mr Colman" which perplexed you is to our *publisher*). It contained a very polite & complimentary letter from the French editor, in which he noticed Gibbs, whom I introduced to him, as "a young man of merit & amiability, whom he saw often & regretted that he did not see oftener." A letter, which I have recd from Gibbs is written in fine spirits & is full of proper feeling.[3]

Thus much for the vague chat & unilateral colloquy of friendship; now, let me trouble you with something akin to business, asking yr pardon for the liberty I take, yr patience while I communicate what I wish & yr *confidence* & *silence* as to its nature. At this moment, absorbed as I am in legal engagts I have enlisted in a *speculation* (I give you leave to laugh!) & I appeal to you if possible & convenient to furnish some information which yr residence in N.Y. & acquaintance there may enable you to obtain.—I am an owner to a large amount of stock in a new Compy, just formed & yet unknown in our Boston Exchange, called the

American Land Compy,[4] the object of which is to purchase cotton lands, by means of facilities which they have obtained at the *minimum* price & sell them at an advance of several hundred per cent. The price of a share is $100;—a share is now held by the Boston stockholders at 100 per cent advance—that is, 200 for 100—this is the *asking* price, but the *offers* in our market are few & much below that, as the stock has not yet become known. Those who have the best means of judging of the concern value the stock at several hundred per cent advance. Now, I have heard of several sales in N.Y. at 100 per cent advance. What I wish of you is to inquire of some Broker friend (if you have such or can easily get introduced to one) or mercantile friend, who keeps the run of the Stock market, what the fair value of the American Land Stock is, whether he knows any thing about it, whether he knows of any sales, at what price these sales were effected, whether sales could be effected now, & at what price. If sales can be effected I wish speedy information; & indeed, I would authorize you to put any amount of my stock up to 5 or 8000 dollars into the hands of any broker, who may have an offer at 75 per cent advance, always having an eye to the 100 per cent if it can be obtained. Pardon this thrusting of my concerns upon you; but you must take it from me at some other day. Remember, I do not ask or expect any brokerage duties from you; I simply appeal to you as the friend, whom I feel most willing thus to afflict & who, probably, will have means of assisting me. My Stake is a great one. If I can effect sales in N.Y. at the prices, or any thing near them, at which sales have been effected there, it will be several thousand dollars outright in my pocket. If you have no means of ascertaining any thing for me, please consider this letter as unwritten. In any communication you may make to any broker or other person withold my name. You will see at once my motive for assuming the vizer.

Friends of mine in Boston have already written to brokers in N.Y.; but I have resorted to the present course in order to have another string to my bow.

I hope to hear from you very soon—[5]

Believe yr sincere friend, Chas. Sumner

ALS MH-H (62/072, PCS)

1. William Channing Russel (1814–96), Harvard Law School classmate, then residing in Newburgh, New York.

2. Possibly Joseph Nerée Balestier (fl. 1840–76), New York journalist and lawyer.

3. Jean Jacques Foelix (1791–1853), French journalist. Samuel Colman (d. 1865),

N.Y. publisher and bookseller. George S. Gibbs (1815–73), Harvard L.L.B., 1838, and historian, had recently written CS from Paris (24 May 1835, 1/158, PCS).

4. The New York–based American Land Company proposed to purchase cotton lands from the U.S. government.

5. Russel apparently answered CS on 31 August, but the reply has not been recovered; on 4 September CS informed Russel that he and Henry S. McKean (1810–57, Harvard tutor, 1830–35) had invested together $25,000 in the company. On 20 September CS wrote Russel that he feared none of the stock had been discounted as promised, and that he had lost his money: "I've learned a valuable lesson. Money & business dissolve all the ties & bonds of friendship" (see 62/076, 62/078). According to Pierce, CS lost all he had invested (Prc, 1:155).

To Samuel Gridley Howe[1]

[Boston, c. 1835]

> "The last fruit which comes to late perfection,
> even in the kindliest soul, is, tenderness
> toward the hand, forbearance toward the
> unforbearing, warmth of heart toward the cold,
> philanthropy toward the misanthropic."—

Dear Howe,

I have happened upon the above from Jean Paul,[2] & send it to you, in support of what I said last night. I know that I need charity & candour; God grant that I may always shew them to others.—Truth & virtue must not be trifled with, nor treated with slight; but I know no vice or corruption that can dim their brightness, &, whoever they are, I hope to be able to see them, even if surrounded by worthless matter. I may be thought lax in my views,—wanting in the sterness which is due to mortal offences, tolerant of vice; I cannot help it. He must be of vice & inquity all-compact, who, brought up in refined society, has not something of good in him. Let us try to find it out, to encourage it, to turn it in its proper direction.

I like Jean Paul. He had a soul; big, comprehensive, human as man; & the sentences of his that go round the newspapers throw light, like planets.

Pardon this scrawl, written at the Athenaeum.

Ever Yrs, C. S. Monday—

> "Love one human being purely & warmly, & you will love all. The heart then, like the sun in Heaven, fills all things, from the dew-drop to the ocean with a mirror of itself & the warmth of its rays."
>
> Jean Paul

ALS MH-H (62/084, PCS)

1. Samuel Gridley Howe (1801–76), physician, reformer, and journalist.
2. Pseudonym of Johann Paul Friedrich Richter (1763–1825), German novelist and critic.

To Francis Lieber

Boston Jan 9th 36

My dear friend,

Before you receive this letter you will receive a newspaper containing a slight notice of yr Reminiscences, with references to some English criticisms. Since that was written the Magazines for November have been received at the Atheneum. The Monthly Review—the old Monthly of England supported of old by the first scholars & writers, Burke, Mackintosh—the same Review which noticed yr Stranger in America so handsomely, has an article of 15 pages on yr Reminiscences, written or rather compiled in a spirit of kindness & respect towards you.[1] I have been anxious to take a passage from it for one of our newspapers; but it consists so much of extracts, joined together—interlaced—by an abstract of the intermediate matter that there is not a single paragraph that one can get hold of. It will do you good in England. If any other reviews or notices appear I will promptly apprize you of them. The German Grammar has not yet shown itself above the rolling sea of publications. I am looking out for it, & shall probably descry it on its first kissing the light.

I omitted to send by my last letter & package, which I trust you have received, through Mr Preston, the sheet from Sparks of Washington's letter to his nephew.[2] It is not so much to the point as you hoped, I am inclined to think.

You are in the midst of Slavery—seated among its most whirling eddies, blown round, as they are, by the blasts of Gov. McDuffie, fiercer than any from the old wind-bags of Aeolus. What think you of it? Shld it longer exist? Is not emancipation practicable? We are becoming abolitionists at the North fast—the riots, the attempts to abridge the freedom of discussion, Gov. McDuffie's message & the conduct of the South generally have caused many to think favorably of immediate emancipation who never before inclined to it.[3]

I think yr Stranger in America[4] is not in the Boston market—it was not, I know, a short time since. A young friend of mine—a son of Professor Greenleaf—who read it on my hint, is ravished with it & tried to get a couple of copies to present to his friends. His mother & father were delighted with it.

Shall you lecture before the American Institute? —a dull assembly of old women in petticoats & pantaloons. I know they have invited you.

I don't intend that this scrawl shall pass for anything in payment of the debt I owe you.

I shall write again very soon.

Yrs ever Chas. Sumner

I am looking for yr Inaugural[5]

ALS MH-H (62/088, PCS)

1. Francis Lieber (1800–72), a German immigrant, was then professor of political economy at South Carolina College (1835–56), later at Columbia College (1857–65), and Columbia Law School (1865–72). His *Reminiscences of an Intercourse with Mr. Niebuhr, the Historian, during a Residence with Him in Rome, in the Years 1822 and 1823* (1835), was reviewed in the *Monthly Review* 3, no. 3 (November 1835): 418–29. Edmund Burke (1729–97), British statesman. Sir James Mackintosh (1765–1832), British philosopher and M.P.

2. Presumably William Campbell Preston (1794–1860) of Columbia, S.C., lawyer and U.S. senator (Dem., S.C.), 1833–42. Jared Sparks (1789–1866; historical editor; president, Harvard, 1849–53), was then working on his twelve-volume *The Writings of George Washington* (1834–37).

3. In his second annual message to the legislature, governor of South Carolina George McDuffie (1790–1851) had characterized those circulating antislavery literature as "wicked monsters and deluded fanatics" and advocated capital punishment because these agitators were "enemies of the human race." See Edwin L. Green, *George McDuffie* (1936), 153–54.

4. Originally published as *Letters to a Gentleman in Germany, Written after a Trip from Philadelphia to Niagara* (1833).

5. "On History and Political Economy, as Necessary Branches of Superior Education in Free States. An Inaugural Address delivered in South Carolina College, before His Excellency the Governor and the Legislature of the State, on Commencement Day the 7th of December, 1835."

To Benjamin W. Stone

Boston August 15th 1836

Dear Sir,

I embrace a few minutes before leaving on my journey[1] (which I was prevented from commencing on Saturday) to address you a few lines.

I have been astonished & mortified by the tone of your remarks in regard to my compensation for editorial services on Mr Dunlap's book.[2] It is unpleasant, you know, to have any estimate that one puts upon his services questioned, or undervalued. And I assure you it was particularly unpleasant in the present case, because the estimate was so low, &, I deliberately state, so much less than the same time I devoted to that book would have yielded if spent in professional & other labors, which I was invited to undertake. It is for you & those who act with you to consider whether I am to be called upon to sacrifice near $1000—perhaps upwards of that sum for the reputation of Mr Dunlap. I repeat to you now, what I said in conversation, that I *distinctly declined business offered to me & which would have yielded from $500 to $1000 or upwards, on the express ground that my engagements to the memory of Mr Dunlap & to his Executor were paramount & could not be deferred.* No one acquainted with me will question my willingness to give up my time & labor to my friends. If they, who represent Mr Dunlap, feel that they have a claim upon me to the above amount, let me understand it, & the grounds on which it rests, & I assure you I shall be reasonably prompt to recognize it. As it is I exhibit no bill & make no demand; but leave the whole business to the *justice*, I do not say the *generosity*, of the Executor & heirs. All that I do say is that if I am to receive any thing as *compensation* $500 is the least sum with which I should be content—& that sum will not be equal to the sacrifice of business which I have made.

It should be considered that, in the first place, the whole manuscript of Mr Dunlap was carefully read & examined by me before it was sent to the press & all of his numerous authorities verified & the proofs read *twice*. This was done before his death. After that event the whole Appendix & the Indexes were entirely prepared by me from p. 340 to p 581, & also the preface & List of Cases prefixed to the book. Every thing in the book after p. 420 {was?} written out with my own hand—& every page required great study & care.

If you communicate with any lawyer upon the proper sum I would thank you either to shew my letter or to state its contents —so that he may know what I have done & also what business I declined in order to do it. I feel inclined, as you have made the disagreeable questioning about the *compensation*, to decline receiving a *cent*. But some friends, with whom I have consulted, have suggested that I should be unjust to myself if I did so, & that no persons, especially if they have property, can expect a young man to {sacri}fice $1000 of time & labor for nothing.

Allow me to invite you to settle this business, one way or another, with my friend Mr Hillard, who has full powers from me, & in whose hands I place myself entirely. I mention this so that you need not wait till my *return,* because, whenever it is settled I wish it to be done through him. I shall feel unwilling ever to *speak* upon this subject again.[3]

I am, dear Sir, Yours respectfully, Chas. Sumner

ALS MSaE (65/192, PCS)

1. From mid-August to mid-September 1836, CS traveled to Saratoga, Niagara Falls, Montreal, and Quebec.

2. Benjamin W. Stone was executor of Andrew Dunlap's estate. Dunlap (1794–1835), ill with tuberculosis, had asked CS to help him complete his book, *A Treatise on the Practice of Courts of Admiralty in Civil Causes of Maritime Jurisdiction* (1836).

3. George Stillman Hillard (1808–79), lawyer and writer, was CS's law partner, 1834–47. A draft of a letter from Stone to CS, 26 October, arranging a meeting to settle the fee is in the Dunlap Estate Papers, Essex Institute. After writing several reminders, CS received on 4 November 1836 compensation of $500. See CS to Stone, 30 August, 25 October, 4 November, 65/196, 204, 207, PCS.

To Richard Peters

Boston Nov. 23d 1836

My dear Sir,

It seems an age since I heard from you; whether the fault be with me, or whether I may venture to charge it upon you I will not determine. I owe you an acknowledgment for your 10th vol.[1] which I duly recd; also for yr introduction of Nathl. Hart, though he was none the better for it, as I was absent from the city on a long journey when he called. I felt strongly tempted to embrace Philadelphia in a tour which I took to Niagara, & through Canada, to Quebec & home through Vermont, N. Hampshire & Maine; but it did not seem to fall within the route which I had marked out, so that I was obliged to forego the sight of yr valued family.

My immediate object in writing is, at the request of Judge Story—our dear friend—who has not time to write, to ask you to send him a copy of your Report of the Cherokee case[2] which he is desirous of presenting to a friend abroad. I have on my table to forward to you by the earliest opportunity the 2nd vol. of the Judge's work on Equity which is just published.[3]

What are your impressions & those of the Philadelphia Bar with regard to Taney's capacity for the high office to which he has been called? I have heard nothing about him, since his jacobin speech at the opening of his first court, when he declined to deliver a *charge*, alleging that the people were *now* so well informed as not to need the instruction of charges.[4] This seemed to be the speech of a demagogue. How he will hold the great scales which Marshall bore aloft with such firm & even hands remains to be seen! Perhaps upon him [*Joseph Story*], who entirely deserved the place & was neglected, the duties will in the main fall.

Every thing has gone against us in politics, & the horizon for another four years is to be darkened by the clouds which have overhung it for eight years already.[5] The report from Pennsylvania, so full of cheering intelligence threw us all into rejoicing; but now we are in the midst of the despondency of defeat. Massachusetts has not been conquered; but, as Pyrrhus said of his victories over the Romans, many more such victories will ruin us. There has been a falling-off; & I should hardly be surprized, if at the next state election the Van Buren party triumphed; but many things will intervene before then, perhaps, to alter the complexion of parties, so that it is difficult to make any prophecy, that may be realized.

I should like to visit Washington this winter; but engagements, sovereign, will keep me at home. The winter after I may be called upon to attend ye Supreme Court; though it is sometime to look ahead. And, indeed, before that time, I hope to be in Europe, to stay years, perhaps. Remember me to all yr family & believe me, as ever,

most faithfully Yours, Chas. Sumner

ALS PHi (65/208, PCS)

1. *Reports of Cases Argued and Adjudged in the Supreme Court of the U.S., in January Term 1836*, hereafter referred to as *Peters Reports*.

2. Cherokee Nation v. State of Georgia, January 1831, *Peters Reports*, 5:25–53.

3. *Equity Jurisprudence* (1836).

4. U.S. Supreme Court Chief Justice Taney's charge to the U.S. Circuit Court in Baltimore, 8 April 1836. See Carl B. Swisher, *Roger B. Taney* (1935), 355–56.

5. Although the results were at first uncertain, Martin Van Buren, the Democratic nominee for president, ultimately carried Pennsylvania as well as fourteen other states to gain the presidency.

To Simon Greenleaf

4 Court St. Jan. 9th '37

My dear Mr Greenleaf,

This is the evening of my first day at Cambridge, where I met the students at 10 o'clk in the Library beneath the over-looking eye of Nathan Dane.[1] I spoke to them of the value of Kent's Com.—of the vast field of law which they cover & of the importance of thoroughly mastering them, in all their principles & also in their abundant references; then of the Law of Evidence, of the various works upon it & of Starkie, & also enforced the importance of thoroughly studying this subject;[2] in conclusion I spoke of the high value of reports as the depository of the law, & endeavored to incite the students to peruse them constantly in connection with the text we study. They all listened attentively, & appeared full of good resolutions. I am to meet the respective classes at 10 & 11 o'clk on Wednesday next—day after tomorrow. In the meantime they are to assemble & determine whether to have an exercise every day, or every other day. This choice I proposed to them, telling them that it would be my duty & pleasure to attend them so often as they desired. And so here endeth the first Lesson. I jumped on top of the Omnibus, & in the eye of a cutting wind reached the haven of my office. And here I am, tormented worse than an infant with a pain, which you may never have experienced, or may be too old to remember; but which is truly harassing & beyond the reach of sedatives & almost of patience. "Canst thou not minister to the *gum* diseased"?[3]—Pardon this reference to such an infantile complaint; but it has deprived me of a night's repose (no loss you may say for *me*!) & made me feverish, faint &, I fear, fretful & ill-natured. Of the latter dispositions this letter will make you the victim. Since you left[4] another year of my life has been counted with those beyond the flood; & to me the day of this new addition was full of melancholy. The time wasted, idled & exhausted in this world's vanities came before me like a potent spirit; & the future looked up to me, from its indefinite abyss, with threatenings & sources of despondency. However, I cast myself upon my duties, trusting that, in their daily calls, they will bear me on, "as a steed that knows its rider." But I cannot now achieve that contentment, which once so completely was mine—which made me so deliciously happy in yr society & that of my more than parent Judge Story & in the pines & elms of Cambridge. My blood demands something more stirring than the quiet scenes of the Academy—&, as they almost seem to me, the oaten pipes of those who haunt them. Oh that I could again "be wreathed with the silver crown of clear content." But I check this maudlin vein, which I have no right to greet you with, & throw myself upon yr friendship for full absolution. I have written what I have because the words flowed from my pen & I could not stop them.

Nothing is new in Boston. We have had hearty, [bracing] cold weather, with a clear air, which it was, like elixir, to inhale. I loved to drink it down, as I would a costly liquor—it carried an invigorating refreshment to the inner man. Our Courts of C.P. & Sup. Ct. are dragging their slow lengths along—the cases for the rail-road concession having occupied much time in the latter Ct. but being now settled against the Corporation.[5] Paine, who opened for Plffs against the Corporation enforced Lord Coke's dictum, that a Corporation has no soul, by classic authority—saying that the Corption cld not exclaim with the Latin poet—

—Homo sum, et nihil a me alienum puto.[6]

Affairs are at a stand-still in our Legislature, a preliminary question, which seems pregnant with that master, *talk*, having arisen as to the seats of some Senators from Berkshire, which must be decided before the Governor's Address[7] can come. In the meantime the Codification Report is in the printer's archives. Cushing[8] has altered & amended his *Reading* & sent it to the Governor *de bene esse*.[9] What course the latter will take with regard to it is not known. Give my love to Judge Story & tell him I shall write him immediately. Pardon the melancholy tinge & believe me

affectionately Yrs, C. S.

Stackpole, of our bar & Susan Benjamin[10] got *engaged* last evng!

ALS MH-L (65/216, PCS)

1. Nathan Dane (1752–1835), Massachusetts statesman, had funded a professorship at the Harvard Law School.

2. Kent's *Commentaries on American Law* (1826–30) and Thomas Starkie's *Practical Treatise on the Law of Evidence* (1824).

3. "Canst thou not minister to the mind diseas'd," *Macbeth*, 5.3.40.

4. Greenleaf was then at the U.S. Supreme Court arguing for the defendants in the suit brought by the Charles River Bridge Company against the Warren Bridge. The justices were to rule whether a private corporation, the Charles River Bridge Company, operating a toll bridge over the Charles River, could establish a monopoly there.

5. James Thompson v. the Boston and Providence Railroad Corporation (Boston *Daily Evening Transcript*, 6 January 1837:2). Sir Edward Coke (1552–1634), British jurist.

6. "I am man and I deem nothing foreign to me."

7. Edward Everett (1794–1865), governor of Massachusetts, 1836–40.

8. Luther S. Cushing (1803–56), Boston jurist.

9. "Such as it is."

10. Joseph L. Stackpole (1808–1847), Boston lawyer. Susan Benjamin (1815–96).

To Joseph Story

4 Court St. Feb. 5th '37
Sunday-night

My dear Judge,

Your letter was a perfect treat. I was glad to hear that affairs went on so harmoniously, & that the term would end so soon; & I was particularly glad to hear of Greenleaf's success. We are all waiting anxiously for the judgment of the court; & I am expecting to see Greenleaf to-morrow. I think it probable that he arrived at his *domus et placens uxor*[1] last evening. If so, my labors at Cambridge will speedily close. I have gone over the 1st vol of Kent, comprizing International & Constitutional Law; & also more than half of the 1st vol. of Starkie, expounding & commenting on the subject, step by step, & saying every thing which occurred to me by way of illustration from the cases, from practice, history & legal anecdote. I have given some most righteous judgments in the moot-court. The School is in admirable order, most ardently engaging in work, & zealous after knowledge. They enquire after their absent shepherds, & seem anxious again to enjoy their pastoral care. Some will press you, I fear, to hear a class in Equity on yr return. Do not, however, be tempted into too much work.

I have passed several evn'gs with Mrs Story, & have found her in remarkably good spirits. Mary, I think, is better than she has been. William is, of course, well, & apparently attentive to his studies.[2] We have had some good-natured disputes about College affairs & the government. I am very much struck by his power of argument & the ability with which he makes the worse appear the better side. It is sometimes with no little difficulty that I find myself able to maintain my ground, so adroit is he in making his points, & so quickly does he turn upon me. I fancy that in the law his powers will be eventually developed, & that you will find great joy in his success.

Mr Ellis Loring[3] has recd a letter from Miss Martineau, full of interesting things. Her book is to be entitled, *The Theory & Practice of Society in the U. States*, under which title you see she will be able at once to trace the theoretical perfection of our institutions (which she very much admires) & the practical discrepancies, which she very much condemns.[4] She writes that American affairs, & particularly slavery are constantly discussed in English society, & that we are universally & strongly condemned, so that she is obliged to act as *moderator*. David L. Child[5] is well recd in London.

I have heard tonight a long letter from Ticknor to Mr Wm Prescott,[6] giving a detailed account of several visits to Prince Metternich. The conversation of the Prince was very interesting, frank & pregnant. He said that if he were in the U. States he should be of the party opposed to Van Buren—that he should belong to the Old Conservative Party founded by Washington. It is astonishing how much these Germans find out about us. They seem to grasp our party distinctions & detect the narrow lines, almost with the instinct of those "to the manner born." He conversed much on the difference between a monarchy & republic, & seemed to be very kind & humane. Ticknor's letter occupies two sheets. I feel that if I should attempt to [detail?] to you what I can call up from my poor memory, it would lose all its original flavor, & I must, therefore, commend you to the letter on yr return home.

Codification is at a stand-still. The Committee will certainly all agree to codify the Criminal Law. But the subject seems to have lost somewhat of its old interest. The Report has so little that is *extreme*, that neither party can screw themselves to decided opposition. We are all talking about Webster's resignation, & his successor. The candidates mentioned are Ed. Everett (strong opposition) Hoar, I. C. Bates, Wm Baylies, & Abbott Lawrence.[7] The editor of the Atlas[8] mentioned Lawrence's name to me in conversation last evng. A fifth judge is to be given our Supreme Court. Questions run, who will it be? Wm Sturgis[9] is said to have been [dieting?] for the Senate; but he cannot expect to succeed. Gov [*Levi*] Lincoln is completely "shelved," in theatrical language. Have I not written a letter worthy of a common gossip or quidnunc?

As ever Yrs most affectionately, C. S.

The Address I sent to Mr Brockenbrough,[10] as desired.—No new[s] from England. Rand's article in N. American on the bar[11] is quoted & printed in the Legal Observer.

ALS DLC (65/224, PCS)

1. "House and pleasing wife." The defendants in the Charles River Bridge case received a favorable 5–2 decision from the Supreme Court, with Story dissenting.

2. Sarah Waldo Story (1784–1855), Story's wife, and his children, Mary Oliver Story (1817–49) and the sculptor William Wetmore Story (1819–95).

3. Ellis Loring (1803–58), Boston lawyer and antislavery activist.

4. The work, *Society in America*, by British writer Harriet Martineau (1802–76), was published in 1837.

5. David L. Child (1794–1874), lawyer, journalist, and husband of the writer Lydia Maria Child (1802–80).

6. George Ticknor (1791–1871), former professor of modern languages at Harvard, was traveling in Europe with his wife, Anna, and their two daughters. Ticknor met with the Austrian diplomat Klemens, Fürst von Metternich (1773–1859), in June 1836. William Hickling Prescott (1796–1859), historian.

7. After an outpouring of Whig support, Webster eventually changed his mind about resigning his U.S. Senate seat. See DW, 4:181. Possible successors mentioned were Samuel Hoar (1778–1856), U.S. congressman (Whig, Mass.), 1835–37; Isaac C. Bates (1779–1845), U.S. congressman (Whig, Mass.), 1827–35; William Baylies (1776–1865), U.S. congressman (Dem., Mass.), 1833–35; and Abbott Lawrence (1792–1855), Boston merchant, U.S. congressman (Whig, Mass.), 1835–37, 1839–40, and U.S. minister to Great Britain, 1849–52.

8. Richard Haughton.

9. William Sturgis (1782–1863), intermittent member of Massachusetts House of Representatives, 1814–46; Massachusetts state senator, 1827, 1836.

10. Story had requested that a copy of his "Discourse on Chief Justice Marshall" be sent to John A. Brockenbrough of Philadelphia (Washington, 25 January 1837, 1/306, PCS).

11. Benjamin Rand (d. 1852), Boston lawyer, was traveling in Great Britain. His unsigned article, "The Legal Profession in England," had appeared in the *North American Review* 42 (April 1836):513–49.

To Joseph Story

4 Court St. July 13th 1837

My dear Judge,

You will think it habitual with me, I believe, to introduce most topics in which I am interested by letter, rather than by word of mouth, & I must plead guilty to the charge; for I feel a repugnance to a first breaking of a subject orally, & rather leave it to the unblushing paper. I have so often spoken with you with regard to my visit abroad, that I can hardly hope to say any thing more which can alter your views of its expediency; & yet I wish I could bring you to my side. Do, then, think of my strong desire, which dates back to my earliest days of memory—amounting almost to an instinct—to visit those scenes memorable in literature & history & to see, so far as it may be given to one so humble as myself, the great men that are already on the stage—think, then, of the desire, which has arisen in maturer years, of obtaining a knowledge of languages, of observing the manners customs & institutions of other people than my own, particularly of noting in France & Germany the administration of justice & the course of legal instruction & in England frequenting Westminster Hall & drinking at the very bubbling fountain of the common law. A tour for such purposes, I submit & I think on consideration you must agree with me, is not for *display* but for *purposes of education*; it should, therefore, be undertaken, before the mind, absorbed in business, has lost its freshness, & its capacity for receiving impressions, while the spirits are still elastic & hope is high & ambition prompts to the full & profitable enjoyment of every privilege. The knowledge derived from such a tour, I regard as a kind of *intellectual capital*, into the use & possession of which I long to enter, sincerely hoping that if I am enabled to, my friends (even Presdt Quincy) will not find occasions of regret. In this object all my affections are enlisted, to such a degree as to withdraw my attention from my profession & studies & to prevent me from doing that justice to myself which shall vindicate yr constant friendship & approval. I am in love; but as you once said, *it is with Europa*. Now, my dear Judge, I wish to talk with you on this subject, explain to you more at large the object &

course of my proposed journey, & particularly to let you know the means on which I expect to rely for funds, & to ascertain if you are so situated as to be able to render me any assistance. I know the generosity of your nature so well, that I have long hesitated to break this subject, for fear that, under the impulse of friendship you might make some offer not entirely consistent with yr circumstances. But I have determined to rely upon your frankness & upon the free relations of mutual confidence which exist between us to call the subject to your attention & to explain to you fully my situation, hoping that you will deal with me with equal frankness. That you may not be influenced by a fear that, without assistance from you, my hopes of going will be blasted, I will add that I have funds more than sufficient at my disposal; but that *I should prefer to be indebted to you before all other men*; & should, therefore, be extremely happy, if, on hearing my whole case, my wants, my security, & the probable time of my absence, you should find it entirely consistent with all yr circumstances, to lend me a part of the sum which I shall need for my expenses abroad. I shall see you very soon & in *private* conversation I will lay open all my affairs.[1]

To you, my best friend, I owe constant gratitude, & I hesitate to allow the alloy of money to enter into our friendship; but human affairs cannot be conducted, or human desires gratified, without many contacts which jar the finer nerves & sensibilities. Nothing, however, can jar the attachment by which I am bound to you & with which I subscribe myself yr affectionate friend,

Chas. Sumner

ALS DLC (65/256, PCS)

1. No written response from Story to this request has been recovered. According to Donald, CS received $1,000 from Story as well as equal amounts from Samuel Lawrence (1801–80), Boston businessman, and Richard Fletcher (1788–1869), U.S. congressman (Whig, Mass.), 1837–39; judge, Supreme Court of Massachusetts, 1848–53 (DD, 1:44).

To John Gorham Palfrey[1]

4 Court St. July 31st '37

My dear Sir,

One who has failed in fulfilling his promises so often as I have may well hesitate to renew them; but, notwithstanding my hesitation I feel emboldened to offer again. Mr F. A. Grund[2] has expressed a strong desire that I should write a notice or review of his work on our country in the North American. I have read part of the work; in the English edition, &, though I dissent from some parts of it that I have read, yet I think it an able, grave & eloquent production, without scandal or small-talk &, therefore, without that condiment which is so tasteful to the American palate. It is a disquisition on & a defence of our Institutions & Character. If it is agreeable to you I should be pleased to write an article, which should have from 7 to 10 pages of original writing & about the same amount of extracts—say, in all 15 or 20 pages. It would be strictly a Review & not a dissertation or defence. If you have not that space I will write a notice. Perhaps yr number for October is already full; or perhaps, it will not be agreeable to you to notice the work. In either alternative I shall not be disappointed by yr declining my offer.

Mr Grund is a very able & eloquent man both with his pen & tongue; but very [tiring?], in my opinion, on some subjects, & quite democratic. His faith in our Character & Institutions is mighty. His work has been well received in England, & has been translated *three* times into German, in different states of Germany,—once by himself. About 6000 copies were sold in Germany, as he has informed me.

Will you be good enough to let me know at an early date, what you will have me do, &, be assured that, for this time, you may rely upon my promises.[3]

I am my dear Sir, very truly Yrs, Chas. Sumner

P.S. I shld praise him some, rap him over the knuckles some, & comment upon & extract some.

ALS MH-H (65/259, PCS)

1. John Gorham Palfrey (1796–1881), Unitarian clergyman; editor, *North American Review*, 1835–43; U.S. congressman (Whig, Mass.), 1847–49; postmaster of Boston, 1861–67.

2. Francis J. Grund (1805–63), Austrian journalist then living in Philadelphia, had written *The Americans in their Moral, Social, and Political Relations* (1837). CS saw Grund frequently in June in Boston (CS to Hillard, 24 June 1837, 62/126, PCS).

3. CS's unsigned review appeared in the *North American Review* 46 (January 1838):106–26.

To Charles Stewart Daveis[1]

Boston Oct. 26th '37

My dear friend,

You may wonder at my absence from Portland, or rather at my failure to present myself there at the proper time. Business, with its hydra heads, has prevented me hitherto. I fondly hoped at this time to have been rejoicing in the blue waves of the Atlantic, & wooing the Zephyrs for friendly aid on my way. But what mortal ever accomplished what he expected in the time in which he expected to accomplish it. My date of departure has receded constantly from grasp. I have, however, now fixed on Monday, week from next Monday. I can not, however, think of going without seeing you for a few hours, & also, perhaps, making the acquaintance of Mr Neal.[2] Unless something, in the shape of storm or imperative engagement, occurs, I shall take ye boat Tuesday evng next, & return in ye Wednesday Evng boat. I wish yr good advice, & parting benizon before I go. Your letters, too, I rely upon much. All yr introductions I shall appreciate, & hope not to dishonor. Mr Hoffman has introduced me to Sir Robt Inglis, Mr Sergeant D'Oyly;[3] Rand will give me letters to Denman, Park, Solicitor General, Geldart, Coventry &c;[4] Judge Story to Mr Justice Vaughan, Wilkinson, Stuart Wortley &c;[5] Alex. H. Everett; to Ld John Russell & several others;[6] Edward Everett to, I dont know whom; Dr Lieber has already sent me a dozen to France, Germany & England; Mr Pickering[7] will give me letters to all he knows; Washington Allston to Wordsworth; Then I may also rely upon Mr Binney[8] in Phila; upon Chancellor [*James*] Kent, if he knows any body—I shall write him immediately; also upon Mr Sparks, to whom I have not yet spoken; & upon many others. All of which things we will ponder together when we meet.

I shall go direct to Paris, where I shall meet the Ticknors, & pass two or three months; then go to England, to pass several months. If you have any communication for the Ticknors prepare it for me. Can I procure letters from Prof. Cleveland to Sir D. Brewster[9] or any other characters that it may be desirable to see? You may think me *exigeant*; but my whole soul is garnered up in this project; & I wish to have all ye materials & means for seeing, enjoying & understanding. England is my great passion & admiration. Her history I have studied & throbbed over from boyhood; & her scenes & characters I regard with a feeling kindred to that of patriotism. Excuse this exuberance of feeling, & believe me,

as ever, affectionately Yours, Chas. Sumner

ALS NNCB (65/288, PCS)

1. Charles Stewart Daveis (1788–1865) of Portland, Maine, lawyer and friend of CS's father, Charles Pinckney Sumner (1776–1839), then sheriff of Suffolk County.

2. John Neal (1793–1876), writer, editor in Portland.

3. David Hoffman (1784–1854), professor of law, University of Maryland. Robert Inglis (1786–1855), British M.P. Thomas D'Oyly (1774–1855), British lawyer.

4. Thomas Denman (1779–1854), British jurist. James Parke (1782–1868), British jurist. James W. Geldart (1785–1876), professor of civil law, Cambridge. Thomas Coventry (1797–1869), British lawyer.

5. John Vaughan (1769–1839), British jurist. James John Wilkinson (d. 1845), British judge. James Stuart-Wortley (1805–81), British solicitor-general, M.P.

6. Alexander H. Everett (1790–1847), U.S. diplomat, editor, brother of Edward. Lord John Russell (1792–1878), Whig foreign secretary and prime minister.

7. John Pickering (1777–1846), Boston legal scholar.

8. Washington Allston (1779–1843), American painter. Horace Binney (1780–1875), Philadelphia legal scholar.

9. Parker Cleaveland (1780–1858), professor of chemistry, mathematics, and mineralogy at Bowdoin College. David Brewster (1781–1868), British editor, writer.

To Francis Lieber

Boston Oct. 26th '37

My dear friend,

Yrs of Oct. 17th arrived this morning, & found me still in Boston & just decided on a further delay of a few days. Business, with its hydra heads, overcomes me from day to day. I shall leave Boston *Monday Nov. 6th*, & proceed to Washington; so that you will have ample time to write me, either at Washington or New York, after ye receipt of this. Do not send the *original* of Story's letter; but simply a copy. My acquaintance with Judge Story & my word will be sufficient to vouch it.

Did I write you that, sometime ago, I received a cordial letter from Mittermaier? I have ordered the Jurist to be sent regularly to him, & I shall also send him my Reports in 2 vols.[1]

I've read & pondered yr views about sovereignty.[2] I only wish I could talk with you one hour about that. My mind labors some in adopting yr explanation; & yet I believe you are right. Some discussion would confirm both of us. *Sovereignty* is exercised by *society*. Should you not then, explain *society*? In the sense in which you use it, it is *all human beings*; because all these contribute to public opinion, & indirectly to laws, by influencing fathers & husbands & brothers. You make revolutions rather *co-ordinate* manifestations of *sovereignty*, with public opinion; whereas, are they not *subordinate*. Revolutions are the natural result of the suppression of, opposition to, or interference with, *public opinion*. If the gentle changes, which are perpetually suggested by what Lord Bacon calls, "the great revolutionist Time," are adopted there will be no revolutions. England demanded reform—the whole country had outgrown the ancient institutions. The opposition to this suggestion of public opinion caused the great palpitations of 1831, & 1832, & nearly a revolution. Macaulay rightly said—"*by* parliament, *through* parliament, or *over* parliament reform must be carried."[3] However, this view does not differ materially from yours. The great *director* of sovereignty, is the *public will*, or ye *will of society*; this will exhibiting itself in different ways & under different modifications in different countries. In *free countries* the public will is controlled, only by the primal laws of our nature & of God; & countries are more or less free, according as the *will of society* is more or less unrestrained. In Turkey society has no *will*, or it is circumscribed very much by the despotism of the Sultan. Assuming, then, that the public will is the *director* of sovereignty; we may next find the exponents or manifestations of the public will; viz—*public opinion*, which insensibly operates every where, like the gentle droppings of water & produces mighty results; & *the laws*. And yet I am not sure that I have not made an identical proposition, when I say public opinion is a sign of the public will. But usage has given public opinion a meaning—being the *unwritten* expression of public will, composed of the will of young & old, male & female combined. Usages & customary law would come under this head; & the statutes under the head of *written*. Now revolutions appear to me *subordinate* manifestations; viz such are resorted to, when the others fail. I write in haste, & with my first thoughts. I repeat, if I could see you, a few minutes' conversation would make every thing clear. But miles intervene, & we shall not meet for a long time. Yr dear wife's kindly interest I most cordially reciprocate.[4] Give her my best love.

Perhaps yet again I shall hear from you. I cannot sail before the 18th Nov. perhaps, the 24th. Leaving Boston Nov. 6th, I shall be in Washington Nov. 10th or 12th, where I shall expect a letter to Gilpin.[5]

Yrs ever, Chas. Sumner

ALS CSmH (65/290, PCS)

1. Karl Joseph Mittermaier (1787–1867), German legal scholar. The *American Jurist; Report of Cases Argued and Determined in the Circuit Court of the United States for the First Circuit, by Charles Sumner, Reporter of the Court* (1836–37).

2. Working at that time on his *Manual of Political Ethics* (1838–39), Lieber had no doubt sought CS's views. For further discussion of sovereignty in *Political Ethics*, see Frank Freidel, *Francis Lieber* (1947), 157–58.

3. "In peace or in convulsion, by the law, or in spite of the law, through the Parliament, or over the Parliament, Reform must be carried," speech on the Reform Bill by Thomas Babington Macaulay (1800–59), historian and M.P., House of Commons, 16 December 1831, *Speeches* (1854), 81.

4. Matilde Oppenheimer Lieber (b. 1807), married Francis Lieber, 1829.

5. Henry D. Gilpin (1801–60), Philadelphia lawyer and U.S. attorney general, 1840–41.

To Joseph Story

Sunday Dec. 3d '37
on board Steamer Robert Morris

My dear Judge,

Here am I violating the Sabbath by travelling; but necessity knows no law,—"nor does Lord Anstruther," according to the old adage. Since I wrote you from Phila I have seen much & have volumes to communicate, & I long for an opportunity of speaking face to face. I have seen Mr Hoffman, who received me very cordially, & talked a great deal about you. He seemed much pleased to get a letter from you, & said that he had begun to feel morbid at your long silence, & afraid you, too, had deserted him. I, however, undeceived him. He told me of a very long conversation which he had with Lord Denman about you & yr work on Bailments, in which he bore down upon his Lordship with great vigor. When you see him again, take the trouble to call his attention to it. Mrs Hoffman[1] enquired after Mrs Story, & Miss Hoffman after Mary, & hoped that you would bring her on South with you. Mr Peters's daughter [*Eliza?*] expressed the same hope. In Washington I called on the President [*Van Buren*], & spent a portion of the evening in his drawing-room, sitting on the Nation's sofa. Forsyth & Woodbury were present, besides Mr Gilpin who introduced me & a vulgar New York partizan editor, by name Mumford, who has been made Secretary to the Commission of Spanish Claims.[2] The conversation was partly on the resumption of specie payments & the bank convention in [New?] York, in which they appeared to take a lively interest. The subject of Canada,[3] however, occupied considerable attention; & on this they talked like children. I held my tongue; but I could not but wonder that men, to whom the affairs of a great people had been entrusted, should be so utterly ignorant of the situation of affairs in a province adjoining us & implicated with us by a thousand ties. Woodbury actually inquired, with the gravity of a school-boy, what the grievances of the Canadians were, & on what point the disturbances hinged. And, then, to hear the President instruct his pupil was a scene! I had supposed that our Government must have applied itself to the Canadian crisis; but the scanty knowledge which I had with regard to it gained no addition from this interview. An anonymous article, which appeared in the New York American on the resumption of specie payments, was discussed,

& attributed to John Duer,[4] whom the President pronounced to be an "exceedingly clever-headed man."—On the next day I called on J. Q. Adams, & sat with him sometime. He abused General Jackson & his administration most violently; but said that the present one had not shewn its character decidedly at present. He enquired of me about the Law School; on which I took occasion to speak of yr manner of lectures & also of Mr Greenleaf. I can assure you I lose no opportunity to bring forward my nurse in the law. Being in Baltimore on the next day (yesterday) I called with Mr Hoffman upon the Ch. Justice. He was not at home; but I went into his study, a raw ill-furnished apartment, with a paltry collection of books, which seem to be very seldom used—indeed, without any of the signs of the jurist about him. His library would have been an ordinary one for an humble Boston Attorney. In the evening I called & found him at home. He received me in a quiet way, & seemed slightly complimented by the visit. I remained about ten minutes, during which I spoke in a measured way, without any particular glow; for my awe for his station & his own quiet—I will hardly call it coldness—subdued me. He enquired after you. I mentioned, in a general way, the state of Mrs Story's health—her past illness, yr anxiety about her & her present convalescence. He hoped that her situation would not prevent yr attendance at Washington—he apparently spoke with great sincerity. He said that there were only 34 actions on the docket for the next term. He was in a great quandary about engaging rooms for the *nine* judges; & had about concluded to take rooms at Gadsby's at the rate of $26 a head—which, with corkage & judicial wine (if that has not lost its flavor since Marshall's death) will make something of a bill. The Ch. Justice was pleased to say that my labors were familiar to him, at which I felt much gratified.

I do not despair of hearing from you & Mrs Story's health before *Dec. 8th* at the *Astor House*, N.Y. The boat is in sight of Phila.

Ever Yrs C. S.

ALS DLC (65/339, PCS)

1. Mary Murray Ogden Hoffman, married David Hoffman, 1837.

2. John Forsyth (1780–1841), U.S. secretary of state, 1834–41. Levi Woodbury (1789–1851), U.S. secretary of the Treasury, 1834–41; U.S. senator (Dem., N.H.), 1841–45; U.S. Supreme Court justice, 1845–51. John M. Mumford, ed. *Merchant's Telegraph*, 1830s (William C. Bryant and Thomas G. Voss, *Letters of William Cullen Bryant*, vol. 1 [1975], 333).

3. A Canadian insurrection led by William L. Mackenzie against British authority was threatening Americans along the Canadian border in New York and Vermont.

4. John Duer (1782–1858), New York City Superior Court judge, 1849–58.

To George S. Hillard

Astor House Dec. 8th '37

My dear George,

It is now far past midnight, & I sail tomorrow forenoon. But I must devote a few moments to you. Yr three letters have all been received & have given me great pleasure. I have a fresh copy of Wordsworth, as my cabin companion, & I hope that I may be penetrated with his genius. Sea-sickness now stares me in ye face; & ye anxiety arising from ye responsibility of my course quite over-comes me. I have in my letters to several of my friends alluded particularly to my feelings, & also defended my plan of travel; but to you I need start no such idea. Yr mind goes with me; & yr heart jumps in step with my own.

I passed a pleasant day in Phila, where I dined with [*Richard*] Peters & supped with Ingersoll,[1] & met all ye first lawyers; then a delightful *homelike* day (such alas! as *home* has never been to me) in Burlington, where Sarah Perkins[2] received me with sisterly regard, I may almost say; & the whole family made my stay very pleasant. In New York I have been exceedingly busy, for ye day I have been there, in arranging my money affairs & writing letters of all sorts. I shall take with me about $150 in French gold; & a bill drawn by ye Bank of America on the Rotschilds for 4,000 francs; all that I have taken making about $1025, with my passage-money ($40) included; for this sum I have drawn on [*Samuel*] Lawrence. The residue of my funds in his hands I wish [*Henry R.*] Cleveland to use, if he desires, till. next spring, when I shall wish remittances to England. But I shall advise you of ye course to be pursued from Paris.

John O. Sargent[3] owes me $60 which he will send to you in the course of a few weeks. Keep yr eye upon it. You have doubtless received a list or memorandum of matters to be attended to by you. Keep yr eye upon that.

Keep yr courage up, my dear Hillard, have hope, & do not [bate?] a jot of heart. The way is clear before you & you will bowl along pleasantly & speedily. Be happy. Remember me affectionately to all my friends & to yr wife,[4] & believe me,

ever affctnly Yrs, Chas. Sumner

P.S. Unless qualms of sickness overcome me, I shall write you by ye pilot, after I have embarked; thus giving you [*a*] last hailing sign.

ALS MH-H (62/148, PCS)

1. Joseph R. Ingersoll (1786–1868), U.S. congressman (Whig, Pa.), 1835–37, 1841–49.
2. Sarah Perkins Cleveland (1818–93), married Henry Russell Cleveland (1808–43), Harvard A.B., 1827, and writer.
3. John O. Sargent (1811–91), Harvard classmate and Boston lawyer.
4. Susan Howe Hillard (1808–79).

To Joseph Story

Paris, Feb. 7th 1838—

My dear Judge,

It is now two months since I left the United States, &, when I consider what I have seen & the new impressions I have received, it seems like two years. And then the time is miserably lengthened by another consideration—the sense of my solitude & the cessation of intercourse with these friends to whom I am so tenderly attached. Give me letters; the olive branch in the lips of the dove was not more grateful to the second progenitor of our race, a cup of water not more inspiriting to the battle-worn soldier, than is a letter to me at this distance from friends. But I will not send things so dull as complaints on the long journey across the Ocean. In my last I told you of Foelix.[1] Do you wish to hear of a French dinner?—I mean of a dinner in a *family*. Any body may tell you of a dinner at a *table d'hote*, & its long procession of dishes, steaming hot, notwithstanding their number, or of a dinner at one of the brilliant *restaurateurs*, where every thing that can please the palate is served in the most exquisite style, or of a dinner with Americans resident in Paris, where, of course, more or less of the customs of our own country prevail; at any rate you cannot be sure of meeting *continental* customs. I will tell you of a thorough continental dinner, with Foelix, who, you know is a German by birth, so that I doubt not there was a German tinge to all the proceedings.—It was on Sunday. My invitation, received the day before, designated the hour as 5½ oclk, which is the every day dinner hour throughout Paris. I promptly accepted the invitation by a note, written in my best French; &, punctual at the time appointed, presented myself. The *salon* where I was received was furnished in a common French style, with rich curtains, chairs, & couches, but without a carpet—I should add, however, that carpets are invariable in the best houses of Paris, & that I attribute the absence of them at Foelix's to his German extraction. There was in the room, when I entered, one of my host's sisters & a Member of the Chamber of Deputies. Subsequently appeared a German, of some age, & of a great deal of information, as well as good manners, & two young men.[2] My host & his other sister also soon appeared. We talked, as we should in America, on some odds & ends of things, before going in to dinner. The Member, who proved to be man of a good deal of ability & character inquired of me with regard to de Tocqueville's book & also Chevalier's.[3] The latter I had not read. When dinner was announced, ignorant whether the custom of the Continent was to offer your arm to a lady in passing to the dinner-room, & being unwilling to commit myself, I lingered enough to allow both the ladies to be handed in by the Deputy & the German—as, indeed, was proper, considering my juniority. Arrived at the dinner-room, there was a round table; of course, without head or foot; with cards at each plate designating the seats of the several persons. Mine was between the two ladies, one of whom speaks a little English. The dishes were French—soup, first, of course; for a dinner in France without soup, would be like a man without a head; & then, a succession of common French dishes—tongue made tender instead of hard, as it always is with us, chicken, hare & a dessert of some little trifles; for the French never have puddings & would look with astonishment at our pies. Their dessert has in variety what it lacks in substance, preserves of different kinds & other contributions of the confectioner. The wines were all French or Corsican. They were all but little stronger than water, so that there was no danger of any undue excitement. Since I have been in France I have seen no other wine than the light wines of the country, except on one occasion Sherry at Mr {*George*} Ticknor's. These light wines are excessively cheap; much that is drunk not costing more than 12 or 20 sous a bottle. My host seemed to be too much of a philosopher to carve himself; & this duty appeared to be devolved upon his eldest sister by whose side I was placed. Of course, here was an occasion for my assistance; & you must imagine me most lustily discharging this duty, smoothly dissecting the tongue, tearing apart the chicken, &, as for the hare, (an animal whose bones & dimensions I was entirely ignorant of) mangling it in the most wolfish manner. While this last operation was going on Foelix called the attention of the company to my handy-work, by saying *voila un veritable artist!* I committed blunders, of course, & introduced, till I was corrected, the Americanism of supplying each guest myself from the dish, instead of sending the dish the circuit of the table, after it has been carved, & leaving each guest to select for himself. You may have some idea of the course of things at a French table from this sketch. No healths were drunk; & no persons took wine together. This, indeed, is exclusively an English & American custom, I believe. At table, after a while, the conversation turned upon America, & then my time came. I can assure you Monsieur le Deputé was as ignorant of my country as I was of his language, though he was curious about it. I was interrogated with regard to the present state of parties—the duration of Congress—the qualifications of electors—the relations of the states & the National Government—the character of our jurisprudence &, particularly with regard to the law of *alluvion*, the Deputy, having just introduced some provision on that subject into the Chamber. You may well imagine that I had text enough for my dis-course; &, then, my French, it was the most amusing hodge-podge & gibberish ever heard, presenting in every sentence a violation of every rule of grammar. However, it served the main purpose of language, the conveyance of thought. As benighted as the Deputy appeared to be with regard to our country, he yet appeared to have a glimmering knowledge of you. All left the table at once—gentlemen & ladies—& adjourned to the *salon*, where coffee was served, being the only poor coffee I have seen in France; this I attribute to the German extraction of the family. The French seem to have a sort of natural talent for making coffee. The *salon* proving cold, we, in the most informal manner, adjourned to the study or office of Foelix, which was on the same floor, where we talked & heard German airs on the guitar. After several songs the guitar was handed to me for a song! In the study, after some time, tea was brought in—I believe it was not a [decoction?] of the Chinese plant, but of some French one. Here the ladies interrogated me with regard to the state of society in my country; & I astonished them by talking of Lyceums & evening lectures, [&] learned ladies; & you must understand that I was addressing a lady who had read the French code. I left about 11 o'clock; & so much for a French dinner. I have written this long scrawl, because I thought it might interest you & Mrs Story. The French, you know, rarely give dinners; indeed, Mr Ticknor, who has been in Paris six months, & who has circulated, I believe, more freely in the highest circles than any other American traveller, perhaps even minister, told me that he had never dined at the table of a Frenchman. Mr Ticknor is engaged, literally, *all the time* in society. He passes from one palace to another; & in one evening often attends several *soirées*. And yet he is attached to Boston & is anxious to return. This he will do at the close of the summer. Remember me affectionately to yr family, & believe me as ever

most affectionately yours, Chas. Sumner

Mr F. Gray[4] is at Paris. We are all very anxious about the relations between our country & Grt. Britain. The news has just come of the *Caroline* affair.[5]

ALS MHi (TTR, 65/375, PCS)

1. 21 January [1838], 65/367, PCS.

2. In his journal, CS confided that he was unable to catch the name of either the Chamber of Deputies member or the German, the latter whom he met again on 14 February (Prc, 1:243, 251).

3. Part 1 of *Democracy in America* by Alexis de Tocqueville (1805–59) had been published in both French and the Reeve translation in 1835. Michel Chevalier's (1806–79) *Lettres sur l'Amérique du nord* was published in 1836.

4. Francis C. Gray (1790–1856), Boston writer and prison reform activist.

5. In their rebellion against British authority, Canadians, led by William L. Mackenzie, had used a U.S. ship, the *Caroline*, to transport supplies from the U.S. to Canada. On 29 December 1837 British representatives boarded the ship, killed an American, and destroyed the *Caroline*.

To George S. Hillard

Paris March 8th 1838—

My dear Hillard,

I feel astonished when I think that a month has passed since I have written you; & yr two letters have been running through my mind every day. A twig of olive was not richer to old Noah at the close of his watery pilgrimage. How I long for news of distant Boston, & how I picture all its clean streets, its sensible people & my dear friends. Stands my office where it did & all Court Street, is it still firm on its foundations? State St, if I may believe the reports, which, perhaps, have been magnified by the distance, has been rocking to its centre.[1] I trust, however, Boston will come out of its trials sound; though, at this distance, it does not sustain to the eye a very creditable position. Prescott's book, however, relieves the commercial discredit, & I rejoice to hear from various quarters of its reception in our country.[2] I have seen a copy, & glanced through it. By the way, the American edition is every whit as well printed as the English, & has some plates more appropriate than those prefixed to the English. The book reads beautifully, & I am glad that we have produced a work with so much of research, learning, suavity & elegance. A few days since, at dinner at the Baron Degerando's,[3] I met the *Procureur Général* of Spain. I was full of Prescott's book, & I took the occasion to endeavor to scatter some seed on Spanish ground. I described the work & the labors of Mr Prescott to the Spaniard, who appeared particularly interested & inquired the name of the author. He was quite astonished when I told him that he had drawn from unpublished manuscripts & documents. Ticknor has placed a copy of the book in the hands of one or two French *litterateurs* who have promised to review it in some of the French Journals. Ticknor leaves for London, in a few days. I am sorry to lose him & his family. You will gain them soon in Boston; & I believe you will bear me out in the voucher that they are *Americans*. Mrs Ticknor will carry home some of the most beautiful scraps of pencil sketches by some of the Italian artists, & even one *super-delicious* production of Retsch,[4] all in his own divine pencilling, that have ever been seen in America; also a collection of drawings of the productions of Raphael, which will give a better idea of that artist than any thing that has yet reached our country. You have a treat before you, particularly in that little rich, minutely finished pencilling of Retsch, which is as mellow & as expressive as the finest colouring. It seems as if you could bathe in it.

You have written about the article on Cooper in the Quarterly. It was a savage cautery, written, I am told, by Croker; not by Lockhart, as some of our Journals have thought.[5] Among my acquaintances in Paris is Mr O'Donnell an Englishman and Tory, who like 20,000 of his country men, lives in Paris, because it is cheaper than mammoth London. I had a letter to him from Baltimore; &, being an Englishman, he dined me. We talked of tories, toryism, & tory writers. It seems that O'Donnell is one of the principe writers in Blackwood, having an article every month, &, of course, could tell much that was interesting in the machinery of that Journal. He says that Wilson the editor never reads the article of one of the regular corps.[6] For instance, my friend always sends his article directly to the publisher. A new correspondent's article is examined by the editor & is either adopted or rejected *in toto*; there is no alteration. O'Donnell told me that Croker wrote the article on Cooper, & he appeared to relish it very well. Have I told you about Cass?[7] Certainly I have. But I have commenced a gadding letter & so I will e'en continue in the same mood. He has given two or three semi-diplomatic dinners, with great splendor, for he has one of the handsomest hotels in Paris, & superb table furniture. At one of them I was present. At another Mr Ticknor was. The Count Dapurey[8] & the Pope's Nuncio were there with Mr Ticknor, neither of whom spoke a word of English; whether Mr Cass spoke more French will be developped. In the course of the dinner Mr Cass, addressing the Count Dapurey, said, *M. Ticknor savoir parler Francais et Allemagne also*. Have I not told you this story before? I fear I have & that I repeat myself.

Since I wrote you last I have again changed my lodgings & am now in the *Place des Italiens*, very near the Boulevart of the same name, & Tortoni's[.] If you wish to taste Tortoni's best ice, which is Vanilla, go to Mad. Nichol's in Cambridge St. Her Vanilla is a duplicate of Tortoni's. I should not know them apart, with my eyes closed. I have attended 50 or 60 lectures at the Sorbonne & the School of Law, & have met some of the Professors of Law. As soon as I get my French talking tackle in better order I hope to profit more by the introductions which I have had. None of the French professors of law are remarkable, though all of them, I believe, are more or less of authors. I amused one immensely by telling him of our blue laws in Connecticut; it was Bravard,[9] whose works you have heard of. Write me about the Jurist; & all other things.—

Believe every thing you hear of the immorality & total depravity of Paris. It is a perfect Sodom; without religion & without any morality between the sexes. I never understood it till I reached Paris. I used to hear Cleveland talk it; but you must actually be here, to understand it—I shall stay in Paris till the middle of April. I find ten times as much here to interest me as I anticipated. The lectures, the Courts, the arts, each would consume a year, to say nothing of the language which I am trying after very hard. I have funds enough to be in funds for *two months* or more after my arrival in London. I wish some remittance, say one or two hundred pounds to *reach* me at the end of May; & before I leave England I shall wish to have either a remittance or a letter of credit for all the funds of which you have on account left by me.—Love to all.

As ever affctnly Yrs,   Chas. Sumner

I have recd 2 letters from you; one from Greenleaf for which I shall especially thank him, & another from Lieber, Dr Palfrey &c—

ALS MH-H (62/164, PCS)

1. In the Panic of 1837, numerous U.S. banks suspended specie payments.

2. William Hickling Prescott's *Ferdinand and Isabella* was published in the U.S. in December 1837, in England, January 1838.

3. Baron Joseph Marie de Gérando (1772–1842), French philosopher.

4. Moritz Retzsch (1779–1857), German illustrator.

5. The review of James Fenimore Cooper's *England, with Sketches of Society in the Metropolis* (*Quarterly Review* 59 [October 1837]: 327–61) stated, "we never met such a phenomenon of vanity, folly, and fable, as this book exhibits" (327). John Gibson Lockhart (1794–1854), biographer of Sir Walter Scott and literary critic. John Wilson Croker (1780–1857), a Tory politician and frequent contributor to the *Quarterly Review*.

6. O'Donnell (b. c. 1798), British writer, then living in Paris (Prc, 1: 248). John Wilson (1785–1854).

7. Lewis Cass (1782–1866), U.S. minister to France, 1836–42; U.S. senator (Dem., Mich.), 1845–48, 1849–57; U.S. secretary of state, 1857–60.

8. Possibly Louis I. Duperry (1786–1865), naval officer and scientist.

9. Pierre Claude Jean Baptiste Bravard-Veyrières (1804–61), law professor and member of the Legislative Assembly.

To Henry Russell Cleveland

Paris April 14th 1838

My dear Hal,

I hasten to take back what I wrote in my last letter. Yrs of Feb. 18th came to hand yesterday, & with it the information that there was yet another for me at Hottinguer's. Be assured I lost no time in getting it, & in devouring its contents. There it has been *perdue* in the drawer of Hottinguer for two months, & I have been anxiously raising daily questions with regard to yr unaccountable silence. I read it with as much interest as if it were fresher, for it was full of feeling & friendship & these are always fresh.—You have my congratulations, & has yr happy wife—I need not repeat them again—they are always understood.[1] Many a time in this full city, communing with myself, have I summoned before my mind, the whole scene which you have described—not only the happy attendants at the altar, but the impertinent gaping crowd which environed it, & converted what was a private solemnity into a public show. *Eh bien! N'importe.* Let them look on, & gape & publish silly articles.—

Did you ever attend the *Reunion des Nations*, a society at Paris, of which old Jullien,[2] the private secretary of Robespierre, is Presdt. I have been invited twice; once I attended—there were the American & Greek ambassadors & many *savans*, amounting in all to upwards of 100; & a poor dinner & bad Champagne. Not withstanding the Presdt in a long speech, told them that on that occasion they were honored by the presence of Mr Sumner—*un de plus celebres jurisconsults et savans des Etats Unis*, & made my *eloge* at as great length as a Yankee epitaph. They expected a speech in reply, & had the grace to give a round of applause when the Presdt was fully delivered of his monster. But I was determined to be guilty, neither of the absurdity of making a speech in *English* to a *French* audience, nor yet of making one in *French* to a *French* audience. So I blushed, & held my tongue; while *savans* cried out—*c'est bien cela*, as M. le Presdt ceased speaking.—You have been kind enough to send me an illustration of the folly on your side of the water; I think that I have returned the gift. The French language is the language of compliment & eulogy; & I can assure you these words of the Presdt did not lack the superlatives which come so readily to a Frenchman's tongue. I give you leave to laugh in a friendly way at this scene. Imagine me at a great table, with a Spaniard, a Deputy of the Cortez & *Membre de l'Institut of France* on one side, & a *medecin* from Switzerland on the other, each of them anxiously giving their cards to the distinguished American whom they found near them, & you will have a *scene*, at which I will give you leave to laugh at, with yr loudest laugh. Would that I could hear that laugh, & echoe it back!—*Quam parâ sapientia regitur mundus.*[3]

A few days since I was presented to Madame Murat,[4] the sister of Napoleon, widow of Murat (the prince of cavalry) & ex-queen of Naples. They address her as *Madame la reine*. She recd me in her bed-chamber. Indeed, you know that the bed-chamber is one of the handsomest rooms of a French establishment. There were two or three young ladies—*Mademoiselles*—rendering their homage to Madam. Madam, among other things, asked if I was *married—etes vous seul*. I had to content myself with a very short answer, different from, & less honorable than, that, which you would have rendered. On my return, perhaps I shall vindicate myself; but I doubt & feel more & more every day, that I am to live a *bachelor*. By accident, I have touched upon one of our old [notes;?] I will not prolong its sound.

I have seen much of the Ticknors, while in Paris. They are now in London. I recd yesterday a letter from Ticknor,[5] in which he writes me that he leaves London for Scotland *today*. They will return home by August, & will be glad to see you & Sarah; they will have a large store of delicious things in the way of paintings, sketches & the like. You will find weeks of luxury in seeing their importations. The Warrens have just arrived from Italy—Emily looks prettier—much *prettier* than I ever saw her in Boston. She has acquired a beautiful colour in the cheeks. The Cabots[6] have also just arrived, & all will spend six weeks here previous to going to London. I met Mrs Cabot under the arches of the Rue Rivoli, with that daughter of hers, & have been *very polite* to her—I always take my hat entirely off *à la Française* when I see them.

Ralph Emerson[7] has removed to Paris. His wife is very anxious to hear from you. Mr [Cames?], whom you must have known, has been obliged to flee the country at *half an hour's* notice, to save himself from the *galleys*. He had forged or imitated a *stamp* on certain goods which he had sent to America—an offence which is visited very severely here. Good bye. You will next hear from me in London. With love to yr wife—

as ever affctnly Yrs, Chas. Sumner

ALS NNCB (65/409, PCS)

1. In his letter of 18 February 1838 (65/378, PCS) Cleveland described his wedding to Sarah Perkins on 1 February.

2. Marc-Antoine Jullien de Paris (1775–1848), military administrator under Napoleon.

3. "Since the world is ruled by pure wisdom."
4. Caroline Bonaparte (1782–1839), widow of Joachim Murat, King of Naples, 1808–15.
5. 10 April (1/393).
6. American visitors were John Collins Warren (1778–1856), Boston surgeon and professor of medicine, Harvard, and family, and Henry Cabot (1783–1864) and family, including his daughter, Anna Cabot Lodge (1821–1900).
7. American merchant formerly living in Le Havre (Prc, 1:218).

To Sarah Perkins Cleveland

Combe Florey August 6th 1838
Somersetshire

The last time I had the pleasure of seeing you, my dear Sarah, was at St Mary's Parsonage under the hospitable roof of yr mother.[1] If I could ever forget yr kindness then, I could not now, when I find myself again within the protecting walls of a parsonage. I am now staying, with one of the most remarkable men of England, in one of the most beautiful spots of this delicious country. I am the guest of Sidney Smith[2] at his sweet seat in the very garden of England. Truly, I was never before in so sweet a spot, with a trim garden about me, a neat & well-filled conservatory, a closely wooded park & an open lawn stretching behind. This is a little Eden. The House has all the comforts of ye city in the quiet seclusion of the country. There is the Library, where I sat a good portion of yesterday (Sunday) with my distinguished host, listening to his merry tones; & the drawing-room & dining-room, with all the elegancies & comforts of the most luxuriously furnished Town house, &, then, chambers without number, in one of which I am installed. The pen, ink & paper, which I find on my table, have seduced me into writing you this note, & I feel persuaded that it will not be the less acceptable, because it is written in this sylvan retreat & under the roof of one of the great writers of the age. Alas, that I cannot carry away some of the genius & attainment of my host! But the village itself is beautiful; all are common laborers, living in humble cottages, overshadowed by trees & surrounded by a towering hedge; & then, the Church, over which Centuries have passed, looks through its surrounding grove, & discloses its brown walls, & its tasteful arches. As the clergyman walks along, all bow on courtesy, & if they address him, it is always by the title of "*Your Honor*." He drove me, two in hand, through the park of his neighbor Sir Thomas Lethbridge;[3] &, then, for the first time did I see the Squire chasing the deer. There was Sir Thomas himself, on a mettlesome hunter, & attended by his huntsmen pursuing the deer through his own park, in order to select a fat buck for the day's repast. The luxury, comfort & splendor of an English country seat you cannot conceive. Nothing that I have ever seen in any part of America can serve as a model. Consider that very often the house stands one, two, three or four miles from the road, & all the way you pass through a beautiful park, entirely the property of the lordly resident. *One* of the porter's lodges belonging to the Marquis of Westminster, cost upwards of $50,000. But I have strayed from my parsonage, which is of itself a gem. We dined at 7 o'clock, &, if I had sat down to a London feast I could not have fared better, & all the company was myself. Mr Smith & his wife & myself composed the table. It sounded odd to hear Mrs Smith, herself a most agreeable woman, calling her husband a man of 67, "Sydney." I should like to send you the good things he uttered, but I find it difficult to catch & detain the "winged words" which came out in the warmth & confidence of social intercourse.

In yr most agreeable letter of May last, which I found as a welcome on my arrival in London, & for which I cannot sufficiently thank you (I first read it in an omnibus, while the great historian Hallam was sitting opposite me) you ask for a sketch of Lockhart. He has been out of town, nearly all the time I have been in London. I may meet him in Scotland; if I do, I shall not fail to communicate to you my impressions of him. I know many of his friends, & I hear him spoken of constantly as an unamiable man. But [*George*] Ticknor can tell you all about him. As you have the Ticknors at home now, it will almost supersede my writing. They have seen society in its various shapes, & may be to you a living fountain of interesting conversation. I doubt not you will find in Mrs Ticknor an admirable friend. She is a fine-souled creature, & at once abounds in heart & accomplishment, both of which I hold to be necessary in woman. I met at a great party at Lady Lansdowne's[4] the greatest heiress of the world, Miss Burdett Coutts,[5] who is reported to have about *seventy five millions* of our money. I think it will be difficult for all her fortune to purchase a decent husband. Shall I say that she had a red nose, a most unhealthy countenance, & a face devoid of expression? —Forty times her fortune wouldn't tempt me unless she would consent to live in one hemisphere, & let me be happy in the other. Pardon this *badanage*, which however contains a truth, & believe me, with no common love to Henry,

as ever most affectionately Yrs, Charles Sumner

I am now on my way North to visit Scotland, & Ld Brougham[6] at Brougham Hall. His Lordship has invited me to his country seat & given me letters of introduction to his friends.

Aug. 12th. I send this letter at Liverpool, & shall direct it to Burlington, as Henry's letter of July 1st says you will be there in Sept. Remember me to yr mother & the Bishop & the boys,[7] who, doubtless, have forgotten me by this time.

ALS NNCB (65/478, PCS)

1. Eliza Perkins Doane, married to George Washington Doane (1799–1859), Episcopal bishop of New Jersey.

2. Sydney Smith (1771–1845), British journalist and rector of Combe-Florey, and his wife, Catherine.

3. Probably the father of Thomas Prowse Lethbridge, who succeeded Smith at Combe-Florey.

4. Louisa Emma Fox-Strangeways, married, 1808, Henry Petty-Fitzmaurice Lansdowne, third marquis (1780–1863), lord president of council, 1830–41, 1846–52.

5. Angela Georgina Burdett-Coutts (1814–1906), British philanthropist and daughter of Sophia and Francis Burdett.

6. Henry Peter Brougham, baron Brougham and Vaux (1778–1868), British reformer and M.P.

7. Cleveland's letter, 1 July 1838 (1/493, PCS). Sarah Cleveland's brothers, Edward N. Perkins (1820–99) and Charles C. Perkins (1823–86), later, art critic.

To Sarah Perkins Cleveland

Edinburgh—Sept. 17th 1838

You have asked me, my dear Sarah, to tell you about Lockhart, if I should chance to meet him. You may suppose that the death of his wife[1] would keep him out of general society in London, & this is true, so that, though I once met him with Millman,[2] yet I never saw him in company, & he is not a man whose acquaintance I should seek in any way. I have, however, met him this evening (& have just parted with him) under the very circumstances which I would have chosen. It was at Lady Gifford's,[3] the dowager of the late distinguished peer of that name. There was nobody at dinner but Lockhart, another gentleman & myself, forming, with her Ladyship a company of *four*, & I did not know that I was to meet Lockhart till one minute before dinner was announced. He is rather tall, but well-made, with a countenance rather thin & sharp, but fresh & fair; in these last respects not unlike Stackpole's. His hair, which must have been a rich black, begins to be sown with grey, so indeed as to give it quite a grisly appearance. His manner is awkward & constrained; neither is it cordial frank or energetic. It is, however, simple & full of repose. I should agree with all the world in calling him cold, & his repose is that of a man who makes no exertion & shews no interest in what is passing. If I may judge from what I have heard others say—I mean Englishmen & Scotchmen, his own friends—I should think he conversed with more freedom to-day than usually. In conversation he shews no readiness or tact—perhaps, I should say, he shews a decided want of them. He first spoke with animation when abusing some person, whose name had been mentioned. Speaking of a common friend of ours—& I may say a dear one of mine—a member of Parliament he said he was too much of a gentleman to be a Radical; I was not a little amused at his attempt to vindicate Capt. Hall[4] for his most unjustifiable book on his visit to the Countess in Hungary (I have forgotten her name) in which are detailed the occurrences of a private family. He acknowledged that it was wrong, but he said that Hall was not like other men —that he did not know that it was so. Think of this from the author of the savage article on Willis in the London Quarterly—.[5] Lockhart said that all persons who kept journals should be excluded from society. In the course of a long evening we discussed a variety of things, the proper scite for the great monument to [*Walter*] Scott, London society, mutual acquaintances &c—under this last head Mr Ticknor was mentioned in most gratifying terms.—I left him without regret, & with little desire ever to meet him again, though his conduct towards me personally was sufficiently gracious.—

Only yesterday I dined with an old friend of Scott's[6] & in company with the clergyman who christened his children. The latter told me that he had met Lockhart frequently at Scott's house, & once sat opposite him at table, but that Lockhart never addressed a word to him. Since I have been in Scotland I have found myself among the old friends of Scott, & I have heard but one opinion expressed with regard to the *injudiciousness* of Lockhart's biography. Sir David Brewster expressed himself very strongly on this point.—Think of two days that I passed with this amiable & distinguished man at Melrose, with the silver Tweed, the venerable abbey & the Eildon Hills in sight from my bedroom window, besides the greater portion of the woods planted by Scott's hands. Here I met that staunch friend of Scott's, whose name will be most familiar to you, Sir Adam Fergusson,[7] a hearty jolly old man. Lady Brewster[8] assured me that the reports were not true, that Lockhart was cold or harsh to his wife. Mrs L. once said to her, in a laughing way—"you know they say my husband beats me."—

I have written this dull account with a villainous steel pen, that refuses to shed ink, & am now most entirely out of patience. I hope yours (which is a woman's full portion) will hold out better than mine.—

I have met in Edinburgh my most delightful friend Lady Stratheden[9]—the most pleasing woman, perhaps, that I ever encountered. Tomorrow I dine with Lord Jeffrey at Craigcrook Castle. On leaving Edinburgh I am to visit the Lord Advocate[10] at his seat in the Highlands.—My love to Henry.

As ever affctnly Yrs, C. S.

You doubtless have heard that Lockhart is *engaged* to a Miss Alexander, an old friend of his wife.—Enclosed are autographs of Scott & of the Duke of Hamilton, the latter the premier Duke of Scotland.[11]

ALS NNCB (65/505, PCS)

1. Sophia Scott Lockhart (d. 1837), daughter of Sir Walter Scott, married Lockhart in 1820.
2. Henry Hart Milman (1791–1868), English clergyman and poet.
3. Harriet Maria Drewe Gifford (d. 1857), wife of Robert Gifford, first baron, British attorney-general.
4. Basil Hall (1788–1844), navy captain and travel writer, author of *Schloss Hainfield, or a Winter in Lower Styria* (1836).
5. Lockhart's unsigned review (*London Quarterly Review* 54 [September 1835]:445–69) of *Pencillings by the Way* by the New York journalist and novelist Nathaniel Parker Willis (1806–67) concluded that Willis's book "is the first example of a man creeping into your home, and forthwith printing—accurately or inaccurately, no matter which—before your claret is dry on his lips—unrestrained *table-talk on delicate subjects, and capable of compromising individuals*."
6. Probably Sir John Robison (1778–1843), inventor; founder and president, Scottish Society of Arts.
7. Sir Adam Fergusson (1771–1855), British army captain and keeper of Scottish regalia.
8. Juliet Macpherson Brewster (d. 1850), married David Brewster in 1810.
9. Lady Stratheden, Mary Elizabeth Campbell (1796–1860), married in 1821 John Campbell, M.P. for Edinburgh and attorney general.
10. Francis Jeffrey (1773–1850), Scottish M.P. (Whig), editor, *Edinburgh Review*. John A. Murray (1779–1859), Scottish judge and M.P.
11. Alexander Hamilton Douglas, tenth duke of Hamilton (1767–1852), Scottish M.P.

To William Wetmore Story

Wortley Hall Oct. 21st - 1838
Yorkshire

My dear William,

I received your kind letter of August last evening. Strange to say it bears the post-mark of Marseilles, &, evidently, from the time it has been on its passage, has been beating about the world. If, like wine, it had not derived an additional flavor from these travels, it had certainly risen to a higher cost. Its postage was more than *a dollar & a quarter*. However, it was worth *four times* that. There are two things I never scruple about—*postage* & *good paper*. The difference between a small & a large postage bill, & between using good & bad paper is very small; whereas the comfort & pleasure from *both* are incalculable. Try if you can't fix me with a *two dollar postage* next time. I will make some future client settle it; so, do not be afraid.—

You have expressed a capital sentiment in your letter, which I am glad has crossed your mind—You say to me—"You must have found, or I am a very stupid observer, that the little concerns of home are still interesting for the heart, & that the province of the affections is one, wherein the intellect never intrudes."—Well said, my boy. Amidst all that I have seen & enjoyed in this glorious country I think of home & the friends of my bosom; even now, in one of the proud halls of Old England, I am trimming my midnight lamp, in order to send these hasty lines to my young friend who is far away. I am now the guest of Lord Wharncliffe[1]—your father will tell you all about him—the descendant at once of Lady Mary Wortley Montagu & of Lord Bute.[2] The hall & spacious staircase & apartments are adorned with portraits by Godfrey Kneller,[3] & Sir Joshua Reynolds. As I have surveyed these I thought of you. I wish that you could have a view of them. And you will, if you work, study, think & prepare yourself. Banish from your thoughts or even desires the coming to Europe at present. Consider yr youth, inexperience, your unfinished education, your unformed character, yr undetermined position before the world, & say that you will wait for some of the gravity & experience of maturer years, & for the full development of your character & the determination of yr position. *Be unwilling to go abroad at present.* I assure you, though I had the strongest desire to travel, when I was of yr age, yet so well was I convinced of its utter unproductiveness at that period, that I would have declined going abroad, if I could have gone for nothing. I then wished to wait till I was a man; till I had so studied & labored that my friends at home could conscientiously recommend me. The result has been beyond my most sanguine expectations. I have been received—not as a boy, not as a young man—but as a person of established position. Now, I need not say to you, how sensibly I feel all this kindness, & also how I am oppressed by the sentiment of my own unworthiness which rises & greets me at every step. Now, my dear William, I wish you to visit Europe—in the fullness of time; but not until time has ripened your character & given you such a position that you will be able to make your way in Europe. I cannot conceive of anything more disheartening than to travel in a country—particularly one like England—& not enter its society or know its glorious country establishments, except by paying half a crown to the house-keeper to shew you round. And yet are shoals of our countrymen who come abroad, scamper round this beautiful country, are shewn some of the country seats, survey a lord at a most respectful distance—& then return, having completed their travels, & are, forsooth, lionized in our society as *travelled men*! Do not, my dear boy, get your honorable name into this list. Study, then; make yourself master of your profession; get yourself fairly embarked in it; keep yourself a bachelor; & then for Europe! Perhaps, at that time, I may be able to contribute to your facilities abroad in the various ways derived from my experience & already most extensive acquaintance. I shall pass a few days here; & then go to the magnificent seat of Earl Fitzwilliam; from there I go to the Earl Leicester at Holkham.[4] In both of these places are some of the finest pictures in England

The vignette, with which this sheet is enriched, is (half of it) Dryburgh Abby—the burial place of Sir Walter Scott. I visited this with Sir David Brewster & mused with melancholy, as I beheld the arch under which repose the remains of that mighty spirit.—

When you write, acknowledge the receipt always of my previous letters, mentioning the date. Tell yr father to do the same.

As ever affectionately, Yours, Chas. Sumner

ALS TxU (65/520, PCS)

1. James A. Stuart-Wortley Mackenzie, first Baron Wharncliffe (1776–1845), British M.P.

2. Lady Mary Wortley Montagu (1689–1762), British writer. John Stuart Bute, third earl (1713–92), British statesman.

3. Godfrey Kneller (1646–1723), anglicized German painter.

4. Charles William Wentworth Fitzwilliam, third earl (1786–1857), British M.P. (Liberal). Thomas William Coke of Holkam, first earl of Leicester (1752–1842), British M.P. (Reform).

To Lord Brougham

2 Vigo St—Regent St.
Nov. 15th 1838

My dear Lord,

I trouble your Lordship with these lines to assure you of my gratitude for your hospitable reception of me at Brougham Hall this Autumn.

This assurance may be entirely unimportant to yr Lordship, but it a gratification to me to tender it, as I now do, with sincerity & respect.

When at Brougham Hall, I heard yr Lordship express an interest in the speeches of Lord Chatham[1] & the manner in which they had been reported. It did not occur to me at that time to mention that we have in America a report of his celebrated speech on American affairs, made, I think, Jan. 20th 1775, which has, probably, never reached England; perhaps, it has not met your Lordships's eyes. Mr Josiah Quincy Jr,[2] a lawyer, & an ardent eloquent man himself, who had taken a leading interest in affairs in Massachusetts was sent to England by that Province in 1774 as its agent. He was in the House of Lords the night of Lord Chatham's speech, & took notes of it, which he wrote out & sent home. These have since been published, in a memoir of Mr Quincy, by his son.[3] It is quite clear that they have not received any correction from Lord Chatham, & they have a freshness about them, which seems, like a record, "to import verity." It may not be uninteresting to yr Lordship to be aware of the existence of this Transatlantic report of one of the greatest speeches ever made in the British Parliament.

Allow me to repeat the assurance of my gratitude for yr Lordship's kindness, & believe me, with the highest consideration,

very faithfully yr Lordship's, Charles Sumner
of U.S. of America

The Right Honorable Lord Brougham &c

ALS GBUCL (65/537, PCS)

1. William Pitt the Elder, first earl of Chatham (1708–78), British statesman, spoke on withdrawing British troops from American colonies.

2. Josiah Quincy, Jr. (1744–75), father of Harvard president Josiah Quincy, and Boston lawyer, who was sent to England in 1774 to represent the American colonies' position.

3. *Memoir of the Life of Josiah Quincy, Jun., of Massachusetts* (1825).

To Charles Stewart Daveis

Holkham House—Nov. 2nd [*and 6 December*] 1838

My dear friend,

Since I last wrote you I have seen Lord Jeffrey & Lord Fitzwilliam, & from both had enquiries about you;—how much pleasure it gave me to answer them I need not say. Lord Fitzw. had received the copy of the Annual Register, containing yr. obituary notice of his Father,[1] the late

Earl; he said there was one mistake in that, which should be corrected in justice to another person. You have given Lord Fitzw. the credit of first introducing Sir James Mackintosh into Parliament. It belongs to the late Duke of Devonshire, for one of whose boroughs he first sat.[2] I passed three days at Wentworth House & was kindly invited by his Lordship to remain longer & to visit him again at his other seat, *Milton*. You will be pleased to hear that the Ticknors have made a most agreeable impression upon all the family. Miss Anna is regarded as something little short of a prodigy—a clever girl she certainly is &, as an Englishman would say, a very *nice* one—. Lady Mary Thompson, one of the elder daughters, said that she wished her young sister *Lady* Dorothy were as clever as Miss Anna. The young Lord Milton has just married the Lady Frances Douglas,[3] the daughter of the Earl Morton, who resembles Anna Ticknor very much—so much so that I could hardly believe that my young friend was not returned to wear an English coronet. I am now staying with Lord Leicester at his most delightful place, where you find every thing to interest & charm the choicest productions of the pencil & of the chisel,—&, above all these, the most valued society. Here are Lord Spencer & lord Ebrington, & Edward Ellice,[4] come down to enjoy their partridge shooting. And since I have touched upon the Ticknors, & I know you take such interest in them, I must tell you that Lord Spencer speaks of Ticknor in the warmest terms, & broke out in the praise of Miss Anna in language that you would have hardly have expected from a whilolm Chancellor of the Exchequer & peer of England. I doubt not these little things will please your daughter, of whom I have heard as at school in Boston. Lord Spencer said that Miss Anna was one of the cleverest & best informed young ladies he ever knew. A description of the mode of life in an English country-house, where you find more of the appliances of the most refined luxury even than in Armida's Garden under the warm touches of Tasso, would hardly interest you; &, besides, you may have them from the living lips of your friends now returned home. I will now stop my galloping pen, & close this letter in London, whither I go this afternoon, in order to sit out the Michaelmas Term in Westminster Hall. I shall be much disappointed, if I do not find a generous epistle from you awaiting my return. But I fear that you have forgotten me.

London Dec. 6th 1838

This sheet has been in my port-folio, awaiting letters missive from you; but it is as I augured, I am out of yr books. You are not, however, out of mine; & so I will e'en blot it with a few more words. Since my return to town I have been in a constant round of society, literary or legal—judges, lawyers, politicians, writers or authors—not a day that has not brought its plural invitations. I wish I could take ye wings of ye morning & speed across the sea, to talk my English budget; for it will fade from my mind in ye oblivious depths of Germany, whither I go from here. But I begin to think of home & my profession now. Tell me, as my friend what are my chances at home. Will it be said that I have forgotten that law, which some have before given me ye credit of knowing—that I am spoiled for practice & for this work-a-day world. True I should be glad to be able to hold constant communion with ye various gifted minds that I nightly meet—to listen daily to the argts of Talfourd & Follett,[5] & so, indeed should I rejoice in more ennobling society still to walk with Cicero over Elysian fields & listen to the converse of Plato & Socrates. But I well know that neither the one nor the other is given to me, & that I have duties to perform, which will be anything but such as this. Welcome, then, labor in its appointed time!

If you write me immediately on ye receipt of this, I shall get yr letter before I leave England. Do not fail to tell me ye *exact* position and prospects of ye Boundary question,[6] for I am often interrogated about it, & I should be glad to be so instructed as to answer questions.

Judge Story's name is spreading daily here, & is doing much to extend ye knowledge of our jurisprudence. This is a matter which I have near at heart, & I hope that ye conversations I have had with some of ye most eminent members of ye bar & bench will not be without its influence.

Croyez moi, affectueusement,

Tout à vous, Charles Sumner

ALS NNCB (65/550, PCS)

1. The notice of William Wentworth Fitzwilliam, second earl of Fitzwilliam, (1748–1833), British statesman, was published in the *Annual Register for the Year 1833*, appendix to chronicle, 205–7.

2. William Cavendish (1748–1811), fifth duke of Devonshire.

3. Anna Ticknor (1823–96). William Thomas Wentworth (1815–1902), British M.P., married Frances Douglas (1819–75), September 1838.

4. John C. Spencer, third earl (1782–1845), British M.P. (Whig). Hugh Ebrington, second earl of Fortescue (1783–1861), British M.P. Edward Ellice (1781–1863), British M.P., deputy-governor, Hudson's Bay Company.

5. Thomas Talfourd (1795–1854), British judge and writer. William Webb Follett (1798–1845), British solicitor-general, 1834–35, 1841; attorney general, 1844.

6. Great Britain and the U.S. were disputing the boundary between New Brunswick and Maine. The state of Maine had granted land to Americans along the Aroostook River; during the winter of 1838–39, Canadians also claimed it.

To Henry W. Longfellow

Athenaeum Club, Jan. 24th '39

My dear Longfellow—

"Is not this good!—Charly will come home & marry one of the daughters"!—No such thing. Do not disturb yr imagination by supposing that I have any design, wish or intention in that quarter—although, I know full well, that nothing but the distempered jealousy of a lover would do me the credit of supposing that all my designs, wishes or intentions could be of any avail, particularly against yr march. The way is now clear to you—march on—you have a friend in the camp—why not honestly make her a *confidante*. I need not tell you that Harriet S.[1] is a fast friend of yours, & I doubt not, she would be too happy to serve any of yr wishes in her new house. I found yr letter on my arrival in town from Milton Park. I wrote you from that place; but my letter, with the wreck of those proud packet-ships, has been probably lost on the sounding sea-shore. If it reaches you, it will doubtless wear the tincture of the sea. I rejoice in this unexpected flash of light upon a darksome house. It must have come as upon a journey to Tarsus.[2] And I dare say the people of Boston have been busy with this subject ever since. One who mingles in the broad society of London & Paris must be reminded, by sad contrast, of the narrow impertinence that characterizes our town, where the colour of a gentleman's coat, & the habit of his shirt-collar or cravat are cardinal topics of criticism. It is true—that which we have often been told—that there is more liberty of action, conduct & opinion abroad, than with us. Society here is not so censorious as in America; I cannot but confess however, that this trait of our character brings with it some attendant good; it preserves society very much from the taint of impurity; but it lowers it by making it a petty prying observer. A friend invited me to breakfast with him last Sunday at Lincoln's Inn, & asked some pleasant men, & gave us a sumptuous French *dejeuner*. One said to me—"Should you dare to give us such a breakfast at this hour on Sunday in Boston?"—"No," of course I replied. Is there such a thing as a French *dejeuner* of a Sunday in the Annals of the town, beginning with the first refreshment snatched by the hardy settler?—And yet I will not disparage my home. There is much in it that is good & refined to no common extent. There is a general intelligence & morality, which I do not believe exists to such a degree in any other place of the same size. Why can not this intelligence be chastened by charity? & why will not our people confine themselves to regarding the essentials, & cease to watch the unimportant things of life? But why interrogate you on this subject? To you travel has unfolded all & more than it has ever shewn me.

While I now write, Bulwer—he now rejoices in Sir Lytton[3]—lies stretched on a sofa before me devouring one of the paltry new French novels, the bastard product of a bastard literature. He still cultivates the imperial, & dresses in the *ultra* extreme of fashion.—

I wish you had sent me some sketch of yr Romance.[4] I should rejoice to do something for you here, if I could, but you have given me no *data*. I have talked with Bentley; he spoke kindly of you, would be pleased to publish for you, but would make no arrangement until he had more specific information. I have got from him a statement with regard to yr "Outre-Mer," which I enclose. He would be glad to have you write for his *Miscellany*. I have also talked with Colburn,[5] & have foundered with him, in the same way, through want of proper information.

Present to Harriet Sumner—perhaps I should write Mrs Appleton—my most cordial felicitations, & say that I much regret that I am not at home to tender them in person. I think, however, I shall write her myself; though she had not the grace to send me the tidings under her own hand.—Yr letters seem warm as a lover's heart. I can almost feel the heat as I break the seal. Direct to me in future, care of Draper & Co—20 Hautville St. Paris.—Be earnest, & success will be yours.

As ever affectionately Yours, C. S.

P.S. I have heard in London, from some of his friends, that young Mackintosh, who has just gone to U.S., is in love with one of the Appletons.[6] From the description I thought it was Mary. How is this?

ALS MH-H (65/570, PCS)

1. Harriot Sumner Appleton (1802–67) married Nathan Appleton (1779–1861) in 1839. The poet Longfellow (1807–82) in 1838–39 was courting (then in vain) Frances Appleton (1817–61), Nathan's daughter (see HWL, 2:123).

2. The apostle Paul's conversion took place on his journey from Tarsus to Damascus (Acts 22:1–16).

3. Edward Bulwer-Lytton, first Baron Lytton (1803–73), British M.P. (Reform), novelist, dramatist.

4. *Hyperion*, published August 1839.

5. Richard Bentley (1794–1871), London publisher and founder of *Bentley's Miscellany*, 1837. Henry Colburn (d. 1855), in partnership with Bentley after 1830–32.

6. Robert James Mackintosh (1806–1864), son of the philosopher James Mackintosh, married Mary Appleton (1813–89) on 26 December 1839 (HWL, 2:193).

To Jared Sparks

Athenaeum Club, Feb. 18th 1839

Dear Mr Sparks,

I wrote you from Scotland, apprizing you of the existence of three letters from [*Benjamin*] Franklin to [*David*] Hume; but I told you nothing new, as I supposed at the time, & as yr last volume of the letters of Franklin has made me know. I saw only a few days ago another letter of our philosopher, which was very characteristic. I think its date is 1775 from Paris; it is addressed to Dr Perceval.[1] It was in the possession of Miss Hannah More, & with her very valuable collection of autographs passed to Sir Robert H. Inglis, in whose hands I saw her. I have asked him for a copy of it; & have been much surprized at his hesitation to give it to me. He has ever been very kind to me since I have been in England; & I felt emboldened to ask this favor. He says that he has not yet determined what to do with the whole collection of autograph letters from distinguished persons, & he may wish to publish this letter in a vol. with all the others. The letter is about *duelling*; & though, I think we have Franklin's opinion on this vice & folly in several places, yet I cannot but think that this piquant letter, if published, would do go[od]. My interest in yr labors has induced me to apprize you of its existence.

Before I left home you asked me to ascertain what had been done with [*Edmund*] Burke's papers. The bulk of them are in the hands of Ld Fitzwilliam, forming several large chests-full, I think, & containing, of course, a great number of valuable letters, & also tracts that have never seen the light. The Hon. Mrs Ramsden, the sister-in-law of Ld. Fitzw. told me that she also had a large body of Burke's papers; but I have forgotten how they came to her. I ventured to suggest to his lordship to give them to the world, either by editing them, or drawing up a life of Burke in which they should be embodied. He seems to be not disinclined to the former course, & his eldest daughter the Lady Charlotte offered to rise at 5 o'clk in the morning or at any other hour agreeable to her father to act as his *amanuensis* in this business. Mrs Ramsden seems anxious [that? *MS torn*] the Earl should do this, & thanked me for pressing it upon him. I do not think, however, that he will ever undertake it. The labor will be too serious for one, who, though an industrious person, has not addicted himself to literary occupation.

You will not be sorry to hear that your books have been received by Lds Lansdowne & Holland.[2] The latter told me that he valued the present very highly, both on account of its intrinsic value, & as coming from you. A piratical publication of the Life of Washington, & of some of the public documents has introduced a portion of the work very extensively to the public. I recently received a letter from Dr Sheppard[3] of Liverpool, the old friend of Roscoe, who had commenced reading it on my suggestion, & was very much pleased with it. He will write a review of it for the Edinburgh [*Review*], if Lord Brougham does not, & if the Editor will allow him to do it. I have already spoken to Ld. B. about it several times, & Dr S. has written to his lordship to induce him to undertake it. What may come of this, I cannot tell. Allow me to mingle my felications with those of yr friends at home on your approaching marriage,[4] & believe me,

ever very faithfully Yours, Charles Sumner

P.S. It may not be uninteresting to you to know that the little book on the American Revolution, published by the Br. Society for the Diffusion of Useful Knowledge was written by Dr Sheppard, that it was read in *MS* by Lord John Russell, & in proof-sheet by John Randolph of Roanoke.[5]

ALS MH-H (65/577, PCS)

1. This letter to Thomas Percival (1745–1833), 17 July 1784, was published in Sparks, *The Works of Benjamin Franklin*, vol. 10 (1840). CS's interest in autograph collecting continued through a good part of his life, and he bequeathed three volumes of autograph letters to the Houghton Library.
2. Henry Richard Vassall Fox, third Baron Holland (1773–1840), British diplomat.
3. William Shepherd (1768–1847), Unitarian minister, writer, and Radical Reformer, wrote CS 26 December 1838, Liverpool, 2/023, PCS.
4. Sparks married Mary Crowninshield Silsbee, 21 May 1839.
5. John Randolph (1773–1833), U.S. congressman and senator (States Rights Democrat, Va.) intermittently, 1799–1833.

To Edward Everett

Paris—April 6th 1839
Rue de la Paix

My dear Sir,

My last letter to you from London was written at the first blush of the intelligence from the United States, & before it had assumed the grave aspect that it now seems to wear. I fear that I wrote in a tone, which may ill accord with the solemn feelings at home; certainly, I felt little anxiety, except for the *honour* of our country, which was threatened by the rash & vulgar proceedings of Gov. Fairfield.[1] Since then, however, the curtain has been further drawn up, & we now see the doings of Congress. I need not say with what anxiety all Americans on this side of the water regard what has been & may be done; & I now trouble you again, partly to remove the impression which I fear may have been excited by the apparent levity of my last letter, & partly to communicate what seems to me interesting with regard to the opinions of *Englishmen*. I mentioned to you in my last, I think, that *every Englishman* I have met ⟨(& they are legion)⟩ who has *examined* the subject is with us. The *Solicitor General* [*Follett*] of the crown volunteered to me his own favorable opinion; Lord Jeffrey (who is now luckily in London) *thinks Great Britain has not a shadow of a claim*; it was mainly owing to Ld J. that Brougham went to the Lords & made the declaration he did just before the Easter recess.[2] My conclusion from all that I have heard in England is that *we must in some way make the English study the case*, & *go, au fond*; & I feel confident that, then, nothing can interrupt our relations. Ld Brougham is now in Paris. I have had many conversations with him on the subject; & when I submitted to him that all we wanted was a *hearing*, or, in other words, that somebody, who understood our case, should present it to parliament, he said—"By God, it shall be discussed."—"That damned Melbourne,"[3] he added, "has never read a paper upon the subject." He says there never was a clearer case; & that Great Britain has not a hair's breadth to stand on. I have put papers in his hands, which he has undertaken to read. Mr Hume & Mr Leader,[4] & several other influential Englishmen, are here. I know Hume & Leader very well, & they entertain the most friendly sentiments towards our country. Mr Hume has undertaken to have some matters on our side published in the London papers. Lord Lyndhurst[5] is also here; but I have not ventured to broach the subject with him; he is, however, truly friendly to us, but *does not understand the case*. Edward Ellice, who, as you doubtless know, has more influence with the present Administration than any other man, talks in *innuendoes*, & leaves me in doubt where to find him on this question. The result of my conversations with Englishmen is that, if the State of Maine does not embroil us by its rash conduct, the two great countries will settle it by amicable negotiation. *There can be no war; if the subject is discussed*; for it must, then, be seen that there are ample grounds, either for concession or some honourable compromise. *And, that it will be well discussed I feel confident*. I shall not leave Paris until I have addressed on the subject a large number of my personal friends & acquaintances in Parliament, soliciting their earnest & conscientious attention to it. The privileges I have from any personal relations with many distinguished Englishmen I feel anxious, according to my humble ability, to turn to the benefit of my country. I should add that Brougham says the course of the present Govt will depend very much upon the views of Lord Ashburton, who has extensive possessions in the disputed territory. Ld. A. is now on his way from Florence, where he has just lost his daughter (poor Mrs Mildmay)[6] who was burnt to death; but Brougham will exert himself to see him as soon as possible, in the hope of influencing his judgment. How he is disposed at present is not known.

I cannot repeat too often that our cause labors in England from the fact, that it is not understood. If the same question concerned a single manor in an English county, it would be thoroughly canvassed & understood; but, concerning a wild tract in a distant hemisphere, as it does, scarcely anybody has interested himself enough about it to make any enquiry; & prejudice, & national partialities take the place of reason. I have looked into the case since I have been in Paris, & I cannot doubt our *title* to the full territory as claimed; but it seems ungracious conduct to offer to negotiate with England, declaring at the same time that *we will not be content with anything less than the whole*. Maine, by her proceedings, has hurt the great cause of liberal institutions in the world, & has brought our national government into derision. To-day I conversed with Leon Faucher, the editor of the *Courier Francais*,[7] one of the most influential political writers in France, & he was fully persuaded that our *central* govt is fast losing its *little strength* (I will say *illud totum nihil*),[8] & that we should soon be broken to pieces. A case exactly in point, as you are doubtless well aware, has just occurred in France. Anticipating some *sympathy* among the warlike Aslatians, or the surrender of Limbourg & Luxembourg, a considerable army was marched from other parts of France in order to controul the *national guard* of Alsace. Would that Van Buren would do the same *in casu consimili*;[9] to the end that we might shew the world that our government is as ready to resist disorganization from *within*, as invasion from *without*.

You will observe that the tone of the London Press has essentially changed within a few days with regard to the U. States. It is much more subdued. I have been most troubled by the hostile tone of the *Morning Chronicle*; but there is a prejudiced pen [concerned?] in that paper. Mcgilvray, who is largely interested in the British & Candn North West Compy, is the writer of these articles, though the other political leaders are now from *Fox*,[10] the Unitarian clergyman.

I hardly know what right I have to inflict upon you this long scrawl, written in great haste; but I venture to think that your interest in the question pending might make you not unwilling to receive even in this rough way the impressions of a countryman in Europe.[11] If there is any thing here, which you think worth mentioning to any friends, you are perfectly at liberty to do so; but I am anxious to prevent any thing like *personal* remarks from getting to the *press*. You will pardon my making such a superfluous suggestion; but I am this moment smarting under a betrayal of confidence on the part of an Englishman in the London press, & I am afraid almost of a shadow.[12]

In France all is uncertain. Lady Granville,[13] whom I have just left, is fearfully anxious; but I think all will go smoothly.

As ever, very faithfully Yours, Charles Sumner

ALS MHi (65/623, PCS)

1. CS refers to his letter of 18 March 1839 to Governor Everett, in which he wrote that British leaders were generally ignorant of the Northeast boundary dispute (65/606, PCS). As that dispute continued, in January 1839, John Fairfield (1797–1847), governor of Maine, asked the Maine legislature for an armed force to disperse the Canadian settlers in the Aroostook region. An American land agent was seized, and both New Brunswick and the U.S. Congress threatened war. Major General Winfield Scott (1786–1866) arranged a truce in March between Fairfield and the lieutenant governor of New Brunswick.

2. In the House of Lords, 26 March, Brougham declared his hope that Britain would make every effort to negotiate the boundary dispute, and to admit that Britain was "undeniably, clearly, and manifestly in the wrong" (*Hansard's Parliamentary Debates*, 3rd series, 46: 1219).

3. William Lamb, second Viscount Melbourne (1779–1848), British prime minister.

4. Joseph Hume (1777–1855), British M.P. (Radical). John Temple Leader (1810–1847?), British M.P. (Radical Reformer).

5. John Singleton Copley the younger, Baron Lyndhurst (1772–1863), lord chancellor, 1827–30, 1834–35.

6. Alexander Baring, first Baron Ashburton (1774–1848), British M.P., commissioner in Washington, 1842, for settlement of Northeast boundary dispute; his daughter, Anne Eugenia, was the wife of a Foreign Service official, Humphrey Mildmay.

7. Leon Faucher (1803–54), political writer, *Courier Français*, 1836–43; reformer and economist.

8. "All of this is nothing."

9. "Extremely similar."

10. William Johnson Fox (1786–1864), British M.P. and journalist.

11. Replying to CS's earlier letter of 18 March (Boston, 20 May, 2/344), Everett agreed with CS that the British had no claim to the disputed territory. He thanked CS for the article he had written on the boundary question, published in *Galignani's Messenger*, 12 April 1839.

12. Later that spring CS became embroiled in a dispute with Robert Walsh, an American newspaperman living in Paris. According to Pierce, CS originally suggested that Walsh write an article on the boundary issue, but Walsh declined. CS apparently believed that Walsh supplied the London *Times* with the charge that CS had inordinately influenced Lord Brougham's 26 March criticism of Britain's land claims. CS wrote the *Times* 23 May denying any such influence over Brougham, and

Walsh answered CS's letter (unrecovered) denying he had leaked any information to the *Times* (Prc, 2:86–87, London *Times*, 7 May 1839:7, 14 June 1839:6, Walsh to CS, Paris, 8 June, 2/350).

13. Harriet Elizabeth Cavendish (1785–1862), wife of Granville Leveson-Gower, first earl of Granville, British ambassador to Paris, 1824–41.

To Daniel Webster

Rome June 24th 1839

My dear Sir,

I had learned from the American papers & from letters from Mr Peters & Mr Ticknor of yr determination to come abroad; the English paper[s] that I have just seen, have announced your arrival in our dear father-land. Allow me to give you joy on this occasion, & to say how truly happy I am as an American to know that you are in England. It has [happened] to me to see English society quite widely, & to enjoy in no moderate measure that hospitality which it understands so well. I can truly say that yr distinguished name has gone before you, & that you will find large numbers of the best people anxious to make your acquaintance. Lords Lansdowne & Holland enquired of me about you with great interest; Lord Fitzwilliam has the first volume of yr speeches in his Library at Milton Park, & he told me with what pleasure he had read yr Discourse at Plymouth.[1]—Stuart Wortley & Ld. Wharncliffe will rejoice to receive you. I fear that I may seem too bold in offering my humble intervention; but I feel anxious that you should not leave England without personally knowing a friend—I may say an affectionate friend,—of mine, who takes a great interest in our country, & who will be truly happy to make yr acquaintance—I mean Lord Morpeth.[2] It is more than probable that you will meet him, even before you receive this letter. I shall, however, write Morpeth by the same post that takes this letter, to request him to leave his card upon you. [*inserted in margin*] As Ld Morpeth may not know yr address, it may be most proper for you to leave yr card upon him *No 11 Grosvenor Place*. [*end insert*] He is of great simplicity of [character and?] kindly disposition. Circumstances [*MS damaged*] me acquainted with many, if [*MS damaged*] leading lawyers, & I would fain [*MS damaged*] them [know?] of yr being in London, [*MS damaged*] you [the] opportunity of seeing them. But you will be in better hands, & yr own card will be a general letter of introduction every where. Allow me to say, however, if it should occur to you that I can be useful to you in any way, I shall be most happy to know of it. A line from you sent to *Draper & Co Paris*, will always reach me, wherever I may be on the Continent.

I well remember Mrs Webster[3] in Boston, & would present my respectful compliments to her.

Renewing my salutations, & wishing you great joy in Europe, I am, my dear Sir,

very faithfully Yours, Charles Sumner

P.S. Among the lawyers you should see *Follett* & *Charles Austin*;[4] the last as decided a *liberal*, as the first is *Tory*. Austin is, probably, the most accomplished man at the English bar.

ALS DLC (65/655, PCS)

1. "A Discourse Delivered at Plymouth," 1820.
2. George William Frederick Howard, later seventh earl of Carlisle (1802–64), M.P.; lord lieutenant of Ireland, 1855–58, 1859–64.
3. Caroline Le Roy Webster (1797–1882), married Daniel Webster, 1829.
4. Charles Austin (1779–1874), British lawyer.

To William Wetmore Story

Rome July 6th 1839
Piazza di Spagna

Dear William,

I fear from yr letter of April 18th, which I had the pleasure of receiving shortly after my arrival at the *Eternal City*, that some of the letters I have written you have not come to hand. Two long ones, I wrote from England—one filling two sheets; but of this no more. I have thought of you often in these wonderful galleries of painting, & in the noble collections of antient art. How you would revel here! How your eye would delight to taste the rich sights offered to it on all sides! How your soul would expand into worship of those beautiful things that Old Time has spared to us from the Antients. What delicacy, what proportion, what expression, what niceness of finish, & what grace & beauty do you find in these once blocks of marble. I have stopt for hours before the Apollo; the marble is still unsoiled, & though some parts of it are modern, it stands proudly, yet gently—every inch a God. You see before you the God of the silver bow, & almost hear the winged shaft that he has sped. Pass to the next room; there is Laocoon—the same figures that Pliny admired. From the heavenly looks, beaming from the countenance of the Apollo, you pass to the terrible Hell of struggles, where the father & his sons are expiring in the folds of serpents. At the Vatican these are the two great pieces of antient art; but in that vast collection, so full of beauty & interest, there are many others, which excite no little attention. There is a small bust of Augustus—not so large as one of Frazee's[1]—which I have stopped before twenty times. It has been broken in pieces, & put together. It is entirely simple—there are no deep lines—none of Frazee's sharp cuts—the cheeks are smooth; & yet, in the long line of a thousand, where it stands, you are struck by its magnificent beauty, its perfect grace & expression. All the gold & silver of America could not purchase that little piece of broken marble. There is a full-length of Demosthenes that has been found in some comparatively recent excavations; it still bears the marks of the soil in which it was discovered; yet under this dirty exterior you cannot fail to see that it was great artist who put his hand to this work. I wish you were here to walk with me through the immense galleries where these things are kept—to tread the floor inlaid with the antient marbles or [pretious?] mosaics, & to admire the antient columns of porphyry, & of marbles of all sorts with which they are adorned. Pass to the Capitol, & there you will see the Gladiator, the drops of blood just welling from the fatal stab, & the breath leaving his body.—How inapproachable the antients would seem—*if Torwaldsen had not lived.*[2] This artist is a Dane, who has passed all his life in Rome, as every artist must, who aspires high, in sight of the great masters of Antiquity. These he has made his constant study. Their simplicity he has imitated; & he has almost reached their beauty. Much that Torwaldsen has done would do honor to the antients. His King has recently become conscious of the glory he has reflected upon his country, & invited him to visit Denmark, placing a vessel of war at his disposal. This invitation he accepted; & he is now in Denmark, though expected in Rome very soon again. Canova was a great artist; but very much inferior to Torwaldsen; & Chantry[3] should not be mentioned in the same century. Rome is full of artists; & some of them are very good; but all together do not make a *Torwaldsen*. We have a countryman here—a young man by name, *Crawford*, of New York,[4] who has pursued his art under singular discouragements, but who has devoted himself with a classical spirit to the *antique*. I think he will do our country great credit. He is now modelling a large piece representing *Orpheus descending into Hell* after Eurydice. He has seized the moment when the musician, with his sweet lyre, had charmed the fierce Cerberus. *Crawford* first worked in the studio of Frazee & there was engaged on the head of your Father. He is poor & I feel anxious to do something for him. If I could induce any body to order this large piece he is now engaged upon, *his fortune would be made*. All that he needs is to be *known*. I wish you to aid me in this matter. I shall write a full letter to Hillard & Longfellow about him. *I wish you would put all yr heads together & see what can be done. Remember these are not vain words. Poor, & full of genius, & devoted to his art—he deserves patronage—*

But not half the attractions of this place are yet told. I have been studying the works of the great masters of the brush; I have gone from picture to picture often, & have read several works to assist me, among others, one, which you must read, before you come abroad, *Storia Pittorica* by Lanzi.[5] It is in *five* volumes; & the Italian is not so agreeable as the silver notes of Ariosto & Tasso, or the high strains of Dante, or even the prose of Machiavelli[;] *still it must be read*, for the knowledge it contains. In painting *Raffael* is what the *antients* are in sculpture. The wonders of this great artist's pencil fill me with admiration whenever I look at them. The more you study Raffael, the more you find to study—there are deeps below deeps, vistas revealing other vistas, which you find in no other works of painting. I envy you the enjoyment of Allston's gallery. Ticknor wrote me that it reminded him more of an European gallery than any thing he ever saw in America. Do me the favor to preserve for me one of the *Catalogues*, that I may see it on my return home. I wish I could borrow the wings of the morning & fly there.—But over & above all the attractions of art, antient & modern, that make this place so interesting, here are the remains of the antient Queen of the earth. How often have I walked down the *via Sacra* with Horace, & entered the forum where Cicero convened the Senate to judge the Affair of Catiline. This *forum* once the mighty centre of the world, whence went forth mandates to the East & the West, the *North* & the *South* is now a pasture; & I have seen oxen & asses rubbing themselves against columns of Pentelican marble. If I take a carriage to drive to this place, I tell the coachman to go to the *Campo Vaccino*; the word *forum* he would not understand. All these things you will see & enjoy in good time. Study well, get yr profession; & prepare yr mind properly. I hope you know French & Italian & German well. You may know when you know French by this test; take up an English book & *at sight read* it into French; then *write* it in French. If you cannot do this; you don't know French. Don't forget the *law*. Ah, the *law*, with which I must grapple soon. To feel myself again in its embrace I fear will be too much like that iron man of Nabis.[6] But up! courage! man!—I heard from your father in a PS of Greenleaf's which I received yesterday.[7] He has almost forgotten me. Remember me to all, & believe me

as ever affectionately Yours, C. S.

P.S. I have already seen life in considerable variety. I am about to retire to *convent* to live with some Franciscan monks in a beautiful place, which hangs over the Alban lake.—"far from the madding crowd's ignoble strife."[8] I shall overhaul their library, study Dante, & drink their wine. Don't report me to the Temperance Society.

2nd PS. How is Frank Tuckerman?[9] Remember me to him & to his family if you see them.

I have written you a crowded letter about art, when I should have written you about the *law*, & given you a great deal of good advice, not one word of which you would have listened to!—

ALS TxU (65/660, PCS)

1. John Frazee (1790–1852), American sculptor.
2. Albert Bertel Thorvaldsen (1770–1844) lived in Rome after 1797.
3. Antonio Canova (1757–1822), Italian sculptor. Francis Legatt Chantrey (1781–1841), English sculptor.
4. Thomas Crawford (c. 1813–57).
5. Luigi Antonio Lanzi (1732–1810), *Storia Pittorica dell'Italia* (1795–96).
6. Nabis (d. 192 B.C.), Spartan king and warrior.
7. CS noted "July 3 '39" on the letter he received from Greenleaf, dated 17 May 1839, but no P.S. is present (2/342, PCS).
8. Thomas Gray, "Elegy Written in a Country Churchyard," stanza 19.
9. John Francis Tuckerman (d. 1885), Harvard A.B. 1837, M.D. 1841.

To George Sumner

Florence Sept. 6th 1839

Dear George,

I have just re-read yr letter from Constantinople of the 2nd July.[1] Doubtless ere this you have received my reply to it of the 28th July from Rome. Though I have heard nothing from you since then, yet I can not forbear again troubling you with my opinion on several points suggested by what you have written. Bear with me; for I write from the interest I feel in you, & from my desire to assist you in your plans. I shall criticise you, in order to save you from the criticism of others. I might suggest that as your [*MS torn for 2 lines*] prerogative. However, I presume you will be slow to recognize this feudal quality; & I hope never to exercise it in a manner that will induce you to call it into question.—

You have determined to write a book.—Study your subject thoroughly.—Collect all necessary facts & information, whether by observation, conversation, or books.—Digest, arrange & classify these in that way that will present them most clearly & philosophically to the reader. Invest them with a style, clear, correct & elegant. To do this will require time. It cannot be done *en route*, as one would write letters for a Yankee newspaper. If you content yourself with such a concoction as would be the result of the *extempore* labor of a traveller, you may produce a book that shall be lively & interesting, & sell for a year or two; but you will not give us a work that will live. Not so are written the volumes that find a permanent place on the shelves of a library, & give their author a reputation that is truly desirable. *De Tocqueville's* work on Democracy in America was not published till *four* or *five* years after his return to France; & he has another work on *Society in America*, which is not yet published;[2] & which has occupied the greater portion of his time during the four last years. He writes—not for the readers of *one* year & *one* country; but of *many* years & *many* countries. His work already published has given him a world-reputation. You will not think me going too far, I trust, when I suggest that your youth; (for you [are] young) your inexperience; (for till recently you had seen the world only in a contracted sphere) your want of education; (for you have never received what in all civilized countries is called *an education*) your slight practice as a writer; (for the chance newspaper production [*MS torn*] counting-room hardly rise to the dignity of compositions); [*MS torn*] what is called the *society* of your own country (for [*MS torn*] never seen any; & in [*MS torn*]—all these circumstances, which I have thus presented freely & boldly, make it particularly incumbent on you to give the most anxious care to the preparation of a work, like that you have in view, where the government policy, & society of a great nation are to be considered. You may imagine that you have the subject well-digested in your mind. Believe me, you will see it more clearly two years from now. Keep it constantly in your thoughts; turn it over & over; fashion & arrange it, according to the increasing distinctness with which you perceive it. And, then, the style; this must be carefully elaborated. You never will lack force, or clearness of style; you must study to acquire correctness, grace & elegance. In your last letter to me you say—"So long as the world chooses to eat *swill,* the cook [*MS torn*] would have no higher rank *than that of a scavenger*."—I have itali[cized] [*MS torn*] original. The word *swill*, which you raise into the bold relief of a [*MS torn*] according to the effect of those lines with printers, of capitals, is disgusting. [*MS torn*] think of using another word that begins with S.—John Wilkes's[3] famous [*MS torn*] speech was going far; but you get beyond him. In your sentence I should have forborne underscoring any word. I should have employed *dirt* instead of *swill*; & should have omitted "*himself*" after "Apicius", & "that of" after "than." But this is an incidental criticism which I make chiefly to warn you against such words as "*swill.*" A correct, pure & undefiled English style comes only from conversance with the best authors, & considerable practice as a writer. I might also add that it may be improved by intercourse with people who habitually speak correct & pure English, & who understand their language. A writer of our day should reject words & terms, even though sanctioned by the classics of another day, which are no longer in vogue among the best authors & speakers of our time. Language, as well as dress, has its variations. You would be thought an odd fellow, if you went into a London drawing-room with the huge ruff of Queen Elizabeth's time, or the jerkin of the Puritan—though, in their day & generation, these were quite fashionable. And so in the best society of England, & among the few carefully-educated people of America, would you be thought anti-diluvian & provincial, if you used words that are not the current coin of the present time. Cicero avoided the hard terms of *Eumius*[4] & it was the great fault of Livy (with all his glorious merits) that his style was tinctured with the provincialisms of the little town where he was born or lived, & that he did not rise to the purety & correctness of the Roman diction. Shun, then, *Americanisms*. And to do this will require much care. A late English critic, after praising Prescott's work, has charged him with provincialisms & Patavinity.[5] Few persons in our country have endeavored to guard against these faults more than Prescott. After all, his work is the greatest literary production of our country. Few Americans are aware of the *isms* which they use. The best way of correcting the tendency, or the habit, is by carefully reading the best authors & by observing the conversation of the educated English you may meet. As you have never written more than articles for a newspaper, why not try your hand by an article on the *present state, policy & prospects of Russia* for the *North American Review*? This would give you some experience & make your name known in some circles where it might not be unwelcome to you to be received. The editor Dr Palfrey is quite a friend of mine, & a correspondent; & I think I might render you a slight service in introducing you to him. Such an article you might write in Europe & send home for publication; & it would be a sort of harbinger of the book.—But enough of this.—

You will not be in Italy till winter—I am told that the best place for passing *Quarantine* is Malta. From there you can pass to Naples where there is much to see in the way of art &c & from Naples to Rome. While in Italy I hope you will study *art*. Do not content yourself with [*MS torn*] statues & paintings; but *study* them, & in connection with this, study the [*MS torn*] Of course, you should read Sir J. Reynold's Lectures & Flaxman's[6] [*MS torn*] if you read Italian as you doubtless will) Lanzi's

Storia [*Pittorica*] [*MS torn*] which is in French. I have announced your coming to my friend *Greene*,[7] [*MS torn*] present you to the Pope. *Greene* is one of the most [accomplished?] [*MS torn*] the preparation of a great historical work to which he proposes dedicating 20 or 25 years. I ought to add that he is poor; so you will be careful not to subject him to any expense on your account; if, for instance, you go any where in a carriage with him, you must pay for it. I need not say, that *his fees* are his *property*—what he lives on; & you, I know, would not wish to rob him of them. I hope you are not of the vulgar tribe of American travellers, who question consul's fees & demur at paying them, or try to beat them down. The fee of $2.00 is established by law, as also another fee on going from Rome to Naples. Persons should stay at home, or at least should not aspire to rank with gentlemen, unless prepared silently & respectfully & without wrangling or question, to pay the fees of travellers. May I venture still further in the liberties I have taken with you in this letter, & give you some hints derived from my experience as a traveller.—1. Make it a rule to read or study *every day*, whether *en route* or not, in a carriage, steam-boat or howsoever, at least *six hours*. Perhaps you already do this. If you do, your experience will confirm mine, in the conclusion that one can do this, & still have time for conversation, sight-seeing & pleasure. Most American travellers literally read nothing while travelling. You should read the standard French classics. I suppose you have already read Moliere, Corneille, Racine &c; but you will always find cheap editions of French works at book-stalls, which you can buy, & afterwards give away, or exchange for other books. 2. As a general rule avoid your own countrymen. They are the least educated of all the travellers one meets. Always alter your journey in order to get rid of them. I have been so fortunate as not to have travelled with one in Europe; though I have had some "hair-breadth scapes"—The English are more agreeable & instructive companions; but I should avoid these also. If you have companions from other countries, you will have the advantage of practice in foreign languages. 3. Whenever you arrive at a town, where you contemplate staying a few weeks, as Rome or Naples, for instance, engage an *instructer* in the language. This should be the first thing, after ordering your dinner. [4. In] conversation, avoid speaking of yourself, of attentions you have received & of the great people you have [known.] These things, if told, would only excite the admiration of the vulgar. Bury the *acorn* story as deep as possible, so that it may never shew the smallest *sprout*. 5. In manner, always be frank & cordial; but cultivate a [*reticence?*]. You know Americans are charged with being bold, forth-putting & impertinent. I hope that nothing from you will contribute to fasten upon us this disagreeable imputation. I was sorry to read the sentence in your letter—"All the secret of success in this world consists in knowing *when* & *where* & *how far* to *push*" &c. One should never *push*—except in a crowd. And be assured, that any temporary success that you may get by *pushing*, will be at the expence of yr reputation in the long run. "Oh! he has the Yankee *pushing*"! Do not let this be said of you. The few of my friends at Boston who had seen you thought that you were free & bold in your manners. Their opinion joined with my own recollections makes me anxious to get you to reconsider this principle of conduct which you have laid down for yourself. You have talents & conversation that will naturally, quietly & gracefully carry you to your proper place, without pushing. [*inserted in margin*] (a) In conversation with Englishmen, never say No *Sir* or Yes Sir; but simply *yes* & *no*. The "*Sir*" is left for the use of servants generally, being employed by gentlemen only in conversation with a Prince of the Blood.—Endeavor, if you can, to get rid of the Yankee [drawl &] pronunciation. [*end insert*] 6. As a general rule, avoid asking for introductions; & be careful not to address people to whom you are not introduced, unless some peculiar circumstances, as close contact or the like, should make it entirely proper. 7. In dress, always dress well; but cleanest possible linen is more important than dress. Look after your shirts, gloves, & stockings; & the rest will take care of itself. In the evening, or at dinner always wear a body coat; & shoes & nice silk stockings. Many people, particularly on the continent, wear at dinner & in the evening dress boots; but the better way is shoes & silk. If you wear shoes in the street, the stockings should always be silk, unless covered by your trousers. The shirt should always be changed at least *once a day*; in London, if you go into society, *twice*. It is an American idea, that of *clean-shirt day*; every day should be *clean-shirt day*. Alfieri[8] (one of the greatest men that ever lived) in his amusing autobiography describes his savingness & avarice at a time when he supposed he had lost nearly all his property; but he says he never gave up his daily change of linen. I well re [*MS torn for 3 lines*] days which I looked for [*MS torn*]. A clean shirt, next after a clean conscience. No matter where you are travelling, if out of sight of human kind, do not forget that *every day* is "*clean-shirt day*." 8. Remember the bath, once or twice a week, or oftener. If you pretend to shave at all (I don't know but what you have a beard & moustachios) *shave every day*. Use a finger-brush to clean your nails always when you wash. [*MS torn for one sentence*] Always have fresh & clean gloves, particularly for the evening.—

And here ends, my dear George, this homily.—I hope you will receive it, as it is written, in a brotherly spirit of love. I wish I could talk with you for one half-day; I could explain my views, particularly with regard to yr book in a way that should avoid mistake. There is, probably, no other person in the world who would venture to make to you the suggestions in this letter. I judge others by myself; & I should be truly grateful to any friend, whose relations with me justified suggestions on such delicate subjects, who exercised the same freedom towards me that I have now used with you.—*Veniam damus, petimusque vicissim.*[9]—I hope you have already written home stimulating matter in the education of the children. Lend me your influence. Teach yr brothers & sisters to be *ambitious*, to aspire, & to look up.—You can do a great deal of good in this way. I hope that Horace {*Sumner*}, when grown up, will not smart as I do, under the mortification of a defective education.

Ever yr affectionate brother, Chas.

P.S. There is an American sculptor at Rome, *Mr Crawford*, who has great talent in his profession. He is poor, & well deserves mo[re] than he has; though his way to fame is clear. I have spoken of you to him. He will be glad to make yr acquaintance, {*MS torn*} you to visit the sculpture of Rome.—When you write to *Chichacheff*,[10] remember me to him; & tell him that I shall be glad {*MS torn*} him under address to *Draper & Co*, Paris, which is my general continental address. I wrote him from Marseilles at the {*MS torn*} May; but as I have not heard from him since, I think there may have been some miscarriage—I shall send this {*MS torn*} paying the postage to that place. Are you *personally acquainted* with our Consul at Alexandria? If not, how do you venture {*MS torn*} letters addressed to his care? This is Yankee impertinence, to which our consuls are too often subjected; those of no other {*MS torn*} treated. I know that some of our consuls are displeasd at the liberty. For myself, I should as soon think of ordering my {*MS torn*} care of Ali Pacha, as of a Consul, with whom I was not on terms of considerable personal familiarity. I {*MS torn*} or letters always {*MS torn*} the care {*MS torn*} or {*MS torn*} or letters from Boston down to July 29th—nothing new—Hillard's edition; {*MS torn*} completed—it had cost him a good deal of labor. Longfellow's romance {*MS torn*} Prescott engaged on a new Historical work, which will occupy {*MS torn*} I suppose 10 or 12 years. Felton engaged on a translation from Ger {*MS torn*} I believe still at home—fancying that he is enjoying himself.[11]

P.S. I shall be in *Vienna* till Oct. 15th, where my address is *chez Arnstein & Eskeles*, banquiers. I hope to hear from you there. If your letter will not reach Vienna by the above date, direct to my standing address, *Draper & Co, Paris*.

P.S. Let your card be *Mr.* George Sumner; not George Sumner. The latter denotes an unfled[ged? Y]ankee, or a Quaker—Wherever you are, if you have acquaintances, & expect to be called upon, you must have *at least* t[wo roo]ms, so as not to receive a person in your bedroom. A person passing as a gentleman must not bury in a hole [but? alwa]ys dine in a respectable place.—

I am anxious to hear from you, to know yr plans of travel; & also what you propose to do on yr return to America. Write me immediately. Before you go to France & England, I shall have another dish of advice; if this be not too unpalatable.

ALS MH-H (62/407, PCS)

1. In all their years of correspondence, only seven letters from CS's brother George (1817–63), a journalist, have been recovered; this one was not. CS's letter was forwarded to George Sumner in Alexandria from Smyrna.
2. *Democracy in America*, vol. 2, published in 1840.
3. John Wilkes (1727–97), British M.P. and reformer.
4. Eumaeus, Ulysses' faithful swineherd, *Odyssey*, books 15–16.
5. Unsigned review by Richard Ford of "A History of the Reign of Ferdinand and Isabella the Catholic of Spain," *Quarterly Review* 64 (June 1839): 1–58.
6. John Flaxman (1755–1826), *Flaxman's Lectures*, 1829.
7. George Washington Greene (1811–83), U.S. consul at Rome, 1837–45; writer, historian.
8. Vittorio Alfieri (1749–1803), Italian dramatist.
9. "We give kindness and we ask the same in return."
10. Chichacheff, a "young Russian" whom CS had met in Paris (Journal, 20 January 1838, Prc, 1:242).
11. Hillard's *The Poetical Works of Edmund Spenser*, 5 volumes, 1839; Prescott's *History of the Conquest of Mexico*, 1843. The classical scholar and later Harvard president, Cornelius C. Felton (1807–62) was translating Menzel's *German Literature* (Longfellow to George Washington Greene, 23 July 1839, HWL, 2:162).

To Francis Lieber

Florence Sept. 12th '39

My dear Lieber,

Our correspondence seems to be question & answer; for yr letters—always interesting & agreeable—contain so many interrogatories that I am compelled to make mine responses to yr catechism. I have now before me *three* of yr favors—of March 24th recd by me at Rome May 24th; of April 21st recd at Rome June 22nd; & of 18th June, recd in

Florence August 25th.—Now for them in succession. And first that of March 24th; several of the topics broached in that have been disposed of in previous letters; particularly that about your friendly correspondents, who had been startled by a report connecting them with me. Perhaps, I need say nothing at present with regard to that, as I have already expressed myself to you in the most decided terms. I shall either live a bachelor, or marry the prettiest daughter of the Grand Duke of Tuscany,[1] who is now just 17, & speaks all sorts of languages with infinite grace. If the latter takes place I shall take the *Careggi Villa* about 3½ miles from Florence, the favorite residence of Lorenzo di Medici, & will make that great hall the witness of literary festivities, in which the spirits of Politan & Mirandola shall rejoice.[2] There is a fine suite of rooms in a wing which I destine to you; how we will study & talk & weave the web of thought—in that retreat, from the slope of the Appenines looking down upon Florence & the lovely valley of the Arno. Here I hope still for your friendship, as much as if settled down in Yankee land with all of yr Yankee girls.—

If you have four or five copies of the *Hermeneutics*[3] to spare send them—Wm Burge Esq Queen's Counsel &c &c &c, Lincoln's Inn; Joseph Parkes Esq, Great George St. Westminster; Right Honorable Baron Parke &c &c &c, 57 Park St London; A. Hayward Esq 11 King's Bench Walk, Temple (Editor of Law Mag.);[4] Charles Austin Esq, Temple. All these are my friends, & you may make such use of my name as you see fit in sending them copies of the Hermeneutics. You enquire about C. Austin. My acquaintance with him arose from repeatedly meeting him in society, sometime before I knew [Miss?] A;[5] & the latter I had met several times & been invited to her house, before I presented the letters of introduction I had to her. She spoke very kindly of you.—I am inclined to think the English form of publishing the notes of the *Polly* [*Manual of Political Ethics*] is the best—Don't trouble yourself about the Boston Review; & as to being told to write no more—Hume was so admonished after the publication of the first volume of his History. Read his autobiography, & also the *critique* in the old *Monthly Review*.[6]—

Next, for the letter of April 21st—*De Tocqueville's* address for letters is 12 *Rue de Bourgogne*, Paris. You can probably send him parcels through the bookseller *Hector Bosange*,[7] who has established relations in America.—

As to Wm lst of Orange. Have you ever read *Bentivoglio's* history of the Dutch war?[8] You have, doubtless.—

The copies of yr *Polly* that were sent to the *reviews* &c, I think, came out of the publisher, leaving you a clear 25 for literary friends. Smith, the publisher,[9] seemed a very fair-minded man—honester & more liberal than any of the press-gang I saw. Colburn & Bentley are sharks.— As to avoiding the calamities of postage in England, give yr books to some book-selling or trading house in America, to be forwarded to their correspondent in London, who will distribute them according to instructions.—

As to the discussion of the *representative* system, to which you allude, have you ever read the discourse of *Savonarola* to the people of Florence about 1490,[10] in which he proposed a *representative* system, in contradistinction to the *democratic*? the first promulgation of this potent idea—is it not?—I long to read yr discussion of the right of [distinction?]. It is a good question, & fit to occupy the highest powers. I hope you will establish the pillars of this subject on which the country may lean.—I see that *Mr Baring Wall*,[11] M.P., an acquaintance of mine has just addressed a pamphlet to his constituents on independence in an M.P.—It was well-done by you, refusing to *lend* your chapter to the politicians. Let them use it when it is before the world; but save yourself from the suspicion of party bias while yr work is still unpublished.—

If I meet Chancellor Harper I shall be happy to see him on yr account, & will do anything that my experience of Europe may enable me to do for him; but Southern judges & lawyers (always excepting Wm Gaston of N.C.) are to me sounding vessels.[12]—

De Tocqueville is elected, & has made a good speech. His work on *Society* as *affected by Democracy* is in press. *Beaumont* is not elected; but he has done better; he has written a book on Ireland, which is spoken very highly of.[13] —I have already written you that there is a good *Weekly* paper which gives the debates, & *critiques* of all new books, & editorial sketches of politics, written with admirable ability. I have lost my love for the *Examiner*; the *Spectator* is so much more complete.[14] You should get the *Spectator*. The [*Boston*] *Atlas* would not answer yr purpose—

There is a plan of the *Chambre des Deputés* at Paris; & I have written to some of my friends to procure it, & forward it to you. On that you will see the actual seat specified of every member. Generally speaking, the deputies sit according to the terms *Gauche, Centre Gauche* &c, but not invariably & I have been puzzled to know where the dividing line between the different sections was—all being blended together most prismatically. *Lafitte* who is *Extreme gauche* sits by the side of Odillon Barrot, who is simply *Gauche*.[15] These terms originally derived from the seats of the deputies now stand for party appellations, & denote, by exacter shades than any party nomenclature in England or America, the opinions of those to whom they are applied. And they are applied not simply in the Chamber; but every where; for instance, a friend of mine, with whom I conversed about politics—said *Toute France à present est gauche*. By these [words?] the French are able to denote *eight* different *nuances* of party, whereas we have but *two* or *three*.

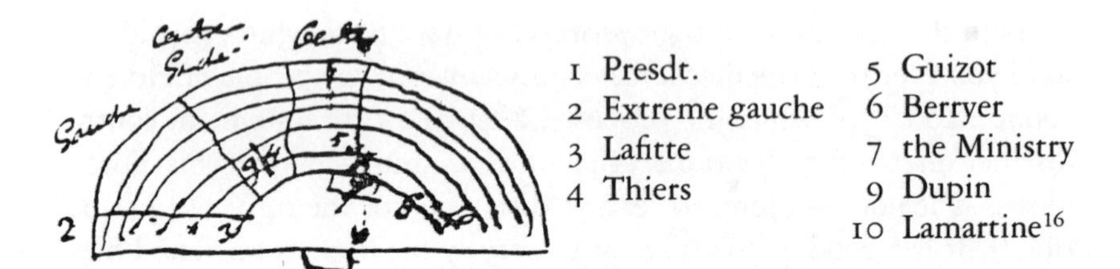

1	Presdt.	5	Guizot
2	Extreme gauche	6	Berryer
3	Lafitte	7	the Ministry
4	Thiers	9	Dupin
		10	Lamartine[16]

This is a rude sketch from memory; but you will doubtless receive very soon the engraved diagram. Members certainly do not take their places invariably with reference to these divisions; for I have always seen Jouffroy[17] by the side of Berryer. The following is a rude sketch of things in England.

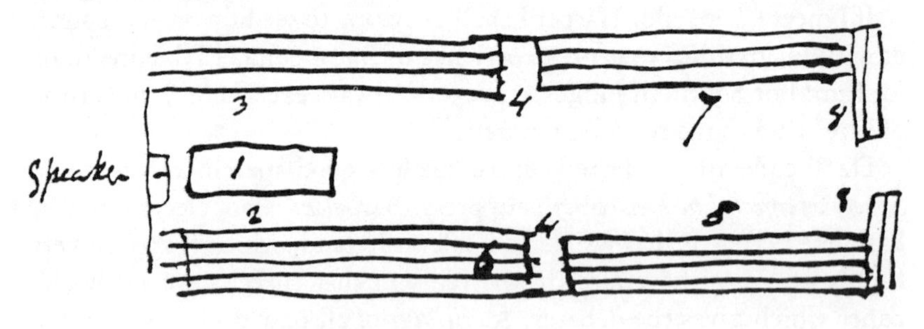

1 Clerk's table
2 Ld J. Russell & the ministry
3 Sir R. Peel, Stanley, Burdett &c[18]
4 called the "gang-way"

All persons who sit above the *gang-way* (that is towards the Speaker) are considered as espousing the side of the Ministry or Opposition. All below the *gang-way* are undecided. The radicals generally sit on the benches marked 5, on the same side with the Ministry, but below the gang-way. O'Connell[19] & Hume sit above the gang-way at the place marked 6. The stoutest supporters of each side are supposed to sit directly behind their leaders (nos. 2 & 3). The benches below the gang-way on the Tory side are generally occupied by undecided persons inclining to Opposition. The cross-benches are used merely to lounge upon. But when we meet I will explain these things to yr heart's content. The following is the House of Lords

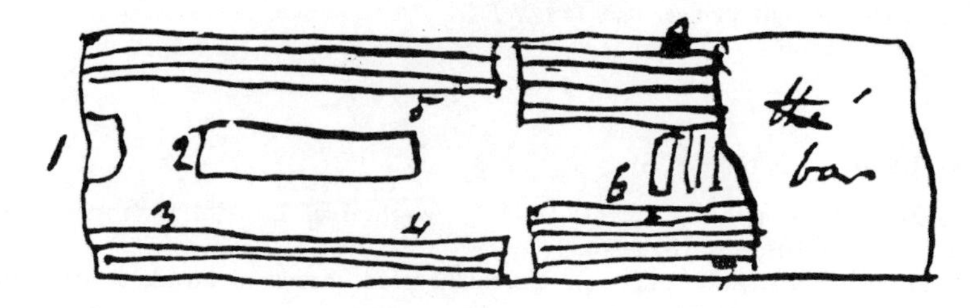

1 The Throne
2 The Ld Chancellor
3 Bishops
4 Ministry
5 Duke of Wellington
6 Ld Brougham
7 Ld Durham[20]
8 Ld Lyndhurst.

Why Ld Lyndhurst sits in his distant corner, I cannot tell; & I never met any body who could.—

I have heard in the French chamber very eloquent speeches, where there was no reading *les cahiers*. I think the peers *read* oftener than the *deputies*. The late debate in the French chamber on the affairs of the East must have been grand. The deputies speak *en bourgeois*; & were very much laughed at winter before last for an attempt to bring back the *uniform*. The peers always wear a uniform—not unlike the diplomatic dress of the U.S.—blue coat, with a stand-up collar, trimmed with gold-lace.—

And so, my dear Lieber, I am at the end of yr questions & of my paper. Where is the room to pour out my soul about Italy? I tenderly love this country, & hope some time again to be permitted to see it. From here I go to Venice, then to *Vienna*, where I expect to be at the end of Oct. Alas! I must make a hurried visit to yr country.

I shall return home in the winter. I could cry to think of leaving Greece unvisited; & then your language & literature & mind I long to master. I have read nearly all the Italian classics, poets, & prose-writers, from Dante & Mach.[*iavelli*] to Alfieri & Manzoni.[21] Would that I had done the same with German. My tour has stimulated my ambition—taught me my ignorance—& enabled me to direct my future studies.

Good bye, God bless you C. S.

What say you to this letter? Does it not contain enough. The Arno flows beneath my windows! What would you give to see the Arno?—Would that I had yr *German tongue!*

ALS CSmH (65/681, PCS)

1. Marie Caroline Auguste (1822–41), daughter of Leopold II (1797–1870), Grand Duke of Tuscany, 1824–59.

2. Angelo Poliziano (1454–94), Florentine poet. Giovanni Picodella Mirandola (1463–94), Florentine philosopher.

3. Lieber's *Legal and Political Hermeneutics*, 1839.

4. William Burge (1797–1850), British legal scholar. Joseph Parkes (1796–1865), British solicitor and reformer. Abraham Hayward (1801–84), British lawyer and essayist.

5. Possibly a sister? According to the *Dictionary of National Biography*, Austin did not marry until 1856.

6. David Hume (1711–76), *History of England*, 1754–78; *Life of David Hume, Written by Himself*, 1777.

7. Hector Bossange (b. 1795), member of French family of publishers and booksellers that published the first French editions of James Fenimore Cooper's novels.

8. Guido Bentivoglio (1579–1644), *1632–1639; The Compleat History of the Warrs of Flanders*, 1654.

9. William Henry Smith (1792–1865).

10. *Tratto circa el reggimento e governo della citta di Firenze*, c. 1498.

11. Charles Baring Wall (1795–1853), British M.P. (Liberal).

12. William Harper (1790–1847), U.S. senator (Dem., S.C.), 1826; chancellor of South Carolina, 1828, 1834–47. William Gaston (1778–1844), U.S. congressman (Fed., N.C.), 1813–17; judge, Supreme Court of North Carolina, 1833–44.

13. Tocqueville was elected to the Chamber of Deputies 2 March 1839. Beaumont was later elected in a special election of December 1839; *L'Irlande social, politique et religieuse* was published in 1839 and 1842.

14. The British periodicals the *Examiner* and the *Spectator* were both Radical.

15. Jacques Laffitte (1767–1844), French banker; president, Chamber of Deputies, 1830; prime minister, 1830–31. Odilon Barrot (1791–1873), member, Chamber of Deputies; prime minister, Second Republic, 1848, 1849.

16. Louis Adolphe Thiers (1797–1877), historian; prime minister in July Monarchy, 1836, 1840. François Pierre Guillaume Guizot (1787–1874), historian; prime minister in July Monarchy, 1840–48. Pierre Antoine Berryer (1790–1868), member, National Assembly in Second Republic. André Marie Dupin (1783–1865), member, Chamber of Deputies, July Monarchy; president, Legislative Assembly, Second Republic. Alphonse de Lamartine (1790–1869), poet; historian; member, Chamber of Deputies, 1833–48.

17. Théodore Simon Jouffroy (1796–1842), philosopher and member, Chamber of Deputies.

18. Robert Peel (1788–1850), prime minister, 1834–35, 1841–45, 1845–46; founder of Conservative Party. Edward John Stanley (1802–69), British M.P. (Whig); secretary of the Treasury, 1835–41. Francis Burdett (1770–1844), British M.P. (Reform and Conservative).

19. Daniel O'Connell (1775–1847), Irish M.P.

20. Arthur Wellesley, first duke of Wellington (1769–1852), British soldier and statesman. Edward Maltby (1770–1859), bishop of Durham.

21. Allesandro Manzoni (1785–1873), Italian poet and novelist.

To Victor Cousin[1]

Florence Sept. 15th 1839

My dear Sir,

When in Paris in the winter of 1838, I prepared a memoir concerning the life & words of my countryman M. Joseph Story, with the view of aiding in presenting his name as a candidate for the high honor of foreign correspondent or associate of the *Institute of France*. Since then I have caused a copy of his numerous works to be presented to the Library of the Institute; at the same time, the memoir above-mentioned was laid before the *Academie des Sciences Morales & Politiques*.[2] I now presume to take advantage of the slight acquaintance I had the honor of forming with you during my visit to Paris, to ask your favorable attention to the name of my countryman, M. Story, as a candidate, and, if you will not think me too bold, to solicit your powerful influence in procuring his election. I will add that I have been encouraged in taking the present course by my friend M. Warden[3] of the *Academie des Science*. M *de Tocqueville*, who has visited the United States can bear testimony to the exalted character which M. Story holds in his own country, both as a judge & as a writer on juridicial subjects. In both these characters he seems to have gained almost equal consideration in England, where his judgments & works are cited with great respect. In the memoir which I have prepared, I have presented a short sketch of his life, & of his principle works.

I ask a thousand pardons, my dear Sir, for the great liberty I have presumed to take in intruding myself upon your notice.

Allow me to add that I remember with lively gratitude your kindness to me when at Paris, & am, with great regard,

Your faithful servant, Charles Sumner
of Boston—United States of America.

P.S. Since I had the pleasure of seeing you, *Mr Brownson*,[5] in whose writings you were interested, has received a small appointment under government—I think it is curator or superintendant of a hospital—with a salary of 6 or 7000 franks. I should not think the duties would greatly interfere with his literary labors.

M. Cousin Pair de France[4]

ALS FPSb (65/685, PCS)

1. Victor Cousin (1792–1867), French historian and philosopher.
2. A learned society, created in 1795, part of L'Institut de France.

3. David Baillie Warden (1772–1845), U.S. consul at Paris; member, L'Institut de France.

4. Cousin was made a peer of France in 1832.

5. In his meeting with CS in Paris, Cousin expressed interest in a number of American writers, especially Orestes Brownson (1803–76) (CS, Journal, 9 March 1838, Prc, 1:264–65).

To George S. Hillard

[*Munich*] 18 Sept. [*October and* 26 *October*] 1839

Dear Hillard,

The day after I wrote you from Venice, I made a painful discovery in my bed-room—or rather suspicions which I had been lead to indulge were sadly confirmed—it rained very hard, & promised a dismal night for travel—my mind, however, was at once made up to escape—I hastened to the post-office, & inscribed my name for a place in the Malle-Poste for that evening as far as Milan. We started at 8 o'clk—it poured down cataracts—my companions a countess "fat, fair & forty" who snored like a chambermaid, & an honest father with his son a boy of 14 going to a school in Switzerland to prepare for trade, by learning bookkeeping, geography, history, arithmetic, to speak English, French, German & Italian—all that night we rode in the midst of a tremendous storm—it is exciting to rattle over the pavements of villages, towns—& cities in the dead of night—to catch, perhaps, a solitary light shining, from the room of some watcher, "like a good deed in this naughty world"—&, when you arrive at the gates of a city—the postillion [winds?] his horn, & the heavy portals are swung open—it seems like a vision of romance—nor is it less exciting in earlier evening, when the shops & streets are all bright with light & people throng the streets, to dash along—all the next day we rode, & the next night, stopping one half hour only for dinner—we passed through Padua, Verona, Brescia, Bergamo—& at nine o'clk on the morning after the 2nd night entered Milan. This is a great place for encountering friends—it is such a thorough-fare. I had just entered the room which contains *Leonardo's* last Supper,—a painting truly divine—when I heard a voice—"By God—there is Sumner"—I turned, & saw Sir Charles Vaughan.[1] He is on his way to Rome. A friend here, who is travelling alone, *à la Beckford*, in his own carriage, urged me to take a place with him to Munich—a distance of nearly 500 miles. This luxury of travel, faring richly & easily, I at once declined—

Dashed down that cup of Samian wine[2]—wishing to lose no opportunity of seeing the people & talking the language—at once inscribed myself again for the Malle poste by the passage of the Stelvio, to Innspruck—started Sunday morning at 11 o'clk & arrived at Innspruck Wednesday morning 10 o'clk—sleeping out of the carriage but 3½ hours during those three days & three nights—the pass over the Alps is magnificent, dwarfing infinitely anything I have ever seen among the mountains of New Hampshire or Vermont—it is the highest road in Europe, being 8900 feet above the level of the sea, in the region of perpetual snow & amidst flashing glaciers—we stopped for a little sleep at 12 o'clk at night at Santa Maria a thousand feet below the summit—it was the 5th Oct—we had left the plains of Italy warm with sunshine—here was sharp winter—the house was provided with double windows—my bed had warm clothing to which I added my heavy cloak—& yet I was bitter cold, & before daylight was glad to stir my blood by ascending on foot—the sun was just gilding the highest snow-peaks when we reached the summit, & crossed the boundary line of Italy. My sole companion was an elderly, lean, learned, pragmatical German. I have travelled with all sorts of people, gentlemen, scholars, soldiers, priests, monks, saints & devils—& I have never failed to get something good out of all, even the two last. The villages of the Tyrol were beautiful. I wish that I could waltz. There was a fair Tyrolese who did me the honor of inviting me, through an interpreter, to this dance, while some wandering Hungarians played. After one day at Innspruck, again took the *Malle-Poste* for Munich,—a day & night—in the *Malle-Poste* found a very pleasant Englishman, quite a linguist, an antient friend of Cleveland's.—At the *table d'hote* here encountered our Mrs Otis.[3] She is *toute Française* in her dress & manners, & affects continental [*inserted in the margin*] I should not say of the *Continent*, but France. [*end insert*] manners & usages, particularly in her *coiffure*. She speaks French with great facility, & even grace, though I have heard her trip on her genders. She appears at the *table d'hote* in the dress of a dinner-party, making a great contrast with the simple costume of the English here. D'Israeli & his ugly wife[4] (whom he has taken for £5000 a year) were here. Mrs Otis said to D'Israeli (the conversation had grown out of Vivian Grey): "there is a great deal written in the garrets of London." Putting his hand on his heart, D'Is. said—"I assure you Vivian Grey was not written in a *garret*." D'Israeli speaks execrable French. Mrs. O. is attended only by her *femme de chambre*, & though she does not depart *perhaps*, from the *convenances* of the Continent, yet I doubt if there be another American & Englishwoman who could play the part she does. I respect her much for the pains she has taken with the education of her boys—She returns to Boston in the spring. My pen moves with such difficulty on this wretched paper, that I will abandon it for the present, to resume it at Vienna.

Vienna, Oct. 26th—At length in the Imperial City—left Munich in the Eilwagen for Passau—rode a day & night—at Passau, with an English friend, chartered a little gondola or skiff down the Danube 70 miles to Linz—dropped with the current through magnificent scenery till towards midnight, & stopped at a little village on the banks—to our inquiries, if they ever saw any English there, we were told "they should as soon expect to see God Almighty," & I was asked if America was not "in the neighborhood of Odessa"—at Linz took a carriage for Vienna—two days & a half—where I arrived yesterday. Have been refreshed by yr two letters of *Aug. 19th, & Sept. 23d.*—Do be of good cheer. Why don't you review Longfellows [??] Romance for the *N. American?* That would be a pleasing labor that would animate yr soul, & give play to the warmth of friendship.—You are becoming too much of a Cato—I have not seen L's book; but I would wager my reputation upon it. I am sure that in any fair balance of criticism it must be found—whatever may be its defects—full of high & singular merit. I do not write now for you to repeat it to Longfellow, but I assure you, as I look at my country at this distance, I see him distinctly in my mind, rising far above the herd of people to whom you at home have given reputation, whether for politics, law, or literature. Ah! "a ministering angel will he be" while those labellers, detractors & critics "lie howling."[5] I am vexed to the heart when I hear of the remarks to which he has been subjected, both in print & conversation, from persons, who are not worthy to lay their hands on his garment. I hope you will write an article on his work—& you can include the Poems, which shall put to flight those indecent harpies.—

You have doubtless heard of Webster's reputation in England. I have just recd a letter from my friend Morpeth (to whom I sent a letter for Webster), who says he "was much struck by him; there seemed to be a sort of colossal placidity about him." All appear to think him reserved & not a conversationist. *Sydney Smith* calls him the *Great Western*. My friend *Parkes*, whom I encountered with his family at Munich, says that his friends, such as *Chas. Austin & Grote,*[6] were disappointed in his attainments; nor did they think him as "true American." Parkes insists that on my return to London, I shall stay with him in his house in Great George St. He was highly gratified to know the author of that article on Milton, which he says is the ablest & truest appreciation of Milton's character ever published—entirely beating Tom Macaulay's or

Dr Channing's. *Parkes* wishes me to take to Emerson the copy of Milton edited by him in 1826 (Pickering's edition).[7] He has a collection of upwards of 100 works about Milton, & contemplates a thorough edition of him, & also of Andrew Marvel. But politics and £8000 a year in his profession bind him for the present.—

In your letter of *April 23d*, you mentioned that you had deposited £100 to my credit with Howe. *I have received no* notice *of it from the* Barings; & though I am not in want of it, yet I wish that you would be certain that *all is right*, so that I may avail myself of it on my arrival in London.

As ever C. S.

P.S. Morpeth says "no violent affection seemed to exist between the Stevensons[8] & Websters"!—

Send yr letters to the care of *Coates & Co* & London. Tell my friends of this.

ALS MH-H (62/415, PCS)

1. "A good deed," *Merchant of Venice*, 5.1.90. Sir Charles Vaughan (1774–1849), fellow of All Souls, Oxford; British minister to the U.S., 1825–31, 1833–35.
2. Lord Byron, *Don Juan*, 3.86.16.
3. Eliza Henderson Bordman Otis (1796–1873), widow of Harrison Gray Otis, Jr.
4. Benjamin Disraeli, earl of Beaconsfield (1804–81), Conservative prime minister, married Mary Anne Evans Lewis (d. 1872) in 1839.
5. "A minist'ring angel shall my sister be / When thou liest howling," *Hamlet*, 5.1.264.
6. Morpeth's letter, London, 13 August 1839, 2/357, PCS. George Grote (1794–1871), British historian, M.P.
7. Hillard's "The Poetical Works of John Milton," *North American Review* 47 (July 1838): 56–73. William Ellery Channing (1780–1842), Unitarian clergyman. Ralph Waldo Emerson (1803–82).
8. Andrew Stevenson (1784–1857), U.S. minister to Great Britain, 1836–41, and his wife, Sarah Coles Stevenson.

To Henry W. Longfellow

Vienna Nov. 10th '39.

Dear Henry,

Well said; you deserve little from me; but I will pour coals of fire upon yr head. Indeed, I cannot be still, when I read yr warm heart-to-heart letter. You should have written earlier; but such a letter wipes away a heavy score of delinquencies. When did it reach me, you ask? Ah! not in Italy, amidst those fields Elysian in my memory, nor was it my pocket companion when I passed the Alps, clambering high among snows & glaciers, & hugging precipices. I found it in Vienna on my arrival; & my soup stood before me untouched till it was cold, & the *hors d'oeuvres* were removed, while I devoured the repast which you had sent me. You still love.—*Miror magis.*[1] I wrote you from among the monks—a fit place to discuss a subject of love—giving you my views & feelings with a fullness & frankness that will require all yr friendship to pardon. I cannot differ now from what I wrote then. If she would not love me, I would not love her; & we should be at "quits."[2] But I have read enough of the page of life—that great book never fully unclasped to him who stays at home—& of those other pages, where are set down the experiences of men & women in affairs of this sort, to know that all cannot do as I suggest, & that a persevering heart often wins the fair lady who at first inclined another way. You are the best judge. I am as much surprized that she fails to love, as that you continue to love. Which will be the most persevering spirit—yr love or her indifference? The question will be answered before I return, I trust. Ah! Let me find you happy—rejoicing in friendship, & higher & stronger than this, the love of her who has yr love. Hillard writes me letters of distress, almost. I fear to find him drooping, & refusing to be consoled. His health seems bad; & his spirits far worse. I know you & all our friends do all that you can to lighten his burthens & to make him glad.—

Yr "Hyperion" I am burning to see, & should sit up all night to read it, wherever I may be, when it first reaches my hands. What I can do in London, I shall gladly do; but I shall be there so short a time, that I can hardly expect, in that mammoth place, to have an opportunity of conversing with many, whose voice would have much weight. But I shall be happy to write to several well-known to you by reputation; & I am not sur[e] that this would not be the more effective means; for if I simply speak about you & [yr] writings, what I say may be straightway forgotten; but a letter will remain. Be assured I shall do all that I can, when in London, & on my return, I will write to any persons with whom I may be acquainted, [to] whom you should like to have yr writings particularly introduced. I am ve[xed] with *Ford*, for his petty & pedantic article on Prescott in the Quart. Rev. In [??] &, the general impression it is calculated to leave upon a reader's mind, it is very unlike his letters & conversation. But he was, doubtless, obliged to pay his tithe to Toryism. I should be glad, nevertheless, to put into his hands yr [two? little?] translations from [Spanish?]. Did I ever write you that my friend Ingham[3] M.P. once took up a little collection called the *Columbian Lyre*, & was so much pleased with a piece of yours, that, when I told him you were my friend, he went & bought the book, & carried it on a journey as his travelling companion?—

I am glad you are resolved to devote yrself to literature. I look forward to the pleasure I shall have in yr success. I hope the "*Voices of the Night*" & "*Hyperion*" are already in the hands of a London house; not for money's sake, but to extend their circulation. I know well that English criticism is decisive with us. Do you remember the *trunk-maker*, whose powerful blows in ye Gallery as described by the *Spectator*—breaking benches, partitions &c—were considered the regulator of applause in the old London theatre. The management cheerfully undertook to repair all his nightly damage for the benefit of his potent knocks. Such is English criticism with us.—If I return to Paris, I shall execute yr order for the coats &c; if not, I shall probably, write to some friend to do it for me.—

Do you remember Vienna? Crowded streets, gay shop-windows, prancing horses, proud equipages, women innumerable in the streets, a [vitious?] dialect almost a *patois*, the best *cuisine* I have seen since I left Paris,—weather dismally dark, damp & cold—I have been knocked up with a cold, have kept in the house several days; taken warm tea before going to bed, have now discarded that & adopted the more masculine punch—do not report me to any of the Temperance Societies to which you belong,—bundle myself up with great coats & wollen scarfs when I go out, & am getting well again. Our Legation here is a bird of high feather. Van Buren was asked what Muhlenberg[4] had to qualify him for this post. "Oh" was the Presdt's reply "he speaks a little bad German." They tell me it is the dialect of the Suabian peasants; &, that when his excellency is at all excited, he talks like a farmer.—"*Das is kein Deutscher man*"—French is here the language of Society; but none of his family have a word of this. They have just returned from Italy. I asked his Excellency what he thought of this country—"Oh! it is all a humbug—it has got a name through a parcel of English writers who have exaggerated its merits & written it up—figs are not so good as pappaws, & they are obliged to water their orange-trees." Of all the cities, & he visited all from Genoa to Naples, he was best pleased with *Trieste*! This is too bad. But that is a specimen of our sorry representation abroad. Can we expect consideration, equal to our deserts, from people to whom we send such Ministers?—I wish to see Americans for Ambassadors, who, by their talents, education, & attainments, will command the respect—& not excite the derision—of courts & princes. It makes me sad to go from capital to capital, & note the ignorance, & bad breeding of those who represent us. I do not know how you were struck in yr travels, by our own countrymen; to me they seem illiterate, dull & uninteresting beyond endurance. I was told there were some four or five in the house where I am; but I have not asked their names, & live [in] hope of not meeting them. Their acquaintance would only occupy time without imparting any thing interesting or useful. There are two here among the best I have met[;] one of them, I gladly say, from what I have seen of him is a credit to us, full of various information, a correct appreciation of life & society, & great simplicity—his name is *Bissell*—a good scholar—speaks Latin, Spanish & French—& knows very well Italian & German. The other is a gentleman from New York;[5] well-known in society there & in Boston, of an agreeable address; but the conversation of the most interest to him is about the U.S. Bank stock. I own no stock; & [never?] expect to. What in the devil do I care about that? *Hallam* once asked me pleasantly in London, if in all my dining out there, I had ever heard a question about the "price of cotton"?—

I shall soon be with you; [&] I now begin to think of hard work—of long days filled with uninteresting toil & humble gains—I sometimes have a moment of misgiving when I think of the certainties which I abandoned for travel & of the uncertainties to which I return. But this is momentary; for I am thoroughly content with what I have done. If clients fail me, if the favorable opinion of those [on] whom professional reputation depends, leaves me, if I find [myself] poor & solitary—still I shall be rich in the recollection of what I have seen, & will make companions of the great minds of these countries visited. But it is to my friends that I look with unabated interest, & in their warm greeting & renewed confidence, I hope to find ample compensation even for lost Europe. Then will I work gladly; & look with tr[ust] to what may fall from the ample folds of the future.

Veggo, pur troppo
Che favola e la vita
E la favola mia non e compita.[6]

I hope people will not say that I have forgotten my profession, & that I canno[t] live contented at home. Both of these things are untrue. I know my profession better now than when I left Boston, & I can live content at home.—

I have been generous to Felton; but he niggardly to me. I wrote him from the South of France at the end of *April*—from Rome in *June*—

from Florence in Oct. None of these letters have been acknowledged. Has he re[ceived] them? I deeply hope he will come to Europe; but I fear that B. Whit [*MS torn*] failure may affect his arrangements. It should not.—I trust Mrs H.[*arriot*] Appleton is well by this time, & has a fine boy.[7] If you see her remember me to her, & tell her that her promises are like those of all her sex—easier made than kept. Not a line have I had from her since I have touched *outre-mer.*—

How is the *Scan. Mag.*?—That & Hyperion must have made even Nahant hot this last summer. Have you seen *Grattan*?[8] I trust my friends like him.—I hope, among you, something has been done for *Crawford*. Whatever may be lisped or said, I assure you, I am not mistaken, & that he is the honor to our country. The Muhlenbergs thought higher of him than of any other artist in the country. Tell this only to the Democrats; for it would [make?] against poor Crawford with people of taste. What a misfortune to be praised by an Ambassador!—

You alone are left to me, dear Henry. All my friends, save you alone, are now engaged or married. What shall I do?—I will beat you all.—I have my eye on a fair Jewess, who will bring me a warm nature, black eyes, & pearl necklaces for a dowery. She has an exquisite hand to boot, which, in the scales of love, outweighs the Sword of the old Gaul;—*bianco piu que latte.*[9] And now, good night; read all this trash with charity; & then burn it; & believe me

as ever Affectionately Yrs Charles Sumner

My address is Coates & Co, 13 Bread St., London—What are those beautiful lines of Ariosto describing a beautiful hand?—

ALS MH-H (66/008, PCS)

1. "I'm greatly astonished."
2. In his letter of 26 July 1839 from the Convent of Palazzuola (65/666, PCS; Prc, 2:106–7), CS advised Longfellow to "woo [*Fanny Appleton*] or abandon her."
3. Robert Ingham (1793–1875), British M.P. (Liberal).
4. Henry A. Muhlenberg (1782–1844), U.S. minister to Austria, 1838–40.
5. A Mr. Miller (CS to Greene, 30 December, 66/017).
6. "I see unfortunately that life is a fairy tale and my fairy tale is not finished."
7. William Sumner Appleton (1840–1903).
8. Thomas C. Grattan (1796–1864), novelist and historian; British consul in Boston, 1840s.
9. "Whiter than milk."

II

EARLY REFORM ACTIVITIES

July 1840 – April 1851

In the early 1840s Sumner advocated disarmament and prison reform. He helped Horace Mann build normal schools, wrote articles on international legal issues, and practiced law intermittently. Not surprisingly, Sumner regarded the law as a means of bringing about reform and employed his legal and scholarly talents to that end.

As he applied legal principles to the growing problem of slavery, Sumner clearly believed that the institution could be undermined by legislative means. He wrote his friend Congressman Robert C. Winthrop that under the common law a resident of the United States, black or white, was a citizen (9 February 1843). Common law, wrote Sumner, entitled fugitive slaves to trial by jury and due process of law (to Mann, 3 June 1850). In the Roberts case, Sumner contended that Massachusetts statutes had established a single integrated school system. For Sumner, slavery was only a "local institution" (to Lieber, 10 February 1842) and a state could not "extend its *injustice* to the *citizens* of *another* state" (to Winthrop, 9 February 1843). Later Sumner distinguished between legal crimes and moral crimes (see to Joshua R. Giddings, 6 May 1848). Slavery was indeed "legal," but its immorality spurred Sumner to work to change and stretch existing laws in order to weaken the institution. Sumner would not break the law himself, he wrote Giddings, but he "could not condemn those" who had broken a law they deemed unjust. In a similar vein, Sumner wrote Winthrop that the "Govt. cannot expect support when it ordains injustice" (9 January 1846).

Sumner's interest in disarmament and prison reform led him to follow European events closely and to correspond with other reformers there. His optimism flourished as he wrote to Richard Cobden (1 April 1848) about the fall of the July Monarchy in France, "I feel sure that this Revolution will promote human happiness." Events like the "unjust" Mexican War, he wrote his brother George, then residing in Paris, "seem tame by the side of these great events" (14 April 1848). When the revolutions of 1848 failed to secure democratic reforms, Sumner's attention turned back to the United States. He optimistically wrote the Scottish astronomer John Pringle Nichol (17 September 1849) that the U.S. "Govt. will change from its inward & pro-slavery course to a moral & anti-slavery course."

Indicative of his politics and personality were Sumner's feuds with the Boston establishment over prison reform, disarmament, the Mexican War, and finally and most importantly, New England tolerance of slavery. He opposed Louis Dwight's conservative leadership of the Prison Discipline Society. More significantly, he took on such worthies as his former friends Winthrop, Nathan Appleton, and Samuel Lawrence (a financial backer of Sumner's 1837 European trip). Sumner joined with other Conscience Whigs to lambaste Winthrop for his support of the Mexican War. Obviously politically motivated, Sumner's attacks on Appleton and Lawrence were also deeply personal. They reveal his naïveté, his rigidity, and his insistence on having the last word in any quarrel. *"I will not speak from a pulpit,"* Sumner wrote George P. Marsh (4 September 1847), yet Sumner's speeches were often sermons. He permitted no one, especially old friends, to impugn his speeches, even remarks delivered for rhetorical effect, such as the notorious "lords of the loom" phrase uttered in June 1848 (see to Appleton, 31 August 1848, note 3). In a letter to Lawrence (29 November 1848) Sumner defended this phrase as merely "the natural expression of an intensive sentiment of indignation." He could enjoy such language, but his opponents could not. In his letter to Lawrence, Sumner complained that Lawrence was "under ye influence of a sentiment so bitter as yr nature can well enlist," and that Lawrence should have refrained from using such vehement words against Sumner.

Though Sumner remained officially an outsider in politics, he became increasingly a strategist, adviser, and polemicist. Beginning with the Massachusetts protest against the annexation of Texas, Sumner went on in 1847–48 to urge his two congressional friends, Mann and John Gorham Palfrey, to move more aggressively against conservative Whigs and the proponents of slavery. Regularly he fed Mann legal arguments and citations for his congressional speeches and tracts. In December 1846 he began corresponding with two Ohio antislavery activists, Salmon P. Chase and Joshua R. Giddings, and sounded out Ohio moderates like Thomas Corwin. Declining to take a public role at the Buffalo Free Soil Convention in 1848, Sumner privately tried to pull Whigs like John McLean, Edward Everett, and George Briggs into the Free Soil party.

Did Sumner really want to remain behind the political scenes? To his brother George, Sumner wrote (30 September 1845) that he was "too much of a Reformer in law" to become a law professor, yet he would not seek political office because "in office my opinions will be restrained." He refused to run for Congress in 1846 and continued to express disdain for politicians and to maintain loftily, "I have never been accustomed to think highly of political distinction" (to Charles Francis Adams, 16 December 1850). Gradually, however, Sumner gravitated toward the center of antislavery politics, despite an overwhelming defeat as a candidate for Winthrop's old congressional seat in August 1850. His letters to Howe and Chase that month hint at his opportunity to become a U.S. senator. Colleagues and biographers have agreed that Sumner was not personally ambitious. Yet once Sumner embraced a cause—as by 1848 he had embraced antislavery—with no little vanity he considered himself its fitting leader.

To Richard Monckton Milnes

Boston July 31st 1840

Dear Milnes,

One word to you by this noble steam-ship, the Britannia,—one of the great shuttles to weave the bonds between our two countries—which sails from Boston tomorrow—or rather this day, as it is already after midnight. I think of you often, & wish that we could meet. Yr article on Emerson[1] has been most extensively read in this country (you know there is a Yankee reprint of yr Reviews) & gives great satisfaction. Emerson was highly pleased. It was the Rev. Dr Henry Ware, who wrote the article on yr Poems in the N. American—a person of respectable attainments, severe taste, a professor of Divinity at our Cambridge, about 50 years old. He was quite sorry, when I told him that you were annoyed by the first paragraph.[2] I see you are again in the field—"Poems for the People."[3] I am anxious to see them; for next to talking with a friend, is reading him. What can I write you, from my Western exile, that you will read?—Here I am, beyond the setting sun, returned home, with prosaic, work-a-day American life about me, still thinking, dreaming of Europe, & of the pilgrimage I there made—

Et outre mer fait mon pilgrimage. The old troubadour said this of the journey to the Holy Land.—Every thing here is on a small scale—my standard of comparison has changed, & what once seemed spacious

& magnificent I now know to be small. So much for eating of the tree of European life!—Our politics are vulgar. The candidate for the Presidency at the next election (*Nov.*) against Van Buren, is Genl. [*William Henry*] Harrison, whose face adorns a corner of this sheet, a person whose great recommendation is, that he beat you English at Tippecanoe (spirits of Marathon, Platea & Zama[4] think of this!) He lives in Ohio, in very humble circumstances—a very Cincinnatus. A Van Buren paper ridiculed him, as living in a "log-cabin" (see the print!) & drinking "hard-cider." Harrison's friends at once adopted these terms, as their watch-words, & present their candidate as the log-cabin & hard-cider representative. The vulgar appeal has succeeded beyond expectation. *Webster* has let himself to it, & every where is this election-cry—The Whigs (opposition) are confident of success. If they have it (& the chances are now in their favor) there will be a general change of office-holders, from the Presdt to the tide-waiters. Of course, our troop abroad will be recalled, *Stevenson* leading the dance home. Webster will, probably, go to London.—Fanny Elssler's success[5] has been transcendant. She will make by her 3 months trip $30,000—say £6000 pounds. Yr verses about her were much admired—The *Websters* speak of you with kindest recollections; & Mrs Paige[6] was much gratified by yr message to her. She regretted only that you had not seen fit to write it—*Prescott* is engaged upon his history of the Conquest of Mexico & Peru—& has already written about 200 pages of an introduction on the manners, customs &c of the natives. He is a sweet soul, with all sorts of gentleness, upon whose shoulders sits most gracefully, because worn unconsciously, that mantle of many colors—his European fame. You once told me that you had marked some 30 or 40 Americanisms on the margin of yr copy of the history of Ferd & Isabella. *Prescott* asked me to request you to send them to us. Pray do this.—Robert Mackintosh has returned to England with his Boston bride—a clever & accomplished woman. You will be pleased to make her acquaintance, as she would be, yours. What is Mac's chance in the *carriére* of diplomacy?—Answer me this. Remember me to Carlyle, & yr clever French friend, Rio.[7] Ah! I cannot forget you—any of you. Write me about every body & thing—

"Give all thou canst & let me dream the rest"[8] I kiss my hand to Old England!—Believe me, ever & ever,

Sincerely Yours, Charles Sumner

P.S. Can't you persuade *Moxon*[9] to republish my friend Longfellow's Poems—Voices of the Night? The Psalm of Life is the most beautiful thing ever produced here.

ALS GBCTC (66/041, PCS)

1. Richard Monckton Milnes, later first Baron Houghton (1809–85), British M.P., poet, and critic, had written "Emerson's Works. American Philosophy," *London and Westminster Review* 33 (March 1840):345–72.

2. Henry Ware (1764–1845), Harvard divinity professor, wrote in "The Poems of Richard Monckton Milnes," *North American Review* 49 (October 1839):348–54, "some have that ambiguous air of half-real, half-fictitious, which renders it doubtful to the reader, whether they have any true meaning or not" (348).

3. *Poetry for the People, and other Poems*, 1840.

4. Athenians defeated Persians at Marathon, Greeks defeated Persians at Plataea, and Scipio defeated Hannibal at Zama.

5. Fanny Elssler (1810–84), Austrian ballet dancer then touring the U.S.

6. Harriette Story White Paige (1809–63), wife of Boston merchant James William Paige and sister-in-law of Daniel Webster.

7. A. F. Rio (James Pope-Hennessy, *Monckton Milnes: The Years of Promise, 1809–51* [1949], 109–10).

8. "Give all thou canst; high Heaven rejects the lore . . . ," Wordsworth, "Ecclesiastical Sonnets," 3.43.

9. Edward Moxon, publisher of Milnes's poems.

To Henry Russell Cleveland

4 Court St. Sept. 23d '40

My dear Hal,

I write you from my elbow chair, where I am regularly at 9 o'clk in the morning. Things begin to assume their ancient aspect; I can see ordinary people, without disgust; & listen to the stories of clients with a patience that may fairly vie with Hillard's. I have already disposed of one weighty matter (say $50,000) by my opinion, which turned on a point that had escaped Rand & some other lawyers to whom the case had been submitted. So! *allons!* avaunt, ye croakers! who said I could never [file?] my mind to the business of my office. I can always do my duty; & *always will*.—You know I am liable for that Mckean[1] for some $1200; a bad tune to dance to on my return from Europe. To day I paid an installment of $240 on this; being my first money, over & above my expenses.

I fear, my dear Hal, I have compromised you & Sarah. You remember you were kind enough to give me permission to drive through yr grounds with Fanny Elssler. Last week, I presented Dr *Howe* to the fair *danseuse*, & he invited her to visit the Blind Asylum! I could not well avoid going with her! "In for a penny; in for a pound" thought I; so I offered to shew her the environs of Boston.—We drove by Grove Hall; then to Jamaica Plains, where, mindful of yr permission, I told the coachman to drive through yr grounds.[2] We passed yr house, where *Mademoiselle* seemed ravished by the place, & I invited her to descend;

we walked to the Summer House, & then to the margin of the lake, where we scaled stones, & made circles in the water (nothing more horrid than this), & then returned to Boston; she being enchanted with the spot, & saying *on pourrait* bien *être amoreux là.*[3] To-day I have heard a report, that I had had the effrontery to take Fanny E. to my friend Mrs Cleveland; & this first of Christian places, forgetting the first of Christian virtues, without which [it] is a tinkling cymbal, has talked of me, as if I had committed the great offence. I can bear well enough (though not with indifference) the scandal from my attention to Fanny; but I am troubled by a report that takes such a shape as this.[4] I know you & Sarah will do me the justice to believe that I would not take any improper advantage of your friendship for me; but, I fear, that some of her relatives, & perhaps, Mrs Perkins, not understanding me, or this affair, as well as you do, will think I took an undue liberty. I hope Sarah will hold me blameless. Perhaps, you will write me soon. Love to Sarah;

& Ever & ever Yours, Charles Sumner

P.S. I have tried to discourage Charley & Ned from going to the theatre so much

---

ALS NNBe (66/062, PCS)

1. Probably Henry Swasey McKean, Harvard tutor (See CS to William C. Russel, above, and 4 Sept 1835, 62/076, PCS).
2. At Pine Bank, Massachusetts.
3. "One would be able to be loved well there."
4. In a letter to Lieber (1 Sept 1840, 62/460) CS asked, "What can I do for her in this puritan place? T'were social death to be seen in public with her." Cleveland replied from Burlington, "be assured that if anybody is fool enough to suppose that you had brought her to be introduced to me and mine, I care nothing for such a supposition" (27 September, 2/576).

To George Sumner

Boston Oct. 30th '40—
Friday Evng—

Dear George,

"Once more into the breach!" Politics are raging; newspapers teem with stump speeches, election reports, & inflammatory editorials. Banners are waving in our streets; the front of the Atlas office is surrounded by earnest crowds; the Whig Republican Reading Room (in Scollay's buildings—Pemberton Hill) is wreathed with flags & pennons; this very day the Presidential election takes place in Penna. & Ohio, on Monday in Maine—in one fortnight we shall know who is to rule over us for the next four years. Though, there seems to be little or no doubt at present on the subject; the local elections that have taken place this autumn appear to have settled it. Without lending myself to the exulting anticipations of the Whigs, I can no longer hesitate to believe that Van Buren will lose his election, & by a very large majority.[1] I fear the coming six months will be a perfect *Saturnalia* in our poor country; the Whigs, elated with success, hungry by abstinence from office for twelve years, & goaded by the recollection of ancient wrongs, will push their victory to the utmost; of course, the example set by Jackson will be followed, &, perhaps, improved upon; there will be a general *turn-out* of all present office-holders at home & abroad; the war of parties will have new venom; & it is even intimated that the present party will do some mischief to the government, offices or country, when it finds that it must go out, as an evil spirit is said to rend & tear the body from which it is exorcised, or as a retiring enemy spikes its guns & throws caltrops in the streets to founder the horses of the victor. There is so much passion, & so little principle; so much devotion to party, & so little to country,—in both parties—that I think we have occasion for deep anxiety. Harrison's success will be the signal for a new organization of an *Opposition*, which will, probably, be the most vulgar, jacobinical, & furious that has ever appeared among us. Van Buren will be thrown aside, & Amos Kendall,[2] or Benton started as leaders—God save us from such Presidents!—They will underbid the Whigs in *vulgarity*; & to do this, they must descend into the lower deep. The Whigs have met with their present surprising & most unexpected success, by means of their low appeals—to hard cider, log cabins & the like—they have fairly beaten the Locos[3] at their own game, & pelted them with their own stink. This course has been deliberately adopted as the effectual way to meet them; the high-minded portion of the party regret it very much, & there are some (among whom I am willing to be counted) who think success, obtained by such vulgar means, of very doubtful value. But the greater part think nothing of these things, & are now in full cry—running down their game. I do not anticipate any very decided change in principles by Harrison's advent. One thing, however, will take place—namely, a practical alteration of our Constitution, so that no President shall be elected for more than *one term*. Harrison comes in pledged not to be a candidate a *2nd time*. His example will establish a precedent which will operate like Jefferson's determining not to be a candidate a 3d time. As his election is favoured by the merchants, I think it probable, trade will take a new start; there will be new confidence, which is the muscle of credit, & business will extend its arms freely again;—perhaps, we may have another speculation mania. I have already written you, I think, as to some of the probable changes. *Webster* to London; but the news of today is that Webster is very ill on his farm in New Hampshire, where he had gone *a stumping*; *Ewing* of Ohio, *John Davis* of Massach., *Preston* of S. Carolina, *Crittenden* of Kentucky, &, probably, *Rives* of Virginia into the Cabinet; *Legaré*[4] of S. Carolina will have a mission abroad; it is doubted if *Ed. Everett* will have any thing; in Boston, the collectorship will go to *George Bond* or *Isaac C. Bates* (the latter of Northampton); the District Attyship to *F. Dexter* (if he will take it); the District Judgeship (for old Judge Davis only awaits the rising of our sun to resign) to *Peleg Sprague*.[5] And so the offices are partitioned. Abbott Lawrence has been obliged from ill health to resign his seat in the present Congress; R. C. Winthrop has been nominated in his stead, & will, of course, be elected. I think him little more than a *formula* of a man; I shall, however, vote for him. Of course, *Morton*[6] will lose his election; he will, probably, resume the practice of the law at Taunton; his jacobinical conduct, since his election, will prevent his ever being restored to the bench. He is a vulgar fellow.—

I ask yr pardon, dear George, for filling so much of this sheet with politics; particularly as I am uncertain how you will receive all this narrative. If you ever were a loco, now is the time to shuffle off this coil; would that you could erase from the memory of all that last unfortunate letter in the *Post*![7]—There is another correspondent of this high-toned journal in Europe, now writing letters from London, full of bad grammar, vulgarity & Americanisms; of course you have the reputation of these, as you are the only *known* foreign correspondent of the Post. L. S. Cushing (who has recently taken a wife—Miss Lincoln, a cousin of Hillard, & daughter in law of James Savage,[8] with about $35,000) is quite concerned for yr politics; he has a sincere regard for you, & says that he is distressed to see you throw yourself away. You will excuse me, if I again allude to my own personal feelings. I [*MS torn*] & wish to sp [*MS torn*] silence [*MS torn*] warm or [*MS torn*] posely [*MS torn*] grieved [*MS torn*]. I would not have you act contrary to yr principles, or yr fixed convictions; but are you sure that you understand the real state of things here? do you know the character of the men with whom you are fraternizing? have you not been seduced by some slight personal attentions shewn to you a youth by the people in power? Perhaps, these queries will not affect you; but I am sure, if you resolve to continue with the locoes—if you think you are called upon to express publicly yr political faith—you will do it with dignity, decorum & gentlemanliness, & in a style corresponding with yr abilities, character & hopes; not in the language of oyster-cellars. Enough however of this stale topic; it is the last time I shall touch it.—

Now, as to the article on Greece; I have approached *Hale* in various ways, but to no purpose; I met *Greene* accidentally in the street, & was bold enough to tell him that you desired its insertion in the *Post*;[9] he said that he had laid it bye for insertion after the elections (three weeks from now); this is, probably, the last he will think of it; Park Benjamin promised Albert[10] to insert it in his mammoth sheet the *World* at New York, but failed, & then trumped up an excuse that his competitors inserted *Poor Jack* instead, without consulting the editor! You have placed yr light under the bushel. Further, if you trust to a rotten concern, you must expect to fall to the ground; I have written to the *editor of the Dem. Rev.*[11] asking for copies on yr account, also to have yr name enrolled as a subscriber; of course, no notice is taken of this; & Albert has undertaken to purchase in New York *three* copies to send to you. On the first page of this letter is a list of persons, to whom I have directed Albert to send the article, should it ever appear in a newspaper. What are yr plans of travel? how long shall you continue abroad? I do not enquire as to yr means; but I much fear, that you will spend an undue portion of time in the East, Italy, & Germany, so that you will be straitened both in money & time, when you reach France & England, the two countries the most exhausting of both these. I trust you will not travel one moment longer than you can with dignity. What are your views for life now? & what do you propose to do on yr return? I do not wish to impose my advice upon you; but I wish you would let me know enough, to give you a brother's sympathy. Tell me something of yrself. How are you in the languages? Which do you speak? read? How is yr health? How do you divide yr time? What studies pursue?—Do not believe that I put these questions, from any motive, except a sincere desire to know yr condition. I rejoice in yr improvement & success, & look forward with earnestness to meeting you.

Ever affectionately Yrs, Chas.

If this finds you at Vienna remember me to Clay, to whom I owe a letter. I shall write him immediately. I have announced you to my friend Fay[12] at Berlin. It is possible, if I knew yr plans & desires better than I do, that I might be able to give you some advice, the result of my own experience in the country you are about to visit.—*Henry* does no more than usual. I am annoyed, perhaps too much, by his calm indolence.—*Julia*[13] is as active & bright as he is the contrary. I shall let you know the result of the elections by the next steamer.

Greene at Rome; Greenough, Wilde, Edw. Everett at Florence; Thorp at Naples; Schwarz, our Consul at Vienna, & Clay, our Chargé; *Fay* at Berlin; General Cass, & Mr Wilkes, & Mr Warden, M. de Tocqueville, M. Foelix, M. Ledru,[14] at Paris; to M. Mittermaier at Heidelberg, in Baden[.]

German you will find difficult; but you will not hesitate to do battle with it. Take an instructor the first moment you arrive in any town to stay. I wish I could pass six months in Germany. I was not there long enough. But, don't give time to the examination of things, without looking to the future bearing of yr labors. Consider, whether you would not be doing more good, at home, in studies or business, rather than ranging abroad.

ALS MH-H (62/464, PCS)

1. Harrison defeated Van Buren, 1,275,017 to 1,128,702 popular votes.

2. Amos Kendall (1789–1869), U.S. postmaster general, 1835–40.

3. Locofocos, a radical wing of the Democratic party, advocating hard money and limited bank influence.

4. Thomas Ewing (1789–1871), U.S. senator (Whig, Ohio), 1831–37, 1850–51; U.S. secretary of the Treasury, 1841. John Davis (1787–1854), U.S. senator (Whig, Mass.), 1835–41, 1845–53; governor of Massachusetts, 1834–35, 1841–43. John Jordan Crittenden (1787–1863), U.S. senator (Whig, Ky.), 1817–19, 1835–41, 1842–48, 1855–61, (Unionist, Ky.) 1861–63. William Cabell Rives (1792–1868), U.S. senator (Dem., Va.), 1832–34, 1836–39, (Whig, Va.) 1839–45. Hugh Swinton Legaré (1797–1843), U.S. congressman (Dem., S.C.), 1837–39; U.S. attorney general, 1841–43.

5. George William Bond (1811–92), Boston manufacturer and merchant. Franklin Dexter (1793–1857), Boston lawyer. John Davis (1761–1847), judge, U.S. District Court in Massachusetts, 1801–41. Peleg Sprague (1793–1880), U.S. senator (Natl. Rep., Maine), 1829–35; U.S. district judge of Massachusetts, 1841–65.

6. Robert C. Winthrop (1809–94), U.S. congressman (Whig, Mass.), 1840–42, 1842–50; U.S. senator, 1850–51. Marcus Morton (1784–1864), governor of Massachusetts, 1840, 1841, 1843, 1844; Massachusetts Supreme Court judge, 1825–40.

7. CS may be referring to a letter dated 10 April addressed "Dear Brother" from Jerusalem, which appeared in the *Boston Morning Post*, 27 August 1840:1, or a letter, also to "Dear Brother," from Beirut, 3 May 1840, appearing in the *Post*, 1 September 1840:1. Both letters are travel descriptions, however; neither contains any political observations. The other *Post* correspondent CS refers to is one signing himself "P," writing from London.

8. Mary Otis Lincoln Cushing (d. 1851). Probably James Savage (1784–1873), Boston banker.

9. Nathan Hale (1784–1863), editor, *Boston Daily Advertiser*, 1814–54. Charles Gordon Greene (1804–86), publisher, *Boston Morning Post*, 1831–75.

10. Park Benjamin (1809–64), Boston lawyer, 1830s; journalist, *New Yorker, New York Evening Signal*, 1834–64. Albert Sumner (1812–56), brother of CS.

11. John Louis O'Sullivan (1813–95), editor, *United States Magazine and Democratic Review*.

12. John Randolph Clay (1808–85), U.S. secretary of legation, 1838–46. Theodore Sedwick Fay (1807–98), U.S. secretary of legation, 1837–53; U.S. minister to Switzerland, 1853–61.

13. Henry Sumner (1814–52), brother of CS, seaman. Julia Sumner Hastings (1827–76), sister of CS.

14. These names are the list CS refers to regarding George's proposed article on Greece. Richard Henry Wilde (1789–1847), writer and former U.S. congressman (Dem., Ga.). John George Schwarz, Vienna consul, 1829–53. John Wilkes (d. c. 1844), British journalist. Charles Ledru, French lawyer whom CS met in 1838 (Prc, 1:266).

To Sir Charles Vaughan

Boston—Feb. 28th '41

My dear Sir Charles,

The steam-ship sails tomorrow, & I cannot let it go without my thanks for your most agreeable letter from Oxford of Dec. 29th. It was very kind in you to send me the extract from the Quarterly Review,[1] which I feel to be most exaggerated praise. You will doubtless see in the newspapers the construction of the new cabinet, which commences on the 4th March. Webster Sec. of State; Ewing, a brawny man from Ohio, Sec. of the Treasy; John Bell, of Tennessee Sec. of War; *Badger*, of N. Carolina, a lawyer, who has never been in Congress, or known out of his state, Sec. of the Navy; Crittenden, of Kentucky, Atty Genl; & Francis Granger, of New York, Postmaster General.[2] The newspapers extoll this selection as comprising an unrivalled amount of ability, & as the most efficient Cabinet since the days of Washington. There are some, however, who lisp in conversation, that, with the exception of Webster, none are characterized by great ability or peculiar fitness for their posts. Upon Webster's Atlantean shoulders, it is said, all will devolve, & he must carry the country through the next four years. All Webster's associates are supposed to be friends & partizans of Clay, so that, if there be any difference in the policy of the two leaders, that of the latter will be represented. It is still unknown, who will succeed Stevenson. Report has fastened upon Mr John Sergeant of Phila;[3] but during this last week an impression has gained ground that Clay will be sent to London on a special mission, that he may have the honour of arranging the difficulties & healing the soreness between our two countries. It is doubtful whether Cass will be recalled. It is said that he desires to stay at Paris. I recently received a letter from him [in?] which he says that he abstained from sending you a copy of his little book, on the Court & King of France, from a motive of delicacy, as there were several things in it, pointed at England.[4] To speak the truth, it never should have been written. If you have not seen it, & have a curiosity to encounter it, I shall have great pleasure in sending you a copy.

You will see Pickens's Report on the Caroline affair, & war with England.[5] I think it has been repudiated by the whole country. It is a document which will do us great discredit[.] It is really afflicting to see that such an important topic, touching so many great relations, may fall into the hands of such a *Bombastes*. I think *Webster* will exercise a salutary influence over the negotiations that will ensue between the two countries. He loves England well. He has formed personal friendships there. His studies during his whole life & his tastes will conspire with these to make him guard our relations on the most amicable footing.— Perhaps, both nations will be obliged to keep before them the precept—"bear & forbear."—

Believe me, ever, dear Sir Charles,

very sincerely Yours, Charles Sumner

ALS GBOAS (66/144, PCS)

1. In his letter, 29 December 1840, 2/655, PCS, Vaughan included a passage from "American Orators and Statesmen," *Quarterly Review* 67 (December 1840):33–34. There Abraham Hayward wrote that CS showed how an American "by mere dint of courtesy, candour, an entire absence of pretension, [and] an appreciating spirit . . . may be received on a perfect footing of equality in the best English circles."

2. John Bell (1797–1869), U.S. congressman (Dem., Whig, Tenn.), 1827–41; U.S. senator, 1847–59; U.S. secretary of war, 1841. George Badger (1795–1866), U.S. secretary of the navy, 1841; U.S. senator (Whig, N.C.), 1846–55. Francis Granger (1792–1868), U.S. congressman (Whig, N.Y.), 1835–37, 1839–41, 1841–43; U.S. postmaster general, 1841.

3. Henry Clay (1777–1852) was then U.S. senator (Whig, Ky.). John Sergeant (1779–1852), U.S. congressman (Federalist, Natl. Rep., Pa.), 1815–23, 1827–29, 1837–41, declined the appointment.

4. Lewis Cass wrote CS about his pamphlet, *France: Its King, Court and Government* (1840), 20 November 1840 (Paris, 2/625, PCS).

5. Francis Wilkinson Pickens's report on the *Caroline* affair, 13 February 1841, stated that the House Committee of Foreign Affairs, while hoping "that harmony may long be preserved by both Governments," believed the *Caroline* was not illegally shipping supplies to Canadians. The report affirmed the right of the state of New York to try Alexander McLeod for murder. McLeod (1797–1871), a Canadian deputy sheriff, had been arrested on charges of murdering an American when the British seized and burned the *Caroline* (*Globe*, 26th Cong., 2nd sess., 1841, 170–71).

To Francis Lieber

Boston March 23d '41—

My dear Lieber,

Pray forget the past. You know me negligent, remiss, perhaps unfaithful; but you cannot doubt my sincere attachment to you, & my wish to serve you. I am sorry that aught should have occurred to ruffle anew our relations. Pray *have faith*, even as I have.—You will see the defeat of Talfourd's bill; & that by a semi-treacherous stab from that rhetorician Macaulay.[1] The *Examiner* (Fonblanque's) of Feb. 28th (I think) contains an admirable refutation of M's speech.[2] Poor Talfourd will be enraged. It is the bill he has nursed through several successive parlts, & where his heart was; & now to be overthrown by unexpected opposition from a scholar, & friend of scholars, will make him furious. It will not be grief, but downright rage that will absorb his soul. I shall send him my sympathy.—Macaulay seems a thorough failure—the sky-rocket, come down a stick. Milnes, in a letter recd yesterday, calls him "poor Macaulay" &c, & says that it is a great matter of regret to the Govt, that they did not take Charles Buller instead.[3] Milnes thinks of visiting us next autumn. The present Govt., it is acknowledged by all sides, will out-ride the present session. Ld Morpeth, of the Cabinet, writes me that he "has strong confidence in their vitality" &c, & other authorities, radical & tory accord them longer life.[4] We have been upon the verge of war; but Webster understands our difficulties, & the law of nations, & will not lack judgment or boldness; so I fear not. The English were unquestionably justified in the burning of the *Caroline*; but whether justified or not, if they have adopted it as a national act (as they have) all individual liability is merged in the grand responsibility of the nation. Suppose the Duke of Wellington visits France, & is prosecuted for a murder committed in entering France after the battle of Waterloo; this would be Mcleod's case. The only difficulty seems to be as to the *quomodo*[5] by which Mcleod shall be let off. How shall the court be informed of the fact that the British Govt. have adopted the burning of the *Caroline* as their act?—

Judge Story has returned from Washington, with more health & spirits than I have known him blessed with for a long time. He has gained new life from the death of the late Administration, though he is much vexed by the appointment of *Daniel*[6] to the Supreme Bench. He is described as no better than a 5th rate County Ct. lawyer. With our dear Judge will perish the Supreme Ct. of the U.S. Learning, high character, dignity, all will then have taken their flight. There is not a learned lawyer on the bench, after Story.—Greenleaf is putting to press his long-pondered work on the *Law of Evidence*. I have read portions of it, & am very much pleased. It will take the lead of all the English works on the subject, & be the manual of the student & practitioner. It will not be through the press before next autumn. Judge Story is taking up his work on Partnership, which he will carry on slowly through the summer.[7]

Prescott has completed his introduction to his history of the Conquest of Mexico, comprising an elaborate survey of the manners, institutions & origin of the ancient Mexicans. He was on the point of going to England with the Appletons, to pass the summer & enjoy his triumph in English society; but, after much debate & doubt, he has given up the plan. Fanny & Tom Appleton sail in the steamer of the 1st May.—How is yr Oscar?[8] Do you get cheering news from him?—Mrs Brooks always talks of you, when we meet. I heard Brooks, the husband I mean, make yr *éloge*.[9] Marsh Capen & Lyon are embarrassed; perhaps, have failed. Hillard had seen them about yr affairs. They will endeavor to account according to yr contract; the book has sold well;[10] but Hillard thinks they may be totally bankrupt. Hillard sends regards to you. He does not write because he is not well, & does nothing that he is not obliged to do. The past notwithstanding,

Yrs ever & ever, Charles Sumner

ALS MH-H (62/478, PCS)

1. In the House of Commons, 5 Feb 1841, Talfourd's bill to extend the copyright from 28 years from the date of publication to 60 years from the date of the author's death was defeated 45–38. Macaulay spoke at length against the bill (*Hansard's Parliamentary Debates*, 3rd series, 56:342–60).

2. "The Defeated Copyright Bill," *The Examiner* no. 1726 (28 February 1841): 130–31.

3. Milnes's letter, 1 March 1841 (2/690, PCS). Charles Buller (1806–48), Radical Reformer, M.P.

4. The Melbourne government remained in power until August 1841. Morpeth's letter is dated 13 Jan (2/630).

5. "In what manner."

6. Peter V. Daniel (1784–1860), Supreme Court judge, 1841–60, from Virginia.

7. Greenleaf, *A Treatise on the Law of Evidence* (1842–53); Story, *Commentaries on the Law of Partnership* (1841).

8. Thomas Gold Appleton (1812–84), brother of Frances Appleton and later a philanthropist. Francis Lieber's son, Oscar (1830–62), had been left with friends in Germany when the rest of his family returned to the United States.

9. Probably Charles Timothy Brooks (1813–83), Unitarian clergyman and German scholar, who married Harriet Lyman Hazard in 1837.

10. Marsh, Capen, Lyon, and Webb, Boston publishers of Lieber's *Great Events, Described by Distinguished Historians, Chroniclers, and Other Writers* (1840).

To Richard Monckton Milnes

Boston—U.S. of America
May 1st '41

My dear Milnes,

This morning of the *first* of May is as disagreeable as bad poetry—cold, gloomy, & with no ray of sunshine, or shew of flowers. It is such mornings that belong to *our* May days, & yet we, children of yours, repeat your verses about the 1st May, &, scouting the genial bed, sally forth to find flowers & green things, as if we were in merry England. Here is one of the signs of our intimate relation. We are fastened to you by all the many cords of literature & sentiment, which bind as strong as that iron chain of self-interest. And yet you talk of war. We cannot go to war. It is out of the question. No reflecting people here have supposed for a moment that there was any danger of it. *Webster* is our Secretary of State, in whose department falls the foreign affairs. He will see that all is arranged amicably, & that the republic receives no detriment. The last Administration have left our relations with you very much embroiled, & it will require all possible prudence & skill to unravel the tangled skein. They made, through Mr Stevenson, as long ago as when I was in London, a demand of satisfaction for the burning of the *Caroline*, which, I thought at the time (for Mr S. read me his long note to Ld. P.) unreasonable & untenable.[1] Lord P. took no notice of this demand. So far as I understood the facts, you were justified in what you did. It were better, perhaps, if you had not done the deed; but it seems defensible, not on the ground of hot pursuit of an enemy into a neutral's territories, but as an act of *high necessity* for *self-defence*. Van Buren's Administration kept this question open between the two countries, to use it as political capital in the New York elections. As it was, however, they lost these elections. I have no doubt the new Administration will see it very much in the light in which I have put it; at all events, they will discuss it frankly, fully & with a view to its adjustment on proper grounds of international law.—*Mcleod* is safe. He will be ultimately discharged; but this cannot properly take place, except in a judicial way, as he has been indicted. His defence is a valid one, namely that he was engaged in an act of national hostility, for which his Queen is responsible. There, then, remains only the old outstanding boundary dispute which must be settled by umpirage. The Report of Featherstonhaugh & Mudge,[2] we consider a very trashy production—pardon the freedom of my language.

Emerson has published a vol. of Essays [*Essays, First Series*], which *you* will read with pleasure; they abound in fine thoughts & expressions, with striking oddities side by side. I would send you a copy, if I did not suppose that Emerson has reserved that pleasure to himself. There is a little vol of poems—"a year's life," written by a young man of 21, being the chronicles of his love, which I have sent you by a friend. You will find some of them very pretty, particularly "Irene."—When shall you come to us? We shall all be glad to see you, & give you of our plain fare. Seriously, I can hardly find it in my conscience to urge you to come. I fear much that you would be disappointed. Write me more fully as to yr plans. You would wish to be at Washington during the session of Congress; that will commence the first Monday in December. Niagara is still safe!—I have given a young friend of mine Mr Appleton a line of introduction to you. He goes out with his sister Miss A. (one of our most agreeable American women) to visit Mrs Robert Mackintosh for the summer. If you meet them about, let me commend them to yr kind notice, as friends & fellow townspeople of mine. Appleton will assist you in planning yr journey to America.—Sparks has just returned, having been completely successful in the object of his visit, namely, the collection of materials for the English & French archives for a History of the American Revolution.[3] He speaks of yr kindness to him, & of that breakfast, where there were *eight* poets!

Farewell! ever & ever Yours, Charles Sumner

ALS GBCTC (66/157, PCS)

1. On 22 May 1838 Andrew Stevenson wrote Henry John Temple Palmerston, third viscount (1784–1865), then British foreign secretary, that Britain was responsible, under the law of nations, for the deliberate attack on the *Caroline (Diplomatic Correspondence of the United States: Canadian Relations*, vol. 3, ed. William R. Manning [1943], 449–56).

2. This British surveyors' report of George Featherstonhaugh and Lt. Col. Mudge, submitted by Palmerston to Henry S. Fox, British minister to U.S., 3 June 1840, favored the British claims along the Maine–New Brunswick border (Edward Everett to Lord Aberdeen, 13 August 1842; ibid., 779–781).

3. Never completed.

To Francis Lieber

Boston June 3d 1841

My dear Lieber,

Thanks for yrs of May 21st, & its multifarious contents. You have pleased a warm friend of mine very much. Dr Howe will be happy to have you make any use you see fit of his *report*, on Laura Bridgman;[1] he would be glad if you would quote from the *2nd* edition, which is now forthcoming. I am very much attached to Howe. He is the soul of disinterestedness. He has purged his character from all consideration of *self*, so far as mortal may do this; & his sympathies embrace all creatures. To this highest feature of goodness add intelligence & experience of no common order, all elevated & refined by a chivalrous sense of honor, & a mind without fear. I think of the words of the Persian poet, when I meet Howe—"Oh God! have pity on the wicked. The good need it not; for in making them good, thou has't done enough."—We are together a good deal. Both have been wanderers, & both are bachelors; so we drive fast & hard & talk, talk, looking at the blossoms in the fields, or those fairer in the streets.—You have doubtless seen the Edin. Rev. ere this.[2] The tone is good & respectful; but all reviewers aim to seem wiser than their authors. They try to *write down* upon their subject; & happy he, who can do this with what he attempts.—You do not do Bancroft justice.[3] I like his history very much. It is not complete, perfect, or entirely satisfactory to the calm truth-seeking mind. It is eloquent, fervid, brilliant, & calculated to excite the patriotism of those who read it, & to stimulate the love of liberal institutions. It makes a deep impression. The reader is kept excited. He travels from mountain to mountain, from peak to peak, & never finds the repose of a valley, or a canter over a level plain. Sparks will give us an anatomy of history, with red sealing wax poured into all the veins, & every fibre at its full tension; but the heart will not beat. Let them both work in their vocation. They have grand themes; & the country will gain by them.—We do not differ much about *Mcleod*. I trust *Minos* will teach the Lockport judge[4] some of the duties of the bench. Where would Dante doom him?—The English, you say, were right in destroying the *Caroline*. I am disposed to think so, on the facts, as we have them. But their course can only be vindicated by the *necessity* of *self-defence*. Now what a *nation* does, under this *necessity* & for this *object*, is justifiable, as if the same were done by an individual. But in *Mcleod's* case the enquiry cannot be pushed to the question of *necessity* & *self-defence*. The English govt. acknowledge the act of the burning of the Caroline, & take the responsibility for it. To a certain extent, this was a warlike incursion upon our territory. Now, all engaged in it, I admit are *prima facie* guilty of murder &c. They are, therefore, properly indicted in our courts. And being indicted there is no *prerogative* here or in England to arrest the course of judicial proceedings. Ld. Palmerston was too hasty in demanding the immediate discharge of Mcleod.[5] It would not be done in England, land of the common law, & of liberal institutions. But on his trial, I think Mcleod will have a sufficient defence, in shewing that the act in which he was engaged was undertaken by him, in military subordination to his superiors, & that it was an act of *national* & not *individual* aggression. The questions you put about the Duc d'Enghien[6] perplex me somewhat. But when we meet, we will solve these.—I saw Mrs Ellett of yr University, at Bancroft's the other evng, & talked to her about you. I did not like her. I do not like women who have written books & articles. Commend me to that female soul, that throbs with all that is feminine, that, knowing books well, knows human affection better, & that *writes* love letters, rather than books. Mrs E. seemed to think nothing of me, because I had never written a book. She has a scowl, like the horseshoe of Redgauntlet. Pardon me for dealing so freely with yr neighbour.[7] Hillard has recd yrs; & will attend punctually to all yr affairs. Goodbye—

Ever & ever yrs, C. S.

ALS MH-H (62/486, PCS)

1. At the Perkins Institute, Samuel Gridley Howe had been working with the deaf and blind girl Laura Bridgman, and had recently issued a report on her educational progress. Lieber's *On the Vocal Sounds of Laura Bridgman* was published in 1850.

2. Review of Lieber's *Political Ethics*, *Edinburgh Review* 73 (April 1841):55–76.

3. *History of the United States* (1834–75) by George Bancroft (1800–91), U.S. secretary of the navy, 1845–46; U.S. minister to Great Britain, 1846–49; U.S. minister to Germany, 1867–74.

4. Samuel Nelson (1792–1873), New York Supreme Court judge (later on the U.S. Supreme Court), became ill and was replaced by Philo Gridley (Howard Jones, *To the Webster-Ashburton Treaty* [1977], 63).

5. Palmerston declared that since the raid on the *Caroline* was an official British act of self-defense, McLeod should be released. McLeod was indeed acquitted by the New York courts on 12 October 1841 (ibid., 29–30, 65).

6. On 1 April 1841 Lieber had written CS, "If what McLeod's prosecutors maintain be true as to his act, it is the case of the Duc d'Enghien" (*The Life and Letters of Francis Lieber*, ed. Thomas S. Perry [1882], 150). Louis-Antoine Henri de Bourbon, Duc d'Enghien, was executed in 1804 by Napoleon on false claims that he sought to overthrow the French government.

7. Elizabeth F. Lummis Ellet (1818–77), literary critic, translator, travel writer. Redgauntlet, a zealous Scottish Jacobite in Walter Scott's 1824 novel by that name. Despite CS's preference for "that female soul," he did assert that wives should hold property independently of their husbands (CS to Howe, 30 September 1844, 63/057, PCS).

To Ralph Waldo Emerson

4 Court St. August 23d '41

My dear Sir,

Since I had the pleasure of seeing & hearing you at the State House, I have received a letter from Milnes, wherein he writes as follows;

"The 'year's life' is a little volume full of grace & power, & Emerson's Essays delight me so much that I am about to write a little notice of the English reprint of them in Frazer's Magazine. x x x *I* have committed nothing but a theological brochure (anonymous) called "One Tract more," of a nature too occasional & local to claim any ultra-Atlantic interest, but which I would send you were I in town, & had any copies by me." [1]

Is the above *sentence* worth the postage between Boston & Concord?—The weights in yr scales are not of the nice Utilitarian measures, guaging profit & loss by hairs-breadth; so that I am emboldened to play my communication against 6¼ cents. Believe me, my dear Sir,

very faithfuly Yours, Charles Sumner

ALS MH-H (66/173, PCS)

1. 27 July 1841 (3/60, PCS).

To Joseph Story

Boston Jan. 31st '42

My dear Judge,

What can I write you from Boston? We are living in peace, undisturbed by the wars & tumults of Washington. Hospitalities to Dickens are the most interesting circumstance that I can communicate. He has brought a letter & pamphlet from Ld Brougham for you, which he hopes to be able to deliver to you in Washington. He had two letters for me; & I have seen much of him. [1] He is a most delightful person, overflowing with genius, cordiality & kindliness. Under *thirty* (he will be 30 next month), & a more than conqueror of the world. The whole country seems prepared to rise up to do him honour. In Boston he has been oppressed by calls, & invitations; & has been obliged to engage a private secretary, who will accompany him, to write notes & letters, in answer to the numerous invitations & compliments he receives. The dinner is to be given tomorrow. I shall not be there; Hillard goes, & will make a beautiful speech. William [*Story*], of course, is in all his glory. I introduced him to Dickens, & they both rattled very fast together. I think you will like him very much. He is a very *lovable* person.

I enclose two letters by the last packet, one from *Ingham*, the other from *Parkes*. You will see how Ingham speaks of you. [2]

Pray remember me most kindly to Mr [*Richard*] Peters, whom you see daily. I trust he is able to bear with composure his great bereavement.

This letter is short, & does not go for much; but it gives me another opportunity of subscribing myself, as ever

most affectionately Yours, Charles Sumner

P.S. Hillard joins in remembrances to you.

Chancellor Kent wrote me that he my article on the Right of Search[3] was "sound, logical & conclusive—I have no hesitation in subscribing to it—there can be no doubt of it." So thinks Judge [*John*] Davis, Judge Prescott.[4] I understand Mr *Legare* thinks otherwise. How does *Webster* think? How does *Legare* succeed? & what manner of man is he?

ALS MiUc (66/232, PCS)

1. Dickens's visit to Boston is described in his *American Notes*, chapter 3, and in *Letters of Charles Dickens*, ed. Graham Storey et al., vol. 3 (1974), 15–51.
2. London, 15 December, and Westminster, 4 October 1841 (3/150, 116, PCS).
3. The 1841 Quintuple Treaty (to which the U.S. was not a party) had outlawed the slave trade. CS's article "Right of Search On the Coast of Africa," *Boston Daily Advertiser*, 4 January 1842:1–2, responded to a recent allegation by President John Tyler that Great Britain violated international maritime law in stopping ships sailing under the American flag which she suspected might be slave traders in disguise. CS defended Britain, stating, "The right of a belligerent cruiser to detain and search, in order to ascertain whether the ship or cargo are liable to capture, naturally carries with it all the means necessary to its exercise." For CS's summary of his argument, see his letter to George Sumner, 29 March 1842.
4. William Prescott (1762–1844), Boston lawyer and father of the historian.

To Francis Lieber

Boston Feb. 10th '42

I was glad, Dear Lieber, to receive yrs of Jan. 30th, & hope that you will still *understand* me in the same spirit in which that is written. I know very well that I fail often in duty to friends & strangers; but I claim a candid appreciation of my efforts, at least from my friends.[1] But a-truce to all this.

I am sorry that you mis-judge Longfellow's book [*Ballads and Other Poems*] so widely.[2] I think it contains some of the most beautiful gems of American poetry—I would almost say some of the most beautiful in

English poetry. The description of the wreck in the ballad of the *Hesperus* is one of the most beautiful things in English ballad literature. *Excelsior* is a noble poem, which cannot die, & which, as long as it lives, will fill with new energies those who read it, besides exciting the highest admiration of the writer. Endymion is a most poetical thought, beautifully wrought; "It is not always May" is a most melodious composition—said by some to be a sort of *stern-chaser* at a fair friend of ours.—A Rainy Day is a little pearl—Maidenhood is a delicate, delicious, soft, hazy, composition—God's Acre is a very striking thought. Then, the hexameters. I do not like the measure in English. Our language has too many little words to bear this dactylic & spondaic yoke; but Longfellow has written the best that have been written in the language. How could you say there was nothing clever in the book? Get you gone, & repent! Four editions in little more than a month attest something; to say nothing of the concurring testimony of our best critics here. Read the book again. Howe writes me from Frankfurt Ky, where he has every prospect of all he wishes—that he has "read L's book over & over & over again, & read it to his boy also."[3]—

I return you yr notes on the Right of Search. I sent you sometime ago a reply to my article which appeared in the Daily Adv., written by J. C. Perkins of Salem, a lawyer of great attainments & acuteness in his profession. I have taken up the subject again, partly to rejoin to him, & partly to consider several points which I have heard stated in various places on the subject. In my 2nd article[4] I have taken the liberty of stealing something from you. You will recognise yr property when you see it. Tell me how the question stands on this last article. The *Natl Intell.* I am told has published my *first* with some notes of praise, while the *Globe* & *Madisonian* has come out against—I have not seen either. I do not belong to a reading-room, & see very few papers.

I long to see yr letter on the *Creole*; & wish I could send you a copy of one I wrote to Mr Harvey of New York about a month ago who wrote to me asking me what I thought of the case.[5] My opinion is very clear—1st—Whatever might have been expected of England prior to August 1st 1834, *since then* she cannot be called upon to recognise slavery *nor* to afford the machinery of her justice & state to sustain it in any way. She has pronounced it immoral, & unjust; & no country can be called on to enforce the immoral & unjust laws of another. This disposes of the case of the slaves, who took no part in the mutiny & murder. 2nd—Slavery is a local institution, deriving its vitality from local laws—unknown to the common law, to the law of nature, & to the law of nations. It can have force only on the soil over which these local laws, from which it is derived, extend. If a slave-master voluntarily takes his slave beyond this jurisdiction, as into another state, or on the Atlantic ocean, he manumits him. On the ocean he is a free-man. The courtier of Queen Elizabeth said the air of England was too pure for a slave to breathe in; so it is with the breezes of the sea. The *Creole* slaves on the ocean were remitted to their original rights—all restraint was unlawful; & they committed no crime *cognizable* even by *our* laws. They are, therefore, in the same predicament with the others who took no part in the mutiny. 3d—Even if the slaves were guilty of a crime according to *our* jurisprudence; still they were not according to any law administered by England; nor, under the law of nations, or treaties, can we call upon England to surrender them up.—I have thought of discussing this subject; but I will leave it to others.—

I have the Laura [*Bridgman*] MS safe in my drawer; but have not yet received the books from the *Harpers*. I will write them to-day. Remember me to yr wife—I wish I had such a wife—any body in the world to love me as she loves you.

Ever yrs, C. S.

Mary,[6] if she knew I was writing, would send her love to Mrs. L. & her best regards to you. She has been expecting a letter from you.

ALS MH-H (62/527, PCS)

1. CS and Lieber had recently exchanged several letters about the lack of faith CS alleged Lieber had toward him.

2. Lieber wrote CS that "there is nothing clever" in Longfellow's recent book and he particularly criticized Longfellow's "awful would-be hexameters" (21 January 1842, 66/225, PCS).

3. Letter of 30 January, 66/230.

4. Responding to CS's reliance on Palmerston's statements as support for CS's discussion of the right of search in his 4 January article, Jonathan C. Perkins (d. 1877) stated that Americans needed more than the British foreign secretary's assurance that the right of search would be practiced according to international law (*Boston Daily Advertiser*, 21 January 1842:1). In his second article, CS further distinguished between the wartime right of search and a peacetime "right of *inquiry*" (ibid., 10 February 1842:1–2). See CS to George Sumner, 29 March 1842.

5. On a voyage from the U.S., slaves on the American ship the *Creole* mutinied and forced the vessel to dock at the British port of Nassau. When British there freed all the slaves except the mutineering crew, Secretary of State Webster demanded that all the crew be returned to the U.S. for criminal charges; the British, however, demurred. CS's letter to New York lawyer Jacob Harvey (14 January 1842, 62/521, Prc, 2:199–200) presents essentially the same analysis of the *Creole* case as this letter to Lieber. On 1 August 1834 the British had emancipated all slaves in their West Indian possessions.

6. Mary Sumner (1822–44), CS's sister.

To George Sumner

Boston March 29th [*and 1 April*] '42

Dear George,

The steamer of the 4th March has at last arrived, after a tempestuous passage & the breaking of a shaft, without any news of you. I hoped you would let us hear from you by every steam-packet at least, & tell us something about yourself. We would all give more for a hearty letter about your own plans, your pursuits, your studies; your friends, the way you employ yr time, than for the largest & most elaborate discussion on steam boats or any question of the law of nations. Hillard would have been better pleased by a letter of friendship, than a letter for publication. Mr Hale was glad to print the letter from Brussels,[1] of which I send you 2 copies; I shall also send copies to Mr Maxcy at Brussels, Mr Van de Weyer in London, & Mr Bates, of the house of Baring all of whom I know very well.[2] The letter on the right of search shared a different fate. Mr Hale did not incline to publish it; indeed, he thought it would be better to suppress it entirely. We on this side do not respond to yr warmth; we differ from Genl. Cass entirely & regret very much the course he has taken.[3] I have read his pamphlet carefully, & have been pleased with its ready flow, its agreeable style, its patriotic fervour & its general ability; but I must say to *you*—not to be repeated, however, that its argt seems to me unworthy a statesman & a diplomatist. He has mixed up questions which are not all related—he has introduced the old questions of impressment & other grievances growing out of the belligerent right of search, into the discussion of the late claim of England, which is entirely distinct in its nature from all others.

This claim turns upon a nice point in the law of nations, almost technical, certainly juridicial in its character. It is simply this. If an English cruiser commits a trespass on board an American vessel, suspecting this vessel *not* to be an American, & also, suspecting her of being engaged in the slave-trade, what is the *measure* of *liability* for the commander of the cruiser. He has committed a *trespass* unquestionably in setting his feet *without permission* on any ship with the *true* American flag; but the *maritime law* of the civilized world, a part of the law of nations, says that the officer shall not be liable in damages provided he had *probable cause to suspect* the ship of being liable to capture. *Probable cause* is a sufficient defence for any marine tort. This has been several times declared by the Supreme Court of the U. States—the highest & most authoritative expounder of the law of nations so far as we are concerned; but I will not trouble you with an argt. on the question. Perhaps, you have received an article I wrote on this subject in the *Advertiser* of Jan. 4th. My own opinion is of very little consequence, though such as it is, it was the result of considerable study & reflection, & is my most sincere & conscientious opinion. I followed up my first article with another & longer one, more technical, which I was not able to send you, as all the copies were taken up. Judge Story coincides *entirely* in the view I presented; & Chancellor Kent wrote me, on reading my first article, that he subscribed to it *without hesitation*.[4] So also did Judge Prescott, & Mr Jeremiah Mason,[5] Mr Choate & Dr Lieber. I feel disposed to discuss the question in a pamphlet; but I shall wait till the arrival of the next steamer to see how the question stands on yr side of the Atlantic. Entertaining these views you may imagine that I did not sympathize strongly with yr fiery article. I, however, gave Mr Hale the opportunity of publishing it; when he declined, I sent it to the *Morning-Post*, which presented it gladly to the public.[6]

April 1st—Dr Channing has put forth a glorious pamphlet on the *Creole* in reply to Webster's sophistical despatch.[7] One feels proud of being a countryman of Channing. His spirit is worthy of the republic, & does us honour abroad. His is a noble elevation which makes the pulses throb. The paltry, uncertain, shifting principles of Webster's letter are unworthy of him. The question of slavery is getting to be the absorbing one among us, & growing out of that is that other of the *Union*. People now talk about the value of the Union, & the North has begun to return the taunts of the South. But let drop to personal affairs. [*MS torn for half a page.*] [re]fined sugar by a duty of 27 to 30 percent, while a very low duty of 10 percent is levied on raw sugar, so that the manufacturer may get his raw article cheap, while the rival manufactured article is excluded from the market. Unless some legislation takes place on this subject before June, they will obliged to suspend work at the Refinery, turn the key of the door & put it in their pockets, to await the legislation of next winter. Mother[8] is in great anxiety, fearing that she will be stripped of all that she has, & not knowing how each year will [*MS torn for one-third page.*] which excite interest or admiration—

You correct me for my opinion about Rail Roads. When you return (if that ever takes place) you will be a better judge. I thought as you, when in Europe; but remember what I say, that the *worst* European road is *better* than the *best* American; & when I use the word *better* I refer to the *road*, the *speed*, the *carriage*, & the accommodations in general—

My dear friend Longfellow, whose fame has increased vastly since you left the country, sails in the packet for Havre on the 24th April to be absent six months for his health. The chief of his time will be passed at one of the German baths. Perhaps he will pass through Paris. Two young friends of mine Edward Perkins & Saml. Eliot will be in Paris in May; & Mrs Wm H. Eliot[9] leaves Boston soon for Europe. Tell me who you know in Paris. Whose *soirées* do you attend? How does Cass live? How are his dinners? Have you explored the *Roches*, & the chief places of the *Palais Royal?* Felton has been very ill, but is getting better. Before you visit Spain, read *Prescott's Ferdinand & Isabella*. Before you leave Paris provide yourself with an ample store of French boots, & if you could send me several pairs—from 2 to 6 pairs—made on my last at *Forr's* in 1838–9, I shall be glad. *Forr* is *Rue St. Honoré* nearly opposite the Palais Royal. Have you visited at Thorn's?[10] & danced with his youngest daughter? She was very beautiful. What beautiful & attractive women do you see, or have you seen?—So ends my catechism.

Ever & ever affctaty Charles—

If it is true that *Cass* has *protested* against the Quintiple Tr. he has taken an extraordinary step, which, I have some reason to believe, will not be approved by *all* of [the] [*MS torn*] If Mr [*Henry*] Wheaton is in Paris make my complts to him [*MS torn*] I have read his *Progres du Droit de Gens*, & am read[ing] [*MS torn*] with great pleasure & instruction.

ALS MH-H (62/533, PCS)

1. "Belgian Steam Packet," *Boston Daily Advertiser*, 18 March 1842:2.

2. Virgil Maxcy (1785–1844), U.S. chargé d'affaires at Brussels, 1837–42. Sylvain Van de Weyer, Belgian representative to Great Britain, and son-in-law of Joshua Bates. Joshua Bates (1788–1864), American banker, Baring Brothers partner.

3. In *An Examination of the Question, now in Discussion, Between the American and British Governments, Concerning the Right of Search* (Paris editon, 1842), Cass argued that the Right of Search (provided for in the recently negotiated Quintuple Treaty) would give the British grounds for impressment (26–37). He urged the French not to ratify the treaty, which outlawed the slave trade. Although not a slavery proponent, Cass stated that slavery and the slave trade were not internationally illegal; thus Britain could not declare the slave trade illegal for all nations (65–69).

4. 6 February 1842, 3/197, PCS; Prc, 2:192.

5. Jeremiah Mason (1768–1848), U.S. senator (Fed., N.H.), 1813–17; Boston legal consultant, after 1838.

6. George Sumner's article, in the form of letters from Paris entitled "Foreign Correspondent of the Post," appeared in four issues of the *Boston Morning Post*, 17, 19, 21, and 22 March 1842. In these letters, he criticized Britain for hypocritically abolishing slavery in the West Indies and stated that Britain could not survive a war against the U.S. and the European powers.

7. In his letter of 29 January 1842 to U.S. minister to Great Britain Edward Everett, Webster stated the U.S. case regarding the *Creole*. These slaves on the ship, wrote Webster, were recognized by the Constitution as property of American citizens,

and the British authorities at Nassau should have restored the captain and sent the mutineers to the U.S. for trial. British law was not enforceable on an American ship, and Britain should maintain a "doctrine of non-interference" (*Writings and Speeches*, 14:373–81).

In *Duty of the Free States; or Remarks Suggested by the Case of the Creole* (1842), William Ellery Channing criticized Webster's version of the *Creole* mutiny for its "morally unsound and pernicious doctrines" and its tendency "to commit the free States to the defence and support of slavery" (*Works of William Ellery Channing* [1877], 853–71).

8. The Compromise Tariff Act of 1833 provided gradual reduction in duties until 1842, when they were reduced sharply (Frank Taussig, *The Tariff History of the United States* [1892], 110). CS wrote his brother Henry that his mother's (Relief Jacob Sumner, 1785–1866) refinery stock was "little better than a drag." He wished she had not invested so heavily in sugar refining (14 April, 62/535).

9. Samuel Eliot (1821–98), writer, historian, and educator, and his mother, Margaret Boies Bradford Eliot (1796–1864).

10. The American Herman Thorn (c. 1784–1859) had married Jane Mary Jauncey, daughter of a wealthy Englishman, and entertained lavishly in Paris (HWL, 1:549).

To William Ellery Channing

Boston May 31st 1842

My dear Sir,

I have just received a letter from Ld Morpeth under the date of May 22nd 1842 from the Sulphur Springs of Virginia, I venture to copy a passage for yr eye.[1]

"I have to thank you very much for sending to me Dr Channing's publication, [*on the* Creole *case*] which I wanted extremely to see, & Dr Howe's very interesting notice of Laura Bridgman. I was very much delighted with Dr Channing, with the logic, the eloquence, the whole spirit, & I think that unless his countrymen are more under the evil spell even than he supposes, it must do real good. I wish that my countrymen too might have the grace to profit by the admonitions to them which he conveys. I am very glad that he does full justice to them on the subject of Slavery because I think it their due, & it is the point on which they are now subject to such general, I cannot honor it by thinking it altogether such bona-fide misrepresentation; & on that account, & still more, if it should incidentally assist the reception of his high truths & noble aims by those to whom they are addressed, I will not grudge one or two expressions with respect to England, which I, not an impartial judge I admit, do believe to be somewhat beyond the mark; I allude to our being objects of dislike to *all* other countries, to our being at hostility with the world.[2] If I were called upon, as I certainly am not, to take up my country's cause, without presuming to interpret the feelings of America, I should like very much to abide the issue of a poll, upon the relative estimation & favor between England & France, the two most prominent European countries, by the whole German nation, the Spanish nation (Dr C. would not ask me to include the sugar-growers of Cuba), the Greek nation (I will let the Sultan & Mehemet Ali pair off together), & I will even add the Emperor of Russia himself, who virtually, & on the whole favorably, represents his whole people. However, all this is little to the purpose, & all I have further to say respecting Dr C's work, is to beg you to send a copy by the next steamer to the Duchess of Sutherland &c"—[3]

—The *second part* will be printed to-day, so that I hope to be able to send some copies to England by the packet tomorrow. I think the whole forms a tract of very great interest. It cannot fail to do a great deal of good. If the spirit of yr writings could animate our country a new order of things would arise. I hope that you will find the text free from any very annoying mistakes.[4]

You will see that Mr Winthrop has resigned his seat in Congress.[5] This is on account of the illness of his wife, who has a consumption.[6] It was proposed at first to send Mr Abbott Lawrence, but he excused himself on account of ill-health; & Mr Nathan Appleton was nominated by the party caucus last evng. I presume he will accept, though it must be much against his inclination to leave his home for a session of Congress during the long & hot summer. He has in every way such a stake in the country, that the people have a right to his services.

Hillard joins me in regards.

Ever sincerely Yours, Charles Sumner

ALS RHi (66/298, PCS)

1. 3/276, PCS; Morpeth was on an extended tour of the U.S.
2. Channing praised Great Britain in *The Duty of the Free States. Part I* for her emancipation policies, but added, "Great Britain, with all her progress in the arts, has not learned the art of inspiring confidence and love. She . . . has made the world her foe" (*Works of William Ellery Channing* [1877], 869).
3. Harriet Elizabeth Leveson-Gower (1806–68), British antislavery activist.
4. CS and Hillard were editing and assisting in the printing of part 2 of Channing's pamphlet, "The Duty of the Free States" (1842). Channing wrote them from Germantown, Pennsylvania, that "this part seems to me of more value than the former" (2 May, 66/285). In part 2, Channing proposed that the free states should propose constitutional amendments that would enable them to discharge any obligation to the support of slavery (*Works*, 871–906).
5. On 25 May.
6. Eliza Blanchard Winthrop (1809–42).

To George Sumner

[*Boston, before 14 September and 14, 16 September 1842*][1]

[*MS damaged*] (who do [*MS damaged*] you). As none of these are so fortunate as [*MS damaged*] has not occurred between us. I ought not to omit Judge Story? [or Pro] fessor Greenleaf. The latter has enquired about you; I am not awa[re] that Judge Story has alluded to you since I have been home. You will see, then, that the circle in which I have ever spoken of yr plans has been a very narrow one. Have you not done injust[ice] to me in charging me with a violation of yr *confidence*

But, my dear George, if you felt to me as the paragraph I have quoted indicates—if I had violated yr confidence in a "saucy" manner &, in early years, had treated you so as to impair that respect which is the foundation of confidence, why could you ask me to introduce you to my friends—much more, why could you complain of me for not extending my introductions further?—I trust you will pardon me when I say it—but I think your letter shews a want of candour &, a degree of feeling, in phenological language, of combativeness, which does me great injustice.

Let me pass to another sentence of yr letter—"Can I tell you names? In a letter to Mary [*Sumner*] I ventured to mention one or two, & that very letter you singled out to publish, thus holding me up in the position which of all others I would shun." This is the first intimation I have had that the publication of that letter was disagreeable to you. I had it published, thinking that there was nothing in it improper for pub [*MS missing*]

Sept. 14th——I have already announced to you that the Presdt nominated Mr Howard Payne to the Consulate at Tunis. This nomination you will have seen was confirmed by the Senate, while that of [*Francis*] *Grund* at Bremen was *rejected*. I cannot disguise that I was glad that the confirmation of Mr Payne removed from me the disagreeable duty of applying in yr behalf. I observe that in your last letter you say—"I should never beg or *seek* for the office." Let us not deceive ourselves by *words*. To be an office-*seeker*, it is not necessary to employ the word "*seek*" in conveying our desires to the proper quarter. I have before me your letter to Mr Webster in which you say—"*I take the liberty of offering myself to the Depart. of State as a Candidate for that office*." It seems, also, that you engaged in yr behalf, Mr Everett, Mr Wheaton, & Mr Hodgson,[2] who have addressed letters to the Department. It would be rather difficult for me—as I understand language & things, to say that you did not *seek* to be Consul at Tunis. And glad am I, that it was not {so} ordered that you should receive such an exile. I think & trust that better things are in store for you; but the tide must be taken at its ebb. I had hoped that you would be willing to study in some place, & acquire certain departments of knowledge to use on yr return home. Ticknor was of yr age when abroad for the first time. He then passed 4 years in Europe, in which time he acquired a mastery of the French, German, Italian & Spanish languages—so as to speak them {all?} with elegance & fluency—& also a considerable acquaintance with the literature of all these languages—in Spanish he made himself the first scholar of the age—& while in Spain, collected his present library of works & MSS, which is the best private library on Spanish subjects in the world. He was also adopted as a member of several learned societies. On his return to America he was chosen Professor at Cambridge; Longfellow passed 3 or 4 years in Europe—commencing when he was {19?}—during which time he laid the foundations of the admirable & elegant scholarship by which he is so distinguished. On his return he became Professor at Bowdoin from whence he was translated to Cambridge. I have always hoped—since I saw that you had wandered in yr tastes from trade, & as I knew that you were without a professional education—that you would prepare yourself for some chair in one of our Colleges. To live upon *public office*, either diplomatic or otherwise, I have regarded as out of question, as, I trust you will regard it so. Lieber is now in Boston, & in my office. He just asked to whom I was writing. I told him to you. He said—"give your brother my best regards, tell him that he must return prepared to work very hard or to marry a rich girl"—tell him he ought to return soon—he has been absent "long enough." I did not venture to open to him any of yr longings for a diplomatic career; but without any suggestion from me he said that you would be adapted for such a life, if you were of any other country, but that no American could have any assurance of being continued in a career which he had commenced; of all which I am most devoutly convinced—so much so, that situated as I am now, without fortune, I would not accept the highest post in diplomacy. I had rather enjoy a competency of which I am sure from year to year, than accept a post from which I might be discharged at some new turn of the wheel, & be left without any thing to depend on. Who would willingly embrace the anxious life of Mr Wheaton, living in perpetual fear of losing his place. While writing of this, I ought to add that Mr Webster's views on this subject are different. The last time I saw him I had a conversation with him on this very topic. I said that no competent person was encouraged to enter our diplomatic service because there was no *avenir*. He replied that there would be an *avenir* to those who were worthy of it. But how can he say this? How long will Mr Webster be in power? & will his successor sustain his nominations—especially as some of them, as Mr W. confessed, were of notoriously incompetent persons. Will Mr Tyler in one year sustain the men nominated by Mr Webster? & will the loco focoes sustain those nominated by Tyler? I am most strongly of the opinion that no young man, who looks for peace, happiness, & the means of usefulness, will enter the diplomatic service of the U.S.—certainly unless he has a fortune which will render him *independent*. I am also convinced that it would be very difficult, *if not impossible*, for a young man to obtain any foreign appointment, unless *he* or his *friends* had rendered *essential* political services to the Powers that be. My friend Howe, whose various claims to public & private regard you recognise—who was seven years in Greece—who was by the side of Lafayette during the three days—& who has led a life of singular chivalry & philanthropy—in many respects one of the most remarkable men of the age—speaking French, German, Italian, & Greek—in a moment of restlessness allowed himself to apply for the place of Secretary of Legation at Madrid (one year ago)—his application was urged by the warmest letters from Prescott (who had been invited by Webster to designate some fit person for this place), Ticknor, (who is, perhaps, Webster's warmest personal friend), Choate (who has W's place in the Senate), & Abbott Lawrence—no notice was taken of the application, & Howe has regretted very much that he brought himself to make it. His letter was not unlike yours in its language—he "offered himself as a candidate."—

You will read Webster's letters to Ld Ashburton. They are the poetry of diplomacy. I know of no such papers in our history, in dignity & strength of composition, in the stately pace of the argt, & the firmness of the conclusion. The letter on impressment is magnificent. He thinks it his best. The former letter on Mcleod was a great production. The two on Mexican affairs are equally so.[3] The demand for the surrender of the Santa Fe prisoners is epic. If I find leisure I will write an article for the North American on these despatches as a new era in state papers. The only one in our history comparable to this is, perhaps, the famous paper of Jefferson,[4] in which he announced the *neutrality* of the Administration of Washington; but I have not read this lately, & I doubt if it can be compared with Webster's. You will see that Ld Ashburton has used the word "*apology*" with regard to the Caroline affair.[5] I understand that Webster spent 2 days & a night with Ld A. before he brought him to the important word. It is fortunate for the country that a person of Webster's knowledge & power had the management of this negotiation. Under Forsyth, there never would have been any settlement. Who excells, who equals Webster in intellect? I mean in the mere dead weight of intellect. With the moral elevation of Channing he would become a prophet—Webster wants sympathy with the mass, with humanity, with truth. If this had been living within him he never could have written his *Creole* letter. Without Webster's massive argumentation Channing sways the world with a stronger influence. Thanks to God, who has made the hearts of men respond to what is elevated, noble & true! Whose position would you prefer, that of Webster or Channing? I know the latter intimately, & my admiration of him grows constantly. When I was younger than I am now, I was presumptuous enough to question his power. I did not find in him the forms of logical discussion, & the close continuous chain of reasoning—& I complained. I am glad that I am wise enough to see him in a different light. His moral nature is powerful, & he writes under the strong instincts which this supplies; & the appeal is felt by the world. In England he stands at the head of American writers. The elevation & purity of his views always diffuse about him a saint-like character. You asked me to call Channing's attention to a matter stated in yr article on Afghanistan. The last time I saw him, his daughter was speaking of Hillard's beautiful & most successful article in the *North*;[6] & I asked him if he had read it. He told me that he never read the *North American*!

I should like to send you my friend Mann's[7] Oration on the 4th July.—It is the most noble production ever called forth by that celebration. An edition of *twenty thousand* has already been exhausted & more are printing. I doubt not that 100,000 copies will be circulated in the country. It is a *plea for education*. To this cause Mann has devoted himself as an Apostle. It is beautiful to see so much devotion, & such exalted merit, joined to such modesty.

Oct. [*Sept.*] 16th—In haste I close my sheet. Lieber is still here. He likes Mary [*Sumner*] very much, & has been to see her often. He is a good friend of yours. He asked yesterday whether he had ever seen you. I told him that *you* had doubtless seen him.—Longfellow will be in London in the middle of October or beginning. His address will be care of John Hillard—Messrs Coates & Co—13 Bread St—[*MS damaged*] Mr [*MS damaged*] one of our ablest & most accomplished divines, [*MS damaged*] active wife & daughters I know whose house is on every [*MS damaged*] a mile from the Colleges, I think, has read yr article on Afghanistan. He said the other day—"where did yr brother acquire his knowledge of Eastern affairs?"—But his daughtrers—they are among the charmers of our time here[.] Mr & Mrs Sydney Brooks sail for England 27th Sept—Brooks is the brother of Mrs Everett[8]—& his wife is one of our sweetest women—they are both friends of mine. Mrs Brooks would bear a high palm for beauty & cleverness at any European court—Horace has commenced as a farmer—He is with Mr Ripley[9] 8 miles from Boston—he picks tomatoes, cucumbers, beans, upsets a barrell of potatoes, cleans away chips, studies agriculture, rakes hay in a meadow, & is pleased with his instructers & associates. When shall you return to dissolve [*MS damaged*]? There is now too much [*MS damaged*]

Ever ever Yrs, Chas

ALS MH-H (62/564, PCS)

1. Parts of this manuscript are severely torn; the letter has been pieced together according to the best evidence.

2. William Brown Hodgson (1801–71), U.S. consul general, Tunis, 1841–42.

3. In the spring of 1842 Lord Ashburton came to Washington to negotiate the Northeast boundary question, which on 9 August became the Webster-Ashburton Treaty. The *Correspondence between Mr. Webster and Lord Ashburton . . . on McLeod's case . . . on the Creole case . . . on the subject of Impressment* (1842) contains Webster's letter of 8 August 1842 to Lord Ashburton (26–31), in which Webster stated that British jurisdiction was limited to British territory. "The ocean is the sphere of the law of nations; and any merchant vessel on the seas is, by that law, under the protection of the laws of her own nation, and may claim immunity, unless in cases in which that law allows her to be entered or visited" (27). On the Alexander McLeod case, Webster's letter of 24 April 1841 to Henry S. Fox, British minister to the U.S. (*Correspondence*, 3–8), stated, "And when an individual comes into the United States from Canada, and to the very place on which this drama was performed, and there chooses to make public and vainglorious boast of the part he acted in it, it is hardly wonderful that great excitement should be created, and some degree of commotion arise." Webster's two letters on "Mexican affairs" are probably his instructions of 3 January 1842 to Powatan Ellis (envoy extraordinary in Mexico, 1839–42) and of 5 April to Ellis's successor, Waddy Thompson (*The Writings and Speeches of Daniel Webster*, vol. 12 [1903], 96–99 and 101–14).

4. Thomas Jefferson to Gouverneur Morris, 16 August 1793, *American State Papers, Foreign Relations*, 1, 167–72.

5. After presenting the British view of the *Caroline* dispute in great detail, Ashburton wrote Webster, "I am instructed to assure you that her majesty's Government . . . would unfeignedly deprecate its [*the destruction of the U.S. ship*] recurrence. . . . [W]hat is, perhaps, most to be regretted, is, that some explanation and apology for this occurrence was not immediately made" (letter of 28 July 1842, *Correspondence*, 13).

6. George Sumner's "The English in Afghanistan" was published in the *North American Review* 116 (July 1842): 45–72; Hillard's article is probably "Recent English Poetry," *North American Review* 116 (July 1842): 200–245.

7. Horace Mann (1796–1859) was then engaged in educational reform.

8. Sidney Brooks (1799–1878), New York merchant, and his wife Frances Dehon Brooks (d. 1871). Brooks's sister Charlotte Gray Brooks had married Edward Everett in 1822; another sister, Abigail (1808–89), married Charles Francis Adams in 1829.

9. George Ripley (1802–80), Unitarian clergyman who established Brook Farm in 1840.

To Maria Weston Chapman

4 Court St. Nov. 30th [*1842*]

My dear Mrs Chapman,

I ought long since to have thanked you for your kind note of Nov. 17th, & for the important suggestion it contains.[1] I have hoped to be able to join with my thanks some intelligence, in which you would have great pleasure, as well as myself. It may not be deemed expedient for the bar to adopt a rule, according to which each member shall refuse his professional assistance to reclaim a fugitive slave. Still I am not without hope, that, in some form or other, such a rule may be promulgated by a large & most respectable number of the profession. I shall sign it, vote for it & rejoice in it; & I am most happy to know that there are many other lawyers who feel as warmly in its favor as I do.

You kindly asked me to send you something for the Liberty Bell.[2] In default of nothing of my own, let me enclose you a letter from a friend, which contains a most harrowing sketch of a scene which he witnessed in a Southern prison. The letter, you will see, was written as from friend to friend, without the most remote idea of its being seen by any other eye than my own. The writer (Dr H.[*owe*] of the Blind Asylum) visited New Orleans last winter, with the view of interesting the Legislature of Louisiana in the education of the Blind. His visit to the prison, described in his letter, was made in company with a gentleman apparently of humane & enlightened character, but a *slave-owner*. This gentleman stood by his side, while the stripes fell upon the back of that poor slave; he seemed to be moved by it (so Dr Howe has told me) & said he "was glad that no Abolitionist saw the scene"; & he hoped that Dr Howe would not tell of it. But Dr Howe does not consider a transaction which he witnessed in a public prison as *confidential*, & he is entirely willing that his account of it, written when the scene was fresh in his mind, should be published as testimony against Slavery.

The letter refers to other matters, which may have no interest for you; but Slavery appears about the middle of the 2nd page. I have thought that it might not be without interest to the readers of your little book to furnish them so authentic a story of oppression by so unimpeachable a witness.

Believe me,

Yours very sincerely, Charles Sumner

ALS MB (66/386, PCS)

1. In her letter of 17 November 1842 (3/392, PCS), the antislavery writer Maria Weston Chapman (1806–85) had asked CS to call a meeting of the young lawyers of Suffolk County in order to prepare a declaration that they would never help a slaveholder capture a fugitive slave.

2. Regarding the antislavery periodical she was then editing, Chapman asked in her letter of 24 September 1842 (3/375), "May I not depend on you for *the Cause's* Sake, for a page or two for the Liberty Bell?" She thought CS "able to bear the present discredit of being counted an abolitionist."

To Francis Lieber

Boston Dec. 8th 1842—

Dear Lieber,

Who is *en retard* in our correspondence—you or I?—My debt is unquestionable for that most delightful letter from yr wife, which 20 of my scrawls cannot adequately repay. There are some suggestions of hers worthy of much reflection.

You have doubtless heard of Longfellow's return. Felton, Howe & I went to New York (my visits are so frequent to N. York as justly to awaken suspicion) to greet him on his arrival. Our rejoicing with the Trinity of Bond St[1] was great, & who should I catch in playing Blind Man's Buff, but the lovely Louisa? & who should catch me, in the same game, but the same paragon of loveliness? If yr wife knows this, she will think herself more than justified for the insinuations of her letter. Annie is my delight—gentle, simple, sweet, confiding, she is formed to lean upon some one for life, to cling to him. Happy he on whom she rests the tendrils of her heart! To me she has all the sweetness, & sensibility of Fanny Appleton, without that stateliness which bars approach & those gleams, which make you shiver, while you admire their brightness. Am I not right at least about the angelic Annie? Fanny has lost her grandmother—old Mrs [*Maria Marsh*] Gold—& her mourning garments sweep the ground. I was with her an evng or two ago, & she spoke of a long unanswered letter from you. Young Alex. Inglis was sitting by her side, apparently wrapt by her charms.

The Inglises are here, & the Calderons now. Madame C's letters on Mexico, in 2 vols will be published in January, with a short preface by Prescott, & will appear at the same time in London. The Jany number of the North American will contain a review of them by *Prescott the kind.*[2]

Longfellow is quite well, & we all rejoice in his health & fine spirits. He has written some *Poems on Slavery*, which will be published next week; I admire them very much; *you* will not find any poetry in them. L's reputation is rising, rising, soon, I prophecy, to illumine the whole horizon. Have you read his Spanish Student? It contains some very beautiful poetry. Freiligrath, whom L calls the first of the young poets of Germany, is about publishing a translation into German of L's poems, with an engraving of the Author for frontispiece.[3]

I suppose Howe has sent you the 17th Rep. of the Prison Discip. Soc. Think of the [enquirey?] of that Soc. being [converted?] to the circulation of an orthodox tract, for what else are the first 20 pages of the last Report?[4]—Dwight has been very civil to me lately; he has called at my office repeatedly. Yesterday he came for me to read to him a French letter from Geneva; for he cannot read any of the living languages, except English. I fear that Howe allowed himself to be deceived with regard to his place, its desirableness, & the chances of getting rid of Mr Dwight. I have found that several persons were strong partizans of his;—then, he is obliged to solicit subscriptions for the society—ostensibly for the society, but in reality for himself—for his salary absorbs the larger part of the funds of the society. This you could never do, & I should be most unwilling that you should consent to it.[5] [Wherefore?], be of good cheer in Carolina. *Le jour viendra*.

On Saturday we all (Hillard, Longfellow, Felton & myself) dine with Howe on oysters—& nothing but oysters—in various shapes, beginning with the *raw*—then with oysters for soup—for fish—for boiled—for the roast—for *entrées*, & for game—& lastly for the pastry & dessert. You shall not be forgotten at our symposium.

Judge Story has been quite ill, but is now quite well. [*Henry R.*] Cleveland has gone for his health to Cuba.

I have had a very pleasant letter from Morpeth since his return, written among his family, under the towers of Castle Howard.[6] He wished me to send him some *canvass backs* which I have done. Two days ago we dined with Felton, Washington Allston was there, & we enjoyed canvass backs.

My brother George is still in England—when he will return I know not. In his last letter he spoke of going over to Paris in December.—

Mary [*Sumner*] wonders that she does not hear from you.

Choate leaves Boston tomorrow for Washington. The locoes have gained power in our state; so poor Choate must stay in till the wheel turns round & the Whigs are again uppermost. Why does Preston resign?—& Calhoun?[7]—

Ever ever Yrs, C. S.

Howe feels as cool towards New York & all therein, as a North wind. Felton thinks him a great blockhead. I am not sure that he is not a very wise man.

ALS MH-H (62/572, PCS)

1. The Ward sisters were Julia Ward Howe (1819–1910), writer, married Samuel Gridley Howe, 1843; Louisa Ward Crawford Terry (1823–97), married Thomas Crawford, 1844, and Luther Terry, 1861; and Anne Eliza Ward Mailliard (1824–95).

2. Frances Erskine Inglis Calderón de la Barca (1804–82) and Don Angel Calderón de la Barca (1790–1861), Spanish minister to the U.S. and Mexico. Frances Calderón's *Life in Mexico During a Residence of Two Years in that Country* (1843) was reviewed in the *North American Review* 118 (January 1843): 137–70.

3. Ferdinand Freiligrath (1810–76), German poet, had already published translations of a few of Longfellow's poems (Longfellow to Samuel Ward, 6 August 1842, HWL, 2:454).

4. CS's reference is not clear. Pages 113–34 describe the conversion of a black prisoner, Jack Hodges, while at Auburn State Prison (*17th Annual Report of the Managers of the Prison Discipline Society*, 1842).

5. Among the positions Lieber repeatedly sought outside South Carolina was that of Louis Dwight (1793–1854), founder of the Boston Prison Discipline Society (see DD 1:121–22; CS to Lieber, 13 October 1837; Lieber to CS, 8 March 1842, 65/284, 66/265, PCS).

6. 30 October, 3/387.

7. William Campbell Preston resigned from the U.S. Senate, December 1842; John C. Calhoun's resignation was effective March 1843.

To Robert C. Winthrop

Boston Feb. 9th 1843

My dear Sir,

Your favor of Feb. 1st, & the accompanying documents reached me late this afternoon. I had already read in the Courier your admirable Report,[1] which seems to me to put the argument of the Northern States with unanswerable force & distinctness. You will allow me to say, that I have not read any document from Congress for a long time, which gratified me so much by its tone, its composition & its matter. The views you maintain are presented with that blended firmness & decorum, which, take from the South all cause of offence, at the same time that you shew yourself tenacious of our rights. I am most heartily glad that so good a cause has fallen into so good hands.

I have read this evening the Minority Report.[2] It seems to me more moderate in its tone than is customary with documents from Southerners on any subject connected with slavery. Nor is it destitute of a certain form of logic. But I have not found anything in it, which is not amply anticipated by your Report. The decision of Judge Daggett I remember very well. I think it was at *nisi prius*,[3] either in summing up to the jury, or in the course of the *ex tempore* rulings of a trial. Of course, it is but the ruling of a *single* judge, in haste, without deliberation, & without consultation with his bretheren. And this judge too is a *State* judge—

not one of the justices of the U.S. whose province it is to pass on questions of Constitutional law. It might be added, that Dagget, though Chief Justice of Connecticut, & Professor of Law in Yale College, is far from an accurate lawyer.

When this judgment of Dagget's was first promulgated, it excited much sensation & ridicule. It was proposed to carry the question to Washington, as one, under the Constitution of the U.S. & therefore within the cognizance of the Supreme Court. This was never done. I remember speaking with Judge Story, with regard to this decision, &, though his opinion cannot properly be used in debate, yet it may not be uninteresting to you. He treated the decision as utterly untenable, &, indeed, worthy of little more than ridicule.

If it be urged that the *African* cannot be a citizen of the U.S., it may be asked if the Constitution was intended to apply only to the *Caucasian* race. Is the *Indian* race also excluded? Is the *Mongolian* excluded?—How can you "curtail of their fair proportions," & limit words, which of themselves express no limitations derived from color or race? The genius of our Institutions invites immigration; but it does not say "come," & then add "but all who come must be of the purest white, or you cannot have offspring entitled to privileges & immunities of citizenship." For whatever may be the condition of the foreign immigrant under the Acts of Congress, I cannot doubt that his children, *born in the U. States*, are *citizens* thereof.

We have no general law determining *citizenship*. This is left to the unwritten law of the land—the vital principles of the common law, prevailing in all the states individually, & adopted by the Constitution & the Acts of Congress, so far as necessary to explain what is uncertain in this matter. Thus Lord Coke's famous judgment in *Calvin's*[4] case is constantly referred to, in determining questions of *alienage* in our country, & the niceties of the English law on this subject have received the sanction of the Sup. Court of the U.S.

The American *citizen* corresponds to the British *subject*. And you are doubtless aware that the latter term was employed in the Constitution of Massachusetts, as originally adopted in 1780, though the Convention of 1820 did not approve of the language of Samuel Adams & James Bowdoin.[5]

Who, then, is the *subject* under the British laws? Clearly, every one, high or low, peer or peasant, *born* within the *allegiance* to the British crown—*the old phrase is* infra ligeantiam.[6] *The accident of* birth impresses upon the infant this indelible character. The Rebellion of '45 presented a case which put this principle to the test. I refer to the case of *Macdonald*[7] (Foster's Crown Law 59), who was born in England, but when quite young went over to France, where he was educated, & passed his riper years. He joined the French forces, was taken prisoner by the English, was tried & convicted of *high treason*, on the ground that he was a British *subject*, & had violated his *allegiance*.

But the duty *of allegiance carries with it the correlative duty of protection* on the part of the crown. This is *feudal*, at the same time that it finds its support in the principles of natural justice.

Who, then, is the *citizen* of Massachusetts? Clearly every one, *born* within the *jurisdiction* of the Commonwealth, & owing *allegiance* to its Constitution & laws. Such a person, be he *Caucasian* or *African*, would be liable for *treason*, if he should "levy war against the Cwlth, or adhere to the enemies thereof, giving them aid & comfort." And shall it be said that this *allegiance* does not, as in the country from which we have derived the rules which govern it, carry with it the correlative right to *protection*?

It is immaterial to this view of the case, that the person of African race, is regarded as of a despised caste, that he is not advanced to office, or that he does not find a seat among the jury. It would be immaterial, even if it were true, as it is not, that the negro was not *legally* entitled under our laws to the privileges of a white man. He becomes a *citizen* by *birth* within the *jurisdiction* of the Commonwealth; for then the Cwlth treats him as one owing *allegiance*. He is one of her children. He is not a *resident*; but a *citizen*.

I do not know that his privileges or immunities in other States are enhanced by his enjoyment of *political* privileges in Massachusetts. It is sufficient that he is a *citizen*. Being a *citizen*, he carries with him, wherever he goes the *protection* of his state, & of the whole country, of which his state forms a part. If he goes to a foreign country, he bears with him, as a humble seaman, the *letter of protection*, which has never been refused, within my knowledge, on account of *colour*, from Officers of the United States; or he takes a *passport* from the Govt. of his State, or of the U. States. And in a foreign country the Federal Govt. assumes the obligations of the Commonwealth. If he goes to another State of the Union, the Constitution of the U.S. *protects* him, by declaring that he shall be entitled to the same "privileges & immunities" as in his own state. If the state to which he goes declines to respect this provision of the Constitution, our Comwlth should address a *reclamation* to it, in order to *protect* its *citizen*.

It is idle to reply that free blacks, natives of S. Carolina, are treated to imprisonment & bondage. The Constitution of the U.S. does not prohibit a state from inflicting *injustice* upon its own citizens. As the Duke of Newcastle[8] said with regard to his rotten boroughs; "Shall we not do what we will with our *own*"? But a state must not extend its *injustice* to the *citizens* of *another* state. Unfortunately, the poor slave of S. Carolina, & the free blacks, natives of this state, are *citizens* thereof; they owe it allegiance, if a slave can owe allegiance. Of course, they have no other power, under Heaven, from whom to invoke protection. But the free negro, born in Massachusetts, & still retaining his domicile there, wherever he finds himself, may invoke the protection of his native state.

I have been betrayed beyond my intention into this very hasty & discursive view of the question about which you enquire. I cannot flatter myself that any thing of mine can aid yr elaborate studies. The matter does not seem to me to rise to the dignity of a debatable question. All reasoning under the Constitution is on our side, & all the instincts of justice too.

All the learning on the subject of alienage is collected & arranged by Kent in his Lecture on Aliens vol 2nd; & Mr Wirt, in his masterly argt on the Impeachment of Judge Peck[9] (the greatest published juridical argt. in English or American history) has thrown great light upon the influence of the common law over the Constitution & laws of the U.S.—a topic that may not be unimportant in determining the meaning of the word *citizen*. Believe me, my dear Sir,

very faithfully Yours, Charles Sumner

P.S. There was a company of blacks during our Revolution, &, I think, some of them have drawn pensions.

Robert C. Winthrop Esq. &c &c

ALS MHi (66/418, PCS)

1. The report of the U.S. House of Representatives, Committee on Commerce, *Free Colored Seamen* (House Report no. 80, 20 January 1843, serial set 426), submitted resolutions that free black seamen on either U.S. or foreign vessels could not be prohibited from entering any port in the U.S. "in the prosecution of their rightful business"(6). Winthrop argued that detention of such men violated their rights of citizenship guaranteed by the Constitution.

2. This report stated that South Carolina and other states had a right to protect themselves against insurrection from outside their borders, and that blacks generally had been "excluded from the privileges of citizenship" in most states (ibid., 37–49).

3. Ruling in the case of a white schoolteacher, Prudence Crandall, who enrolled black children in her Connecticut school, David Daggett (1764–1851), chief justice of the Connecticut Supreme Court, stated blacks were not citizens under the Constitution. *Nisi prisus*, "unless before," i.e., a writ that sets a trial on a certain day in the central court, unless before that day the trial has been heard in the county.

4. Edward Coke ruled that Robert Calvin, born in Scotland in 1606 after its union

with England in 1603, was not an alien and stressed the bond of allegiance a subject owed to his or her ruler (*Blackstone's Commentaries*, vol. 1, ch. 10). Coke wrote that "an alien is a subject that is born out of the ligeance of the King, and under the ligeance of another"; every man was thus either an alien or a subject ("The Famous Case of Robert Calvin, A Scotsman; As Contain'd in the Reports of Sir Edward Coke" [1705], 16–17).

5. Revolutionary statesmen Adams (1722–1803) and Bowdoin (1726–90) helped write the 1780 constitution, revised in 1820–21.

6. "Within the liegeness," a latinized legal term used in Coke's decision.

7. This case is described in Kent's "Of Aliens and Natives," *Commentaries on American Law*, vol. 2 (1827), 33–63, which CS cites in this letter.

8. Thomas Pelham-Holles, first duke of Newcastle (1693–1768), British statesman.

9. In his defense of Federal District Court Judge James Hawkins Peck before the U.S. Senate, 22, 25 January 1831, former attorney general William Wirt (1772–1834) argued for the independence of the American judiciary (*Register of Debates in Congress*, 21st Cong., 2nd sess., 34–39). He stated that "a blaze of moral *glory*" surrounded judges, a blaze that transcended regular laws (John P. Kennedy, *Memoirs of the Life of William Wirt* [1850], 277).

To Charles Francis Adams[1]

Court St. March 1st 1843

My dear Sir,

I owe you many thanks for yr kindness in sending me a copy of yr very interesting Report on Fugitives from Slavery[2]—I owe you still greater thanks for your willingness to make the Report. It cannot fail to do much good in correcting & shaping public sentiment.

I have not examined the case of Prigg[3] with any special attention. But—perhaps from professional habits, or from the great confidence I am accustomed to place in the judge who pronounced the opinion—I cannot but regard the judgment in that case as legally, I may say, *scientifically* correct. It seems to me to flow legitimately from previous decisions, & established rules of construction. That it leaves all persons in the Free States defenceless, that it takes away trial by jury & the *habeas corpus*, are considerations shewing the injustice of the system, of which this judgment is now a great part. I fear that the Court were right in annulling the legislation of the States. But they leave the Act of 1793 standing, like a grim fortress from which inroads may be made upon our liberties. Is it not important that this should be overturned?—I must confess that I am disposed to remove the blame from the Sup. Court & place it upon Congress, which does not abrogate the law immediately, or add to it provisions in harmony with the spirit of the Constitution.

I beg to assure you of the pleasure & admiration with which I have read yr Report, & of my joy that Slavery has in you so able & earnest an opponent. Believe me, my dear Sir,

very faithfully Yours, Charles Sumner

C. F. Adams Esq

ALS MBApm (66/442, PCS)

1. Charles Francis Adams (1807–86), U.S. congressman (Rep., Mass.), 1859–61; U.S. minister to Britain, 1861–68; *Alabama* claims negotiator, 1871–72.

2. In February 1843 Adams presented to his colleagues in the Massachusetts State Legislature a petition requesting the legislature to enact laws prohibiting Massachusetts citizens and public institutions from assisting in the recapture of fugitive slaves. Adams's *Report of the Joint Committee* acknowledged the legality of U.S. constitutional provisions and Supreme Court decisions, but declared that a state should protect its own free black citizens and proposed that a constitutional amendment change the Constitution's basis for congressional representation (article 1, section 3), currently based on three-fifths of the slave population. The report was adopted by both houses of the Massachusetts legislature (Martin Duberman, *Charles Francis Adams* [1960], 80–84).

3. The Supreme Court, in the case of Prigg v. Pennsylvania (1842) affirming the constitutionality of the federal fugitive slave law of 1793, ruled that its execution was only to be carried out by federal authorities. The decision, written by Joseph Story, also declared unconstitutional state laws that forbade the return of fugitive slaves.

To John Jay[1]

Boston May 25th 1843

My dear Sir,

It was only this morning that I learned from Longfellow that I was indebted to you for the most interesting pamphlet on "Caste & Slavery in the Church," which I had the honor of receiving some days ago, marked "from the Author." I lose no time in expressing to you my sincere pleasure in being remembered by you in this way &, allow me to say, my higher gratification that the slave has in you so able & earnest an advocate.

Is it not strange that the Church, or any body of men, upon whom the faintest ray of Christianity has fallen, should endeavor to exclude the African, "guilty of a skin not coloured as their own," from the freest participation in the privileges of worshipping the common God? —It would seem as if prejudice, irrational, as it is uncharitable, could no further go. Professing the religion of Christ, they disaffirm that *equality*, which he recognises in all his presence; & they violate that most beautiful injunction (which infolds so much philanthropy & virtue) "Love thy neighbor." I am truly glad that you have been willing to lend the just influence of your name & talents to reclaim them from their error.

The Catholic Church is wiser & more Christian. On the marble pavements of their cathedrals all are equal; & this Church invites the services of all colours & countries. While in Italy it was my good fortune to pass four days at the Convent of Palazzuoli on the margin of the Alban Lake, not far from the supposed site of *Alba Longa*. Among the bretheren of this convent was an Abyssinian very recently arrived from the heart of Africa, whose most torrid sun had burned upon him. To one, accustomed to the prejudices of colour which prevail in America, it was beautiful to witness the freedom, gentleness & equality with which he mingled with his bretheren. His dark skin seemed to give him an added interest in their eyes, over his great claims as a stranger & brother.[2]

It was a Cause of not a little regret, as the steamer parted from the wharf (where you had so kindly come) both to myself & my friends, that we had not enjoyed the good fortune of seeing more of you. If you & Mrs Jay[3] should visit Boston—perhaps, Nahant may be an attraction in the heats of summer—we all count upon renewing our acquaintances with you. You will, probably, find Longfellow a married man, for he is now *engaged* to Miss Fanny Appleton, the Mary Ashburton of Hyperion, a lady of the greatest sweetness, imagination & elevation of character, with the most striking personal charms.

I wish you would present my most respectful compliments to your Father,[4] whose pen has entitled him to so much gratitude, & to your sisters; & believe me, my dear Sir, with sincere regard,

faithfully Yours, Charles Sumner

P.S. I hope you will not forget to send a copy of yr pamphlet to Ld Morpeth.

John Jay Esq. &c

ALS NNCB (66/484, PCS)

1. John Jay (1817–94), New York lawyer and antislavery activist.

2. Jay wrote CS from New York 28 June 1843 (draft, 66/505, PCS) that he would include CS's anecdote in the next edition of his pamphlet.

3. Eleanor Field Jay (b. 1819), married John Jay in 1837.
4. William Jay (1789–1858), judge and antislavery writer.

To Thomas Crawford

July 16th '43 Sunday—

My dear Crawford,

I had just sat down to write you a most hasty note (the last chance of sending by this packet passes away in a few minutes) when yr letter of May 30th was recd. Let me first say that the superb bust you have made arrived about a month since.[1] I cannot tell you how grateful I am to you; nor can I say how you humble me by undeserved expressions of thanks on your part for services which I have had the highest pleasure in performing.

The moments pass, & I can only say, that Allston is dead—he died suddenly, having passed a very happy evng, & suddenly at 12 oclk at night snatched away to heaven. I have just started a subscription for a monument, & hope to raise $2000, or $2500. I suppose there will be a general disposition to consult Greenough about this; he was the friend of Allston.[2] I shewed Allston yr letter to me. He has always taken a very warm interest in yr success. There are serious difficulties in the way of a *proper place* for the Orpheus; but I shall do as well as I can for you. Dixwell is my friend. There will be a disposition to do every thing that can be done. Count upon this.[3]

Longfellow was married last Thursday—he is very happy.[4]

We shall all be rejoiced to see Greene. The money shall be sent according to yr desires. The £400 did not stand for $2000; but simply for £400 whatever that sum may be. I shall hope to send you more.[5] *Nous verrons*. In a hurricane haste,

Ever Yrs Charles Sumner

In May no. of Democratic R. I wrote an account of you, & of Orpheus,[6] to accompany a very good sketch of the Orpheus.

ALS MLNHS (PL, 66/531, PCS; Prc, 2:264)

1. Rome, 30 May 1843 (3/491, PCS). The bust of CS is now at the Boston Museum of Fine Arts. See Lauretta Dimmick, "Thomas Crawford's *Orpheus*: The American *Apollo Belvedere*," *American Art Journal* 19, no. 4:47–80.
2. Washington Allston died 9 July. Horatio Greenough (1805–52), American sculptor.

3. John J. Dixwell (d. 1876), Boston merchant and banker. CS was arranging for an exhibit of Crawford's statue at the Boston Athenaeum in the fall of 1843, but the exhibit was delayed until May 1844 (DD, 1:80; Dimmick, 75).

4. Longfellow married Frances Appleton 13 July.

5. George Washington Greene returned to the U.S. from Italy in the summer of 1843 (HWL, 2:549). CS organized a subscription fund among wealthy Bostonians to buy Crawford's *Orpheus* for the Boston Athenaeum (see DD, 1:80–1; CS to Abbott Lawrence, [19+ September 1843], 66/588; to Longfellow, [16? October 1843], 67/020; to Greene, 20 October 1843, 67/024).

6. In the *U.S. Magazine and Democratic Review* 12 (May 1843): 451–55, CS described seeing Crawford's statue when he visited Rome in 1839.

To Francis Lieber

Court St. July 21st [*1843*]

Dear Lieber,

When shall we expect you?—The Longfellows are very happy—Felton & I have dined with them. One of the dishes was *pigeons*, which Felton insists were *doves*. Fanny said that, if she had known of yr being so near at hand, she should have urged you to her wedding. But you will come to *mine*. Willard Phillips[1] tells me that I am not old enough yet to be married. I am not solid enough yet, he says. He was married at 48, which is a very good age. Somewhere about 1860 I shall send you a summons; we will have a gay evening.

I long for yr views on Mackenzie's case, & desire you to read mine. Sam Ward has a copy of my article.[2] I have none, except in the Review. But I sent you a cop[y]. Did I tell you, that Choate said he wa[s] at first startled by the view I took, but was convinced that it was the true vie[w,] so much so, that, as Counsel of Mac[ken]zie, he would not rest the defence on [that?] ground. But we will discuss the[se] things when we meet. Good bye—

Ever Yours, Charles Sumner

I have promised an article for the ne[xt] *North American* on Judge Story's juridic[al] character.

ALS MH-H (62/590, PCS)

1. Willard Phillips (1784–1873), Boston lawyer and insurance executive.

2. On 1 December 1842 Philip Spencer and two other seamen were hanged for an attempted mutiny aboard the U.S. ship *Somers*. A later court of inquiry upheld Alexander Slidell Mackenzie's decision to proceed with the trial and execution of the accused mutineers at sea. CS's article, "The Mutiny of the 'Somers,'" in the *North American Review* 57 (July 1843): 195–241, defended Mackenzie's actions. Sam Ward (1814–84), brother of Julia Ward Howe, was an adventurer and writer.

To Richard Monckton Milnes

Boston August 1st '43

Dear Milnes,

I can not let this packet go without thanking you earnestly for yr most flattering kindness to my friends the Howes.[1] He wrote warmly of yr hospitality, & of a breakfast where he was much pleased with Charles Buller. I cannot forget your breakfasts.

I am glad that you propose another edition of yr Poems, & an addition to them.[2] They will be received with great warmth by yr admirers here. Do you remember that the idea of the story of the monk & the pictures on the wall appear in some verse by Locke? As you may not have them in mind I venture to quote them from Locke's Life of Shaftesbury vol. 2nd p. 13—[3]

> To Mr Greenhill, with
> Cowley's Poem by Mr Locke.
>
> For in yr matchless pieces may be seen
> Strength, vigor, beauty, humour, life & mien;
> Which when we view, & sadly find that they
> Are than ourselves subject to decay
> We think ourselves *the shadows which do fade*,
> And should be lost, but for yr timely aid.

I shall write you carefully on the subject about which you enquire; & will say nothing at present.[4] Our politics are uncertain. We have a President who has shamefully deserted the party & politics to which he owes his election, surrounded by a Cabinet in whose character & principles there is no general confidence. I dined in company with Webster last week. He seems happy in his escape from power; he certainly could have had little sympathy with those he has left behind. Of the Cabinet, Spencer is an acute & able lawyer, & unwearied manager. Upshur, the Sec. of State, is the gentleman of the set.[5]

In the last North American Review there is a long article by me on the *Mutiny of the Somers*, & Mackenzie's unhappy position. The view that I have presented seems to have satisfied the minds of a large number of persons with regard to that tragedy, & the justifiableness of the act.

The post closes, & I must close.

Ever sincerely Yours, Charles Sumner

P.S. My friend Longfellow is a most happy married man; Miss Appleton is his beautiful wife. Have you seen his "Spanish Student" a Play?—

ALS GBCTC (66/538, PCS)

1. Samuel Gridley Howe had married Julia Ward 26 April 1843, and soon after they sailed for sixteen months in Great Britain and Europe; CS refers to Howe's letter of [15] June (66/497, PCS).

2. *Poems, Legendary and Historical* (1844).

3. "Memoirs relating to the Life of Anthony, first Earl of Shaftesbury," in *Posthumous Works of Mr John Locke* (1706).

4. In his letter of 29 May (3/489) Milnes asked CS for information on the change from public to private executions in various American states.

5. John C. Spencer (1788–1855), U.S. secretary of war, 1841–43; U.S. secretary of the Treasury, 1843–44; father of Philip Spencer, mutineer on the *Somers*. Abel P. Upshur (1791–1844), U.S. secretary of state, 1843–44.

To Samuel Gridley Howe

Boston Dec. 31st '43

"A happy New Year"! dearest Howe, to you & yours! But what need you of any such salutation! Is not happiness yr own? Has not the coy goddess descended, & made her home in yr soul? An eventful year has closed—a year which has witnessed yr engagt., marriage, & happy travels—which has witnessed the revival of long buried hopes in Longfellow, his engagt. marriage, & establishment in a happy home. When I think of these things I am penetrated with the thought of what changes may take place in that short span of time. Changes of character may also be wrought. I know that, in no lapse of time, can you lose yr love for truth, virtue & right. I see before you a beautiful career, which fills me with envy—a fireside sacred to domestic love, constant & increasing usefulness, the recognition of yr name & services by the world, & the blessings of all good men upon yr head. But you deserve it all, dear Howe, & more, if Heaven has anything more for its most deserving children.

I saw Mann to-day. He boards in Bowdoin Square in the house, called the Coolidge House, next the Baptist Church. He has been preparing what I think will be a very elaborate report on his foreign travels, from which I anticipate great good. I have not seen his wife,[1] but I understand she is very well. Mills is well, & expresses himself in a characteristic style. Longfellow's eyes are no better; but his wife's are bright for him. Felton is happy as the morn; life with him is a march of exultation. When will happiness gild the days of poor Hillard?—I saw Fisher[2] the other day; he sat with me sometime. I wish him a happy New Year!—

I know not what to write you. You will be glad to see that the old Sentinel, Mr [*John Quincy*] Adams, at Washington has at last produced such an impression on the House of Reps, that the obnoxious 21st rule will probably be repealed, & the petitions of the country on slavery will not be stifled.[3] The present Congress has shewn a different mood on this subject from previous Congresses. I exalt in the continued health & power of old Adams. Through all his various errors, & eccentricities, I have been fast in my admiration of him; for he possesses two things which cannot be extolled too highly, particularly in our country—unquestioned purity of character, & remarkable attainments, the result of constant industry. These I prize more than genius. I trust he may be spared to guide & enlighten the land. We fear some insidious movements in favor of Texas. The South yearns for that immense cantle of territory, to carve into great slave-holding states. We shall witness in this Congress some animated contest on this matter. The question of Oregon[4] promises some trouble, though the whole country is not worth a groat to us; for we can never exercise any practical dominion over it. How can we plant our *representative* system in the valley of the Columbia? Imagine a representative crossing the Rocky Mountains to find his way to Washington! I wish that our people & Govt. would concern themselves with *what we have now*—let us fill that with knowledge, & virtue, & love of one's neighbor; & let England or Russia take the rest—I care not who. There has been a recent debate in Congress in which Mr Chas. Ingersoll said *he wld go to war, rather than allow England to occupy Cuba*.[5] I say, take Cuba, Victoria, if you will—banish thence slavery—lay the foundations of Saxon freedom—build presses & school-houses. What harm can, then, ensue to us? Mr Ingersoll proceeds on the idea of preparing for war. He adopts the moral of the old fable of Esop, which, you know, I have always thought so pernicious, where the wild boar was whetting his tusks, though no danger was near, that he might be prepared for danger. I wish our country would cease to whet its tusks. The appropriations for the Navy last year were 9 millions. Imagine half—nay a tithe of this sum given annually to objects of humanity, education & literature! I know of nothing in our Govt that troubles me more than this thought. And who can talk lightly of war? One year of war would break open & let loose all the imprisoned winds,—now happily imprisoned by that great Aeolus, Peace—& let them rage over the world. But I prose, you will say. I have touched the chords, & you must listen to the tedious notes that ensue.

I have nothing to say of gaieties. My last chronicle gave you a supper of them. It is Sunday night now. I have been for the first time at Mrs Lee's in Mt Vernon St—a resort of yours. Mrs Otis & Mrs Minot were there. A few days since, I passed an evng at Mrs Bruen's—Fanny was pleasant & pretty—Caroline Fleming was there[6]—I had not seen her for 2 months—good, sensible, conscientious girl, who admires you with a fervor that makes me warm to her. Prescott's "Conquest of Mexico" has complete success. I send you an article of 2 columns on it which I wrote in the Advertiser.[7] Mrs Bates enquired of me to-day "who wrote the *pretty* notice in the Advertiser"? As I draw to the end of this sheet, so do I draw to the close of the Old Year. Its last sands are running out. Midnight is at hand! Fare well.

Ever affectionately Yrs C. S.

ALS MH-H (62/613, PCS)

1. Mary Tyler Peabody Mann (1806–87), married Horace Mann, May 1843.

2. Probably Arthur Mills (1816–98), a British lawyer who was visiting the U.S. in 1843–44. John D. Fisher (1797–1850), Boston physician who headed the Perkins Institute for the Blind in Howe's absence.

3. "Gag rules" to prevent antislavery petitions from being discussed in the House of Representatives were enacted at every session of Congress from 1836 to 1844.

4. Oregon settlers had petitioned the U.S. government for a territorial government, exacerbating the long-standing uncertainty between the U.S. and Great Britain as to the precise latitude for the northwest boundary north of the Columbia River and south of the forty-ninth parallel between the U.S. and Canada.

5. Charles Ingersoll (1782–1862), U.S. congressman (Dem., Pa.), 1813–15, 1841–49. *Globe*, 28th Cong., 1st sess., 27 December 1843, 76.

6. Probably Louisa Davis Minot, wife of William Minot, Boston lawyer. Mary Bruen, mother of Fanny Bruen Perkins (1825–1909). Caroline Fleming Hare (1825–1893).

7. CS, "Prescott's History of the Conquest of Mexico," *Boston Daily Advertiser*, 27 December 1843:2.

To Richard Monckton Milnes

Boston May 1st '44

My dear Milnes,

Many thanks for the new vol. of poems [*Palm Leaves*], which are graceful & refined, & full of beautiful truth & sympathy. Longfellow has the copy, which you were good enough to send him; but I have not seen him, since I heard of his wife reading it to him. I liked much yr gentle & pleasant dealing with *Custine*. It gave repose, after the clangour of Macaulay's article. It seems that he followed you in the debate in Ireland—you follow him in the Review.[1]

My special object in writing now is to ask yr countenance for the publication of a vol. of yr Poems in the U. States. I have long hoped to see an American edition of yr Poems; but untoward circumstances have interfered till now; among these was the considerable importation of English copies, which was thought to have drawn off part of the American market. The same publisher—Ticknor & Co—who has recently brought out Barry Cornwall, now proposes a selection from yr *four* vols. Pray see Procter;[2] for he has a copy of the Boston edition of his songs. You will not be dissatisfied with the appearance of the book. Now, my dear Milnes, if you take interest enough in this reprint, pray send me a list of the pieces, which you would prefer to see in a collection of one or two vols. You would add to the obligation, if you would arrange the pieces on yr list in the order of preference. And if any suggestions occur to you, connected with the proposed edition, I hope you will make them freely. As the publisher is desirous of bringing the volume out very soon, I hope I may have an answer from you by the return of post.

You will see that Pennsylvania has at last resolved to tax herself—to find the interest already accrued & to pay interest after August next. I regret very much that Sydney Smith sold out at 40 per cent. "The drab-coloured men of Pennaya" have done their duty. But why have they been so dilatory about it?—[3]

Folly, *dementia* & vulgar weakness now rule the country. Tyler is as contemptible, as his conduct is discreditable to the land. The attempt to absorb Texas is one of the most bare-faced acts of political profligacy, that has ever occurred in the country.[4] His object is 1st. *self*—hoping by this new & startling question to draw public feeling to him—particularly the two most debasing feelings in the country—the hatred of England, & the love of slavery—both of which he ministers to. If Tyler thinks of anything beyond himself & the chances of a re-election, it is 2nd. the strengthening of the power of the slave-owners.

The Treaty will be rejected by the Senate; & perhaps an end may be put for the present to the whole project, though I fear that it will be brought forward again, & at a future day may succeed. *We are doomed to have Texas*, as I fear.

Clay's prospects brighten; & I begin to feel sanguine that he will be our next Presdt. He is a noble character, & with the instincts of greatness—with a heart that flows out like water, & a voice of richest melodies. I wish that Webster & he were better friends.

Ever & ever Yours, Charles Sumner

ALS GBCTC (67/150, PCS)

1. Milnes and Macaulay, both speaking on 19 February 1844, supported forming a committee to look into the present crisis in Ireland and strongly criticized the

government's present policy (*Hansard's Parliamentary Debates*, 3rd series, 72:1158–94). Macaulay's review of *Mémoires de Bertrand Barère* (275–351) was followed by Milnes's review of *La Russie en 1839, par Marquis de Custine; Un Mot sur l'Ouvrage de M. de Custine, intitulé 'La Russie en 1839'; Encore Quelques Mots sur l'Ouvrage de M. de Custine, La Russie en 1839* (351–96) in the *Edinburgh Review* 79 (April 1844).

2. The American edition of Milnes's poems, *Poems of Many Years*, appeared in 1846. Bryan Waller Procter (1787–1874), British novelist, pseudonym Barry Cornwall.

3. In the 1830s many states, including Pennsylvania, had sold state bonds abroad to finance internal improvements. Financial difficulties had forced Pennsylvania to stop interest payments in 1842, but these were resumed in 1845 (Margaret G. Myers, *A Financial History of the United States* [1970], 143–44). In his letter of 20 November 1843, Milnes had criticized Sydney Smith for "howling" at his debtors, because they now seemed inclined to pay (3/596, PCS).

4. A treaty to annex the Republic of Texas had been negotiated between Texas and the United States on 12 April and submitted to the Senate 22 April.

To Lord Brougham

Boston May 15th 1844
U.S. of America—

My dear Lord Brougham,

Mindful of your hatred of slavery, & of your kindness to me some years ago, while I was in Europe, I take the liberty of enclosing a few printed pages, which expose the errors in the late census of the U. States, on which Mr Calhoun has founded his infamous defence of slavery. The author is Dr Jarvis, a most respectable physician, born in a free state, for sometime a resident in a slave state, now a resident in a free state. He has devoted much attention to the condition of the Insane, & had published the enclosed correction of errors in the census, sometime previous to Mr Calhoun's letter.[1] Strange *dementia* that should lead this advocate of slavery to offer such an issue! But the Southerners, & slave-owners are Chinese in character; theirs is the celestial empire; & all who do not buy & sell human sinews are outer barbarians.

I also forward by this packet a newspaper, containing a formal memorial,[2] addressed to Congress by the *American Statiscal Society* (established at Boston) pointing out other errors in the census. This memorial was drawn up by Dr Jarvis.

I anticipate at least one auspicious result from Mr Calhoun's letter; the distinct & authoritative refutation of its abominable doctrines, so that they shall no longer be proclaimed in debate & in public documents, or skulk in conversation. The single point of the blessings of freedom, in comparison with slavery, has never been so clearly before the world. The issue of Mr Calhoun is, that emancipation is less humane than slavery; & the U. States, who have for the [fountlet?] between their eyes, the declaration that "*all men are born free & equal*," now, by a high functionary, stultify themselves & their fathers.

Loving my country, I cannot subscribe to the wicked opinions, which weak men, & men mad with prejudice, put forward in her name; & I trust that the world will believe that the great mass of the American people repudiate Mr Calhoun's letter. It is hoped that it will receive a proper rebuke from Lord Aberdeen.[3] Delicacy may make him hesitate to refer to the errors of the census; but it will be observed that they appear on the face of the census, & are not ascertained by evidence *dehors*. So that Mr Calhoun's own evidence, introduced by himself, tumbles in pieces, on a slight examination.

If you would add yr eloquent condemnation of a doctrine, which I feel persuaded has already excited yr detestation, the hope of the friends of emancipation would be strengthened, & we should all be happy to recognise a new debt of gratitude to one who has laid his age under such deep obligations.

Believe me, dear Lord Brougham,

very sincerely Yours, Charles Sumner

The Right Honorable, Lord Brougham &c &c

ALS GBUCL (67/163, PCS)

1. In a confidential letter of 18 April 1844 to Richard Pakenham (1797–1868), British minister to the U.S., 1843–47, Secretary of State Calhoun defended the U.S. intention to annex Texas and went on to justify slavery. Stating that "the census and other authentic documents show that, in all instances in which the States have changed the former relation between the two races, the condition of the African, instead of being improved, has become worse," Calhoun cited statistics showing that deafness, blindness, and idiocy had all increased among free blacks in northern states (*Works of John C. Calhoun*, vol. 5 [1856], 337–39). Calhoun's letter was leaked to the New York *Evening Post* on 27 April. Edward Jarvis (1803–84), Massachusetts physician and statistician, author of *Insanity among the Coloured Population of the Free States* (1844) and "Remarks on the Inaccuracies of the Census of 1840."

2. Jarvis's memorial for the American Statistical Society asked Congress to correct errors in its 1840 census data, which reported a high number of blacks as lunatics.

3. George Hamilton Gordon, fourth earl of Aberdeen (1784–1860), was then foreign secretary in the Peel government.

To Ezra Stiles Gannett[1]

Court St. Tuesday—[*November 1844*]

My dear Sir,

Let me return [*Thrush?*] *on the Unlawfulness of War* with many thanks.[2] It is a book calculated to do much good. It has the power of *sincerity*, even if it cannot claim the merit of presenting its important theme in a new light.

When shall we become worthy of the name of *civilization?* The spirit of war is the unworthy legacy of Heathenism & barbarism. Literature has handed it down, & invested it with charms that do not belong to it. I long for the *Iliad* of Peace. The next great Poet, that charms the world, must not describe battles or any triumphs of force. I am happy to believe that such things will no longer find any response in the human heart; & this circumstance is, indeed, a token that we are in advance of our fathers.

But why do I write this to you? Let me thank you again for the book you were good enough to lend me, & believe me,

Very sincerely Yours, Charles Sumner

P.S. I have never let you know sufficiently my sister's grateful feelings to you for your kindness to her.[3]

Revd Mr Gannett

ALS MH-H (67/219, PCS)

1. Ezra Stiles Gannett (1801–71), Unitarian clergyman.
2. *Unlawfulness of War to the Disciples of Christ; in Several Extracts from Authors of the Society of Friends*, no. 22 (1817), issued by the Tract Association.
3. At her request, Gannett presided at the funeral of Mary Sumner on 13 October 1844 (CS to George Sumner, 15 October 1844, 63/061; Prc, 2:321).

To Sarah Perkins Cleveland

Boston Jan. 31st 1845

My dear Sarah,

If I have not written you before, it is not because I have failed to have a constant interest in your "travel's history." I have followed you, seeing you always with the mind's eye, & enjoyed your emotions, as the scenes of Europe broke upon you, in the mazes of Parisian life, in the Alps crested with snow, & in dear sunny Italy, where at each step you set your foot on some reverend history, where the Past has put its choicest seal, & where the soul is warmed & ennobled by the precious influences of Art & Literature. Oh! I love Italy. But to other lands, even to England, I can only feel as a friend.

Your little missive,[1] a golden arrow, from the Alps, came to me in Berkshire, where I was enjoying the delicious sensations of returning strength, &, what I valued more than these, the sympathy of friends.

Many thanks for that little note, which assured me that I had not passed entirely from your mind. It bore what was more grateful even than the recollection of myself, a message of love to my sister. On my return home, that I might be near her, while the last sands of her most beautiful life were fast running out, I mentioned to her, that I had received a note from you with a message for her. She asked me to read it to her. I read her the whole note. It was the last words I had the happiness to read to her—almost the last words she heard from my lips. Her soul had already communed with angels, & soon passed away. I had long expected this blow; but no preparation could render it other than bitter. I dwell often on the image of her beauty, of her sweet nature, & of her most serene soul, & feel that it would have been far better, had the health, which was unexpectedly renewed in my veins, been bestowed upon her in my stead.

At Lenox I enjoyed the conversation & voice of Mrs Butler.[2] She is a noble nature, touched to the finest issues, with a heart that beats for every thing that is true, elevated & humane. I was entranced by her genius & character; while, from the bottom of my heart, I sorrowed for her unhappy lot, a wife without a husband, a mother without her children. Her griefs are peculiar, admitting of little solace, whether from the sympathy of friends, or the passage of time. For what can friendship offer to the wounded soul of a wife & mother? And where are the consolations which Time so generously affords in most cases? While with the scythe He mows down her joys & hopes, He refuses, with his glass, to measure this period of her trial. She read Shakespeare in the evngs; & sang some of those songs of our own language, which I am innocent enough to love. I could listen to these songs, made vital by her voice, longer than she had strength to sing. She dreams that she may some day build a cottage by that beautiful lake-side in Lenox. I enjoyed very much the sudden friendship, which warmed at once into vigorous life, between her and Mary Dwight.[3] Their two natures seemed to me, in many respects, not unlike; in both there is a prevailing intensity, while to both is accorded that sensibility, which is the attendant of genius & too often the fore-runner of unhappiness. But I doubt not, you have already heard of these things. I know you have scribes here, so that you may almost say with Macbeth,

> There is not one of them in whose house
> I do not keep a *servant* feed.[4]

I hear of the constant tribute from Park St. & Shady Hill. Jane most blithely tells me the latest tidings of you, &, I always long to hear from Mary Dwight more than she chooses to impart. I do not see her very

Sumner's home on Beacon Hill until 1867. Courtesy of the Colorado College Library.

often; but I never meet her, without being animated by her conversation, & cheered by her kindness.

There was an Anti-Texas Convention held this week in Boston, in which Hillard & myself took a strong interest.[5] A powerful Address to the People of the U. States was prepared by Mr Webster, in which Slavery is denounced in terms as strong as any that Channing employed. Hillard made an exquisite speech. His words descended in a golden shower; but Garrison's fell in a fiery rain. It remains to be seen, if this

Convention will have any effect to prevent the Annexation of Texas. You will see that the measure, by a most iniquitous vote, has passed the House of Reps;[6] it is doubtful what will be its fate in the Senate.

I wish I could make this letter pleasant by any special tidings of yr friends. My own circle is contracted. I see only those with whom I am most intimate. Hillard's winter has been full of occupation, &, I think, he has been stronger & better than heretofore. He has just written a Lecture, which he will deliver Feb. 5th before the Mercantile Liby. Assoction. The Longfellows have a delightful home. For them the meridian sun of happiness stands still as on Ascalon. The Howes continue most energetic lovers; & I am delighted now by the happiness & confidence which subsist between Louisa & Crawford.[7] I have seen them several times. He is now engaged in modelling, in a small size, an equestrian statue of Washington. Prescott is well, & seems to be rallying from the severe bereavement which he suffered in his father's death. Little Edith Forbes is rounding into girlhood, while her eyes continue *lampeggio*.[8] Farewell, & let me not be entirely forgotten.

Ever Yours, C. S.

Remember me most kindly to Ned & Charley. I hear from Crawford much of Charley's elegant tastes. And pray, if you see [*George Washington*] Greene; let him not forget me among his friends here.

ALS NNBe (67/248, PCS)

1. Freiburg, Switzerland, 27 August 1844 (4/119, PCS).
2. Fanny Kemble Butler (1809–93), British actress and writer, was at that time separated from her husband, Pierce Butler, who had custody of their two daughters.
3. Mary Eliot Dwight (b. 1821), married Samuel Parkman, 1849.
4. "There's not a one of them but in his house / I keep a servant fee'd." *Macbeth*, 3.4.131.
5. The Convention of the People of Massachusetts, held in Faneuil Hall 29–30 January 1845, protested the annexation of Texas, still pending in Congress. Only the first part of the "Address to the People of the United States" was written by Webster, the rest by Charles Allen (1797–1869; U.S. congressman [Free Soil, Mass.], 1849–53) and Stephen C. Phillips (1801–57; U.S. congressman [Whig, Mass.], 1834–38, and Salem antislavery activist). The address, adopted by the convention, argued that annexation was both unconstitutional and proslavery. In his speech William Lloyd Garrison (1805–79) moved that the convention should declare the annexation of Texas to be null and void if "the infamous plan be consummated." Massachusetts should then consider the Union dissolved, and form a new government with other free states (*The Liberator*, 31 January and 7 February 1845:5, 18, 22).
6. A final version of the Texas annexation treaty was passed by joint resolution of Congress on 28 February 1845 (*Globe*, 28th Cong., 2nd sess., 372).
7. Louisa Ward Crawford had married Thomas Crawford 2 November 1844.
8. "To flash like lightning."

To Wendell Phillips

Court St. Feb. 4th 1845

My dear Phillips,

I have read yr pamphlet[1] with the best attention that I could command, & regret that, agreeing with you in so much that concerns our relations to Slavery, I must differ so decidedly from your conclusions with regard to voting, & otherwise acting under the Constitution of the United States.

I know of no Constitution or form of Government, in the world, from the ancient rule of China to the most newly-fashioned republic of our hemisphere, which does not sanction what I consider injustice & wrong. All of these Governments, for instance, sanction war, which is a sin as hateful & mischievous as that of slavery, productive, like the latter, of immoralities of the worst character, subverting the happiness of thousands, dissolving families, dooming to death women & children, & poisoning the soul with bad passions.

But because Governments lend their sanctions to what I consider unjust, shall I cease to be a citizen? Shall I not rather, so far as in me lies, according to the humble measure of my ability, by the various modes in which I may exercise any influence among my fellow-men, by speech, by the pen, by *my vote*, endeavor to procure an alteration in the Constitution, to expurgate the offensive passages? I think that you would *speak* in favor of an alteration of the Constitution, why not *act* in favor of it? Take your place among citizens, & use all the weapons of a citizen in this just warfare.

You already support the Constitution of the U.S. by continuing to live under its jurisdiction. You receive its protection, & owe it a corresponding allegiance. In simply refusing to vote or to hold office you proceed only half-way under your own theory. You should withdraw entirely from the jurisdiction; you should sever the great *iron cable* of allegiance, & not content yourself with cutting & snipping the humbler cords, by which some of your relations to the Constitution are regulated.

But what new home will you seek? Where, in the uttermost parts of the sea, shall you find a spot which is not desecrated by the bad passions of men, embodied in acts & forms of Government?

Our lines are cast under a Constitution, which, with all its imperfections, secures a larger proportion of happiness to a larger proportion of men, than any other Government. Let us, then, continue to live under it; but, living under it, to strive in all ways for its purification. I am mindful of what our master Lord Coke says: "Blessed be the *amending hand*"!

Do you not feel animated by the result of the recent Convention? The people of New England will be lifted up to the new platform of Anti-Slavery, & all must join in the reprobation of Slavery.

I listened to Garrison with an interest, hardly ever excited by any other speaker. His position before that audience, as well as his words, spoke eloquently for him. I voted against his motion;[2] but was most sincerely glad that he made it, & that he had so good an occasion to explain his views.

I abhor the bravado, & threats of the South. I hope we shall not imitate them in launching these *bruta fulmina*;[3] but when the occasion occurs, let us *act*. If Texas be admitted, let us *then* consider, whether we can properly remain in the Union. It may be that this conclusion against Garrison's motion is to be referred to my native hue of *ir*resolution, which leads me to postpone action on important matters.

But in earnest opposition to Slavery, I may almost assume the complacency of a veteran, while I survey the new-born zeal by which we are surrounded.

To you & your friends belong the honor & the consolations springing from the great spread of Anti-Slavery.

When shall I see you, to converse on these things?[4]

Pardon my freedoms & believe me, dear Phillips, with great regard,

Sincerely Yours, Charles Sumner

ALS MH-H (67/254, PCS)

1. In his pamphlet "Can Abolitionists Vote or Take Office Under the United States Constitution?" (1845), the antislavery leader and former Harvard classmate Wendell Phillips (1811–84) reaffirmed the May 1844 resolution of the American Anti-Slavery Society: every abolitionist should secede from the Union and no abolitionist should vote or hold office (3). Phillips stated that the Constitution allowed 10,000 slave-owners holding 50,000 slaves equal representation with 40,000 Massachusetts residents (11); it also compelled all citizens to treat fugitive slaves as criminals (18). Therefore a citizen could join the government or not as he saw fit (26). Phillips concluded, "Voting *under our Constitution* is appointing a man to swear to protect, and actually to protect slavery" (34).

2. See letter of 31 January 1845 to Sarah Perkins Cleveland.

3. "Senseless strokes."

4. In his reply to CS (17 February 1845, 4/227, PCS), Phillips termed CS's first point a "flat non sequitur" and argued that there were other ways besides voting to influence governments: "to vote a man into office is morally the same as filling it oneself." Of CS's second point, Phillips wrote that he failed to see "what right *you* have to set up a Govt., & *force* me to pay taxes, & then tell me that I must leave the country or be guilty of all the sins you incorporate into *your* Govt." He "rejoiced," however, that CS was so favorably impressed by Garrison's motion.

To Horace Mann

Boston June 23d 1845
Monday

My dear Mann,

I have this moment received yours of 21st.

I am ready to do what you think proper, under all ye circumstances.[1]

Mr James[2] thinks that the Board should be called together *expressly* to determine where the Western School should be placed; that we may have the benefit of contributions from the selected town; & that our payments should be made *afterwards*.

Still, if you think proper, I am ready to take advantage of Mills's offer, & advance the Board the $5,000, on *condition* & with the express understanding that the sums, now offered by the towns where the Schools are to be placed, shall be paid to us, to be applied to indemnify the above advance. I anticipate some difficulty in this course.

I do not think the Govnor[3] or the people of Northampton have appreciated our motives in this matter. When we commenced this movement, we did not contemplate being made responsible for the whole sum; & it does not seem to me just or generous to attempt to crowd this responsibility upon us.

I agree with you that something should be done *immediately*; but I do feel that the first step is the determination of the place of the School. Then we shall be able naturally to make our collections & redeem our pledge, according to the spirit in which it was given.

But I refer the whole to yr better judgt. You know the facts; you know Mills; & you can determine, whether, under the circumstances, such an advance might not be precipitate, & entail upon us a responsibility beyond our calculations.[4]

Ever Yrs, Charles Sumner

P.S. My Oration will not come out, Minerva-like; for it will have no *armour*![5]

ALS MH-H (63/083, PCS)

1. CS had been assisting Mann in raising funds for construction of new normal schools in Westfield, Northampton, and Bridgewater, Mass., and $5,000 for that purpose had been voted by the Massachusetts State Legislature with the stipulation that an equal amount be privately raised (DD, 1:102–3). In his letter of 13 June 1845, CS told Mann that James Kellog Mills (1799–1863), a Boston businessman who had previously lent Mann money for both private and school expenses, was willing to advance the whole $5,000 needed to match the legislature's $5,000. But

CS feared that no subscriptions would then come from residents in Northampton or Westfield (67/198, PCS; Jonathan Messerli, *Horace Mann* [1971], 300, 402).

2. J. W. James of Boston (Mann to James, 24 December 1847, Mann Papers, Massachusetts Historical Society).

3. George N. Briggs (1796–1861), governor of Massachusetts, 1844–51.

4. On 2 July CS alone signed an agreement with the Massachusetts State Board of Education stating that, in order to hasten construction, CS and his associates would advance the board the matching sum of $5,000. CS stated that sums raised for the schools would then be paid to him and his associates (63/085). Two years later, after the schools had been constructed, CS still had not been repaid by many of the subscribers, and found himself seriously in debt. See Prc, 2:326–28, DD, 1:102–3, and CS to Robert C. Waterston, [1847?], 63/208.

5. CS's "The True Grandeur of Nations," delivered in connection with Boston's Fourth of July ceremonies.

To Robert C. Winthrop[1]

Sunday July 6th 1845

My dear Mr Winthrop,

It has occurred to me that you may have thought me wanting in frankness, when I avoided expressing a positive opinion with regard to the righteousness of the resistance of our Fathers to taxation by the British Parliament.[2] I am very desirous, on many accounts, of not disturbing that question; "Let the Dead Past bury their Dead." I wish to confine myself to the Present & the Future.

There is one conclusion, following, with irresistible force, from the assumption that our Fathers were justifiable in their course, which neither of us would wish to have promulgated. It relates to the present condition of *our* Slaves. At the time of the Stamp Act & Tea Tax the population of the Colonies amounted to about *two* millions (according to Mr [*Edmund*] Burke, though our writers have called it *three*); their grievance, their slavery, was the necessity of paying a few pence more or less on certain things, under the direction of a Parliament in which they were not represented. No just or humane person can fail to perceive that all this was as a feather compared with the rod of oppression, now held by our country over *more than three millions of fellow-men*. If *two millions* were justified in resisting by *force* the assumption of the British Parliament, as contrary to the law of nature, the principles of the common law, & the rights of Freedom; then *a fortiori*[3] the *three millions* of blacks, into whose souls we thrust the iron of the deadliest slavery the world has yet witnessed, would be justified in resisting by *force* the power that holds them in bondage. Can we proclaim such a truth?

To me the more humane, the more Christian, the more expedient course, seems to be to leave that great question undisturbed in the coffins of our Fathers. There are minor rules of propriety, not to say of politeness & good breeding, that seem to indicate the same conclusion. The customary tone of reference to the war of the Revolution is in a spirit which would be considered indelicate with regard to any private or personal experience; &, it seems to me, well worthy of consideration, whether the time has not come for nations to put aside their habits of boasting, as indecorous, if not unchristian. It seems to me that the propriety of this course must commend itself, not only to those, who may regard the conduct of the Fathers of the Revolution as questionable, but even to those who think it entirely justifiable. Even if the great *trial by battle* be regarded as a rational mode of determining *justice* between nations, it should be held rather as a field of execution, than of triumph. We do not erect monuments to commemorate the scenes of public executions.

There is another topic to which I venture to draw your attention. You observed to me that, in your opinion, I had gone too far in my condemnation of Dr Vinton.[4] Perhaps, you did not distinctly understand the terms which I applied to him. They consisted of a strong expression of regret that any person, who had *voluntarily* become a *preacher* of *Christian truth*, should in a pulpit advocate war, of any kind, as consistent with the teachings of Christ. Now, I have nothing to say with regard to any statesman, or public character, a layman, who, on grounds of human experience, of reason, of policy, advocates *defensive war*. My position was merely that such a war is not sanctioned by the Gospel; a truth of which the earliest history of Christianity affords many beautiful illustrations. Not being sanctioned by the Gospel, but, on the contrary, being *expressly forbidden* by the Gospel, is it not improper for a professed *preacher* of the Gospel, to inculcate an opposite doctrine, however strong this doctrine may be founded in the received opinions of men, in worldly ideas of duty, & in the great law of self-defence which seems to be ordained by nature?

I think that life may be defended at the cost of human life; in the weakness of my nature, I cannot ascend to the requirements of the Gospel; but my tongue should cleave to the roof of my mouth, if, after consecration as a minister of the Gospel, I was unable to preach its truths. I would not ingraft upon the Divine Tree a branch which I had found in my perigrinations on the earth.

But the question, perhaps, may be asked, does Xtnty absolutely forbid all wars. I presume no one supposes that Christ or his Apostles, or St Paul [would?] have drawn a sword under any circumstances. Since I saw you, I have read a tract, which I had never read before, which seems to place this matter on impregnable grounds. You mentioned that you had read Dr Vinton's sermon. Mr Gurney's[5] little tract is much shorter, & less argumentative; & I take the liberty of sending it, with this note which has extended so much beyond my intentions. You need not return it. As I propose to allude to Dr Vinton directly in a note to my Oration when printed, I should be truly happy to be able to modify in any way the expressions which I deemed it my duty to employ. I should, therefore, regard it as a favor, which I have no right to ask, if, after reading Mr Gurney's tract, you would suggest any change, consistent with exact truth, of the [reprehension?] of a *professed Xtian teacher*, who, with subtle logic, in a Xtian pulpit, advocates any kind of war.[6]

Asking yr pardon for this unwanted intrusion, believe me,

very faithfully Yours, Charles Sumner

Hon. Robert C. Winthrop

ALS MHi (67/305, PCS)

1. The first three paragraphs of this letter were added, with the addressee's name omitted, to later editions of CS's antiwar oration, "The True Grandeur of Nations."

2. In his address, CS had declared that "Marathon and Bannockburn and Bunker Hill, fields held sacred in the history of human freedom, shall lose their lustre." Washington would be remembered, not for his Revolutionary War victories but for later "upholding the peaceful neutrality of the country" ("The True Grandeur of Nations" [1845], second edition, 77).

3. "With stronger reason."

4. In the oration, CS criticized the enthusiasm with which the Christian Church had endorsed war. He cited a recent sermon by Alexander H. Vinton advising Christians "*to serve the God of Battles, and, as citizen soldiers, fight for Peace*" (ibid., 32).

5. Probably *An Essay on War, and on its Lawfulness under the Christian Dispensation* (1833) by Joseph John Gurney (1788–1847), British philanthropist and Quaker leader.

6. In his reply of 9 July 1845 to CS from Saratoga Springs, Winthrop wrote that he would study CS's letter when he had more leisure. Any response, however, would be "too late to say more or less" since the oration would already be printed (4/354, PCS). CS's comments on Vinton's sermon were appended as "Note D" to the second pamphlet edition of "The True Grandeur of Nations" (88–92).

To Sarah Perkins Cleveland

Cambridge, Aug. 15th '45

My dear Sarah,

I have thought of you most solemnly at each packet, & have thought of my negligence during all the intervals. That kind letter of yours[1] which has remained so long unanswered, rises to call me "wicked." I am now with Felton at his *palazetto*, which you have not forgotten yet; for several weeks I have passed my nights under the [sh]elter of his roof. It is the College vacation; part of the time, his two children have been away, so that we have lived together much *en garçon*. He is as ever genial, mirthful & kind, though his joys have all been chastened by his bereavement.[2] In the constant intercourse which I have with him in his own house, I find new occasions to admire & love the rich qualities of his nature, & his rare attainments.

The Longfellows are at Brattleboro, that he may undergo the *wasseau* for his eyes. Mr Appleton hoped to detain them both at Pittsfield; but they hied away; & when I said, that perhaps Longfellow would not find accommodations good enough for Fanny, the *beau-pere* replied; "but she has taken him for better & for worse."

What can I write you, that will not be dull & stale? You have heard of Longfellow's great book on the Poets & Poetry of Europe, which is one of the most important contributions our literature has recently received. It affords a most instructive *coup d'oeil* of the poetical literature of modern Europe. It is the best book that has been published for a long time in America, to give as a present to a European friend.

Among new publications is an Oration delivered July 4th by C. S. It is almost a book, containing upwards of 100 pages. It was delivered to a large & applauding audience, & has been received, since it was printed, by some persons with very great favor, & by others with condemnation. It is admitted on all sides to be bold & fearless, & many, who condemn its sentiments, praise its style. I send you a copy by the Dr, so that you shall judge for yourself. It is sufficient for me that I have the approval of my own conscience, & the cordial assent & sympathy of all our immediate circle of friends. The sentiments that I put forth have been cherished long & are the result of much careful thought & observation. Have I not said enough of myself?

I have been disturbed by the idea of your premature return, leaving so much of the original plan of travel unperformed. I fear that at Pine Bank there will be longings unsatisfied; that the fine phrenzy of travel will stir the blood even in that beautiful retreat. Why not linger abroad another year? Let Ned be married, without coming home. But my advice comes after the resolution has been taken.

Hillard continues to prosper in worldly affairs, though his health droops under the heats of summer. He is to repeat at Hartford next week his beautiful lecture on Geography, & is to visit New Haven, where he is to charm the *alumni* of Yale with a short address.

Howe looks thin & worn, from excessive labor. I wish he were more disposed to enjoy life—as if, indeed, there is much enjoyment to be had in it, except by a pair of lovers. Remember me to Ned & the sweet *promessa sposa*, & take perfect care of the Dr, not forgetting a kiss for Sir Peter Lilly.

Ever sincerely Yours, Charles Sumner

ALS NNBe (67/313, PCS)

1. Rome, 17 March 1845 (4/240, PCS).
2. Mary Whitney Felton had died 12 April.

To Wendell Phillips

Court St—August 19th '45

My dear Phillips,

Many thanks for yr kind letter of sympathy. I am happy to think, that, in your judgment, I am further on than in those days when I fed so ravenously on the husks of the law. Life is unsatisfactory & unhappy enough; but one of its chief consolations is the idea of *progress*.

I note your comment on the principles of penal laws.[1] I have long thought, that a prison should be a Hospital for the morally Insane; & that the criminal should be treated as unfortunate, & his cure carefully studied. I think it should be the pride of Massachusetts to carry this idea into practice.

I confess that there is great difficulty in sustaining the distinction which I set up between the Force of Police, & the Force of Armies, on the principles of the Gospel.

I felt it my duty to dwell on the faithlessness of the Xstian clergy with regard to war; but you will observe, that, in the arrangement of my subject, I class it among the prejudices by which war is sustained. My argt. against war is founded on the paralell with The Trial or Ordeal by Battle; & I submit that I have shewn, that, at this day, questions between nations are determined by the same monstrous & impious *ordeal* which once determined questions between individuals. The bare statement of this proposition shews a crime which, to be hated, needs only to be seen. I should like to brand all war with the title of *Trials by Battle;* & I hope that our disgraceful contest with Mexico, about the title to Oregon, will always be called by this designation, suggestive of the dark ages & of barbarism. To make this paralell more impressive I have collected in a note some details with regard to the trial by battle.

At present I have no copies of the Oration; there is a 2nd edition in press, which will be printed in a few days, when I shall be happy to send Mr Ballou a copy.[2]

What can be done against Texas? S. C. Phillips is anxious to do something more. I was glad to hear him say the other day, that he thought the present crisis greater than that in which our Fathers found themselves before the Revolution.—Ours, however, must be *moral weapons;* not the foul cowardly weapons which accompany epaulettes & martial music.

Ever sincerely Yours, Charles Sumner

ALS MH-H (67/319, PCS)

1. In his letter of 17 August 1845 (4/409, PCS) congratulating CS on his oration, Phillips asked CS if he agreed that humans should not "be made the mere *means* to an *end*. . . . *A* is never to be imprisoned merely in order that *B* & *C* may be secure:—but the morally insane A is to be cured—so surrounded with moral influences as to develope [him?] higher & bring under his animal propensities—this the State *owes* him."

2. Adin Ballou (1803–90), Universalist clergyman, headed the Hopedale Community, 1841–68.

To George Sumner

Boston Sept. 30th '45

My dear George,

Enclosed is a letter from Hodgson, who is kindly inspired with the idea of installing you as dragoman at Constantinople.[1] He spoke to Charles G. Greene on the subject, who desired me to say that any influence of his was at yr service. I replied that I had no reason to know that the office would be acceptable to you.

I have to-day recd a proof of yr article on the Pilgrims, which, I think, promises to be an admirable paper. It is thorough, & apparently accurate, though it appears that you have not always quoted from Prince, Hubbard[2] & others with perfect precision; yr departures from the text have, however, been noted & corrected. I think this paper will be read with interest & will shew you to be a master of historical research.

I am sorry that I have not yet sent you copies of my Oration. I presume you recd a newspaper which contained an abstract of it. The edition by the City Printer was the largest ever made of a 4th July oration; this has been exhausted, & another of 3000 copies is, I believe, nearly gone. It is vehemently praised, & vehemently condemned; I receive newspapers, which express these extremes. After you have read it carefully I should like to know your judgment; I hardly venture to count upon your assent.

By the last packet went the news of Judge Story's death, which makes an immense void in my circle. I hope you have recd the article in which I endeavored to express, in most hasty words, my sense of the loss sustained.[3] Woodbury has been appointed to the vacant seat on the bench. He knows absolutely nothing of the important branches of Equity, Admirality, Patent, & Commercial Law, which he is to administer. The professor's chair is still vacant. To whom it will be offered, I know not. Many tell me it will be offered to me, & Judge Story always hoped I should be his successor. But I doubt if it will be offered to me; I have so many idiosyncracies of opinion, that I shall be distrusted; I am too much of a Reformer in law to be trusted in a post of such commanding influence, as this has now become. But beyond all this, I have my doubts whether I should accept it, *even if it were offered to me*. I feel that I can only act, as I could wish, in a private station; in office my opinions will be restrained, & I shall be no longer a free-man.

I have just returned from a little journey in the course of which, I passed a night with Chancellor Kent, who has always been a most kind friend to me. He is still hale & well under the burthen of 82 winters. I wish you had seen more of his son,[4] who is a sterling character, with a morbid sensitiveness, & delicacy on a point, in which our countrymen so often fail, I mean, introductions to foreigners.

Everett has just returned. He has been offered the Presidency at Cambridge, & hesitates whether to accept it. Caleb Cushing[5] enquired of me after you. He thinks of going to Paris to publish his work on his Chinese negotiations. If he goes, it will be at the close of the autumn.

I hope you have seen Mr Ruggles of New York, who is concerned more extensively, than any body else in the *industrial* movements of the country.[6] I think you can aid him much. I am afraid you will think I send people to you without end; but you must come home, & in this way cease to be a target.

Thanks for the sight of yr clever letter to Albert [*Sumner*]; but I cannot subscribe to yr view about Texas. It seems to me (perhaps, I am mistaken, however!) that you have fallen into the error of public characters, who look too often only to what appear to be the *material* interests of the country. It may be that these are to be promoted by the accession of Texas; but I know that *right, justice* & *sound morals* are overthrown by it. Here I stop. Let me hear from you.

Ever Thine, C. S.

ALS MH-H (63/094, PCS)

1. Boston, 27 September 1845 (4/517, PCS).

2. "Memoirs of the Pilgrims at Leyden," *Collections of the Massachusetts Historical Society*, series 3, vol. 9 (1846), 42–74. Works cited by George Sumner were William Hubbard, *A General History of New England* (1815), and Thomas Prince, *New England Annals* (1736).

3. "Tribute of Friendship: The Late Joseph Story," *Boston Daily Advertiser*, 16 September 1845, and Wks, 1:133–48.

4. William Kent (1802–61), New York judge; professor of law, Harvard, 1846–47.

5. Caleb Cushing (1800–79), U.S. congressman (Whig, Mass.), 1835–43; U.S. minister to China, 1843–45; U.S. attorney general, 1853–57; *Alabama* claims negotiator, 1872.

6. Most likely Samuel B. Ruggles (1800–81), lawyer, canal and railroad entrepreneur.

To Francis Lieber

Boston Nov. 19th '45

My dear Lieber,

I feel as a sinner, when I think of my long silence. I have had it on my mind to write you for a long time.

All yr friends think that it is in yr power to open a school, to prepare boys for College or to give them an education that shall be a substitute for College, that shall be very successful. I have spoken with Hillard, Longf. & Felton about it; & Detmold,[1] of N.Y. who is now here joins in the same opinion. It should be in the neighborhood of N. York—on Staten Island—Detmold thinks at Orange in N.J. If you have a boarding school, you may make a large profit; & in ten years retire with an ample property. Your own name will not require recommendations; but you can command the best in the country. You may issue a circular, developing yr views, & yr scheme of instruction, that cannot fail to interest a large circle of parents & guardians.—Consider the large number of persons who are perpetually seeking places for their children, & who would rush swiftly to a school under yr auspices.

Two days ago the long suspense was ended, & Everett intimated that he would accept the post of Presdt. of Harv. Col. which had been informally tendered to him. This is most agreeable to the friends of the college. If he had refused, it would have been difficult to find a person on whom the public sympathies would unite. By this acceptance, it seems to me that Everett renounces 2 things—politics, & the opportunity of executing an elaborate work of literature. The duties of his office will absorb the working portion of his time for the remainder of his life.

Webster has talked of resigning his seat in the senate. His debts annoy him very much; & he is unwilling to go to Washington unless these shall be paid. The debts that must be paid amount to about $30,000. If he should resign, it would be difficult to determine his successor. The Anti-Slavery element is becoming the controlling power in our State, &, I doubt, if any person could be sent who was not in favor of earnest efforts for the abolition of slavery under the Federal Constitution. Ever since you left the North this topic has assumed a great importance in Massachusetts. S. C. Phillips & Wm B. Calhoun (formerly of the House of Reps.)[2] & several other prominent Whigs have entered the field, & will labor to bring the Whig party of Mass. to the Anti-Slavery platform. This will, of course, put them out of communion with the Southern Whigs. These efforts are discountenanced by Abbott Lawrence & Nathan Appleton. I doubt if the Whigs of Mass. will ever again vote for a slave-holder as Presdt.

We have commenced an agitation against the admission of Texas *as a Slave State*, which promises to light a powerful flame. S. C. Phillips has delivered a couple of lectures on the Texas question, & on Slavery, which present a masterly development of the relations of Massachusetts to these matters. They have elevated immensely my estimate of his character, moral & intellectual.

Everett is cold & kind. Alex. H. is with his brother. Prescott is happy in his new house. I look each morning now-a-days for tidings of another occupant of the Craigie House. Mrs Story has removed from Cambridge, & the Judge's establisht. has been entirely broken up. Let me say that she was touched by yr note of kindness on the death of her husband, & has given me for you the ink-stand, which he used at his death, also a pen from his desk. At her request I selected for you a volume from his library. There were *very very* few books which contained his autograph, so that I was restrained to a narrow range. I have selected a copy of Locke on Govt. bound in old morocco, with his autograph on the title-page. How shall I send these? also a book which has been sent for you from some bookseller & which lies at my office?—

George at his last letter was at [Burgos] fraternizing with the Infanta of Don Carlos.[3] Hillard has not been very well. Let us hear from you soon, & remember me kindly to yr wife. I observe that my tribute to Judge Story (which you did not care to read) has been copied into several of the London papers &c.

Ever Thine, C.S.

ALS MH-H (63/100, PCS)

1. Christian Detmold, a leading German-American (Frank Freidel, *Francis Lieber* [1947], 221).

2. William Barron Calhoun (1796–1865), U.S. congressman (Whig, Mass.), 1835–43, and Springfield lawyer.

3. CS probably meant the infante, or Don Carlos VI (1818–61), who succeeded his father as a pretender to the Spanish throne.

To Nathan Hale

Boston Nov. 29th 1845

My dear Sir,

I read in yr paper of Nov. 28th the letters of Mr Appleton & Mr Lawrence, with some comments approving of their sentiments.[1]

Believing, as I do, that those letters are inconsistent with the declared opinions of the Whig party, as they appear in various legislative resolutions, & anxious that the other view shall be presented, I enclose a copy of the Free State Rally,[2] containing an answer to both these letters, which I hope you will be willing to publish in yr paper.

As a member of the State Anti-Texas Committee, & as one of the persons to whom one of these letters was addressed, I further desire the publication of the answer *as an act of justice* to myself & my associates—particularly to those who act politically with the Whigs. I am desirous that it should be known that we are acting in conformity with the *prescribed course* of the Whig party, & also according to the principles already declared by the leaders of all parties in 1819.

I am emboldened to ask the insertion of this answer, because I have always understood that it was your habit to allow a hearing to both sides.[3]

I remain, my dear Sir,

faithfully Yours, Charles Sumner

Hon. Nathan Hale

ALS NcD (67/364, PCS)

1. In his letter of 7 November 1845 to C. F. Adams, Abbott Lawrence stated that continued protest of Texas annexation was "useless"; Appleton essentially agreed in his letter of 10 November to Adams, Palfrey, and CS: "I cannot think it good policy to waste our efforts upon the impossible." The *Boston Daily Advertiser* called the letters "entirely satisfactory" (27 November 1845:2).

2. The *Free State Rally and Texas Chain-Breaker* was a newspaper organized by CS and other "Young Whigs" to oppose the admission of Texas as a slave state (DD, 1:139).

3. In an editorial, the *Advertiser* (10 December 1845:2) asked, "What right has an ephemeral journal, of only four weeks' anonymous existence, to take the Daily Advertiser to task for not condescending to follow its lead, in attempting to preach up a hopeless crusade, against an act of the National Government?" The *Advertiser* criticized the Massachusetts State Anti-Texas Committee for its unwillingness to entertain opinions that differed from its own and stated, "True, we declined, on deliberate consideration, publishing their reply to those gentlemen. We thought it, we must confess, too puerile to deserve publication."

To George Sumner

Sunday Evng—Nov. 30th [*1845*]

My dear George,

Yr interesting letter from Nantes came by the last packet.

The paper on the Pilgrims is printed, so that it will be impossible to send you proofs. I hope to be able to send you a parcel containing some copies of that & of my Oration, through Bossange.

If you will send me a sketch of Navarrette,[1] I have no doubt it will arrive in time; but I have not spoken to the Committee on the subject, because I had my doubts of the expediency of publishing it in the doings of the Histor. Soc. You had better write it, (perhaps, in ye shape of a letter) &, if you desire it, I will communicate it to the Society, or to the Daily Advertiser, or to any other journal that you may indicate. Send it home immediately.

I was much interested in what you say of George Sand. I had just read Consuelo,[2] which shews a soul, instinct with humanity, & with virtue. I felt that she must be pure & noble, with irrepressible desires & capacities to serve & bless mankind. Such a work cannot fail to accomplish great good. It will awaken emotions in bosoms that would not be reached, except by a pen of such commanding interest as hers. How she makes us detest the age & the society through which such actors could stalk with impunity. I have felt the atrocity of Frederick's character more than ever in her impressive pictures. I wish she would paint the military system of our own day, the *slavery* of a soldier's life,

& the cruelties & atrocities of the war-system. Pray take advantage of the favor with which she regards you to recommend this theme. I wish you would give her a copy of my Oration (when you get one) with my complts *de la part de l'Auteur* —that is, if you think it worthy of her acceptance.

We are all anxious as to Polk's message.[3] J. Q. Adams holds our title to be good up to 54°. He does not think Polk was sincere in his declaration on ye subject, but means to hold him to his pledge. I have be[en] sorry to find, by conversation with Mr Adams, how energetic he is in his determination. He dislikes Mr Webster's views on the subject, & will probably, take ground against them in Congress. It is understood that Calhoun & Webster agree on this subject. My own conviction is that Oregon is not worth to either country the diplomacy that has been expended upon it; to fight about it would be infamous to both countries; it would be on a grand scale, a resort to the *ordeal by battle*, to determine a title to a piece of territory.

A Prof [Vethope?] in Phila. has undertaken a supplt. to Lieber's Encylop., which, I should think, will supersede any other.

The spirit of Anti-Slavery promises soon to absorb all New England. Massachusetts will never give her vote for another slave-holder. The cotton lords will interfere; but they will at last be borne away by the rising tide; but this cannot be immediately. You will be home, & an actor in the conflict that approaches.—Healey, the artist, who is here speaks kindly of you, & of the honor you do us all. In Dr Ray you have made a valuable friend; he wishes to be gratefully remembered to you.[4]

Ever thine, Chas.

P.S. I hope you will see Kent, if he shld be in Paris again. He is the most important & interesting character whom we have sent abroad for a long time. What is J. T. Austin about?[5]

ALS MH-H (63/102, PCS)

1. George Sumner had met Martin Fernandez de Navarette, Spanish writer on Spanish explorations, in Spain in 1843 ("Letters of George Sumner," *Proceedings of the Massachusetts Historical Society* 46 [1913]:365).

2. George Sand (1804–76), French novelist. Her novel *Consuelo* (1842–43) narrated the adventures of a young gypsy singer in Austria who retained her innocence despite many villainous assaults.

3. In President James Polk's first message to Congress, delivered 2 December 1845, he advocated that Congress assert U.S. claims to all of the Oregon Territory to 54° 40′. Webster believed the U.S. should claim no territory above the forty-ninth parallel.

4. George Peter Alexander Healy (1813–94), Boston portrait painter then living in Paris. Isaac Ray (1807–81), physician and psychiatrist.

5. James Trecothick Austin (1784–1870), Boston lawyer and conservative Whig.

To George Sumner

Boston Dec. 16th '45

My dear George,

At a meeting of our Prison Disc. Committee Howe submitted a Report, which arraigned the whole course of the Society, & advocated or set forth the merits of the Separate System.[1] It is feared that he & I will be left alone, & that the majority of the Committee will prevent our Report from being published. We insist that the Society has done wrong, & it must retrace its steps; that it is necessary that it should do this in order to set itself right abroad. Its influence, we think, has been perverted. I wish you would do us the favor, by an early post—by the next post after you receive this letter—to let me know, as definitely as you can, what is thought in Europe, in Paris, in Berlin or elsewhere, of the course of our Society, & of the character of its reports; & make any suggestions that occur to you with regard to our course.

Boston will build a new jail this year at South Boston, & I am much concerned, that it should be on a true system. I have written an article for ye Xstian Examiner, which will appear Jany 1st, in which I express myself warmly in favor of the Separate System.[2] I was much instructed by ye book you were so kind as to send me.

The idea of *war* or of a *war feeling* on account of a fraction of a worthless territory is horrible;[3] & yet we seem to many on the brink of war.

Let me hear from you soon. How is Foelix. Remember me to him kindly. What are you about? & when shall we see you at home?

Ever Thine, Chas—

Albert, wife & daughter are here,[4] & help fill our house, which resembles a bee-hive. Horace does nothing; but talks about "fulfilling his mission."

ALS MH-H (63/106, PCS)

1. Howe's *Report of a Minority of the Special Committee of the Boston Prison Discipline Society* was ultimately published in 1846. In his preface, Howe expressed regrets that, in its annual reports, the Boston Prison Discipline Society never discussed the merits

of the Eastern Penitentiary of Pennsylvania system, which practiced separate housing for its prisoners. Instead the society wholly favored the Auburn system, advocating that prisoners be housed together and mix with each other (iii–xi).

2. "Prisons and Prison Discipline," *Christian Examiner and Religious Miscellany* 40 (January 1846): 122–39.

3. War threatened between the U.S. and Great Britain over the Oregon Territory boundary.

4. Catherine Barclay Sumner (d. 1856) and Catherine Sumner (c. 1842–56).

To Robert C. Winthrop

Boston Dec. 22nd 1845

My dear Sir,

Let me intrude upon you with my thanks for the noble resolutions you have introduced, proposing Arbitration instead of War.[1] I envy you not a little the opportunity you have of setting forth the superiority of reason, & justice over the Ordeal by Battle. I hope most sincerely that the speech you give us reason to expect from you will become classical in the history of the progress of this question.

Even if the country should not be ready to receive *all the truth* now, it will soon grow up to it. I have been obliged to feel, in my observation of public men & of politicians, that they are *behind the moral sense* of the people; & I believe, that a manly earnest Christian protest against war, as wicked & unjust, would find a response throughout the country. I have heard but one remark on the Cass debate in the Senate;[2] that it was disgraceful to the *morality* of the country, that not a single Senator was found to throw himself with resolution on the side of Peace, to utter that famous cry, which has immortalized Ld Falkland, "Peace!, Peace."[3]

There were some, undoubtedly, who felt the importance of Peace; but they feared to risk a temporary popularity, not thinking that one vigorous plea for Peace, on this emergency, would confer immortality, besides being the performance of a sacred duty, which would be better far than fame or office.

Pray pardon my freedoms. When I commenced, I proposed merely to thank you earnestly & sincerely for the step you have taken.

It has occurred to me that the tracts on "Arbitration" on "War as a Judicial Redress" & on a "Congress of Nations" may contain some thing to assist you & I send them accordingly.[4] In the Appendix to my Oration (I wish you had been less displeased by it!) there are a couple of notes, the result of some research on the Trial by Battle, & on Arbitration as a substitute for War. I venture to send a copy of this, thinking that you may not have it with you, with the desire of facilitating your study of the history of these matters.

It seems to me that it would be glorious for our country to propose to refer the present dispute to Mr [*Henry*] Hallam, on the English side, Prescott or Sparks, on the American, with Guizot as umpire. Let our republic *neglect* crowned heads, & select as its judges those who have earned the real crowns of merit. Why should not the question about Oregon be decided as that between Rhode Island & Massachusetts is to be decided this winter?[5]

Very sincerely Yours, Charles Sumner

Hon. R. C. Winthrop

ALS MHi (67/379, PCS)

1. On 19 December 1845, Winthrop proposed a four-part resolution for peaceful settlement of the differences between Great Britain and the U.S. over the Oregon Territory boundary (*Globe*, 29th Cong., 1st sess., 86).

2. In the Senate, 16 December, John J. Crittenden challenged Lewis Cass as to whether, in his speech of 15 December, he really meant that war with Britain was inevitable. Cass replied he did believe war would take place, because Britain would assert her claim to the whole of the Oregon Territory (ibid., 55–56).

3. Fighting with the British Royalists against Cromwell, Lucius Cary, second Viscount Falkland (1610–43) was reported to have cried for peace amid the war's heartbreaking destructiveness.

4. Two of these tracts can be tentatively identified as "Arbitration as a Substitute for War," Boston American Peace Society, n.d., and "Congress of Nations for the Amicable Adjustment of National Differences, by a Friend of Peace," 1832.

5. The boundary dispute, Rhode Island v. Massachusetts, was scheduled for a hearing before the U.S. Supreme Court (DW, 6:281–82).

To Elizabeth Bliss Bancroft[1]

Boston Jan. 9th '46

My dear Mrs Bancroft,

You will think that I never appear, except as a *beggar*. Very well. I never beg for myself. But I do beg now most earnestly for another; for a friend of mine, & of your husband's; for a man of letters, of gentleness.

I have heard to-day of the poverty of Hawthorne.[2] He is very poor indeed. He has already broken up the humble & inexpensive home, which he had established in Concord, because it was too expensive. You know how simply he lived. He lived almost on nothing; but even that nothing has gone. Let me say to your husband, not to you (for I would not quote Latin to a lady)

Nil habuit Codrus. Quis enim negat?
et tamen illius: Perdidit infelix totum nihil.[3]

Some of his savings were lent to Mr Ripley at Brook Farm; but he is not able to repay them, & poor Hawthorne (that sweet, gentle, true nature) has not wherewithal to live. I need not speak of his genius to you. He is an ornament of the country; nor is there any person of any party who would not hear with delight that the author of such Goldsmithian prose, as he writes, had received honor & office from his country. I plead for him earnestly, & count upon your friendly interference to keep his name present to the mind of your husband, so that it may not be pushed out of sight by the intrusive legion of clamorous office-seekers, or by other public cares.

Some post-office, some custom-house, some thing, that will yield daily bread,—any thing in the gift of yr husband—or that his potent influence might command—will confer great happiness upon Hawthorne; &, I believe, dear Mrs Bancroft, it will confer greater upon you; feeling, as I do, that all true kindness blesses him that bestows it more even than it blesses the receiver.

I wish I could have some assurance from yr husband that Hawthorne shall be cared for.[4]

You will be glad to know that Maria Eldredge had a ball, which was brilliantly thronged. She appeared lovely, as, indeed, she is.

I wrote yr husband lately on Peace; but he will not heed my words.

Believe me, dear Mrs Bancroft

Yours sincerely (provided you do not forget Hawthorne)
Charles Sumner

P.S. I saw your younger boy making himself very agreeable to Mrs Paige at Miss Eldredge's ball. The elder preferred more *juvenile* beauty.[5]

ALS DLC (67/392, PCS)

1. Elizabeth Davis Bliss Bancroft (1803–86), wife of George Bancroft, then U.S. secretary of the navy under Polk.

2. Nathaniel Hawthorne (1804–64), with one child and another on the way, was then living in his mother's home in Salem (James R. Mellow, *Nathaniel Hawthorne in His Times* [1980], 267–71).

3. "Codrus had nothing. Who could deny it? and therefore the unhappy one lost everything."

4. George Bancroft wrote CS 13 January 1846 (4/647, PCS) that, regarding Hawthorne's prospects, he was "most perseveringly his friend. I am glad you go for the good rule of dismissing wicked whigs & putting in Democrats." Bancroft said that unless he had no influence at all, Hawthorne would soon have a position. In March Hawthorne was appointed surveyor of the Salem Custom House.

5. Alexander Bliss (1827–96), then a Harvard student, later in the foreign service. William D. Bliss (d. 1886), also a Harvard student, class of 1846.

To Robert C. Winthrop

Boston Jan. 9th 1846

My dear Sir,

I owe you many thanks for yr kind letter, many more for the speech which you made, much of which I read with admiration & gratitude.[1] It will not be unwelcome to you to know that Abbott Lawrence, Nathan Appleton & Judge [*Peleg*] Sprague (whom I happened to meet yesterday) had read it with great pleasure. The *defence* of Peace will find a response in many hearts.

But you will pardon my frankness if I mention that there was one part of yr speech which has been read by many with sorrow. You say, in the outset, that in the event of a war, the whole country will be *united*, whatever may be the previous differences of opinion. Now, if I understand this sentiment correctly, it supposes that Congress can make that *just* & *right* which is intrinsically *unjust* & *wrong*. I do not believe in *Act of Congress morality*; nor do I see how it can be expected, or declared, that an unjust war, a war for the whole of Oregon, will find the country *united*. Some there are who adhere to the Decatur toast, *our country be she right or wrong*;[2] but immense masses now feel that there is a higher allegiance due to justice.

I never knew Judge Story more eloquent or earnest than when inveighing against this sentiment; nor do I know a person, among those with whom I have discussed this sentiment, who does not join in its condemnation.

With this feeling I cannot but regret that you were willing to leave it to be inferred that the country would be *united* in wrong. If there should be a war for Oregon there are thousands, who would do their utmost to impede the war, & to weaken its forces.

Believing that the truth should be told, I regret, that it cannot be proclaimed earnestly, conscientiously from the floor of Congress, that the *people* of this country will *not* sustain the Govt. in an unjust war; that the age has come in which Govt. can claim allegiance only by keeping itself within the right.

I hope you will pardon my freedom; & let me add that I hope not to be regarded as impracticable or ultra in my views. Most earnestly, as a Whig citizen, would I support Govt. & our Constitution; but Govt. cannot expect support when it ordains injustice. A war for Oregon will be murder by wholesale; & no form of legislation can give it any other character. It can have in it no element of self-defence.

Mr Adams's course had been expected. His allusion to Frederick's invasion of Silesia will do our national character infinite harm abroad.[3]

The rumors of war from Washington have not disturbed the general confidence here that Peace will be preserved; & I cannot but feel that there is a *vis inertia* in favor of Peace, which cannot be overcome.

Thanking you again for yr kindness, & for your eloquent words for Peace, I remain, [my] dear Sir,

very faithfully Yours, Charles Sumner

Hon. Robert C. Winthrop
&c &c &c

ALS MHi (67/396, PCS)

1. Although in his speech of 3 January 1846 Winthrop continued to argue for arbitration, not war, to settle the Oregon boundary question, he also stated that "if the controversy with Great Britain should result in war, our country, and the rights of our country . . . are to be maintained and defended with all the power and all the vigor we possess" (*Globe*, 29th Cong., 1st sess., appendix, 98).

2. Stephen Decatur (1779–1820), naval officer, after successful negotiations with the Barbary Powers in 1815, had made the famous toast "Our country! . . . may she always be in the right; but our country, right or wrong."

3. On the Oregon question, John Quincy Adams argued for first giving notice to Great Britain that the existing treaty was to be terminated, then occupying the disputed territory. He did not advocate negotiation only to avoid war. "We might negotiate after taking possession. That was the military way of doing business. It was the way in which Frederick II of Prussia had negotiated with the Emperor of Austria for Silesia" (ibid., 2 January 1846, 126–27).

To George Bancroft

Boston April 22nd '46—

My dear Bancroft,

From my desk in Court St, let me send you & Mrs Bancroft greetings & thanks for yr kindness to me, a stranger in Washington.[1] Our visit continued to be full of interest to the last; & now, that I am again returned to my narrow office, all that I saw seems like a vision.

Among the pleasant recollections of Washington is Mrs Polk, whose sweetness of manner, won me entirely. I am also happy to be undeceived with regard to Benton. I was not prepared to find him so much a courtier in his manners, & so full of the stores of various learning. Mrs Fremont had a pleasant wild strawberry flavor.[2]

You will be glad to hear that Prescott's eyes are much stronger than they have been. They were benefitted by the bright lights & good cheer of Washington. In New York Dr Elliott[3] treated them for a week, & promises, if he can have him for 3 mos. to render his single working eye permanently fit for literary labor.

With kind regards to Mrs Bancroft;

Ever sincerely Yrs, Charles Sumner

Hon. G. Bancroft

ALS MHi (67/446, PCS)

1. Traveling with W. H. Prescott, CS visited Baltimore, New York City, and Washington in early April.

2. Sarah Childress Polk (1803–91), wife of James Polk. Jessie Benton Frémont (1824–1902), Thomas Hart Benton's daughter, who had married John C. Frémont in 1841.

3. Samuel Mackenzie Elliott (1811–73), oculist.

To Sir Charles Vaughan

Boston May 1st 1846

My dear Sir Charles,

I have felt for a long time how much I was yr debtor for a kind note from Oxford.[1] It brought before me the pleasant memories of my three days' sojourn in venerable All Souls, & of the choice companionship of that monastery.

I am happy that the clouds of war seem for a while scattered. The partizans of 54° 40′ might be put into an omnibus, without a close squeeze. Their leader is Allen, a wild man from Ohio, tall, gaunt, tobacco-chewing, spitting, of unbridled passions, & ignorant democracy. With him is [*Lewis*] Cass, commonly called *Gas*, who has a most pestilent Anglophobia which manifests itself on all occasions. He is weak & timid. At their back is Hannegan, a furious red-faced Irishman from Indiana, & Breese; an unimportant lawyer from Illinois.[2]

I have recently returned from Washington, where I saw something of these characters. I liked [*Richard*] Pakenham very much. He is prudent, grave, with the phlegm of his country. He told me that he felt "no anxiety with regard to the settlement of the question." You have doubtless seen Webster's remarks on the proper basis of settlement.[3] The whole country & a large portion of the Senate are in favor of 49°, leaving the questions of the navigation of the Columbia, & the straits of Fuca to be arranged by such convention as can be agreed upon. It is important, however, that the whole strife should be [composed?] *before autumn.* It must not be allowed to enter into our next elections. If it is then unsettled, it will be made a prominent topic of stump speaking at the West, & a flame may be excited which will be difficult to control. I hope that England will not hesitate, on any ground of diplomatic etiquette, to speed the final & immediate adjustment.

You will read Charles Ingersoll's base attacks on Webster.[4] The latter seems to be winning popularity under this abuse. He is received every where with especial rapture. Everett was inaugurated yesterday Presdt. of Harvard University. His Address was an admirable effort, & the whole day was a triumph for him.

In Baltimore I met yr friend McTavish. We talked of you. I shall send you by a private hand the Eulogy of Story on Marshall.[5] Can I do any thing for you in this nether world? I liked young Ponsonby[6] the attaché very much. He is amicable & intelligent. Believe me, dear Sir Charles,

Very sincerely yrs, Charles Sumner

Right Honorable, Sir Charles R. Vaughan

ALS GBOAS (67/458, PCS)

1. Most likely Vaughan's letter of 28 December 1845 (4/614, PCS).

2. William Allen (1803–79), U.S. congressman (Dem., Ohio), 1833–35; U.S. senator, 1837–49. Edward A. Hannegan (1807–59), U.S. congressman (Dem., Ind.), 1833–37; U.S. senator, 1843–49. Sidney Breese (1800–78), U.S. senator (Dem., Ill.), 1843–49.

3. In Senate remarks 30 March 1846, Webster stated that the "49th parallel must be regarded as the general line of boundary" in the Oregon Territory and that the settlement should be promptly negotiated (*Globe*, 29th Cong., 1st sess., 567–68).

4. Ingersoll had criticized Webster in Congress for giving in to Britain on the issues of the *Caroline*, and the Maine and Oregon boundaries (DW, 6:127–28), calling Webster "a delinquent, a public defaulter" in his handling of the Oregon boundary issue (9 April 1846, *Globe*, 29th Cong., 1st sess., 636).

5. Joseph Story, "A Discourse Upon the Life, Character, and Services of the Honorable John Marshall" (1835).

6. Spencer Cecil Brabazon Ponsonby (1824–1915).

To Francis Wayland[1]

Boston July 7th 1846—

My dear President,

Yr letter makes me feel that we cannot disagree as to the course of our Society; & yet there are some suggestions in it, which invite comment.[2]

You say that you "cannot persuade yourself that I look at the subject before us in the true light;" & you add in that connexion, that I spoke of Mr Dwight in such a way "that if what I said of him were true he must be a notorious rogue." "You spoke of him to be sure" you say, "several times as the *indefatigable* Secretary; but every one who knows you is perfectly aware that you think his labors for the society very much the reverse of indefatigable."—Now, in the first place, as to what I said of Mr Dwight. I began by an account of the good he had done, & in this connexion I called him *indefatigable*. I thought that in the early stages of our society, in combating abuses, he had been so, & I gave him the credit accordingly. When I came to speak of the evil that had been done I did not allude to Mr Dwight but to the *Society*. —I constantly referred to the *Society*, avoiding all reference to the *Secretary*. In introducing quotations from others I was obliged to follow their language, & in one of these the *Secretary* was mentioned. I gave no sanction to those disagreeable imputations; but deemed it my duty to bring them forward, that the Society should know into what disesteem it had fallen. Was I wrong in this? If what Moreau-Christophe, Adshead[3] & others said, is true, the secretary must be "a notorious rogue;" but ***I*** said nothing suggesting any thing of the kind.

I send you a copy of my Remarks, as written out by myself. Let me ask you to read them. I have recently perused them, & I can find no such suggestion with regard to the Secy. as you suppose; nor do I perceive anything in the course of them, which is not fully sustained by the facts & authorities adduced.

And now, as to our Report. I repeat, that I do not see how we can disagree with regard to it. Our Committee should review, according to the terms of the Resolution, our former Reports. In doing this, they will be aided by Dr Varrentrap's pains-taking article, just published in the Law Reporter.[4]

(1) If they find any thing in the nature of *misrepresentation*, or a withholding of truth which in fairness should be made known, it will be their duty, to point it out.

(2) If we have spoken wrongfully of others, we should retract it.

(3) We should recognise the Society at Phila. as fellow-laborers in the cause of Prison Discipline, honest, virtuous, humane as ourselves, & should volunteer to them our fellow-ship in their work, & ask them to forget the asperities of the past.

(4) The Society should divest itself of its uncandid & partizan character, & seek to recover the ground, occupied by its Constitution, of exertion for the improvement in Prisons.

(5) It should cease to be an *Auburn* Prison Discipline Society, & become a *Prison* Discipline Society, setting forth the good that is

wrought by both systems, the history & progress of both, & the means of improving both.[5]

(6) It should withdraw all opinions on the subject of Capital Punishment, expressing itself neither *for* nor *against*.

In asking the Society to adopt these conclusions, or something like them, I think I do not ask too much. By doing so, it will place itself on the high ground of a just impartiality.

I shall send you Varrentrap's Review, which seems to shew our Reports to be unworthy of credit. It may well put us to shame, that a German should be so much better instructed with regard to our own prisons than we are.

I have a letter now before me received by the last steamer from England which says—"the good work of reform is steadily & effectually advancing, & I may say, that important measures are contemplated for the better ordering of *all* our prisons. About *forty* counties have adopted, or are in course of adopting the Separate system."

On the other hand from Prussia comes contrary views. A correspondent writes "The Prussian Govt. has stopped all further extension of the Penna. System in consequence of the violent opposition to it by the Communists. The Auburn men, I suppose, on the one hand, & the Rhenish Catholics, with the acting Archbishop of Cologne, loudly protesting at their head on the other. —— The Eremitic system has yet many battles to go through, & Mr Dwight will work up such things very showily & blabberingly."[6]—

Have you read the article in the North Am. Rev. on Whewell's Morality?[7] I thought it was yours, & was on the point of thanking you for one of the most admirable criticisms of an ethical work that I have ever read; but I learn that it is by Peabody of Portsmouth. He rebukes the *merely Anglican standard* of Whewell.

Pray pardon the trouble I give you. You must not desert us as President. At least see the Society through its present difficulties. Yr candor is required very much.

Believe me, my dear Sir,

very sincerely Yours, Charles Sumner

ALS RPB (67/495, PCS)

1. Francis Wayland (1796–1865), Baptist clergyman; professor; president, Brown University, 1827–55; president, Boston Prison Discipline Society.

2. In a speech at the 26 May 1846 business meeting of the Boston Prison Discipline Society, CS strongly criticized Dwight and the society's "partizan warfare against the Philadelphia system" (*Boston Courier*, 27 May 1846:2; DD, 1:124–25).

CS and Wayland exchanged several letters about the minority report that the society had refused to print (see CS to George Sumner, 16 December 1845). Here CS answers Wayland's most recent letter, 1 July (5/135, PCS).

3. Louis Mathurin Moreau-Christophe (1799–1883), French economist; inspector-general of French prisons, 1837–48. Joseph Adshead, British penologist (DD, 1:121).

4. The *Report of a Minority of the Special Committee of the Boston Prison Discipline Society* (1846) concluded with resolutions that parallel the first five that CS lists in this letter (90). The article by Georg Varrentrap (1809–86), a German physician, was published in the July 1846 *Law Reporter* (Wks, 2:105).

5. In his letter of 1 July 1846, Wayland wrote, "Our gentlemen have united together to promote a knowledge of the true doctrines of Prison Discipline. They have been convinced that one system is better than another & they desire to promote it" (5/135).

6. These letters from England and Prussia to CS have not been recovered. The writers were possibly Adshead, who supported CS's criticism of the Boston Prison Discipline Society, and Nicolaus H. Julius (1783–1862), physician and penologist, also critical of the society.

7. Review of "The Elements of Morality, including Polity," *North American Review* 63 (July 1846): 1–28, by Andrew P. Peabody (1811–93), then Unitarian minister. William Whewell (1794–1866), British mathematician and philosopher.

To Robert C. Winthrop

Boston August 10th, 1846

My dear Sir,

Your favor of August 7th reached me yesterday (Sunday). I need not add that I have read it with pain, because it seems to shew on your part personal & unfriendly feelings. In the great public question, on which we are, for the moment, separated, I had hoped, perhaps ignorantly & illusively, that an honest, conscientious, & earnest discussion, such as the magnitude of the occasion seems to require, might be conducted without the suggestion of personal unkindness on either side.[1] When more than a year ago I heard of the unambiguous voices of condemnation, which you widely scattered with regard to certain sentiments of mine on a cause as Christian & holy as Peace, I did not allow myself to believe you personally unkind towards me. I regretted our difference of opinion; but gave to you the credit, which I doubt not you deserved, of a conscientious, though earnest & decided reprobation of my course. I ask similar justice at your hands now. I have no personal motive to gratify in this controversy. I seek no office of any kind for myself, or for any friend. Towards yourself personally I have no feeling, except of kindness. It would please me more to listen to your praise than yr censure.

But the act, with which yr name has been so unhappily connected, is public property. Your conduct is public property. Especially is it the property of yr constituents, whose conscience you represent. I do feel, my dear Sir, that, holding the sentiments on this subject, which I do, & which seem to be general in our community, it was a duty to direct them distinctly, unequivocally, & publicly *against* the act. This was rendered, at a later day, more imperative by the fallacious & immoral apology, which the Advertiser set up, keeping out of view the *fact of facts*, that the representative from Boston had voted for an *unjust war*, &, arguing, that two or more votes against a propostion, unfounded in truth, would justify a *final* vote for it.[2]

Long before any thing was written on the subject, much had been said in conversation. One of your predecessors—still another than he who said that he would not obey patriotism when it told him to lie—spoke to me earnestly with regard to your vote, shortly after it had been given. He said, "Mr Winthrop ought to be rebuked." I proposed to him at once to call a meeting at Faneuil Hall, & promised to arrange the preliminaries of the meeting, if he would preside. He declined to do this, & suggested to me to write in the papers. I was disinclined to this; for I much preferred an open expression of my opinions.

Weeks passed, when Mr Adams, without any consultation with me, & without any previous knowledge on my part of his intended course, published his first article, on yr vote, in the Boston Whig. Sympathizing with him entirely in his view, & glad that the conscience of the community had at last found a voice, I addressed to him the communication, signed *Boston*,[3] which I wrote with pain, under the conviction of duty. *Amicus Plato, amicus Socrates, sed magis amica Veritas*.[4]

At a later day, Mr Buckingham of the Courier called at my office. Finding from conversation with him that he took the side of Mr Adams in his controversy with the Advertiser, I asked him why he did not say something about it in his paper. He at once invited me to discuss it. I hesitated; he urged. He came to my office again for the communication, which I had written, after consultation with friends, whom you would be unwilling not to consider as yr friends also; & it was finally published with his entire approbation.[5]

Such is my connexion with this unpleasant question. I hope that I have not in my communications "perverted your words or acts, or falsified your whole conduct." I aimed to be rigorously within the Truth.

I cannot disguise from you that, when I listened to yr speech & toast in Faneuil Hall last year, I felt a pang.[6] I said to myself at the time, that "I would have cut off my right hand, rather than utter such a sentiment, setting *country* above *right*." Not long after, I saw you in the groups of mourners at the funeral of Judge Story. He was a great Jurist, & a true Whig. I wished, then, that his spirit could speak *to* you, as it had spoken *of* you, only a few days before his death, to arrest you in the path which you seemed to have adopted.

When at a later day [*April 1846*], I saw you personally at Washington, I longed to converse with you frankly on the subject. I witnessed with pride the position which you occupied in the House, & hoped that it might always be exerted in the highest causes of Humanity & Right, believing that any notability, acquired in the displays of party politics, or in the service of *mere* material interests, is little better than pinchbeck, or sounding brass.

I hope, my dear Sir, that we may always meet as friends. It will not be easy for me to be pressed into any other relation.[7]

I remain, my dear Sir,

faithfully Yours, Charles Sumner

Private. When I marked my other letter *private*, I only desired to designate it as not for publication. I cannot be offended by yr mentioning to any body that I wrote the article Boston, & the leader in the Courier, with its still unpublished supplement,—if Mr. B. should see fit to publish the latter on his return from his journey.[8]

Hon. Robt. C. Winthrop &c &c &c

ALS MHi (67/511, PCS)

1. Since Winthrop's vote supporting the Mexican War in May 1846, he had been criticized in the *Boston Daily Whig*, a newspaper recently organized by the Young Whigs, later called the Conscience Whigs, with Charles Francis Adams as editor (DD, 1:141–44). In his letter to CS (Washington, 5/196, PCS), Winthrop wrote he found it hard to believe that CS had attacked him in the *Whig* and the *Boston Courier*, because the articles were "so utterly inconsistent with those personal relations which had recently existed between us." Winthrop told CS that to friends he had characterized CS's articles as "ungenerous & unjust," and that he stood by these charges. He hoped their friendship could be restored.

2. In its editorial (27 July 1846:2) the *Boston Daily Advertiser* called Adams's attack on Winthrop "a personal attack which is not only unmerited and unprovoked, but grossly slanderous and indecent." Winthrop was only carrying out his responsibility, said the *Advertiser*, and had gained even more support from his constituents.

3. Adams stated that in voting for the Mexican War bill, Winthrop was "voting a positive sanction of that policy, involving a moral deliquency in sustaining a falsehood" (*Boston Daily Whig*, 16 July 1846:2). In his letter to the *Whig* (22 July 1846:2) CS praised the *Whig's* editor (Adams) for criticizing congressional Whig support for the Mexican War, especially the vote on the preamble blaming Mexico for the war. Winthrop's act, wrote CS, was "a suicidal blow to the Whig party. It has taken from us our moral strength."

4. "Plato is a friend, Socrates a friend, but Truth is more a friend."

5. Joseph T. Buckingham (1779–1861), editor, *Boston Courier*, 1824–48. CS's article (*Boston Courier*, 31 July 1846:2) expressed "extreme sorrow" over Winthrop's support of the war, which he saw as a "series of well-planned and elaborate efforts to *fortify and extend slavery.*"

6. At a dinner after CS's July Fourth oration, 1845, Winthrop had declared, "*Our Country*—However bounded, still our country—to be defended by all hands" (*Boston Daily Advertiser,* 7 July 1845:2).

7. Winthrop's reply of 17 August (5/211) to this letter stated that CS's articles not only condemned Winthrop's actions, but also his "motives" and his "integrity. They seem to arrogate for their author an exclusive privilege of pronouncing upon matters both of truth & of conscience, & to deny me all right of judgment as to either." Winthrop wrote he was "compelled . . . to decline all further communication or conference, while matters stand between us as they now do."

8. CS's third attack on Winthrop appeared in the *Boston Courier,* 13 August 1846:2. Its main points are stated in CS to Appleton, 11 August. In a preface to the article Buckingham stated that he "leaves the writer to himself,—neither affirming nor denying what he says."

To Nathan Appleton

Boston August 11th 1846

My dear Sir,

I have this morning received your letter of August 8th, & the enclosed communication for the Whig, which I have handed to Mr Adams. He will publish it, with commentaries. He did not need any suggestion from me, that all that he should say should be gentle, kind & respectful; for he has no personal feelings toward you, except of respect. He proposed to shew your communication to Dr Palfrey, before he published it.[1]

I think you are not aware of the influence which your letter, joined with Mr Lawrence's, had on the Annexation of Texas, particularly in encouraging the *esprit de corps* among slave-holders.[2]

I have always voted for Winthrop, & have known him from College life, when I looked up to him as my senior, & as a person of pure life, & good scholarship. *But he has done the worst act that was ever done by a Boston representative*. He voted *for* a measure, which may be viewed under *five* different aspects; (1) It was a *Declaration of War* against a sister republic; (2) it was an *unjust* war, for even *he* will not *say*, though he did seem to insinuate, that the conduct of Mexico created a *casus belli*; (3) it provided for "the *successful* prosecution of the war," in other words for the triumph of *injustice*; (4) it asserted that the war was commenced "*by the act of Mexico,*" which was a National Lie; (5) it had its source & origin in efforts to *extend* & *fortify* slavery.

You say that "his friends should not be ready to censure him, *because his decision in a most difficult case* has not been precisely according to their views."[3] Surely the case submitted to him had *no* difficulty. *Five*-fold *Right* was on one side; *five*-fold *Wrong* on the other side. Of the two caskets before him, he chose the blazing one of the *majority*, filled with a death's head.

I regret very much that he did so. He has dissolved the charm of his character. I have heard this act spoken of by all sorts of men; men in State St, & in Court St, scholars & clergymen, & always with condemnation. It seems to me that it is wrong to keep him under the illusion that he has not done wrong. His friends should loyally & frankly let him know that he has done wrong; & he should have the magnanimity to retrace his steps, so far as he can.

I know of no person who wishes to disturb him in his office. I have sometimes said to myself; "Cassio, I love thee; but henceforth be no servant of mine." But I would not give the thought voice; nor could I bring myself to vote against him, or to think unkindly of him. I hope always to meet him as a friend; but I cannot help thinking that he has done an Act, which he will regret, both on earth & in heaven.

I intended to write you a letteret as Charles Lamb calls it; but it has swollen to an epistle. I envy you all the retreat at Berkshire, & am sorry that the children are visited by any ailment.

I would write to Henry [*Longfellow*]; but have nothing to say. Howe has returned, in translucent health, from the waters of Brattleboro, believing in the efficacy of that treatment of disease.

Ever sincerely Yours, Charles Sumner

P.S. The Whig newspaper has produced a strong impression, & awakened a response, particularly among the young Whigs. Adams has his heart in it, as have a considerable body of writers. It is hoped that the Whig party of Mass. will be enabled to recover the ground which it occupied two years ago, & take the lead in a series of firm but temperate measures for the overthrow of slavery.

Hon. N. Appleton

ALS MHi (67/515, PCS)

1. In his letter of 10 August 1846 (Pittsfield, 5/198, PCS), Appleton wrote that he had written an answer to the *Boston Daily Whig*'s article of 1 August 1846 blaming Appleton for supporting the Mexican War. He asked that CS refrain from printing the letter if it were likely to "provoke any harsh commentary." Appleton's reply appeared in the *Whig*, 14 August 1846:2.

2. See CS to Nathan Hale, 29 November 1845.

3. In his letter to CS, Appleton also expressed regret for the *Whig*'s "severe" attacks on Winthrop.

To Henry W. Longfellow

Court St Wednesday
[*12 August 1846*]

Dearly beloved Henry,

I send you a Whig, which contains a piece of poetry by Dr Frothingham.[1]

I saw Putnam last evng, recently from London. He talks glowingly of the Hutchinsons in England. He heard them *six* times, & saw Dickens, Foster, Milnes & others, among their audience.[2] Their Anti-Slavery songs commended them; but yr Excelsior was more popular than all else. He felt elated by its success. It was always sung with triumph.

I wrote a long political letter to Mr. A[*ppleton*] yesterday. I *do* wish that I could agree with him more than I can on this great question of slavery & war. It seems to me Winthrop's friends ought gently & kindly to put him *right*; not defend him; not let him deceive himself into the belief that he has done any thing but *wrong*. He has certainly done the *worst act*, that has ever been done by a Rep.'tive from Boston. How different from Quincy. Those were noble words of his, which Adams quoted against Winthrop.[3] I wish you would mention to Mr Appleton that the articles in the Whig, on the Policy of the Administration, originally published in the Essex Register, are by a distinguished member of Congress, whose name is a secret, but who lives far away from Salem.[4]

Mr Adams will publish Mr Appleton's letter, with comments, of which I know nothing, & from which I shall keep myself entirely aloof. Love to all,

Ever thine, C. S.

Corny [*Felton*] sits here & sends his best love, & Hillard also.

ALS MH-H (67/519, PCS)

1. The poem, "The Old Man's Song" by Nathaniel L. Frothingham (1793–1870, Unitarian minister, Boston) was published in the *Boston Daily Whig*, 12 August 1846:2.

2. George Putnam (1807–78), Harvard classmate; pastor, First Religious Society, Roxbury; coeditor, *Christian Examiner*. The Hutchinson family singers were connected with antislavery and temperance movements (HWL, 3.121). John Forster (1812–76), British biographer and critic.

3. In "The Daily Advertiser and Mr. Winthrop" (*Boston Daily Whig*, 6 August 1846:2), Adams compared Winthrop unfavorably to his "predecessor," Josiah Quincy, who had said, "If patriotism ask me to assert a false hood, I have no hesitation in telling patriotism, 'I am not prepared to make that sacrifice.'"

4. A series of articles called "The Policy of the Administration" appeared in the *Whig* on 10, 11, and 13 August 1846:2. In them the writer criticized a weak and obsequious North, as guilty as the South, he said, on the slavery issue.

To Nathan Appleton

Boston August 22nd '46

My dear Sir,

I have just received your letter of Aug. 20th, & have read it with grief, as I could not fail to read any thing from you, which seemed to shew that we were so wide apart on a matter in which each is interested.[1]

I do not wish to reply to the details of your specifications in behalf of Winthrop. And yet you will pardon me if I say, with the freedom employed by you towards myself, that they do not seem to me to disturb *one* of the five points of his wrong-doing. It is *certain* that we are now engaged in war with Mexico, *legalized* by Congress, & report says that *three* invasions are moving upon Mexico. If this be true, it can be only by virtue of the act for which Winthrop voted.

Believing, as I do, that an *unjust war* is the greatest *crime* a nation can commit, drawing in its train murder, & offences of all kinds, I think it was the *imperative* duty of every Xtian representative to oppose it, even if he stood *alone*. Above all, it was ye duty of ye representative of Boston, a place of conscience, & morality, to see that the influence of the city of Channing was not thrown on the side of injustice.

I regret much—very much—large numbers regret very much—that our representative was found wanting in the high moral character which was needful on ye occasion. His toast at Faneuil Hall, "our country, *howsoever bounded,*" caused Judge Story to say of him, that he was "as *bad* as Decatur," & to call him "*traitor* to morals & freedom." His vote seems to me the dark *consummate flower* of that toast.

Feeling this, in my inmost conscience, seeing no excuse for his act, finding my own views echoed by all whom I was in ye habit of meeting, I deemed it my duty, a most painful one, to call public attention to his act. In this matter I have no private feelings to gratify. My relations with Winthrop have always been amiable. It is bitter to me, that they should cease to be so. But on reviewing the past I see nothing to regret. My articles were read & approved by *others*, before they were published, & I have received from many quarters most unexpected expressions of the sympathy which they have awakened.

I know of no disposition among my friends to oppose Winthrop for Congress. There are doubtless many persons, who will feel unable to vote for him; but I know of no persons, who would organise any opposition.

And now, my dear Sir, I have written with freedom—certainly not greater than you have directed towards me when you allude to "a sublimation of morality incompatible with a perfectly sound judgment."[2] I confess that I do regard morality, in private & public, as sacred; nor do I believe that any judgment can be sound, that is not inspired by it.

You may remember the feelings which I expressed when you told me what you had from Winthrop's lips, that *one* of the considerations which entered into his vote was, that he "did not wish to see *all* Mass. going with ye Abolitionists." And so, he votes for war! What he said in the Whig caucus, as reported to me from another source, shewed that he was not looking *singly & exclusively* at the justice, the *righteousness* of the measure.

Let us not remember, my dear Sir, that we differ on this question. I cannot forget yr kindness & friendship, & hope that you will be willing to dwell on our many points of sympathy. Pardon this long letter, which is not so long as it seems to be, but which has unexpectedly swollen under my rapid pen.

Believe me, ever, my dear Sir,

gratefully & sincerely Yrs, Charles Sumner

P.S. I hope you will be able to be present at the Φ.B.K.[3]

ALS MHi (67/526, PCS)

1. In his letter (20 August 1846, 5/215, PCS) Appleton said he did not agree with any of the five reasons CS had advanced in his letter of 11 August in condemning Winthrop's vote for the Mexican war and answered them point by point. He considered CS's *Boston Courier* article attacking Winthrop (13 August 1846:2) "inconsistent with a proper Christian charity," and advised CS to "recall your charges against Mr. Winthrop."

2. Nathan Appleton wrote, "But the assumption that one's own opinion is the only right one in a complicated case of this kind, implies, it appears to me, a sublimation in any organ of morality incompatible with a perfectly sound judgment" (5/215).

3. On 27 August CS delivered "The Scholar, The Jurist, The Artist, The Philanthropist" to the Phi Beta Kappa Society at Harvard.

To John Quincy Adams

Boston August 28th 1845 [*1846*]

My dear Sir,

I was touched more than I can tell by your kindness to me yesterday, & especially by those words at the dinner,[1] in which you associated my name with those whom I had undertaken to commemorate. To have won such a tribute from you fills me with happiness. Let me thank you from my heart again. When as a boy, with a silver medal & blue string, it was my fortune to listen to you in Faneuil Hall—you were then President of the United States—it little occurred to me that I could ever receive praise from those lips on whose accents I hung with such interest.

Let me subscribe myself,

Sincerely & affectionately Yours, Charles Sumner

Hon. John Quincy Adams

ALS MBApm (67/327, PCS)

1. Adams attended the Phi Beta Kappa celebration at which CS delivered his address (John Quincy Adams's Diary, 27 August 1846, Adams Papers, microfilm reel 48). In answering CS's letter, Adams repeated his praise of CS's address, both in subject matter and delivery. Adams predicted, "you have a mission to perform," but added that CS would have to learn to compromise (letter of 29 August [*1846*], 5/226, PCS).

To Daniel Webster

Boston Sept. 25th 1846

My dear Sir,

In the course of some remarks which I addressed to the Whig Convention in Faneuil Hall, I ventured to introduce your name.[1] I trust that I shall not be thought to have transcended the line of courtesy, respect & kindness, which I can not fail to feel towards you.

I have long desired, in public or in private, to approach you with the sentiments which I then expressed, believing that there now lie before you fields of usefulness & glory, which you have not yet entered.[2]

Believe me, my dear Sir,

Faithfully Yours, Charles Sumner

Hon. Daniel Webster &c &c

ALS DLC (67/552, PCS)

1. In his speech "Antislavery Duties of the Whig Party," 23 September 1846, CS proposed that Whigs should work toward a constitutional amendment abolishing slavery and called on Webster to lead in this effort (Wks, 1:304–16).

2. Webster's holograph reply has not been recovered. In his reply (Prc, 1:129; Wks, 1:316) Webster stated his regret that in politics, the two differed regarding "the line of duty most fit to be pursued in endeavors to obtain all the good which can be obtained," but professed the highest "personal regard" for CS.

To Nathan Hale

Private

Hancock St Saturday Evng.
[*31 October 1846*]

My dear Sir,

I enclose a short statement addressed to the public, which I hope to have inserted in the Advertiser on Monday morning.[1] I have sent copies to the other papers.

Allow me to ask yr attention to yr remarks with regard to me in yr paper of Friday.[2] I reached home about 11 o'clk on that evening, after a long & weary day, & found yr paper of that date.

I do not complain of any thing but simply invite yr attention to what you have stated.

Mr Andrew informs me that you have given an erroneous idea of what he said, & has read to me his own report of it, by which it appears that he declared explicitly, that I had no knowledge or suspicion of any purpose to nominate me, & that I had always declined to be a candidate. This is most certainly the case.

Four weeks ago I declined a formal nomination, & have since persevered in repelling all proposals addressed to me on the subject, saying, that, so far, as I knew myself, I would not go to Congress, if I could go by a *unanimous* vote.

Under these circumstances, I think yr remarks with regard to me were hasty, & not justified by any thing I have done.

I have nothing to say with regard to any criticisms on what I have said or done. That is, of course, open to the severest comment. Nor am I sure, that the disagreeable *tone* of yr article with regard to me, was not entirely proper, when I consider the character of political comments & the circumstances in which I was placed.

I pray you, dear Sir, to believe me to speak *ex pectore*[3] when I say, that I have no desire for public life. If it should be my lot to exert any influence (& I know full well how little it must be) I wish it may be always as a private citizen.

Yours sincerely, Charles Sumner

P.S. Mr Andrew tells me that his remarks all appear in Monday's Whig.[4] Perhaps, it would not be too much to expect that his own version of what he said, *so far as it regards me* should appear in yr paper, where he thinks it has been misapprehended.

ALS NcD (67/579, PCS)

1. "Refusal to Be a Candidate for Congress" (67/581, PCS; Wks, 1:331–32). Although CS had repeatedly declared he did not want to contest Winthrop's seat in Congress, a committee chaired by John Andrew (1818–67) nominated him anyway as an independent candidate (DD, 1:149).

2. Of CS's candidacy, the *Boston Daily Advertiser* (30 October 1846:2) wrote that Andrew was "quite confident" that CS would agree to be a candidate, and, if he did, "the citizens of Boston may at last have an opportunity to vote for—as member of Congress—a man who really understands their interests as connected with those of the nation at large,—who is a statesman while he is their friend." The *Advertiser* went on to state, however, that if CS had decided that "the principles which have made the name of the Whigs of Boston known throughout the land, are to be sacrificed for a temporary and isolated purpose; if in fine he has consented to throw the influence which his friends have garnered and saved for him into the scale against that other well known Boston man,—well known and well tried,—*Robert C. Winthrop*, we shall turn our backs upon the neophyte, almost self-proposed, and cling to him whose qualities, whose services and whose motives we know."

3. "From the heart."

4. At the Independent Rally, 29 October 1846, Andrew stated that CS's nomination was against CS's wishes. However, given the *Boston Daily Atlas*'s "harsh and unjustifiable" attack on CS, Andrew declared that he should be defended, and therefore nominated (*Boston Daily Whig*, 2 November 1846:2).

To Salmon P. Chase[1]

Private

Boston Dec. 12th '46

My dear Sir

I am obliged by yr letter announcing Mr Vaughan's mission.[2] He is now here. What can be done to promote his views is still uncertain. Those, who are engaged most warmly in this cause of Anti-Slavery, have had, & still have, at home, ample occas[ion] for all the funds which they are [able?] to devote to that purpose. This you readily understand. Small minorities rarely command superfluous wealth.

But the regular Whigs in Boston have always professed a strong interest in the cause of Emancipation, while they objected to our movement, as impracticable & impertinent. Nothing can be done here, they say. Mr N. Appleton said to me at the Whig Convention, as I came down from the stand, after speaking; "Yours would have been a good speech in Virginia."[3] He did not recognise, that *we* were in Virginia, as to the Slave-Power. It has occurred to us, that an opportunity should be given them of shewing the sincerity of their professions; & we hope to enable Mr Vaughan to lay his case before them. If they are so disposed, they can easily place his paper on a permanent footing. I am curious to know what they will say.

I hope the time will come,—(I wish that it had come)—when the Friends of Freedom may stand together. There must be very soon a new chrystallization of parties, in which there shall be one grand Northern party of Freedom. In such a party I shall hope to serve by yr side. Meanwhile, the opponents of Slavery should aim at Union together. They should look upon each other with good will, & generosity, & direct their powers,—never against each other—but always against the common enemy.

The feud between the Garrison party, & the Liberty Party,[4] seems to me (pardon my candor) discreditable to our cause. Powers of argument & eloquence, which should be pointed at Slavery, are employed by earnest assailers of that Institution, upon their bretheren, who are equally earnest with themselves. Must this be so always? Then again, (pardon my freedom) the Liberty party seem to depart from their principles when they oppose such men as Giddings, J. Q. Adams, & Palfrey,[5] all three staunch & uncompromising friends of the Slaves. It is important that these men should be sustained by large votes; their usefulness will be increased thereby. But some of my friends of the Liberty Party here—though not all of them—have prevented the return of Palfrey, & swelled the triumph of the Pro-Slavery Whigs, who secretly exalt over his defeat, though they do not venture to oppose him openly, because he is the *regular* candidate of the party. Anxious for the platform of Liberty, on which we can *all* stand together, it seems to me we can reach it only by cultivating a kindly spirit among one another. There is no *real* question now before the country, except as to the Slave-Power. John Quincy Adams said to me a week ago, as he lay on his sick-bed, "the Tariff is an obsolete idea."[6] What other questions could *seem* to separate us? I know nothing of the currency, or Sub-Treasury. Opposition to Slavery is the idea which I wish to carry practically into politics, regarding it as paramount, to all others; & I believe that I have yr sympathy in this. Grateful for yr kind appreciation of what I have done, & happy in this opportunity of communicating with you, believe me, dear Sir,

very faithfully Yrs, Charles Sumner

S. P. Chase, Esq.

ALS DLC (67/595, PCS)

1. Salmon P. Chase (1808–73), then a lawyer and antislavery activist in Ohio.

2. Chase had written CS that John C. Vaughan would come east seeking funds in order to continue the *True American*, a Lexington, Kentucky, antislavery newspaper (Cincinnati, 26 November 1846, 5/362, PCS).

3. "Antislavery Duties of the Whig Party."

4. In the *Liberator* and his speeches, Garrison attacked the Liberty Party, a party in which Chase was then active, for its moderation, asserting that slavery could not be abolished through political action. In return, the Liberty Party denounced Garrison's pleas for dissolution of the United States. See Walter M. Merrill, *Against Wind and Tide* (1963), 201–5, 212.

5. Joshua R. Giddings (1795–1864), U.S. congressman (Whig, Free Soil, Ohio), 1838–42, 1842–59; consul general to Canada, 1861–64. Palfrey, a Conscience Whig, had been initially prevented by Liberty Party votes from being elected to Congress. In a run-off election, however, he achieved the necessary majority (F. O. Gatell, *John Gorham Palfrey and the New England Conscience* [1963], 136–37).

6. The Walker Tariff of 1846, opposed by the Whigs, lowered import duties on manufactured goods. CS had argued in his speech to the Whig convention that the antislavery cause was more compelling than that of tariff repeal (Wks, 1:304–16).

To Joshua R. Giddings

Boston Dec. 21st '46

My dear Sir,

I feel happy in your approbation of any thing which I have been able to do, & thank you much for the kindness of yr letter to me.[1]

Let me thank you still more for yr free voice on the floor of Congress. Yr speech has been received, as reported in the Intelligencer.[2] It will, probably, appear in the Whig tomorrow.

The speeches which have been made seem to fall below the occasion. They are superficial, & do not really grasp the question. Mr Winthrop's seemed a party speech, in which he avoided the discussion of all ultimate principles. I should add, that I have not yet read Mr Hudson's.[3]

I am curious to know, whether we may expect any sympathy from Mr Clayton.[4] You led me to think, that he might be found with us.

As we parted at Springfield, you pressed upon my attention the important question, whether the relation of Slavery was not dissolved, when the Slave escaped upon the Ocean. I had often thought of this question before, & have considered it somewhat since. Certainly, the Ocean ought to be *free* in every sense—*mare liberum*[5]

There is one difficulty to which I venture to call yr attention. The laws that sanction slavery are *local* & *municipal* in their character. It is clear that, by the common law, & the law of nations, the *status* of slavery is divested, when the slave passes under a *municipal* jurisdiction, which does not sanction slavery, as if he reached England or France. But is the *status* of slavery divested on the Ocean? The slave has fled from the *local* laws, which sanction his slavery; but has he reached the influence of other institutions, which will discharge him? The writers on the Conflict of Laws, treating of the *Capacity of Persons* (a fruitful theme) assert that it attends them on the sea. Though Slavery should derive no sanction from the Constitution of the U. States, I fear, that, in accordance with the principles of public law, governing the *capacity of persons*, it is so deeply impressed on the person, that it can be dissolved only by the strong action of a *municipal* jurisdiction, within which the slave may be brought. The slave becomes free, not merely by escaping from his own laws, but by virtue of other laws, which shall *actively* pronounce him free, as if he comes under another jurisdiction, as by getting on board a ship of war of a foreign state, or touching the soil of a foreign state.

It seems to me clear that the Slave cannot be held on the Ocean, by virtue of the Constitution of the U. States. That ground is dismissed at once. But I do fear, that looking at his condition, in the light of jurisprudence, the subtle thread of the *municipal* law, by which he was held in slavery, would continue to bind him, until it was cut or snapped asunder, by the operation of some other *municipal* law.

I have ventured to throw out these suggestions with diffidence, submitting them to yr better judgment.

We all watch yr course with interest & gratitude. Believe me, my dear sir,

Faithfully Yours, Charles Sumner

P.S. I think Presdt. Adams is gaining strength as fast as could be expected. He sits up now, & walks across his chamber. I conversed with him two evenings ago as much as two hours.

Hon. J. R. Giddings

ALS OHi (67/599, PCS)

1. In his letter of 13 December 1846 Giddings thanked CS for sending his Phi Beta Kappa address, "The Scholar, The Jurist, The Artist, The Philanthropist" (Washington, 5/387, PCS).

2. In his speech 15 December (*Globe*, 29th Cong., 2nd sess., appendix, 47–52), Giddings declared, "the civilized world will hold the advocates of that measure [*the Mexican War*] responsible for all the crimes, the misery, and suffering, which have resulted from it" (48). Since the Mexican War was "a wicked and unjust war, it follows, that the longer it is carried on the greater will be the wickedness and the injustice of those who continue it" (51).

3. Winthrop protested the U.S. occupation of the conquered territory in Mexico with the intention of annexing it, and feared that President Polk, in his annual message, "had taken care to suppress that which the people had a right to know" (9 December 1846, *Globe*, 29th Cong., 2nd sess., 17–18). Charles Hudson (1795–1881; U.S. congressman [Whig, Mass.], 1841–49) declared on 16 December 1846 that the various alleged charges that Mexico had instigated the war were all spurious: "there was no just cause of war in this case" (ibid., 49).

4. John Middleton Clayton (1796–1856), U.S. senator (Natl. Rep., Whig, Del.), 1829–36, 1845–49, 1853–56; U.S. secretary of state, 1849–50.

5. "A sea open to all."

To Joshua R. Giddings

Boston Dec. 30th '46

My dear Sir,

I am grateful to you for the kindness & confidence of yr letter of Dec. 25th.

The question of *freedom* on the Atlantic Ocean I shall consider in the light of yr suggestions. Your speech I read at the time it was first printed, & I well remember Mr Duer's argument.[1] It is, certainly, so much in accordance with my feelings, to incline to the side of Liberty, that I cannot be an unwilling listener to yr views. If there should be any occasion to apply them here, I shall not fail to do it.

I send you a Boston Courier, containing an article on Mr Sears's Plan of Emancipation, written by Henry Lee,[2] the gentleman, who received the votes of South Carolina for the Vice Presidency in 1832. You will perceive that he believes with us that Slavery must be abolished.

Another agreeable indication of sentiment in Boston is the reception of Mr Vaughan, of Cincinnati, who is soliciting help for the True American. Some of our "old Whigs" have taken hold of the matter, & are subscribing in sums of $100 each. Towards $3000 have already been subscribed. This shews a softening on their part. I think several have been induced to subscribe for *appearance sake*; that they might seem disposed to take part in what they call *a practical measure*. It is a good sign. It shews that public opinion is moving on.

I send also a Courier of to-day, in which I have endeavoured to call attention to yr position against the war.[3] I hope to follow it with a similar notice of Mr Hudson.

It seems to me that you are right in opposing all supplies.[4] Our position is an extreme one. We can preserve it only by standing on *principle*. With our feet there we shall be firm. If we abandon any *principle*, we shall lose the confidence of the country, & our own self-respect. Let the minority be small or great, I would oppose the war in every form. I would never lend it any sanction from my vote.

Can I aid yr views by any action here? —We are all disappointed by the silence of Greeley in the Tribune.[5] Why does he not speak out?

I passed two hours last evng with Presdt. Adams. He has gained very much, & incidentally, spoke of taking his seat at Washington.

Yours very faithfully, Charles Sumner

Hon. Joshua R. Giddings

ALS OHi (67/612, PCS)

1. In his letter of 25 December 1846 Giddings stated that he believed that a ship "entering the high seas [*is*] national in character, . . . and that laws of the state have no more influence [then?], than they have in the District of Columbia or the Territories of the United States." Giddings referred CS to his speech of 3 June 1842 on the *Creole* case, and [John?] Duer's support of Giddings's stand (Washington, 5/391, PCS).

2. Henry Lee (1782–1867), Boston merchant, publicist, and free trade proponent, wrote "Plan of Emancipation," 24 December 1846, which appeared in the *Boston Courier* 29 December 1846:2. In it Lee discussed the "blighting effects of slavery" and commended David Sears's plan, which showed how slavery was detrimental to the U.S.

3. CS's article, "Mr. Giddings's Speech" (*Boston Courier*, 30 December 1846:2), warmly praised Giddings's speech opposing the Mexican War: "it is a source of gratification that [*his protest*] has been uttered by a Whig."

4. Giddings wrote that he thought a majority of Whigs in the House would vote "against all appropriations for its [*the Mexican War's*] prosecution."

5. Horace Greeley (1811–72), editor, *New York Daily Tribune*, 1841–72; U.S. congressman (Whig, N.Y.), 1848–49.

To George Sumner

Boston Dec 31st '46

My dear George,

I wish you a happy New Year. I have recd. yr letter to the Mayor. It is admirable & much to yr purpose. He has read it; so has Hillard, who has more influence in City affairs than any other person; so has Mr Sampson one of the Common Council.[1] All are struck by it, & say it shall be printed—sometime in Jany—, after the organization of the new Govt. I shall distribute copies widely. I am glad that you have done this. It will help us in our efforts for a jail of a proper character, & also in the war with Louis Dwight. He has returned, much incensed, I am told, with me. He has considerable salary & does nothing. But next May, I shall call him to account.

You will see by the papers which I have sent you something of the part I have taken in our public affairs.[2] I do not know where yr predilections would be; & yet I am persuaded, that no party biases could render you insensible to the atrocious injustice of this war with Mexico. It is bad in every respect. It is without legal cause. It was unconstitutional in its inception. It is wasteful of life & treasure. It is demoralizing in its influence. As such, it ought to be arrested at all hazard. Winthrop & a large portion of the Whigs were drawn to its support, contrary to the principles of the party. In contending with the prevailing sentiment of Boston, I have, of course, exposed myself to much asperity of feeling.

The affairs of our country are now in a deplorable condition. The Mexican War & Slavery will derange all party calculations. The Anti-Slavery principle has acquired such force as to be felt by all politicians. In most of the Free States it will hold the balance between the two parties, so that neither can succeed without yielding to it in a greater or less degree. The Abolitionists have at last got their lever upon a *fulcrum*, where it can operate. It will detach large sections from each of the other parties.

Both parties are not controlled in their conduct, even on the Mexican War, by a reference to the next Presidential election. The Whigs shrink from opposing it, for fear of unpopularity at the South & West; & the leaders of both parties act mainly with a view to maintain the force of their party. —— The question of Slavery advances upon the country with great strides. Come home, & give us the advantage of yr counsels. —— Prescott has completed his [*Conquest of*] Peru in 2 vols., & made his contract with the Harpers who are to print 7500 copies in the 1st year.—Hillard & Wm Story will visit Europe for a year, leaving next July. —— I hope Greene is well & properous. Mrs Hayward talks of you with admiration. She thinks you "the most interesting person she has ever known." I am glad of it. Mrs Lee talks with praise & gratitude. You have bewitched those 2 old women. Would it were one younger.

Henry [*Sumner*] is at home, crisp, curt, taciturn toward all of us. Albert [*Sumner*] is in New York.—Every body says, when is yr brother George coming home?—I do not know.

Ever Thine, Charles

ALS MH-H (63/142, PCS)

1. "Mr. Sumner's Letter on the Subject of Prison Discipline in France" (1847). Josiah Quincy, Jr. (1802–82), mayor of Boston, 1845–49. George R. Sampson (d. 1895).

2. Besides his criticism of the Boston Prison Discipline Society and his newspaper articles attacking Winthrop, CS had delivered a speech, "Slavery and the Mexican War," at Tremont Temple, Boston, 5 November 1846, supporting Samuel Gridley Howe as a congressional candidate against Winthrop (Wks, 1:333–51).

To Joshua R. Giddings

Boston—Jan. 21st '47

My dear Sir,

I agree with you entirely in yr views of the proper course towards the Democrats. You will see something on this matter in an article which I wrote in the Whig of last Tuesday, entitled "The Boston Atlas & Southern Influence."[1] It is evidently the present design of the ultra Whigs to discredit the Democratic movement & to denounce its authors as "turncoats." But it seems to me that they have come nearer to our position, than our associates the Whigs. They have proclaimed Slavery to be *wrong*, & have pledged themselves with force against its *extension*. It is difficult to see how they can longer sustain themselves *merely* on that ground. Their premise sustains a broader conclusion, that is, the duty of no longer allowing the *continuance* of the evil any where within our constitutional action. They must become Abolitionists. It seems to me that our great object should be to encourage *union* among all who are against Slavery. The disputes between Anti-Slavery men are unseemly.

I hope that our friends will stand firm with regard to the candidates for Presdt & Vice-Presdt. It seems to me that we must not have a National Convention. We cannot expect a Convention to adopt candidates who are *true* on our questions. We must not consent to any who are *not true*. I have supposed that it would probably end in a multiplicity of candidates as in 1825, & in our defeat. The term after next our chance will be pretty sure. *But we must stand firm now*.

I do not know Mr Marsh the correspondent of the Tribune. I am told that he does *not* incline to our views. But why did Greeley take him? I am glad the Tribune has spoken at last.[2]

Mr Cushing's Resolve[3] will be rejected by a large vote. The discussion has turned much upon the question of the character of the troops—whether militia or army.

I am glad you are to speak again. Whatever may have been the opinions as to justice of the war of 1812 with England, it is very clear, from the character of that Power, that when it was once commenced, it was to us a war of *self-defence*.[4] I send you a copy of C. F. Adams's speech on that point. It is on the hand-bill, which you have already had.[5]

Yours faithfully, Charles Sumner

ALS OHi (67/629, PCS)

1. In his letter of 18 January 1847 (Washington, 5/410, PCS), Giddings proposed "taking ground a little more liberal toward the northern democrats than heretofore . . . extending to them the hand of fellowship in consequence of their late position" (i.e., a split from the southern Democrats). CS's article in the *Boston Daily Whig* (19 January 1847:2) protested the "*slaveholding* influences which predominate in the Atlas." He rejoiced that Democrats like Preston King and Hannibal Hamlin ("turncoats") supported the Wilmot Proviso. Wrote CS, "Welcome to such turncoats! . . . [T]ies of *mere* party [*were*] . . . no more than threads of gossamer, compared with the adamantine claims of duty by which we are bound to our high endeavor."

2. Probably Charles M. March (Donald Ritchie, "Press Gallery," unpublished manuscript, 1988). Greeley devoted several columns on the front page of the 20 January 1847 issue of the *New York Daily Tribune* to antislavery messages, including a poem, "Epistle," by John Quincy Adams.

3. On 14 January a majority of a Massachusetts House committee chaired by Caleb Cushing voted $20,000 to support a regiment from Massachusetts in the Mexican War. But the resolve was defeated on 28 January by the full House (Claude M. Fuess, *Caleb Cushing* [1923], 2:36–38).

4. Giddings said in his letter to CS that in a forthcoming speech he would "try to draw the distinction between the war of 1812 and the present, between offence and *defence*, and to answer Mr Winthrop's views in regard to the precedent set us by British statesmen" (5/410).

5. No speech by Charles Francis Adams has been located, but his editorial, "The War," appeared in the *Boston Daily Whig* 15 January 1847.

To Joshua R. Giddings

Boston Feb. 19th '47

My dear Sir,

Should not some steps be taken, before our friends leave Washington, to bring forward Corwin *at once* as a candidate for the Presidency?[1] *They* will try to head us. Let *us* try to head *them*. I throw this out for yr consideration. By commencing an agitation on his name now, it has occurred to me that we might give a direction to public sentiment.

But, perhaps, you will think it better to stand still on our principles. I am not confident that this is not the better course, without committing ourself *even* to Corwin. If we should bring him forward, the old Whigs might fasten upon him a slave-holding Vice-Presdt.

We must stand *firm*. Mr S. C. Phillips is in favor of taking steps at once for Corwin. He said that he would write you on the subject.

I have just read Delano's speech[2] which I like much. It is clear & energetic.

Mr Adams has not yet returned from Washington.[3] I shall hope from him an encouraging account of affairs in Washington.

The Presdt Adams, I trust, is well. I am very anxious that, in some way,—by speech or letter, he should express his *present* opinion on the subject of Slavery. He could not leave a better legacy behind; but, in the present state of his health, he can not do it.

Yours truly, Charles Sumner

ALS MH-H (63/154, PCS)

1. Thomas Corwin (1794–1865; U.S. senator [Whig, Ohio], 1845–50; U.S. congressman [Rep., Ohio], 1859–61) had on 11 February 1847 vigorously denounced the Mexican War (*Globe*, 29th Cong., 2nd sess., appendix, 211–18). Giddings wrote CS that Corwin "retires this night in the proudest attitude of any man in the nation" (11 February, 5/449, PCS). The Twenty-ninth Congress would adjourn 3 March 1847.

2. In his speech, Columbus Delano (1809–96; U.S. congressman [Whig, Rep., Ohio], 1845–47, 1865–67, 1868–69) argued for withholding supplies for the Mexican War (2 February 1847, *Globe*, 29th Cong., 2nd sess., appendix, 278–82).

3. Charles Francis Adams accompanied his ailing father from Boston to Washington in February 1847 (*Memoirs of John Quincy Adams*, ed. Charles Francis Adams, vol. 12 [1877], 280).

To Francis Lieber

Boston March 22nd '47

My dear Lieber,

Night before last, in the dream of a heavy sleep, I visited Columbia. I seemed to arrive by a railway, & to stop at a hotel,—hesitating whether to repair at once with all the baggage of a long journey to the home of my friend; but at the hotel I passed the night. From my bedroom windows I seemed to see the town—of brick, with two large edifices surrounded by imposing doors, one a theater, & the other a court-house, or state-house. You may tell me that no such edifices exist in yr Columbia—but I saw them, & sure I ought to know—in my dream. The next day was lost in yr hospitality & kindness; but I have no image of yr home; & remember rather my longing to see you, as I lay at the hotel, than any impression of you.

And now today comes the impression. I have been happy in receiving yr letter, charged with kindness. It is so pleasant to hear from a friend. I have read yr letters to Hillard, & in this way have kept pace with yr doings, & thoughts. I liked much yr scheme of a party.[1] Consider me a volunteer in support of yr principles. The Mexican War has hastened by 20 or 30 years the question of Slavery. The issue is now made. It will continue, until Slavery no longer has any recognition under the Constitution of the U.S. I tell you—what you already know—that preparations are now maturing to make the *grand issue* in the next Presidential contest on slavery. The chief part of the Ohio & Massachusetts Whigs are ready for this. I do not think it possible to stave this off. Clay, Webster & Taylor[2] *cannot* be the candidates of the *united* Whig party. Secret efforts have been made by Webster's friends in the Mass. Legislat. within a few weeks to have him nominated for the Presidency; but it was ascertained *that the nomination could not be made*. This has caused disappointment in some quarters. —I think [*John*] McLean is out of the question. The Anti-Slavery Whigs think him too much of a *politician*, & have no reliance on his firmness in the war with Slavery & the Slave-Power. Corwin seems to be the man; but our present object is to lay down principles, which must be the standard of fitness; & we are less anxious as to our candidate than the principles which he is to represent. I think we may now see *le commencement du fin* of the Slavery contest. Massachusetts is fast becoming, if she be not now, a thorough uncompromising Anti-Slavery State.

Hillard's lectures on Milton are a triumph, greater than was ever before enjoyed in Boston.[3] The large Tremont Temple is crammed with an audience of fashion & intelligence, charmed by his exquisite delivery, & his clear & consecutive history of Milton's life & genius. Last evng he lifted his audience to a state of rapt attention & admiration, as he sketched Milton's condition at the time of the composition of Paradise Lost. It was magnificent. It swept over my soul with thrilling effect. Next comes the discussion of the Paradise Lost, which is his most careful effort. I wish you were here to listen & to enjoy. He hopes to see Europe in July.

Julia Howe has been ill with the scarlet-fever; but is now convalescent. Longfellow is with his wife, waiting for the fall another ripe apple from his family tree.—Benedict says "the world must be peopled."[4]— I am alone—more alone than ever—becoming more so—with little to hope in this world. Felton has a new wife.[5]

If you were here, I could tell you much of Everett.[6] *Entre nous*, he seems to have disappointed every body. He is *ultra* conscientious in the discharge of what he thinks the duties of his post; but he is unhappy there, & makes others unhappy about him.

[*William*] Kent is most acceptable to pupils, & to all the professors. Every body is in love with him The young men tell me his lectures are most interesting.

Prescott's Peru is printed. He is joyous & even talks of an excursion to London. He challenges me to join him. I might if I were independent in condition; but I must drudge, drudge, drudge.

I see nothing of *Nathan der Weise* [*Appleton*]. Politics have parted us. Much displeasure has been directed against me. I could have wished it otherwise, but cannot regret any thing I have done. Let me hear from you, & remember me to yr wife.

Ever Yrs, Charles Sumner

P.S. I shall send yr letter to George. Cushing's book[7] is not yet finished.

ALS MH-H (63/160, PCS)

1. In his letter of 15 March 1847 (67/651, PCS) Lieber enclosed a "trifling publication" of his, which has not been recovered.
2. Zachary Taylor, then major general in the Mexican War.
3. George Hillard delivered a series of twelve lectures for the Lowell Institute (Longfellow to Lieber, 23 February 1847, HWL, 3:131–32).
4. *Much Ado About Nothing*, 2.3.250.
5. Mary Louisa Cary Felton (1821–64), married Cornelius Felton, 16 August 1846.
6. Edward Everett remained president of Harvard until 1849.
7. Possibly Luther Cushing's revision of his 1844 edition, *Manual of Parliamentary Practice*, 1848.

To Joshua R. Giddings

Boston May 24th '47

My dear Sir

On my return from New York, where I had been for a few days, I found yr favor, dated April 12th, postmarked May 13th. A letter from me, written at about the last date, will have answered somewhat yr inquiries.[1]

Taylor has disturbed all parties, & at the present moment seems to be the most popular person in the U.S. I think Massachusetts stands as firm against him as any state, or part of the country. Her resolutions[2] have made her position strong. But the current in his favor is strong even here. I have had no intimate conversation with any of the leading

Cotton Whigs with regard to him; but I presume from what I observe & hear that they would be willing, if not glad to support him. Union under him puts the slavery question in abeyance, which they desire above all things. I heard of John Davis talking in his favor, & saying that Mass. would support him. It would certainly be difficult to oppose him, as he would draw a large part of the Locoes. Still I should not despair. It is said now, that Webster will run as Vice-Presdt. on the ticket with Taylor. If he should, it would embarass us here, unless we confined our opposition to Taylor.

In New York I was much struck by the war-spirit; all, locoes & Whigs, seemed penetrated by it. In a long conversation with Greeley, he avowed warm opposition to Taylor, but thought it better to allow the feeling in his favor to subside with time, & to be neutralized by the rising claims of [*Winfield*] Scott. He prefers Corwin; but said that he should support Mclean with a hearty goodwill if nominated by the convention.—He perceived *feelers* for Winthrop as speaker. The latter is now in Europe.

I conversed with several of the other side, all of whom assured me that they should stand firm on the Wilmot Proviso; & give "our Southern friends" as John Van Buren called them, a lesson.[3] The latter told me, however, that if he were obliged to vote tomorrow, he should vote for Taylor! —He thinks politics in inglorious confusion, & looks to some changes in the course of the year. Sedgwick, Field, & Bryant,[4] all talked warmly against the extension of Slavery.

Our true course, it seems to me, is loyalty & perseverance. Our principles are correct. They will not allow us to support Taylor. We must watch our opportunity for bearing our testimony.

Yours very faithfully, Charles Sumner

ALS OHi (67/678, PCS)

1. In his letter (Jefferson, Ohio, 5/497, PCS) Giddings had asked about the Cotton Whigs and Winthrop's stand regarding Taylor's presidential candidacy, and expressed concern about the *New York Daily Tribune*'s hesitancy.

2. A resolution opposing annexation of Mexican territory and condemning slavery was signed by Governor George N. Briggs on 26 April 1847, *Acts and Resolves of the General Court of Massachusetts in the Year 1846, 1847, 1848*, 541–42.

3. Proposed on 8 August 1846 by David Wilmot (1814–68; U.S. congressman [Dem., Pa.], 1845–51), the proviso called for the prohibition of slavery in any territories acquired as a result of the Mexican War. John Van Buren (1810–66), lawyer, son of the U.S. president.

4. Theodore Sedgwick (1811–59), New York attorney. David Dudley Field (1805–94), New York lawyer and reformer. William Cullen Bryant (1794–1878), poet; editor, New York *Evening Post*, 1829–78.

To George Sumner

Boston July 31st '47

My dear George,

I shall put this note into Liebers which was enclosed to me unsealed. You will see that he has done what you wished in Phila. You were too nervous with regard to that. Come home, & be rubbed as we all are constantly, & you will be less sensitive to such things. Lieber's views of Taylor's chances are founded on the public opinion of the South, which is coalescing in his support, in order to ward off the Slavery question.[1] But the best part of the Northern Democrats & Whigs will not allow this, I think; but all is uncertain. There are some persons familiar with political movements, who now declare that Taylor cannot carry a single Free State. But this will be decided by the revelations of the autumn & winter, particularly after the meeting of Congress.

I think you are mistaken in saying that, in the Prison movements, I felt the recoil of the 4th July Oration. It was the opposition to Winthrop that aroused personal feelings against me. No development, not calculated to bear immediately upon politics, seriously disturbs people; but the cotton lords, whose nominee Winthrop was, were vexed with me for [that] just & righteous opposition. It has cost me friendships which I value much. I *was* pained, dear George, by yr judgment of my effort on the 4th July; but hardly surprized. I think that you & I at present look at many things with different views. I am indifferent to what is called political success; I am satisfied, if I can in an effective way bear my testimony to a great truth. Now, it seems to me, one of the greatest causes—perhaps the greatest in which one can labor (greatest because it applies to all nations) is the doing away of war. I know this cannot be done at once; but this is the *age for effort*. What I said has not fallen idle to the ground; nor was it written for old maids. It has been circulated & read more probably than all other 4th July addresses together. Within a few weeks a stereotype edition of it has appeared in Phila[2]—in addition to the many editions of it, which have been already published. I mention this, only to shew the influence that it must have produced. I have received thanks & gratitude for it, which have touched me. Yr position will be one of commanding influence over the *Peace Question*. Familiar with foreign nations, & with yr keen & practical eye, you may present it in a manner, that shall do incalculable good—far surpassing any trumpery political success. But we will talk of these things yet, I trust. When shall you return. One of my friends, James K. Mills, the merchant, said last night to me, that he desired to see you very much—that he thought yr career most remarkable. I should not forget that Sparks was much pleased with yr Lamartine letter. He says you will find stronger confirmations of yr views about Vergennes in the Franklin correspondence edited by him.[3] There are one or two letters there that settle the matter. He says you are right, & told me to say to you—to go on. He has an admirable body of papers & Mss. culled by several months labor in the archives of France, illustrating the Foreign Revolutionary history of our country. If he dies, leaving his work on that period undone, he wishes me to take those papers & write the book.

I suppose you are now in England. Remember me to my friends. You must see Morpeth. Be sure to let him know you are there, by sending yr card to him.

Ever Thine, Chas.

Mr Warren goes by this packet. He asked me for a letter to you, & I thought you might be glad to know his story. He is nephew of Dr W. & the representative of Morton in the Ether Controversy.[4]—Mr Ricketson also has a note from me. He is of N. Bedford & a friend of Swift's.

I send to Bancroft some more copies of yr Idiot letter. The first batch I sent to Paris by Mr Fields, which was the best opportunity I had.[5] Don't [*gronder?*] me.

ALS MH-H (63/185, PCS)

1. In his letter of 25 July 1847 (68/009, PCS) Lieber sent an open note to be forwarded by CS to George but did not refer to its contents. Regarding Taylor's possible presidential candidacy, Lieber wrote, "I suppose what I have written about Taylor to George will be a horror to you; but you will have to swallow his election."
2. New edition of "The True Grandeur of Nations," published by H. Longstreth.
3. George Sumner's letter to Lamartine, 28 May 1847, pointed out inaccuracies in American history in Lamartine's *Histoire des Girondins* (*Boston Daily Advertiser*, 7 July 1847:2). Charles Gravier, Comte de Vergennes (1719–87), French foreign minister.
4. John Collins Warren's nephew. William Thomas Green Morton (1819–68), a dentist, had recently used sulphuric ether and wanted to protect his development of the anesthetic from unrestricted use by others.
5. George Sumner's "Letter on the School for Idiots in Paris." James Thomas Fields (1817–81), publisher, Ticknor and Fields; editor, *Atlantic Monthly*, 1861–70.

To George Perkins Marsh[1]

Boston Sept. 4th '47

My dear Sir,

Strange to say—I forgot to ask you, whether there was a stage, or any thing like it, at Schenectady—any thing in short, not a pulpit. *I will not speak from a pulpit.*[2] It is a devilish place. I do not wonder that people in it are dull. Let me know what the state of things is at Schectady.

I was glad to hear to-day, that Little & Brown are to publish yr address. They also will publish Wheaton's.[3]

I lost sight of you in Providence, after passing you in that protracted procession.

Faithfully Yrs, Charles Sumner

ALS VtU (68/026, PCS)

1. George Perkins Marsh (1801–82), U.S. congressman (Whig, Vt.), 1843–49; U.S. minister to Turkey, 1849–53; U.S. minister to Italy, 1861–82.

2. The prospective address to the Phi Beta Kappa Society of Union College must have been postponed. CS did not deliver "The Law of Human Progress" there until 25 July 1848.

3. Marsh's address, "Human Knowledge: a Discourse Delivered Before the Massachusetts Alpha of the Phi Beta Kappa Society, at Cambridge, August 26, 1847"; Henry Wheaton's address, "The Progress and Prospects of Germany: A Discourse Before the Phi Beta Kappa Society of Brown University at Providence, R.I., September 1, 1847."

To Thomas Corwin

Boston Sept. 7th 1847

My dear Sir,

I have received yr favor of Sept. 2nd. & lose no time in acknowledging its kindness. The resolutions to which you refer were also received at the same time. I had already read them in our newspapers today.[1]

Our friends have been pleased that a Convention, embodying so much old Whig strength as that at Warren, has declared sentiments so strong & staunch & seasonable as it has done. We have been struck by the 6th Resolution,[2] as clinching together the two issues of "no more territory" & the "Wilmot Proviso"; nor have we failed to note the careful & proper limitation to any annexation "either directly by conquest, or indirectly as a payment of the expenses of the war," leaving untouched the question of annexation by purchase or by way of indemnification for claims antecedent to the war. (You will see, that I write with frankness) It seems to me, however, that the latter part of the resolution might have contained with effect a few additional words, so that it would read;—"but if additional territory be forced upon us, [[or be acquired by purchase or in any other manner]] we will demand & c [[the Wilmot proviso]]"

It cannot be doubted that territory will be acquired. The iron hand which is now upon California will never be removed. Mr Webster's efforts when Secy. of State, to obtain a port there are too well known; so that, even if a large fraction of Eastern Mexico should not become ours—still there will be territory acquired on which the Wilmot proviso must operate. It is then of vast importance, that we should be prepared for this alternative, & not be cajoled into the simpler cry of "no more territory."

The 7th Resolution,[3] expressing opposition to "an improper interference with slavery" seems to be a "negative pregnant," asserting all *proper* interference with it under the Constitution. This is probably, as explicit as could be expected from any party not exclusively devoted to the cause of Abolition.

The 8th Resolution, calling for the withdrawal of the troops is pointed & just.

I observe that you omit any explicit declaration of the right & duty of Congress to stop the supplies which feed the unjust war. Perhaps, this is expedient, in order to avoid the offensive misinterpretation, which make us leave our poor servants & soldiers already in the field a prey to famine & death. And yet the line is sufficiently clear between those *active* appropriations which sustain the war, & the *passive* appropriations which only contemplate the support & safety of our troops.

The 9th Resolution[4] recapitulates the Whig principles of former years. Can these awaken any echo now. The [means?] required by the war which must be raised by the revenue will place the question of a Tariff in abeyance for several years. The Currency seems to be right enough now. The sub-treasury scheme will not be understood by the people. The demand for internal improvmts particularly in the Rivers & Harbors ought to be heard. It seems to me, however, that little remains for us to contend for before the people, except the stopping of the war & of the extension of slavery; or rather these two matters, by their gigantic importance, dwarf all the others.

An interesting question here arises which has occupied much of our attention, & which seems to be contemplated by the 10th Resolution,[5] what will be our duty if the National Convention shld postpone, or evade, or negative these questions. Our policy has been adherence to the Whig party, believing that through that organization we might accomplish the greatest good, most effectively advance our sentiments. But, if that Convention under slave-holding influence, should decline to sanction what seem to us cardinal truths, placed [also?] in the foreground [of?] yr resolutions, can we sustain its course? It seems to me, & to our friends here that we should then be driven to the most disagreeable alternatives of inactivity or opposition. It would be impossible, for instance, for us to support General Taylor. I do not know yr views on this point further, that they appear from the resolutions; but I do hope, in such a result, you would be willing to be our leader.[6]

It has appeared to us almost vain to expect a Whig Convention or the Whig party throughout the country at present to sustain our views;—which are substantially set forth in yr resolutions. It has, however, seemed to us not impossible, that many of the Northern Democrats, & perhaps all of the Liberty Party would join us, if we stood firmly on the ground which we have assumed.

Our State Convention will meet Sept 29th. It is still uncertain which course it may take. Mr Webster's friends have made a strong effort to bring about his nomination there for the Presidency. I have understood this evng, that the plan has been at last abandoned. Others would like to keep the State unpledged, so as to be open to any future influences. Others still are very desirous that you should be nominated at once; & Mr S. C. Phillips, in one of our private conferences, has proposed that an effort for this object shall be made; & that, in the event of a failure, that our friends shall organize, after the convention, expressly to nominate you, sustaining in ⟨other respects⟩ the other regular Whig nominations. I mention these things, as not unimportant, in this frank communication.

I send herewith an article by Mr Adams in the *Whig*, which expresses the views of those with whom I am in the habit of acting.[7] I shrink from troubling you, & from intrusion upon yr confidence; but I cannot disguise that it would give us pleasure—particularly at this juncture before ye meeting of our Convention, to know more fully that we do how far our views harmonize with yours as to the binding nature of the proceedings of the Nat Con. A separation from customary party ties—it might be called in our case a movement to *Mons Sacer*,[8] —is not to be contemplated without anxiety. And yet may we not profit by the lessons of the South? They already refuse in advance to support any person friendly to the Wilmot Prov. Must we not refuse to support any person who is *not* in favor of the proviso & against the war? [*inserted in margin*] Yr views on our duties in this respect wld help materially to guide our cause. We all honor you much for what you have done & regard yr speech in the senate as our platform. I trust that we may soon read yr great speech in Warren Co. [*end insert*]

Let me thank you for yr generous appreciation of the trifles of mine to which your refer. The Amherst Address[9] I shall have great pleasure in sending you, so soon as it is printed.

Dft MH-H (63/187, PCS)

1. With his letter of 2 September 1847 (5/606, PCS) from Lebanon, Ohio, Corwin enclosed thirteen resolutions (unrecovered) from the Warren County Convention of 28 August and asked CS's opinion. He hoped to meet CS soon and to discuss CS's "schemes, views, and hopes." The *Boston Daily Whig* (6 September 1847:2) carried an account of Corwin's speech at the convention, and printed resolutions six, seven, and eight.

2. The sixth resolution stated the convention's opposition to any annexation of territory. If, however, "additional territory be forced upon us," the convention would then "demand" that no slavery should exist there.

3. The seventh resolution protested both an "improper interference with the question of Slavery where it constitutionally exists" and any extension of slavery.

4. The ninth resolution stated that the convention supported Whig principles of sound currency and tariff protection and opposed "executive usurpations" (*Boston Daily Whig*, 11 September 1847:2).

5. The tenth resolution stated that "no man who is not a thorough Whig, approved by a Whig National Convention, can receive our support for the Presidency, now or hereafter" (ibid.).

6. In his reply of 20 September (5/617) Corwin stated that no nomination should be made until the close of the next congressional session. He pleaded for unity among Whigs, believing that southern Whigs would be forced to join with northern Whigs on the war issue.

7. In the *Whig* (1 September 1847:2), Adams wrote that only Taylor and Corwin represented for Whigs "the great public questions now at issue," and that Massachusetts "friends" looked to Corwin for leadership supporting the Wilmot Proviso.

8. A hill near Rome where plebeians retreated in the fifth century B.C. until granted certain concessions by the patricians.

9. "Fame and Glory," delivered 11 August at Amherst College.

To Alexis de Tocqueville

Boston. U.S. of America
Sept. 15th 1847

My dear Sir,

I have received your important & interesting letter of Aug. 6th.[1] Let me thank you much for this prompt & authoritative expression of opinion in a way that cannot fail to exert great influence. Feeling unwilling that it should be confined to those only, who could peruse your manuscript, I have ventured to regard it as for the public, & have accordingly translated it & caused it to be printed in one of our newspapers. It has already been extensively copied by the newspapers of the country. Your name is so familiar to the enlightened minds among us that nothing from you can fail to attract attention & inspire confidence

The discussions which have recently taken place in Boston on the subject of Prison Discipline[2] have been the means of diffusing much information, & awakening an interest, which will be productive of good. Every thing relating to it is now read with avidity.

The Government of our Society is in the hands of a few persons who are strongly prejudiced against all change. I think, however, that its course will now be altered. Mr Dwight the Secretary has become insane —whether incurably so, I do not know.

The New York Society promises great usefulness. Its last Report[3] is a document of great research & candour & contains some remarkable admissions, particularly when we consider that it belongs to a state which is the cradle of the Auburn System.

I cherish a lively recollection of my brief intercourse with you in Paris.[4] It will always be a source of gratification to me to hear from you, & to be of service to you in any way in my country.

Believe me, my dear Sir,

very faithfully Yours, Charles Sumner

Monsieur de Tocqueville &c &c &c

ALS MH-H (63/191, PCS)

1. Tocqueville's letter (Tocqueville, France, 5/592, PCS) shared CS's displeasure about the Boston Prison Discipline Society's preference for the Auburn system. See CS to George Sumner, 16 December 1845, and Francis Wayland, 7 July 1846. CS's translation appears in Wks, 2:148–50.

2. The struggle continued between the Prison Discipline Society and CS, Howe, and Hillard over the Pennsylvania versus the Auburn system. Debates between the two factions took place 25 May–23 June 1847 in Tremont Temple; CS spoke in favor of the Pennsylvania (separate) system on 18 June. Ultimately the issue was tabled (DD, 1:124–28).

3. *Correctional Association of New York. Report*, 1846.

4. CS had met Tocqueville probably in May 1838 (Tocqueville to CS, 18 May 1838, 65/441).

To Salmon P. Chase

Boston Oct. 1st '47

My dear Sir,

I found yr letter of Sept. 22nd on my return yesterday from our Whig Convention. I am gratified by yr kind & partial estimate of the little I have been able to do against Slavery.

I cannot disguise that I have looked to Mr Corwin as a possible, I might say, probable leader in the approaching contest. Yr communication, & the article in the National Era, just received, make me fearful that he is not an Anti-Slavery man.[1] But the sentiments of his speech against the war are so magnanimous & just, that I felt that their author must be with us. The courses, which look to the welfare of man, through practice & benevolence, are kindred; so that it is difficult to perceive how any person like Mr Corwin can earnestly embrace one without adopting another.

You will perceive by the enclosed paper what some of us have tried to do in our Whig Convention. Our effort has been defeated. I think it doubtful whether we shall ever enter another Convention of the party. It was, however, only the peculiar influence, caused by Mr Webster's presence (he was not, however, in the hall when our debate occurred) at the Convention; & Mr Winthrop's earnest exertions[2] that defeated us. I think the heart of the Convention was with us.

I hope yr nominations will be postponed till next spring.[3] In the course of the winter unexpected combinations may occur. At all events, all of us, who are in earnest in our opposition to Slavery, should cultivate kindly relations with each other in view of some future association.

You will perceive that Mr Webster has adopted at last our view with regard to witholding supplies.[4]

I was happy to become acquainted with Mr Ball,[5] & hope you will remember me to him.

I should be pleased to know how much Anti-Slavery there is in Judge McLean. I have strong personal predilections in his favor. I honor his character. Believe me, dear Sir,

sincerely Yrs, Charles Sumner

ALS DLC (68/032, PCS)

1. Chase stated that Corwin's recent Carthage speech with its "attack upon the Abolitionists" had convinced Chase that he must "leave him, until he comes to a better mind" (Cincinnati, 22 September 1847, 5/619, PCS). The *National Era* (30 September 1847:2) stated that antislavery Whigs were mistaken in considering Corwin one of them. Corwin had "good impulses, general Anti-Slavery sympathies" but lacked "any definite Anti-Slavery principles."

2. At the Whig Convention in Springfield, 29 September 1847, Conscience Whigs had tried both to prevent an endorsement of Webster as Massachusetts' favorite son in the 1848 presidential campaign and to ensure that any nominee declare himself against slavery. A supporter of Taylor for president, Winthrop engaged in debate with CS on whether a Whig presidential nominee should declare himself against the extension of slavery (*Boston Daily Whig*, 1 October 1847:2; DD, 1:158–59).

3. Chase wrote CS that, although the Liberty Convention would be held in October, he would try to put off any nominations until spring, organizing then, he hoped, "a powerful party of Independents."

4. In his Springfield address, "The Mexican War," *Writings and Speeches of Daniel Webster*, ed. James W. McIntyre, 1903, 13:364.

5. Flamen Ball (b. 1809), Chase's law partner in Cincinnati, had recently visited Boston.

To Joshua R. Giddings

Boston Nov. lst 47

My dear Sir,

Yr favor marked *confidential* was duly received. Since then I have received a letter from Mr Corwin, in which he shews some anxiety on account of the reports of the Carthage speech.[1] I regret that speech very much. The passage with Mr Chase was unfortunate. It has undoubtedly disaffected the Abolitionists, who already inclined to Mr Corwin. His shrinking from the Wilmot Proviso, as a *dangerous question* was another mistake. That question, when rightly understood, is a source of safety. It is the beginning of the rally against the Slave-Power which will save the Union. I wish Mr Corwin could see this as we do. I had begun to feel a personal attachment for him, & shall be unhappy if we cannot act under him.

The courage which he shewed against the war ought to inspire him to active demonstrations against slavery.

Meanwhile the democrats in N.Y. are in motion. I have assurances, on which I rely, that they are *in earnest*. Preston King says he does not care whether the Presidential candidate is a Whig or a Democrat, *but he must be a Wilmot Proviso-man*.[2] I may say *confidentially* that a letter has been received here from Albany, inquiring if J. Q. Adams will join with Martin Van Buren & others in a call for an Anti-Slavery Convention to nominate a Northern candidate. Mr Adams was asked yesterday, if he would do it. He expressed great pleasure in the plan; but pleaded that he was so old & infirm, that he could not *do* what might be justly expected of him if he were to sign such a call. He was not urged.

It seems to me that the continuance of the war will prevent such a call immediately; but when that ceases, nothing can prevent the coalition of the two Anti-Slavery sections. Let us try to prepare the way.

I regret J. P. Hale's acceptance of the Liberty Nomination.[3] I urged him in vain to a contrary course.

Yr anticipations with regard to Palfrey will be fulfilled. He is true as steel. As a new member,[4] of marked opinion, he will be exposed to trials. I know he may count upon yr friendship & sympathy.

I see that the Whigs will continue to vote supplies.[5] Before going into caucus on the speakership should you not understand their proposed course?

Faithfully Yrs, Charles Sumner

Hon. J. R. Giddings

ALS OHi (68/052, PCS)

1. In his letter to CS (Lebanon, Ohio, 25 October 1847, 5/641, PCS) Corwin wrote that if the Whigs "go into convention, we *must* abide the result," and any Whigs unwilling to do so should not attend the convention. He saw a split of the Whigs as a "fearful alternative." Corwin stated his first priority was opposition to further territorial conquest, rather than support of the Wilmot Proviso. Corwin decried the press accounts of what he termed a "perfectly good natured colloquy between Mr Chase & myself" when Corwin asked Chase if he "repented" of his vote against Clay in 1844. (After Chase had answered that he did not repent, Corwin had stated, "I do not question your sincerity, *but I pity your ignorance*" (*Cincinnati Morning Signal*, quoted in *National Era*, 30 September 1847:2).

2. At their Syracuse convention in September 1847, the Democrats had split into Hunkers, those against opposing slavery in the territories, and Barnburners, those supporting the Wilmot Proviso. Preston King (1806–65), a Barnburner, was U.S. congressman (Dem., N.Y.), 1843–47, (Free Soil, N.Y.), 1849–53, and senator (Rep., N.Y.), 1857–63.

3. John Parker Hale (1806–73), U.S. congressman (Dem., N.H.), 1843–45; U.S. senator (Free Soil, Indep., N.H.), 1847–53, (Rep., N.H.), 1855–65; U.S. minister to Spain, 1865–69. He was nominated for president at the Liberty Party's convention in November 1847.

4. Palfrey had narrowly been elected to a seat in the U.S. House of Representatives as a Conscience Whig.

5. For continuance of the Mexican War.

To Henry W. Longfellow

[*Boston*]
[*22 November 1847*]

Beloved Longfellow,

I send the Whig of to-day with an article by Charles F. Adams on Evangeline. He is slow to praise & admire; but he *does* praise & admire Evangeline.[1] You have seen doubtless the Harbinger. I sent my copy to yr father, thinking it would gladden his heart.[2]—I never read any verses or extracts from that poem, without loving it better than before! It is a sweet, a truly glorious poem. True Glory! You have really [moved?] the waters—as with an angel's wing.

I send a note from Mrs Forbes,[3] which I received sometime ago & which explains itself.

Have you heard of Charlotte Everett[4] trying to read Evangeline to her father?

Ever Thine, C. S.

ALS MH-H (68/091, PCS)

1. Adams wrote, "albeit little used to deal in unqualified praise, we must plead guilty to great admiration of this new poem" (*Boston Daily Whig*, 22 November 1847:1).

2. John Sullivan Dwight wrote a laudatory review of the poem in the 13 November 1847 issue of the *Harbinger*, a Fourierist newspaper (Longfellow to Alexander W. Longfellow, 27 November 1847, HWL, 3:144) which CS had sent to Stephen Longfellow (1776–1849).

3. Possibly Sarah Hathaway Forbes, wife of John Murray Forbes (1813–98), Boston merchant and railroad entrepreneur.

4. Edward Everett's wife and daughter were both named Charlotte; CS probably refers to Everett's daughter, Charlotte Everett Wise (1819–69).

To Joshua R. Giddings

Boston Dec. 1st '47

My dear Sir,

I find that the person who wrote to ascertain whether Mr Adams would unite with the Van Burens & others in the call of an Anti-Slavery Convention, was not authorized to speak for the latter. He saw Mr M. Van Buren, who said that he was in favor of the Wilmot Proviso, but that he must keep himself aloof from the agitation of that question. Old fox!

You will be able to communicate directly with the Northern Democrats at Washington. I trust you will do what you can for *union*, sooner or later, with them. At all events, extricate us if possible from our present uncomfortable position of political association with those who really hate us more they hate Locofocoes. Let the lines be drawn.—The sooner the better.—I hope this may be *in the organization of the House*.[1]

Palfrey has left to-day for Washington. He has been seriously ill; but is happily restored, so as to be able to commence his journey. He is firm as adamant. I hope that he may have some early opportunity to shew his character. He is not, however, without sensitiveness, & I know he will appreciate any sympathy or friendship which you & yr friends may shew him.

You & Palfrey are our only sure hope & anchor at Washington. I know both of you will stand firm.

We shall be glad to know, if any light is struck out with regard to the organization of the House.

Yrs faithfully, Charles Sumner

ALS OHi (68/065, PCS)

1. Giddings had written CS 8 November 1847 (5/656, PCS) that all antislavery congressmen should take the Wilmot Proviso as their platform and repeal any congressional law that supported slavery; Congress should "leave [*slavery*] altogether with the states in which it is situated." Giddings wrote that if a "war Whig" were elected Speaker of the House, he would have locofoco votes; he thought that the Whig Party would be "*remodelled*" at the beginning of the next Congress. The term *locofoco*, originally applied only to antimonopoly Democrats, had now become a Whig reference to all Democrats.

To John Gorham Palfrey

Circuit Court Dec. 10th '47

Dear Dr,

The papers bark, people talk—but they cannot rail away the virtue of yr act. I admire yr courage, firmness & *conscience*. Yr single vote struck a strong blow for freedom. It was strong in itself, stronger in the assurance of what you would do hereafter. The *Atlas* & *Advertiser* may utter their maledictions; but good men cannot fail to sympathize with you.[1]

Mr [*Richard?*] Fletcher came to me here in court yesterday, & expressed his warm admiration of yr course. He said you ought to be defended, & that he would write an article on the subject. He admired a man who followed his own conscience rather than the lead of party. Mr Edward Brooks[2] last evening expressed to me his warm sympathy with you. Mr S. C. Phillips, as you may imagine, appreciates yr noble position.

I regret very much that Mr Adams & Mr King did not stand with you. And yet I suppose you may count upon their support & countenance always.

I trust yr health is confirmed. If it be so, I hope we may soon hear from you on the floor of Congress; in such a way as to shew yr colleagues that you can do more than vote. There is no man in the House, who can develop his views with more effect, if with so much effect, as yourself. I long for *two* speeches from you, one on some topic of general interest, the other developing so far as can be done with propriety, our *faith*. But be careful of yr health & strength.

Can any thing be done here?—Let me know how I can be of service. I do feel *ex uno pectore*[3] an obligation to you for your sacrifices.

There is schism among the Boston Whigs on the Mayoralty; but mark how gently the schismatics are treated by the sachems. A Committee of Old Whigs (!!!) called on me last evng to ask me to speak at their meeting Saturday Evng! I shall be happy to support Quincy.[4]

I have sent to you the Mass. Quartly Review (with which I have no connection though newspapers have said I had)—thinking you may like to read Theodore Parker's article on the Mexican War, with its stinging conclusion against the course of the leading politicians. Wayland's Sermons (which I have sent also) contain an able Christian argt. against War.[5]

Ever Yours, Charles Sumner

P.S. Don't trouble yourself to write to me, unless you have nothing better to do. I have written this in court, while Stanton is replying. Hallett[6] still insists that you are the only true man of the delegation.

ALS MH-H (68/069, PCS)

1. Winthrop was elected Speaker of the House on the third ballot, 6 December 1847, with Palfrey, Giddings, and Amos Tuck of New Hampshire the only Whigs voting against him (*Globe*, 30th Cong., 1st sess., 2). The *Boston Daily Advertiser* stated in a "Letter from Washington" that in no way could Palfrey's vote be defended; another correspondent wrote that Palfrey had dishonored the Whigs (10 December 1847:2, 11 December 1847:2).

2. Edward Brooks (1793–1878), Massachusetts state legislator, brother-in-law of Edward Everett.

3. "From my heart."

4. Josiah Quincy, Jr., was re-elected mayor of Boston.

5. Theodore Parker (1810–60), Unitarian theologian and reformer, had assumed editorship of the *Massachusetts Quarterly Review* in the summer of 1847 (Henry Steele Commager, *Theodore Parker* [1936], 131–34). His article "The Mexican War" can be found in *The Works of Theodore Parker*, ed. Frank B. Sanborn (1911), 12:1–47. CS may be referring to Francis Wayland's "The Duty of Obedience to the Civil Magistrate, Three Sermons Preached in the Chapel of Brown University," 1847.

6. In Hovey v. Stevens, Circuit Court of U.S., Henry B. Stanton represented the defendant (*Boston Daily Advertiser*, 7, 11 December 1847:2). CS and Benjamin F. Hallett (1797–1862; Boston journalist and Democratic leader) represented the plaintiff.

To John Gorham Palfrey

Boston Dec. 30th '47

My dear Dr,

Adams tells me to-day that you have relaxed in yr purpose to reply to Mr Clingman. I have entire confidence in your judgment of the proprieties of time & occasion. It did seem to me, however, on hastily glancing at his speech that it gave you an opportunity of developing yr position.[1] But I am very anxious that you should not speak until yr health shall justify you, & further, not until you feel a *strong & special movement* to speak. I would not have you speak, if yr heart is not in it. I hope too when you do speak, that you will see that what you say is amply & completely reported in the Intelligencer. I need not say that yr speech will be full as much for the country—Buncombe, if you please—as for the House. I want you to make a *great speech* that shall become a text for our side.

I have recd yr favor containing a copy of yr note to Winthrop. It is as I supposed. I regret that you have not explained to Mr Adams the reasons of yr course.[2] I think C.F.A. regrets it. I hope you will have an *épanchment* with the Ex-Presdt. He is on our side. By conferring with him & communicating freely the reasons of yr course you will be enabled to act with him hereafter.

I observe that Schouler in the Atlas of to-day is aroused by my article of last week in the Courier. He promises a review of it. Let it come. That is the best sign of its effect. Phillips's articles in the Whig are much to the purpose.[3]

You will observe that I write with great freedom, & express myself with plainness. I endeavour to do by you, as I should have you do by me.

Ever sincerely Yrs, Charles Sumner

ALS MH-H (68/088, PCS)

1. On 22 December 1847 Thomas Clingman (1812–97; U.S. congressman [Dem., N.C.], 1843–45, 1847–58; U.S. senator, 1858–61) delivered an address, "The Slavery Question," in the House of Representatives (*Globe*, 30th Cong., 1st sess., appendix, 41–48). He declared that the Constitution did not prohibit the extension of slavery into territory acquired from Mexico and that the Constitution's guarantee of a republican form of government to states meant that slavery could not be excluded from states or territories (43). Clingman blamed the "agitation" over slavery on antislavery groups who were inclined to deceive others and ignore facts (45), and used Nathan Appleton as an example of an upstanding citizen who had been abused by antislavery groups. He said the question of slavery should not be divided along party lines (46).

2. Palfrey enclosed his actual letter to Winthrop explaining his vote (6 December 1847, in the Winthrop Papers at the Massachusetts Historical Society) with his letter of 28 December (68/084, PCS), instructing CS to "keep it for me carefully." In his letter of 25 December (68/078) Palfrey stated that John Quincy Adams had, via other House members, asked Palfrey to vote for Winthrop for House Speaker, but Palfrey had not yet found it convenient to explain his reasons for voting for Hudson instead of Winthrop.

3. CS's article "Honor to John Gorham Palfrey" praised Palfrey's vote against Win-

throp: "It may be the harbinger of a better period, when the egotism of party shall be controlled, and adherence to *principles* shall be regarded rather than the political elevation of *men*" (*Boston Courier*, 23 December 1847:2). William Schouler (1814–72; editor, *Boston Daily Atlas*, 1847–c. 1853) wrote from Washington that CS's article was "a labored defense" of Palfrey. The *Courier* writer had "labored . . . to *decry* and *misrepresent* Mr. Winthrop" (*Boston Daily Atlas*, 30 December 1847:2). Schouler's fuller review appeared in the *Atlas*, 3 January 1848:2. Meanwhile in the *Boston Daily Whig*, in articles signed "A Massachusetts Whig," Stephen C. Phillips criticized Winthrop's compromising tendencies in Congress (29, 30, 31 December 1847:2).

To Salmon P. Chase

Boston Feb. 7th 1848

My dear Sir,

As I look at yr favor of Dec. 2nd, now open before me, & think how long it has been unanswered, I cry *peccavi.*[1] It was so important & instructive, that I ought long ago to have expressed my gratitude for it. Yr vivid sketch of the position of the opposing camps of party, disturbed by the cry of Freedom, awakened hopes that something true & earnest might be done in the approaching canvass.

I *do* trust that we may yet be able to arrange our lives so that all the friends of *Liberty* may act together. I am tired of the anomalous position which is forced upon dissenting Whigs here in Massachusetts. Let us have an open field, & direct battle, instead of private assassination & assault, which is our lot here—suspected, slandered, traduced by those who profess & call themselves Whigs.

Of course, we cannot & will not under any circumstances support General Taylor. It would be impossible for us to support Mr. Clay, unless he takes the ground distinctly, that Slavery which he regards as a "wrong" shall not be extended. We cannot support any body who is not known to be against the extension of Slavery. We are disposed to select this single point, because it has a peculiar practical interest at the present moment, while its discussion would, of course, raise the whole question of Slavery.

There are omens, I regret to see, that it will be abandoned by the two great parties. I should not be surprized if it was left in the hands of those few, who are known for their opposition to Slavery under all circumstances. If Judge McLean could be induced to take any practical ground against the extension of Slavery, he would be a popular candidate in that part of the country. I have heard him often mentioned for Presdt. & J. P. Hale for Vice-P.—That would be a strong ticket.

It is a source of great satisfaction, that we have such representatives in Congress as Hale & Palfrey. I think you will enjoy the keen dialectics of Palfrey's speech, as well as its courageous & high-toned vindication of the political movement against Slavery. He seems to have despoiled poor Clingman of his honors.[2]

I ought to add that there is a strong sentiment among our friends here towards Corwin. I suppose, however, that his strong *Whiggishness* would prevent the Barnburners of N.Y. from supporting him. But can we hope much from the latter?

I read yr argt. in the Van Zandt[3] case, as I have already assured you, with delight, & shall be happy in an opportunity of circulating a few copies in Westminster Hall.

Sometime ago I sent you, I believe, my Amherst Address. I hope that I may soon hear from you, with glad tidings promising united action

Faithfully Yours, Charles Sumner

S. P. Chase Esq.

ALS DLC (68/141, PCS)

1. "I have sinned." In his letter of 2 December 1847 Chase expressed his fear that "a great effort be made to keep both parties together upon their old platforms." He hoped a "great Convention of all Anti-Slavery men" might take place in May or June 1848 (Cincinnati, 5/684, PCS).

2. Palfrey's speech, "The Slave Question," delivered 26 January, emphasized the increasing influence of slavery with a table showing that U.S. officials from slave-holding states were frequently twice as often represented as those from free states. Slavery had discouraged emigrants from settling in the South, asserted Palfrey, and only one-fiftieth of the U.S. population (not one-half, as Thomas Clingman had claimed) actually supported slavery. Referring to a recent Massachusetts state resolution declaring slavery "a great calamity," Palfrey concluded that, if the South insisted that the Union and slavery could not coexist, then the Union must prevail (*Globe*, 30th Cong., 1st sess., appendix, 133–37).

3. Chase unsuccessfully defended John Van Zandt in both the Ohio and U.S. Supreme Courts against the charge that Van Zandt had illegally aided escaped slaves from Kentucky.

To William Henry Furness[1]

Boston Feb. 12th 1848.

My dear Sir,

I have to thank you for a pleasant note, in which you expressed a desire that Mr Giles's name should be mentioned to Mr Lowell in the hope that he would be invited to lecture before the Institute.[2] I lost no time in doing this. Mr Lowell's reply was, that his courses were all filled up for the present season; but that he should consider Mr Giles's name among the candidates for the next. Meanwhile I observe a statement that he is to deliver his lectures in Boston in March. From what I hear of them, I anticipate for him a great success. Yr sympathy & commendation make me believe that I shall like them much.

I trust you have read & enjoyed Palfrey's speech. Thank God we have a man there at last! Though I can never think of Congress, without gratitude to Mr Giddings for his incessant advocacy of Freedom.

I think Palfrey's speech has won many of the luke-warm to sympathy with him.[3] Its temper & argument are much admired. We who are sometimes termed "Conscience Whigs" feel grateful for such an authoritative exposition of our principles. I anticipate for him a distinguished career of championship. Would that those sentiments, which he so well represents, might prevail, throughout the land! I thank you my dear Sir, for the words of Christian cheer with which you welcome them.

Believe me,

very faithfully Yours, Charles Sumner

Revd. Wm. H. Furness

ALS PU (68/157, PCS)

1. William Henry Furness (1802–96), Unitarian theologian and antislavery activist.

2. Probably Henry Giles (1809–82), Unitarian lecturer. John Amory Lowell (1798–1881), Boston banker and trustee of the Lowell Institute.

3. In his letter of 15 January 1848 (5/728, PCS) Furness expressed appreciation for CS's *Boston Courier* article on Palfrey (probably that of 6 January 1848:2): "How I thank you & him."

To Joshua R. Giddings

Boston, Feb. 20th 1848
Sunday—

My dear Sir,

Adams tells me that he wrote you yesterday suggesting the publication of yr proofs & statement without further delay. I had intended to write to the same effect; but was prevented by a pressure of engagements. I enclose to you, however, the Daily Advertiser of yesterday, which again & more distinctly, denies yr charges, *in behalf of Mr W.*[1]

The points in question seem to be as follows:

Was there a Whig caucus on the War Bill?

Did Mr W. attend it?

Did he speak at it?

On which side did he speak?

What did he say?

Did he go among the Mass. delegation to prevail upon them to vote in favor of the Bill?

To whom particularly did he go?

What did he say to each?

Did he influence any?

Important as it seems to be, that yr publication should take place *at once*, I am anxious that it should not appear, until you have obtained such letters as, in yr opinion, substantiate the facts *beyond dispute*. If you may justly expect other letters by delay I trust you will take time; but if you have already sufficiently fortified yourself on all points in question, then it seems to me the publication may properly be made

Have you sifted the recollections of any of the Southern members? They ⟨are sometimes generous⟩ might be disposed to hold Mr W. to his speech, more firmly that some of our Northern friends.

It does seem most strange that there can be any possibility of question on a matter like the present. One would think that there would be a cloud of witnesses at once.

Not long ago a prominent politician of our state told me that Mr W. on his return to Boston, after the War Bill, said to him, that the reason why he forbore to pursue the idea of a *protest* against the Preamble, which he said he had drawn up immediately after the passage of the Bill,[2] was because "he feared that if General Taylor were actually cut off, the indignation of the country would be aroused against the signers of the Protest, & would doom them to the fate of the Hartford Convention." This sentiment, you will perceive, tallies with what he is supposed to have said in the caucus.

I have said nothing for sometime on general politics. Can it be that Clay will retire in favor of Taylor? The papers say so.

Palfrey's speech grows upon our public here. Mr Dwight in our Legislature, a prominent person, has recently made an elaborate speech on the War Resolutions, taking our ground entirely.[3] He is an important accession.

I am glad to know that you intend to speak? I have been expecting to hear from you in this way; but have hesitated to make any inquiry of you, lest I might seem to urge one who labors so freely.

Faithfully Yrs   Charles Sumner

ALS OHi (68/165, PCS)

1. The "Conscience Whigs" of Massachusetts had been engaged in a widely publicized dispute with conservative Whigs over Winthrop's support of the Mexican War. At issue was whether, as the Conscience Whigs asserted, Winthrop had attended a Whig caucus in May 1846 and insisted that all Whigs support the Mexican War. Giddings had stated that Winthrop was present, but Winthrop's supporters denied this allegation. On 3 February 1848 (68/134, PCS) CS sent Giddings a copy of a *Boston Daily Atlas* article (3 February 1848:2), which defended Winthrop and stated that Winthrop had "authorized" the *Atlas* to deny Giddings's statement that Winthrop "had personally urged his colleagues to vote for the war bill." The *Boston Daily Advertiser* agreed with the *Atlas* and called the Conscience Whigs' defense of Giddings in the *Boston Daily Whig* and *Boston Courier* evidence of "detraction and hostility which had no parallel among us" (17 February 1848:2). The *Advertiser* declared (19 February 1848:2) that its allegation that Winthrop had not attended the Whig caucus "can never be proved, so far as a negative ever can be proved."

2. The bill of 11 May 1846 authorizing funds for the Mexican War contained a preamble stating that Mexico had caused the war. Though supportive of the war, Winthrop had found it difficult to vote for this preamble (*Globe*, 29th Cong., 1st sess., 795, 1214; DD, 1:143).

3. William Dwight, a Massachusetts state legislator from Springfield, stated that the Mexican War had been pursued only for "the extension of slave territory" (*Boston Daily Advertiser*, 18 February 1848:2).

To John Gorham Palfrey

Boston Feb. 22nd '48

My dear Dr,

I have to-day seen yr telegraphic communication with regard to Ex-Presdt. Adams.[1] Charles—his son—has left this afternoon, & will, probably, see you, before this reaches you.

Let me recommend to you to procure a book "The Past the Present & the Future" by H. C. Carey—a work of political economy & speculation.[2] It makes for peace strongly—shewing the true *policy* of peace. Though the writer is a free-trader, he is obliged to admit what he calls *self-defensive* Tariffs; but argues finally for "direct taxes." This is toward the close of the book. I think you will find much in it that will help some of yr present trains of thought.

I have also requested Mr Drew, the editor of the Christian Citizen to send you copies of some articles, written, I think a year ago, by Elihu Burritt, in favor of "direct taxation."[3]

This whole subject of a tariff is to me a Serbonian bog. I am not sure that protection is not expedient now; though I feel confident that the time cannot be far distant when it will cease to be. But that question I regard as strictly within the range of *expediency*. No sacred principle, or right seems to control it.

Yr little speeches have been most happy.[4]

You have doubtless seen G. T. Curtis's article in the Advertiser, which is a tissue of mis-representations & mistakes. I have written to him, & told him so, & added that it was particularly indecent in him to *mis-represent me*, as during the last two years I have exerted myself not a little to promote his welfare in certain important family matters.[5] *Inter nos*.

Ever faithfully Yrs, Charles Sumner

P.S. I cannot but think how many *rubs* it is my fortune to receive!

ALS MH-H (68/169, PCS)

1. On 21 February 1848 John Quincy Adams collapsed on the floor of the House of Representatives. He died 23 February.

2. Henry Charles Carey (1793–1879), political economist. *The Past, The Present and the Future* was published in 1848.

3. Thomas Drew, Jr., peace advocate, editor, *Christian Citizen*, c. 1848; writer for the *Atlantic Monthly* in the 1860s. Elihu Burritt (1810–79), peace movement activist and U.S. consul in Birmingham, England, 1863.

4. On 10 February Palfrey argued that a petition from the Conferences of Friends asking for a speedy end to the Mexican War be printed, and on 17 February he proposed that the U.S. be required to pay off a loan of $18,500,000 for military expenses from the Mexican War in five years, not twenty (*Globe*, 30th Cong., 1st sess., 330, 368, 370).

5. George Ticknor Curtis (1812–94), Boston lawyer and biographer, had written an anonymous article, "The War Upon Mr. Winthrop," in the *Boston Daily Advertiser* (17 February 1848:2). In it, Curtis criticized the *Boston Courier* writer for his attacks on Winthrop. CS's letter to Curtis is unrecovered but apparently CS persuaded William Wetmore Story to meet certain obligations due Curtis (Prc, 3:153; Benjamin R. Curtis to CS, 24 May 1846, 5/075, PCS).

To William I. Bowditch

Court St. Monday
[*February 1848?*]

My dear Sir,

I am glad that Dr Putnam[1] has found a critic so careful, calm & able, as the author of the pamphlet you were so good as to send me.[2] I think he has well exposed the shallowness of the sermonizer.

But, while I sympathize in his spirit, & am glad that he has written, I feel obliged to dissent from his conclusion as to the necessity of attacking the Union. He says (p. 12) "We seek to effect such a *moral revolution*, as, in its course, shall be powerful enough, *either to relieve the constitution from all taint of Slavery*, or to break it in pieces." In this clause he proposes an alternative, *either* to relieve the constitution, or to break it in pieces. Now, proposing to act by moral means only, it seems to me better, juster, & more consistent with our duty to other high objects, to strive "to relieve the constitution" of slavery—always mindful that the same *moral means*, which can break it in pieces, can modify & amend it.

Let us all do all that we can for the *abolition of Slavery, by moral means*—I would add by *& through & under* the constitution, & not *over* it.

Yrs faithfully, Charles Sumner

ALS MSaE (66/100, PCS)

1. In an article in the *Boston Courier*, 8 May 1847, CS had criticized a recent sermon by clergyman George Putnam for its strident attacks on the Garrisonians and its failure to condemn the Mexican War and slavery. Putnam and CS had recently exchanged charges regarding the severity of CS's criticism in the *Courier* (CS to Putnam, 19 January 1848, Putnam to CS, 26 January, 63/212 and 6/002, PCS), hence the tentative dating of this letter.

2. William I. Bowditch (1818–1909), an abolitionist residing in Brookline, was the anonymous author of "God *Or* Our Country: Review of the Rev. Dr. Putnam's Discourse" (Boston, 1847).

To Charles Francis Adams

Boston March 2nd 1842 [*1848*]

My dear Adams,

I see by the papers to-day, & hear also from Mrs A. that the Congressional Committee is not discharged & that it is their purpose to attend the remains of yr father to Massachusetts. I cannot forbear saying more specifically than in my former letter, that such a cermony seems to me inopportune. It will have the effect of keeping alive this unnatural excitement or ferment in the public mind, without serving any good purpose. Our Legislature will, of course, be called upon to dispense hospitality to this Committee at a period, when all the charm of hospitality will be lost in the melancholy occasion.

I shrink from intruding my opinions; but I feel additional confidence in them, as I find them in entire harmony with those of Mr Brooks, your father-in-law, whom I met at yr house this morning. He thought that you should, *if possible*, discharge the Congressional Committee at

Washington, & permit the remains to be carried to Quincy by the way of Fall River in *entire privacy*.[1]

I believe that this course will be most agreeable to all persons here, except the thoughtless, who are always seeking some new excitement, and the vain who are anxious for some occasion of display. I feel confident, from what I see & hear, that it will be most agreeable to the Legislature.

I wrote to Palfrey yesterday on matters connected with the approaching election in the 8th district & I presume he will see you.[2] I will not repeat what I then said.

I hear to-day that Dwight's resolutions have been rejected only 39 voting for them. Bullock helped this work.[3]

Yrs sincerely Charles Sumner

ALS MBApm (68/183, PCS)

1. Peter Chardon Brooks (1767–1849), Boston merchant and Adams's father-in-law. CS regretted in his letter to Palfrey (6 March 1848, 68/196, PCS) that "the public, by their intervention in various ways & in different places, have now taken this whole affair into their own hands."

2. No letter of 1 March has been recovered. In his 6 March letter to Palfrey CS expressed his hope that Adams could be elected to his father's seat; however, CS feared that Adams's residency outside the eighth congressional district might create difficulties.

3. Dwight's resolutions opposing the Mexican War were rejected in the Massachusetts House of Representatives, 32–212 (*Boston Daily Advertiser*, 3 March 1848:2). Alexander H. Bullock (1816–82), Worcester lawyer and state legislator; later governor of Massachusetts, 1866–68.

To Joshua R. Giddings

Boston March 4th '48

My dear Sir,

I have yours of March 1st.[1] I have not supposed you inattentive to the subject to which you refer, nor have I wished to make any suggestion to you.

The death of Mr Adams seems to throw a pall over our anxieties & struggles. Would that it could cause harmony! But the great cause of difference still remains. Winthrop's *system* of action is entirely different from ours.

Then this special issue, affecting you personally, & myself also, can not be left untried. He [*Winthrop*] has travestied what you have said. Of course his troops must be withdrawn, or yr proofs must proceed.

I cannot forget that this whole matter has been made the grounds of personal charges against me of a most offensive character, in print & in private. In all this unhappy controversy there has been on Winthrop's side a peculiar personal feeling—amounting almost to malevolence—; on his side has been the *personality* while his friends have charged it upon us.

I long to read yr speech, & yr new catechism to Taylorites.[2]

Mr J. Q. Adams's successor[3] will stand by yr side & Palfrey's in Congress. No other man can come—so those familiar with the District say.

Faithfully yrs, Charles Sumner.

ALS CSfHS (68/190, PCS)

1. Giddings's letter (Washington, 6/050, PCS) raised hope that Winthrop might recall his denial of Giddings's claim. If not, Giddings wrote he would send his "proofs" to the *Boston Daily Atlas*.

2. In his 28 February 1848 speech, "Deficiency of Appropriations" (*Globe*, 30th Cong., 1st sess., appendix, 380–83), Giddings stated that the new issues of upholding and extending slavery might lead to a realignment of political parties. For example, Whigs voting for further appropriations for the Mexican War or for slave trade in the District of Columbia did not differ from Democrats. Giddings described Taylor as "one whose hands are dripping with human gore" (381), and stated that Taylor's supporters had no real idea how their candidate stood on such issues as the tariff, free trade, internal improvements, and the extension of slavery. He declared that Whigs "*shall not again be Tylerized.*"

3. At this time the Massachusetts Whigs had not yet chosen the successor. On 15 March 1848 the Whig caucus nominated Horace Mann (Jonathan Messerli, *Horace Mann* [New York, 1972], 453–54).

To John Gorham Palfrey

Boston March 9th 1848

My dear Dr,

I see by the Atlas that Giddings's paper has been recd. though not yet published. I await its publication with anxiety.[1]

I heard yesterday, that Mr Grennell had written to Theophilus Parsons,[2] suggesting a nomination by the Whigs of Mass. of Taylor for Presdt. & *Webster* for Vice Presdt. Yes! Webster for Vice-P. The plot thickens. Our best energies are needed—especially in the Whig, to counteract it.

I am placed in a dilemma, which is most trying. Adams appeals to me to take charge of the Whig. His present relations with Winthrop, & his new & absorbing duties make him think that he cannot continue to conduct it.

It is very hard for me to decline this duty; but I fear that it would be harder still to assume it.

To conduct the Whig at the present crisis will require the best strength of a strong man. He must write much. But more than this, he must keep himself thoroughly familiar with all the movements of all the papers & politicians in the country. The course of the paper must be uppermost in his mind.

Now, I am a professional man—without future—dependent upon my profession. Besides my ordinary professional duties, which in themselves are not absorbing, I am at present the trustee of Judge Story's copyrights,—superintending the editions of these works. I have just published an edition of Equity Pleadings, adding some 50 pages of my own, which is incorporated into the text as notes.[3] Besides these engagements professional & judicial, I have many others—some of which you can comprehend—multifarious & incessant. I am now engaged to deliver the Address at Schenectady College in June. Have I time to take the Whig? I feel that I have not. And yet I do not like to decline. I fear that Adams may think me indifferent to his comfort & to our cause[4]

For a long period my desire has been to withdraw my *time*, from our movement, rather than to embark still more in it.

I write all this to you—because I cannot help it. And yet why should I annoy you with my anxieties?

I have spoken to [*Joseph T.*] Buckingham with regard to Webster's speech.[5] He has no copy of it. I shall try to find it.

Yrs ever, C. S.

In the *Courier* of tomorrow will be an article by Whittier, commending C. F. Adams.[6]

ALS MH-H (68/198, PCS)

1. *Boston Daily Atlas*, 8 March 1848:2. The full correspondence was published 17 March 1848:2.

2. George Grennell, Jr. (1786–1877), U.S. congressman (Whig, Mass.), 1829–39; Massachusetts judge of probate. Theophilus Parsons (1797–1882), professor of law, Harvard, 1848–69.

3. *Commentaries on Equity Pleadings*, 4th ed. (1848).

4. CS wrote Giddings (14 April, 68/225, PCS) that he could not take on this added responsibility. However, Pierce states that the *Boston Daily Whig*'s leaders of

1, 9, 10, 16, and 23 March 1848 "bear intrinsic evidence of being written by Sumner" (Prc, 3:150).

5. In his letter of 2 March (68/187) Palfrey asked CS for a copy of an 1844 Webster speech to the farmers of Pennsylvania arguing for import duties.

6. Whittier's letter (signed "Carver") stated that Adams should take his father's seat in the House of Representatives (*Boston Courier*, 10 March 1848:2).

To Horace Mann

Sunday [*20 March 1848*]

My dear Mann,

In great haste, & at my cold office I write to say, that I hesitate to express any opinion with regard to yr acceptance of the nomination. I shall be sorry—sorry indeed—to know that you go to Washington unwillingly—yr heart elsewhere—*duty* calling in other directions. Ponder this well; & if you feel constrained by circumstances to accept, then write a *triumphant* letter. No man can do so much by a letter as yourself—especially at the present moment. You can shew, as no other man can how supreme is duty—above all the suggestions of "*expediency*" or the urgency of party dictation. You can vindicate the importance of the individual. Avowing a hatred of slavery, you can well renounce the slavery of party. Such a letter will strengthen *all* Massachusetts. Write it. Do.[1]

Ever Yrs, Charles Sumner

ALS MHi (68/208, PCS)

1. In his letter of acceptance, 21 March 1848, Mann wrote that he agreed with the three stipulations of the nominating committee: first, that the nominee be faithful to the principles of John Quincy Adams; second, that the nominee be faithful to freedom; and third, that he work for "extending and securing liberty to the human race." Mann stated that he would not be "a slave of party. . . . [I]n the last resort, my own sense of duty must be the only arbiter" (*Slavery: Letters and Speeches* [1851], 1–9).

To Joshua R. Giddings

Boston March 25th 1848

My dear Sir,

Constant pressure upon my time has compelled me to intermit during the last fortnight much of my correspondence. I have, therefore, seemed to neglect yr favors.

You have doubtless seen the Whig containing yr letter, & our comments. I cannot disguise my feeling that the evidence adduced by you, *independent of yr own assertion*, that Winthrop was present, & spoke, at the caucus, seemed to me less strong than I had anticipated.[1] I have not been astonished that many persons have regarded it as inadequate. Believing, as I do, that you must be right, from the circumstance that this was stated by you to Mr Adams *shortly after* it took place, when yr memory was fresh & not liable to be deceived, I am able to remedy in my own mind the seeming defect of yr proofs. In the Whig I endeavored to set them forth analytically, & in such wise as to give them their strongest character. I avoided the discussion with the Atlas—partly for want of room & partly because it seemed to me of doubtful policy to prolong it. This is the *Winthrop region*. His friends are dominant here, controlling opinion. They have done much to prejudice our whole movement, by charging a vindictive personality upon us, though you well know how impossible it has been to proceed a step without encountering Winthrop's influence.

I have recd. yr favor with the criticisms on the Atlas; but the reasons, which are given above, have made me hesitate to open the subject anew.[2] I should like yr views with regard to it.

It seems to me clear that Taylor is to have the nomination of the Whig Convention. You must rally the Proviso forces. Where is Corwin? He should speak now in the Senate.

You have read Mann's letter. *He is with us*. Ardent pursuits in other directions have prevented him from being very familiar with the details of our position. But I have entire confidence in him. He consulted Dr Howe & myself with regard to his letter before sending it. This may go for something. I put it to him—that he must go to Washington to struggle against the Taylor movement. *This he will do*. Furthermore he read yr speech before writing his letter, & subscribed to all that you said. Is not this enough? He sympathises entirely with Palfrey. The Atlas, which began with warm commendations, is now silent. It is caught. A Hunker Whig on the evng of the nomination said he liked Horace Mann—"there is nothing of *"conscience"* in him." I told this to Mann, who was much edified by it. He is a thorough *"Conscience"* Whig.

Mr Root's speech is a gem.[3] I have rarely read anything with more pleasure.

Yours faithfully, Charles Sumner

J. R. Giddings Esq.

ALS MH-H (63/229, PCS)

1. Giddings had gathered letters from five congressman which were published in the *Boston Daily Atlas* (17 March 1848:2). Four agreed that Winthrop had attended the May 1846 Whig caucus, but evidence as to Winthrop's advocacy of the Mexican War was contradictory and imprecise. The *Atlas* concluded that Giddings's proof was "a most lamentable failure." If these letters were all the evidence Giddings could produce, "how frivolous it is!" In the *Boston Daily Whig* (18 March 1848:2) CS stated that Giddings's letters showed that Winthrop's denial of attending the caucus was "distinctly overthrown," because the assertion of one or two members recalling Winthrop's presence was stronger than his denial. The *Whig* also published Giddings's letter to Winthrop of 7 February asking him if he indeed denied Giddings's allegation and Winthrop's one-paragraph reply, 7 February, stating he did not desire to be "drawn into any correspondence or controversy with you on the subject."

2. In his letter of 20 March (6/070, PCS) Giddings criticized what he claimed were inaccuracies in the *Atlas* editorial. He affirmed the statements of his colleagues: "They stand as high as Winthrop."

3. Speaking on "The Return of Santa Ana" 15 March, Joseph Mosely Root (1807–79; U.S. congressman [Whig, Ohio], 1845–49, [Free Soil, Ohio], 1849–51) attacked the constitutionality of the Mexican War and the peace settlement, both of which disregarded the rights of Mexicans. He declared that the acquired territory should be treated as that under the Ordinance of 1787, with slavery excluded (*Globe*, 30th Cong., 1st sess., appendix, 394–96).

To Richard Cobden[1]

Boston April 1st 1848

My dear Sir,

I have ventured to send through Mr [*George*] Bancroft for yr acceptance another pamphlet, which touches some of the topics connected with the Peace Question. I am well aware that this is to be treated, in legislative assemblies, very much in the light of economy; for in this age the pocket argt. is most potential with those who guide public affairs. Still, there are other considerations, of a moral character, which may properly reinforce the argt. of economy. It is one of these which is treated in the pamphlet which I send you.

It seems to me that the French Revolution is to render Europe like wax, to receive the impression of new ideas. Why may not that of *Universal Peace* be stamped there? Lamartine must be open to receive this?[2]

I am astonished at the course of the Spectator.[3] I have always read that paper with sympathy & admiration. But it is now going astray. It is positively Heathenist. Suppose England should abandon half of her armaments, & appropriate the means thus saved to *Schools*. Would she not be better *defended* then than now? And would not happiness be increased immeasurably—& power too?

I was thankful for the kindness of yr letter[4]—& trust that your want of confidence in the Future of France may give place to Hope & Satisfaction. I know that the Conservatives of Europe & America (for we have some of the most rabid here) will condemn France, whatever may be the result. But I feel sure that this Revolution will promote human happiness.

I write in great haste, that I may not miss the opportunity.

Believe me, my dear sir,

very faithfully Yours, Charles Sumner

Richard Cobden Esq.

ALS GBWSR (68/217, PCS)

1. CS had met the liberal statesman and reformer Richard Cobden (1804–65) at a London dinner at the home of Joseph Parkes in 1838 or 1839 (CS to Cobden, 12 February 1848, 68/155, PCS).

2. On 22–24 February a republican and workers' demonstration precipitated the abdication of King Louis-Philippe and the resignation of the prime minister, Guizot. Lamartine was then chosen leader until elections for the Constituent Assembly were held in April.

3. *The Spectator*, in an article, "The Militia," satirized newspapers protesting use of military force (4 March 1848:215) and in "A National Force" stressed the need for a strong defense; recent events had provided "a cogent refutation of the assumptions of the pseudo Peace party" (11 March 1848:251–52).

4. Cobden's letter of 9 March (6/055) had expressed doubt about the future of a French republic.

To George Sumner

Boston April 14th '48

My dear George,

Yr letter to Dallas came duly. I read it to Austin. We both agree that yr suggestion would have an important influence in France.[1] I wrote on the subject to the Vice-President—enforcing yr views. I await to hear of the introduction of the measure before writing to others. But you must be prepared for disappointment. This unhappy war has absorbed our finances, so as to prevent us, in the view of many, from being generous. People begin to clamor for a higher Tariff. Will the administration venture to reduce the present in any particular? If they should consent to yr measure, how can they protect themselves against calls from other quarters? Besides we are deeply in debt & can we help France, until this is removed? Such questions will arise in the minds of many, who do not feel that a generous idea is worth more than a Tariff. I wish success for you; but cannot expect it.

I send you papers describing a meeting in Boston to express sympathy with France at which the Mayor presided. It was a fatherless meeting, called anonymously. I was asked to go & speak; but declined, as I was unwilling to compromise myself by the possible extravagances of a meeting convened in such a manner. The Resolutions are trivial. The Address to the People of France is capital. I am glad that such a document will go there. And though here the meeting may be disregarded, yet in France, it will have as much influence as if the chosen spirits of Boston had attended it. I observe that my name is on the Committee; but I did not attend the meeting, nor was I consulted by the Committee.[2] Certainly, this is a license.

The feeling in Boston is counter to the Revolution. This movement is in advance of the sentiment here. The commercial interest is disturbed by the shock that property has received. John E. Thayer,[3] the rich broker, who has risen since yr day, tells me that he regards France as a "wreck." I suspect that he speaks the opinions of his class. Mr [*Henry*] Cabot told me that I was the first person he had seen, who had hope in the Future of France. I do not disguise my anxiety. France has fearful trials in store, the necessary incident of a *transition-state*. She is moving from one house to another. Indeed it is more than this; she is fleeing from a burning house; so doing, she must feel present discomfort; but I do not doubt the Future of that great country.

Lamartine's position excites unbounded admiration. Let him be the *pacificator*, & guide of these stormy elements. His firmness has thus far been beyond all praise. I trust it will continue. I do wish that he would make a resolute effort in his vivid phrase, to reverse the French "ideas of Glory!" Let him put forth the True Grandeur of Peace. I count upon yr influence with him to present these views to his mind. I trust that the patronage of the new Govt will be given directly to the people in their localities. I should not center at Paris. If the whole apparatus is there, & all the secret springs, then a mob may at any time overturn it; but if the prefects, & offices of the provinces are all chosen by the people where they live, then the central power will be shorn of that peculiar influence which it has thus far exerted, while the whole Govt. will be strengthened; because it will be sustained equally by all France. I hope you have the recent New York Constitution,[4] which seems to be working very well.

I am constantly struck by the vigor & tone of Louis Blanc's book. Mrs Coolidge has just lent me his French Revolution, which I expect to read with great interest.[5] Lamartine's Girondins is a marvellous production. These two writers must have strongly influenced the mind & heart of France.

Our domestic politics seem tame by the side of these great events, with which Europe teems. An unjust peace will, probably, close the unjust war. Many think now that Polk will be the democratic candidate. This is not improbable. It may be Woodbury. The democrats are sanguine of success. Clay is now distinctly in the field. Whether the Whig Convention will adopt him or Taylor, I cannot say. —— All that I hear said of yr letter on the French Revolution is much in its praise.[6] It is admitted that you have furnished the only account that has yet appeared of the constitutional grounds of the Revolution. You have said nothing of Gray's book.[7] I should like to know how it impresses you. What is the state of the Prison Question in Europe? Let me know by return steamer—as I may wish to speak on the subject in the last week of May.—I see that Chamber's Edinburgh Journal has a long & agreeable article on my Address on "Fame & Glory."[8] I long to talk with you face to face on the interesting events of which you are a spectator.

Ever Thine, Chas.

My last letter, I sent directly to the Rue des Beaux Arts—also sundry newspapers. This time I send to Greene & Co.

P.S. Hillard, I suppose, is still in Paris.[9] He will refresh you with authentic tidings of Boston. There are no persons here with regard to whom I do not agree with him—unless perhaps the Ticknors, who are vipers & vultures. They are the only persons in Boston against whom I would put *you* on yr guard. I do not use strong language with regard to people; but I know them to deserve my epithets. I wish that Hillard was not blinded to their true character. He would be a happier & better man. I am not alone in this opinion.

ALS MH-H (63/235, PCS)

1. George Sumner had met George Mifflin Dallas (1792–1864; U.S. vice president, 1845–49; U.S. minister to Great Britain, 1856–61) in 1838 when Dallas was minister to Russia ("Memoir of George Sumner," *Proceedings of the Massachusetts Historical Society* 18 [1880]: 192–93). Edward Austin (b. 1803) was a Boston businessman. Evidently George Sumner hoped for some U.S. financial support for the new French republic; CS wrote George on 18 April 1848, enclosing an unrecovered reply from Dallas that, CS stated, was "more encouraging" than he had expected, but Dallas did not promise "*instant* legislation which is so desirable" (18 April 1848, 63/237, PCS).

2. At the meeting CS was named to a committee to draft resolutions supporting Lamartine and the "birth of European liberty" (*Boston Daily Advertiser*, 13 April 1848:2).

3. John E. Thayer (c. 1803–57), Boston investment banker.

4. Ratified in 1846, this constitution instituted universal male suffrage and judicial reform (DW, 6:196).

5. Jean-Joseph Charles-Louis Blanc (1811–82), French utopian socialist and member of the provisional government, Second Republic, 1848, had written *Histoire de Dix Ans, 1830–40* (1841–44), and was working on *Histoire de la Révolution Française* (1847–62). Mrs. Coolidge is possibly Ellen Wayles Coolidge (1796–1876).

6. Probably the letter from a "Boston Gentleman" dated Paris, 29 February 1848, which appeared in the *Boston Courier*, 1 April 1848:1.

7. Francis C. Gray's *Prison Discipline in America* (1847).

8. The favorable review appeared in *Chambers's Edinburgh Journal* 9, no. 218 (4 March 1848): 155–57.

9. CS's law partner toured Europe from July 1847 to September 1848 (HWL, 3:132).

To Joshua R. Giddings

Boston April 21st. '48

My dear Sir,

It seems to me advisable that you should join in interrogating Clay, or at any rate, that you should promote the plan. An answer in our favor would help that public sentiment which we chiefly seek to forward. It would help us in another contingency. Suppose he shall be nominated by the Convention?[1] It will be difficult for us, who have always supported him, to *organise* a revolt against him. We may be content to remain inactive. Anticipating such a contingency I shall be happy to see him take such a position as will indispose us to any formal opposition, in the event of his nomination.

A distinct declaration from him in favor of the Wilmot Proviso—not a jesuitical juggling Janus-faced expression—would have great influence in fortifying our cause. It would help shut the gates of the North upon Taylor. This would be its direct influence. Indirectly, it might help Clay's personal views. But I am willing to forget this indirect influence in the direct good. I am also desirous or at least willing to give Clay every opportunity of putting himself in a position, which will take from us the necessity of organising an opposition, in the event of his nomination. Of course, if Taylor is nominated, it will be our duty to revolt.

Efforts are now making here to have Webster nominated by our Legislative caucus.[2] I have been asked to favor it. I replied, that I did not regard him as the representative of our sentiments—that I did not see how we could ⟨help promote his nomination now⟩ join in presenting him as a candidate—that if he were nominated by the Convention, it would be difficult, if not impossible, for us to oppose him. I think he will be nominated by the caucus. His friends say that, united New

England can carry him through the Convention, & that if he is nominated, he can be elected. They are very sanguine. It is their purpose to have something done at once in Connecticut & Vermont.

I am filled with shame at the transactions in Washington.[3] I honor you much for yr constant efforts in behalf of the oppressed. I trust that no day will pass without some motion, that shall bring this hypocritical sin before the country. In Europe they *mob* for Freedom, in Washington for *slavery*. But all these occurrences prepare the way for the final success, which I know we shall yet achieve.

Webster has recently said that the Wilmot Proviso is the great question for the next campaign. He says he will not formally oppose any nominee of the Convention; but if Taylor should have the nomination, he "will not ask his fellow-coutrymen to vote for him." *In short he will not sustain Taylor*.

Ever Yrs, Charles Sumner

P.S. Should not C. J. Ingersoll's motion about duties on French goods prevail?[4] *It seems to me it should*.

ALS OHi (68/232, PCS)

1. The Whig convention was scheduled for 7–9 June 1848 in Philadelphia.

2. Ebenezer Rockwood Hoar (1816–95; Massachusetts judge; U.S. attorney general, 1869–70; joint high commissioner for Treaty of Washington, 1871–72; U.S. congressman [Rep., Mass.], 1873–75) and Charles Train were organizing a movement to nominate Webster with an address "setting forth the Wilmot Proviso as the platform," CS wrote Palfrey. If Webster were nominated, CS had told Hoar, "our present policy would be silence" ([23 April 1848] 68/243, PCS).

3. On 17 April Daniel Drayton and William Sayres had sailed from Washington with 78 slaves, bound for freedom. The ship was captured by the U.S. Navy, the slaves sold, and Drayton and Sayres jailed without being specifically charged with any crime. Giddings visited the two men in prison and defended them in the House on 20 April. At the same time, proslavery mobs in Washington clamored for the lynching of Drayton and Sayres (*Globe*, 30th Cong., 1st sess., 654–55; James B. Stewart, *Joshua R. Giddings and the Tactics of Radical Politics* [1970], 152–53).

4. On 17 April Ingersoll had proposed a 50 percent decrease on duties on imported French goods in order to assist French industry "at this crisis in French Government" (*Globe*, 30th Cong., 1st sess., 638).

To Joshua R. Giddings

Boston May 6th '48

My dear Sir,

I think the effect of the debate in the Senate & the House has been admirable. I hear it often spoken of. I long to read yr closing speech.[1]

Such another debate would deepen the impression. *And the subject must be pushed*, until the House entertains it, like any other subject,—as the Mexican War, or the annexation of Texas.

I am not prepared to say, how I should have answered the question put to you,—whether you thought Capt. Sayres wrong?[2] In the first place, I am not entirely satisfied of the constitutionality & legality of Slavery in the District; & in the second place, assuming its legality, I am not prepared to say that I can condemn those, who, in obedience to the great law of Humanity, have striven to extricate their fellow-men from unjust laws. I have always said, when speaking of such cases, that, as at present advised, I would not myself be a party to any efforts to remove a slave from the custody of his master; but that I could not condemn those who engaged in them—nay more, that it was difficult for me not to regard them with honor. Who can doubt that the day will yet come when Torrey[3] & Capt. Sayres will be regarded as martyrs of Liberty?

It seems to me that Hale should bring forward some *agressive* measure on Slavery—I would suggest a Bill for the Abolition of the Slave-trade in the District. In support of this let him set forth all the enormities of the system, as we have them in [*William*] Jay & other writers. What he says or reads in the Senate is reported at length, & thus circulates over the whole land.

I fear [*Winfield*] Scott. I believe you have confidence in his Anti-Slavery. If you have, I am content; but I cannot disguise an [inimicable?] repugnance to support for high office the man who bombarded Vera Cruz, & otherwise acted as the instrument of this atrocious war. Webster's friends are sanguine. They quote Thurlow Weed[4] as saying that he is the most "available" Whig at the present moment. I passed a half-hour with him this morning; talking all the while of European politics—not a word of American. I did not think it best to introduce the latter.

I have written to Mann, urging him to make a demonstration against Slavery very soon.[5] Dr Howe will call on you in Washington. He is very intimate with Mann. I feel that every new voice against Slavery on the floor of the House helps mightily to create a Public Opinion. I trust that you will be able to enlist others yet; but Mann must speak soon.

Ever faithfully Yours, Charles Sumner

ALS OHi (68/266, PCS)

1. Congress debated 20–25 April 1848 on matters relating to the Drayton and Sayres arrest. In the Senate on 20 April John P. Hale introduced a bill providing for

restoration of property damage from "riotous or tumultuous assemblage." The House debated Palfrey's motion to appoint a committee to investigate the need for legislation protecting congressmen and other citizens from mob violence (*Globe*, 30th Cong., 1st sess., 649–56, 657–64, 665–73). In his speech 25 April, "Privileges of Members of Congress," Giddings declared that he did not advocate interference with slavery in present slaveholding states, but that slavery in the District of Columbia was a violation of the Constitution. He decried the slave dealers from nearby cities who led the mobs in Washington, prodded by House members. Giddings concluded that the slavery issue must and would be discussed in Congress (ibid., appendix, 518–23).

2. When asked on 20 April by William T. Haskell of Tennessee whether Drayton and Sayres had broken the law in stealing slaves, Giddings replied that they had committed a "legal crime" but not a moral crime (*Globe*, 30th Cong., 1st sess., 654–55).

3. Charles T. Torrey, a clergyman and abolitionist, had been jailed for helping an escaped slave and died in a Maryland prison in 1846.

4. Thurlow Weed (1797–1882), Albany journalist and Whig politician.

5. 4 and 5 May (68/258, 264, PCS).

To George Washington Greene

Boston May 10th '48

Dear Greene,

I have sent you my last copy of the ϕ.B.K. Address. I have none of the Amherst.

I shall be glad to hear from you on the subject of our conversation.[1] I am curious to know any thing in literature or history illustrative of the great *Law of Progress*. I am disposed to regard this as a *discovery* of our age—heralded indeed by Xtianity, but not practically recognised till our own time; &, indeed, even now recognized by comparatively few. That Law is the tocsin of monarchy & of injustice of all kinds. But while it shews that no change is impossible in the Future, yet, when properly understood, it shews that all change must come gradually,—I am tempted to add peacefully.

I am curious to know whether there was any recognition of this in Antiquity, except in the prophecies of the Jews & the promises of Xtianity? Is there in China?—Why has the Chinese civilization continued immovable?

The idea of Vico is still common.[2] We hear much talk of the *old age* of nations, their decline & fall, assimilating them to short-lived mortals.

If there are any books or speculations on this theme which occur to your mind, let me hear from you.

Ever faithfully Yrs, Charles Sumner

ALS MH-H (68/273, PCS)

1. Greene was then living in Providence, having lost his consulship in Rome in 1845 (HWL, 3:10). CS's speech "The Law of Human Progress," delivered at Union College 25 July 1848, essentially argues the points he lays out in this letter.

2. Giovanni Battista Vico (1668–1744), Italian philosopher whose work "The Principles of a New Science Concerning the Common Nature of Nations" (1725) CS lauded as having first systematically put forth the idea of a law of progress. According to CS in his speech, Vico did not, however, realize that such a law would lead humanity "through unknown and infinite stages" ("The Law of Human Progress," 1849, 15).

To George Sumner

Boston May 30th [*and 31st*] 1848

My dear George,

The last steamer brt yr letter of May 11th; but you say nothing of Hillard. Surely you have seen him. I counted upon yr fresh impressions of him after so long a separation. I doubt not you have been of incalculable service to him in Paris. But I must repeat what I have said before, that I feel great qualms as to any further *exploitation* of yr time by Americans. I fear, that you may say of them as Rogers once said to Kenyon[1]—"These Americans are pleasant people—but don't we see too much of them." Still all this does not touch Hillard. I trust yr next letter will give liberal accounts of him.

I have admired Lamartine's two speeches much. They are both in the right direction, & contain sentiments which have the breath of regeneration. Can Europe abide King's speeches after these? And yet they "squint" in one or two places at the besetting insanities of France—the love of "Glory" & of War.—My interest in Louis Blanc the historian is so great that I am pained by the treatment he receives at the Tribune.[2]

You will see the nomination of Cass.[3] That does not settle the question. There are the *ultra* Alabama slave-holders, & the New York Barnburners both recalcitrating. What will be the consequence? But the Whigs are no better off. They are in no condition to take advantage of the feud; for the same Slavery question lies athwart their organization. Two days ago Taylor's nomination seemed inevitable. The strengthening opposition, however, makes me believe that a Northern candidate may yet succeed in the Convention. Webster's friends are making great exertions, & some of them are very confident. Then there is Scott & Mclean, both with many friends. In the event of Taylor's nomination there will be an organized revolt at the North. We in Massachusetts are maturing it in advance; the same is doing in Ohio. It is possible, that we may all join with the Barnburners. If so, there will be a new party, having some *principles*, & looking to the good of Humanity.

Bancroft writes me, in some apparent dissatisfaction, that Lamartine quoted some opinion of mine on the Mexican War.[4] I am curious to know what it was. Tell me. I am happy if he is willing to receive his impression from me. I supposed, of course, that whatever it was, it must have reached him through you.

The Prison Discipl. Socty.[5] have had no public Anniversary this year. So they have avoided criticism & debate. This was to escape from us. In a certain sense, it is a triumph of our side. I am not sorry for it. The weight & influence of the Society abroad have already been broken—partly through our exertions; the continuance of the controversy would cause bitterness at home without accomplishing any good commensurate. This should not prevent other exertions. I wish you would write yr letter about Gray's pamphlet. That would do good.

I gave Howe yr message. He would not hesitate on account of his past course. He has always been assured by the Poles, that they did not seek power over their serfs.[6]—Was Brougham crazy when he proposed to be naturalized in France?[7]—I do not know that I have told you that Dr C. T. Jackson threatens an Ether pamphlet. It will require evidence stronger than he possesses, as I believe, to shew that he has not been most unwise, hasty, careless & reckless in his claims. Opinion here awards the praise to Morton[8]

May 31st. I have recd. a letter this morning from N.Y. which shews the "confusion" of the democrats there.[9] It is all uncertain what they will do. Some are in favor of Taylor. This will be a detestable profligacy.

I send this letter direct to Rue des Beaux Arts. As I remember that street I should think it very convenient. It is retired, & yet central. When I was in Paris, Wolowski[10] the Editor of the Journal of Jurisprudence lived there. Is he the Wolowski with whom you had the passage? How is Foelix now? And how is Charles Ledru? Tell me something of both.

Ever Thine, C. S.

ALS MH-H (63/251, PCS)

1. Samuel Rogers (1763–1855), British poet, and John Kenyon (1784–1856), British writer, both patrons of the arts.

2. Lamartine's account of the Provisional Government as of 5 May 1848 and his "Report of the Minister of Foreign Affairs" were printed in the *New York Daily Tribune*, 29 May 1848:1–2. On 20 May, a *Tribune* editorial criticized Blanc for having adopted one of the "radical errors of Communism" in advocating equal pay for all

workers; on 23 May, "H. B.," the foreign correspondent, stated that Blanc had "shamefully deceived" the working people with unfulfilled promises (ibid., 20 May 1848:2; 23 May 1848:2).

3. In December 1847, with the presidency in mind, Lewis Cass wrote a public letter stating that the Constitution had no authority to interfere with slavery in the territories; residents of a territory should determine themselves whether or not slavery was allowed (Frederick J. Blue, *The Free Soilers* [1973], 48–49). When Cass was nominated on 22 May by the Democrats at Baltimore, Barnburners left the convention in protest.

4. George Bancroft wrote from London 3 May, "I was sorry a copy of something you have written or said on Mexico, reached Lamartine; for he has not time to inquire into particulars & [form a] judgment of his own on minor points of fact or policy; & his generous nature is liable to be swayed by sentiments even in opposition to reason & even without due regard to facts" (6/117, PCS).

5. Boston conservatives George Ticknor and George T. Curtis had been elected to the board of the society and the board voted to hold no more public meetings (DD, 1:128).

6. In 1846 Polish gentry had rebelled against Austrian rule and promised emancipation of serfs. The serfs, however, backed by the Austrian government, fought against their landlords and the gentry's revolt collapsed.

7. The *New York Daily Tribune* (10 May 1848:1) printed correspondence from the *Journal des Débats* between Brougham and the minister of justice, Adolphe Crémieux, about Brougham's request to become a French citizen.

8. Charles Thomas Jackson (1805–80) claimed he, not Morton, had first discovered ether as an anesthetic.

9. Writing on 29 May, Theodore Sedgwick stated that the Democratic Barnburner behavior depended on the Whig nomination (6/150).

10. Louis Wolowski (1810–76), law professor, member Constituent Assembly, 1848–49.

To Frances A. Longfellow

Court St. Friday afternoon
[*May 1848*][1]

My dear Fanny,

Your note of true friendship written on Wednesday was received on that day; but absorbing engagements have prevented me from doing more than glance at it till this moment.

I am grateful for all kindness, & desire to have the advantage of advice from those I love. I have not read yr note without deep sensibility. It has almost disarmed me. And yet, I am persuaded, that you could never have written it, if you had read what I have written, & understood my true position.

I dislike controversy. It is alien to my nature; but I do love what seems to me true & right; nor do I speculate much with regard to personal consequences in their maintenance. Believe me now, dear Fanny, as I look back upon all that has passed during the last year—

groping among the wrecks of friendships that might have been argosies—I feel that I have done nothing but a duty, poorly, inadequately, but a duty which my soul told me to perform. In that time I have been mis-represented—treated unkindly by some—coldly by others—condemned bitterly by many who have never read what I have written—while I have had few or no friends, who understood my position, to speak for me. I make no complaints; least of all do I ask any friend to undergo unkindness on my account.

In criticising Mr Winthrop's course at first I was prompted by a desire—not unworthy it seems to me—to do something to arrest this hateful War. The position I then took drew upon me bitter personalities from Mr W—to which I never replied—& malignant abuse both in public & in private from his friends. To all this I have never replied. If people derive pleasure from this, let them go on.

Some of my friends, mingling much with those interested for Mr W. have expressed a warm sympathy for him. I have never heard them express any concern with regard to the repeated personal attacks levelled against me. I never invited it. Perhaps they did not know their existence.

The discussion this winter with regard to Mr W. was accidental in its origin. Mr Palfrey voted against him as Speaker. He was attacked most cruelly in leading papers. I wrote two articles in his defence in the Boston Courier[2]—most moderate & guarded in their tone—setting forth the reasons of his vote & defending it. It is these articles—which might have been preached as sermons—that have aroused the feeling against me anew. I thought Mr Palfrey right. He was attacked. He was my friend. May this hand lose its cunning, if it ever fails to defend a friend who is right!

I sent you a paper two days ago which contained a summary of the controversy, &, as I hope, its close. But I trust that I shall never shrink from any responsibility of renewing it, if the occasion shall seem to require it. It is now evident that General Taylor is to be forced upon the Whigs as their candidate; & it is said that Mr W. is a promoter or favourer of this scheme, by which the party is to abandon its principles. I will not vote for Taylor; & I shall do all in my power to oppose his election, believing that it will be most hurtful to all those views which I cherish so strongly. In this probable contest there is a prospect of still other collisions. I do not close my eyes to them. But I trust that I may meet them in a becoming spirit. Take from me the pleasures of friendship, &, I have small satisfaction left except in the performance of my duty. To the latter, God willing! I will hold fast. Without personal hostility to any one—seeking to temper all differences by kindness of manner on my part—cherishing friends though they may not accord with me in all things—I trust that I may be able to encounter the alienations that may be yet in store for me.

I have sought little for myself—not office or wealth—or worldly favor. No small chance for all of these I have dismissed. Who can say, then, that in striving against asperities of condemnation—such as is now my lot—I have selected a path, which can have any attraction except that of duty? I am said to be ambitious. But I have sacrificed what ambition chiefly seeks. I am said to be malignant. Read what I write. My fixed principle is to allow no difference on public matters to influence my private relations; nor do I ever make any suggestion with regard to the motives of men. I would say to all,—if we cannot agree, let us at least *agree* to *disagree*. In this spirit I trust to live & labor. What of disappointment & sorrow may yet be in store for me I know not; but I do fervently confide in the constancy of yr friendship,—with Henry's too. If I ever do aught in *spirit* or *act* unworthy of it, then may God forget me!

I have written this hastily longing to let you know that I was not insensible to yr kindness.[3]

Ever affectionately Yrs, Charles Sumner

ALS MLNHS (68/176, PCS)

1. Although this letter bears the notation "March 1848" and was tentatively dated "February 1848" in the microfilm edition, CS's reference to Taylor's imminent nomination seems to place it closer to the date of the Whig convention, 7–9 June 1848.

2. See CS to John Gorham Palfrey, 30 December 1847. In a second article in the *Boston Courier* (6 January 1848:2), CS distinguished Palfrey's politics from Winthrop's: "It will not be disguised that Mr. Winthrop is a devoted member of the 'united Whig party.' His political principles are those of the 'united party.' Nor is it too much to say that he has never shown any disposition to hazard the union of the party, by the support of those 'peculiar' measures which Massachusetts has so much at heart. Here at the outset is a difference between himself and Mr. Palfrey. The latter would not shrink from 'any political hazard' . . . in the maintenance of those measures which Massachusetts has so earnestly commended to the attention of Congress."

3. According to Pierce, Fanny Longfellow's entreaty, combined with others' pressure, caused CS to cease attacking Winthrop (Prc, 3:154).

To George Sumner

Boston June 13th [*and 14*]—'48

My dear George,

I had nothing from you by the last steamer; but by the steamer before yr little letter describing the Hubert affair. I admire yr readiness &

courage, & think they come naturally to you. I was glad to see by the later news that all seemed composed at last. I suspect the Assembly is conservative enough.[1] M. de Borante, who arrived here ten days ago, —I met him at Prescott's—told me that out of the 900 members 800 are in favor of a Regency. I do not believe this, though I did not tell him so. He regarded the whole movement with fear & disgust. On his way to America, he visited Louis Philippe & Guizot.[2] He said that the former had only 12,000 francs a year. À'propos of the King's poverty let me tell you that Mr. I. P. Davis[3] told me recently, that, when in Philadelphia, he ascertained on enquiry that there were $75,000 standing in Louis Philippe's name on the public books—I suppose of the public debt. Some of this was the accumulation of interest. With this sum, he will not starve.

Lamartine's popularity seems to be waning. At this distance I am not able to satisfy myself as to the exact reasons. I should like to know what you think of Ledru Rollin?[4] I have been troubled not a little by the *cockamanie* of Louis Blanc. Admiring him as a writer & an historian I have been solicitous for his success. Perhaps he may recover from that overwhelming defeat before the Assembly on the evng of May 15th, for his genius is great; but only a remarkable genius could hope to rise from such an ignominious prostration.[5] I long to follow him to the close. *His* will be the great work on that theme.

Taylor is nominated at last.[6] A week or fortnight will disclose, whether a new combination will not be effected among the Free States. The effect of a Regular Nomination is potential. It is difficult to oppose it. But it will be opposed in Ohio. There are symptoms now of rebellion in New York. In Mass. we have called a Convention for June 28th to organize opposition. Meanwhile the Barnburners are shaking New York to its centre. We hope to establish an alliance among the disaffected of both parties through-out the Free States, & thus build a new party, which shall be truly democratic. The Barnburner's policy is to defeat Cass, & thus let the Northern Democrats see that they cannot hope for success without adopting the principles of Freedom. I understand that at their Convention at Utica June 22nd, they will lay down their platform & assume the name of *Radical Democrats*.[7]—We have reason to believe that Judge McLean will accept a nomination from the Free States, & we hope to bring this about. The Hunker Whigs are sanguine of success under Taylor. I doubt whether they will have it. But it is impossible to discern any thing clearly now with regard to the next contest. For myself, I should rather see Cass prevail than Taylor. John Van Buren has made a most brilliant reputation during the last few months. I need say nothing of this, however; for you have read his speeches.—I fear that I shall be called upon to exert myself in these matters more than I desire during this summer. I do not seek the honors or emoluments of politics. My only wish is to sustain those principles which I think essential to the well-being of our country.—I have already consented to deliver the Phi Beta Address at Schenectady College at the end of July. I wish you were here to take some portion of these things.

Mrs Coolidge has returned from the South & is here for a few weeks before adjourning to Newport. Her daughter is a graceful refined person; the mother has a fine intelligence.—Scholfield[8] told us of seeing much of you in Paris. Hillard writes of yr kindness in [procuring?] him a sight of the Nat. Assembly. I trust you have seen a great deal of each other. Lodge[9] always inquires warmly after you. —Who is to take Wheaton's place at the Institute?[10] I should be glad to see you in it.—You are old enough for an Academician!—I wish you would write a book—a solid volume—into which you would pour the conclusions & experience of the last ten years. Think of this.

June 14th. The steamer sails this morning. To our astonishment last evng the steamer of June 3d arrived—the shortest passage on record. It is stated that Circourt[11] has been appointed Minister to the U.S.—Nothing from you as yet.—The news this morning shews still further disaffection in the Whig ranks. Still I give no definite opinion as to the course it will take.

It is thought that Everett may still stick to Cambridge. He seems to give himself to his police duties there with a dogged devotion.—I wish I could pass a week in Paris. I should enjoy its sights very much.

Ever Thine, C. S

P.S. The Merc. Lib. Assoc. think of asking Hillard to give a course of lectures on Europe. He is a special favorite with them.

ALS MH-H (63/255, PCS)

1. France's Constituent Assembly, elected 23 April 1848, convened on 4 May. Of the nine hundred representatives, five hundred were moderate republicans, eighty progressive republicans, two hundred Orleanists, and one hundred legitimists. As the assembly tried to establish a government, on 15 May, a crowd of workers and supporters of Polish and Italian nationalism, encouraged by Wolowski, entered the assembly hall. Aloysius Huber (1812–65), who may have been a police spy, stepped forward and declared the assembly dissolved. The crowd then moved on to the Hôtel de Ville to set up a provisional government, but were eventually dissuaded by Lamartine, Ledru-Rollin, and the presence of the National Guard (*New York Daily Trib-*

une, 1 June 1848:1; Georges Duveau, *1848: The Making of a Revolution* [1967], 95, 98–99, 117–24).

2. Louis Philippe and Guizot had both fled to England.

3. Isaac P. Davis (1771–1855), Boston businessman.

4. Alexandre-August Ledru-Rollin (1807–74), minister of the interior in Lamartine's Provisional Government of 1848, stood to the left of Lamartine in politics.

5. The *New York Daily Tribune* (3 June 1848:1) stated that there were "strong grounds for suspecting" that Blanc had joined in the conspiracy of 15 May to overthrow the Provisional Government, but his behavior was hard to assess. Blanc had "expressed his confidence" in the crowd, but then disappeared; later, when he returned to aver his support for Lamartine, he was greeted with "derision and contempt."

6. Taylor was nominated on the fourth ballot at Philadelphia, 9 June.

7. At this convention Barnburners nominated Martin Van Buren for President.

8. Isaac Scholfield, a friend of Henry Sumner, had gone to England on a diplomatic errand (CS to George Sumner, 14 January, 63/210, PCS).

9. Probably John Ellerton Lodge (1807–62, father of Henry Cabot Lodge) or his brother, James Lodge, both Boston shipping merchants.

10. The diplomat Henry Wheaton had died 11 March. CS's notice of Wheaton, written for the *Boston Daily Advertiser*, 16 March 1848, is published in his Wks, 2:215–25.

11. Adolphe de Circourt (1801–79), writer and diplomat, supported the monarchy and the Bourbons (Roger Boesche, ed., *Alexis de Tocqueville: Selected Letters on Politics and Society* [1985], 381).

To Horace Mann

Boston June 21st 1848

My dear Mann,

I am not disappointed in what you write with regard to the French proposition.[1] I think, however, if some other person than Ingersoll had introduced it, a more cordial welcome might have been found for it.

We are busy in preparation for our Convention. Giddings is to be with us—we hope also Roote—perhaps Palfrey. Wilson has been deputed to ask yr presence or at least a communication from you. I cannot disguise that our friends have expressed great solicitude with regard to yr probable course. Keyes[2] this morning, while speaking of you with personal regard, seemed disappointed by the contents of a letter which he had received from you. I have not seen the letter.

We hope that you will join the movement—I am tempted to say unreservedly. I mean surrender to the *Principles*, which we advocate, wherever those may carry us—whether to a greater or less divergence from our old political associates. There is a breaking up of parties, & old names will soon become mere toys. Let us stick to our *Principles* & to the *men* who will sustain them. A cordial word of cheer from you will be of great importance. In yr District, Keyes, Wilson & Russell[3] are with us.

In Middlesex all the best men—so also many on Connecticut River.

I envy your *position* for the opportunity of usefulness which it gives you, by striking a strong blow in the right direction. And let me add, the stronger you strike, the stronger you will be in yr District.

Ever Yrs, Charles Sumner

ALS MHi (68/311, PCS)

1. See CS to Giddings, 21 April 1848. No letter from Mann on this issue has been recovered; CS wrote Mann on 15 June (68/299, PCS) about reducing U.S. duties on French goods to show support for the republic.

2. Whigs who refused to support Taylor, the Whig nominee for President, were convening in Worcester 28 June. Among them were Henry Wilson (1812–75), editor, *Boston Daily Republican*, 1848–51, and Edward L. Keyes, editor, *Dedham Gazette*.

3. Possibly G. R. Russell, a correspondent of Mann's.

To Joshua R. Giddings

Boston June 23d '48

My dear Sir,

I have just received yours of June 21st.[1]

Your name has been advertised among those who are to speak at Worcester. There is an intense desire to see & welcome you in Massachusetts.

Let me exhort you, my dear Sir, to renounce all those compunctions, to which you refer; & to speak to us from your heart. Give us yr views on Slavery, & the duty of the North. Say what you would say in Ohio. Our Convention will be of farmers, & men from the people—comparatively few politicians.

If you should not come, we should be much disappointed, & I fear that our Convention would lose much of the force which we desire to give to it.

I have written also to Mr Roote. We count also on his presence.[2]

Mr Phillips is preparing an Address & resolutions to put forth from the Convention.[3]

I have just met Abbott Lawrence. I said to him—"I am glad you were not nominated for the Vice-Presidency"—"That is a doubtful compliment" said a bystander.—"I would not have Mr L's name" said I, "discredited by association with General Taylor." He then said—"Do you know where you are going—You will have to support Martin Van Buren"—"*I am ready*" was my reply.

So I am. If the Utica Convention nominates him, will he not be our man? He has suffered in the course of Anti-Texas.

Yours most truly, Charles Sumner

ALS OHi (68/316, PCS)

1. Giddings wrote (6/201, PCS) that he did not see how his presence at the anti-Taylor convention at Worcester on 28 June 1848 would help the cause, but he would come if he were not asked to speak.

2. CS also hoped to get William Pitt Fessenden (1806–69; U.S. congressman [Whig, Maine], 1841–43; U.S. senator [Whig, Rep., Maine], 1854–64, 1865–69; U.S. secretary of the Treasury, 1864–65), as well as Horace Greeley and Thomas Corwin to attend, but evidently did not succeed (CS to Fessenden, 19 June, to Giddings, 17 June, 68/303 and 301).

3. Stephen C. Phillips, chair of the committee on an address and resolutions, offered a resolution thanking Whig Congressmen Charles Allen and Henry Wilson for their stand against the Taylor nomination at the Whig convention. The two delegates had left the convention in protest. Phillips's address set forth goals for an organized political party to protest slavery (Wilson, 2:146; *New York Daily Tribune*, 30 June 1848:1).

To Joshua R. Giddings

Boston July 5th '48

My dear Sir,

I enclose $50, which with the $20, we have supposed, may cover yr expenses. I regret that our means allow us to do so little. But you have our warmest thanks. I hear nothing but pleasure & gratitude expressed with regard to yr visit. You have done us incalculable good.

I am glad to hear that Connecticut is moving.—The great Whig ratification meeting at Bridgewater, Mass. turned out a perfect failure.[1] Our friends take courage from this.

Allow me to call yr careful attention to Mr Van Buren's position with regard to the District of Columbia.[2] I find this labors very much. There are many Whigs who are against him on this score, & most of the Liberty-men. The sentence which excites especial displeasure is where he says that the reasons for his course on the District of Col. are "still satisfactory to him." Adams had a letter to-day from one of our active men, who says that this unexplained will cost Van Buren 100,000 votes. I trust you will take it in hand.

Adams thinks that the New York Delegation at Buffalo should be prepared to make the explanation, & that this would be better than a letter. Still the explanation, in some form or other, seems necessary.

There is another passage in the letter which is unpleasant—where he ratifies his past course, impliedly covering the outrages [in] the mail.[3]

I have written to Mann earnestly calling upon him to lose no time in making a demonstration.[4] I think he will co-operate with you. At all events, I hope you will appeal to him to join you. I have asked him to follow you in declaring on the floor of Congress that he will not support Taylor.

Ever faithfully Yrs, Charles Sumner

P.S. Thanks for yr note from Springfield. Adams goes tonight to Norwich.

ALS OHi (68/357, PCS)

1. The *Boston Daily Whig* (7 July 1848:2) reported the ratification meeting of 4 July as failing "to raise the steam" for Taylor.

2. In his 20 June letter to delegates of the Utica Free Soil Convention, Van Buren stated that as a presidential candidate in 1836 he had asserted that Congress had the power to abolish slavery in the District of Columbia. He went on to say, however, that he was "for reasons which were then, and are still satisfactory to my mind, very decidedly opposed to its exercise there" (Oliver C. Gardiner, ed., *The Great Issue* [1848], 110–16).

3. Van Buren said he supported the Founders' compromise on slavery, and subsequent ones regarding the admission of both slave and free states into the Union: "I was determined that no effort on my part, within the pale of the constitution, should be wanting to sustain its compromises as they were then understood, and it is now a source of consolation to me that I pursued the course I then adopted" (ibid., 114).

4. CS sent essentially the same plea to Mann on 2, 3, 4, and 5 July (68/345, 349, 353, 359, PCS).

To Dorothea Dix[1]

Boston July 6th '48

My dear Miss Dix,

I have written to Dr Jarvis for a copy of his pamphlet. I trust I may be able to procure one for you.[2]

Dr Howe has promised to send you through Mr Bell his last two Reports. I hope you have seen his report on Idiots.[3]

I thank you very much for yr perseverance in noble labor. I cannot forbear saying how much higher I regard yr triumphs than any in this Mexican war.

Teach them at Washington the beauty of charity. Shame them for their unholy purposes.

The passage of such a bill as you propose for the benefit of the Insane, would be of incalculable influence for good throughout the country.[4] It would elevate the thoughts, the hopes, & the hearts of the people.

Faithfully Yours, Charles Sumner

ALS MH-H (68/361, PCS)

1. Dorothea Dix (1802–87), prison and hospital reformer.

2. In her letter of 30 June 1848 (6/218, PCS) Dix had asked CS for a copy of Edward Jarvis's "Remarks on the Inaccuracies of the Census of 1840" and Howe's reports on the Perkins Institute to be sent to her, care of John Bell.

3. *Report Made to the Legislature of Massachusetts Upon Idiocy*, 1848.

4. Dix wrote CS that she had just proposed a $5 million program to Congress for relief of the insane.

To Salmon P. Chase

Boston July 7th. 1848—

My dear Sir,

The whole country seems to be arousing at last,—God be praised!

The spirit of Freedom is spreading in Massachusetts now as in the days of the earlier Revolution. It promises to sweep the whole state. The developments of public opinion have thus far gone beyond our most sanguine anticipations. Even in Boston, the stronghold of the commercial spirit, we find most unexpected sympathy.

It seems to me that immediate success—even in the Presidential contest now at hand—will be ours, if we are able to rally all the forces of Freedom, from all parties. Union must be our watchword.

The nomination of Mr Van Buren has favorable & unfavorable circumstances connected with it. His name will draw the Democrats, while it may disaffect some Whigs. But the chief trouble is to arise,—not from differences on old party issues—but from Mr Van Buren's rather superfluous re-affirmation of his opinion with regard to Slavery in the District of Columbia. His language, however, admits of explanation, &, I hope, he will be able to remove some of our difficulties.

It is probable that he will be the nominee of the Buffalo Convention. The retirement of Mr Dodge[1] happily leaves a vacancy which we must fill in a manner to strengthen the union of all parties. I should like much to see J. R. Giddings in his place, but he cannot be spared from the House. Who then, shall it be?

There is one man, who will unite at once Whigs & Democrats, & give to the ticket a commanding force. With his name we should be almost certain of success. I mean *John McLean*. If he were the candidate for the Vice-Presidency with Martin Van Buren, his way would be opened to the Presidency at the election for 1852.

All our friends, to whom I have submitted this matter, feel that it is very desirable for the cause that he should consent to take this nomination—they feel too that the dignity of the occasion may properly commend even the second place—& that the friends of Freedom have a claim upon him to take even that place in a cause so holy, & of such high historic importance.

Governor [*Marcus*] Morton, who, as you know, represents the Barnburners of Massachusetts, tells me that, in his opinion, it is very desirable that Judge McLean should take this nomination.

Can you approach the Judge on this matter? Let him consent; & our principles will certainly triumph. Our Union will then be irresistible.

Ever faithfully Yours, Charles Sumner

S. P. Chase Esq.

ALS DLC (68/363, PCS)

1. Henry Dodge (1782–1867), governor of the Territory of Wisconsin, 1836–41, 1845–48; vice presidential nominee of the New York Barnburners, 1848; U.S. senator (Dem., Wis.), 1848–57.

To Charles Francis Adams

Saratoga Springs
Sunday [*July 30, 1848*]

My dear Adams,

In New York I saw Mr [*David Dudley*] Field, in Albany, Mr [Burwill?] & Mr Benton, thorough Barnburning politicians, in Schenectady Bradford R. Wood. I find from all these a fixed conviction that our Convention must nominate Van Buren. They all regard themselves as pleged to him. Dudley Selden joins in this. He also regards him as the strongest man.[1]

They all say that Mr Van Buren is in favor of the removal of the seat of Govt. from Washington, unless Slavery is abolished; & Dudley Selden suggests that our Convention should, by express resolution, call for that removal, on account of Slavery in the District. In this way that question may be agitated in the coming canvass. Think of this. It seems to me of great importance, & to afford a chance of reconciling our Abolitionist friends.

Let the resolution set forth the evils of Slavery in the District, & the stain upon the country in tolerating it at the seat of Govt, & then call for the removal of the Govt to a Free State. This would be a stroke that will tell far & wide.

B. F. Butler,[2] Bradford R. Wood & others have written to Judge McLean asking him to be Vice-President. They were willing that he should be considered as the candidate for the Presidency in 1852, & would regard the contest now as substantially for his benefit. I think it advisable that as many of our friends as know Judge McLean, should write to him, urging him to allow his name to go *unreservedly* before the Convention. With him as Vice-President, I am sanguine that we shall send our candidates to the House. His only chance for the Presidency depends upon his joining our movement.

The more I hear of Van Buren, the more I become reconciled to him as our candidate. His name gives our movement a national character.

Selden, who is here now, is very earnest on our side; but he is unwilling to move at present, as he may expose himself to criticism on account of his own large Slave ppty in Cuba. I think he is more master of the whole field of our politics than any person I have talked with.—I have been disappointed in him in this respect. He is desirous that our resolutions should leave the moral question of Slavery untouched & should allude only to the inequality under the Constitution for its extension.—This will not do.

I hope you will not send me as a delegate to the Convention. If I am there (& I am not certain now that I shall be) I should rather be a private individual. The Convention promises to be unmanagable in size.

I proposed to Mr Wood that some of Mr V. B.'s friends—Cambreling for instance[3]—should be ready to answer a question at Buffalo with regard to his views about the District of Col. He seemed to think well of this, & promised to talk with V. B. on the subject.

From all that I see & learn, I feel new confidence in our movement. Care & moderation are requisite; but its strength is already great.

I am assured that Pennsylvania will go for Cass. Selden thinks Louisiana, Missippi & Alabama will also.

In haste, Yours sincerely, Charles Sumner

J. C. Hamilton,[4] as I expected, is uncertain. He is unwilling to move forward.

ALS MBApm (68/382, PCS)

1. "Burwill" is possibly Fitzwilliam Byrdsall, a Locofoco; others are Charles Swan Benton (1810–82), U.S. congressman (Dem., N.Y.), 1843–47; Bradford Ripley Wood (1800–89), U.S. congressman (Dem., N.Y.), 1845–47, U.S. minister to

Denmark, 1861–65; and Dudley Selden (d. 1855), U.S. congressman (Dem., N.Y.), 1833–34. The Free Soil Convention was to be held in Buffalo 9 August 1848.

2. Benjamin Franklin Butler (1795–1858), U.S. attorney general, 1833–38; U.S. attorney for south district of N.Y., 1838–41, 1845–48.

3. Churchill C. Cambreleng (1786–1862), U.S. congressman (Dem., N.Y.), 1821–39.

4. John Church Hamilton (1792–1882), New York lawyer and editor of the works of his father, Alexander Hamilton.

To Edward Everett

Saratoga Springs
July 31st '48

My dear Sir,

You are perhaps aware that a Convention is to be held at Buffalo on the 9th August, composed of delegates from all the Free States & also from some of the Slave States, to nominate candidates for the Presidency & Vice-Presidency pledged against the extension of Slavery. That single issue is to be presented in the election.

It is probable that Mr Van Buren will be nominated for the Presidency, though not absolutely certain. My own preferences are for Judge McLean, & many delegates from New England & Ohio will probably have the same partialities. Still I cannot now disguise from myself, that it is most probable that the friends of Mr Van Buren will have a majority in the Convention; nor am I insensible to some of the strong considerations in his favor.

In the event of Mr Van Buren's nomination to the Presidency, it is proposed to bring forward Judge McLean for the Vice Presidency,—in this way effecting a powerful combination between seceders from both the great parties. It is not now known that he will consent to the use of his name for this purpose; though it is certain, that he has expressly declared that he did not consider himself bound by the Philadelphia Convention, & that he should not sustain Taylor. It is supposed that he may appreciate the importance & dignity of the present movement, & perceive that, by being the candidate for the Vice Presidency in 1848, he will prepare the way for his candidacy for the Presidency in '52.

In the event of Judge McLean refusing to take the nomination of Vice-President, several persons interested in the movement have turned their thoughts upon you. Mr Dudley Selden, who is now here, authorizes me to use his name, in asking you to allow yourself to be put in nomination for this office. Next after Judge McLean I can think of no name, that would impart to our movement more of that character which we desire to impress upon it, & which would be more widely acceptable,—harmonizing democrats & Whigs,—than yours.

I have no reason to believe my dear Sir, that you have any disposition to mingle in our movement; but, in my desire to serve the cause, I have made bold to seek yr permission to use yr name, if the contingency should occur to which I have alluded, &, if, under all the circumstances, it should seem advisable so to do.

I ought to add that, whatever may be the fate of the movement, I feel assured from what I have now seen, it will be such as to command the respect of the whole country. There are many who think that it will prevail in most of the Free States. *In 1852 it must succeed.*

If you will address me at Buffalo in answer to this communication, I will follow yr suggestions, whatever they may be. I cannot forbear saying that I trust you will appreciate the delicacy of my own position in making these proposals, & believe me sincerely desirous of yr fame & happiness.[1]

I write this letter in Col. Perkins's[2] room, while visiters are talking. Believe me, my dear Sir,

ever sincerely Yours, Charles Sumner

ALS MHi (68/386, PCS)

1. Everett replied to CS on 4 August 1848, stating that while he sympathized with the Buffalo convention's goals, he had "an extreme dislike of *third* parties . . . to advance some single principle." Believing that he should remain loyal to the Whigs, Everett stated that he had no choice but to vote for Taylor (Cambridge, 6/283, PCS).

2. Most likely Thomas Handaysd Perkins (1764–1854), Boston merchant and founder of the Perkins Institution for the Blind, who spent two weeks in Saratoga Springs in July 1848 (L. Vernon Briggs, *History and Genealogy of the Cabot Family* [1927], 455).

To John McLean

Saratoga Springs July 31st 1848

My dear Sir,

I cannot forbear expressing our earnest desire that you should allow yr name to go before the Buffalo Convention *unreservedly*.

My own strong hope, & that of many others, is that you may be nominated for the Presidency. Still I cannot disguise from myself that Mr Van Buren's friends may probably prevail in the Convention. In that event, we wish to secure a more general & a Whig support by nominating you for the Vice-Presidency.

I should not venture to make this suggestion, if I did not feel that the importance & dignity of the movement are such as properly to enlist the most illustrious names, & still further, if I did not regard yr candidacy for the Vice-Presidency, as a certain introduction to the Presidency in 1852. Whatever may be the fate of the movement in 1848, *it must succeed in the next election*, & all would gladly turn to you at that period as their chief. Indeed, the contest of '48 would be practically a contest, whose triumph would be yours. In saying this, I do not express merely my own opinions.

Mr Dudley Selden, who happens to be now at this place, authorizes me to speak for him, in urging you to allow yr name to be used by the Convention. He will regard you, in the event of yr nomination to the Vice-Presidency, as practically our chief. I understand from him that Mr B. F. Butler takes the same view.

You will perceive that I write with freedom. My interest in the cause must be my apology. I trust that some friend at Buffalo will be authorized to act for you. Let me add that I feel new confidence in our movement. Your name only is wanted to give it a commanding force throughout the Free States.[1]

In Massachusetts, & even in Boston, the movement has spread beyond the most sanguine anticipation of it friends.

Believe me, my dear Sir,

Very faithfully Yours, Charles Sumner

P.S. I write amidst the interruption of conversation, which is going on about me.

ALS DLC (68/388, PCS)

1. No reply from McLean has been recovered. McLean vacillated about the presidential nomination, but eventually decided to stay with the Whig party (Frederick J. Blue, *The Free Soilers* [1973], 63–64). At the Buffalo convention 10 August, Salmon P. Chase stated, according to Dana, that "he was *authorised by J. McL.* to say that he refused to be a candidate, tho' his feelings were with us" (*The Journal of Richard Henry Dana Jr.*, ed. Robert F. Lucid, vol. 1 [1968], 350).

To George N. Briggs

Private

Boston Aug. 28th '48

My dear Sir,

The Free Soil State Convention will meet in Boston on the 6th Sept, to nominate electors for the Presidency, & candidates for Govnr & Lieut Gov. Their candidates will, of course, be exponents of the principles declared at Buffalo, & supporters of Van Buren & Adams.

I am one of many who are desirous of avoiding any opposition to you. Indeed, it would give me great pleasure to continue to vote for you. And it is on this account that I take the liberty, *thus informally*, & acting for myself only, to address you, in order to ascertain your position in this time of change.

I wish to know, whether you will accept a nomination from the Free-Soil Convention, & as an exponent of its principles, & a supporter of Van Buren & Adams. If you should decline this, I hope you will pardon me if I ask, whether it is yr intention to be a candidate for re-election. This last inquiry I am induced to make, with a view to aid the action of some friends in our Convention, who will be reluctant to take any steps, which may seem to conflict with yr personal desires. We have voted for you; we do not wish to vote against you.[1]

I count upon yr frankness to receive this letter in the spirit in which it is written, & remain, with great regard, my dear Sir,

very faithfully Yours, Charles Sumner

P.S. I have not conversed with Mr Hoar or Dr Palfrey on the subject;[2] but I have reason to believe that it will give them great pain to oppose yr re-election, should you be a candidate. I am not authorized to say that they would do it; but you are aware of their deep interest in the Free Soil Movement. We all hope to find you with us—at least so far as not to oppose us.

His Excellency, George N. Briggs

ALS NHi (68/402, PCS)

1. In his reply, 1 September 1848 (6/324, PCS), Briggs stated that he could not back Van Buren and listed a number of proslavery positions of the Free Soil candidate. He did not believe Van Buren had changed, as CS had insisted in his Faneuil Hall speech of 22 August, "The Party of Freedom" (Wks, 2:292). Briggs also informed CS that although he did not want to continue as governor, he would run again if asked.

2. According to Frank O. Gatell, Palfrey had also asked Briggs to run as a Free Soil candidate for governor (*John Gorham Palfrey and the New England Conscience* [1963], 173).

To Nathan Appleton[1]

Boston Aug. 31st 1848

Dear Sir,

On my return to Boston I found yr letter of Aug. 17th. The language of inquiry is now changed to that of denial & challenge, while the lordly tone is still preserved—perhaps unconsciously on yr part. Reasons are not set forth to shew that you have a special right to interrogate me.

In assigning these reasons, you refer to the Boston Whig, & proceed by implication to connect me with certain language said to have been used in that paper with regard to yourself.[2] I shrink from no responsibility for any word that I may write, say, or sanction; nor do I hesitate to declare that the general course & sentiment of the Boston Whig have had my cordial approval. It is, perhaps, not known to you, that, with the exception of a few weeks immediately after the death of J. Q. A., I have never had any editorial connexion with that paper, nor exercised any control over the articles published in it. I have sometimes written in it, though much more frequently in the Boston Courier. If the Whig has contained any remarks upon you, or any allusions to you—as you say it has—I have never in any way been a party to them; nor have I seen or known of them, except as you have, after the *publication* of the paper. To connect me with any such articles is as unreasonable as it would be for me to connect you with the venom of the Atlas, or the personalities of the Advertiser, when directed against me, because you are reputed to be an influential friend of those two papers, & to be a correspondent of one or both.

I make this explanation partly in reply to the insinuations of yr letter, & partly from a regard to the relations which have subsisted between us. I have occasion to remember you with kindness & respect; nor will it be easy for you, by any excess of anger or unfounded imputation, to make me think of you, except as a person, who has been to me a friend, & towards whom, through all differences of opinion, I have always hoped to act as became a friend. But let this pass. I have desired from the first to write to you frankly with regard to the matter of yr inquiry; but yr notes have been couched in a tone which seemed to forbid all correspondence. My first impulse was to leave yr letter of Aug. 17th unanswered; but when I thought that you had pronounced a statement of mine to be untrue, I determined to waive all exceptions to yr manner, & to shew to you the error in which you have fallen. ⟨It will be for you to determine⟩

You volunteer as the representative of a class of persons described in the speech at Worcester as authors of a "secret influence which went forth from among ourselves," & as uniting, or conspiring, with other classes at the South West & North East to promote the nomination of General Taylor.[3] I do not understand you as speaking for the "politicians" of New England, except so far as they are "interested in the cotton manufacture." Alluding to the charge of a combination among these persons, you proceed to say; "believing & professing to know all which can be known in relation to your assertion as connected with individuals interested in ye manufacture of cotton, I pronounce it utterly untrue."

If your denial had been as broad as the charge made at Worcester I should have proceeded, without any explanation, to cite Mr Truman Smith, & Mr John Davis, as "politicians" whose "secret influence" contributed powerfully to the nomination of General Taylor.[4] Whether you will regard them as "individuals interested in ye cotton manufacture" I know not; but you will not question that their public course has caused them to be regarded as representatives of this interest. If you ask for the evidence of this "secret influence," I refer you to Mr Charles Hudson, who will not deny that he wrote to Judge Allen, prior to the Whig Convention, apprizing him "of the manoevres which were going on" in Washington, & mentioning "one individual, Truman Smith, who was doing all in his power for Taylor." With regard to the influence exerted by Mr John Davis in favor of *General T.*[,] I will refer you to the report of the conversation of the Indiana & Ohio delegation with that gentleman, in which to their astonishment they found him "in favor of Taylor." You will find these matters exposed in Judge Allen's speech before the citizens of Worcester.[5]

And here let me remark, that when it is said there was a ⟨union⟩ combination between certain classes in different parts of the country, it is not meant that every individual of these classes participated in it. Not all "cotton-planters & flesh-mongers"—not all the "cotton-spinners & traffickers" united; but individuals so prominent in those respective classes combined in the support of Taylor as to justify the remark that the classes combined. A review of some earlier matters will help us to see this aright.

If we glance at the politics of Mass. during the last 3 or 4 years, we shall find that certain prominent gentlemen "interested in the cotton manufacture" & exercising much influence as "politicians" over our Commonwealth, have generally discountenanced those measures, whose object was to oppose the extension of Slavery & the aggressions of the Slave-Power. They stood aloof from the State Convention, which was convened in the spring of 1845 to oppose the annexation of Texas. It was generally said & believed that they were opposed to the calling of the Convention—partly on the ground of private assurances from a slave-holding Senator. In the autumn of the same year, when efforts were made to rally the people, without distinction of party, against the admission of Texas as a *Slave-State*—the opposition being founded on the identical question of the Wilmot Proviso—these same gentlemen not only stood aloof from these efforts, but by formal letters, addressed to a Committee, discountenanced them.[6] These letters were re-published in New Orleans, & were hailed with satisfaction throughout the slave-holding states. They were considered as the voices of "individuals interested in the cotton manufacture." At the same time that the opposition to the Annexation of Texas was abandoned by these gentlemen, the Tariff was urged by them with especial ardor. It was pressed upon the attention of our State & of Congress, & was treated as the important issue before the country. It was then that a Senator of our Legislature in his place said that "the reign of Cotton had endured long enough. ⟨that of Conscience ought to begin."⟩[7] The Mexican War broke forth. A member of the Massachusetts delegation [*Winthrop*] supposed to be particularly connected with those "interested in the cotton manufacture" voted for the preamble of the War Bill, containing a falsehood, & afterward voted supplies to carry on a war, which has been declared by our Legislature, by solemn resolutions, passed after debate, to be a war for the extension of Slavery & the strengthening of the Slave-Power. In this course he was upheld by "individuals interested in the cotton manufacture." Time advances; & certain "politicians" at the South-West, slave-holders, & friends of the extension of Slavery, bring forward General T. as a candidate for the Presidency. In the discussion which ensues, he is opposed in New England, & particularly in Massachusetts, on the ground that he is the hero of an unjust war, & that he is not known to be opposed to the extension of Slavery. The prominent gentlemen "interested in the cotton manufature" do not unite in this opposition.

Various steps ensue. In Feb. Mr Lawrence addresses a letter to Philadelphia[8] in which he suggests a paralell between Taylor & Washington.

John Quincy Adams dies. His remains are attended by a Congressional Committee, on which was placed the most prominent Southern & South-Western slave-holding partizans of Gen. Taylor. New relations are said to be established between these partizans, & "politicians" & others here "interested in the cotton manufacture." The confidence of these partizans is said to be raised; & on their return to Washington at least one of them is reported as saying in conversation on the floor of the House that certain persons in Boston (mentioning the names of several "interested in the cotton manufacture") had said that Massachusetts [could?] be carried for Taylor. The impression becomes stronger & stronger in the public mind that there are "secret influences" in Boston in favor of Taylor, & *in concert or harmony with those proceeding from the South West.*

At length March 27th, the New York Tribune, in an editorial article, distinctly charged "a section of active & influential politicians" in Boston with "*manoeuvres* to carry the New England delegation at Philadelphia for Genl. T., & *thus* secure the nomination of a prominent & active Bostonian for the Vice Presidency[.]"[9] This charge directly made & widely circulated was so much in harmony with the previous conduct of "active & influential politicians"—particularly of those "interested in the cotton manufacture,"—as to awaken belief in many minds. This belief was strengthened by the appearance shortly afterwards in a New York paper of a letter which was said by the Tribune to be "from an unnamed but well-known Bostonian, who has been proposed for Vice President on the Taylor ticket, affirming that Taylor, if nominated, can carry the Whig vote of New England."

Public report also said, & it was never contradicted, that the Representative from Boston—the Speaker of the House [*Winthrop*]—supposed to be connected with "individuals interested in the manufacture of cotton," was friendly to the elevation of Taylor, & was in confidential relations with his South-Western partizans.

Public report also said the same—& it was never contradicted—with regard to other "individuals interested in the manufacture of cotton."

I am one, Sir, who believed these charges & reports both as to "manoeuvres" & "secret influences." I believed, as I said at Worcester, that there were "secret influences from among ourselves which contributed powerfully to the nomination of General Taylor." Is not this too true?

The public & private history of the Philadelphia [*Convention*] completes this hasty sketch of the evidence of the combination which I have described. [*inserted in margin*] To characterise this in proper terms, it must be borne in mind, that ⟨the nomination of Taylor in such a combination by Massachusetts men⟩ it involved the betrayal of the part of Massachusetts men of the policy & principles, solemnly declared by our Legislature & in successive Whig Conventions, & also the abandonment of Mr Webster, who had been brought forward by the Whig State Convention. It was treacherous to Freedom, & to Mr Webster. [*end insert*] Such a combination, for such a purpose is odious. It is worse than the combination to carry the Missouri Compromise. It is unholy. It may justly be called a conspiracy.

Here I might fitly conclude, leaving it to yr candor to determine if I have not fully encountered yr denial. But I will not leave the matter here. That I may not seem to use too strong language, or to draw inferences too strong from the facts set forth, I propose to communicate some portions of a conversation which took place between Mr Lawrence

& myself on an evening during the last week of May, some ten days before the Convention at Philadelphia. In doing this, I wish to premise, that I have always regarded this conversation as belonging to the confidence of friendship; nor do I consider myself entitled to divulge it to the public. I think, however, that, after the bravado of yr letter, I may be pardoned for imparting it to you. It will be for you to verify it by consultation with Mr Lawrence, & to make such use of it as you shall see fit.

I had passed an ⟨pleasant⟩ evening at Mr Lawrence's, in compliance with an express invitation. No allusion was made to politics till I rose to go. I had carefully avoided them. It was then half past 10 oclk. Reference was made to the Democratic Convention then in session when Mr Lawrence said that he would tell me who the Convention at Philadelphia must nominate for the Presidency. "Who?" said I.—"General Taylor" said he, "for he is the only man who can be elected." I expressed my hope that the Convention would do no such thing. This seemed to open the whole subject, & an earnest conversation ensued, which lasted beyond midnight.

I soon discovered that Mr L. was a warm partizan of Genl. T. I had supposed as much from all that was before the public; but I felt pained to receive such strong assurances of it from his own lips. I ventured, with unstudied plainness of speech, to remonstrate with him. I said to him, "I am yr friend—I have faith in the sincerity, the goodness & generosity of yr nature—I do not believe you actuated in yr present course by a desire for the Vice Presidency—I have often defended you against this charge—; & I now plead with you to withdraw from this movement in which you are involved." I afterward said—"You have recently given $50,000 to Harvard College—I honor you for this munificence; but I cannot forbear saying that the evil which will ensue from yr participation in this movement for Taylor will counterbalance all the good which can arise from yr munificence. As you value yr own good name, & that of yr family, I exhort you to withdraw from the movement." I cannot forget Mr Lawrence's answer. We were then standing in the entry at the head of his stairs. Apparently penetrated by the earnestness of my manner, & yielding for a moment to the urgency of my entreaties, he said;—"*What can I do about it; I am in up to the eyes.*—"Get out of it" I replied, "It is never too late to begin to do right. Your influence is great, & I firmly believe, that, if earnestly exerted from this moment, you might defeat the nomination of Taylor."

The impression which seemed to have been produced lasted but for a moment; for Mr L. soon proceeded to defend the nomination of Taylor. To my remark that the intelligence & morals of the Commonwealth would be against his course he replied buoyantly that I was mistaken. When I said, that I happened to know, that all the professors at Harvard University were against Taylor, &, as I thought, would never vote for him, he said; "I don't wish to know their opinions; I want to know how the truckmen will go." When I told him that, if Taylor was nominated, an opposition to him would be organized at once in this Commonwealth, he said it would consist of very few persons; & when I mentioned that Worcester Co would sustain Charles Allen, he said, *"John Davis & Gov. Lincoln will take care of Worcester Co."*—thus giving me to understand that these gentlemen were friendly to Taylor.

In the course of our conversation Mr L. asked me if I knew Mr Choate's position. "I know nothing about it" was my reply, "but I trust he is for Mr Webster."—*"He is for Taylor"* said Mr L. *"I have not seen him"* he continued, *"but he is for Taylor."* I still repeated my regret at hearing it suggested that Mr Choate was in a movement of so discreditable a character.

Mr L. seemed anxious to explain to me the circumstances, under which he had consented to have his name brought forward for the Vice-Presidency. *I understood that it was to be on the same ticket with Taylor.* He said that, when he received a request to allow his name to be brought forward, *he had called together a circle of his [old?] friends, & in his answer, had followed their advice.*—I regretted that he had not spurned the proposals.

My last words addressed to Mr L. from the steps of his house were to this effect—"It is not too late; do abandon this movement. Give up Taylor."

I cannot furnish this sketch of my conversation with Mr Lawrence without renewing the expression of my confidence in the many virtues of his character. I do not believe that he intrigued for the Vice Presidency—nor am I inclined to believe that he desired it. Of course I do not believe that there was a "bargain" between him & the partizans of Taylor. But I cannot disguise my conviction, that, in an unhappy hour—unhappy for our country & for his own fame—he surrendered to the desire of fraternity with slave-holding politicians, even at the cost of principle, which as a son of Massachusetts, he should have guarded to the last. I believe that he will yet regret his course.

Thus much in answer to yr challenge I think, after this review, you will pardon me, if I repeat the charge I made at Worcester. I do not question yr denial, so far as it relates to yourself. I must say again, that no persons familiar with the politics of the country can doubt that such a combination existed as I have described; & that Massachusetts "politicians" & "individuals interested in the cotton manufacture" were *"in up to the eyes*[10] ⟨You are right in supposing that I meant "to attach something dishonorable to the parties concerned"⟩

Dft MH-H (63/272, PCS)

1. Although an LS exists (68/404, PCS), CS's draft (one of his few in the entire correspondence) has been included instead, since the cancellations reveal some shifts in his thinking. The LS bears CS's complimentary close, "Faithfully yours" in his own hand, and his signature. Except for more frequent paragraphing, the text is essentially the same as this draft. CS's letter is his final reply in a heated exchange with Appleton, beginning 6 July 1848. See Appleton to CS, [6 July], 31 July, 17 August, and 4 September (6/228, 277, 291, 331), and CS to Appleton, 8 July and 12 August (68/366 and 394). Appleton declared in his letter of 17 August (6/291) that CS's remarks about the "lords of the loom" in his speech at the Free Soil Convention at Worcester, 29 June, were "utterly untrue." In his letters CS objected to Appleton's "tone" and defended his charge against the cotton manufacturers. After Appleton's reply on 4 September (6/331), the two apparently did not correspond again.

2. In his 17 August letter, Appleton stated that the *Boston Daily Whig* "repeatedly brought me before the public, and justified the doing so because it considered me the living embodiment of the cotton manufacturing policy." For example, *Whig* attacks on Appleton for his support of Texas annexation and cotton manufacturing had appeared in the 8, 14 August, and 12 November 1846 issues.

3. In his charge on 29 June that a conspiracy existed between slaveholders and New England cotton manufacturers, CS declared, "I cannot forbear alluding, however, to the aid which his [*Taylor's*] nomination derived from a quarter of the country which should have encountered it with an inexorable opposition,—I refer to New England, and especially to Massachusetts. I speak only what is now too notorious, when I say, that it was the secret influence which went forth from among ourselves, that contributed powerfully to this consummation. Yes! it was brought about by an unhallowed union—conspiracy, rather let it be called—between two remote sections of the country—between the politicians of the South-West and the politicians of the North-East; between the cotton-planters and flesh-mongers of Louisiana and Mississippi, and the cotton spinners and traffickers of New England,—between the lords of the lash and the lords of the loom" ("Union Among Men of All Parties Against the Slave Power and the Extension of Slavery," *Orations and Speeches* [1850], 2:256–57).

4. Truman Smith (1791–1884), U.S. congressman (Whig, Conn.), 1839–43, 1845–49; U.S. senator, 1849–54. In his reply of 4 September 1848 (6/331) Appleton stated that both Smith's and Davis's actions were "open and aboveboard," not secret, and that Smith had no ambitions to be the Whig vice presidential nominee.

5. Allen's speech, published in the *Boston Daily Whig* (24 June 1848:1–2), stated that Taylor's nomination "was made NOT AT PHILADELPHIA, BUT AT WASHINGTON, and through the influence of members of Congress at Washington, from all parts of the country."

6. See CS to Nathan Hale, 28 November 1845.

7. Probably E. Rockwood Hoar. See Moorfield Storey and Edward W. Emerson, *Ebenezer Rockwood Hoar: A Memoir* (1911), 43–44.

8. Abbott Lawrence's letter to the Philadelphia Whigs of 17 February, printed in the *Boston Daily Atlas* (25 February 1848:2), stated that if Taylor were the Whig nominee, he would be elected president and serve the nation well. Lawrence praised Washington in paragraph 1 and in paragraph 2 indicated his "highest respect and regard for General Taylor." Thus a parallel was implied.

9. The *New York Daily Tribune* (27 March 1848:2) stated that Massachusetts' sup-

port for Webster was only a cover for its real choice, Taylor; *Tribune* readers should decide for themselves if the *Boston Daily Atlas* was a "party" to this "game."

10. Appleton's reply of 4 September to CS discounted CS's remarks as insubstantial; he said CS's only real complaint against the "lords of the loom" was that they supported Taylor. He saw no connection between CS's lengthy description of his conversation with Abbott Lawrence and CS's accusation that Lawrence's behavior was part of a "conspiracy." Stating that he openly tried to help Lawrence secure the nomination for Whig vice president, Appleton once again denied that his efforts implied any conspiracy with the South. He regretted that CS's talents were "more than thrown away" with his Free Soil advocacy.

To Joshua R. Giddings

Boston Sept 3d '48

My dear Sir,

I was gratified by yr favor of Aug. 24th, & the encouragement it afforded.[1] I received it a short time before one of our meetings, & could not forbear reading some passages from it, which I see the papers have mis-represented. I expressly said that you forbore to express any definite opinion with regard to the vote of Ohio.

Our ratification meetings have been large & enthusiastic beyond expectation.[2] Our meeting at Faneuil Hall was prodigious in numbers & in determination. I have never seen so powerful a demonstration in Boston. That at Salem surpassed any political meeting ever held in that place. And so throughout the State Free Soil meetings & speakers seem to excite overwhelming favor.

Many of our friends are sanguine that we shall carry Massachusetts. This is my own belief. The people every where are with us.

Mr Webster's speech at Marshfield, so far as I can judge from what I hear, will not damage our movement. He was described by those who heard him, as talking like a man angry with every body.[3]

Still I cannot disguise that Mr Van Buren's past course puts a load upon the cause, which I regret that it is obliged to bear. Here in Massachusetts that is felt more than, perhaps, any where else. With McLean we should have swept the state easily. I cannot express to you how easily. Is it too late for him to write a letter approving what was done at Buffalo? Think of this.

Our State Convention takes place Sept. 6th & 7th. John Van Buren is to be here. We anticipate a great gathering.

[*George N.*] Briggs & Reed[4] both sustain Taylor. We shall be obliged to oppose them; & shall have candidates of our own every where. *We are a new party*—entirely.

Yrs faithfully, Charles Sumner

ALS OHi (68/411, PCS)

1. Giddings wrote from Jefferson, Ohio, that attendance at Free Soil meetings was three times that at Whig rallies. He expected Van Buren and Adams to carry the county and district, but was doubtful about the entire state (24 August 1848, 6/304, PCS).

2. Both Free Soil ratification meetings on 22 August 1848 at Faneuil Hall and 30 August at Salem were described as crowded. The Boston *Daily Evening Transcript* (23 August 1848:2) called the Faneuil Hall audience "enthusiastic and intelligent." The *Boston Daily Atlas* (31 August 1848:2) said that most attended the Salem meeting out of curiosity.

3. In his "Speech At Marshfield," 1 September 1848, Webster declared that, although the Taylor nomination displeased Massachusetts Whigs, the nomination was fairly conducted and was the choice of Whigs in many nonslaveholding states. Webster listed a number of proslavery actions taken by Van Buren, and reiterated his original intention not to oppose the Whig nominee (*Writings and Speeches*, ed. James W. McIntyre [1903], 4:123–44.

4. John Reed (1781–1860), U.S. congressman (Fed., Whig, Mass.), 1813–17, 1821–41; lieutenant governor of Massachusetts, 1845–51.

To Henry Gilpin

Boston Nov. 8th '48

My dear Mr Gilpin,

I am obliged by yr kind & pleasant note.[1]

The urn has been shaken, & our fates have come forth. The papers will tell you what we have done in Massachusetts. I am inclined to think this has been the scene of the closest contest—that there has been more force in the field on both sides, or rather on all sides—more speakers—& more money spent here than in any other state. The *money-power* has put forth all its Briarean arms.

Our friends feel satisfied with Massachusetts. The Taylorites are defeated for the present. Their ticket, if chosen at all, must come in through the Legislature. By our law, a majority—not merely a plurality—is required; & if it is not obtained the choice devolves upon the Legislature.

Next Monday we choose Governor, State officers & members of Congress. You kindly refer to me as candidate. I am put up as a mark; for there is no chance for us here in Boston. I am exposed, perhaps, to as strong a pressure as can be encountered in the whole country.

If Taylor is elected, as seems probable now, we must rally our forces on the basis of the Northern Democracy. We must plant ourselfs on the Declaration of Independence & the Constitution of the United States, & insist upon bringing back the Govt. to the true spirit of these instruments, so that it shall be administered, not in the spirit of Slavery, but of Freedom. Here is something truly conservative & reforming. We shall be the party of Conservative Reform.

It seems to me that our friends ought to hold a consultation speedily in order to mark out our future course, which should be developed in an address to the people of the U.S.

It is supposed here that Pennsylvania has gone for Taylor.[2] Believe me, my dear Sir,

very faithfully Yours, Charles Sumner

Hon. H. D. Gilpin

ALS NSyU (68/438, PCS)

1. Gilpin wrote (2 November 1848, 6/375, PCS) to congratulate CS on his nomination by the Free Soil caucus, district 1, Massachusetts, for the congressional seat held by Winthrop. CS's letter of acceptance of 26 October 1848 is published in Wks, 2:301–15.

2. Gilpin had written that he thought Cass would carry Pennsylvania; in fact Taylor did.

To Salmon P. Chase

Boston Nov. 16th 1848

My dear Sir,

Our contest is at last closed—for the present. I have been so deeply engaged in it, that I have had no time for correspondence. You also have been constantly occupied.

Looking over the field now, I feel that we have cause for high satisfaction. We have found a large number of men through all the Free States, who are willing to leave the old parties & join in a new alliance of principle.[1] The public mind has been stirred on the subject of slavery to depths never before reached; & much information with regard to the Slave-Power has been diffused in quarters heretofore ignorant of this enormous tyranny.

What shall we do in future? Here in Mass. the old Democratic party is not merely defeated—but, as it seems to me, irretrievably broken. Is it not in the same state throughout the country? In Ohio & the Western States, it has a numerical superiority,—but it has no *principles* on which it can rally. It must seek safety upon our Buffalo platform. The only opposition that can be formed to Taylor's Administration will be upon our platform.[2]

It seems to me that an Address to the People of the U.S. should be issued as soon as possible, summing up the results of this contest, & rallying our friends to continue firm in their new organization. Unfortunately we have no National Committee. It might be prepared by delegates from the State Committees or by our friends at Washington on the opening of Congress. It seems to me important that such a document should be put forth.

I would have it develop fully the encroachments of the Slave-Power—its monopoly of office—& its gradual usurpation of our Govt, so that it has come to be administered, not in the spirit of Freedom, but of Slavery. And it should propose as our object—the prevention of the extension of Slavery—the [deviance?] of the National Govt from all support of Slavery—& finally, the overthrow of the Slave-Power, or in other words, the establishment of such a prevailing public opinion, that Slavery shall no longer in any way influence our National Govt. I am thus particular in dwelling on these latter points; because some persons suggest, that with the settlement of the question of the Wilmot Proviso, our whole platform will disappear. This is not so.

I am curious to know how the field seems to you at the present moment, from yr point of view.

In Massachusetts I think the battle has raged with more ardor than in any other part of the country. The force brought into the contest on all sides has been great. The Money-Power (now in combination with the Slave-Power) has put forth all its energies. The sums said to have been subscribed in Boston are prodigious. The Taylorites are jubilant; but I think they will lose something of their harmony in determining who shall have the "spoils."

It seems to me not improbable, that Genl Taylor will lean for support [upon] the South & South-West; & I should not be surprized if he was sustained by that part of the country almost without distinction of party. Joined to this will be the *sea board*. But the Great North West (greater by the "All Hail Hereafter") will be against him, & also the interior of the Northern States. In these we shall find the elements out of which to construct an oppostion.

Surely the Whigs have a difficult office to organize their party to sustain Taylor, & especially with a view to the succession. Our mission is simple, to stand by our principles.

I hope yr health has stood firm through yr labors, & that you are still fresh for duty. Much will be expected from you.—I am sorry that Corwin has surrendered to false gods.[3] I do lean to him warmly. Let me hear from you soon.

As ever faithfully Yours, Charles Sumner

P.S. What is Judge McLean's position now?[4]

S. P. Chase Esq.

ALS DLC (68/443, PCS)

1. The 1848 presidential election, 7 November, gave Taylor 163 electoral votes, Cass 127, and Van Buren none. Taylor had 1,360,099 votes, Cass 1,220,544, and Van Buren 291,263. Van Buren ran second to Taylor in Massachusetts, New York, and Vermont, and was instrumental in giving New York to Taylor, and Ohio to Cass. In Massachusetts, 45 percent voted for Taylor, 28 percent for Van Buren, and 27 percent for Cass. Two senators and twelve representatives were elected to Congress as Free Soilers (Frederick J. Blue, *The Free Soilers* [1973], 141–46, 302).

2. The Free Soil platform of 1848 contained fourteen resolutions, among them that Congress should not interfere with slavery within a state, that Congress had no power to establish slavery in any territory, and that Congress should make this limitation explicit by means of a congressional act (ibid., 293–96).

3. Corwin had campaigned actively for Taylor in Ohio (ibid., 116).

4. McLean did not publicly support Taylor in the election (ibid., 116–17).

To Samuel Lawrence

Boston Nov. 29th 48—[1]

My dear Sir,

The volcanic flames of the election, upheaving the whole land, have now subsided, & even its heats are giving way to a more salubrious atmosphere. I will take advantage of the change to appeal once more to the candor of an old friend.

Yr letter of Nov. 7th was duly recd.[2] I need not say, that I read it with pain. It seemed to me [this?] most unworthy of you. I shewed to two friends of yours & mine. One said—"if Lawrence sees this five years from now, he will be mortified at having written it." Another said; "his better nature will soon return to him, & he will regret what he has done."

I thought of answering it at once; but was unwilling to take my pen while under the first influence of yr ungenerous words; nor did I believe that you would be in a mood to receive with candor what I should write. Persuaded that I can now address you with calmness, I venture to believe that you may not be entirely insensible to the [claim?] of justice.

What are the facts? Sometime before ye election, in public addresses, at Lowell & elsewhere, I read an extract from a letter of yours, dated Sept 26th 1848 in the papers,[3] in which you assign reasons for the embarasments in the wollen manufactures. I read all of yr letter that bore on the subject[;] I quoted it fairly & fully; & then dwelt particularly upon the closing sentence, that "all the old & new machinery would be in full operation *within a year*."—that is as early Sept 26th 1849—*before* ye meeting of ye new Congress for which a change in ye Tariff might be hoped.

I made no allusion to the question of Free Trade.[4] I certainly have never been its advocate; &, so far as I understand the subject, I think there should be at the present moment a Tariff furnishing moderate protection to our manufactures.

But I did draw the conclusion from yr letter [*26 September 1848*], that in yr opinion, the wollen business, would rally without a Tariff. In this conclusion I have been sustained by others.—by newspapers & public speakers. You probably know that Mr S. C. Phillips often discussed yr letter & drew from it ye same conclusion; & a paper which I send herewith will shew you that Mr Huntington of Northampton[5] also did ye same.

If I did you wrong, then, it was in common with others.

You authorized the Atlas to say that ye letter of Mr Lawrence as quoted by Mr S. is a perversion of his "meaning, as any one who will read it will himself see."[6] If I perverted your meaning, then, of course the speakers and newspapers, who have used yr letter as I did, have "*perverted*" it also.

Now, in truth, nobody has "perverted yr meaning"—nobody has misquoted you—nobody has done you the slightest injustice.

If any person is to be blamed it is yourself; for not saying in yr letter what you wished to say, or what you now wish you had said! The letter itself is plain, & explicit. You now say you "based yr predictions of better times on the belief that G. T. wld be elected & that a new Congress wld make a new Tariff at the session of 1849–50." And yet in yr letter [*26 September 1848*] you make no allusion to the influence of the Tariff & expressly say that "all the old & new machinery would be in full operation in one year"—from Sept 28th 1848; thus seeming to exclude the idea of influence from a new Tariff.

Most certainly Mr Phillips & Mr Huntington & myself have not all "perverted your meaning." We may have *mistaken* the idea you intended to convey; but,—you would hardly be willing to say now, I believe, that we had "perverted" it.

It was with the feeling that, in a hasty moment, you had done me injustice, that I wrote my letter of Nov. 6th.[7] I thought you would see it much as I did, & that you wld be swift to repair the wrong ⟨you had done me⟩, knowing full well the "truth of what was said of old, that he who has done a wrong—& not who has received it—is to be pitied."

In yr letter of Nov. 7th you did not withdraw or explain the original charge; nor do you expressly repeat it; but insinuate it. [*inserted in margin*] This is a repetition of yr original injustice [*end insert*]. You then proceed, to animadvert [on?] me in connexion with other matters,—in no respect affecting the question of my use of yr letter. ⟨Out of that fullness the heart speaketh; & I might [add?] you apply to me an epithet⟩ Of course, by so doing, you do not in any respect fortify the original charge against me, nor do you excuse the wrong you have done me. For, my error on other ocasions can have no bearing on the point to which I called your attention.

Departing then from the subject in hand—& apparently under ye influence of a sentiment so bitter as yr nature can well enlist—you proceed to speak of certain language used by me last June at Worcester. You do not quote the whole passage, shewing the context; nor do you lead me to believe that you did me the justice when you spoke at the City Hall, to quote the whole passage.[8] It does not appear that you took exception to the charge which was contained in that passage [[Worcester speech]] against certain persons in two remote sections of ye country, but simply against certain phrases, which, according to you, "every lover of his country must regard with a feeling of abhorrence." You do not say why this feeling should be excited; but leave it to be inferred that there is something in these phrases, ⟨independent of the original charge against the parties⟩ which is most exceptionable. And you then volunteer to speak of an old friend in language ⟨which seems to deny those qualities of truth, sincerity & benevolence⟩, personally offensive, which you would apply to very few enemies.

I will not now undertake any vindication of the phrase, to which you refer. It is—at the present—probable that you & I could not be brought to regard them in the same light. They were the natural expression of an intensive sentiment of indignation at the unhallowed union as it seemed to me, which had taken place, between two different classes of persons, in abandonment of all those sacred principles which every American & every Xtian should have at heart. As such they came from the depths of my inmost sentiments & convictions. You certainly have [many?] a right to differ from them—to question them, to condemn them. And I certainly should also welcome any kind & honest expression of difference. But a regard not merely for the sanctity of friendship, but for the courtesies of private life, should have made you hesitate to employ the language which you did.

[*inserted in margin*] I might borrow a [string?] from those words of ye late P. T. Jackson,[9] as quoted by Mr [Downer?] "I fear" said he at yr [stand?] of ye annexation of Texas, "that ye *moral principle* of ye people of Boston on polit. subjects is not strong enough to resist the *money influence*." [*end insert*]

Most certainly I will not imitate your [[bad]] example. But you will easily see, that if I were so disposed—if I would descend to any such work—I might borrow from the [well?] some of the epithets, & which, it unhappily applies to you & those [particularly?] with whom you act, might find some justification in ⟨your exclusive advocacy of a Tariff⟩, your ⟨political answer⟩ position & opinions. In this way, I should do no good, & I should do you injustice. You are honest in your opinions; but you are not more honest than those with whom I have acted. I say now, as I always said in public—as I said at Lowell, that I claim but this one thing for my opinions,—that they are honestly entertained, & what I claim for myself I cheerfully [concede?] to those from whom it is my misfortune to differ. Let me not then return to you any of the words which you were willing to address to me.

Not content with volunteering offensive epithets to me, you next volunteer to express yr pain at the part I am acting. If this seemed to proceed from a sentiment of good will, I should be churlish not to welcome it. The warnings of a friend are precious; but you will pardon me if I do you injustice, when I say, that it seems to be infected by the bitterness of your whole letter. It certainly has not the pleasant odor of friendship. And you then proceed to rebuke me "for taking hold of this one idea of Slavery," & tell me that I am "in a fair way of becoming severed from a very large circle of friends, who give dignity & honor to our [common?] country." "I could name" you say, "scores & scores of men whom you have honored yr whole life, who regret & condemn the course you have taken."

Let us look at this one moment. I might well deny that I taken hold of "this one idea of Slavery." Beyond my profession, & my customary pursuits, much of my thoughts have been given to the cause of Peace, & still further to efforts to introduce into politics the principles of Xstianity. It is especially in carrying out these latter principles, that I have been induced to oppose Slavery. But admitting what is not true that I have taken hold of this *one idea* of Slavery, I might well ask, whether this is not better & more Xtian than to take hold of the *one idea* of the Tariff—whether, whatever may be the judgment of "the scores & scores of men" to whom you refer, I am not more truly obeying those high behests, which you & I both recognise as a rule of life. So doing I can well afford to be indifferent even to those "scores & scores." The world with ignorant or intolerant judgments may condemn; the countenances of companions may be averted; the hearts of friends may grow cold; but ye consciousness of duty done will be sweeter than ye applause of ye world, than ye countenance of companion, or ye heart of friend.

And what humane man wld put this great question of ye extension of Slavery in companion with ye Tariff—important as the latter may be. Let me bring the case home to you. You love your wife & sweet children—infinitely more than all the mills in Lowell. If any tyrant should propose to carry away this beautiful wife & happy children, & separate them from you forever, I know how yr heart would throb with irrepressible anxiety; nor would you hesitate to sacrifice every dollar which you possessed to save yourself from this bereavement. You would rejoice in poverty thus obtained. But a tyranny in our Govt. proposes to separate not one family but many families, & to carry them away into distant slavery. It is true these miserable victims are not of color; but they are our bretheren, children with us of the same Father; & it is difficult to see how any person, who feels the Xtian truths, can regard their separation as less atrocious than would be that of yr family. Should we not then exert ourselves to prevent this, in disregard even of the mills of the Lowell? "Do unto others as you would have them do unto you." Let us in wealth or comfort, do now towards those poor slaves, as we would have them do unto us, were our situation theirs.

I am not insensible to the kindly regard of my fellow-men. I have always treasured the delights of friendship; but these I willingly sacrifice if need be, to bear my testimony in this great cause. How small, indeed, is my offering, compared with what we are required to make. The favor or yr friendship that is lost on account of such efforts—even if it be from "scores & scores of men," can be of slender value. [[In this cause I have no personal interests to promote—no selfish desires to gratify]]—. ⟨I see only my duty⟩

And now in conclusion, let me say frankly; You have done me injustice; [[first in your original aspersion through the Atlas upon the fairness with which I quoted on yr letter; & next in yr apparent perseverence in the original wrong; & then again, in addressing to me a letter, which in its tone is entirely inconsistent with true friendship.]] I do not know that you will yet perceive this; but I cannot doubt, that, if hereafter, you should revert to this correspondence, you will look upon your part with ⟨lively⟩ regret.[10] For myself, there is one rule which I have steadily pursued. The records of kindness & friendship, of which I have been the partaker, are engraven [on?] my heart; the wrongs I have received are written in water.

F—— Y——

Dft MH-H (63/286, PCS)

1. Lawrence dated CS's actual letter, which has not been recovered, 30th November 1848 (4 December, 6/398, PCS).

2. Lowell, Mass., 6/380.

3. Printed in the *Boston Daily Republican*, 3 November 1848:2. In his draft of 6 November 1848 to Lawrence 63/280, CS stated he used Lawrence's letter of 26 Sep-

tember 1848 to counter the argument that the current economic "derangement" was due to the Tariff of 1842 (i.e., 1846), inferring from Lawrence's letter that no new tariff was needed. The *Republican* claimed CS had used Lawrence's letter "honestly and fairly."

4. In his letter to CS of 2 November (6/377), Lawrence declared a free trade policy to be "suicidal."

5. Probably a Massachusetts state legislator from Northampton.

6. In his letter to CS of 7 November, Lawrence stated that he had told William Schouler, editor of the *Boston Daily Atlas*, that CS's quotations from Lawrence's 26 September letter intimated that Lawrence approved of the Tariff of 1846, and he asked Schouler to correct that impression.

7. CS asked Lawrence, in his draft of 6 November, whether Lawrence had initiated the *Atlas* statement that CS's use of Lawrence's letter was "a perversion of his [*Lawrence's*] meaning." He hoped Lawrence would redress "the injustice which has been done me by the Atlas, & also by yourself."

8. Lawrence declared in his 7 November letter that his speech at Lowell on 6 November was necessitated to explain his position, after CS's misuse of his letter of 26 September. Lawrence stated that he then criticized CS's reference in his Worcester speech to "the unhallowed union . . . between the lords of the lash & the lords of the loom" because CS had appeared as a "demagogue" in uttering such words. On CS's Worcester speech, see CS to Nathan Appleton, 31 August 1848.

9. Patrick Tracy Jackson (1780–1847), Lowell cotton manufacturer.

10. In his answer to CS's letter of 30 November, Lawrence stated that CS must stand as the "libeller of your immediate neighbors." Lawrence criticized CS's allies like Wilson, Keyes, and Van Buren, no models, he said, of Christian behavior. Abolitionists were responsible for slavery in four states, for the admission of Texas, the Mexican War, and would eventually break up the union. Concluded Lawrence, "You and I can never meet on neutral ground" (4 December 1848, 6/398).

To Henry W. Longfellow

Court St—Tuesday
[*5 December 1848*]

Dear Henry,

I am to lecture—as Emerson says "to read a lecture"—this evening at West Cambridge—say at 7 o'clk. I shall count upon leaving there before 9 o'clk—earlier I trust—it may be later however,—& reaching your roof for the night. I bespeak a bed & a welcome.

Ever thine, C. S.

P.S. I heard Emerson last evng on Plato[1]—a most curious cluster of fancies & philosophies, sometimes deep & most suggestive, then wild, vague & unsatisfactory, but expressed with a beauty, which ravished me. As I listened, I thought of the lotus-eaters. After him, I feel almost a nausea at all that I can do—at my scarlet, green-baize, holyoke-flower stuff.

ALS MH-H (68/450, PCS)

1. "Plato," at Freeman Place Chapel, Boston, 4 December 1848 (William Charvat, *Emerson's American Lecture Engagements: A Chronological List* [1961], 23).

To John Greenleaf Whittier

Boston Dec 6th '48

My dear Whittier,

Yr poem in the last *Era*[1] has touched my heart. Are you well? I fear that you are not. May God preserve you in strength & courage, for all good works.

I have yr new volume.[2] It is a precious collection, but where are the Poems of Labor? I rejoice that this volume is published. We will set our poets upon the slave-holders. These they cannot withstand. How much more powerful is a song than a bullet!

The literature of the world is turning against Slavery. We shall have it soon in a state of moral blockade. Then it must fall. We will treat it like a besieged city—cut off from all supplies.

I admire Bailey[3] as an editor very much. His articles shew infinite sagacity & tact. That in the last number on the old Democratic party is perfect.

Do you see the efforts to wriggle away from the Wilmot Proviso?[4] I fear that the artful dodgers will yet prevail; But I took my pen merely to ask after yr health. There are few to whom I would allot a larger measure of this world's blessings than to yourself,—had I any control; for there are few, who deserve them more. I trust to hear that you are strong in body, & happy in heart. Adieu.

Ever sincerely Yours, Charles Sumner

ALS MiMp (68/453, PCS)

1. "The Wish of Today" in the *National Era*, 30 November 1848:190.
2. *Poems by John G. Whittier* (1849).
3. Gamaliel Bailey (1807–59), editor of the *National Era*, 1847–59.
4. In his annual presidential message 5 December, Polk urged different sections of the U.S. to compromise in order to preserve and strengthen the Union. He stated that residents in the newly acquired southwest territories should themselves decide whether or not slavery should exist there; Congress should not interfere. Polk advocated use of the Missouri Compromise line, 36° 30′, if necessary, as "a middle ground of compromise" (*Globe*, 30th Cong., 2nd sess., appendix, 3–4).

To John Gorham Palfrey

Boston Jan. 4th '49

My dear Dr,

We all rejoice in our success through you & Allen. I wish much that an additional 100 or 200 had placed yr election beyond present question. But another time will do what is still left undone. You will succeed easily on the next trial.[1]

I note the wriggling efforts at Washington. The reconsideration, or postponement (the latter I fear) of Gott's resolution must be prevented.[2] I trust Mann will speak on that. I doubt not you are watching your opportunities.

I note also that the signal has been given to attack & run down Giddings & our other friends. This is the cue of Schouler, whose letters from Washington, so far as I have seen them have been the productions of a malignant viper.[3]

I have not seen Adams for several days. The Everetts propose to continue in Cambridge, which has given occasion to an old politician to observe—"My beloved Middlesex"!—And he added that Mr E. wld be brought forward against you. I mention this, because I thought you might hear it from some other quarter, & I wished to express my opinion most distinctly & unequivocally, that I do not think this within the range of probabilities. I came to this conclusion at once on hearing this, & have been confirmed in it by Mr Sparks, who mentioned to me a conversation with Mr Everett, which excludes all such idea. I do not know that he could resist the temptation of the Senate.[4]

You must be happy in Allen's triumph. His alliance with you & Giddings will give you great strength.

Ever Yrs, Charles Sumner

Hon. J. G. Palfrey—

ALS MH-H (68/478, PCS)

1. The Free Soiler Charles Allen defeated the Whig Charles Hudson for the congressional seat in the Worcester district. In his campaign for reelection, Palfrey refused to court the Democrats. Although he won more votes than any other candidate in the 1 January 1849 election, he failed to get the necessary majority (Frank O. Gatell, *John Gorham Palfrey and the New England Conscience* [1963], 178–80).

2. On 21 December 1848, Congressman Daniel Gott (1794–1864; Whig, N.Y.) moved that slave trade be prohibited in the District of Columbia. The motion to table failed twice, but Gott's resolution was eventually defeated (*Globe*, 30th Cong., 2nd sess., 83, 105, 107–8).

3. Giddings's bill to have a referendum on slavery in the District of Columbia with all males, including blacks, voting was criticized by Jacob Thompson (Dem., Miss.) and Patrick W. Tompkins (Whig, Miss.) and eventually defeated (ibid., 55–56). Schouler wrote that Giddings's bill was "clearly agitation" and that "fanatical demogogues" such as Giddings hurt more moderate efforts like the Wilmot Proviso. "When the Union is dissolved, we shall have King Giddings ruling the Northern dominions, and King Calhoun those of the South" (*Boston Daily Atlas*, 29 December 1848:2).

4. Everett had stepped down as Harvard's president and was succeeded by Jared Sparks. According to Gatell, Everett did have his eye on the Senate, and he did not run against Palfrey (*Palfrey*, 187–88).

To Salmon P. Chase

Boston Feb. 27th '49

My dear Sir,

It is then all true! I can hardly believe it. Ignorant as I am of the details of yr local politics I can only imperfectly comprehend the movement which has given our cause so triumphant a triumph in yr election.[1]

It does seem to me that this is "the beginning of the end." Yr election must influence all the Great West. Still more yr presence in the Senate will give an unprecedented impulse to the discussion of our cause. It will confirm the irresolute, quicken the indolent, & confound the trimmers. I know you will grapple at once with John C. Calhoun on any issue that he shall venture to make.

By the papers this morning I see that Mr Giddings was voted for to the last. This increases the perplexity with regard to yr local politics. I do honor Giddings so much, & confess my obligations to him so fully for his lead against Slavery, that I am sorry that he should be disappointed in any reasonable expectations. I trust he has not been. We have *him* already, & now we have *you*.

In my last I asked you to be good enough to send me another copy of yr Van Zandt argt, as I have given my copy away. And Judge Allen, who was with me a few days since, expressed a desire to possess a copy of it. Will you send one to his address—Charles Allen, Worcester, Mass.?—

It seems to me General Taylor will have a hard rub in the Senate. The elements of opposition will be strong, while his supporters will be of the most confused character. I am curious to know what course Seward[2] will take. I have always honored him for the generous sympathies which he avowed, & for his ability—I regretted his retrograde Taylorism—I trust he may be animated anew to an earnest unequivocal support of Freedom.

Ever sincerely Yours, Charles Sumner

Hon. S. P. Chase

ALS DLC (68/504, PCS)

1. Chase had secured a fusion of Free Democrats and Free Soilers in the Ohio legislature, who on 22 February 1849 elected him senator over the other leading candidate, Giddings. For a detailed discussion of these maneuvers, see Stephen Maizlish, *The Triumph of Sectionalism: the Transformation of Ohio Politics, 1844–1856* [1983], 124–46).

2. William H. Seward (1801–72; U.S. senator [Whig, Rep., N.Y.], 1848–61; U.S. secretary of state, 1861–69) had voted for Taylor in 1848 (Frederick J. Blue, *The Free Soilers* [1973], 112).

To Charles Timothy Brooks

Boston March 29th '49

My dear Brooks,

I have just learned the newspaper stir which my lecture occasioned in Newport. I regret that you should have suffered in it, though most grateful for yr apt defence.[1]

I spoke in my lecture[2] of two kinds of conservatism—one I called "proper" or "just"—& added that "though it may not always satisfy our judgment, it can never fail to command our respect." The other I called "bigotry"—That is all.

I am used to these things. I trust that you are not. I know, from experience, the misrepresentations to which a public speaker, who touches debatable matters, is exposed—particularly from those who take counsel of prejudice, rather than reason.

Yr opponent must be some cis-Atlantic Bob Acres.[3] I hope you have not been drawn into a duel by him. Don't.

I have delivered that Newport Lecture in a large number of places; but was not aware of any disturbance, hardly of any difference of opinion which it aroused. Verily, Newport must be a strange place. I had thought it dull. But this cannot be. It is sensitive. Like the gymnotus, it gives a shock to a man who barely touches it.[4] I shall be careful in future.

Ever sincerely Yours, Charles Sumner

P.S. My brother [*Albert Sumner*] sent me the papers containing the whole Iliad.

Revd Charles Brooks

ALS MH-AH (68/529, PCS)

1. Brooks had taken on CS's defense in the Newport *Daily News*, against a "Major G" who characterized CS's attack on conservatism as "*impious blasphemy*." Writing under the pen name "Paul," Brooks stated that G's attack was unjustified; he had taken CS's criticism out of context. The series of letters was published in a twenty-seven-page pamphlet as "The Sumner Controversy: A Series of Articles Published in the *Daily News* Relative to the Lecture on 'Human Progress' in 1849."

2. In "The Law of Human Progress" (1849) CS had described two kinds of conservatism: a "principle of moderation, honestly pursued, from motives of justice and benevolence, and promising the 'well-ripened fruits of wise delay'" versus another "which performs no good office, and cannot secure our respect. Child of indifference, of ignorance, of prejudice, of selfishness, it seeks to maintain things precisely as they are. . . . Such a conservatism is the bigotry of science, of literature, of jurisprudence, of religion, of politics" (36–37).

3. A character in Sheridan's *The Rivals* who challenges Captain Absolute to a duel.

4. Brooks replied (2 April 1849, 6/464, PCS) that the criticism of CS was atypical and that CS's address had been "universally welcomed" in Newport.

To Henry D. Gilpin

Boston June 5th '49

My dear Mr Gilpin,

A note from you is always pleasant, & your last is particularly so because of its friendly criticism.

I have not lately referred to Pope or Bolingbroke;[1] but I have a strong impression, that neither had any comprehension of the Law of Human Progress, & that the phrase *Whatever is, is right* was in part an expression of their want of faith. They inculcated submission to Providence, & harmony with its laws. But I did not suppose that they recognised the progressive improvement of man as ordained by one of these laws.

The phrase of Pope is often quoted as an excuse for blind adherence to the Present, & is doubtless pressed beyond the meaning of its author. I am glad that you have directed my attention to it.

I agree with you, that Mr Jefferson was an advocate of Progress of all kinds, & a believer in the Law.[2] It was not my purpose to throw any doubt upon this. In grouping several illustrations of doubts encountered by efforts for physical improvement, I could not resist the temptation of quoting the example of Mr Jefferson, as shewing at least how such doubts are apt to beset the most generous minds.

With many thanks for yr kindness, Believe me, my dear Sir,

very faithfully Yours, Charles Sumner

Hon. H. D. Gilpin

ALS NCD (68/573, PCS)

1. In his letter (2 June 1849, 6/515, PCS), Gilpin thanked CS for his address, "The Law of Human Progress," but said that CS did not do justice to Pope, whose argument in his "Essay on Man" Gilpin considered a "vindication of the great scheme of Providence." In his address, CS denounced the second kind of conservatism (see CS to Charles Brooks, 29 March 1849), stating that "it plants itself upon the irreligious sophism of Bolingbroke and Pope, that *Whatever is, is right*, or vainly exalts all that has been done by our ancestors as beyond addition and above amendment" ("The Law of Human Progress" [1849], 37). These references do not appear in CS's later version (Wks, 2:243–90). Henry St. John Bolingbroke (1678–1751), philosopher.

2. Gilpin wrote that CS had also been unfair to Jefferson. In criticizing those who defend the status quo, CS said of Jefferson: "Even Mr. Jefferson (and I cannot mention him as an immoderate conservative), when told that the State of New York had explored the route of a canal from the Hudson to Lake Erie and found it practicable, . . . replied, that 'it was a very fine project, and might be executed a century hence'" ("Law of Human Progress," 41–42).

To Amasa Walker[1]

Boston June 29th '49

Dear Walker,

Here is the Address.[2] I know yr friendship & candor, & ask only a careful perusal of what I have said. I think that you will see that I have presented our cause in such a way as not to *traverse* any principle which you hold, while I have avoided *traversing* any principle held by the conservatives of Law & Order. I hoped to reconcile all the friends of Peace & to point out a common ground on which all might meet. I will not yet dispair of this.

You will understand that I shall complain of no candid & honest & judicious criticism by any friend of Peace.[3] My views are now before the world—for criticism, if they will—for adoption, if they will. But I hope my critic will first understand me, before he criticises.

I believe that some will find that they misapprehended my positions. All who comprehend them will do me the justice to admit that they are in entire harmony with all that I have said before. Look at my letter to the Mayor preceding the 4th July Oration, & my admissions in that Oration, that the Navy might be employed as a *police*.[4] See also my Phi

Beta Kappa address at Cambridge, & my Amherst Address, & my substitute for Burritt's Pledge.

It seems to me of vast importance to our cause, to shew that it is thoroughly *practicable*. This is done by shewing that we aim to introduce among nations the same principles which prevail among towns & states. It would be wrong for Boston & Charlestown to fight, in order to determine a litigation between them, but it would not be wrong for Charlestown to defend itself against a mob of ruffians from Boston who might come over to rob, or to burn a Convent. At any rate, in condemning War, & in endeavors to induce nations to learn War no more, we assume a superfluous burthen, if we undertake to say, that it would be wrong for Charlestown, or any other place, or individual, to defend itself against riotous & offensive intervention from a neighbor. It is enough for our cause to say that the Institutions of War, & the whole War System is outrageous, unchristian, & radically wrong. There is ground enough—conservative enough,—radical enough.

Think of this.

Ever sincerely Yours, Charles Sumner

ALS MHi (68/600, PCS)

1. Amasa Walker (1799–1875), professor of political economy, Oberlin, 1842–48, and Amherst, 1859–69; U.S. congressman (Rep., Mass.), 1862–63. Walker was soon to attend the second General Peace Conference at Paris.

2. "War System of the Commonwealth of Nations," given to the American Peace Society 28 May 1849 (Wks, 2:329–429).

3. CS had written Walker on 11 June (68/583, PCS) about "misrepresentations" in *Burritt's Christian Citizen* (2 June 1849:2), criticisms he thought Walker endorsed. In reviewing CS's address the *Christian Citizen* regretted that its tone was "more conservative" than expected. The *Citizen* hoped it erred in inferring that "Mr. S. is not one of those who are willing to plant their feet upon the Christian law as the great foundation stone of the temple of Peace." Walker, however, replied that he liked CS's address and would soon write a review of it (12 June, 6/530).

4. In his letter to Thomas A. Davis, 10 July 1845, added as a preface to the second edition of "The True Grandeur of Nations," CS wrote that he did not intend to argue that "Force may not be employed, under the sanction of Justice, in the conservation of the laws and of domestic quiet." About the navy CS said, "So far as it may be necessary, as part of the *police* of the seas . . . it is a proper arm of Government" (56).

To Frances A. Longfellow

Boston Monday—[*July 1849*]

Dear Fanny,

I have just finished Lamartine's *Confidences* & also his *Raphael*. I do not remember whether you condemned the latter or the former or both.

The latter belongs to the school of *Werther*, & of *Jacopo Ortis*; but the *Confidences* are most interesting. The story of Graziella seems as touching as that of Paul & Virginia.[1] Read it, if you have not. Make Henry read it. Perhaps the beginning is too diffuse; but the residence at Naples is bewitching. I confess it—I cannot help it. All that sensibility & love move me much.

The news from Europe is of less importance than was anticipated. The Romans still hold out. My brother George writes me that he has recd a letter from Madame de Tocqueville, "in which she abjures for her husband all connection or sympathy with the Roman expedition."[2] And yet de Tocqueville is minister of Foreign affairs! They all begin to be ashamed of themselves!—George has met Dickens & [*John*] Forster, & breaks out against their vulgarity! I send you a French illustrated paper.

I hear nothing of Mr [*Stephen*] Longfellow's health.

I took up my pen merely to enter my protest against yr condemnation of the *Confidences* of Lamtine. Love to Henry.

Ever Thine, C. S.

ALS MH-H (68/649, PCS)

1. Lamartine's autobiography, *Les Confidences*, and the novel *Raphael* were both published in 1849. CS compared *Raphael* to Johann Wolfgang von Goethe's *Sorrows of Young Werther* (1774) and *Paul et Virginie* (1787), a romance by Bernardin de Saint-Pierre.

2. Mary Mottley de Tocqueville (1799–1864), British wife of Alexis de Tocqueville, who was appointed minister of foreign affairs 2 June 1849 by Louis Napoleon. At this time French forces were assaulting Rome in an attempt to defeat the recently formed Roman Republic. In a letter of 26 July (68/635, PCS) CS wrote Fanny Longfellow that he was "disgusted more & more with the present French Govt. It is a despotism in disguise of a republic."

To Joshua R. Giddings

Boston Aug. 20th '49—

My dear Sir

I regret very much, in common with all the friends of Peace here, that you did not go to the Convention.[1] I perceive that your probable presence there had been announced by the foreign papers. But there [will?] be many occasions hereafter for a good word in our cause.

I cannot imagine any cause grander—not even our Anti-Slavery cause—than that of the *Disarming of the Nations*. And I believe that the day has now come for a practical agitation of this question. I can see no other way of meeting *socialism*. Let nations *disarm*, & they will then have means, which they can acquire in no other way, for the potent remedies required by the ills of European society.

I am glad that an effort will be made to stop the enormous expenditure for our military & naval armaments.

It seems to me impossible at this moment to determine what course the Free Soilers should take on the speakership.[2]

This will be best determined on consultation after arrival in Washington. It remains to be seen how many will stand firm in a separate organization. I am inclined to think that there must be a complete *break-up* in the Dem. party. The Northern Democrats cannot harmonize with their Southern allies.

There will be another trial in Palfrey's district Sept. 10th.[3] I am not sufficiently advised at present to speak confidently of the result. The District Committee of 1[8?] met last week, & resolved to make their best efforts. It will probably depend upon the resistance made by the Democrats, of whose temper at present we are not certain. Their voters agree with us; but 2 or 3 of their leaders are so implicated in the pro-slavery policy that they cannot join us.—Mr [Wilson?] has just come in, & tells me that Palfrey's chances are increasing—he knows that some people will vote for him who have heretofore held back.—I am happy that our friends stood firm against the "Gauls" at Rome.[4]

Ever sincerely Yours, Charles Sumner

Hon. J. R. Giddings

ALS DLC (68/668, PCS)

1. CS wrote Giddings at least seven letters in June and July urging him to attend the Paris Peace Convention. See PCS, reel 68, frames 585–644 passim. In his most recent, and final, refusal Giddings wrote that a combination of the fear of cholera in Europe and the expense of the trip had prevented him from attending (Jefferson, Ohio, 13 August 1849, 6/633, PCS).

2. In his 13 August letter, Giddings asked CS's opinion on the upcoming election of a House of Representatives Speaker. Giddings hoped the Free Soilers in the House would "stand firm to their principles," and thought it "far better" for other parties to unite to elect a Speaker than for the Free Soilers to unite with either party.

3. Palfrey still failed to get a majority of the votes in his congressional district (Frank O. Gatell, *John Gorham Palfrey and The New England Conscience* [1963], 185).

4. Most likely a reference to the separate conferences 16–25 August 1849 of the Democratic (Hunker) and "Free Democratic" (Barnburner) parties held in Rome, New York. The Barnburners refused to drop their support of the Wilmot Proviso, while the Hunkers tried to remove the slavery issue as a political test (Frederick J. Blue, *The Free Soilers* [1973], 157–58).

To John Pringle Nichol

Boston Sept. 17th '49—

My dear Nichol,

By every packet I have hoped to write you an abundant answer to yr inquiries; but various engagements & the spirit of procrastination have interfered. I trust you have not set me down as indifferent to yr requests.[1]

In the first place, I have already speeded to you through Mrs Follen,[2] & the post, pamphlets & newspapers, containing matters which I thought might interest you. The Madison Debates, & the vol. of the Life of Hamilton which you desired, I do not possess myself, & they are not to be procured by any bookseller. I have been obliged, therefore, to forego the pleasure of sending those. And now for yr questions most briefly.

1st. As to the real tendency of things. We are a republic. I have met one or two persons who desired a king or at least an hereditary aristocracy here; but it may be said, that for all practical purposes, those institutions find no recognition here. Nobody could openly advocate them for us, without being considered a madman. In this respect we are in advance of Europe. Our present struggle is not with a feudal aristocracy; but with a modern substitute, the Slave-Power, which for years has given a tone to our national Govt. A rally is making against this. Its animating sentiments are justice & benevolence. And I cannot but look to the triumph of the Anti-Slavery cause as the herald of the recognition of those sentiments by our Govt. more completely than they have ever yet been acknowledged by any political power. Of course, we should then have something of a Xstian Fraternity, without an impossible [communism?]. Education, & Peace would then be thoroughly organized; & the enormous means that now go to armaments, & destructive industry will go to beneficence, & productive industry.

To all this, the great opposing force, is the selfishness of men, as displayed in business & in the old combinations of party. I could dwell on this topic at length; but must hasten on.

2nd. As to whether the character of our course is already indicated by the past. In some respects, yes—in other respects no. The industrial progress will continue as heretofore; but the Govt. will change from its inward & pro-slavery course to a moral & anti-slavery course. If you will read an Address prepared by me for the Free Soil Convention at Worcester Sept 12,[3] & which I send with this steamer, you will see something of the way in which I should answer you, if I had time.

3. The Dorr. trial. I have already sent you all the documents I could collect bearing upon that.[4]

4. S.C. Nullification: I have sent you a pamphlet containing Mr Webster's speech against Nullification, usually considered his greatest effort, also Mr Hayne's defence of it.[5]

5. Selection of judges. All my prejudices have been in favor of the English or British System of appointment by the Govt; but the experience of New York, where the judges are now chosen by the people directly, & of Vermont where they are chosen by the Legislature, has shaken my early ideas. An experienced lawyer, who has been familiar for 30 years with the courts of the two adjoining states of Vermont & N. Hampshire, tells me that the courts of Vermont have been always the better of the two; & in N. Hampshire the judges are appointed by the Govt. In New York, I think the change has worked well. The original friends of it are satisfied & many who were against it are agreeably surprized.

6. The passion to *transmit* money is not so strong with us as in other countries. But it is strong. The absence of any law of primogeniture promotes equality among the children, & secures the division of large estates.

And now, dear Nichol, as I have answered these with a flying pen, I feel how crudely & inadequately I have done what I had hoped to do fully, &, according to the measure of my ability, satisfactorily. But you must pardon me. Howe & Longfellow, if they knew of my writing, would join me in regards to you. We are looking for yr book with much interest.[6] To yr liberal mind I trust willingly the statement of our great cause.

Ever sincerely Yours, Charles Sumner

ALS NIC (69/008, PCS)

1. John Pringle Nichol (1804–59), professor of astronomy at Glasgow University, had recently made a lecture tour of the U.S. In his letter of 13 June 1849 from Glasgow (6/532, PCS), he asked a number of questions on the internal politics of the U.S. and "the course your society is running." The numbered items in CS's answer, below, indicate his responses to Nichol's specific questions.

2. Nichol wrote CS that "our friend" Elisa Lee Follen (1787–1860), writer and wife of abolitionist Charles Follen, could bring with her to Great Britain the materials Nichol sought. These were "Debates in the Several State Conventions on the Adoption of the Federal Constitution," published 1836–59, and the *Life of Hamilton*, vol. 2 (1840), by John Church Hamilton.

3. The convention was officially called the "State Convention of the Free Democrats." In "The Free-Soil Party Explained and Vindicated" CS stated: "The whole weight of the Government would then be taken from the side of Slavery, where it has been placed by the Slave Power, and put on the side of Freedom, according to the original purposes and aspirations of its founders" (*Orations and Speeches* [1850] 2:312).

4. Thomas W. Dorr (1805–54) was tried and sentenced in June 1844 for insurrec-

tion in Rhode Island. Dorr and his followers had protested stringent suffrage requirements in Rhode Island, and formed a separate government in 1842.

5. In January 1830 Robert Y. Hayne (1791–1839; U.S. senator [Dem., S.C.], 1823–32) and Webster debated in Congress the constitutional aspects of states' rights versus federal intervention. Hayne argued for state sovereignty and nullification rights against Webster's claim that federal courts should settle differences between states and the federal government (*Gales and Seaton's Register of Debates of Congress*, 21st Cong., 1st sess., 58–80).

6. Nichol published two works in 1848: *The Planet Neptune: an Exposition and History* and *The Stellar Universe: Views of its Arrangements, Motions and Evolutions*; neither was published in the U.S.

To Salmon P. Chase

Boston Sept. 18th '49

My dear Chase,

Many thanks for yr letter of Sept. 15th from New Haven, & especially for the words of sympathy. And yet I am unwilling to pass into the limbo of mere theorists. A student of the *ideal*, I trust never to lose sight of the *practical*.[1]

Our Convention was very large & respectable. Persons older in political wars than myself said that it was the best political convention they had ever attended. Certainly, it was most enthusiastic & harmonious. In the course of the day you were more than once called for, & I was gratified once by the report that you had been seen in Worcester. Judge Allen read to the Convention yr note, by way of excuse.

We are all much disquieted by the occurrences in New York.[2] I do not judge our friends hastily; but I confess to a feeling that our cause has been sacrificed to a vain desire for the harmony of that ancient omnibus the Democratic party. Politics in New York seem always full of pit-falls; I trust that our friends have not fallen into one.

It seems to me that there is no state in which our cause stands so firmly as in Mass. You will find in the Address & resolutions a full statement & vindication of the Buffalo Platform, in short of the old Liberty party. I am curious to know how it will strike you. The Atlas has fallen foul of the Address several times already.[3]—Judge Allen's speech is very much to the purpose. Burlingame[4] let fall some things which I regret. I do not think it right to abjure slave-holders socially or politically. Keyes made an eloquent, & Adams a most [racy?] speech. But you will read our doings in the paper I send.

I leave tomorrow or next day for a short journey, & shall be in New York at the Irving House Saturday or Sunday. Let me hear from you there; tell me what you think of the New York consummation.

Whatever Hunkers & Barnburners do, let us stand together. We in Massachusetts shall keep to our Ancient Anti-Slavery ways, & shall try to consolidate our party. I think you must do the same in Ohio. I doubt if you can throw yourself so completely as you hope on the old democracy. Our party is composite, & you must try to harmonize all sections. With us the fusion is complete.

You will note in the Address, that I have sought to heed those persons, who, like George Ashmun, say, that when California is admitted as a state, our "occupation" will be gone.[5]

Palfrey actually wrote a note to the Chairman of the District Com. withdrawing. This was shown to me, & I appealed to him again, for the sake of the cause, & for his own sake, to stand firm. So did Adams also. *He has withdrawn his withdrawal.* I think our Convention, & its doings have contributed to this.—You mistake very much if you suppose I could take his place without encountering an opposition more bitter, if possible, than that he has had.[6] Write.

Ever sincerely Yours, Charles Sumner

P.S. Remember me kindly to Mr Cleveland,[7] & do not forget how much of our cause is confided to you.

ALS DLC (69/010, PCS)

1. Chase had urged CS not to become discouraged in their cause, and expressed his admiration: "I find no man so congenial to me as yourself, though I do not pretend to be *up* to your theories in all respects" (6/673, PCS).

2. At the New York state convention, 17 September 1849, the Barnburners, who had left the New York Democratic Party in the presidential election of 1848 to join with the Free Soilers, settled their differences with the conservative Democrats, or Hunkers, and rejoined the party (*Boston Daily Advertiser*, 18 September 1849:2).

3. In his convention address, "The Free-Soil Party Explained and Vindicated," CS stated that the party intended to serve as a national party, that the slavery issue overrode all other issues, and that Congress should prohibit its extension (Wks, 3:7–45). The *Boston Daily Atlas* (15 September 1849:2) criticized the fact that CS had not helped meet the costs of the 1844–45 anti-Texas convention while he now called those Bostonians who had paid "'the selfish, grasping, subtle, tyrannical, money-power.'" In another editorial, the *Atlas* called CS's address "long-winded" and declared it useful only if abridged (17 September 1849:2).

4. The speech by Anson Burlingame (1820–70; U.S. congressman [American, Mass.], 1855–61, U.S. minister to Peking, 1861–67) was published in the Boston *Emancipator & Republican* (20 September 1849:1). Burlingame called upon Free Democrats to refuse to shake hands with slaveholders or to introduce them to friends or relatives.

5. In addressing several "objections from various quarters," CS stated that the Free Soil Party sought to achieve wider goals than preventing the extension of slavery in the territories. The party wanted, he declared, "to bring back the administration of the Government to the standard of a Christian Democracy, with a sincere and wide

regard for Human Rights—that it may be, in reality as in name, a Republic" (*Orations and Speeches* [1850], 2:320). George Ashmun (1804–70), U.S. congressman (Whig, Mass.), 1845–51.

6. Palfrey's election to Congress was still unresolved.

7. Charles D. Cleveland (1802–69), Philadelphia library scholar; U.S. consul to Cardiff, 1860s.

To Horace Mann

Boston Sept. 20th 1849

My dear Mann,

The enclosed letter, it seems to me, was addressed to me by mistake. It should have been addressed to you. I put it aside some time ago to speak of when we met, & forgot it. I now send it, for you to do what seems best in the [premises?].

The question propounded involves a volume; but I suppose you can send him some documents that will cover the ground.

I have sent you our State Address,[1] which I hope you will read. There are many reasons for my faith. I belong to a party pledged unequivocally *to place the Federal Govt on the side of Freedom*. In sustaining any other party, it seems to me I should jeopard this vital principle—the only principle of national politics that is worth contending for, or that could have drawn me from other pursuits. Think of this. Oh! I wish you were with us. Howe and I sigh over you, but are,

Always Yours, Charles Sumner

P.S. I think that the Free Soil party of Mass. is the best political party of the size this country has ever seen, containing a larger amount of talent, principle, & sincere unselfish devotion to the public good than has ever before been brought together in any similar number of persons acting politically. It will yet leaven the whole union.

ALS MHi (69/019, PCS)

1. CS's Worcester speech, "The Free-Soil Party Explained and Vindicated" (Wks, 3:7–45).

To Jared Sparks

Court St. Oct. 6th '49

My dear President,

Many thanks for yr kind letter of Sept. 24th, which I found on my return home, after an absence of two weeks.

I have already sent you a paper containing a copy of a letter of the Atlas, which I sent from New York. You will see that I corrected the error in the date of Washington's letter.[1]

I am daily struck by the bitterness, & the spirit of misrepresentation which animate party politics. I did not fully know it, until I had felt it in my own person. But my skin is thick. I can endure.

Ever Sincerely Yours, Charles Sumner

President Sparks

ALS MH-H (69/029, PCS)

1. In his letter (Cambridge, 6/690, PCS) Sparks remarked on a "blunder" in the 24 September 1849 *Boston Daily Advertiser*, but said he was not sure of the correct date of a letter of George Washington's. CS's letter of 27 September 1849 (Wks, 3:46–50) responded to the *Boston Daily Atlas* (25 September 1849:2). The *Atlas* stated that, in his Worcester speech, CS exaggerated George Washington's desire to abolish slavery; Washington was "opposed to the intermeddling of such men as Mr. Sumner with slavery." In his letter CS pointed out the *Atlas*'s error dating Washington's letter to Robert Morris and asked the paper to include his extracts from Washington's works supporting his argument that Washington had favored an abolitionist political party. The *Atlas* printed CS's letter and accompanying documents but added that it did not support CS's contention. The paper stated that it considered CS's address "a labored attempt to magnify the sins of the South" (1 October 1849:1, 2).

To Francis Lieber

Boston Oct. 13th '49

Dear Lieber,

In recently reading some vols. of Rousseau I have met with a passage of several pages, which has pleasantly reminded me of you & yr able disquisition on Veracity. It is *IVme Promenade*, immediately following his Confessions, in which he discusses at some length, & with a variety of illustrations & distinctions, your topic.[1] If you have not seen it—but you doubtless have—you will be pleased to refer to it.

I arrived in New York from Newport the very Sunday morning that you left. Before getting breakfast I went round to White St, & learned that you had gone to Bordentown. I had a very happy vacation of a fortnight, which I finished by a visit to the sage of Lindenwald [*Martin Van Buren*]. I found him very courteous, & any thing but non-committal—conversing freely on all persons & things. During two days he was agreeable & communicative. I found that he took a strong interest in Col. Benton's struggle.[2]

Mrs Pringle asked me at Newport why we Free Soilers did not get Mr Poinsett[3] into our party; & when I asked whether he was with us in sentiment, she said, he was with any body that was against Calhoun, whom he regarded as thoroughly dishonest, & indeed, he said, he *knew* him to be so. Some other talk with her would have shocked the nerves of S. Carolina.

Caleb Cushing telling me to-day the secret history of all the appointments to Taylor's cabinet, said that Genl. T. was urged to appoint Ballard Preston, to please W. C. P. & his friends, that he had never heard of him before, but, at once came into the idea.[4] I think it probable there will be a change in the cabinet very soon. Things cannot go on as they are now. Taylor must do as Jackson did—*chasser* the present set. To get rid of [*Thomas*] Ewing I understand the Depart. of Interior is to be abolished. I do not like this. There is also talk of opposing Lawrence's confirmation.[5] I do not see how this can be done. They cannot make a case against him.

The Longfellow's are well & happy. Howe was to leave this morning for the water-cure at Northampton.

Ever & ever Yours, Charles Sumner

P.S. Remember me to yr wife, & to that boy, who didn't know me.

ALS CSmH (69/032, PCS)

1. In his "Fourth Walk" Rousseau asserted that any words contrary to truth which "hurt" justice cannot be justified. In analyzing his own youthful lies, Rousseau wrote that he followed his "conscience" rather than abstract notions of truth and falsehood (*The Reveries of the Solitary Walker*, ed. and trans. Charles E. Butterworth [1979], 43–61).

2. Proslavery elements in Missouri threatened Thomas Hart Benton's Senate seat. He was defeated by the Whig Henry S. Geyer in January 1851 (William M. Meigs, *The Life of Thomas Hart Benton* [1904], 411–14).

3. Joel Roberts Poinsett (1779–1851), U.S. congressman (Dem., S.C.), 1821–25; U.S. minister to Mexico, 1825–29; U.S. secretary of war, 1837–41.

4. William Ballard Preston (1805–62), U.S. congressman (Whig, S.C.), 1847–49, and cousin of William Campbell Preston, served as secretary of the navy from 7 March 1849 to 19 July 1850.

5. Abbott Lawrence had been temporarily appointed U.S. minister to Great Britain on 20 August 1849; he was confirmed 24 June 1850, and served until 1852.

To Joshua R. Giddings

Boston Oct. 19th '49

My dear Sir,

Since I last heard from you many things have occurred to distract our friends. The New York Union had a very bad look. But some of our friends have made it worse than it is. The Boston Republican has been very unfortunate in its course. Wilson has set at naught the counsels of our best friends. Adams, Allen, Palfrey, Phillips all condemn him. I have most earnestly protested. His course has embarrassed us very much.[1]

I have been in New York, & seen many of the Barnburners. I am satisfied of their sincerity, & earnestness. They hope to make the united Dem. party of New York an Anti-Slavery party. It remains to be seen, whether they can succeed. Meanwhile we should adopt with regard to them the rule of *non-intervention*. At all events, do not embarass them.

The recent union in New York, & the way in which the Republican has treated it have embarassed our position in Massachusetts very much.[2] The day after our Worcester convention we stood firm & confident; never more so. At this moment, there is a little uncertainty as to several matters connected with our organization[.] I think it very probable, that there will be a union with the Democrats, in most if not all the counties on the senatorial ticket; but this has not yet taken place. If it should take place, the Democrats will probably withdraw their opposition to Palfrey.

I anticipate a very bitter contest here for the last week or two preceding our elections the 12th Nov.

Horace Mann has shewn signs of choosing Whiggery rather than our party. *Inter nos*, I have written most earnestly, telling him to beware of *timidity*, & putting it to his conscience to meditate well before he leaves us.[3] He lacks courage.

I was glad to see so much of Chase as I did here a month ago. He is a very able senator. I trust the friends of Freedom in Ohio will forget old feuds, & old party names.[4] Let us all stick together.

Ever Yours, Charles Sumner

ALS OHi (69/034, PCS)

1. According to Frederick J. Blue, many of the elitist Conscience Whigs such as Adams and Palfrey resented Wilson's democratizing political schemes and opposed his plan for joining with antislavery Democrats (*The Free Soilers* [1973], 211–12). The *Boston Daily Republican* (formerly the *Boston Daily Whig)*, edited by Wilson, ran an editorial, for example, on 6 October 1849, stating that "the people are sick of this annual cry—*this wail of Corporations and Capitalists*." The *Republican* warned against a tariff favoring wealth or special interests.

2. Wilson also edited the weekly Boston *Emancipator & Republican*, which in an editorial (27 September 1849:4) stated that the union of New York Barnburners and Hunkers "is now complete." While the paper regretted that the Barnburners had sacrificed some principles, the editorial stated that antislavery activists should wait for results of the union, and not simply condemn it.

3. See CS's letter to Mann of this same date.

4. CS refers, no doubt, to the Giddings-Chase contest for the U.S. Senate earlier in the year (see CS to Chase, 27 February 1849). On 29 October 1849, Giddings replied, "Chase is an able man, and will prove an able Senator. He lacks a knowledge of popular feeling and of popular sentiment and is not qualified to lead a party. His policy last winter came near to ruining us in this state. . . . But that is now passed" (6/721, PCS).

To Horace Mann

Boston Oct. 19th '49

My dear Mann,

Yr letter was forwarded to me in N. York. Since my return, I have been entirely occupied in grinding professional labor. Otherwise I should sooner have written to you.

Let me write frankly. I was pained by yr letter on two accounts; *first*, because it seemed to shew anger, if not bitterness towards me personally. This I knew I did not deserve. Again & again, when I have heard unwelcome charges against you, I have defended you, according to the measure of my ability. When your fidelity to Freedom has been questioned, I have pledged myself for you. I have been known, whenever my opinions were of any consequence as yr attached friend. But I pass this by.

I was more pained by the *partizan* Whig tone into which you had unconsciously fallen. I think unconsciously, for I am persuaded that if you could see your own image, you would shrink from it. In other days, you would have been the partizan of high truths, of noble causes, of Humanity. Yr letter shewed that you were about "to give to party what was meant for mankind."

In yr criticism upon the test[1] established by the Free Soil party you seemed to forget that a similar test is practically established by the Whig party.

I do not know that it would be profitable for us to discuss these matters. My course is taken, & I shall pursue it without fear. I believe the paramount objects under our Govt. are the principles of the Free Soil party, coincident as they are with all the sentiments of Humanity, so that, in joining this ⟨party⟩ movement, we do not give to party what was meant for mankind. We aim at the highest interests of mankind.

Nothing but my deep conviction of the importance of sustaining these principles would have impelled [me] into the strife of affairs. I had always kept aloof from politics, until drawn into them by this sentiment; & I cannot forget how gratefully yr words of encouragement to *persevere* fell at different times on my ear. I see nothing now in the politics of the country worth struggling for, except the principles of the Free Soil party.

We propose to place the Fed. Govt. actively on the side of Freedom, instead of being as it has been heretofore actively on the side of Slavery. Of course the *national* Whig party cannot be the organ of this sentiment. Think of the importance of this. Imagine the Fed. Govt. the great spokesman for Freedom, instead of the spokesman for Slavery. Who that has a heart, will not work for this? And who that has a head will entrust this high cause to the *national* Whig party?

Knowing yr conscientiousness, & yr humanity, I had supposed that you must be always with us. I had supposed that you would find sympathies with a great moral movement, which promises to regenerate the country. I had supposed that you would be too true to all yr past life even for one moment to hesitate, after you had laid down yr official duties, which were the excuse for neutrality in the presidential contest. I had supposed that you would surely impart to the movement the quickening influence of yr sympathy, & energetic co-operation—that you would be as active for Freedom as you have been heretofore for education.

I infer from yr letter, & from other things which reach me, that I am to be disappointed. It is already reported that you are to be the next Whig candidate for Govr.—that with you they are to sustain their sinking organization, & that with you they are to crush the Free Soil party. —— I am sorry to differ from you. But on the present occasion, I am free to say, I do it without any distrust of my course. And I am persuaded, that in some happier moment, you will regret the opportunity you abandon of serving *bravely* a noble cause.

Nobody questions yr integrity, or humanity. Every where I hear question of yr courage. I tell you this with freedom, & ask you, in all friendship, to search yr heart, & see if there is any thing to sustain this suggestion. Timidity is unworthy a nature like yours.[2]

I heard a report yesterday that you had signified yr determination to vote for Winthrop. I denied the report, on the strength of what you said at my office.

When you publish yr Essay on Party Spirit, & use me as an illustration, I shall write a supplement & introduce you as an unconscious victim of Whiggery. But I have written too much. Come & see me, & let us talk of these things, & believe me, as ever, most anxious for yr fame & usefulness, &

sincerely Yours, Charles Sumner

P.S. I handed yr letter to Howe a week ago, & he has not yet returned it to me. This is my excuse for not answering its suggestions more categorically.

ALS MHi (69/036, PCS)

1. In his September speech at Worcester, CS delineated several provisions of the Free Soil Party; the most exacting were that Free Soilers support the Wilmot Proviso and demand that the federal government oppose slavery wherever the government was responsible for it. In his letter (now unrecovered) Mann may have been referring to these conditions.

2. No reply from Mann has been recovered, but in his letter to Howe of 4 November 1849 (Mann Papers, Massachusetts Historical Society) he laid out his reasons for holding "myself in reserve." He thought the Free Soil attacks on the Taylor administration "premature" and he waited to see what actions it would take regarding slavery in the territories. "Until he [*Taylor*] gives proofs that he intends to defeat the great principles of freedom, I have no right to oppose him."

To Joshua R. Giddings

Boston Nov. 3d '49

My dear Sir,

Mann writes me as follows: "I have never to any mortal given the slightest indication whom I should vote for for speakership—never; I have long ago made up my mind, on what principles, I shall vote, when the facts are more fully before me, but the person for whom I shall vote is another thing."

I have seen him since he wrote this, & I read to him what you wrote about his vote.[1] He says further, that he will oppose any state constitution, which has not a prohibition of Slavery. I represented to him that an effort wld be made to admit California with a constitution silent on slavery. He said most solemnly that he would oppose all such efforts.

Our State election is at hand. There are unions in many of the counties on Senatorial tickets between Free Soilers & the Old Democracy. It is very probable, that these may succeed, & that our combination may control the Senate, perhaps the whole State Govt.[2] But all is uncertain.

Ever Yrs, Charles Sumner

ALS OHi (69/042, PCS)

1. Giddings wrote CS on 29 October 1849, "Mr Mann has always appeared unwilling to enter into the free soil movement. I think he has not confidence in our success." Still, Giddings continued, he would be surprised if Mann would "vote for

the re-election of a man [*Winthrop*] who has thus [exited?] himself to save the slave trade from abuse" (Jefferson, Ohio, 6/721, PCS).

2. The Free Soil gubernatorial slate, Stephen C. Phillips and John Mills of Springfield, a former Democrat, came in third in the fall election (Frederick J. Blue, *The Free Soilers* [1973], 211).

To Horace Mann

Boston Dec. 29th 49

My dear Mann,

As the struggle on the speakership is now over, I cannot forbear writing to you one word, partly of regret, & partly of explanation.[1]

I have been pained more than I can express, that you did not feel it a duty to cast yr vote in a way to express, as it seems to me, a more decided & uncompromising hostility to the Slave-Power, & to all combinations which do not make the cause of Freedom paramount.

It seems to me that you have missed a remarkable opportunity of strengthening & consolidating the public opinion which is now growing against Slavery. Such an opportunity may never occur again.

It is evident that you have deeply grieved the Free Soil party, every where throughout the country, from Maine to Wisconsin. These are the true reformers of the country, yr natural friends & allies.

There are large numbers of yr constituents who feel more than grief with regard to yr course.

I write this frankly, because I wished you to know it. I now wish to add, that I have never to any person, made any remark on yr course, *except that it gave me great pain*. I never shall say any thing else. Though asked by some of yr constituents what course they ought to take, I have declined to advise them. *I shall not advise them*. Whatever they do will be without any suggestion from me.

The band of Free Soilers at Washington are the harbingers of nobler destinies for the Republic. Would to God that Horace Mann would take his place among them!—A conservative Whig, who has often heretofore spoken harshly of you *now* calls you "a noble philanthropist," & uses you against me. I tell him, if he will only stick to his praise of you, I will pardon him something of his Whiggery & his Slavery.[2]

Ever yrs Charles Sumner

ALS MHi (69/056, PCS)

1. On 22 December 1849 Howell Cobb (1815–68; U.S. congressman [Dem., Ga.], 1843–51, 1855–57) was finally elected Speaker of the House on the sixty-third

ballot. Mann had voted alternately for Winthrop and U.S. Congressman Thaddeus Stevens (1792–1868; Whig, Rep., Pa., 1849–53, 1859–68), his final vote being for Winthrop. See *Globe*, 31st Cong., 1st sess., 3–22 December, 2–66, and Jonathan Messerli, *Horace Mann* (1972), 505–6. Free Soilers had not united behind one candidate, some voting for Wilmot and later for the Democratic congressman from Indiana, William J. Brown (1805–57) (Frederick J. Blue, *The Free Soilers* [1973], 193–94).

2. Mann replied to CS on 9 January 1850, agreeing that the slavery issue was "paramount" but not "exclusive." Mann argued that Congress needed the "right officers" to effect legislation against slavery, and while Winthrop "does not come up to my mark" he would have been a better Speaker than Cobb. He stated that Winthrop would have been "fair" and seen that a congressman more hospitable to the antislavery cause chaired the important Committee on the District of Columbia (7/072, PCS).

To Salmon P. Chase

Boston Dec. 31st '49

My dear Chase,

Let me begin by wishing you a happy new Year, & constant strength to sustain the warfare before you.

The papers say that the slave-owners court a discussion of slavery. If so, they ought to have it. Nor should they be let off with a handling of the Constitutional question only. This is important, as creating a basis for the discussion. But I believe the country will be aroused by the moral considerations. These will press hard upon them. The opinions of the fathers, which you have used already, should be put before them. I wish to see yr old Liberty address re-produced as a speech in the Senate.[1]

What assistance do you expect in the Senate? I count upon Seward. I trust he will be true to his past Anti-Slavery. But I fear his ultra Whiggery.

The Brown business[2] in the house was an affair, not to be thought of with entire self-complacency. I should have hesitated having any thing to do with such a character.

I am anxious to see the Globe report of Giddings's passage with Winthrop.[3] Our friend must be very careful in all his statements; for he will be watched. The *mot d'ordre* has evidently gone forth to all the party scribblers to put down Giddings. He cannot be put down, but he must use supreme care in all that he says.

I am glad of the motion to cut off Austria, though our Govt sanctioning slavery, will expose itself to a most biting retort. Let it come. "Our withers are unwrung."[4]—Thanks for your favor of Dec. 14th.[5] I hope soon to hear again.

Ever Yrs, Charles Sumner

ALS DLC (69/058, PCS)

1. Most likely "The Address of the Southern and Western Liberty Convention held at Cincinnati, June 11 & 12, 1845, to the People of the United States" (1845), in which Chase cited statements from revolutionary leaders favoring the abolition of slavery. He also discussed the founders' change of *freeman* to *person* in the due process clause of the Bill of Rights, stating such a change "prohibits the General Government from sanctioning slaveholding, and renders the continuance of slavery, as a legal relation, in any place of exclusive national jurisdiction, impossible" (3).

2. In the protracted struggle for Speaker of the House, December 1849, Giddings and other Free Soilers had temporarily supported William J. Brown of Indiana with the understanding that Brown would constitute House committees to satisfy the antislavery constituency. On 12 December, after stating he would have, as Speaker, honored sectional interests of both North and South, Brown withdrew his name (*Globe*, 31st Cong., 1st sess., 21–22).

3. On 27 December Giddings asserted he could vote for neither the Whig Robert C. Winthrop nor the Democrat Howell Cobb for Speaker and criticized Winthrop for supporting the Mexican War after previously opposing it (a charge Winthrop denied). Giddings gave his final vote to David Wilmot (ibid., 66, appendix, 36–37).

4. Senator Cass had recently moved that the U.S. look into suspending relations with Austria because of Austria's oppression of Hungary (*Globe*, 31st Cong., 1st sess., 54–58). CS's reference to *Hamlet*, 3.2.253, means "we are innocent."

5. Washington, 7/041, PCS.

To Thomas Crawford

Boston Jan. 18th 1850

My dear Crawford,

My anomalous position in politics makes me hesitate to write to persons with whom I have not at present *political sympathies*. Hillard, who prefers the winning side, must make up for my deficiencies. He will send you a letter for Mr Webster.[1] I have also spoken to Howe.

I send a letter for Mr Chase, a senator from Ohio, & an able man,—a friend of mine.

Mr Corwin & Mr Seward, of the Senate are auspicous men. They have always written to me in friendly terms. If you should see them, you can use my name as you please. But I do not feel authorized to write to them.

I fear you will find few persons at Washington now who know or care any thing for art. I regret this very much.

Howe seems very much better, & all are well. I await with anxiety the result of the Richmond verdict. God send you a good deliverance!

In the present mood of the Virginians, they will not give the prize to a sculptor who does not openly avow his belief in the divine right of the master over his slave, & especially in the right to carry slavery into free territory under the Constitution of the U. States![2]

Ever Yours, Charles Sumner

ALS MH-H (63/332, PCS)

1. Crawford wrote CS from Washington, 14 January 1850 (70/083, PCS), asking for letters of introduction and support of his bid to sculpt a statue of George Washington in Richmond. Crawford especially sought a letter from Webster, whom he had met five years ago.

2. Despite CS's doubts, Crawford won the commission for the statue.

To Salmon P. Chase

Boston Jan. 24th '50

My dear Chase,

If I did not believe that Truth in the end must prevail, I should be disposed at the present moment to despair of our cause. Both the old parties are coming together on substantially the same principle—*non-action* or *non-intervention*. I trust to Calhoun's influence to drive them from this shelter.[1] Can he do it?

Cass's speech[2] will prevent for the present the Northern Democracy from joining with us. And yet his leading supporters in our Legislature now in session said yesterday *in private* that they would not sustain him for the Presidency.

The course of the Democrats in Ohio is also disheartening.[3] I think even you must despair of them.

Would it not be well to bring out in the Senate 20 or 30 of the Advertisements of run-a-way negroes in order to shew the character of Slavery? What is uttered in the Senate is now uttered, through the press to the whole country. These advertisements speak trumpet-tongued against the deep damnation.

Have you Judge Jay's last tract—An Address to the Inhabitants of New Mexico & California.[4]

Who will answer Cass? Give me a word of hope.

Ever Yours, Charles Sumner

P.S. I suppose Parker is with you in Washington. My regards to him.

Hon S. P. Chase

ALS DLC (69/065, PCS)

1. Calhoun finally spoke out in March against compromise measures and for Southern hegemony in the Mexican territory ("The Compromise," 4 March 1850, *Globe*, 31st Cong., 1st sess., 451–55).

2. On 22 January Senator Lewis Cass stated that he could not support the Wilmot Proviso (ibid., appendix, 67–74).

3. The Ohio Democratic convention had recently voted against endorsing the Wilmot Proviso (Eugene H. Roseboom, *The Civil War Era*, vol. 4 [1944], *History of the State of Ohio*, 257).

4. William Jay, "Address to the Inhabitants of New Mexico and California, on the Omission by Congress to Provide Them with Territorial Governments and on the Social and Political Evils of Slavery," written August 1849, in *Miscellaneous Writings on Slavery* (1853), 491–551.

To Henry W. Longfellow

Court St—Thursday
[*24 January 1850*]

Dear Henry,

Whittier is here on a short visit. I go tonight with Miss Bremer[1] to hear Wendell Phillips, & tomorrow evng dine out, or I should insist upon taking him to you. He is staying at the Quincy Hotel in Brattle St.

I regret the sentiments of John Van Buren about mobs[2]—but rejoice, that he is right on Slavery. I do not know that I should differ very much from him, in saying that we have more to fear from the corruption of wealth than from mobs. Edmund Dwight[3] once gave, within my knowledge, $2000 to influence a single election. Other men whom we know very well are reported to have given much larger sums. It is in this way, in part, that the natural Anti-Slavery sentiment of Massachusetts has been kept down—it is *money, money, money*, that keeps Palfrey from being elected. Knowing these things it was natural that John V. Buren should say that we had more to fear from wealth than from mobs.

Van Buren is a politician, not a philanthropist or moralist, but a politician, like Clay, Winthrop, Abbott Lawrence, & has this advantage, that he has dedicated his rare powers to the cause of Human Freedom. In this I would welcome any person from any quarter.

Ever & ever Thine, Charles Sumner

ALS MH-H (69/068, PCS)

1. Frederika Bremer (1801–65), Swedish novelist then lecturing in the U.S.

2. Van Buren represented Isaiah Rynders and others who were charged with inciting the Astor Place Riots on 10 May 1849, when a mob tried to drive the British actor William Macready from New York City. In his summation at the trial, Van Buren said that mobs posed no serious danger in the U.S. "It is from the congregated wealth of the country there is danger, which would control and coerce, as in this case, bringing council to aid to reverse the decision of the people" (*New York Daily Tribune*, 19 January 1850, Supplement:2, and 21 January 1850:2).

3. Edmund Dwight (1780–1849), Boston merchant.

To John Gorham Palfrey

Boston—Friday—
[*15 February 1850*]

Dear Dr,

I write to let you know of our doings to-day, & yesterday.

At a meeting of several gentlemen yesterday, at my office, Gov. Morton, Hopkins, Adams, S. C. Phillips, Spooner, Keyes, Wm Jackson,[1] Dana & myself were appointed a committee to make arrangements for our Convention. All concurred in the opinion that you should be our President, & *you* were accordingly designated for that post.[2]

At a meeting of our committee to-day further arrangements were made. Dana was commissioned to prepare the paper on resolutions to be put forth by the Convention. Other men were selected for vice-presidents. We missed you among our counsellors, as it was understood that Mr Keyes had written to invite you.

We hope for a strong demonstration, confining ourself to the actual issue at this moment—the Wilmot Proviso. There is no question of elections or party alliances.

Ever Yours, Charles Sumner

Hon. J. G. Palfrey

P.S. [*Joseph M.*] Roote has been sent for.

ALS MH-H (69/085, PCS)

1. Erastus Hopkins (1810–72), antislavery activist from Northampton. William B. Spooner (1809–80), Boston businessman. William Jackson (1783–1855), U.S. congressman (Whig, Mass.), 1833–37, and a founder of the Liberty Party, 1840.

2. Palfrey agreed to head the Massachusetts Free Soil Convention, held in Faneuil Hall, 27 February 1850 (Wilson, 2:249).

To Joshua R. Giddings

Boston Feb. 19th. '50

My dear Sir,

Here is our circular calling our Convention. We count upon Roote. He must come. You must, if need be, *molliter manus imponere*,[1] & compell him to the North. It is important to know, so that his coming may be announced.

We wish to know whether to propose at our convention a National

Convention in June. In this we must be governed very much by the advice of our friends in Congress.

Of course, it must not be called, unless the occasion shall promise to be of such interest as to secure a powerful convention.

If called, where shall it be? We have thought of Washington. Think of this. A descent of several thousand Free-Soilers upon the District would have a good influence. It would be a movement of our lines of attack nearer to the enemy. Our own friends would be stimulated by the idea of proclaiming liberty to the captive at the very seat of Govt.

I hear of Winthrop's *dodge* during Roote's speech, & *miror magis*,[2] his appeal to Root to notice his absence from the House during the allusion to him.[3] I hope Roote will put in a note or in brackets, at that part of the speech where W. left his seat [[here Mr Winthrop left his seat]] & then afterwards, add at the part alluding to him, that Mr W. requests it to be known that he was out of his seat at this time, or something like this.

Ever Yrs, Charles Sumner

ALS OHi (69/091, PCS)

1. "Lay your hands on him gently."
2. "Wonder of wonders."
3. On 15 February 1850, after Root spoke supporting his bill prohibiting slavery in the California and New Mexico territories, the House voted to table it. In his speech Root declared, "It is bad enough for gentlemen representing constituencies in favor of the proviso to vote against it, but it is worse . . . for such to refuse to vote on the question. Better, sir, vote wrong than dodge" (*Globe*, 31st Cong., 1st sess., 276; appendix, 108). The *Boston Daily Atlas* (16 February 1850:2) defended Winthrop's courage in "withholding" his vote on Root's bill against Free Soilers' criticism of Winthrop for walking out of the House as the vote was being called.

To George Sumner

Boston March 18th 50—Monday—

Dear George,

I write on Monday in order to be sure of my letter going by the steamer. My last did not reach N.Y. in season, & went by a sailing packet. Perhaps it has not yet reached you. It contained the 1st of exchange for 250 francs. I now enclose the 2nd—I deposited with T. W. Ward & Co agent of the Barings on Saturday £40, which will be payable in 60 days from March 16th.—I have recd. yr letter containing Hugo's speech which I have read with great interest. It has been translated & published in the Xstian Register of Boston.[1] Mrs Coolidge, whom I met last Friday at a superb banquet given by Bartlett,[2] seemed pleased by yr attention to her & wished me to thank you. She said, she had already written to you. Her daughter is not well. Bartlett enquired kindly after you. Coolidge will sail for Europe in April.—I note yr inquiry with regard to the Gray matter. As that was originally committed to Albert {*Sumner*}, I have not seen as yet the way to interfere. Albert, who is now in Washington with Julia {*Sumner*} will be here in the course of the week, & we shall then be able to confer upon it & to take such steps as seem advisable in concert or separately.[3]—Mrs Hayward enquires constantly about you.—I am pleased with the tone of Horace's letters from Florence.[4] Mother was much disturbed by the idea of his passing his winter there, but I calmed her, telling her it would do him good. Any thing that teaches self-dependence, & practical ideas will do him good—Mr Amory seemed very happy at the idea of yr undertaking to pursue his claim. There has been an unexpected delay in the execution of the necessary powers of Attorney, owing to the absence at Washington of one of the parties. Mr Wm Appleton,[5] who represents one of the parties, has executed his power. I advised, however, delay until *all* can be sent together. Whether this will be by the present steamer, I know not.—I enclose a letter from Dr Harris,[6] the Librarian of Harv. Col. which will explain itself. If you can attend to its request, you will oblige a modest & worthy man, who devotes his leisure to science. Perhaps you are aware of his eminence as an *Entomologist*. I believe he is the first in the country.—

Tomorrow Dr Webster's trial commences.[7] More than 50 applications have been made to the Shff, for Reporter's tickets. The New York papers, & others at the South will have reporters present. There seems to be very little doubt in the public mind, so far as I can judge, that he is guilty. Many doubt whether he will be convicted.—Meanwhile another Webster has been set to the bar of public opinion; & many feel against him a warmer indignation than against Prof. Webster. You have doubtless read his speech. To me it seems a heartless apostacy. Its whole tone is low & bad, while its main points are untenable & unsound. He is another Strafford or archangel ruined.[8] In some moods, I might call him Judas Iscariot or Benedict Arnold. I have been glad to observe the moral indignation which has been aroused against that speech. The merchants of Boston subscribe to it; it is their wont to do such things; but Gov. Briggs expressed himself against it in conversation with me, as warmly as I do & said that the people of Mass. would not sanction it. David Henshaw[9] says that it is the cunningest & best bid for the Presidency which Webster has ever made. I should not be astonished if he were Sec. of State within a short time.—No man can tell how this contest is to terminate. It is clear that there is to be a good deal of speaking before any important votes. I anticipate much from my friend Chase in the Senate. He is an able lawyer & of admirable abilities otherwise.

Hawthorne has just published a Tale entitled the *Scarlet Letter*,—a story of adultery—which some persons admire very much. Longfellow's poems, & indeed, all his writings, are very extensively circulated. Edward Everett is preparing an edition of his Addresses[10] & lives quietly at Cambridge. The last time I saw him he inquired kindly after you.—You have never told me whether you ever inquired after *Mr O'Mally*, No. 5 rue Faubourg St. Honoré. He was kind to me. He must be now an old man, if he is alive. I should like to send him my regards & to know how he does.—I should like to know also what you think of the republic. Have you seen [*Francis*] Bowen's article.[11] Mrs Coolidge thought you ought to answer it.

Ever Thine, C. S.

Since I last wrote you I have not been well. But Mr Cowdin[12] was able to report to you that I was again at my office. He was so kind as to take any thing to you. I had nothing but a pamphlet to send.—I admired Victor Hugo's speech on education,[13] almost as much as that at the opening of the Peace Congress. The latter I think a masterly address.—Dr [*Nathaniel L.*] Frothingham has resigned his pulpit.

ALS MH-H (63/336, PCS)

Enc: Thaddeus William Harris to CS, Cambridge, 8 March 1850.

1. Speech to World Peace Congress in the *Christian Register*, 16 March 1850:1.
2. Possibly Sydney Bartlett (1799–1889), Boston lawyer.
3. In several letters at this time, CS referred to George's claim against a Mr Gray (e.g., 16 April 1850, 63/344, PCS).
4. Horace Sumner had gone to Italy in the fall of 1849 for his health.
5. Thomas Coffin Amory, Jr. (1812–89), a Harvard classmate, wrote CS 28 November 1851 (63/466) asking him to see that George presented certain unidentified papers to the U.S. minister in Paris, William C. Rives. William Henry Appleton (1814–99) was a Boston lawyer.
6. Thaddeus William Harris (1795–1856) wrote CS asking if George could get for him seeds of various French plants to compare with American species.
7. John White Webster (1793–1850), Harvard chemistry professor, was accused, and later convicted, of murdering George Parkman, uncle of historian Francis Parkman.
8. Daniel Webster's famous 7 March 1850 speech in the U.S. Senate in support of Henry Clay's compromise measures was a plea for reconciliation of sectional differences between North and South to preserve the Union. Especially offensive to Free Soilers was Webster's endorsement of the Fugitive Slave Law, which called for severe

punishment for those aiding runaway slaves (*Globe*, 31st Cong., 1st sess., 476–83). Thomas Wentworth, earl of Strafford (1593–1641), chief advisor to Charles I, was charged with attempting to raise an army against the existing Parliament. "Archangel ruined" refers to John Milton's Satan, *Paradise Lost*, 1.1.591.

9. David Henshaw (1791–1852), U.S. secretary of the navy under John Tyler; Massachusetts Democratic party leader.

10. *Orations and Speeches on Various Occasions*, 2nd ed. (1850).

11. "The War of the Races in Hungary, Review of *De l'Esprit Public en Hungarie, depuis la Révolution Française* par A. Degerando," *North American Review* 70 (January 1850): 78–136, by Francis Bowen (1811–90), Harvard professor of philosophy.

12. Elliot C. Cowdin (1819–80), a Boston merchant conducting business in France.

13. On 15 January, Hugo delivered a speech before the Legislative Assembly arguing for universal compulsory education, and attacking France's clerical establishment (Matthew Josephson, *Victor Hugo* [1942], 308–10).

To Cornelius Felton

Court St. April 9th '50

My dear Corny,

I gave yr message to Howe, & at the same time read him yr note to me. Of course, it excited painful feelings in both of us. It impressed both of us in the same way. It seemed to me one of those unhappy expressions of passion, which it were better to leave unnoticed.[1] I said so. But Howe thought that justice to *others*, whom you have blackened &, as we think, misrepresented, rendered it a duty to answer it briefly. I could not but concur in this. Justice to the absent friend is a sacred duty, &, as I have, of late had occasion to say something in extenuation of yr public course in politics when impeached, I must now say something for others, who are impeached by you.

I have read the Liberator, more or less, since 1835. It was the first paper I ever subscribed for. I did it in the sincerity of my early opposition to Slavery. I have never been satisfied with its tone; I have been openly opposed to the doctrines on the Union & the Constitution which it has advocated for several years.[2] It has seemed to me often vindictive, bitter & unchristian. But let me say frankly I have never seen any thing in that paper at any time so vindictive, bitter & unchristian as yr note. You beat Garrison.

But I do not know that I should be tempted to say anything even for the Liberator; but you proceed to speak of a personal friend of mine, whose acquaintance I first made, in those former days of confidence & friendship, under your roof. You say that you are "profoundly disgusted with the bad taste, worse temper, & *atrocious disregard of truth* manifested by T. P. in his libel upon Mr W[*ebster*]." Now, I have read Mr

Parker's speech twice—once last evng since I recd yr note—& I can perceive nothing to justify yr words.[3] To yr note they would unhappily seem to be too applicable. Allow me now to ask you, in all sincerity, what single passage or sentence in that speech shews "an atrocious disregard for truth"? Believe me, I ask this in no bravado, but with an earnest desire to know what in that careful & well-sustained document can justify such a charge. If there is nothing to justify it, then surely the charge must rebound upon the passionate man who makes it.

You complain that you have been made the subject of "a shameless attack" in the Republican.[4] I am always sorry to see any friend of mine alluded to any where, especially in public, except in connexion with what is pure & good. I was very sorry that there was any occasion to allude to you. But you are doubtless aware that your name has been quoted in the Washington Republic, & also in New York & Boston papers, as among the distinguished literary characters, who had given their sanction to Mr Webster's speech. You had signed a public document, thanking Mr Webster for "recalling you to a sense of your constitutional obligations." In subscribing to this speech in which Mr Webster pledges himself to support Mr Mason's bill,[5] with its amendments, "to its fullest extent & all its provisions," you had pledged yourself to that bill; yes, to surrender a panting fugitive without trial by jury, & yourself to become, at the call of the marshall a slave-catcher. *Alone of all the professors of Harvard, you, Cornelius Corny Felton, enrolled yourself in advance in this troop of man-hunters.* Doing so, it seems to me that you expect too much, if you suppose that, while some newspapers praise you for the act, others should not condemn you.

No person of ordinary intelligence or honesty could have signed the address to Mr Webster, without desiring to be understood as a supporter not only of more stringent laws with regard to fugitive slaves, but of the specific bill with the offensive amendments to it, which Mr Webster so positively supports. I can—[6]

AL MH-H (63/340, PCS)

1. CS returned Felton's letter to him and it remains unrecovered (CS to Felton, [10? April 1850], 63/342, PCS).

2. From its outset, Garrison's paper had denounced any union with slaveholding states and repudiated the U.S. Constitution, which permitted the coexistence of free and slave states.

3. On 9 April CS wrote Longfellow that he had sent Theodore Parker's "Reply to Webster," 25 March 1850, which had been published in *The Liberator*, to Felton. The "Reply" [misdated 1853] is in *The Slave Power, Works of Theodore Parker*, ed. James K. Hosmer (1907), 11:218–47. CS described Felton's reply as an attack on Parker: "Nothing of rage or Billingsgate does he spare" (Boston, 69/134).

4. Felton had been one of nine hundred signers to a letter to Webster thanking him for his speech. In an editorial condemning the signers of this letter, the *Emancipator & Republican* wrote: "We did not expect the name of . . . Professor Felton, who has made great pretentions to anti-slavery sentiments." The editorial expressed a hope that, when the U.S. marshal set out to arrest the next fugitive slave, he would "first call upon Pres. Sparks, Prof. Felton . . . as the *posse comitatus,* for aid" (11 April 1850:2. This paper was published weekly and it is likely Felton referred to an earlier version of the editorial in the *Semi-Weekly Republican*).

5. James Murray Mason (1798–1871; U.S. congressman [Dem., Va,], 1837–39; U.S. senator, 1847–61; Confederate emissary to Great Britain, 1861–65) had introduced a bill to enforce the Fugitive Slave Law (*Globe*, 31st Cong., 1st sess., 4 January 1850, 103).

6. The rest of CS's letter is missing. According to CS's letter of [10? April], Felton's reply (also unrecovered) did not address CS's charges but instead recalled "past matters." In his [10? April] letter CS stated he ranked a supporter of "Mr Mason's bill" even lower than Calhoun and would say so publicly if necessary. "I break off no friendship. In anguish I mourn yr altered regard for me." The two ceased communication until 1856.

To Horace Mann

Boston April 28th 50
Sunday—

My dear Mann,

I enclose some sentences from the Life of Wilberforce, which will give you what you want. It was from Liverpool that the petitions came.[1]

Yr treatment of Webster's anti-proviso argt. dwells in my mind, as most felicitous from its simplicity & clearness. It is like geometry. I hope you will go on, & finish the production in the same spirit, sparing no topic. As you propose to review the apostate speech, I would do it completely in all its points—some of them more briefly than others, but I would not leave him so much as a rag or fig-leaf.

In one brief paragraph you can make his fling at the Abolitionists appear to be contemptible as it really is.

Ask him to shew any legislation at the North inconsistent with the Constitution as interpreted by the Supreme Court. Where has been Northern aggression? Juvenal describes the relations of the two sections, when he says——— 'ubi tu pulous, ego vapulo tantum.[2] And Shakespeare has pictured it beautifully in the play of Julius Caesar. Read Act. IV scene 3d—imagining Cassius to be the South & Brutus the North. The image is perfect. I send a copy. If you wish to use it as an illustration, do not fail. I have no occasion for it.

The Texas mare's nest seems to me opened to a succession of exposures;

1st—The Act of Annexation was unconstitutional. As *against* Webster this point is strong. No person has expressed it stronger than he has. See Anti-Texas State Address. I enclose a passage[3]

2nd—If valid now, it is so only to the extent of *acquiescence* —not a jot further.

3d—Admitting that such a pledge might be made by treaty (which deny) it cannot be by legislation. No Congress can tie up its successors to this extent.

4th—The pledge is in violation of the spirit of the Constitution, & of its Anti-Slavery founders.

5th—The very resolutions, referring to the Constitution, require the *consent* of Congress for ye admission of new states.[4] This, of course, opens the whole question of, whether consent shall be given.

I hope you will reconsider the first part of yr letter.[5] Loyalty to you, & to a great cause compells me to call yr attention to this again.

You accepted a nomination for Congress from the Free Soilers, knowing their distinctive organization, & receiving from them at the time resolutions explaining it. You were chosen in part by their votes. The first part of yr letter will be offensive to them in its tone, besides presenting an argt. against the *very organization* whose support you had accepted.

It will be offensive to all yr Free Soil associates in Congress.

The position you take, it seems to me, is unworthy of you, as a moralist. You seem to ignore the vital distinction between a question of morals, & of cotton. One may be compromised, & the other not.

I take it that the main object of yr letter is not *personal defence*, but to rally Massachusetts, & to *unite* Anti-Slavery men. You call for a *union* in the 4th District. But the part of yr letter to which I refer will introduce heart-burning, & discord. It [*rest of letter missing*]

AL MHi (69/145, PCS)

1. The biography of the British abolitionist, *The Life of William Wilberforce* by Robert I. Wilberforce and Samuel Wilberforce, was published in 1838. CS enclosed three pages of quotations on Wilberforce's efforts against Liverpool businessmen to abolish the slave trade. Mann used these excerpts in his 3 May 1850 "Letter to the Hon. James Richardson et al," *Horace Mann's Letters on the Extension of Slavery into California and New Mexico* (1850), 13–14. Although a copy has not been uncovered, Mann apparently sent CS a draft of his letter to Richardson, which was a reply (published in the *Boston Daily Atlas* 6 May 1850) to Webster's 7 March 1850 speech.

2. "When you are struck, I cry out as one who is also beaten."

3. In his speech Webster had argued that Congress had approved the annexation of Texas, with full understanding it would become a slave state. CS enclosed a para-

graph from Webster's "Address to the People of the U.S. from the Mass. Anti-Texas Convention," 29 January 1845, which stated that there was no constitutional provision allowing the federal government to annex foreign territory.

4. In a letter to Chase, 22 March (69/114, PCS), CS also cited this argument, based on Seward's speech of 11 March. See *Globe*, 31st Cong., 1st sess., appendix, 261–69.

5. In the fourth paragraph of his letter, Mann stressed his political neutrality, that he was "exclusively bound to none" of the existing parties (*Horace Mann's Letters*, 1).

To John Jay

Boston May 13th '50

Dear Jay,

At the end of last week I forwarded to you the packet of books which you were kind enough to send me last autumn. I trust that they have come safely to yr hands.

I used them in my argt in the coloured school case before the Sup. Ct—as you have probably seen—unsuccessfully. I am sure, however, that the court in their opinion, have not answered my argt. If the opinion goes into the report, I think the profession will confess this 10 years from now.[1]

I hope soon to read yr father's address[2] at the meeting of the Anti-Slavery Society. Every thing that he does is an important contribution to our cause.

I am sick at heart when I observe the apostacies to Freedom, which these trials disclose. There is one thing needful in our public men—*back-bone*—In this is comprized that moral firmness, without which they yield to the pressures of interest, of party, of fashion, of public opinion.

I have been happy to hear that Mrs Jay is restored to health. My friend Parker spoke with gratitude on his return of yr kind hospitality.

In reading the life of Wilberforce I was pleased to follow the references to yr grand-father,[3] who seems to have seen much of the Great Abolitionist.

Ever Yours, Charles Sumner

ALS NNCB (69/165, PCS)

1. CS and a black Boston attorney, Robert Morris, argued the Roberts case before the Massachusetts Supreme Court. Sarah C. Roberts, the daughter of a black Boston printer, Benjamin Roberts, had been expelled from a white public school because of her color. CS's brief, 4 December 1849, "Equality Before the Law: Unconstitution-

ality of Separate Colored Schools in Massachusetts" (Wks, 3:51–100), argued that Massachusetts statutes had established but "one Public School . . . equally free to all the inhabitants" (68) and that *equality* meant black children were entitled to attend the school geographically closest to them (70–73). The court denied the appeal in April 1850, but in 1855 the Massachusetts legislature declared segregation in public schools illegal. See DD, 1:180–81; J. Morgan Kousser, "The Supremacy of Equal Rights," Social Science Working Paper 620 (March 1987), California Institute of Technology.

2. Probably William Jay's "Address to Inhabitants of New Mexico and California." See CS to Chase, 24 January 1850.

3. John Jay (1745–1829), first U.S. Supreme Court justice, had negotiated the Jay Treaty in Great Britain in 1794.

To Horace Mann

Boston June 3d '50

Dear Mann,

I wrote you on Saturday, touching one or two important points.[1]

If I were writing on the subject, I should use every thing, appropriating all that I could get from all quarters. Several things I should shew—
1st. The distinction between the case of fugitives from justice, & fugitive slaves, under the Constitution. The first are delivered up on being *charged* simply; the second only to the person to whom service is *due.* Final trial is necessarily implied from this phraseology.[2]
2nd. What is the *trial implied.* It is not a criminal trial; nor in equity, or admiralty. It is a *civil proceeding* to determine an alleged *legal* right.
3rd. The words of the Constitution, securing trial by jury "*in all suits at common law,*" were intended to secure it in all cases "in which legal rights were to be ascertained." These are the very words of the Sup. Ct in Parsons v Bedford, 3 Peters 446 to 449. *Mem* don't fail to read that opinion. It is very important. See also 3 Story on the Const. p. 645—[3]
4th. But at the very time the Constitution was made, among the recognised "suits at common law" was one to determine the title to a "negro," as to determine the title to a "horse." See my letter of Saturday.[4]
5th. The question of *human liberty* is essentially a proceeding at *common law.* It is not in equity, or admiralty; but at *common law.* Congress cannot make it otherwise. If so, they could nullify the amendments to the Constitution, by transferring an important matter from the common law side to a side of the court which did not require trial by jury.

The more I reflect upon this last point, the more it seems to me unanswerable. It is not in the power of Congress, under the amendments to the Constitution, to make such a question, other than a "suit at common law."

6th. The other clause of the Constitution—"trial by jury & due process of law"—also secures it.

Mem. Don't forget to read the decision of the Sup. Ct; there is a passage you must use; beginning "The phrase common law &c & ending same suit"—See 3 Story p. 645.

I think you can find Alvord's report in the Congress Library, or at the Secy of States's office.[5]

Don't be too long; but don't leave a stone of Webster's heathen structure, one upon another.

Ever Yrs, C. S.

The phrase "is *due*"—is like *debt*—a phrase of the common law. For the best explanation of how far the common law is adopted under the Constitution, see Wirt's argument on the Impeachment of Judge Peck—at the end of the vol.[6]

ALS MHi (69/201, PCS)

1. In a letter dated 15 May 1850 to Edward Sprague Rand et al. citizens of Newburyport, appearing in the *Boston Daily Advertiser*, 31 May 1850 (DW, 7:85–95), Webster specifically attacked Mann's ignorance of the Constitution, lamenting that Mann was "crude and confused in his legal apprehensions" (91). CS sent Mann three letters on 1 June advising Mann on appropriate response to Webster's letter (see 69/189, 195, 197, PCS).

2. Using the Fugitive Slave Law of 1793 as historical precedent for the federal government's power to reclaim fugitive slaves, Webster wrote that no jury trial was necessary because "the reclaiming of a fugitive slave is not a criminal prosecution" (DW, 7:91).

3. Richard Peters, *Reports of Cases Argued & Adjudged in the Supreme Ct of the US. in January Term* (1830), 3:432–57; Story, *Commentaries on the Constitution of the United States* (1833).

4. In his letter of 1 June 1850 (69/195) CS cited legal precedents for this "recognised suit."

5. James C. Alvord, *Report on the Powers and Duties of Congress upon the Subject of Slavery and the Slave Trade* (1838).

6. See CS to Winthrop, 9 February 1843.

To Horace Mann

Boston June 10th '50

Dear Mann,

Yr letter appears to-day. An ardent Free-Soiler Dr Stone, has just left me. He says he has done nothing but read it this forenoon.[1] He thinks it "magnificent." At his boarding-house, he is surrounded by Webster-men, one of whom says "Horace Mann is a formidable antagonist."

I stopped my pen just now to speak with Peleg W. Chandler, who came in to speak about the Letter. He says it is "a great document," & that you have put Webster completely down. Downer is in great delight.[2] He says it reads smoothly, from beginning to end.

There is a typographical error, which I have mentioned to the Traveller & Journal—Noyes—for *Noy*.

I perceive you took another version of Fortescue than that I sent you. I think mine was from Amos's translation. That you adopted was from the very loose translation published more than a century ago. I enclose a literal translation which I have myself made from the original Latin. In taking the old version you lose something of the point of the admonition to Webster.[3]

In revising the proofs I took the liberty of introducing a few sentences, which seemed to me important to bring out yr own ideas. I shall send you a copy, marking them.

Yr telegraph communication about Blackstone on reprizals came too late, through the *negligence*, I doubt not, of the office here. I called Sunday Evng about 7 o'clk at the office, & hearing the noise of somebody in the inner office called out, "is there any communication for Mr Sumner." No answer, & again I called out. No answer; & I then went to the Atlas office, which I did not finally leave till after midnight. On getting home I went at once to bed. In the morning I found at home a Tel. communication, which had been left after dark—after my call at the office—& after I had left home for the Atlas office. This little history will relieve me of any charge of negligence.

I am curious to know the effect of yr document at Washington, particularly on Webster, so far as it may be known.

I trust that you will ratify my doings about the Letter. I hesitated at every stroke of the pen, which I introduced; but I did by you, strictly as I would be done by.

Ever Yours, Charles Sumner

ALS MHi (69/219, PCS)

1. Mann's second letter responding to Webster's speech of 7 March, "To the Editors of the Boston Atlas," Washington, 6 June 1850 (*Horace Mann's Letters on the Extension of Slavery into California and New Mexico* [1850], 15–24). James W. Stone (1824–63), a Boston Free Soil Party organizer, was later a Republican Party ward boss.

2. Peleg W. Chandler (1816–89), Boston attorney. Samuel Downer (1807–81), Boston merchant.

3. Mann quoted from *de Laudibus Legum Angliae* (c. 1470) by Sir John Fortescue (1394?–1467?), chief justice of the King's Bench, who wrote that slavery was created by man, liberty by God (17). In his letter of 12 June from Washington (69/221, PCS), Mann thanked CS for his editorial changes and said he would use CS's translation of Fortescue in subsequent editions of his reply to Webster.

To Samuel Gridley Howe

Boston June 25th '50

Dear Howe,

Now I know you are gone, I miss you much.[1] I lack the consciousness of yr presence, & the sense of security, which it gave me. But I trust you are gaining health & strength. Surely you should. No person deserves them more. When I think of you, & your labors, I feel my own littleness, & the little that I do—"muddling away" my life in writing letters, & in doing infinitesimal things of little avail.

I send you Webster's 2nd attack on Mann.[2] He exposes himself much more than before. Mann has already corresponded with me on the subject of his reply, by telegraph & letter. I have sent him some 20 pages of notes & suggestions. I think he has a chance to put Webster—down—down finally. Chase writes me, that by the most careful calculation of our friends the Compromise will be defeated in the Senate by 4 majority; but he says, that the other side count upon carrying it by 4 majority. Giddings writes that, if it reaches the House, as things now stand, it will be laid upon the table by 20 majority.[3]

My own impression is that it will pass the Senate, & probably, the House. Clay is determined, & potential, & he is daily shewing what a strong *will* can do. Such a person with such a *will*, & such capacity as a *leader*, would have carried Freedom long ago. If it passes the Senate, then Clay & Webster & the successful senators will commence their pressure upon the House.

But let us hope for the best!—The telegraph tells us that [*Abbott*] Lawrence is confirmed, on the motion of Webster.

I have no news. I am alone, quite alone—more & more so, every day.—Mary Dwight Parkman has been in a wretched condition, since the birth of her child—not expected to live—but I am told to-day is out of danger.[4]—The Longfellows go to Nahant next week.

Did you note that Charles Augustus Murray had arrived in London from Egypt, while Miss W. was leaving America.[5] The fates have them in keeping, & will bring about a conjunction.

Write me a generous letter. Tell me of yr plans, of yourself, & of what you see. When you have an *address* I will see that papers are sent. Love to Julia.

Ever Thine, C. S.

P.S. Yr Halifax note came to-day, as I was sitting down to write you.

ALS CSmH (69/257, PCS)

1. Howe left with his family 12 June 1850 for England (Howe to CS, at sea, 13 June, 69/223, PCS).

2. Webster's letter of 17 June to Robert H. Gardiner et al., known as the "Kennebec letter," appeared in the *Boston Daily Advertiser* 22 June 1850. See *Writings and Speeches of Daniel Webster*, ed. James W. McIntyre (1903), 12:240–49.

3. Joshua P. Giddings's letter, Washington, 21 June, 7/254. In his letter of 22 June (Northampton, Mass., 7/256) Chase also stated his hope that a fusion of Democrat and Free Soil parties would elect CS to Webster's Senate seat.

4. Mary Dwight Parkman was alive in 1874 (HWL, 5:759).

5. Later that year Charles Augustus Murray (1806–95) married Elizabeth Wadsworth (1815–51), a young woman in whom CS had been interested. See HWL, 2:242–43.

To Horace Mann

Boston June 26th '50

Dear Mann,

It has occurred to me that I did not notice in my last yr inquiry about the article on Cass in the *Era.*[1] I noted that article, & was at no loss to attribute it to you. As I read it, I regretted that it was not spoken or published in such a way as to follow Cass's slander. What he says in the Senate, through various reports goes every where, & passes also into the permanent history of the country.

The saying of Fisher Ames is now verified.[2] "A lie will travel from Maine to Georgia while truth is putting on her boots." But when Truth gets her boots on for you, she has not the same opportunities for a run, that Cass has; as all that he says is reported in the great *party organs.*

Oh! when, oh! when shall this dynasty of Slavery be overthrown, & the press at Washington be *openly, actively & perpetually on the side of Freedom.* Never until both these old parties are overthrown.

To convert our Federal Govt. to *Freedom* is a grand aim for a statesman, or a citizen.

I have sent my last *Era* to Howe; so I cannot refer to yr article on

Cass; but I think, from my recollection of it, it should be circulated widely.

I fear if you confine yourself to a P.S. to a new edition, yr views will not obtain the desired circulation.[3] If you address them at once to the Atlas, they will obtain a start here, & can then be published with the rest.

The P.S. to yr last letter about Webster's bill has excited comment in conversation. I do not precisely comprehend yr purpose in it; nor can I agree in yr emphatic praise of Webster's bill. Even with yr amendments, I cannot regard it as a "perfect bill."[4]

A fundamental principle of our constitution & of the common law is *Nemo tenetur accusare se ipsum.*[5] Now, this maxim, I know, has been restrained to criminal matters; but it was originally established as a security of the subject against oppression & power—in short against men acting like slave-masters. According to the genius of our institutions, it ought to be extended to the fugitive slave; nor can I consider any bill as "perfect" which compells that slave under oath to perjure himself, or to admit himself to be a slave in the state from which he has fled. He should be allowed, as in all other cases, to deny it, by the General Issue, & compell the dealer in human flesh to prove every part of his case. Think of this.

Ever Yrs, C. S.

ALS MHi (69/261, PCS)

1. Mann asked CS in his letter of 23 June 1850 (Washington, 69/253, PCS) if he had seen Mann's answer to Cass in the *Era*. In a speech supporting the compromise on 11 June 1850 (*Globe*, 31st Cong., 1st sess., appendix, 803–10) Cass had criticized Mann's first reply to Webster (letter to Richardson et al. 3 May 1850), ironically singling out Mann's "bravery" and "philanthropy." According to Cass, Mann's protests were a "tissue of bad taste, bad morality, and bad logic" and would only "hasten on this fearful agitation" (806). Mann replied under the pen name "Quere" ("Gen. Cass's Last Speech," *National Era*, 20 June 1850:98) that Cass had "altered the Constitution" when he stated that a higher power than the Constitution, "moral necessity," conferred upon Congress the power to legislate for inhabitants of the territories, and Cass was inconsistent regarding congressional authority over the territories.

2. Fisher Ames (1758–1808), U.S. congressman (Fed., Mass.), 1789–97.

3. Mann had written on 23 June that he would not answer Webster "at length," but rather add a "Note" to the new edition of *Horace Mann's Letters on the Extension of Slavery into California and New Mexico*.

4. In a P.S. to "Mr. Mann's Answer to Mr. Webster" (*Boston Daily Atlas*, 10 June 1850:2), Mann praised Webster's Fugitive Slave Bill submitted to the Senate on 3 June for being "as nearly perfect as a bill on such a subject can be." Mann saw the bill as a sign that Webster was becoming more amenable on the fugitive slave issue. He thought Webster's bill could be "slightly altered" in order to allow a fugitive to

"procure testimony in his defence, and to be indemnified if judgment went his way." Mann's "P.S." was omitted, however, in subsequent editions of the "Answer."

5. "No man should have to accuse himself."

To Richard Cobden

Boston. U.S. of America.
July 9th 1850.

My dear Sir,

I have too long delayed acknowledging the kindness of yr letter of last Nov. & the instructive fullness with which you treated our great cause of Peace, & also that other question of Canada.[1] The latter seems for the present to have subsided. Nothing is said about it here. Our Southern concerns have of late absorbed the whole public attention.

But the Peace Question, though appealing less palpably to the immediate interests of politicians, has been winning attention. Burritt has, indefatigably visited distant places, & aroused or quickened an interest in the cause.[2] His singleness of devotion to this work fills me with reverence. Perhaps, with more knowledge of the practical affairs of government, he would necessarily lose something of that hope which is to him an unfailing succor.

As Burritt was leaving America, I suggested to him to leave no stone unturned in order to secure Alexander von Humboldt as President of the Frankfort Congress. If this venerable scientific chief should preside, I should consider the success of the Congress secure. Indeed, his presiding alone would be success. It would put the cause under the protection of his name. From my personal recollections of him, & more particularly from the character of his life & writings, I am led to believe that he must be substantially with us. His *Kosmos* is a Peace tract. Revealing the harmony of the Universe, it pleads powerfully for harmony among men. Though a friend of the king, he has kept aloof, so far as I am aware, from the late political excitements, & I cannot but feel that he can be pressed, with much effect, to crown a glorious life of science by helping to inaugurate Universal Peace.[3]

Burritt spoke of M. Mittermaier as one who had been proposed as President. He is a man of unquestioned learning, &, probably, at this moment one of the first of living jurists. He is a liberal also. For him personally I have a sincere regard. It was my fortune to know him well, while I was in Germany, & I have corresponded with him since. But his name cannot awake the echoes of Humboldt's. If you & our friends in England should be impressed by these things, as they have impressed me & others here, I hope that you will join in trying to secure Humboldt for President. Perhaps Chev. Bunsen[4] would help in the matter. I cannot regret too much, that you missed enlisting [*George*] Bancroft last year. He distinctly said to me, that he would have gone with you, had he been asked. Such another chance will not occur of catching him. And had he appeared at that time, still warm from his diplomatic harness, he would have set an example for men like Bunsen & Humboldt.

I have read Mr Lawrence's speech at the Gough dinner[5] with great regret. He is full of good nature, &, in most things, of strong sense; but he has never sympathized with our cause. In truth he has never thought of it. Since our recent discussions have arisen he has been exclusively occupied by large concerns of money-making business, & of politics; & he has had no time for a cause that made so gentle an appeal as ours. His praise of military chieftains will, of course, find much sympathy among the people about him now. But is there not reason to believe that with the Iron Duke [*Wellington*] this idea of military glory is destined to die out? His funeral will be its great exorcism for England.

We are waiting with some impatience the result of the discussion in the House of Commons on the Greek question.[6] So far as Ld Palmerston thwarted depotism & Russia, I sympathize with him; but I cannot but feel the essential barbarism of that blockade. It is an illustration of the enormity of the whole War System, of which it is a natural consequence, & of the *Laws of War*.

Our American politics, as you well know, have been in a perplexed state. The slave-holders are bent of securing the new territories for slavery; & they see, in perspective, an immense slave-nation, embracing the gulf of Mexico, & all its islands, & stretching from Maryland to Panama. For this they are now struggling; determined while in the union to govern it, & direct its energies; or, if obliged to quit, to build up a new nation, slave-holding throughout. They are fighting with desperation, & have been aided by traitors at the North. Webster's apostacy is the most bare-faced. He is another Strafford. Not only the cause of true Anti-Slavery is connected with the over-throw of the slave-holding Propaganda, but also of Peace. As soon as it is distinctly established, as the unalterable policy of the Republic, that there shall be *no more Slave territory*, there will be little danger of War. My own earnest aim is to see Slavery abolished every where within the sphere of the National Govt, which is the District of Col. & on the high-seas in the domestic slave-trade; & beyond this, to have this Govt for Freedom, so far as it can exert an influence, & not for slavery. When this is accomplished, then Slavery will be taken out of the vortex of national politics & the influences of education, an improved civilization & of Christianity will be left free to act against it in the states where it exists.

It is difficult to say how the present contest at Washington will end. Nobody there can tell. Things look now as if Clay & his Compromise would be defeated.

There are two persons in England, who it seems to me ought to be with us in the Peace Movement—Ld Carlisle & *Mr Milnes*. Sometime ago I wrote to them on the subject;[7] but as lawyers say, "did not take much by my motion." Still, I must think, that they will yet be with us. Both must appreciate the grandeur of the cause, & have many sympathies with it, even if party habitudes may yet hold them back.

Hoping soon to hear from you, believe me, my dear Sir,

very sincerely Yours, Charles Sumner

P.S. I desire to thank you sincerely for yr kind hospitality to Mr Burlingame.[8] He has returned full of gratitude.

Richard Cobden Esq. M.P.

ALS GBWSR (69/277, PCS)

1. Cobden wrote 7 November 1849 (7/003, PCS) that he was heartened by the "visible results" of European peace parties in protesting foreign loans for armament. Cobden also stated he did not oppose U.S. annexation of Canada, if Canadians voted in favor of it, without any U.S. interference.

2. Burritt had organized the 1848 Brussels Peace Congress which had provided a model for subsequent ones in Europe.

3. CS had met the German scholar Alexander von Humboldt (1769–1859) in 1840 in Berlin (Prc, 2:120). An edition of *Cosmos: A Sketch of a Physical Description of the Universe* translated by E. C. Otte was published in 1844. Frederick William IV (1795–1861) was king of Prussia.

4. Christian Charles Josias von Bunsen (1791–1861), Prussian diplomat and scholar then at the Prussian Embassy in London.

5. Three dinners were held in April in London honoring Sir Hugh Gough, first Viscount Gough (1779–1869), commander of British forces in India.

6. Debate continued until 28 June 1850 on a motion to support the Palmerston government's policy in Greece. Palmerston had sent the British fleet to Athens to support the claim of a British subject, Don Pacifico. His action was criticized in the House of Commons by Cobden and others, but eventually won that body's support. See *Hansard's Parliamentary Debates,* 3rd series, 111:104–5, 235–67; 112:102–7, 228–325, 329–444, 478–596, 609–743.

7. CS wrote George William Frederick Howard, Lord Morpeth, now the seventh earl of Carlisle, 8 January, urging him to become active in the peace movement (Castle Howard Collection, Great Britain).

8. Anson Burlingame visited Great Britain in the spring of 1850.

To Samuel Gridley Howe

Boston July 30th '50

Dear Howe,

On my return from New York, I found yours from London.[1] I was delighted to hear of yr health & happiness; & I said, in my heart, "Enjoy yourself."

I sincerely hope you will surrender to fun, frolic, conversation, sight-seeing & pastime. If you do, I shall have hope of you. I am almost tempted to say—do as I do. But I feel how little of an example I should be to any body. Still I am conscious of a power of enjoyment in society, & in the holy-day of life which I do not discern in you.

I have sent papers to you constantly, & by this steamer I send a profusion. Several containing something about the recent wreck of the Elizabeth[2] in which my youngest brother, Horace, perished. He was an invalid, & had passed the last autumn & winter in Italy for his health. He was returning full of hope, & in company with the Ossolis, to whom he was much attached. My mother & sister were anxiously expecting him, & counting much upon his store of experiences. To them especially it is a bitter thing to lose him; & all who knew him speak warmly of his gentle, loving & utterly unselfish nature. He was a companion to Julia, particularly at concerts, & on horse-back, & enjoyed more than I can her musical zeal. I feel painfully my own inability to supply her loss, by sympathy or companionship.

I heard of the wreck by telegraph on Monday at 2 o'clk, & hastened that afternoon to New York. Fire Island, where it occurred, lies at the South of Long Island—some 50 or 60 miles from New York. I visited the island, & traversed its beach. It is a mere sand-bank & beach. This was strewn for miles with fragments of the wreck. The remains of the Ossolis & my brother have not yet been found. It seemed to me, after what I saw of the sea there & its rage, unreasonable to expect to find them; but others thought differently.[3]

My brother was an invalid, & has passed away from a life of suffering. The Ossolis had, as it seems to me, little to hope in our country. I fear their future would have been bitter.

Mann has published his notes on Webster.[4] Many, who are very friendly to him, complain of their *personality*. I regret this; because it gives a handle to his enemies. They judge his personalities, & neglect his facts & arguments. And yet, according to the way of the world, he appears to me to have been justified. He has *retaliated* with a vengeance upon both Cass & Webster. In the Nat. Era, which I have sent, you will find the notes on Webster. I will try to send the pamphlet; in that you will find the note on Cass.

Webster, as I always supposed when he made his speech he intended, has gone into the cabinet.[5] [*George N.*] Briggs has appointed Winthrop his successor. This made me sick at heart. Briggs always *talks* anti-slavery; but at a crisis, when his act can be very effective, he fails. I took the liberty of telling him yesterday, that he had missed an opportunity of doing an act of justice, by appointing Mr [*Samuel*] Hoar; but that, if he took any body from the House, he should have taken Horace Mann. I felt pained for Mann. Briggs has professed to be his friend, & to agree with him in sentiment; & now, when the *tight pinch* comes, where is he? He advances Winthrop directly over his shoulders, & leaves Mann at this moment under a severe pressure. Put not your faith in *politicians*. They may talk fairly; but they will *act always* as politicians. At last I understand them. Good bye, dear Howe; Write to me,

Ever & ever Thine, C. S.

P.S. You never returned Felton's letter, so full of friendship, which I value as a memorial of the olden time. I hope you have not lost it.

ALS MH-H (63/383, PCS)

1. 9 July 1850 (69/280, PCS).

2. The ship ran aground and broke up on 19 July off Fire Island. Also returning to the U.S. were the writer Margaret Fuller (1810–50), her husband, Angelo Ossoli, and their son, Angelino.

3. CS corresponded with Henry Thoreau about the failure to recover the missing bodies, 29 and 31 July (7/297, 69/297).

4. Mann's "Notes," 8 July, were a response to Webster's Kennebec letter (*Horace Mann's Letters on the Extension of Slavery into California and New Mexico* [1850], 24–32).

5. Webster resigned from the Senate on 22 July to become secretary of state in President Fillmore's cabinet.

To Horace Mann

Boston Aug. 5th '50

My dear Mann,

I recd. with gratitude yr letter of sympathy; & now yr letter of August 1st.[1] I have longed to write you. Each day, I have promised to do it. But beyond the anxieties from my recent sorrow, I have had many matters to watch.

I have 2 vols in press of my *Plays*—in contradistinction to *Works*—being Oration & Speeches; & I have spent time & thought in their revision. I also have in press an edition of Story on Partnership,[2] which during the last few weeks I have revised, & edited with notes & additions. To these may be added what the world calls "business"; & you will see that my moments have been occupied.

In the last Register you will see my answer to Mr R—I presume Mr Ticknor, tilting with vizor down.[3] I think he will find it difficult to make another reply; but, besides a special combativeness, he is vindictive, venomous & wicked—all this. I shall not be astonished, therefore, if he returns to the work.

You have, perhaps, seen my two articles also in the *Transcript* in reply to the criticism on *captatores verborum*. You will observe that I confined myself to the classical question. I did not venture to ask permission to discuss the other; for I felt that I should not be allowed to do it except *in vinculis*.[4]

I have communicated with the *Atlas*; & its editors avow a determination to stand by you. They profess perfect devotion to you & your cause. On the other hand the Webster section are specially envenomed. The Courier, as you will perceive, is audacious & ruthless; the Post cold, cutting & scornful. The *Advertiser*, so far as I have seen (I was absent several days & lost the thread) has not noticed yr notes in the least degree. From this circumstance, I infer that they are satisfied that they cannot. And this brings me to the Notes.

You will remember I urged the immediate publication of yr Reply to the Kennebec Letter. I felt anxiously that every day's delay lessened the interest in the controversy, & gave Webster an advantage; & I feared some change of position. His translation to his present post, in its influences, fulfills my worst anticipations. However, this is one of the incidents of controversy with such a person.

In point, pungency, truthfulness & force, yr notes surpass the preceeding parts of the controversy. They strike a *very hard blow*; one from which Webster could not recover, if he were a candidate before the public. They would fell him, as with an iron mace. In dealing with the classical question, it seems to me you erred by using *intensives*. I would not have called it "the most ridiculous blunder"; but simply a blunder. Nor would I, as at present advised, have introduced the special personalities.[5] He has erred in this respect; &, as I said in the Xtian Register, is the *first* offender; but the public will not see this. He has a license which is not accorded to you. This has been the case with him always. His life would have sunk any other public man of New England; & yet he is sustained by men regarded as moral.

I have learned that, in controversy, caution & skill are required, in order not to say things, which, though true, may yet jeopard the main cause. It seems to me you have erred in this respect. Yr notes on Cass are more questionable than those on Webster.

You must expect the coldness & vituperation of *politicians*. This is the tribe I eschew, & detest. *You* do not yet understand them. I think you will yet see them as I do. Their trade compells them to be faithless to principles—provided they are true to their *party* & *themselves*. Our good friend Gov. Briggs, with strong sentiments prompting him to the right unhappily belongs to the class. I told him directly, that he had missed an opportunity of doing an act of poetical justice, by not placing Mr Hoar in the Senate; but, that, if he could not do this, & was determined to take a person from the House, he ought never to have passed over Horace Mann. Winthrop's nomination was a bolt for which I was not prepared; but it is another illustration, that a *politician* in the service of a *party* cannot be trusted. I shall write again very soon. I have written this amidst constant interruptions.

Believe me, ever Yrs, C. S.

P.S. I shall send you that List of Books.[6] I have hoped every day to make it out. I count tomorrow or next day upon finding more leisure. Howe tells me in a letter from London, that he is much better. He seems to enjoy himself.

ALS MHi (69/305, PCS)

1. Washington, 29 July and 1 August 1850 (69/291 and 299, PCS).
2. *Orations and Speeches*, published in November 1850 by W. D. Ticknor and Company (Prc, 3:56); Joseph Story's *Commentaries on the Law of Partnership*, 3rd edition.
3. An exchange of letters between "R" and "X" (CS) appeared in the *Christian Citizen*, 29 June 1850:2, 13 July 1850:2, 27 July 1850:2, and 3 August 1850:2. At issue was whether the Constitution gave fugitive slaves the right to trial by jury. "R" maintained that Mann was wrong in stating the Constitution granted this right, and that Mann's attack on Webster was ineffective. In his latest letter CS argued, however, that sections of the Constitution implied that "a trial by jury is demanded in all cases of *liberty*" (3 August 1850:2).
4. "Enchained." A scholarly quarrel had raged throughout the summer on Webster's use of the phrase *captatores verborum* in his Kennebec letter of 17 June. Both Mann and Webster summoned classical scholars to their defense and CS, signing his article, "Latin School," jumped into the fray. Stating that he did not "wish to enter into the personal or political manners involved in this criticism," CS alleged that Webster's use of the phrase "is not classical, it is counterfeit" (Boston *Daily Evening Transcript*, 29 July 1850:2). CS's second article appeared in the Boston *Daily Evening Transcript*, 2 August 1850:1. See Mann/CS correspondence 21 June–27 September 1850, reel 69, and Jonathan Messerli, *Horace Mann* (1971), 517.
5. CS may have been referring to the so-called authorities on the New Mexico territory, cited by Webster, whom Mann criticized. See "Notes," 24–32, in *Horace Mann's Letters*.
6. In his letter of 29 July, Mann had asked CS for a list of books for a young man's reading.

To William Bates and James W. Stone

Boston August 12th 1850

Gentlemen,

I have been honored by your communication of Aug. 9th, informing me of my nomination as the Free Soil candidate for Congress in this District.[1]

You knew well my general unwillingness, often declared, to be a candidate for any political office. You were informed also of my special desire, expressed in advance, to be excused from taking any public part in the coming election. Not forgetting these things, you yet call upon me to be a candidate, & you set forth reasons why the appeal is now made.

From the bottom of my heart, I wish you had selected another. If it may be given to me to exert, among my fellow-men, any influence for good, let it be in a private station. Here, by act, or by word, written or spoken, something always may be done. To others I willingly leave the more dazzling opportunities of political office.

And yet I could not satisfy myself, if, at the present moment, I failed, at any sacrifice of personal feeling, to assume a post where I was encouraged to hope I might be of service in the cause of Human Liberty. To that cause I offer my best vows. And now that it has been neglected where it should have been cherished, & alas! betrayed where it should have been defended, I confess a new motive to exertion.

The wave of re-action, which, during the last year, swept over Europe, has reached our shores. The very barriers of Freedom are threatened. Statesmen, scholars, writers, speakers,—once its uncompromising professors, have become the professors of compromise. A hideous, Heaven-defying bill,[2] introduced by a senator from South Carolina, avowedly for the recapture of fugitive slaves, but endangering the liberty of freemen, has received countenance at Washington, & even here in Boston. The great Ordinance of Freedom, once considered an essential safeguard to the territories has been [scanted?]; by some as unconstitutional; by others as unnecessary. Slavery, which is the sum of all injustice & all wrong—which includes every outrage to person or property, as the greater includes the less—is prolonged in the Capital of our National Union, by virtue of National laws; nor is any efficient effort made to remove it. Beyond this, a political power, unknown to the Constitution, & existing in defiance of its true spirit, now predominates over the Congress of the United States, gives the tone to its proceedings, seeks to control all our public affairs, & humbles both the great political parties to its will. This is that combination of slave-masters, whose bond of union is a common interest in Slavery.

All this must be changed. Reaction must be stayed. The Federal Government, every where within its proper constitutional sphere, ⟨& without any interference with the states⟩ must be placed on the side of Freedom. The policy of Slavery, which has so long prevailed ⟨over this Federal Government⟩ must give place to the policy of Freedom. The Federal Government must learn to speak for Freedom, as in times past it has spoken for Slavery. The Slave-Power, which is the fruitful parent of national ills, must be driven from its present supremacy. Until all this is done, the friends of the Constitution & of Human Rights cannot cease from constant devoted labors; Nor can the country hope for any repose, but the repose of submission.

It is not uncommon to hear persons declare that they are against Slavery & are willing to unite in any *practical* efforts to make this opposition felt. At the same time they visit with condemnation, with reproach or contempt the earnest souls that for years have striven in this struggle. To such I would say, if you are sincere in what you declare; if your words are not merely lip-service; if in your hearts you are entirely willing to join in any practical efforts against Slavery, then, by your lives, by your conversation, by your influence, by your votes—disregarding "the ancient forms of party strife"—seek to carry the principles of Freedom into the Federal Government, every where that its jurisdiction is acknowledged, or that its power can be felt. Thus, without any interference with the states, which are beyond this jurisdiction, may you help to erase the blot of Slavery from our National brow, & instead there plant the luminous ensigns of Freedom.

To every laborer in a cause like this there are satisfactions unknown to the common political partizan. Amidst all apparent reverses—notwithstanding the hatred of enemies, or the coldness of friends—he has the happy consciousness of duty done. Whatever may be existing impediments, his also is the cheering conviction, that every word spoken, every act performed, every vote cast for this cause, helps to swell those quickening influences by which Truth, Justice & Humanity will be established upon earth. He may not live to witness the blessed consummation which he has at heart. But it is none the less certain. Others may speak of the Past as secure, Under the laws of a beneficent God, the Future also is secure—on the single condition that we labor for its great objects.

Faithfully yours, Charles Sumner

William Bates Esq.
James W. Stone Esq. Comm

Dft MB (69/315, PCS)

1. The congressional election was to be held 19 August 1850 (*Boston Courier*, 13 August 1850:2) for the seat vacated by Winthrop's appointment to the Senate. CS's letter to the two Free Soil activists was published in the *Emancipator & Republican*, 15 August 1850:2.

2. On 16 January 1850 Andrew Butler (1796–1857; U.S. senator [Dem., S.C.]), had asked leave to report from the Judiciary Committee the bill to enforce the Fugitive Slave Law (*Globe*, 31st Cong., 1st sess., 171).

To Samuel Gridley Howe

Boston Aug. 27th 1850

Dear Howe,

I have yrs from Edinburgh, & marvel at the rapidity of yr movements from London to Paris, & then to Edinburgh.[1] I could not have hurried so soon from Paris. I wish I were there.

Since I last wrote you I have passed a week or more with the Longfellows at Nahant, coming to Boston almost daily. This was pleasant; but let me confess to you, that I found the journey to Boston—rocking on the outside of the stage-coach across the beach—& then jolting in the cars—excited my brain, making it swim, so that I was not good for much when I reached my office. You will, perhaps, call this the token of a failing frame. At Nahant I saw familiarly several whom I have not been in the habit of meeting lately. It seems to me that the tone towards us is softening; the early political asperities have somewhat died out, besides yielding to the exacerbations now existing between the Websterites & the anti-Websterites among the Whigs, who hate each other cordially.

I have sent you papers containing the account of the recent election in Boston.[2] I was prevailed upon to stand, &, I could not satisfy myself, that I should do my duty if I declined. My standing was thought of some importance as a rallying-sign to our friends throughout the Cwlth. You will see that personally I can have no other satisfaction from the result of the election, except that I performed my duty.

I have also sent you papers shewing Mann's last labors, & the attacks upon him. I grieve for him. I think he is severely annoyed; more than ever before. Nothing of former controversy equals this present experience. In attacking Webster, he attacked a person who has powerful friends, leagued in a political cordon, ready to defend him "right or wrong." He has been guilty of a characteristic & constitutional indiscretion in the ardor & intensity of his statements; for instance, in speaking of Webster's classical blunder as the "most ridiculous since Ld Kenyon spoke of Julian as the Apostle."[3] Webster was wrong; he made a blunder. If Mann had played with this, he would have exposed himself less. To add to my troubles, an article has appeared in the Advertiser, of a column; bitter, severe & castigatory upon Mann, with a slant which I easily perceive towards me, which, I have no hesitation in referring to Felton.[4] On Mann's account I desire to reply to it in the *Atlas*; but though this paper would be glad to publish it, I have not the heart to do it. I shrink on several accounts. I cannot bear to have a controversy with an ancient friend, like Felton. I do not like to write in the Atlas; I cannot make an anonymous attack upon Mr Webster, who has shewn me hospitality in other days. I wish you were here for my comfort & succor. Felton's course grieves me much. I cannot forbear repeating, that I regret your remissness in not returning his note to me. I wish I had it now; & I fear you have lost it.

There is a strong disposition in many of our friends to unite with the democrats this autumn, with the view of securing a United States Senator, for six years to the Free Soilers. When I think of the insignificance of the state offices, & the importance of Senator, to our cause I confess the strength of the temptation. Let me hear from you.

Ever & ever Yrs, C. S.

P.S. I have sent you papers—more than one a week.—[*Samuel*] Downer is here—ever faithful to Mann, & to you.

ALS MH-H (63/389, PCS)

1. 2 August 1850 (69/301, PCS).

2. On 19 August Samuel A. Eliot (1798–1862; U.S. congressman [Whig, Mass.], 1850–51), a supporter of the Compromise of 1850, won the election for the U.S. House of Representatives seat, with 2355 to CS's 489 votes (*Boston Daily Atlas*, 20 August 1850:2).

3. *Horace Mann's Letters on the Extension of Slavery into California and New Mexico*, 25.

4. Calling himself "Codex Alexandrinus" ("Mr Mann and Mr Webster," *Boston Daily Advertiser*, 24 August 1850:2), the writer described "Latin School's" article as only a "feeble attempt to support him [*Mann*] in fact and philology."

To Horace Mann

Boston Aug. 27th 1850

My dear Mann,

At last I send you a memorandum of books for a young man to read. It is only this evng that I have been able to seize the time. I fear I may have made it too cumbersome. All the books mentioned are substantial works, of acknowledged position in literature. You can cull from them a smaller list.

I have been pained & shocked infinitely by the article in the Advertiser. From internal evidence I cannot doubt the authorship. It is written by a person, with whom I have been in the most intimate & affectionate relations, & who has often expressed for me & my doings, an unbounded admiration—as little deserved I feel as his present position. In an evil hour he committed himself to Webster's speech, signed the letter to him, & has been straying off—off—in a divergent line ever since. I refer to Prof. Felton. His article shews familiarity with the subject; but it is illogical, Jesuitical, false, bitter & vindictive. I am tempted to reply; but I have not the heart for it. I can reply only in the *Atlas*. There are strong reasons why I should not venture there; & then, I shrink from a controversy, that may bring me in public collision with an ancient friend. This new combatant complicates & embitters my position. If I had not become used to these things, I should feel it more than I do.

I cannot disguise from you that Webster's friends have stirred a strong feeling against you. They are bold, fearless, determined, uncompromising; they have means at command. The Atlas is timid, hesitating, & with very little talent to help it. In yr own District, there is a strong undertoe, started in Boston, against you. I am not able to estimate its force; nor whether it can succeed. I am told that Schouler begins to doubt whether yr friends can control the Whig Convention of the District. But you will be sustained warmly by the Free Soilers; & even without a nomination, by many Whigs. I see no other course for you, but to put yourself upon the country. Even if defeated (which you will not be) yr position would be much better than if you withdraw, under the present volley of abuse. Yr election would be a signal triumph of our cause; & your name as a candidate would be a rallying-cry throughout the state.[1] If Briggs were out of the way, I should hope to see you in the field as candidate for Govnr; & then we would put the question of Websterism—not merely to yr District—but to the whole Cwllth. Charles F. Adams will support you earnestly, by word & act. He was angered by Felton's article.

It would be vain to apply to Beck or Anthon for any public expression on the classical question.[2]

Our Free Soil State Convention was called, contrary to my desire, for the 17th Sept. It will probably be put off till the first week of October, after the Whig Convention.—You will have but little vacation. Believe me, dear Mann,

Ever Yrs, Charles Sumner

P.S. I see Downer constantly. He has shewn me yr letters to him. Be of good cheer.

ALS MHi (69/339, PCS)

1. Mann was defeated for renomination to Congress by the Whig party but, running as a Free Soiler, won reelection (Jonathan Messerli, *Horace Mann* [1971], 519–21).

2. Charles Beck (1798–1866), professor of Latin at Harvard. Charles Anthon (1797–1867), professor of Greek and Latin at Columbia College.

To Salmon P. Chase

Boston Aug. 29th '50

My dear Chase,

It is long since I have written to you; but I have been grateful in my thoughts for yr friendship. Yr last letter was full of comfort, & confirmed me in the course I had already taken with regard to the nomination.[1]

Though the vote of the Free Soilers here was, I am told, according to their full proportion, & distanced by double the Hunker Democrats, still it appeared wretchedly small. If I were sensitive to political humiliations, I might feel this; but I do not.

Our State Convention, which, contrary to my advice, has been called for Sept. 17th will be put off till the first week of Oct. By that time the horizon will be clearer, & we shall discern men & things in their true colors & proportions.

The storm has broken ruthlessly upon Mann's head. The Free Soilers here, who, as I have always told him, are his natural allies, have no competent organ, & the anti-Webster Whigs are timid & without talent. He is therefore, without defenders. *Inter nos*, the *Atlas*, which for years has had column upon column abusing me, now invites my assistance. It wishes me to write an article defending him. I long to do every thing possible for him.

I have been glad to see Dr [*Gamaliel*] Bailey here. He is now about 15 miles from Boston on the sea shore.

Our Mass. Politics are all uncertain. There is a strong movement among Democrats & Free Soilers for a union, in order to secure a Free Soil Senator. I doubt if it can be accomplished, though the national offices are so important to the maintenance of our principles, in comparison with state offices, that I feel great indifference with regard to the latter. Whatever may be the final course, I have requested that my name should not be considered among the candidates for any thing. I wish to be in a private station. In this I must be peremptory.

I am in politics accidentally, certainly without design & unconsciously. ⟨If there⟩ Personally I resign all their fruits; their thorns & bitterness I will share.

Ever Yours, Charles Sumner

ALS DLC (69/343, PCS)

1. In his letter from Washington, 13 August 1850, Chase encouraged CS to run for the House of Representatives in the Suffolk District. "You are looked to as a leader. . . . Take the position assigned to you; and if Websterism must prevail in the capital of Massachusetts—if Boston is to be yoked in with the slavehunters and their apologists, let no part of the sin lie at your door" (7/323, PCS).

To John Gorham Palfrey

Boston Oct. 15th 1850

My dear Dr,

I cannot forbear uttering at least one cry of Distress.

The conduct of our friends at Concord seems to me to shew a *dementia* which makes them proper candidates for Dr Bell.[1]

Young Phillips,[2] who was here this morning, thinks you ought, by an immediate public letter, to wash your hands of the whole movement. I do not see the way to this; but I trust that you will not give it any countenance

It seems to me they have done much to jeopard our cause in Mass. & also your position.

Oh! *back-bone—back-bone—back-bone!* This is what is needed; & not to be afraid of any names by which we may be called. For myself, I am neither Whig nor Democrat; but a Free Soiler.

And nothing seems clearer to me than our duty, in utter disregard of all state issues, & placing our Anti-Slavery above all other things—to try to obtain the *balance of power* in the Legislature, at least in the Senate, so that we may influence *potentially* the choice of a senator to Congress. This can be done only by thinning the Whigs. If I must vote for a Whig or a Democrat—I should be sorry to vote for either—let me vote for the Democrat, because in that way we may secure the *balance of power*. Mr [*Samuel*] Hoar would secure a Whig majority in the senate, & render us powerless; so that the nominee of the Whig caucus would walk over the course next winter.

As between the two tickets now before the county of Middlesex, I could not hesitate—distasteful as some of the democrats may be. Let me see you, when in town.

Ever Yrs, Charles Sumner

ALS MH-H (69/411, PCS)

1. Whigs of Middlesex County met at Concord 14 October 1850. They were approached by a group of Free Soilers who wanted to negotiate with the Whigs regarding the forthcoming elections. A joint Whig–Free Soil committee was formed and in the afternoon the committee reported that Free Soilers agreed to support the Whig ticket. All the Free Soilers asked in return was the Whig endorsement of Palfrey for Congress (*Boston Daily Atlas*, 15 October 1850:2). Luther V. Bell (1806–62) headed the McLean Asylum for the Insane in Charlestown.

2. Possibly Stephen H. Phillips or Willard P. Phillips (1825–1901), sons of Stephen C. Phillips ("*Warrington*": *Pen Portraits*, ed. Mrs. William S. Robinson [1877], 403).

To John Greenleaf Whittier

Boston Dec. 3d '50

My dear Whittier,

Some days ago I sent you, through Fields, my two vols., & I am now tempted to write, partly to excuse myself for this venturing.

My *ideal* is so much above any thing *actual* in my poor life, that I have little satisfaction in any thing I am able to do. And I value these things, which are now published, simply as my earnest testimony to truth, which I have most sincerely at heart. They have all been done, because I could not help it—almost unconsciously, I may say.

One of the thoughts, which reconciles me to my audacity is that possibly these volumes may tempt young men, particularly at colleges, to our fields of action. But I have little confidence even in this aspiration.

I have longed to see you of late; for there are several matters that I should be glad to confer with you about. The late elections have given us great advantages.[1] I hope they will be exercised wisely, discreetly, justly, & without any petty proscription.

But in order to make our position tolerable, it seems to me that Boutwell, if he receives our votes, must in his message put himself substantially upon our platform. I believe he voted for the resolutions of last winter.[2] I should be content, if he would repeat those in his message, & say that he abides by them. Without some such adhesion by him to our principles, our whole combination will be routed next autumn.

Of these & other things I should like to talk with you. When shall you be in town?

Mr Hallam has lost his only other son, by sudden death at *Si*enna.[3] The first died suddenly at *Vi*enna. Who will write his *In Memoriam?*

Ever Yours, Charles Sumner

P.S. Yr last article in the *Era* was most interesting.[4]

ALS MiMp (69/433, PCS)

1. The Free Soil–Democrat coalition had reduced the Whigs' representation in the Massachusetts State Legislature: twenty-one state senators were Free Soil or Democrats compared to eleven Whigs, and in the House, 200 to 176 (Prc, 3:230).

2. Since no gubernatorial candidate had received a majority, that election would be decided by the state legislature. Henry Wilson and other Free Soilers had revived their plan of an agreement between Free Soilers and Democrats in the legislature, giving the governorship to the Democrats and the six-year senatorial term to the Free Soilers (DD, 1:189). In the Massachusetts legislature, George Sewall Boutwell (1818–1905; governor of Massachusetts, 1851–52; U.S. congressman [Rep., Mass.], 1863–69; U.S. senator, 1873–77; U.S. secretary of the Treasury, 1869–73) had supported resolutions offered by Free Soilers in February 1850 that instructed U.S. senators from Massachusetts to oppose the compromise proposals (Wilson, 2:250–51, 253).

3. The historian Henry Hallam's son, Henry Fitzmaurice, had died 25 October.

4. "Slavery in Massachusetts," *The National Era*, 28 November 1850:190–91.

To Charles Francis Adams

Boston Dec. 16th 1850

My dear Adams,

I had hoped to write, so as to reach you before leaving Washington; but various matters—business & calls innumerable—prevented; & I now aim at you in New York.

I am particularly moved to this by yr allusion to me in connexion with a certain post.[1] I appreciate yr generosity, & am proud of yr confidence. I am not entirely insensible to the honor that post would confer; though I do not feel this strongly, for I have never been accustomed to think highly of political distinction. I feel that it would, to a certain extent, be a vindication of me against the attacks, to which, in common with you & others of our friends, I have been exposed. And I am especially touched by the idea of the sphere of usefulness in which it would place me. But notwithstanding these things, I must say, that,

I have not been able, at any time, in my inmost heart, to bring myself to desire the post, or even to be willing to take it. My dreams & visions are all in other directions. In the course of my life, I have had many; but none have been in the U.S. Senate.

In taking that post I must renounce quiet & repose for ever. My life henceforward would be in public affairs. I cannot contemplate this, without repugnance. It would call upon me to forego those literary plans & aspirations, which I have more at heart than *any merely political* success.

Besides, even if I could incline to this new career, there are men in our ranks, my seniors & betters, to whom I {defer?} sincerely & completely. Mr {*Stephen C.*} Phillips, by various title, should be our candidate. If he should be unwilling to take the place, then we must look to you. In seeing you there I should have the truest satisfaction. You are the man to split open the solid rock of the U.S. Senate. I shrink unfeignedly from the work. For this I have never "filed my mind."

I shall see you soon, I trust, when we may talk of these things.

Ever Yours, Charles Sumner

P.S. My impression from what I hear is strong that notwithstanding Hunkerdom & the *Post*, a *Free Soiler* will be chosen Senator.

Give my regards to Mr & Mrs S. Brooks, who are always agreeable.

ALS MBApm (69/441, PCS)

1. Adams wrote CS from Washington on 10 December 1850 (69/436, PCS) about the empty U.S. Senate seat. He saw "difficulties in alliances with the democracy" and preferred to remain aloof from a coalition. "But if our friends decide to risk themselves in that ship I trust we may get a full consideration for the risk," Adams continued, and such a "consideration" would be "securing your services in the Senate. If any thing can be done with that iron and marble body you may do it."

To Charles Francis Adams

Court St. Thursday after.
{*2 January 1851*}

My dear Adams,

What you said last night gave me a pang at the time; & I have not been able to banish it from my mind.[1]

I cannot contemplate without emotion that there should be any political separation between us; nor can I anticipate any occurrence to interfere with our general concert in action, as in times past.

At all events, the thought that I should be without your sympathy & co-operation, & without Palfrey's too, adds to the repugnance with which I contemplate the office, which others seek for me. Most certainly, if I should be chosen, & should bring myself to accept, I should feel infinite encouragement in the assurance of yr support; I should be unhappy without it, & Palfrey's also.

Habitually deferring as I do to you on all matters of politics, yet I cannot see the Future as you see it. Nor do any Free Soilers or Democrats, except Palfrey, so far as I know, so see it. Only this morning Mr Bird told me that Griswold[2] & other leading democrats had distinctly declared that they expected each party to have its separate organization. This, I think, will be the case, while we shall absorb some of the Democrats.

But whatever may take place I shall be found with the Free Soil principles, so far as I act in public. No pressure of party can drive me into any combination, inconsistent with their support, or make me forget our confidential political relations.

Ever Yrs, Charles Sumner

P.S. Do not answer this note. I write it because I could not help it. I go to Chelsea to-night to lecture, or I would call & talk it.

ALS MBApm (69/475, PCS)

1. In his diary Adams recorded CS's visit on 1 January 1851. When CS told Adams that some Democrats had pledged to "'*put him through*' as the Senator," Adams replied that such an act meant a re-organization of parties. If so, CS's "ship was launched in democratic seas, and I must, however sorrowfully, bid him Goodbye. Henceforward we should probably each promote our principles in opposite courses and with differing sympathies" (Adams Papers, microfilm reel 72).

2. Francis William Bird (1809–94), Boston businessman, Free Soil and Republican Party organizer. Probably Whiting Griswold (1814–74), Democrat, later Republican, member of Massachusetts legislature from Greenfield.

To Charles Francis Adams

Court St—Tuesday—
[7 *January* 1851]

Dear Adams,

I liked yr letter[1] this morning very much.

It makes a basis for us all, & keeps prominent the idea which brings us all together.

The tribute to Palfrey is deserved. It thrilled me as I read it.[2]

And the vindication of the majority of the party was a grand rebuke to the paper, which sought to sow dissension among us.

Yr letter will help the Future.

Hunkerism, Whig & Democratic, is at this moment in a bloody sweat. Never before has it been so sorely tried.

Yesterday I had another interview with the Democracy, with some elements of the ludicrous, which you will enjoy. They wished me to say that in the Senate I should devote myself to *Foreign* politics!! I said that I wished them all to understand two things

1st, that I did not in any way, directly or indirectly seek the office,
2ndly, if it came to me, it must find me *an absolutely independent man*.

Ever Yrs, Charles Sumner

P.S. Downer has just called. He says you have written a grand letter.

ALS MBApm (69/479, PCS)

1. Without mentioning CS's name, Adams's public letter, 6 January 1851, "To the Editors of the Boston Atlas" (*Boston Daily Atlas*, 7 January 1851:2), stated that the Free Soilers' goal of "securing to our cause the aid of one of our ablest and most honest and most inflexible of advocates in the position of a Senator of the United States" might be worth some negotiating and compromise.

2. In his letter Adams stated that Palfrey had been Adams's model, forcing him to realize he had a "duty" to express his political views.

To John Bigelow
Private

Boston Jan. 21st '51

My dear Bigelow,

I regret yr illness, for your own comfort, & also because I like to know that you are on the watch-tower.[1]

In pending matters I have no personal interest; & my object in writing you before was, that you might understand my position, not in any way to promote my election. Our cause here, & throughout the country, may be staked somewhat upon my present success.[2] But I assure you *ex pectore*[3] I have no personal disappointments. I do not desire to be senator.

You are right in auguring ill from the Fabian strategy.[4] This alone saved Hunkerdom. Had the balloting taken place in the same week with that for Governor, our success would have been certain. When it was postponed for three days I thought our friends had lost the chances. My own opinion now is that they are lost *beyond* recovery. But others do not share this. The leading Democrats, who undertook to carry the arrangement through, are sanguine. Several towns on Monday instructed their representatives to vote for the regular candidate.

On Wednesday the Senate will vote. On Thursday the House return to the task.[5]

The pressure from Washington has been prodigious. Webster & Cass have both done all they could.[6] Of course Boston Whiggery is aroused against me. There were for several days many uneasy stomachs at the chances of my success.

The pinch has been just this. I would not in any way consent to be used by the Hunkers. Four different Committees called upon me—one simply asked me to meet a few Democrats to confer with them—another proposed a conference with Genl. [*Caleb*] Cushing & told me that he had *already* called on me twice—another wished me to say that in the Senate I would devote myself to the *foreign* politics!—& another wished some assurance that I would not agitate the subject of Slavery. To all these I had one answer—that I did not seek the office—& that, if it came to me, it must find me an absolutely independent man. I declined to have any political conversation with Genl. Cushing. Before this time, in caucus, he had spoken, as I have been told, warmly for me.

It is very evident that a slight word of promise or yielding to the Hunkers would have secured my election. It would now, if I would give it. But this is impossible.

The charge used with most effect against me is that I am a *Disunionist*; but the authors of this know its falsehood.[7] It is all a sham to influence votes. My principles are in the words of Franklin "to step to the *verge* of the Constitution to discourage every species of traffic in human flesh."[8] I am a Constitutionalist & Unionist, & have always been.

Long ago I promised Mr Dunlap to write a notice of his edition of his father's book on Admiralty for the *Post*.[9] Many things have prevented me from even looking at the book; but I will try to do it at once & send it to you.

Ever faithfully Yours, Charles Sumner

R. H. Dana Jr. left yesterday for New York, where he is to be a couple of days. He said he should call on you. He will tell you of our affairs.

John Bigelow Esq.

ALS NSchU (PL, 69/490, PCS)

1. John Bigelow (1817–1911; managing editor of the New York *Evening Post*, 1848–61) had written from New York that he had been housebound for eight days (20 January 1851, 7/541, PCS).

2. At their caucus on 7 January the Free Soil members of the Massachusetts legislature unanimously nominated CS for the full-term seat in the U.S. Senate; by a two-thirds majority the Democrats also nominated CS. At its election on 14 January, however, the House failed to give CS the necessary majority.

3. "From the heart."

4. Bigelow wrote he was disappointed at the legislature's vote on 14 January and regarded the Democrats' cautious or "Fabian tactics" as the cause.

5. See DD, 1:194–202, and Frederick J. Blue, *The Free Soilers* (1973), 215–24, for detailed analyses of the political maneuvering that took place between January and April.

6. Webster wrote his ally Thomas B. Curtis, a Boston merchant, on 20 January 1851, advising Whigs in the legislature to unite with "honest conservative Democrats" for a "sound, sensible, Union man" of either the Democrat or Whig party (DW, 7:196).

7. In his letter to Mann, 22 January (69/492), CS wrote that Marcus Morton was responsible for this charge.

8. CS misquoted Franklin, who wrote, "to step to the very verge of the power vested in you for discouraging every species of traffic in the persons of our fellow-man" (Petition to Congress, 3 February 1790, *Annals of Congress*, 1st Cong., 2nd sess., 1198).

9. See CS to Benjamin W. Stone, 15 August 1836. A second edition of Dunlap's treatise, with notes by Samuel Fales Dunlap, was published in 1850.

To Horace Mann

Boston Jan. 28th '51

Dear Mann,

Yr letter & the M.S. reached me yesterday. I have lost no time in attending to yr suggestion.[1]

The argt. is complete & masterly, & exhaustive. To me it is a *diagram*. I have taken the liberty of suggesting a more formal subdivision. The hearer or reader will need occasional rests. This may be obtained by an [enuntiation?] of yr propositions, proceeding to the proof, & when you have disposed of one, then in a formal way taking up the next.

In this way you will present yr argt., so that the reader will feel its march, & onward movement. I think he may be lost in its apparent maze, unless some change is made.

In printing, the careful use of *spaces* may assist the reader. Still I would not forego the great help of divisions & subdivisions.

You make one admission, which I would not—viz. that Congress has constitutional power to legislate on the subject of Fug. Slaves. Webster, you know, questioned this; so has Chase. See his speech.[2] It seems to me that the strict construction applied to all such powers must shew that Congress has not been entrusted with them; but they belong to the states.

At any rate, I would not conclude myself on this point; nor even on Spoonerism.[3]

See my pencil marks on yr MS.

I trust you will make an opportunity to deliver this. Do.

Many of our friends here are sanguine of success at the next time;[4] & I know that many Whigs are very anxious. Mr Wm Appleton said on Saturday in the hearing of a person who told me, that "he thought Mr S. would be elected." His wish was *not* father to the thought.

I have heard from nobody at Washington. I am curious to know how the contest is regarded there, & if my position is understood.

Ever Yours, Charles Sumner

ALS MHi (69/500, PCS)

1. Understanding "how *distraught* you must be" about the unresolved Senate election, Mann nevertheless asked CS to comment on Mann's forthcoming speech against the Fugitive Slave Law: "there is no one in whom, on this point, I have so much confidence as in you" (Washington, 24 January 1851, 69/494, PCS). Mann's speech was delivered 28 February in the House (*Globe*, 31st Cong., 2nd sess., appendix, 237–49).

2. Chase spoke against the Fugitive Slave Law and other compromise measures 26–27 March 1850 (*Globe*, 31st Cong., 1st sess., appendix, 468–80). He asked his fellow senators supporting the Fugitive Slave Law "where they find the power to legislate on this subject in the Constitution?" The "power" and "duty" of legislation lay with the states, not Congress (476).

3. This reference must have been excised from Mann's draft, now missing.

4. On 22 January the Massachusetts Senate elected CS as senator but CS had thus far failed to receive the necessary majority in the Massachusetts House.

To Horace Mann

Boston Feb. 19th '51

Dear Mann,

Here is a copy of the Georgia Resolutions. They will be found, probably, in the *appropriation act* for 1831.

Think of the violation of the post-office laws.[1]

The excitement at Washington about the Fugitive case here is most ridiculous. *A very few unarmed negroes did it all*. Their success shews the little support the law has in our community. The two ring-leaders, I know, were coloured sailors, who *extemporized* the rescue without preconcert. They have already sailed, & are now in the Gulf Stream.

Wright is innocent. The *Byrnes* who testified against him has no character, & has undoubtedly perjured himself.[2]

This case has for a while swamped the senatorial matter. You have seen that the result has been in accordance with my expectations. Meanwhile some of our more active friends are [nurturing?] things for other trials. They think the chances are better now than ever. Banks tells me that it will certainly be carried, if the Free Soilers stand firm. Clifford, Atty Genl,[3] told me that it could not be prevented ultimately; he also told me that Cushing acknowledged the same, saying "some of our men (the bolters) are *tender-footed.*" But I do not yet see the evidence.

One thing I do see. Nothing can tempt me into a contest next autumn. With this session my service closes.

Ever Yrs C. S.

ALS MHi (69/518, PCS)

1. In his letter of 14 February 1851 (69/517, PCS) Mann asked CS for a copy of the state of Georgia's resolution that in 1831 offered a $5,000 reward if William Lloyd Garrison could be arrested and convicted in the state of Georgia. Mann used this example of Southern flouting of law in his 28 February speech (*Globe*, 31st Cong., 2nd sess., appendix, 249), along with charging that some Southern states interfered with the U.S. mail.

2. On 15 February an alleged fugitive slave, Frederick Jenkins, also known as Shadrack, had been freed from the Suffolk County Court House by two other blacks. Elizur Wright (1804–85), editor of the *Massachusetts Abolitionist*, was arrested 23 February for assisting in Shadrack's escape. As attorney for Charles G. Davis, also arrested for assisting in the escape, Richard Henry Dana, Jr., wrote that the only testimony against Davis came from Byrnes, "a broken down man, of an impeached reputation" (*The Journal of Richard Henry Dana, Jr.*, ed. Robert F. Lucid [1968], 2:410–14).

3. Nathaniel Banks (1816–94), then Speaker of the House, Massachusetts state legislature; later U.S. congressman (F.S., Rep.), 1853–57, 1865–73; governor of Massachusetts, 1858–61. John Henry Clifford (1809–76), Whig governor of Massachusetts, 1853; president, Boston and Providence Railroad, 1867–76.

To John Greenleaf Whittier

Boston March 25th '51

Dear Whittier,

I long to commune with you on our cause at large, & particularly on my duty at the present moment. My situation is one of delicacy & embarassment. Personally I am entirely resigned to any alternative; & I shall be grateful if I can be gently dropped to mother earth. But I am unwilling in any way to seem to forsake the cause or our friends.

The Free Soilers have a letter from me, telling them to abandon me whenever they think best, "without notice or apology."[1] Shall I make this peremptory by an absolute withdrawal?

The course which the Free Soilers should pursue, if my name is withdrawn, seems to me very clear; but it does not become me to suggest it.

I wish I could see you. Can you come down for a night, or part of a day—a few hours [*ms torn for three lines*] which may make it more convenient for you to come here, than for me to seek you at Amesbury.

Let me hear from you at once.

Our affairs are all in disarray;—the paper,[2] confusion [*remainder of ms torn*]

AL MSaE (69/539, PCS)

1. CS's letter of 22 February 1851 to Henry Wilson, chairman of the committee of Free Soil members of the Massachusetts Legislature, is printed in Wks, 3:153–54.

2. CS may refer to a new Free Soil paper in Boston, the *Commonwealth*, recently established, with Samuel Gridley Howe heading the editorial board (Harold Schwartz, *Samuel Gridley Howe* [1956], 178).

To Joshua R. Giddings

Boston April 3d '51

My dear Sir,

I am obliged by your good tidings with regard to the position of Mr Wade.[1] I trust that he may be true to the inspirations of his early life. You know better than I the pressure he will be obliged to withstand at Washington. He has a noble place. May God give him the heart to fill it, as becomes a man from the Western Reserve of Ohio.

I have implicit confidence that we shall yet rally the Free States against the Fugitive Slave Bill. Each day discloses its atrocities. The persecutions here in Boston will keep them before our public; & our Convention next week will deepen the impression.

The result of the Senatorial question here is still uncertain. It is now postponed for three weeks. I am told that a more thorough & systematic effort will be made next time by our friends than ever before. There was a defection yesterday of one vote, caused, it is said, by the influence of Marcus Morton.

I have told our friends to abandon me at any time "without notice or apology." But, I believe, that the conviction is pretty general that I am the only person who can be elected. If the bolters should be satisfied of this, it remains to be seen whether they would take the responsibility of throwing the election over to the next year, with the prospect of giving the post to the Whigs for six years.

I believe no person in New England has ever run such a gauntlet as has been my fate. It is odd that this should have befallen one, who had in every way striven not to be a candidate. I am told that, notwithstanding the political ardours which have been aroused, there has been little or no personal asperity. This is not true, however, of the Webster Whigs. They are very bitter. But I have not read the newspapers, teeming with this discussion.

I am always glad to hear from you; & hope soon to know yr further impressions.

Ever sincerely Yours, Charles Sumner

ALS OHi (69/550, PCS)

1. In his letter of 17 March 1851 (7/608, PCS) Giddings announced that his former law partner, Benjamin Wade (1800–78; U.S. senator [Whig, Rep., Ohio], 1851–69), had been elected senator by a Free Soil–Whig coalition. Giddings wrote he "had no distrust of his [*Wade's*] present feelings" (Wade was strongly opposed to the Fugitive Slave Law), but he did question Wade's "determination of purpose."

To Henry Wilson

Craigie-House Cambridge—
April 25th '51

My dear Wilson,

I have at this moment read yr remarks of last night, which I think peculiarly happy. You touched the right cord.

I hope not to seem cold or churlish in thus withdrawing from all the public manifestations of triumph to which our friends are prompted.[1] In doing so, I follow the line of reserve which you know I have kept to throughout the contest. And my best judgment at this moment satisfies me that I am right.

You, who have seen me familiarly & daily from the beginning to the end will understand me, &, if need be, can satisfy those who, taking counsel of their exultation, would have me mingle in the display. But I shrink from imposing any thing more upon you.

To yr ability, energy, determination, & fidelity our cause owes its present success. For weal or woe, you must take the responsibility of having placed me in the Senate of the U.S.

I am prompted also to add, that, while you have done all this, I have never heard from you a single suggestion of a selfish character, looking in any way to any good to yourself. Yr labors have been as disinterested, as they have been effective. This consideration increases my personal esteem & gratitude.

I trust that you will see that Mr B's resolves[2] are passed at once, *as they are*, & the bill as soon as possible. Delay will be the tactics of the enemy.

Sincerely Yours, Charles Sumner

Hon. Henry Wilson

ALS MBNEH (69/565, PCS)

1. On 24 April 1851 the Massachusetts State House, on its twenty-sixth ballot, finally elected CS U.S. senator. Wilson, then president of the Massachusetts State Senate, had spoken at a meeting on State Street celebrating CS's election (Wilson, 2:350). CS himself fled across the Charles River to Longfellow's house.

2. Joseph T. Buckingham's resolutions, presented in the Massachusetts State Legislature, condemned the Fugitive Slave Law as "an infamous and wicked statute." The legislature was considering an act to provide due process, including trial by jury, for fugitive slaves (*Liberator*, 25 April 1851:65).

III
EARLY SENATORIAL CAREER

May 1851 – May 1856

GIVEN SUMNER'S reputation as a founder of the Republican party, it is surprising that its formation does not appear more significantly in his correspondence. Sumner's letters in this period show none of the enthusiasm for the Republican party that he had expressed for the Free Soilers in 1848. In the fluid political scene following the demise of the Whig party in 1854 and 1855, the Know-Nothings' threat, more than any other political force, absorbed Sumner's attention. As he had in the 1840s, Sumner saw politics only as a means to an end, that end being the elimination of slavery. He had written Horace Mann (5 August 1850) that "a *politician* in the service of a *party* cannot be trusted." Publicly as well, Sumner exhibited little enthusiasm. At the first state Republican convention, 7 September 1854, Sumner called on Massachusetts citizens to rally in protest against the Kansas-Nebraska and Fugitive Slave Acts, but only once named the Republican party as the organization to effect such a protest (Wks, 4:266–67). Sumner's May 1855 speech, "The Antislavery Enterprise," which urged all Northerners to unite against the slave power, specifically foreswore all sects and parties and did not mention the Republican party.

Perhaps Sumner did not initially see the Republican party as the preeminent antislavery organization that the Free Soilers had been for him. He wrote fellow senator Julius Rockwell (26 November 1854) that each of them seemed "without a party in the Commonwealth," although Sumner hoped for a "solid, compact & healthy organization." William Gienapp and David Donald attribute Sumner's lack of involvement in the Republican gubernatorial campaign of 1855 to his cautious concern for his political future; Sumner's high-minded statements eschewing politics for principle were not always sincere. Although Sumner expressed enthusiasm for the Republican party in letters to Rockwell, John Jay, and William H. Seward in the fall of 1855, he did not publicly expound the merits of the Republicans until shortly before the November elections. Then, at a Republican rally in Faneuil Hall on 2 November, Sumner declared that the Republican party "now happily constituted here in Massachusetts, and in all the Free States" would ensure that "the Slave Oligarchy shall be overthrown" ("Political Parties and Our Foreign-Born Population," Wks, 5:80–82).

As an elected official, Sumner was obliged to obey the Constitution, an obligation his Southern detractors frequently reminded him of. Although Sumner publicly called slave hunting a "crime," the activity was not a legal crime. In a letter to Heman Lincoln (24 July 1854) Sumner explained his evasion of the federal Fugitive Slave Law, repeating an explanation from a Senate speech of 28 June 1854. "Only in an *exceptional case,* of transcendant importance," wrote Sumner to Lincoln, should one sidestep the Constitution. In a letter to Wisconsin judge Byron Paine (18 January 1856) Sumner fell back on the states' rights argument ("the *self-defensive* power of the states") to deny the federal government the power to pursue runaway slaves and declared that "the authors of the Constitution did not foresee the dilemma presented." Sumner rationalized that he would obey the Constitution as he interpreted it.

If Sumner was too radical for constituents like Heman Lincoln, he moved too slowly for activists like Theodore Parker and Wendell Phillips. Knowing his oratorical gifts, correspondents urged him to summon these powers for an unrestrained attack on the slave power. At first Sumner was cautious. On 5 April 1852 he wrote Samuel Gridley Howe, "I have always borrowed something from Prudence"; he wanted to establish his credibility on other issues in order to send his antislavery message to a wider audience. This series of letters chronicles the pressure imposed on Sumner and his increasing willingness to yield to it. In connection with the Senate's consideration of Kansas's admission, Sumner wrote prophetically to Gerrit Smith (18 March 1856), "We have before us a long season of excitement, & ribald debate."

To John Bigelow

Boston, May 2nd '51

My dear Bigelow,

Let me first rejoice with you in the infant Astyanax of yr house. Believe me that I sympathize cordially in this happiness —— although I am a "bachelor"! I trust that Mrs Bigelow[1] is strong as becomes the mother of such a boy.

Yr greetings, which were among the earliest I received, were particularly grateful; & Mr Bryant's brief Appendix re-inforced even yr full letter.[2] The whole made me proud of the confidence I received.

I would not affect a feeling which I have not, nor have I any temptation to do it, but I should not be frank if I did not say to you, that I have no personal joy in this election. Now that the office is in my hands I feel, more than ever, a distaste for its duties & struggles as compared with other spheres. Every heart knoweth its own secret, & mine has never been in the Senate of the U.S.; nor is it there yet.

Most painfully do I feel my inability to meet the importance, which has been given to this election, & the expectation of enthusiastic friends. But more than this I am impressed by the thought that I now embark on a career, which promises to last for six years, if not indefinitely, & which takes from me all opportunity of study & meditation, to which I had hoped to devote myself. I do not wish to be a politician.

But I have said too much of this already. For the present I must try to be content.

Rantoul & Palfrey will be elected; perhaps, Bishop in the Berkshire District.[3] Should all this occur our Massachusetts delegation will be very strong in the House. Nothing but Boutwell's half-Hunkerism prevents us from consolidating a permanent party in Massachusetts, not by *coalition*, but by *fusion* of all who are truly liberal, humane & democratic. He is in our way. He has tried to please Hunkers & Free Soilers. We can get along very well without the Hunkers, & should be happy to leave [*Benjamin F.*] Hallett & Co. to commune with the men of State St.

The latter have been infinitely disturbed by the recent election. For the first time they are represented in the Senate by one over whom they have no influence, who is entirely independent, & is a "bachelor"! It was said among them at first that real estate had gone down 25 per cent!

I regret the present state of things in New York, because it seems to interfere with those influences, which were gradually bringing the liberals & Anti-Slavery men of both the old parties together. Yr politics will never be in a natural state till this occurs.[4]

I sympathize much in the opposition to the debt, as a violation of the Constitution; but I regret that the question has come to arrest the Slavery discussion.[5] I am confident that the latter has a basis in the hearts & consciences of the people, which will make it a truer platform than any other, connected as it must be with all that is liberal, & in a just sense democratic.

Yr Hunker allies, I fear, will be false, as is their nature, towards yr candidates.

On the 4th page of the *Commonwealth* of to-day is a part of a speech of R. H. Dana Jr, which, like every thing from him, seems to me most felicitous in its clear simple diction.[6]

I desire very much a copy of Mr Coffin's bill, introduced to yr legislature, but never acted on. Sometime ago I wrote for it to Stanton; but he has been too much occupied to answer me.[7] Was it published in the Post? If so can you send me a copy of it? Or can you write to any body in Albany, & ask him to send me a copy?

Remember me kindly to Mr Bryant, with many thanks for those words, & believe me,

Ever sincerely yours Charles Sumner

Private The following message came to me a few weeks ago from Mr Soulé, senator from Louisiana.[8]

"Mr Soulé sends his salutations to Mr S. & hopes he will be elected. He desires to see a senator from Massachusetts, whose opinions he knows."

John Bigelow Esq.

ALS NSchU (PL, 69/582, PCS)

1. Jane Poultney Bigelow (c. 1829–89), married John Bigelow, 1850.

2. Bigelow wrote from New York 24 April 1851 (7/647, PCS) that all the staff of the New York *Evening Post* had rejoiced over CS's election to the Senate. William Cullen Bryant added his congratulations to Bigelow's.

3. Robert Rantoul (1805–52), U.S. senator (Dem., Mass.), 1851; U.S. congressman, 1851–52. Probably Henry W. Bishop, Democrat from Lenox.

4. Bigelow wrote that there was in New York now "almost a complete reunion of the old political parties," with antislavery Whigs and Democrats returning to their respective parties.

5. A bill in the New York legislature to fund the Erie Canal was viewed as unconstitutional by some state senators. The *Post* agreed and had run a series of editorials opposing the Nine Million Bill (28–29 April, 1–2 May 1851:2).

6. The *Commonwealth*, 2 May 1851:4. In his speech Dana criticized Boston officials for enforcing the Fugitive Slave Law.

7. Henry B. Stanton, then a New York state senator, did answer CS 13 May 1851 (Seneca Falls, 8/025), apologizing for not responding sooner to CS's request for the unidentified bill.

8. Pierre Soulé (1801–70), U.S. senator (States Rights, Dem., La.), 1841, 1844–53; U.S. minister to Spain, 1853–55.

To John Greenleaf Whittier

Boston May 4th '51

My dear Whittier,

I am saddened by the thought of yr illness. For myself I am well in body, but sick at heart. I long to commune with you again on all that has passed.

Some of the heaviest hours of my life have been since my election.

More than ever, I now feel my repugnance to the ⟨life⟩ career of a politician. Would that another faithful to our cause were in my place!

I am oppressed also by the sense of my inability to meet the expectations of friends & the importance attached to the result. And, as I read the reports of gratulations, I am filled anew with the conviction of my own unworthiness. The general joy, so far as founded on anticipations, makes me unhappy. But I will try to be content.

I am pressed to speak at suppers & caucuses; but my true policy, it seems to me, is for the present *silence*. The cause is now committed to my discretion, & I feel that I can best promote it by caution & reserve at least until I take my seat. I wish that the public should become submissive to the idea that I am a senator before they hear my voice. Unless this is so, I shall not secure a fair hearing from the country.

I have mentioned these views to some of our friends, who were at first earnest to bring me out, & have been glad to find them in harmony with me. But there are others who may still press me. All this adds to the difficulty of my position.

I trust this will find you restored in strength. When shall I read the verses you have written on the Sims' outrage?[1]

Ever Thine, Charles Sumner

ALS MSaE (69/586, PCS)

1. George T. Curtis, U.S. commissioner in Boston, had ordered that Thomas Sims, a seventeen-year-old slave, be returned to Georgia, and Sims was jailed in a Boston prison. Whittier's poem "Moloch in State Street" appeared in the *National Era*, 22 May 1851:82.

To Ralph Waldo Emerson

Boston May 7th '51

My dear Emerson,

I rejoiced in reading this morning that you had spoken to the public on the great enormity.[1] Allow me to express a hope that you will repeat yr words in Cambridge & other places of Mr Palfrey's District, & afterwards in Boston. Then you must print.

Yr judgment of the Fugitive Slave Bill posterity will adopt, even if the men of our own day do not. But you have access to many, whom other Anti-Slavery speakers cannot reach. Yr testimony, therefore, is of peculiar importance. I thank you from my heart, that you have given it, & I long to enjoy it in that marvellous style which always awakens my admiration.

Believe me, ever sincerely Yours, Charles Sumner

ALS MH-H (69/588, PCS)

1. In his speech, 3 May 1851, "Address to the Citizens of Concord—on the Fugitive Slave Law," Emerson castigated Boston citizens for permitting the arrest of Sims (*The Complete Works of Ralph Waldo Emerson*, ed. Edward Waldo Emerson [1883], 11:179–214). Stating that a "wicked law cannot be executed by good men and must be by bad" (195), Emerson called for a repeal of the law and restriction of slavery to the slave states (207).

To Abigail Brooks Adams

Boston Tuesday 1 o'clk
[*27 May 1851*]

Dear Mrs Adams,

According to all the evidence we now have our very dear Dr has been defeated.[1] I am sad—sad—very sad; for the cause more than for him (for he loses nothing); & I mourn also for myself.

To him, of course, I had looked for support & companionship at Washington. Would that I were not going! I have no joy in what the world calls "honor."

While I am writing a person has called to tell me of a mistake made by the Whigs of Lancaster, which may cause the rejection of 79 votes from that town. If this is true, perhaps our friend may be elected. This is too good to be true. But in this bit of sunshine I mean for a while to try to be happy.

Greet yr husband from me. I know he will feel this result keenly. The way is now paved for the paper. The Dr must be installed as editor.[2] He said last night that he had this alternative "The paper or Europe." It must be the paper.

Goodbye; Ever sincerely Yours, Charles Sumner

ALS MBApm (69/611, PCS)

1. The election in the fourth congressional district had remained unresolved since November 1848, but the 26 May election finally resulted in a victory for the Whig candidate, Benjamin Thompson, over Palfrey. In his letter to Chase of 5 June 1851 (69/627, PCS) CS attributed Palfrey's defeat to his December letter protesting the Free Soil–Democrat coalition.

2. Palfrey agreed to become a contributing editor of the *Commonwealth* (Frank O. Gatell, *John Gorham Palfrey and the New England Conscience* [1963], 201).

To George Sumner

Boston June 17th [*and* 24] '51

Dear George,

I was glad to have even so little as your very small note of May 17th. The more I think of public life, the less I incline to it. There is nothing in the vista of politics which has any attraction for me. To the "honor" of a seat in the Senate, so much coveted by many, I am absolutely indifferent; nor do I care for the political influence which it gives.

June 24th—

I had written thus far, hoping to send by the last steamer, but was prevented from concluding my note. In answer to yr inquiries, let me say, that there are signs of a contest in Mass. such as very rarely occurs. The bitterness of the Whigs is intense, & they will spare no effort or money to regain the control of the state. I do not think they can succeed. The Free Soilers are united & determined. Our paper has just passed into the hands of Mr Joseph Lyman,[1] as editor & proprietor assisted by Mr Palfrey. I think it will be the most powerful organ in Mass. In the coming contest its influence must be considerable.

There will be a coalition in the autumn between the Free Soilers & Democrats, with no disturbing senatorial question.

The Free Soilers have been mis-represented by their opponents; & none more than myself. This, perhaps, was natural from the strong desire to break me down. You will see from my letter of acceptance,[2] that, by simply stating my position, I have spiked their guns—at least for the present.

My course in this discussion, from the beginning, has been most guarded. I am a constitutionalist, & have never taken any position inconsistent with this character. The Garrisonians have criticised my letter with some severity, though they have always known that there were radical differences between us.[3]

I believe you could not hesitate to adopt every principle in our politics which I have ever maintained.

Whatever may be the course of things in Mass. between now & the next Presidential contest I entertain no doubt that from that time forward the Free Soil party will easily predominate in our state. In the nation the contest, of course, will be longer. But there our ultimate triumph is none the less certain. The young man, whose bosom does not stir with sympathy for a noble cause, may be swayed by a selfish ambition to keep on the side of Freedom.

I long for talks with you, & the enjoyment of yr great European budget. What do you say to Free Trade in our country? Write me of this fully.

Mr Irving[4] was in Boston for a day last week. He enquired warmly after you, & wished me to give you his particular regards. He hoped you would write a book. Will you?

But you ought to be a diplomatist. Another motive to me for discontent in my present position is the fear that I may stand in yr way. It would be difficult for an Administration to appoint the brother of one so obnoxious as myself, without pledges or explanations, which you could not stoop to give. If I were a private man, there would be no influence against you on this score.

If you see Henry Parker[5] in London, he will tell you of our politics.

Let me hear from you soon.

Ever Thine, Chas.

P.S. No draft has come from N.Y.—Julia [*Sumner*] is quite well now, & enjoying Jenny Lind,[6] whose music is marvellous.

ALS MH-H (63/427, PCS)

1. Joseph Lyman (1812–71), Harvard A.B., 1830; editor of the Boston *Commonwealth*; in the 1850s active in antislavery representation in Kansas.

2. In his letter of 14 May 1851, read in the two houses of the Massachusetts legislature (Wks, 3:161–64), CS pledged that he would "oppose all *sectionalism*," which might be manifested in unconstitutional efforts in both North and South on the slavery issue.

3. Describing CS's letter as "purely rhetorical" and far too cautious, *The Liberator* stated, "Mr Sumner should have kept nothing back as to what ought to be done, and what might be done, by Congress for restricting the Slave Power to its Constitutional limits" (23 May 1851:83).

4. The American writer Washington Irving (1783–1859) had known George Sumner when Irving was minister to Spain (see George Sumner to CS, Madrid, 26 July 1843, *Proceedings of the Massachusetts Historical Society* 46 [1912–13]:363).

5. Henry Tuke Parker (1824–90) moved permanently to London in 1855, where he became the London agent for the Boston Public Library.

6. Jenny Lind (1820–87), Swedish soprano.

To Thomas Wentworth Higginson[1]

Boston Sept. 5th '51

Dear Mr Higginson,

I am told that you are very much interested in the course our friends should take this autumn. This I rejoice in, & I wish that I could have the advantage of conferring with you on the subject.

It was only last evng that I returned to Boston after an absence from the state of several weeks. More than ever do I feel the importance to our cause of preventing the Cwlth from passing into the hands of Websterized Whiggery. This, of course, can be prevented only by a *combination*—I wish a complete community of principles would allow it to be a *union*—with the Democrats. Regretting that they are not more essentially with us, I feel that we shall throw our staff away, if we reject the opportunity, which seems offered, of their co-operation against the Whigs.

With a mutual understanding of each other, & with a real determination to carry the *combination* honestly through, in the hope of sustaining our great cause, I cannot doubt the result. Webster & Winthrop will be defeated.[2] Perhaps, at the present moment no political event, connected with elections, would be of greater advantage to Freedom. It would resound throughout the country.

To accomplish this is well worthy our effort; & the only effort, practicable, is *combination* with the Democrats. If the latter will completely adopt our principles, then we hail them as brothers. If they fail to do this, then it seems to me that we should not fail to use them, wherever we can, to secure the balance of power in the Legislature, & to overturn the two W.W.'s of Massachusetts. For one, if they will help in this twofold purpose, I will welcome them & will "ask no questions."

I fear from what I have heard that these views may not entirely harmonize with yours; but I feel that our aims are so nearly identical—my sympathy with yr earnestness is so complete—that I do not think we could differ substantially as to the true course to be pursued,—if we could see each other & fully interchange opinions.[3] Shall you be in Boston soon? If so, be good enough to let me see you. If you dropped me a line the day before I should be certain not to miss you.

Believe me, Ever sincerely Yours, Charles Sumner

Revd. T. W. Higginson

ALS NjMo (70/001, PCS)

1. Thomas Wentworth Higginson (1823–1911), Unitarian minister and antislavery advocate.

2. The Whig convention, 10 September 1851, nominated Robert C. Winthrop for governor and passed a resolution placing "undiminished confidence" in Webster (DW, 7:272).

3. In his reply of 6 September from Newburyport, Mass. (8/184, PCS), Higginson supported CS's "combination" with the Democrats. He argued, however, for a stronger moral stand on the part of the Free Soilers and a tougher negotiating stance when they dealt with the Democrats, who he feared believed "we are to be had cheaper than they supposed."

To Salmon P. Chase

Boston Sept. 18th '51

Dear Chase,

While in New York at the *Evng Post* office, I heard that you had been in these parts. Why did you not let me know of yr movements? It would have been a sincere pleasure to me to meet & confer with you, renewing our long talks.

I have just recd. yr missive with regard to the Convention at Cleveland.[1] I do not think it possible for me to attend it, & I find, on inquiry, that all our friends, who have time to spare for their country, expect to be fully occupied in our own state. Besides, it does not seem to us that there is at this moment any sufficient occasion for such a Convention as is proposed. It would act, doubtless, with good effect on local opinion in Ohio; but I do not think it can serve any national purpose to a sufficient degree to tempt us, who are otherwise occupied, to the long journey. But I trust that we shall not seem indifferent to the cause, because we are unable at the present moment to mingle in yr counsels & efforts.

The Coalition will carry Mass. & Winthrop be completely defeated. This is clear, unless Hunkerism breaks out in some unexpected form of treachery.

I have not seen yr recent letter.[2] That of July I liked much.

I regret more & more my official burdens. There is nothing in the vista of office which has any charms for me.

The Democrats will go into the next Presidential campaign on the issue of Cuban Annexation.[3] This we must meet next winter.

Let me hear from you soon.

Ever Yrs, Charles Sumner

P.S. I have thought of securing rooms at Washington the other side of the Presdt's house.[4]

ALS DLC (70/012, PCS)

1. Chase had invited CS to the "National Convention of the Friends of Freedom" on 24 November 1851, stating the need for Massachusetts' representation (Cincinnati, 30 August, 8/178, PCS).

2. Chase's letter of 25 August to C. R. Miller was published in the *National Era*, 11 September 1851:2. In it Chase endorsed the recent Ohio Democratic Convention platform, emphasizing the platform's strong stand that the federal government had responsibility to contain, in fact abolish, slavery in areas it governed.

3. Some Southern slavery expansionists sought to purchase Cuba from Spain (DD, 1:241).
4. CS engaged a bedroom and sitting room on New York Avenue, between 14th and 15th streets (ibid., 206).

To John Greenleaf Whittier

Boston Oct. 7th '51

Dear Whittier,

Dr [*Gamaliel*] Bailey, who was here a short time ago, longed to see you. He hoped you would sustain the Coalition. And I hope so too.

Will not Higginson see this matter in a practical light? I respect him so much, & honor his principles so supremely, that I am pained to differ from him; but I do feel that we must not neglect the opportunity afforded by *alliances*, not *fusion*, with the Democrats, to prevent the Whigs from establishing themselves in the State. Palfrey is now earnestly of this inclining;[1] so is [*Erastus*] Hopkins; also Burlingame; & all these stood off before.

Do help us.[2]

I start tomorrow for Washington, where I shall see Bailey & look about, & then hurry back.

Ever Thine, Charles Sumner

ALS MSaE (70/030, PCS)

1. Palfrey was nominated for governor by the Free Soilers in November. According to Frank O. Gatell, the nomination meant little since the coalition was pledged to reelect Boutwell. Boutwell defeated Winthrop in the November election (*John Gorham Palfrey and the New England Conscience* [1963], 203).
2. Whittier refused CS's request to support the coalition, saying he couldn't "vote knowingly for an open defender of the Fugitive Slave Law" (8/224, PCS).

To William H. Seward

Boston Oct. 22nd '51

My dear Sir,

Many thanks for yr argt. at Detroit,[1] which I have just received. I had already read it & admired the ability, completeness, & skill with which it is wrought.

While thus acknowledging yr kindness, I am glad of an opportunity to say with how much satisfaction I have made yr personal acquaintance. I have long desired to know you face to face; & I hope you will not deem me too bold, if I declare the delight with which I found, in yr familiar conversation, those congenial sentiments, on things higher than party, which involve the *idem sentire de republica*,[2] once pronounced a peculiar bond of friendship.

Beyond the performance of the stated duties of my unwelcome post, I have no objects in public life, except to sustain as I best may those sentiments of Freedom & Humanity, which should be the inspiring ideas of our country. There is nothing in the vista of politics which has any attraction for me. And my own free choice would carry me back at once to private life, to quiet studies, books, friendship & such labors for our cause as a simple citizen may always perform. Cicero, in one of his epistles, says that he preferred to sit in the library of Atticus, beneath the bust of Aristotle, to any curule *sella*; & I cannot refrain from joining with him, except that I would rather place myself beneath the bust of Plato.[3]

Thus reluctant to enter upon my new duties & scenting in advance the noxious vapors of politics, I find solace in the sympathy which you promise me; & I now write, in the frankness of my nature, to say so.[4]

I trust you will pardon all my freedom, & believe me, my dear Sir,

very sincerely Yours, Charles Sumner

Hon. Wm. H. Seward.

ALS NRU (70/037, PCS)

1. *Argument of William H. Seward in Defense of Abel F. Fitch and Others —September 11, 12, 14, 1851* (1851). Seward defended fifty men against charges of destroying company property, brought by the Michigan Central Railroad (Glyndon Van Deusen, *William Henry Seward* [1967], 136–37). CS had apparently met Seward on his recent trip to Washington.

2. "Knowing of the same things in the republic."

3. *Curule sella*, "chair of high office." CS disapproved of Aristotle's defense of slavery in his *Politics*, no doubt; but, as David Brion Davis points out, Plato was not as opposed to slavery as many abolitionists characterized him (*Slavery in Western Culture* [1966], 66–69).

4. Seward replied on 8 November 1851 from Auburn, New York (8/245, PCS), welcoming to the Senate one "imbued with the uncompromising devotion to Freedom and Humanity of John Quincy Adams."

To Henry W. Longfellow

New York—Nov. 26th. [*1851*]
Delmonico's—Thanksgiving-Day—

Dearest Longfellow,

I could not speak to you, as we parted;[1] my soul was too full; only tears would flow.

Yr friendship, & dear Fanny's, have been among my few treasures—like gold unchanging. How much I sacrifice you cannot tell. For myself, I see with painful vividness, the vicissitudes & enthralments of the Future, & feel that we shall never more know each other as in times past. Those calm days & nights of overflowing communion are gone. Thinking of them, & of what I lose, I become again a child.

From a grateful heart, I now thank you for yr true & constant friendship. Whatever may be in store for me, so much at least is secure, & the memory of you & Fanny will be to me a precious fountain. God bless you both, dear, ever dear friends, faithful & good. Be happy, & think kindly of me.

Charles Sumner

ALS MH-H (70/057, PCS)

1. CS left Boston on 25 November for Washington and the opening term of the Thirty-second Congress.

To Richard Henry Dana, Jr.

Washington Dec 8th '51

Dear Dana,

Yr hand-writing was pleasant to see.

You shall have the Daily Globe, if you desire; but the weekly, it strikes me, will better suit yr purpose.[1] Let me know which you prefer.

The Southerners are in high quarrel; Foote & Butler at red-hot words.[2] The scene was theatrical. While they talk there is no opportunity for us; nor can I yet see my way to intervene in this debate. Perhaps I shall. But I do not yet feel that it is the occasion for me to utter the mature & determined word which God willing! I will.

I have nothing but kindness from all. No "cold shoulders" yet! What will Boston Hunkerdom say?

Mittermaier in a letter just recd. acknowledges the copy of Webster's trial. Tell yr father of this with my regards.[3]

I have Jeff. Davis's seat—one of the best.[4]

Ever Yrs, Charles Sumner

Write me; do.

ALS MHi (70/076, PCS)

1. Dana asked CS for the best paper to learn "the actual proceedings of Congress" (5 December 1851, 8/287, PCS).

2. In a debate over enforcement of the compromise measures, Henry S. Foote (1804–80; U.S. senator [Unionist, Miss.], 1847–52) and Butler of South Carolina argued over their respective states' support of the Constitution and the 1850 compromise measures. Foote had presented a resolution on 2 December 1851 that the compromise measures be "recognized as a definitive adjustment and settlement of the distracting questions growing out of the system of domestic slavery" (*Globe*, 32nd Cong., 1st sess., 12).

3. Heidelberg, 30 October, 8/236. Dana's father, Richard Henry Dana (1787–1879), poet and essayist.

4. Jefferson Davis (1808–93) had resigned as senator in November 1851.

To Amasa Walker

Sen. Chamber Dec. 19th [*1851*]

Dear Walker,

I thought myself sure of yr sympathy in advance.[1]

When I spoke the resolution of welcome to Kossuth was in a most precarious state. Many thought it would not pass. I desired to secure its passage. Mr Berrien had already assailed it very ably; & my first effort for the floor was immediately after him; but I did not succeed then. Still when I spoke I replied to him, & I encountered his amendment, by recognizing its principle, but opposing it as out of place.[2]

In thus pleading at once for Kossuth & Peace, I satisfied all the instincts of my nature. You will observe that I am the only person in debate who resolutely opposed belligerent intervention, while I warmly welcomed our guest.

Kossuth has erred in his 3 demands upon our Govt.[3] They are utterly untenable. I have meditated the subject carefully. Enthusiast for Freedom every where, I am obliged, with great reluctance but with entire confidence, to oppose these demands. I regret that he has made them, because they will shock the conservative & peace-loving world, who, by careful measures, might have been enlisted on his side.

Were I willing to see in my speech any thing more than *duty done* I might have satisfaction in the way in which I was received. The most unbroken attention was observed throughout, & many of the elders of the Senate have spoken to me with regard to it in the warmest terms. Our Mr Alley[4] was on the floor of the Senate at the time, & will tell you of these things. Foote is now speaking. He speaks perpetually. Many expect me to speak on the Compromise. I may say a few words by way of fender against any conclusion from my silence; but the time has not come for me to say what is in my heart on Slavery. I am unwilling to be mixed up with Rhett & these Southern extremists[.]

Foote pressed me to speak before he did; but I was not to be so inveigled.[5]

When I left home I had vowed myself to a 3 months silence. But I could not resist the temptation of the Kossuth resolution, & the opportunity of uttering truth which I have at heart.

My time has been very much occupied. I have no sinecure.

Ever Yours, Charles Sumner

The *Cwlth* errs in pressing its warlike notions[6]

ALS MHi (70/109, PCS)

1. Walker wrote from Boston regarding CS's first Senate speech, "we all felt happy that you had spoken so rightly, and proud that you had spoken so ably" (16 December 1851, 8/344, PCS).

2. Louis Kossuth (1802–94), Hungarian political reformer, had led his country's drive for independence from Austria in 1848. After he was driven out in 1849 he embarked on a tour of Great Britain and the U.S. Seward's welcome to Kossuth was amended by John Macpherson Berrien (1781–1856; U.S. senator [Whig, Ga.], 1845–52) to state that Congress would not depart from established policy prohibiting interference in domestic matters of other nations. CS argued that Berrien's amendment was unnecessary (8, 9, 10 December 1851, *Globe*, 32nd Cong., 1st sess., 34, 44, 50–51).

3. On 11 December, speaking at a New York municipal dinner, Kossuth made three requests of the U.S.: 1) President Fillmore should warn the czar of Russia that Russia should not intervene in Hungary; 2) the U.S. Navy should protect trade routes in the Mediterranean; 3) the U.S. should recognize Hungary (*New York Daily Times*, 12 December 1851:1).

4. John B. Alley (1817–96), later U.S. congressman (Rep., Mass.), 1859–67; railroad entrepreneur.

5. R. Barnwell Rhett (1800–76), U.S. senator (Dem., S.C.), 1850–52. Foote spoke 19 December defending the compromise measures (*Globe*, 32nd Cong., 1st sess., appendix, 54–61).

6. In two editorials (12 and 16 December 1851:2) the *Commonwealth* argued for intervention to help Kossuth in Hungary, even at the risk of war. Although the *Commonwealth* generally praised CS's welcome to Kossuth, the paper on 12 December stated that CS would eventually discover that his "darling cause of Universal Peace requires that we should give something more than our 'gushing sympathies' to the side of liberty."

To Charles Francis Adams

Washington Dec. 28th '51

Dear Adams,

I make haste to mention some facts which you will be interested in knowing. On Friday I dined with our friend Warwick, & heard his report.[1] Genl. [*Winfield*] Scott had passed an evening with him, sipping brandy & water, & went so far in anticipation of the future as to indicate the cabinet he should appoint. Warwick told him at once that no President could ever offer him any office which he would accept. The General seemed pleased with all that Warwick said of his prospects. All the cabinet, xcpt Webster, are now decidedly for him, as also are the Whig members of Congress from the South. It is supposed that in a month their constituents will be so also. Warwick has information from N.Y. shewing that all idea of Webster or Fillmore is there extinct. This helps Scott. Indeed, there seems to be a general accord in his support among the Whigs.

The Boston Committee here took directions from Warwick, & among other things, undertook "to strengthen" John Davis, so that he may be re-chosen as senator, or as Governor.[2] He will speak on the Compromise.

On Xtmas-day, I dined with F. P. Blair at his place in the country. He told me that he wrote to Genl. Butler, that, as a man of honor, he could not receive the support of the Free Soilers, if he were so against their measures as to veto them, should they pass Congress; but he told Genl. Butler, that he did not ask any pledge from him.[3] Afterwards, he saw the Genl. who verbally acknowledged the receipt of Mr Blair's letter. At this moment it is supposed that Butler will be the Dem. candidate; but many think a split is inevitable. I think that the Cass & Douglas troop are disheartened. Cass tells me that he does not desire to be President—that he prefers his seat in the Senate. Mr King[4] talked to me in the same *volo episcopar*[5] vein.

The fate of the Compromise resolutions is uncertain, & I am still uncertain what course I shall take upon them.

I begin to be a-weary of this life. The scenes of the Senate have disgusted me. No man, who cares for happiness, should consent to come here unless for the sake of a sentiment, which he feels an irrepressible impulse to support in this way.

The understanding is that Scott shall say nothing. "Mum" is the word. What say you to all these things.—It has been very uncomfortable weather to-day. I was the sole occupant of yr family pew. Remember me to Mrs Adams & yr children.

Ever Yrs, C. S.

ALS MBApm (70/124, PCS)

1. Most likely a sobriquet for William H. Seward, since Warwick was historically known as the "kingmaker." In his letter to Longfellow, 28 December 1851 (Prc, 3:264, 70/134, PCS), CS stated he had dinner with Seward on Friday.

2. The Whig John Davis had been U.S. senator from Massachusetts since 1845.

3. Francis Preston Blair (1791–1876), editor of the Washington *Globe*, 1830–45, and a leading Democrat. William O. Butler (1791–1880), U.S. congressman (Dem., Ky.), 1839–43.

4. Stephen A. Douglas (1813–61), U.S. senator (Dem., Ill.), 1847–61. William R. King (1786–1853), U.S. senator (Dem., Ala.), 1819–44, 1848–53; U.S. vice president, 1853.

5. "I do not wish to be bishop."

To Samuel Gridley Howe

Washington Dec. 30th '51

Dear Howe,

I have just come from Kossuth. He is an inspired man, of stature not large or strong.[1]

Seward & myself are the only persons here who are really his friends. All the rest have political aims to prompt them or hold them back. I should confine my remarks to the senators.

I said to him, when I took him by the hand—"Governor, how do you do"? He said at once, "Let me rather ask you a question. What will you do?" Thus at once, on the threshold, he opened his cause.

I observed that, at our interview, Cass turned the conversation from Hungary to the ease with which he spoke our language! In this way he will be met at every turn.

Do you ask what balks him thus? It is the Slave-Power. Cass fears to take a step, lest this shall be aroused against him, as it is against Kossuth. Slavery is the source of all meanness here from national dishonesty down to tobacco-spitting.

Ever Thine, C. S.

Thanks for yr letter

P.S. Dec. 31st—I forgot to tell you yesterday that Madame Pulszky[2] is with the Kossuths. She is thin & care-worn, but speaks with admiration of you.

To-day they call on the President. Saturday they dine with him. Monday Congressional dinner. Tuesday dinner at Seward's. But he comes not for hospitality. He is in earnest, & wishes an answer to his propositions.

Did you not once lend me a book on the power of Russia, shewing by a map & careful historical xposition, her careers of absorption & annexation of neighbor states. If you can find it, send it to me by Adams's Xpress.

You also had a work on Austria of very important character. Send that if possible.

If you can't send the books, send me the *titles*. *C. S.*

ALS MH-H (63/474, PCS)

1. Howe had written CS two letters from Boston criticizing his "Welcome to Kossuth" speech (26 and 28 December 1851, 70/117 and 126, PCS). He argued that sometimes force and intervention *were* necessary in the face of tyranny, and that the latter part of CS's speech was merely peace propaganda.

2. Terézia Walder Pulszky, wife of Ferencz Pulszky (1814–97), Hungarian writer and politician. Terézia Moszlenyi Kossuth (d. 1863), married Louis Kossuth, 1841.

To George Sumner

Washington Jany. 5th [*1852*]

Dear George,

Yrs from the Hague came yesterday with instructive speculations on French politics. I believe in France, & am assured that this beautiful country with its republic will be saved.[1]

Kossuth is now here. He produces a great impression, by personal presence & speech; but confesses that his mission has failed. It has failed, under bad counsels, from his asking too much. Had he been content with stating his case, without directly proposing any change in our national policy, he would have secured the hearts of the people, & would have prepared them for all that is practicable when the great exigency arrives. But it is a rank absurdity to suppose that our Govt.—at this nether extreme from Russia—can pledge itself to be the *executive power* to enforce a new reading of the Law of Nations against that distant empire. When the time comes, in which we can strike a blow for any good cause, I shall be ready; but meanwhile our true policy is sympathy with the Liberal Movement everywhere, & this declared without mincing or reserve *tout hautment*. What say you?

Kossuth's visit will provoke a discussion of the whole subject of European politics & our policy. Into this I should like to enter. Now here you can help me. Write me at once on the subject fully, & refer me to books. If there is any thing new which is not accessible here, send it to me. I go to-day to the Department of State to [overhaul?] the Library there to see what I can find. The fire at the Capitol has taken away a staff which I had hoped to use.

I have seen K. several times. He said to me that the next movement would decide the fate of Europe & of Hungary for 100 years. I told him at once that he was mistaken—that Europe was not destined, except for a transient moment to be Cossack—that the Republic was inevitable. Of this I am satisfied.

Pulzky & wife are here also in the suite of the Govnor., who carries with him something of the state of a man in power, & this, I am told, Mad. K. assumes also, though I saw nothing of it during the interview I had with her. He is to be recd. to-day by the Senate.[2] Tomorrow dines with Seward; next day with Congress; two days ago he dined with the President. There is a wretched opposition to Kossuth here, proceeding from Slavery. In truth, Slavery is the source of all our baseness, from gigantic national crime down to the vile manners & profuse expectorations of this place.

I have looked anxiously for yr promised communication on Coinage. There is a bill introduced by Hamilton Fish for the establishment of a mint at N.Y.[3] Now, on this I should like to speak as you suggested. It would be a good theme for a beginning, & would take the public where they do not expect me. I hope to reserve myself on Slavery till a late day.

The Presidential intrigues are beginning to be active. At the present moment Genl. Scott seems the inevitable Whig candidate, & it is not impossible that he may be brought forward without a national convention, so as to catch Anti-Slavery votes. Douglas is a strong candidate on the other side; so also is [*William O.*] Butler. But the field is not yet clear. Webster is ridiculously out of the question, & Cass seems out of sight. Strange fate! The men, who changed on Slavery, will fail of their political reward! I am always pleased to meet Cass. Our relations are very agreeable. Mr King is a little reserved but at times quite kindly. His niece always enquires after you. I met them at dinner recently at the President's. Let me hear from you on Coinage & on European politics & our true policy, & believe me,

Ever Yrs, Chas.

ALS MH-H (63/486, PCS)

1. Louis Napoleon, president of the Second Republic, had on 2 December 1851 dissolved the French legislature, and the military had attacked and arrested assembly members on his behalf. On 20 December Louis Napoleon was elected president for a ten-year term.

2. *Globe*, 32nd Cong., 1st sess., 199.

3. Hamilton Fish (1808–1893; U.S. congressman [Whig, N.Y.], 1843–45; U.S. senator, 1851–57) introduced his bill on the mint on 11 December 1851 (*Globe*, 32nd Cong., 1st sess., 61).

To Amasa Walker

Sen. Chamber Jan. 9th '52

Dear Walker,

I note yr suggestions. I anticipate, in the course of the session, & probably soon, a discussion of our Foreign Affairs.[1] You know where my devoted sympathies are; you also know my adhesion to the cause of Peace. At the same I shall yield to no person in the support I shall give to the most explicit declaration of the rights of nations, & of our indignation at all the efforts of tyranny. I am in the freest communication with Genl. Cass, &, I think, that there is no difference between us as to the true course of Congress.

A leading Senator consulted me about a resolution increasing our fleet in the Mediterranean. I told him, without a moment's delay, that I should oppose it. With my consent, our Govt, while proudly declaring its sympathies, its desires, & its sense of the rights of nations, shall not lift a little finger in menace.

The Presidential horizon is still cloudy. But it seems pretty clear that Scott will be the Whig candidate,—brought forward, perhaps, without a national convention. Many democrats consider Douglas now as the leading candidate. I still think Butler stands the best chance. Though, it is not impossible that there may be a "split," & two Dem. candidates.

Our position is difficult. But I exhort our friends to hold themselves *absolutely uncommitted*, except to their principles. Nobody can tell now what our duty to these may require in the coming election. For myself, I keep aloof from all the combinations making, though I am curious to learn all I can with regard to the actual state of things.

Ever Yrs, Charles Sumner

ALS MHi (70/167, PCS)

1. Concerned about the war spirit in the U.S., Walker in his letter of 3 January 1852 (8/438, PCS) urged CS to speak out, extending sympathy to Hungary, yet protesting intervention.

To Henry W. Longfellow

Sunday—Jan 11th—'52

Would that I could claim a dinner to-day with you! My ordinary dinner is at Willard's Hotel with a mess, composed of Govnr. [*John*] Davis,

Mr Clark of R.I., Mr Stanly of N.C., Mr Miller of N.J. & Mr Barney of Baltimore.[1]

Our Congressional Banquet terminated in a miserable drunken rout. I was called by vehement voices to speak, but I was unwilling to address a company disguised by Circe.

The Assembly here which I attended was inferior to our Boston gatherings. Kossuth had been invited & was expected. This kept away all the diplomatists, absurdly enough. But Kossuth was ill & unable to come; so that the ball lost both attractions. The diplomatists deserve a rebuke for their presumptuous egotism.

I have just read an admirable letter by Judge Jay in the Traveller of Friday on Intervention. Read it.[2]

A letter from Wm Story, written in Rome, says; "I hope by this time the Longfellows have determined to join us in the spring. When you see them give our best remembrances. Is his book out?" In Rome are the Lowells, & the Brownings are soon to be there.[3] Better this than Washington!

Ever & ever Thine, C. S.

ALS MH-H (70/179, PCS)

1. John H. Clarke (1789–1870), U.S. senator (Whig, R.I.), 1847–53. Edward Stanly (1810–72), U.S. congressman (Whig, N.C.), 1837–43, 1849–53. Jacob W. Miller (1800–62), U.S. senator (Whig, N.J.), 1841–53. Mr. Barney may be John Barney (1785–1857), U.S. congressman (Fed., Md.), 1825–29.

2. *The Kossuth Excitement: a Letter from the Hon. William Jay* (1852).

3. Story's letter (12 December 1851, 8/318, PCS) described the American colony there, including the poet James Russell Lowell (1819–91) and his wife Maria White Lowell (1812–53). The poets Robert Browning (1812–89) and Elizabeth Barrett Browning (1806–61) were then living in Florence.

To Charles Francis Adams

Washington Feb. 1st '52

My dear Adams,

It is just a month since the date of your valued letter,[1] which has rested ever since unfiled on my table, as I hoped each day to write, not in answer to it, but in acknowledgment of it. My time has been constantly occupied, so that I have postponed almost every thing but what I was obliged to do.

The Presidential field has changed its appearance several times since I wrote you, more on the Democratic than the Whig side. On the latter the movement seems to be determined for Scott. Among the Democrats Douglas was for awhile in the ascendant; I think, however, he has lost his position, never again to regain it. Cass now is stronger than ever. A week or two ago Butler seemed to be stronger than all. Mr Blair told me that every thing denoted that he would be nominated. But Col. [*Thomas Hart*] Benton now admits that he is out of the question—he says that Butler has been "slaughtered" by orders from Washington—that resolutions calculated to take from him his neutral position were prepared in Washington & slipped through the Kentucky Convention.[2] At all this the Col. is indignant, saying that now no Free Soiler can go into the Baltimore Convention without a halter about his neck. He asks how Preston King can go into such a Convention. It is evident, that the course of things is not clear among the Democrats. To combine all their discordant materials will be very difficult—I trust impossible. Meanwhile I rejoice in my independence.

The Compromises have at last appeared again. John Davis's speech produced no effect in the delivery; it was hardly listened to. I suppose it was calculated for Massachusetts. McRae of Mississippi is a mild & pleasant gentleman, with no personality or asperity. Mangum desires very much to cut off further debate—he is afraid of some strong Northern speeches. He will try to move to lay the resolutions on the table, as soon as McRae has concluded his speech; but Borland & Soulé both desire to speak; possibly some others, also, so that the future is uncertain.[3] The tone of the Senate is now such that I should be willing to enter into the discussion, if I did not feel that what I have to say will come with more effect at a later day. There is no practical urgency in the question—it is like a University *thesis*, & I prefer to wait till I have tried other themes.

I note the criticism of the Advertiser on my speech upon Lands.[4] I challenge that paper. It blundered prodigiously in its article, & assumed, from the imperfect telegraphic report, an exaggerated position on my part, & an ignorance too. I did not speak without study, nor without the best counsels of Washington. I mention to you that my fellow-boarder, Mr Rockwell, of Conn., who is very intimate with this whole matter has aided & encouraged me, going over my calculations, & consulting for me the best-informed persons before I spoke. [*inserted in margin*] He conferred with the chairman of the Committee of Public Lands in the House,[5] who professed to be much struck by the view, & said that it had never been presented. [*end insert*] He assures me that the argt. is entirely original & unanswerable, *to the extent to which I have pressed it*. He tells me that the Western members are preparing to follow the lead I have given. Walker of Wisconsin spoke to me on the subject with great warmth, telling me, & others, that it was the most important speech for the West made in Congress for 10 years. Borland of Arkansas expressed to me personally his thanks; but I have heard of his speaking more strongly to others. He said that it would certainly be copied in every paper of Arkansas, though it would be odd enough, coming from a Mass. Free-soiler. Cass & Shields were both very complimentary; so were some of the South Western men. Jones of Iowa[6] said to Mr Rockwell, that he came to Washington with a prejudice against me, but my speech had cured that. He meant to have a county in Iowa named after me. I mention these things that you may understand that I am not without countenance.

I shewed Mr Rockwell the Boston papers that came to-day. He laughed, & said that they would all have to back out.—You will understand that I make no such ridiculous assumption, as is attributed to me, that the nation is under a legal obligation to the states, but simply that there has been a relation between the two parties which constitutes a basis for a generous administration of the Public Lands as regards those states.

Should my speech be sustained by opinion here, you will appreciate the advantage it will give me on other subjects. The pamphlet edition, much corrected, will be published tomorrow. You will have an early copy.

I was glad to see John, who has been chiefly under the auspices of Mr [*John P.*] Hale & Genl. Houston.[7] The latter I find uniformly amiable, &, except where personal vanity interferes, of great good sense. The former goes to N. Hampshire in a fortnight to speak. I think the people about the *Union* expect Rantoul to support the Baltimore nominee. He made a strong hit by his speech.[8] I was present at the time. The House were much excited. Davis is a dishonored man.

With kind regards to Mrs Adams, & all yr house, believe me,

Ever Yours, Charles Sumner

P.S. To-day I dined with [*Thomas*] Corwin, in whom I find more Anti-Slavery than I had expected; but it is sicklied o'er with irresolution. I like Soulé very much. He says he respects my openness on Slavery, & asks, if he can be expected to believe that Cass in his heart is not as much an Abolitionist as I am? He has concealed what I have expressed; so says Soulé.

ALS MBApm (70/190, PCS)

1. Adams's letter of 1 January 1852 (8/418, PCS) expressed his pessimism regarding the influence of a third party in the forthcoming presidential election. He feared

the Free Soilers were not nationally unified; could they "accomplish anything really useful"?

2. Cass supporters in Kentucky passed a resolution at the Democratic state convention, 8 January, favoring the transmission of slaves into any territory in the U.S. Butler, who had hitherto been silent on the slavery issue, endorsed these resolutions (Roy F. Nichols, *The Democratic Machine, 1850–1854* [1923], 87–88).

3. John Davis spoke 28 January in favor of letting the compromise measures stand without further guarantees or agitation (*Globe*, 32nd Cong., 1st sess., appendix, 130–34). John J. McRae (1815–68; U.S. senator [Dem., Miss.], 1851–52) spoke against Foote's resolution, not because McRae opposed the compromise itself, but because the resolution raised improperly a controversy that had apparently been settled in the previous congressional session (ibid., 165–76). Willie P. Mangum (1792–1861), U.S. senator (Whig, N.C.), 1831–36, 1840–53. Solon Borland (1808–64), U.S. senator (Dem., Ark.), 1848–53.

4. CS spoke on 27 January supporting the bill to grant a right of way to the state of Iowa for railroad construction ("Justice to the Land States, and Policy of Roads," ibid., 134–36). In its editorial, "Mr. Sumner and the Public Lands," the *Boston Daily Advertiser* (30 January 1852:2) stated that CS's views on public lands were "questionable," and quoted more fully from the speech than it had in the earlier "telegraphic report." The *Advertiser* claimed that CS had exaggerated the value of the exemption from state taxation which the U.S. government had enjoyed on its lands in "New states."

5. John Arnold Rockwell (1803–61), U.S. congressman (Whig, Conn.), 1845–49; Washington, D.C., lawyer. Willard P. Hall (1820–82), U.S. congressman (Dem., Mo.), 1847–53.

6. Isaac P. Walker (1815–72), U.S. senator (Dem., Wis.), 1848–55. James Shields (1810–79), U.S. senator (Dem., Ill.), 1849–55, (Dem., Minn.), 1858–59. George W. Jones (1806–84), U.S. congressman (Dem., Tenn.), 1843–59.

7. Adams's son, John Quincy Adams II (1833–94), lawyer and aspiring politician. Samuel Houston (1793–1863), U.S. senator (Dem., Tex.), 1846–59; governor of Texas, 1859–61.

8. Robert Rantoul defended the coalition of Free Soilers and Democrats in Massachusetts against charges of a corrupt deal made by Congressman George T. Davis, a Massachusetts Whig (*Globe*, 32nd Cong., 1st sess., 24 January 1852, 382–84).

To Richard Henry Dana, Jr.

Senate Chamber—Feb. 7th '52

Dear Dana,

I am glad of yr letter, & will follow yr bill[1] in the best way practicable.

I am not a little pleased by yr accurate appreciation of my true position in my Land Speech.[2] The attacks of the Whig press seem inspired by the *dementia* of party, without reflection or knowledge. The fact of the exemption of the national domain in the several states from taxation & the unquestionable value of this franchise cannot be questioned. The inference seems to me irresistible from these unquestionable premises that, as compared with the old states, the Land States have a *peculiar equity* in the public domain; & this is all that I have asserted.

All who are familiar with the subject have recognized my view as original & sound. Even the *Republic*, my bitter assailant, has adopted it in two different articles. Felch, of Michigan, Chairman of Committee on Public Lands, said the same in his elaborate speech.[3] Others, I am told, both in the Senate & House, are preparing to follow.

I was aided & encouraged in this speech by a New England conservative, more familiar with the subject than any Eastern man, Mr Rockwell of Conn. He is a friend of the *Advertiser*, but has read its articles with entire dissent. He says, on my account, he is glad of these attacks, because they will help call attention to the speech, which is impregnable.

Yr glimpse at the new Cambridge theatre was very amusing.[4]

Enclosed is a receipt which belongs to you. I suppose you duly receive the *Globe*.

On the back of my chair is that Senatorial robe cut [from?] the same cloth which covers yr back in Court St, & on yr way to Cambridge.

Ever yrs, Charles Sumner

P.S. I commend my speech in the pamphlet—much corrected.

ALS MHi (70/217, PCS)

1. Dana was eager to get a bill enacted in Congress that would enable seamen more readily to collect wages due them (4 February 1852, 8/548, PCS).

2. In his letter Dana termed CS's speech a "hit"; CS had presented the subject "in a new and most forcible manner."

3. In two articles (28 January 1852:2 and 7 February 1852:2) the Washington *Republic* discussed the public lands issue but only in its 28 January article referred to CS. On that date the *Republic* used CS's calculations as support for the debt the U.S. government owed "its western citizens." Alpheus Felch (1804–96; U.S. senator [Dem., Mich.], 1847–53), spoke 3–4 February on "Grant of Lands to Iowa" (*Globe*, 32nd Cong., 1st sess., appendix, 145–54).

4. Dana described an amateur performance of "Box and Cox" in Andrews Norton's Cambridge parlor "before 60 or 80 elite."

To Francis W. Bird

Washington Feb. 8th '52

My dear Sir,

I knew you must agree with me.[1]

As to the Hunkers, I challenge their comment & criticism. The

Advertiser has not touched my argt. The fact of the exemption of the national domain from taxation cannot be denied—nor the value of this exemption. The conclusion irresistibly follows that the states in which this domain is situated have, on this account, a *peculiar equity* which the old states have not, entitling them to the special bounty of the Govt.

I have read Bigelow's article on Story with regret.[2] It is extravagant & unjust. But I have no time for this topic now.

I trust our friends will persevere in keeping themselves in their present position of independence, uncommitted to any Presidential aspirant. Scott will be the Whig candidate. There is no indication of the man on whom the Democrats can unite. It is doubtful if they can unite on any body. There is much in Houston which interests & pleases me. I know him well. He has talked with me freely about his being a candidate. He despises these demagogues & plotters, who are actively engaged in Presidential manoeuvres, & refuses to make a pledge or promise to any person. Curiously enough, Stockton[3] has also unfolded to me his plans & aspirations. He also is a candidate. But enough.

Yours very faithfully, Charles Sumner

ALS MH-H (70/220, PCS)

1. Thanking CS for a copy of his recent speech, Bird wrote that he "disliked the reckless maneuvering of the public lands." He agreed with CS that the western states had an equitable claim to land grants (6 February 1852, 8/561, PCS).

2. The unsigned review of *Life and Letters of Joseph Story* and *The Miscellaneous Writings of Joseph Story*, both edited by William Wetmore Story, stated that Story was only a fair judge and William Wetmore Story's comparisons of his father to Blackstone and Coke were "not only bad taste but ridiculous" (New York *Evening Post*, 29 January 1852: 2, 4 February 1852:2).

3. Robert F. Stockton (1795–1866), U.S. senator (Dem., N.J.), 1851–53.

To Anson Burlingame

Washington Feb. 14th '52

My dear Burlingame,

I know you never could say any thing unkindly of me. Be assured I have absolute faith. And I always leave every person at full liberty to differ from me in opinion, if he will.[1]

But I am satisfied that if I could converse with you, there would be no difference between us as to the course we should take in Foreign affairs. Read my speech, as marked in the copy sent to-day; & then read Cass's, & tell me the substantial difference between us.[2] I have discussed this question with General Cass, &, in point of fact, we do not differ.

You kindly allude to what I have done in the Senate. Receive it simply as the earnest of what I will do. This session shall not close without my touching topics which will awake an echo beyond those I have thus far dealt with. But I shall take my own time. Have patience & faith.

The Presidential Future is all uncertain.

As a member of Congress, to whom resolutions are addressed, I do not think I ought to *intervene* with any suggestions as to the course of our Legislature on Slavery.[3] I trust our friends will keep themselves firm & true, & will do what is best for the cause.

I shall always be glad to hear from you.

Ever Yours, Charles Sumner

ALS DLC (70/236, PCS)

1. Burlingame informed CS 10 February 1852 from Boston (8/575, PCS) that the *Boston Daily Atlas* misrepresented Burlingame when the paper stated he had made an "onslaught" against CS in the Massachusetts State Senate. Burlingame stated that even though he did not agree with the conclusion of CS's Kossuth speech, he had treated CS kindly in his own speech.

2. Cass spoke against the Berrien amendment to the Kossuth resolution (see CS to Walker, 19 December 1851) on 11 December 1851 (*Globe*, 32nd Cong., 1st sess., 66–69).

3. In his letter Burlingame asked CS if the Massachusetts legislature should introduce any antislavery resolutions this session.

To Samuel Gridley Howe

Washington March 10th '52

Dear Howe,

I see that the *Advertiser* has an elaborate article holding up my views upon the Public Lands to contempt.[1] Now, it so happens, *that no single paper in Mass* has furnished any notice of the support I have recd. from other senators & representatives. I doubt if any person in my position was ever before left so *entirely alone in his state*. Other senators have always had large parties & active presses to sustain them. Our party is small, &, from Mr Keyes's resolutions, I should suppose was willing to desert me, while it has no newspaper that seems to care to sustain me.[2] I do not know that any thing can be done; but I would recommend the publication of a brief extract from Mr Geyer's speech & also from Mr Felch's;[3] but particularly from Mr Geyer's.

Ever Yrs, Charles Sumner

Rantoul's speech yesterday produced a great effect.[4] All admitted its power, & Chase who heard it says it was true to our cause.

ALS MH-H (63/505, PCS)

1. The *Boston Daily Advertiser*, 9 March 1852:2, criticized CS's contention that the original thirteen states were in debt to new states for the taxes that the U.S. government had not paid on publicly owned lands in the new states: "is it not mortifying to see a Senator of Massachusetts putting forth such a claim . . . ? It is indeed too absurd for serious argument."

2. E. L. Keyes introduced resolutions in the Massachusetts legislature opposing CS's stand in his "Justice to the Lands" speech and requesting that copies of the resolution be sent to all members of Congress (ibid.).

3. Henry S. Geyer (1790–1859; U.S. Senator [Dem., Mo.], 1851–57) spoke 24 February (*Globe*, 32nd Cong., 1st sess., appendix, 227–38); part of his speech defended CS against Senator Joseph R. Underwood's charges that CS had overestimated the tax rate on the Iowa land under question (230). In his speech supporting the Iowa land grant, 3 and 4 February (ibid., 145–54), Felch also mentioned his agreement with CS (147).

4. Rantoul expanded his attack against George Davis's charges of a corrupt political alliance between Free Soilers and Democrats, saying such an alliance was necessary to contain slavery (*Globe*, 32nd Cong., 1st sess., appendix, 292–6).

To Samuel Gridley Howe

Washington April 5th '52

Dear Howe,

Shall we see you here? Mann inquires always. I am sorry that you have been troubled with my small affairs.[1]

The *Traveller* has already published the closing speech on the Land Bill.[2] When this is done, by the *Cwlth*, I shall have nothing more to ask; nor indeed, do I ask this; but I think the paper ought to have published it when it first appeared.

I note the taunts of the Hunkers because I do not speak against the Fug. Sl. Bill. I say to you as my friend, that I think I understand myself & my strength. My position here is *peculiar*, more so than you suppose. The prejudices against me before I came, not only here, but throughout the country, owing to positive forgeries & misrepresentations, were enormous. I was held up as a man, incapable of public business, of one idea, & a fanatic, though of acknowledged powers in a certain direction. *As a first condition to my usefulness*, & to my final influence on the cause I have most at heart, I am determined to correct that erroneous impression. In many quarters I have already done this; I am doing it daily in others. Only this morning an eminent lawyer of Phila. volunteered to assure me of a great kindliness towards me in that place, founded in part on the disposition I had shewn, contrary to all expectations, to deal with the real business of the country. Another person, much opposed to us, tells me that my course on the Land Question, has overturned a mountain of prejudice. Now, what I desire is *to secure a hearing*; &, if left to myself, in my own time, *I will do* this; while my whole heart is opened on Slavery & especially its recent enormity, the Fug. Sl. Bill.

But before this, I desire to speak on at least one if not two other questions, in this way strengthening my positon, & securing a vantage-ground from which to address the country for our cause. I confide these things to you. I know yr nature is to throw away the shield, & to rush into the contest. But I may look back upon my life, &, I think I can claim the credit of having carried Anti-Slavery truth, & the ideas of Progress, not unsuccessfully, before audiences to which they had never been presented. But in so doing I have always borrowed something from Prudence. I still borrow from her.

I am one of the juniors of the Senate, &, on this account alone, I might be silent; but few of the new members have taken the part I have.

In reply to all inquiries, you can say that I have always known when to speak, & that I shall speak at the proper time.

The Hunkers would like to see me impale myself by some impracticable course. I shall not gratify them. I wish I could talk of these things with you. Much I could say, which I will not write even to you.

Ever Yrs, C. S.

P.S. Mrs Danforth, of N.Y. an interesting lady, recently here, inquired kindly after you & Julia.

ALS MH-H (63/516, PCS)

1. Howe advised CS to ignore criticism that he should deliver an antislavery speech in the future (Boston, 15 and 27 March 1852, 70/279 and 291, PCS).

2. CS spoke in the Senate 16 March (*Globe*, 32nd Cong., 1st sess., 761–2).

To Henry Wilson

Private

Washington April 15th '52

Dear Wilson,

Kossuth is now here. He looks with great interest to Massachusetts. I trust he will be received by the Legislature in such a way as to encourage him to speak out frankly his whole heart. Do not imitate Congress in this respect.

Seward is happy in the course of things here. He regards Scott's nomination as sure, & in such a way as to entitle him to Northern support. I still say *non-committed* to him or any body else.

I desire that *you* should understand that I have not failed in any respect with regard to the petition about *Drayton & Sayres.*[1] It has been the subject of correspondence between myself & Wendell Phillips, to whom I have explained in part the reason of delay.[2] Had I consulted simply my own comfort, it would have been easy to present the petition & thus *at once* rid myself of it. But I have the liberation of these men sincerely at heart, & wish to act for them in the most effective way.

After consultation with our friends in the Senate, & with Drayton himself in his prison, I was satisfied that I should promote their interests by witholding the petition for a while. But I do not desire to throw the responsibility upon them; I take it all upon my own shoulders. Let me say that I have kept it back, from no personal considerations, having reference to myself, but simply & purely, in the exercise of my discretion, for the good of those poor prisoners, whose freedom I desire to secure.

Among other things, I may mention that Mrs Drayton is now here, trying to secure the signatures of the owners of the slaves to a petition to the President. She has already secured a large number, & I have encouraged her to perseverance. Now, it is obvious, that, while this is pending, any allusion to the matter from the North, even by petition, would have an irritating & injurious tendency. Should this fail, then, it may be important to appeal to public opinion.

I mention these things to *your private ear*. It is, of course, a part of my lot to hear misconceptions, as well as falsehood. I know the future will set things right.

When will the Legislature rise?

Ever faithfully Yrs, Charles Sumner

ALS MB (70/328, PCS)

1. Daniel Drayton and William Sayres had been imprisoned in Washington, D.C., since 1848 for trying to help fugitive slaves escape. Many abolitionists had signed a petition, directed to CS, to bring about their release.

2. See Phillips to CS, 2 February and 15 March 1852 (8/536 and 669, PCS); CS to Phillips, 9 March (70/270).

To Charles Francis Adams

Washington April 16th. [*1852*]

Dear Adams,

Another moment shall not pass without at least a brief letter to you. I was glad to hear from you, & shall be most happy when we meet.[1]

From time to time I have sent you papers which seemed to open light on our politics. I have not written, as I had nothing which these papers did not disclose. At last the field looks clear on one side. Scott will certainly be the Whig candidate, & I find Seward in a peculiarly happy frame of mind. He thinks that he has carried the day, & I believe he has. Some of the Southern Whigs threaten to bolt; but this pleases him. He hopes they will. Of course, this would give Scott a Northern front. It is understood that he will write no letters.

It remains to be seen how these developments will affect the democrats. You will see that, in order to hold their ground against Scott at the North, they will be constrained to modify their present position. How can Cass or Douglas run against Scott in N.Y. Ohio or Massachusetts?? What they will do I know not. In such event, I suppose a large portion of our friends would sustain Scott. For myself, I should be very willing to leave the election to go by default, if the election of a Senator did not depend upon it.

Mr Brown, the bookseller,[2] who is now here, tells me that there are many Whigs who will not support Scott. If this should be the case, then, of course, the Whigs should need Free Soil alliance, &, it is possible, that they might be willing to support a genuine Free Soiler for the Senate. To secure this I should be under strong temptation. On the other hand, it is possible that the same thing may be accomplished through the co-operation of the Democrats; nor can I tell, which way our true safety lies. My own position is still of *absolute independence*, without the least committment, & this I have earnestly commended to our friends in Mass.

I think [*Amos*] Tuck is preparing to support Scott. He came to me yesterday for counsel, & seemed quite anxious. He does not wish to be with a third party. Hale is by himself. Chase still hopes from the Democracy.

I can not join with you in anticipating much from Young America.[3] The sentiment of Progress professed by this party ignores our cause. It is hard & heartless, & looks merely to save vulgar annexations. Stanley's letter was virulent, &, its personal attack on me incomprehensible.[4]

I am struck with the injustice & misconception to which I am exposed. Some weeks ago I recd a petition from Wendell Phillips about

Drayton & Sayres. For reasons having no regard to myself, but with a sincere desire to do something for these men—after consultation with all our friends on the floor & with Drayton himself in his prison—I have kept the petition back. It would be easy to present it & there an end. But its presentation now might do more harm than good.—Tell Mrs Adams that I have intended to write to her; but I have become dry as dust. With sincere regard to all yr house.

Ever Yours, Charles Sumner

ALS MBApm (70/330, PCS)

1. In his letter of 7 April 1852 (70/308, PCS) Adams expressed his opinion that the Democrats would gain the presidency. The Free Soilers in Massachusetts should decide on a course of action but Adams feared the party could lose even more of its integrity. He remained opposed to any alliance with either Democrats or Whigs.

2. Possibly James P. Brown (1800–55), founder of Little, Brown & Company.

3. In his letter, Adams noted with approval the rise of the Young America Party, a movement promoting nationalism and sympathy for European revolutionary causes. Adams said that in the party were "some symptoms of a temper which will not much longer abide by the dictation of the ultra conservative slaveholding section of the [*Democratic*] party."

4. In his letter of 6 April to the Washington *Republic*, Edward Stanly supported the Compromise of 1850 and Fillmore as the Whig presidential nominee. He criticized those who attacked the compromise measures and singled out CS as one who should be "excluded from both Democratic and Whig Conventions." Stanly quoted from CS's November 1850 Faneuil Hall speech denouncing the Fugitive Slave Act and called such passages an "atrocious declaration" (*Republic*, 7 April 1852:2).

To George Sumner

Senate Chamber April 28th '52

Dear George,

I forgot to say to you, that you must not confound the opinion of Boston with that of Massachusetts.[1] The Commonwealth is for Kossuth. The city is against him. The line is broadly drawn. The same line is run between my political supporters & opponents. The City is bigoted, narrow, provincial & selfish. The country has more the spirit of the American Revolution.

When shall I see you?[2] How do things seem in Boston? Write.

Ever Thine, Chas.

ALS MH-H (63/530, PCS)

1. Kossuth was officially received by the Massachusetts legislature on 27 and 28 April 1852. The *Boston Daily Advertiser* criticized excessive preparations for Kossuth's visit to Boston (26 April 1852:2, 27 April 1852:2).

2. George Sumner had arrived in Boston on 19 April after fourteen years in Europe, Africa, and the Middle East (Prc, 3:279).

To Horace Mann

Washington June 4th '52

Dear Mann,

This essay promises to be able & most instructive. I hesitate to criticise the skeleton.

I trust you will encourage the author to proceed with it at once.

You see what the Democracy has done.[1] This helps to make our way clear; but nothing can be determined till after the other Convention. Rantoul's course in Mass. may help us. I understand he will declare war upon [*Benjamin F.*] Hallett & the Hunkers. He tells me so.[2]

Of course, Scott will carry the elective vote of Mass. But it seems to me at present, &, if Rantoul perseveres in his rebellion, it should *not* be by our help.

I fear that the legislature & the vacant seat in the Senate may pass into Webster's hands, unless we are careful. Through Rantoul & his friends, we may be able to prevent this.

Think of these things, & keep yourself for *the present uncommitted*.

The Webster-men are tyrannical & inveterate, & will sacrifice Scott, unless they can secure the promise of the Senatorship. This must be counteracted *at all hazard*.

Ever Yrs, C. S.

P.S. When shall you be here?

ALS MHi (70/383, PCS)

1. The Democratic convention, meeting 1 June 1852 in Baltimore, nominated Franklin Pierce for president and William R. King for vice president.

2. At the convention, Rantoul's seat had been contested because he would not adhere unquestioningly to Democratic party principles; he was unseated in favor of a loyal Democrat (Roy F. Nichols, *The Democratic Machine, 1850–54* [1923], 133–34). Speaking on 11 June in the House (*Globe*, 32nd Cong., 1st sess., appendix, 793–97), Rantoul stated he had refused to promise "beforehand" that he would support the Democratic party's platform: "I do my own thinking, and do not allow any convention to do it for me" (794).

To Charles Francis Adams

Washington—Sunday
[*13 June 1852*]

Dear Adams,

I have yours of the 11th.[1] I have pleaded with Seward & others to stand firm. I have pressed it upon Mr. Mangum, who is the most reasonable of Southern men. The pressure on both sides is great, & I cannot forsee the result.

Chase is firm & resolved. He thinks Peirce's nomination, under the circumstances the greatest triumph Slavery has ever had. He thinks he will be defeated in Ohio. He is hesitating now between support of a third candidate & inaction, with a view to secure the election of Scott.

Rantoul waits for developments in Mass.

I feel the advantage of keeping our force in Mass. together, & I am ready for any course, by which our principles can be best sustained. I have not called myself a Democrat; I will not call myself a Whig. I will be independent.[2]

As I view things from this distance, I cannot but think the triumph of the Whigs in our Legislature, *as well as in the Presidential question*, would be fatal to the Anti-Slavery cause in Mass. In the Presidential question they must triumph, &, against Peirce, their triumph, even with Webster & Fillmore, would be desirable. *This iron democracy*, with the Slave-Power, must not, if possible, be fastened upon every branch of the Govt. But God save our Commonwealth from Webster Whiggery.

Ever Yrs, C. S.

ALS MBApm (70/397, PCS)

1. Adams wrote CS from Boston about Free Soil response to the forthcoming Whig convention in Baltimore 16 June. He asked CS to tell Seward to "stand firm" against any Whig support of the compromise measures (70/394, PCS). The convention, however, voted to support the Fugitive Slave Law and to oppose any further discussion of the slavery issue (Frederick J. Blue, *The Free Soilers* [1973], 237–38).

2. CS wrote John Bigelow 9 June 1852, "The political fellowships I had hoped to establish are vanishing. Of course, I can have nothing to do with Peirce or his platform, probably nothing with Scott, or his" (ALS, Bigelow Papers, Union College).

To George Sumner

Washington June 18th '52
Friday noon

Dear George,

It has been hot here—very; it is so still; it is hardly comfortable. I shall be glad to see you; but I hardly have the heart to say more. I envy you the freedom of Newport & the North, without these anxieties of my position.

Corwin is remiss, & the Sec. of War is a weakling. Between the two the letter may have failed.[1] I am sorry for it. Yr presence would, doubtless, prompt it.

Yesterday I abandoned Boulanger, as my habitual resort for dinner; & this very morning, before receiving yr letter of admonition, I stopped my coffee for breakfast, contenting myself with iced water. A light claret, or *Beaune* wine would relish well.

Come; & the red stripe of the cravat shall not annoy you.

On the subject of the Fug. Slave Bill I must make a clean breast. I cannot help it. Reason, feeling, conviction, all prompt me. I care not for favor or popularity, & I am absolutely insensible to the ambition of a *politician*; but I will do my duty, & be true to myself. If you do not come, let me hear from you.[2]

Ever Thine, Chas—

How did Newport seem? Looking at the question on the Will it seems to me that mother has an estate for life, with a *vested* remainder in the children named. This might be devised by Henry.[3]

I send you a batch of fresh documents. The map & the report on mail to California will interest you.

Prescott writes me that you are out for Webster!—[4]

ALS MH-H (63/547, PCS)

1. Apparently George Sumner sought a position of some sort at West Point which he hoped Charles M. Conrad (1804–78; U.S. secretary of war, 1850–53) could arrange.

2. George and CS were reunited at the end of June when George visited Washington.

3. Their brother, Henry Sumner, had died 5 May 1852.

4. Prescott had written CS 14 June 1852 from Boston, "Is it true that your brother has become a stout champion for Webster? So I was told yesterday" (9/172, PCS).

To John Gorham Palfrey

Washington July 2nd '52

My very dear Dr,

Last evng from some unknown friend I recd through the Post-Office the last N. American Review.[1] My attention was at once attracted to the article said to be by you. It is an admirable work of criticism & friendship. Nothing better of the kind has ever been done in our country. I envy you the satisfaction of having done it. It must have been pleasing labor.

For myself I have been constantly occupied—each day in my place—but I feel keenly how little I have done. With pain also I learn the impatience of some of my friends because I have not spoken on Slavery. This subject is always in my mind & heart, & I shall never be happy until I have expressed myself fully upon it. But my silence has been prepense & deliberate. Before leaving home, I declared my purpose—I think among others to yourself—not to speak on this subject until late—very late—unless pressed by some practical question. No such occasion has occurred. I am left to create one, which I shall soon do.[2]

The death of Mr Clay naturally postpones opportunities; & I say to you *confidentially*, I fear that I cannot without indelicacy bring forward a motion against the Fug. Sl. Bill until his [*Cass's*] return, as he has *confidentially* informed me of his desire to speak at the time.[3] Being no longer a presidential candidate, he desires to answer the claim of the South that Slavery goes into new territories simply by virtue of the Constitution. This is a sign of returning reason.

I am glad that you have given yr name again to our rally. But one course seems open to us; *Independence of both the old parties*.

I regret to hear that our friend Dr [*James W.*] Stone goes to the Whigs & Scott. I do not see how he can do so. He is a true man, & should be saved.

Let me hear from you.

Ever affectionately Yours,   Charles Sumner

P.S. Adams in a noble letter, which I have recd from him, touches the ancient cords.[4]

ALS MH-H (70/427, PCS)

1. Palfrey's review, "Lord Mahon's History of England," appeared in the July 1852 issue (75:125–208). In it Palfrey defended Jared Sparks's emendations to Washing-

ton's letters, emendations which had been criticized by Philip Henry Stanhope, Lord Mahon.

2. Replying on 5 July from Cambridge (70/433, PCS), Palfrey reassured CS that he had heard no complaints of CS's silence; he urged CS, however, to speak soon.

3. Henry Clay died in Washington 29 June and was buried in Lexington, Kentucky. CS inadvertently omitted Cass's name (see CS to Howe on the same subject, 63/533, [July 1852]. Cass spoke briefly about the failure of the Fugitive Slave Law to guarantee a trial by jury to captured blacks (26 August, *Globe*, 32nd Cong., 1st sess., appendix, 1124–25).

4. Adams's letter of 23 June from Quincy, Mass. (9/190), criticized both parties for dodging the slavery issue. He hoped the Free Democrats (the name adopted by the former national Free Soil party in 1851) could "rest upon a principle which may compensate for want of numbers." He intended to vote for John P. Hale at the Free Democrat convention, but to stay out of state elections.

To Dorothea Dix

Saturday—N.Y. Avenue
[*July 1852*]

Dear Miss Dix,

Many thanks for yr kind note.[1]

Yesterday I called the attention of the President to the case of Drayton & Sayres, still lingering in prison where they have been for four years. He has promised to entertain it. Now I entreat you to take advantage of the familiar access, which you enjoy to his house.[2] Plead their case with him & with his family. Let them all see how good a deed would be this pardon of those poor prisoners. This intercession will be worthy of you; nay, it belongs to you. Believe me, dear Miss Dix,

Sincerely Yours, Charles Sumner

ALS MH-H (70/458, PCS)

1. In earlier letters ([14? June], [c. June], 70/399 and 420, PCS) CS had asked Dix to intercede with President Fillmore on behalf of the two prisoners, Daniel Drayton and William Sayres. Dix replied that the president awaited Attorney General Crittenden's report; if that was not produced soon, Fillmore would "make himself *a law*" ([June?] 1852, 9/208).

2. Fillmore and Dix had met in the spring of 1850 and corresponded regularly thereafter. On 13 August 1852 the president notified Dix of his pardon, adding, "I should despise myself, if I feared to do right because of popular prejudice and clamor" (*The Lady and the President*, ed. Charles M. Snyder [1975], 136).

To Samuel Gridley Howe

Washington
Saturday—[*7 August 1852*]

Dear Howe,

I thank you again for yr watchful friendship.[1] Strong in my own consciousness of right-doing, I am thunder-struck by the various reports which reach me from Mass.

Parker suggests the taunts of W & E.[2] Never did this thought enter my mind before. I have kept upon my way doing my duty, as I understand it. If through inopportune events I should fail, I could not lose the consciousness of right endeavor. Parker & all attach an exaggerated importance to the whole transaction. I may be put down now; but I cannot always be put down.

But I shall speak this session. It will be late; but at the earliest moment. Nothing but unprecedented injustice can cut me off.

Persons who criticise do not understand *the surroundings* here in the Senate. The remarks I made were conceived to meet the actual condition of things. Nine tenths of the Senate wished me to speak, & I purposely pressed my claim, delicately & cautiously, so as not to afford them any apology for denying me. I wished to secure the floor, when I should have spoken my soul.

The *Liberator* criticises my remark to Mr Butler. He stood in front of my desk while speaking; &, as I intended to confine myself to Slavery & the Fug. Sl. Bill & not to make a foray into S. Carolina, I smilingly said so. But the harshness of the Liberator is constant.[3]

I find that, as a Senator, I am to lose my independence. Political opponents naturally attack me, weak or hasty friends yield to them; & thus an opinion is created to constrain my course. I am most astonished by Parker.

Ever & ever Thine, C. S.

ALS MH-H (63/566, PCS)

1. Howe wrote from Boston 4 August 1852 (70/469, PCS) that CS should ignore public opinion regarding his delay in speaking and that Howe trusted CS's judgment.

2. Theodore Parker's letter (West Newton, 4 August, 9/299) urged CS to speak soon. Without specifically naming Webster and Edward Everett, Parker told CS that his hesitation gave his enemies more cause for criticism; they say, "'always told you so! nothing but a dough-face'!"

3. *The Liberator* (6 August 1852:126) printed with only slight editorial comment the exchange between Andrew Butler of South Carolina and CS when the latter tried to gain the floor to speak against the Fugitive Slave Law on 28 July. Butler said CS

was entitled to speak only if the other side could rebut and he was certain that CS would disparage South Carolina: "Mr. Sumner (in a low voice) I do not intend to do it." A week earlier, *The Liberator* (30 July 1852:121) had criticized CS for remaining for eight months "motionless and dumb, so far as the atrocious Fugitive Slave Law is concerned."

To Robert Carter[1]

Private

Washington Monday
[*9 August 1852*]

My dear Sir,

This morning I recd. from the President a message, informing me that he had pardoned Drayton & Sayres. This is the result of my application & constant pressure of the case.

I was blamed by *ultras* & taunted by others for not presenting a petition to the Senate in their behalf. Had I done so I should have made their liberation impossible. I should have fastened new pad-locks upon their prison-door. I took the subject in a *practical way*; I saw them at once in their prison—I saw the President & organized the application which has now ended happily. At the request of the President I prepared an elaborate opinion on his power to pardon in this case.[2] The delay of late has been owing to the Atty Genl, who gave his final opinion only last Saturday.

The papers have not yet been formally signed. Say nothing of it till you hear by telegraph that they are out of the clutches of this District.

The marshall of the district has behaved to them with great humanity. ——

The statement in the *Atlas* of Saturday that I could have spoken in the Senate since my motion is an absolute falsehood.[3] No such opportunity has occurred. *Be sure* I know my position & my duties.

Ever Yrs, Charles Sumner

ALS MH-H (70/476, PCS)

1. Robert Carter (1819–79), a Free Soiler and an editor of the *Commonwealth*.
2. "Opinion to the President for Pardon of Drayton and Sayres," dated 14 May 1852 (Wks, 3:219–33).
3. The *Boston Daily Atlas* stated that CS had had "half a dozen opportunities" to speak against the Fugitive Slave Law. "The fault, if any there be, lies with Mr. Sumner, and nobody else" (7 August 1852:2).

To Theodore Parker

Senate Chamber. August 11th. 1852

Dear Parker.

I must at least acknowledge your letter of friendship and admonition.

I will not argue the question of *past delay*. To all that can be said on that head, there is this explicit answer. With a heart full of devotion to our cause, in the exercise of my best discretion, and on the advice or with the concurrence of friends, I have waited. It may be that this was unwise; but it was honestly and sincerely adopted, with a view to serve the cause. Let this pass.

You cannot desire a speech from me more than I desire to make one[1] I came to the Senate, on my late motion, prepared for the work, hoping to be allowed to go on, with the promise of leaders from all sides that I should have a hearing. I was cut-off. No chance for courtesy. I must rely upon my rights[.] You tell me not to wait for the Civil Appropriation Bill. I know, dear Parker, that it is hardly within the range of possibilities that any other bill should come forward before this Bill to which my Amendment can be attached. For 10 days we have been on the Indian Appropriation Bill.

With this the Fugitive Slave Bill is not germane.

The Civil Appropriation Bill will probably pass the House to-day. It will come at once to the Senate—be referred to a Committee on Finance—be reported back by them with amendments[.] *After the consideration of these amendments of the Committee*, and ***not before,*** my chance will come.[2] For this I am prepared, with a determination equal to your own. All this delay is to me a source of grief and disappointment[.] But I know my heart; and I know that sincerely, singly I have striven for the cause.

You remember the pictures in the Ancient Mariner of the ship in the *terrible calm*.[3] In such a calm my ship is at this moment I can not move it; but I have not harmed an albatross. But enough of this. I claim the confidence of friends, for I know that I deserve it.

Monday the President sent me a message that he had pardoned Drayton & Sayers and implored me to communicate the result to them. This I had the satisfaction of doing. The formal papers have not yet reached the hand of the Marshall. Do not speak of this *aloud*, until you hear that they are actually beyond the clutch of the District. Here ends one of the miserable charges against me. The others will end soon.

Ever yours, Charles Sumner

P.S. [*James M.*] Mason said to me this morning; "I see my friend Theodore Parker is after you. The Liberator also calls Butler an *overseer*." How gross the interpretation by the Liberator of the little *sotto voce* between Butler and myself. He stood in front of my desk when he spoke. I had no purpose of discussing the South Carolina laws, and promptly said so. There is a time for all things.

C MHi (70/478, PCS)

1. Parker worried that the Senate might succeed in preventing CS from speaking that session. He told CS that if he returned to Massachusetts without having made an antislavery speech, he would encounter "distrust" from the antislavery faction as well as "the scoff and the scorn" from the Hunkers: "your strength will certainly be much impaired." He urged CS to "stand in a *minority of one,*" if necessary, to brave the Senate and speak out against slavery (4 August 1852, 9/299, PCS).

2. The Civil Appropriation Bill was introduced in the Senate 12 August and debate began on it 21 August (*Globe*, 32nd Cong., 1st sess., 2195, 2287).

3. Samuel Taylor Coleridge, "Rime of the Ancient Mariner," 2.115–18.

To Charles Francis Adams

Senate Chamber Aug. 25th '52

Dear Adams,

For two days I have confidently counted on the floor; but the opportunity has not yet arrived. There is a special clause of the Civil & Dipl. Apptn. Bill[1] on which I can take it & hold it against every thing but death. Each day I have been in my seat prepared for the work.

Another responsibility of a grave character has been thrown upon me. An important friend, whose name you can supply, says that my proposed course will defeat Genl. Scott. Of this he has no doubt. He attaches to it at this moment immense importance. But I am not shaken. I shall persevere. When we meet I shall explain this & many other things to you.

Hale will not probably write anything by way of acceptance of the nomination;[2] but I think, that practically he has already accepted it. In the Senate he has often been mentioned as a candidate. Seward, *who thinks he ought to decline*, says that "a nomination, if not declined at once, is accepted."

I was glad of yr letter from Niagara.[3] I shewed it to Hale, in order to strengthen him.

I fear that I shall be detained in Washington for some days, perhaps a week, after the adjournment. I have much business yet undone. Besides my speech yet undelivered must be printed & franked. Petty work all this!—But I long for rest. I am weary. Each day of the session I have been in my seat; & of late, I have had special anxiety from my peculiar position. I wish I were at Quincy. Remember me to all at yr house.

Ever Yrs, C. S.

ALS MBApm (70/498, PCS)

1. On 26 August 1852 Robert M. T. Hunter (1809–87; U.S. senator [Dem., Va.], 1847–61) moved an amendment to the Civil Appropriations Bill for payment of officials to enforce the laws of the U.S. CS then moved an amendment that no expense should be authorized to enforce the Fugitive Slave Act and that the act would therefore be repealed (*Globe*, 32nd Cong., 1st sess., 2371).

2. The Free Democrats had met 11 August in Pittsburgh and nominated Hale for president and George W. Julian for vice president, but Hale had not attended the convention and appeared reluctant to accept the nomination (Frederick J. Blue, *The Free Soilers* [1973], 241–43).

3. In his letter of 15 August (70/487, PCS) Adams, who had attended the Pittsburgh convention, stated, "Mr Hale must not do any thing to forfeit the implicit confidence bestowed upon his *singleness* of *purpose*."

To John Bigelow

Confidential

Senate Chamber—Monday
[*30 August 1852*]

My dear Bigelow,

The world blesses the telegraph for the promptitude with which it carries news; but speakers must curse it for its inaccuracies. In reading the reports of what I say, I am often tempted to exclaim—"give me oblivion rather such a notoriety." My late speech looked strangely in New York.

The kind interest you express in my speech tempts me to the *confidence of friendship*.[1] I shall be attacked, & the speech will be disparaged. But *you* shall know something of what was said on the floor of the Senate. You will see what Hale & Chase said openly in debate.[2] Others are reported in conversation. I know that some Hunkers have felt its force. Clarke of R.I. said "it would be a text-book when they were dead & gone." Shields said "it was the ablest speech ever made in the Senate on Slavery"; and Bright used even stronger language. Cass has complimented me warmly. Soulé has expressed himself in the strongest terms.

Weller, after using strong terms of praise said "it would do more *mischief* than any speech ever made in the Country." Polk,[3] who was sober & who listened for two hours, said "the argt. was unanswerable," though he could not say this aloud. I write these for your *private & friendly eye*.

I throw the speech down as a gage. I believe it presents the true limits of opposition to Slavery within the Constitution. I challenge an answer. The attempts in the Senate were puerile, & ill-tempered.

I send you the outside of the *Era*, which contains 7 columns. The whole will be 18 columns. The next batch you shall have tomorrow. It would please me much to see it in the *Post*; but I did not expect it.[4]

I can not leave here before the end of the week. Many matters, among others the publication of my speech in a pamphlet will detain me after the close of the session. I see that I am announced for Faneuil Hall next Tuesday. This I regret. I am weary & long for vacation. I have been in my seat every day this session.

I shall hope to see you on my way through New York, to converse on many things. I regret very much that John Van Buren has gone into this campaign. If he could not oppose Baltimore he should have been silent. Even Weller, with whom he has been speaking in New Hampshire, says he ought to have gone to Europe. My admiration & attachment for him have been sincere, &, in the most friendly spirit, I regret his course.

Pardon this freedom.

We are now in the hurly-burly of a last day. The pressure is immense.

Ever Yours, Charles Sumner

ALS NSchU (PL, 70/522,PCS)

1. CS delivered his three and three-quarter hour speech "Freedom National, Slavery Sectional," opposing the Fugitive Slave Law, 26 August 1852 (*Globe*, 32nd Cong., 1st sess., appendix, 1102–13). Bigelow wrote from New York that he was "delighted" with what he had seen thus far of the speech, "all mangled and hashed" by the telegraph (28 August, 9/348, PCS).

2. In the debate before CS's amendment was defeated, Hale said that CS "has formed a new era in the history of the politics and of the eloquence of the country"; Chase stated, "his speech will be received as an emphatic protest against the slavish doctrine of finality in legislation which two of the political conventions recently held have joined in forcing upon the country" (ibid., 1119–21).

3. Jesse D. Bright (1812–75), U.S. senator (Dem., Ind.), 1845–62. John B. Weller (1812–75), U.S. senator (Union Dem., Calif.), 1852–57. William Polk (1815–62), U.S. congressman (Dem., Tenn.), 1851–53.

4. The first part of the speech was published in the *National Era* 2 September 1852:141–43. Bigelow wrote, again expressing approval, on 5 September (9/373) to tell CS that the entire speech had been published in the New York *Evening Post* (3 September 1852:4).

To Wendell Phillips

Boston Sept. 15th '52

Dear Wendell,

I must thank you, & tell you how sincerely I prize yr good opinion. It seemed at one time that I had forfeited it. God knows by no infidelity on my part.

When we meet I can tell you something of the *dessus les cartes*,[1] which will make my course intelligible.

I think in conversation we might harmonize even on these two points of criticism. When Slavery is overthrown under the Nat Govt. the Slave Power will tumble, &, as a political agency, it will no more be felt.[2] So it seems to me.

As to the other point, note that I did not assert that the State Ct would be the *final* interpreter, though on this point I suspend opinion.[3] The more I have reflected upon the course of S.C.—while I condemn her tyranny—I am less disposed to question its conformity with the Constitution; but again on this I still doubt. I have spoken with nobody on this question. But I should like to confer with you.

Much I have to tell you.

Ever Yrs, Charles Sumner

In the case of D. & S. I was active in the beginning, & had *peculiar* means of knowing the opinion of the Presdt, on which from the outset I relied.[4]

ALS MH-H (70/534, PCS)

1. *Voir le dessous des cartes*, "to be in the know."

2. Phillips's letter to CS of 3 September 1852 from Northampton (9/369, PCS) was on the whole laudatory. He did not, however, agree with CS that slavery would die out if left to the states, as CS had claimed ("As slavery is banished from the national jurisdiction, it will cease to vex our national politics," *Globe*, 32nd Cong., 1st sess., appendix, 1106).

3. Phillips also objected to CS's asserting that state courts could determine who was a slave ("*Still further, to the Courts of each State must belong the determination of the question, to what class of persons, according to just rules of interpretation, the phrase 'person held to service of labor' is strictly applicable*," ibid., 1113). Phillips asked, "Is there a final interpreter of the Const.?" He believed the Supreme Court played such a role.

4. Phillips wrote that he thought his own procedure for the release of Drayton and Sayres, gaining congressional approval through petition, was preferable. He doubted that Fillmore would have pardoned the men if he had been renominated for president.

To Joshua R. Giddings

Boston Nov. 6th '52

Dear Giddings,

Mr Jewett, the publisher of Uncle Tom will be glad to be yr publisher.[1] He says, that, if you can insure the sale of 1500 copies on the Reserve or in Ohio, he shall not hesitate to undertake it at once. His house at Cleveland can promote the sale there.

He thinks that it will be better to have only one vol.

He desires to help build up an Anti-Slavery literature. This is doing daily. But yr speeches will add to it some permanent arches.

I trust you will lose no time in attending to this.

What say you of the recent election?[2] An organization true to Freedom must spring from the present chaos.

Ever Yours, Charles Sumner

I am disgusted by Greeley's course towards you.[3]

ALS MH-H (63/581, PCS)

1. John Punchard Jewett (1814–84), a Boston publisher, had brought out *Uncle Tom's Cabin* and published Giddings's *Speeches in Congress 1841–52* in 1853.

2. Pierce was elected president by a vote of 1,601,474 over Scott's 1,386,580. Hale received 156,149 votes. In Massachusetts the Whig John H. Clifford had captured the governorship, defeating the Free Soiler Horace Mann.

3. The *New York Daily Tribune* (4 November 1852:4), lamenting the Whigs' defeat, blamed Giddings for the defection of many Whig voters: "Giddings has now persuaded many thousands of voters who were always Whigs until 1848, and are still advocates of Whig doctrines & measures, that Scott is (or was) as much the candidate of the Slavery Propaganda as Pierce, and that there is no material difference in the platforms and views of the two great parties respecting the Tariff or River and Harbor Improvements!"

To William H. Seward

Boston Nov. 6th '52

Dear Governor,

What say you of recent events?

It seems to me that you are the only Whig on his legs.

Now is the time for a new organization. Out of this chaos the party of Freedom must rise.

Remember me to Mrs Seward.[1]

Ever Yrs, Charles Sumner

The Webster men are inveterate as North American savages, in hatred of us & our great cause.[2]

ALS NRU (70/557, PCS)

1. Frances A. Miller Seward (c. 1805–1865) had written from Auburn, New York (18 September 1852, 9/414, PCS), praising CS's "convincing argument" in the Senate against the Fugitive Slave Law.

2. Seward replied from Auburn 9 November (9/479) that "recent events . . . do not disturb me in the least." He wrote, "We shall go on much as heretofore, . . . only that the last effort to connect the Whig Party to Slavery has been made."

To Harriet Beecher Stowe

Boston Nov. 12th '52

Dear Mrs Stowe,

I have thought much of the proper mode of addressing yr Father.[1] This must not be postponed. His testimony in all respects is too important. But I am satisfied that he can be approached by some other person better & more fitly than by myself. Friends with whom I have conferred counsel in the same way.

My interference would be attributed to political plot.

I have seen Re'd. Dr Storrs of Braintree,[2] who sympathizes in our desires, & who will undertake to address yr Father, if it be expedient that he should do it. Some others might unite with him.

Let me urge you to special care in yr statement of fact & law in yr forthcoming tract.[3] You have at this moment a marvellous power, which the enemy will try to break down, by cavil & criticism. Yr pamphlet will carry a knowledge of the legalized enormities of Slavery where nothing else could carry them. Let me be of service to you, if I can. I leave for Washington in the last week of this month.

I rejoice in yr devotion to the cause & the great work you are doing.

I think *White Slavery* will be published with illustrations.[4]

Ever sincerely Yours, Charles Sumner

ALS NNBe (70/564, PCS)

1. In her letter to CS of 7 November 1852, Harriet Beecher Stowe (1811–96) had expressed the hope that CS would ask her father, the outspoken Presbyterian clergyman Lyman Beecher (1775–1863), for a statement against slavery. Although Beecher had never taken a strong antislavery stand, Stowe told CS that "Every drop of blood

in us that throbs for the great cause of humanity came from him" (Boston, 9/477, PCS).

2. Richard Salter Storrs (1787–1873), fervent antislavery Congregational clergyman.

3. Stowe was at that time working on *The Key to Uncle Tom's Cabin*, a collection of firsthand evidence of slavery's evils, which was published by John P. Jewett in April 1853. CS advised Jewett on *The Key* (Jewett to CS, letters of 18 December 1852, 18 January, 2 February 1853, 9/551, 635, 664).

4. CS's 1847 lecture, "White Slavery in the Barbary States," which Stowe had praised in her letter of 7 November, was published by Jewett in March 1853 (Jewett to CS, 24 March, 10/055).

To John Jay

Boston Nov. 23d '52

Dear Jay,

I rejoice in Judge Paine's decision,[1] which presented the question clearly; but I am disgusted by the swiftness with which the supporters of Slavery have rushed to its support in New York.

I remember well that Judge Story on his return from Washington, after pronouncing the Prigg case, said to me with exulting voice, that it was a "triumph of Freedom," & one reason which he assigned was that it established by the authority of the Sup. Ct. of U.S. "the locality of Slavery," so that it could not exist any where except where sustained by state laws, & in the case of fugitive slaves. You will find this opinion told by his son in the chapter of his father's biography on the Prigg case.[2] Read this. Let Greeley have it. This will help shape public opinion.

Did you see in the last *Era* on the 4th page the letter of the Alabama clergyman to me.[3] It purports to be taken from the *Banner of the Cross*. Where is this paper published?

Ever Yours, Charles Sumner

ALS NNCB (70/570, PCS)

1. On 13 November 1852 Elijah Paine (c. 1803–53), judge of the Superior Court of New York, had announced his decision in the Lemmon case, in which Jay had defended eight slaves brought by the Lemmons from Virginia to New York, a free state. Paine ruled that the slaves were persons, not goods, and must be now freed (*New York Daily Tribune*, 15 November 1852:6).

2. See CS to Charles Francis Adams, 1 March 1843, and chapter 9 in *The Life and Letters of Joseph Story*, ed. William Wetmore Story (1851), 2:381–98.

3. An unsigned letter from an Episcopal clergyman in Livingston, Alabama, printed in the *National Era*, 18 November 1852:188, protested not only the "obnox-

ious sentiments" in CS's "Freedom National" speech, but the fact that CS would send copies to Southern residents.

To Edward L. Pierce[1]

Senate Chamber
Dec. 9th '52

My dear Peirce,

I am grateful to Mr Hildreth & also to yr constant friendship; but I should have been better pleased if the columns of the paper at this period had been directed to the support of Mr Adams as candidate.[2] He deserves yr best rally.

I cannot too strongly urge the importance of placing Mr Adams & Mr Wilson in Congress. All our candidates would do good service; but these especially would make their mark here, though each in different ways. Do all that you can.

The *Lowell American* was sent to me; but I did not read it. I was unwilling to run the risk of receiving an impression which might diminish my sympathy with a laborer in our cause so true & effective as Mr Robinson.[3]

Have you seen Ld Carlisle's preface to Uncle Tom?[4] I heard of it before I left home; but looked in vain for it in the papers.

You will be pleased to know that the speech on the Fug. Sl. Bill has been reprinted in England *entirely*. This shews the interest in our cause there. I do not call to mind any Congressional speech which ever before had this honor.

Remember me kindly & gratefully to Mr Hildreth, & believe me

Ever Yrs, Charles Sumner

ALS MH-H (63/583, PCS)

1. Edward L. Pierce (1829–97), LL.B. Harvard 1852, had been corresponding with CS since December 1849.

2. Richard Hildreth (1807–65), Boston lawyer, historian, and abolitionist, was at that time editor of the *Commonwealth*. Pierce wrote CS (6 December 1852, 9/528, PCS) saying he thought the extensive space given to a defense of CS in the *Commonwealth* "not in the best taste." While the *Commonwealth* endorsed Charles Francis Adams for Congress on the Free Soil ticket, it also ran an editorial praising CS's "principles of integrity, justice, and patriotism" and stating that no man had "more valuable scholarship, more inflexible principles, more reliable habits of reflection" (2 December 1852, 9 December 1852:2).

3. William Stevens Robinson (1818–76), antislavery journalist; editor, *Lowell*

American, 1849–53; Massachusetts state legislator ("*Warrington*": *Pen Portraits*, ed. Mrs. William S. Robinson [1877], 42–59).

4. *Uncle Tom's Cabin, a Tale of the Life Among the Lowly. With a Preface, by the Right Honorable the Earl of Carlisle* (1852).

To Charles Francis Adams

Washington Dec. 19th [*1852*]

Dear Adams,

Here is a letter from Bird which you will read with interest, even though you have seen him.[1]

I learned the result of the election with grief & mortification. Yr presence in Washington would have been a pillar to our cause. What shall we do? Alas!—

The question rages here as to the Cabinet. B. F. Hallett writes that no Free Soiler or secessionist should have a place in it. John Tyler[2] takes just the opposite ground. Soulé tells me that among his friends there has been a discussion on John Van Buren. He said—"we accepted his services in the hour of battle it will be dishonorable to discard him in the hour of victory."

I owe Mrs Adams a letter, part of the *deficit* of last summer, & will write her as the season opens.

Ever Yours, C. S.

Seward's Webster speech is very bad.[3] Fish earnestly advised against its delivery.

ALS MBApm (70/598, PCS)

1. Adams was narrowly defeated by the Whig John Wiley Edmands (1809–77) in the run-off election for the U.S. congressional seat (Martin Duberman, *Charles Francis Adams* [1960], 183). In the enclosure, Bird blamed Adams's defeat on "the shameful indifference of our own voters" (to CS, East Walpole, 15 December 1852, Adams Papers, microfilm reel 541). Adams commented to CS (22 December, 70/605, PCS), "Had I been elected, I might by a bare possibility have done some good, but the trial would have been like those of the middle ages."

2. Former president John Tyler had campaigned for Pierce (Robert Seager II, *And Tyler Too* [1963], 401–2).

3. Daniel Webster died 24 October. In his wholly laudatory tribute to Webster, Seward characterized Webster as a peacemaker in the Senate: "Daniel Webster put forth his mightiest efforts, confessedly the greatest ever put forth here or on this continent" (*Globe*, 32nd Cong., 2nd sess., 14 December, 55–56).

To Lord Wharncliffe

Washington Dec. 19th [*and* 24] '52

My dear Ld Wharncliffe,

During the short recess of Congress I was so variously occupied & so little at home, that I omitted to write you, though I daily thought of it; & now that I am here other duties absorb my time. Yr kind & most agreeable letter deserved a better return.[1] Do not condemn me. Try me again.

Genl. Pierce is elected—as you anticipated. His majority is large, but composed of most discordant materials, & his first difficulty will be to harmonize these in this Cabinet. On this there is much speculation in the papers & in conversation here. At present nobody seems to know who will be the men. But one circumstance is observable. The democratic party being about to assume the responsibility of power, its leaders are becoming more & more "Conservative." They now shrink from pressing the Cuban question, & Genl. Pierce is understood to have said that he would put his heel upon all *fillibusterism*.[2] I like that word. It sounds as it means.

The publication of the Cuban correspondence has contributed to this state of things. In my opinion, & I express it frankly, that correspondence was discreditable to the country. The letter of Mr Buchanan,[3] authorizing the purchase of Cuba, was low in character, as it was feeble as a diplomatic paper. I anticipate its condemnation in Europe; but there are many at home who, while grieving that their country should be so exposed, will not wince. One of the democrats, earnest for Cuba, admits that the publication of that correspondence has "put off its annexation 15 years." Several from the South have been suddenly enlightened on the evils which would surely flow from pressing this measure. They see the Slavery question in a new form, more formidable than ever before, arising from the determination of the North; they also see the prospect of emancipation by the Spanish Govt. as a check to our rapacity, &, finally they see that Cuba, if it belonged to the U.S., would drain the plantations of their slaves & impoverish the [??] present, therefore, we hear little of Cuba.

There is a recent anxiety as to the course of Louis Napoleon in occupying Samana in Hayti.[4] But it is difficult as ever to find any flaw in it. Still his neighborhood to us is not regarded favorably by those who, while crushing slaves, are very sensitive to the national honor. Our Govt., though our merchants carry on a lucrative commerce with Hayti, has never yet acknowledged the independence of the Black Republic. Slave-holders cannot consent to this, as we should then be obliged to receive a black minister at Washington! The presence of such a man, even though silent, would be a perpetual protest against Slavery.

Genl. Scott bears his defeat magnanimously. The lukewarmness of Mr Fillmore & the dissent of Mr Webster, powerful members of his own party, might have aroused a nature not very irritable, but he has no word of criticism or reproach for anyone. You remember the confidence with which he looked to be President, when we met him at the Calderons.[5] Now he renounces all expectation of any civil office.

Mr Webster's death removed him from the reproaches of his party, who would have charged upon him the defeat of their candidate. It has blunted the criticism upon his recent diplomacy, particularly the Fisheries & the Lobos affair,[6] & it has for a while almost silenced the deep condemnation of his defection on the Slavery question. It happens to me to hold his seat in the Senate; I cannot openly condemn him, but I cannot praise him. This has caused me many a pang.

Mr King, whom you will remember as the Presdt. of the Senate & who has just been chosen Vice-Presdt of the U.S.,—his term commencing next March—has to-day resigned his present post on account of ill-health. It is feared that he may not live to be inaugurated.[7] Death is thinning fast the elders of the Republic. ——

Dec. 24th. I was interrupted some days ago in this letter, & now gladly acknowledge the kind attention of yr daughter;[8] but I shall answer her more particularly. You express an interest in the speech I made against the Fug. Sl. Bill. You well know that both the great parties were pledged at Baltimore to the support of the Bill (I am unwilling to call it a Law). It was vain, therefore, to expect its immediate repeal; but, my hope was to destroy its character before the country & to strengthen public opinion for some future contest. I believe that many persons have been led by my argument to regard the subject in a new light. Several slave-holding senators expressed themselves to this effect. One of them said that "the argt. was unanswerable," though they could not say this aloud, & another while I was speaking, gave me the testimony of his tears. I mention these things in response to yr special inquiry. You have challenged this egotism.

But I would not conceal the nature of our contest. It will be long and desperate. A pecuniary interest, so enormous as that of American Slavery, fortified by time & even sanctified in many minds by religion, cannot be overthrown in a day. My hope is to tame its aggressive spirit, to banish it from the national govt, & to drive it into the states, so that it can no longer vex our politics. The way will then be open for the consideration of its true remedy, in the light of economy, morals & religion.

It is well for Mr Webster's name that Mr Everett consented to be our Sec. of State. He told me that he felt that a friendly hand ought to close the administration of the former, & on this account, he has left his home & his invalid wife in Boston to labor here till March 4th, when the new President will be inaugurated. Every thing in the Department was behind-hand. All the foreign ministers complained of neglect. Mr Everett has applied himself to the business with rare assiduity, & has won the regard of all who deal with the Department. Besides attending to all its details with great minuteness, he is now negotiating a treaty with Belgium for the extradition of criminals—a Consular Treaty with France—a Convention with England & France on International Copyright & another Treaty with England on the Fisheries & all questions with the Colonies. Quite a budget for 3 months! But enough of American politics. Yours are not without their interest. Two things are sufficiently piquant—the plagiarism of Disraeli & the feat of Palmerston.[9]

Believe me, dear Ld Wharncliffe,

Ever Yrs, Charles Sumner

P.S. The speech about which you inquire [*Freedom National*] has been widely circulated. I know not the number of copies, but much above 100,000. I send you a copy of one of the cheap editions; also a local newspaper printed at one of the Fishing towns.

ALS GBS (70/602, PCS)

1. Wortley Hall, Sheffield, 24 September 1852, 9/428, PCS.

2. Since 1849 various private military expeditions organized in the U.S. had tried to invade Cuba; all these efforts had been thwarted by the U.S. government.

3. The House of Representatives had requested the correspondence of all instructions from the U.S. Department of State to diplomats regarding Cuba from 1822 to 1848. The *New York Daily Times* (24 November 1852:1) published letters between Secretary of State James Buchanan and Romulus M. Saunders, the American minister in Madrid, including Buchanan's of 17 June 1848, offering to buy Cuba for $100 million.

4. Rumors that the French wished to occupy Samana Bay circulated in 1852, and had not been discounted by E. G. Eugene, Comte de Sartiges, the French minister in Washington (Charles Tansill, *The United States and Santo Domingo, 1798–1873* [1938], 172–73).

5. Angel Calderón de la Barca was in 1852 the Spanish minister to the U.S.

6. The "Fisheries" controversy stemmed from a British threat to send armed vessels into Canadian waters to back up Britain's exclusion of American fisheries there.

The issue remained unresolved because of Daniel Webster's ill health (Clyde Augustus Duniway, "Daniel Webster, Secretary of State, (Second Term)," *American Secretaries of State*, ed. Samuel Flagg Bemis 6 [1928]:110). Americans on the island of Lobos, an island claimed by Peru, had requested U.S. protection, and Webster, over the protest of Peruvians, had sent a U.S. warship (Foster Stearns, "Edward Everett, Secretary of State," ibid., 122–23).

7. William R. King died 18 April 1853.

8. 9 December (9/537). Cecily Stuart-Wortley (1835–1915) had accompanied her parents on their visit to the U.S. earlier in 1852.

9. Disraeli had paid tribute to the duke of Wellington in a House of Commons speech 15 November. The *Globe*, a pro-Palmerston newspaper, exposed the speech as plagiarism, noting that one-fourth of it had been borrowed from an article by the French statesman Adolphe Thiers. Disraeli claimed the borrowed passage resulted from an unconscious "association of ideas" (William F. Monypenny and George E. Buckle, *The Life of Benjamin Disraeli*, vol. 3 [1914], 393–95).

To Theodore Parker

Senate Chamber December 27th 1852.

Dear Parker

This morning Seward came to me, and inquired your address. Giving it to him I said, "do you wish to know what he thinks of you?" "Yes" said he,—I then handed him your letter.[1] He seemed absorbed in it, and returning it to me, asked me to forward to you the enclosed letter *already* written. I trust I did not take too great a liberty in shewing it. The tone was kindly though full of regret. He has since borrowed it of me to shew to his wife, *who agrees with us*.

I will speak to Calderon of the Cuban laws. I have a large work, privately printed by the French Government on Cuba, which I think must contain the information you seek.[2] This will be at your command on my return. But I think the *practical* question of Cuba is now suspended.

Seward was engaged in the Supreme Court when the vote was taken to which you refer.[3] It seems to me that the vote in question has been exaggerated[.] I should be unwilling to say that *all* the *nays* were in favor of proscription. The simple question was of *postponement*. Though Chase announced that he wished the vote to be a test on the question of proscription, yet I told him at the time that it would not be accepted as such.

I await your homily on Webster.[4]

Ever yours, Charles Sumner

C MHi (70/618, PCS)

1. Parker, in his letter of 20 December 1852 (9/563, PCS), criticized Seward's tribute to Webster: "Mr S. has so much good in him that I shall not say much about this defection of his, only [avertir?] it, hoping that he will ere long make amends."

2. Parker sought copies of the Cuban correspondence and the Santo Domingo correspondence. He also asked CS to see Calderón about getting books on Mexico.

3. CS, Hale, and Chase were excluded from Senate standing committees. When Hale asked how the committee members had been chosen, Senator Jesse Bright, in charge of the appointments, said Hale had been excluded because "we considered him outside any healthy political organization in this country." Parker wondered why Seward had not voted on Chase's motion, which, as CS explained, was one to postpone consideration of the appointments. The motion was defeated 6–38 (13 December, *Globe*, 32nd Cong., 2nd sess., 39–43).

4. Parker's revised version of his sermon on Webster, "Discourse on Webster," preached 31 October, was published in March 1853.

To Charles Francis Adams

Senate Chamber—
Jan. 26th '53

My dear Adams,

Not *unconsciously* did I touch upon that subject. I knew its delicacy & importance, &, therefore, referred it to yr discretion. I have long been assured of what your father did.[1] I know him as its *fons et origo*.

It occurred to me that perhaps, now might be a fit time for a full exposition of yr father's work, & my friendly interest in Soulé disposed me at once to comply with his request. He has spoken, & I can hardly regret that he had not yr materials.[2] I told him frankly that I could not sympathize with his speech, although I admired his eloquence. He is a generous nature; but sees things from a point of view very different from ours. Personally he awakens in me a warm friendship.

Immediately on the receipt of yr letter I telegraphed that the *Wilson-Warren story was utterly false*. Never to any person have I expressed any preference between A & E.[3] With very few have I spoken on the subject. For obvious reasons I do not intermeddle with it. My simple aspiration is for the man whose presence here will do the least detriment to our cause. I have never ceased to think, in my private thoughts, that [*George N.*] Briggs would be best for us; but, since our conversation here, I have not expressed this to any body, nor have I sought directly or indirectly to influence any body. Any report to the Contrary I wish you would contradict whenever you meet it.—Seward is speaking now.[4]

Ever yours, C. S.

ALS MBApm (70/664, PCS)

1. CS and Adams had corresponded regarding recent discussions of the Monroe Doctrine in the Senate. CS had written Adams (21 January 1853, 70/660, PCS) suggesting that his father's diary might be a source of information for Soulé's forthcoming speech. Adams wrote CS from Boston that, although his father was clearly the author of the doctrine bearing Monroe's name, discussion of John Quincy Adams's role would only make the doctrine more controversial. Southerners were "already shrinking from it in alarm" and should not have "the advantage of attacking its true author" (23 January, 70/663).

2. Soulé spoke in favor of the eventual U.S. annexation of Cuba on 25 January. Attributing the Monroe Doctrine to James Monroe, Soulé declared that it bore "ominous significancy" for the people of the U.S. and was not to be controverted (*Globe*, 32nd Cong., 2nd sess., appendix, 119–23).

3. Adams wrote CS that the Massachusetts legislature would decide the U.S. senatorship on 26 January between candidates George Ashmun and Edward Everett. He said Henry Wilson had quoted Fitzhenry Warren as saying CS favored Ashmun. On 3 February Everett was elected U.S. senator.

4. Seward defended John Quincy Adams's record against Cass's June 1850 pejorative remarks about the former president, and stated that Adams was the author of the Monroe Doctrine (*Globe*, 32nd Cong., 2nd sess., appendix, 125–29).

To Wendell Phillips
Private

Washington—Sunday—
[*30 January 1853*]

My dear Wendell,

The *Standard* came yesterday, as I was starting for the Senate. In hasty glimpses I read yr speech,[1] but reserved its careful perusal for a better time, when the labors of the day were all over. It was half past 1 oclk at night when I finished it, with renewed admiration for yr ability, gratitude for yr devotion to the slave, & a throb of friendship for the kind memories with regard to myself. Sometime ago I was told that "Phillips had abused me." "He may have criticised me" was my reply, "but I know he has said nothing unkind of me." Such was my faith.

Nobody engaged in public discussion has known me so long as you have. I think you can attest to my early—almost autochthonous—hostility to Slavery, & to its constancy at all times, according to my measure of duty. Our system has differed; but it is a source of real joy to me that we have ever been friends.

I wish that I had seen you in the autumn. There is much I could have told you, at least with regard to persons & things at Washington. But that pleasure I shall surely have in the spring.

You have said so much of me that is kind that I do not desire to criticise yr criticism; but you will bear with me, while I write, in no spirit of controversy, for yr private eye.

You say that "no one would gather from any word or argt" of my speech in the Senate that I ever "took such ground as I did at Faneuil Hall."[2] Then, indeed, was I unfortunate. My aim in the speech at Washington was absolutely to cover the other speech, so far as I could without repeating its very language. After assailing the Act by all legal argts. I then denounced it as a violation of the Divine Law, & declared that I could not obey it.

Again you criticise me for saying that I "know no better aim *under the Constitution*, than to bring back the Govt. to the precise point it occupied when Washington took his first oath,"[3] But can we do more *under the Constitution?* Mark the cautiousness of my language, purposely adopted. Let us now scour the National Govt. of Slavery, & there will be nothing more for us to do *under the Constitution*. The back-bone of the Slave-Power will be broken, & the Anti-Slavery sentiment will find a free course.

What I have done I dedicate to the cause. I think less of it than others have done. Should I live I hope to do better. I am glad also to confess my obligations to my predecessors in the argt., & yet there are some points, which I did not consciously take from others.[4] Let me mention the picture of Washington on the day of his inauguration without a slave under the Nat. flag & the whole argt. deduced from that; also the history of the Fug. Sl. Bill (I cannot call it Law); the argt. from the old writ *de nativo habendo*,[5] which seems to me quite conclusive on that point; & the paralell between the Slave Act & Stamp Act—not in their enormity—but in their *peculiar unconstitutionality*. But enough of this. For myself, I am so grateful to all, under whatever name, & of whatever party, who are in earnest for the slave that I have no public criticism for them. I would that all our powers were directed at the common enemy.[6]

Ever Yours, Charles Sumner

P.S. The subscriptions to newspapers shew an [unwanted?] increase of Anti-Slavery sentiment; but *I have not recd. a single Anti-Slavery petition during this session*. I hope that at the next session the old battery will be renewed.

ALS MH-H (70/679, PCS)

1. Phillips gave his speech, "Philosophy of the Abolition Movement" (*Speeches, Lectures and Letters* [1864], 98–153), 27 January 1853, before the Massachusetts Antislavery Society in Boston. He undertook an extended defense of the abolitionist

movement and criticized the recent "timidity" of some political leaders: "they seem to me to lose in Washington something of their old giant proportions" (146).

2. Phillips criticized CS's "Freedom National" speech, saying, "It is all through, the *law*, the *manner* of the surrender, not the surrender itself, of the slave, that he [*CS*] objects to" (139).

3. Phillips continued, "The more accurate and truthful his glowing picture of the public virtue of 1789, the stronger my argument. If even all those great patriots, and all that enthusiasm for justice and liberty, did not avail to keep us safe in such a Union, what will?" (145).

4. Of CS's speech Phillips said, "there is hardly a train of thought or argument, and no single fact in the whole speech, which has not been familiar in our meetings and essays for the last ten years" (121).

5. "By being a native."

6. Phillips answered CS on 7 March (Florence, Massachusetts, 10/030, PCS), saying, "My objection to the tone of your speech was from no doubt of you: but from the effect even its guarded expressions would have on public opinion."

To Henry W. Longfellow

Washington—Sunday
[*13 February 1853*]

Dearly beloved Longfellow,

Here is a letter which I send for yr eye before letting it pass to the budget of things forgotten.

I sat next to [*Washington*] Irving last evng, while Thackeray[1] discussed of Congreve & Addison. The author of the Sketch-Book had a wakeful pleased look throughout & at the end expressed himself warmly in praise of the lecture.

I have heard T. twice. He has a strong tread as he moves over his subject. To listen to him was a most agreeable diversion. The Humanists of a past century sketched by their representative in ours! That is something. We talk over together days or rather nights at the *Garrick* with the wits of London when I was there. He speaks well of Boston but complains that "party runs high there."

Love to all yr house! C. S.

Send me a verse with yr signature for a lady here—wife of my friend Sibbern, the Swede.[2]

ALS MH-H (71/015, PCS)

1. The British novelist William Makepeace Thackeray (1811–63) lectured in American cities from November 1852 until the spring of 1853.

2. Georg Sibbern (1816–1901) was later minister from the joint kingdom of Norway and Sweden to the U.S. (1854–56).

To Nathaniel Hawthorne

Senate Chamber
March 26th—'53

My dear Hawthorne,

"Good!" "good!", I exclaimed aloud on the floor of the Senate, as yr nomination was announced.

"Good"! "good,"—I now write to you on its confirmation.[1] Nothing could be more grateful to me. Before you go I hope to see you.

Ever Yours Charles Sumner

Nathl. Hawthorne Esq.

ALS CSmH (71/045, PCS)

1. The Senate confirmed Hawthorne's appointment as U.S. consul to Liverpool 26 March 1853 (*Executive Proceedings*, 9:109).

To Theodore Parker

Washington March 28th 1853

My dear Parker.

Your discourse is grand.[1] It will travel forever by the side of its subject, judging him before the world.

I do hope that, by some charitable agency, copies will be sent to all members of Congress. They will read it, and its truth will prevail with many.

Howe's pen quickens in the *Commonwealth*.[2] I rejoice in his influence, but I do mourn the feud between brothers in Anti-Slavery. If Phillips (whom I love, as an early comrade and a faithful man) or Pillsbury[3] rail at me or judge me for my small work in Anti-Slavery, I will not reply. To me the cause is so dear that I am unwilling to set myself against any of its champions. I would not add to their burthens by any word of mine.

In proportion as the position of our pioneer friends seems more untenable and less *practical*, they cling to it with absolute desperation. If the skill and eloquence of Phillips, as evinced in his late speech had been directed not against allies but against Slavery and its enormities—against its influence on our Government—against Hunkers he would have struck a good blow, like yourself on that occasion.

Vale! Ever yours. Charles Sumner.

C MHi (71/047, PCS)

1. Parker thanked CS for his praise of "Discourse on Webster" and continued, "Greeley calls my judgment *harsh*; if he knew half the facts . . . he would say '*It is generous*'" (Boston, 31 March 1853, 10/071, PCS).

2. Howe had become political editor of the Boston *Commonwealth* and determined to continue its antislavery message (Howe to CS, 24 December [1852], 70/614; Harold Schwartz, *Samuel Gridley Howe* [1956], 179–80).

3. Parker Pillsbury (1809–98), abolitionist and lecture agent for antislavery speakers.

To William Wetmore Story

Boston Nov. 28th—'52
[2 *August 1853*]

Believe me, my dear Wm.,

I have longed to write to you, often, constantly; but my new duties & the correspondence which could not be postponed have absorbed my days, hours & minutes. During this last year I have written no letters except when obliged to write. But yr friendship I trust & believe, has already pardoned my seeming negligence. A year & more have passed since we parted.[1] All this while you have been enjoying Rome & art; I have been moiling in hard work. Truly I envy you. Congress lasted till September, & during the whole session I was daily in my seat, without absence or vacation. I came home thin & weary; but am stout & strong now, ready to start again for Washington.

Several times I have seen yr mother, who is well & cheerful. One evng she entertained us at supper—the Danas, Frank Parker[2] & his mother & myself.—Mrs Parker is passing the winter with her. The oysters & the wine relished well, & we talked of you. Another evng I dined with Edward Eldredge at his rookery in Dorchester. His new wife is young, fair & intelligent. I believe you have never seen her; therefore, I send my certificate. Of other persons who would specially interest you, I have seen little of late. But I forget; there is James Lowell, just returned. I sat next to him at a dinner given by Emerson at the Tremont House to the English hexametrist Clough.[3] Lowell looked rugged as a Yankee. He talks of lecturing, which he once foreswore.

August 2nd. 53. I take up this old sheet on which nearly a year since I commenced a letter to you. Do not judge me by my short-comings. If I have not written, it has not been from indifference. Only yesterday the Convention for revising our Constitution closed its labors. I was a member for the borough of Marshfield, & have been much occupied in various ways during its session.[4] This is my first day of rest, & I fly to you & Rome. It is so long since we have communicated with each other that I hardly know where to begin. But I cannot err, if I first tell you of yr mother. I passed a night under her roof at Nahant about a week ago. She seemed quite well. Mrs Parker was with her. We talked of you & she told me of her desire to send you $200, to help pay for the marble of the bust of Edith, I think. I undertook this little business for her & to-day deposited this sum at the Wards[5] to be passed to yr credit with the Barings. There it is now to be used. The Longfellows were at Nahant in that low cottage over the general one; but I saw nobody else,—I should except the [*John Ellerton*] Lodges. Yr cottage by the sea looked very attractive, as I saw it from a distance. Yr mother's has the advantage of spacious rooms; but its shape & general appearance & the grounds about it are not fascinating. I have seen yr Uncle Tom[6] frequently of late, that is as often as he has deigned to attend the Convention. He & I sat on the same bench, though we generally voted on opposite sides. But he did not seem to take things much to heart.

Of all the members of the Convention, during our three months' work, Richard H. Dana has gained most in character & fame & [*George S.*] Hillard has lost the most. Dana has shewn talents which I had long been familiar with, but which have taken many by surprize. He speaks with great ease & clearness, & always with good sense & logic. As a debater he is remarkable. I have enjoyed his success greatly. On slavery you know he is decided & constant with us; but on other things he is strongly & sincerely conservative. Poor Hillard seems to have been under evil impulses. I think him at times a beautiful speaker, & he has said some things in the Convention very well; but their influence has been destroyed by follies of speech, which had all the inspiration of Park St. In a passage with Dana he met with a wretched discomfiture. Dana & I sigh over him. His two vols. on Italy are now in press & will soon be published.[7]

You may be curious, dear Wm, to know how I regard my senatorial life. Very much as I anticipated. My earnest councils to all would be to avoid public life, unless impelled by some over-mastering conviction or sentiment, which could best find utterance in this way. Surely but for this I would not continue in it another day. To what the world calls its honors I am indifferent. Its cares & responsibilities are weighty & absorbing. I no longer feel at ease with a book. If I take one to read my attention is disturbed by some important question which will tramp through my mind. How often I think with envy of you at Rome, enjoying letters & art! No such days for me. At Washington I have found much social kindness, beyond any thing I have known of late in Boston. With most of the Southern men my relations have been pleasant, while with Soulé I have been on terms of intimate friendship. The speech which I made on Slavery was received by many of them with a praise equal to any thing from my warmest supporters at the North. They did not know that our cause could be put so strongly. By the way, I have this very evng received a token of regard from a Bostonian—a person in a humble sphere of life—which will interest you. It is a beautiful engraving of the Duchess of Sutherland,[8] framed with great taste, which he sent to England for. This is for my fidelity.—

Here in Boston Hunkerism is very bitter. Webster's friends are implacable. The *Courier*, which is their paper, has attacked Dana & myself;[9] & others like to shew their spite also. The Webster *dementia* has not yet passed away. I think it will soon disappear. Crowninshield told me yesterday in the cars an anecdote which will amuse you. Some of his little children, straying to the bottom of the Common, had fallen in with other children & played with them. On their return home, they were asked with whom they had been playing. They could not tell. "But did they not speak of their father"? was the inquiry.—"Oh yes! they said he wrote Mr Webster's will." Occasionally I meet in the street the writer of Mr W's will but he is too grand to see me. I enjoy infinitely yr letter to [yr?] mother in which you commented on that will. Was such a [document?] ever written before? Surely, the writer of it cannot easily be forgiven.[10]

Two days ago a gentleman stopped me in the street & announced himself as Mr Holmes, just from Rome. He gave me a kind message from Crawford, & then told me of you. The papers occasionally announce Crawford's progress in his great work,[11] & I always read every thing of the kind with interest. Give him my regards; also his wife. Where are you now? I imagine you on the Alban heights in some spacious apartment, enjoying fresh breezes, & the beautiful lake,—with books & pencil,—with pleasant friends, perhaps, under same roof, & with that simple delectable Orvieto for a sherbet. Tell me. How is it? I have said little of public affairs. In writing to you I wished merely to gossip. I have seen something of our new President [*Pierce*], & have found him an agreeable gentleman, affable in manners & prompt in apprehension. The orders to our diplomats to abandon their foreign liveries were issued at my earnest instigation. I trust you approve of them. On this subject, as on others, both the President & Mr Marcy listen to me with flattering attention.[12] I mention these things for yr eye, as I know you will take an interest in any thing which illustrates my position. I do not think Genl. Pierce a great man, but I do not undertake to prophecy with regard to his administration. His Sec. of State Mr Marcy is a person of wisdom & experience, ignorant of foreign affairs; but he knows his ignorance, & in this self-knowledge is his strength. I doubt not he will master most of the questions. Caleb Cushing is a dangerous character, who believes in war. He thinks that the country needs the occupation of a war, & I fear he will try to secure it for us. Guthrie, the Sec. of Treasury, is a tall, large-limbed, strong-minded Kentuckian.[13]

I hear that Palfrey talks of making Italy a home for some time with his family. By & by you will have a considerable circle there. Would that I were of the number. I do not know if Cass[14] will return to Rome. I was glad to hear that you like him. I do not know him; but if you think well of him, I shall also. Before closing I ought to rebuke you for yr long silence. You should not have stood upon the order of our letters, but have treated me generously. Now at last, you must write. Tell me of Rome, of yourself, wife & children, of art & particularly of the statue of yr father. Give my love to yr wife & kisses to the children.

Ever & ever Thine, C. S.

This sheet has been in my port-folio for nearly a year exposed to blots, which are almost infinite upon it. Yr $200 is passed to yr credit as a remittance at 60 days sight. I suppose Edward Eldredge tells you of the books. All well.

ALS CSmH (71/102, PCS)

1. Story returned to Rome to resume his career as a sculptor in September 1851, with his wife Emelyn Eldredge Story (d. 1894) and his children, Edith and Waldo.

2. Francis E. Parker (1821–86) was a Boston law partner with Richard Henry Dana, Jr.

3. Arthur Hugh Clough (1819–61), British poet, visited the U.S., 1852–53.

4. The convention met from 4 May to 1 August 1853. CS had been especially chosen to represent Marshfield, Webster's home town, by antislavery voters wishing to indicate disapproval of Webster's support of the Compromise of 1850 (Prc, 3:327–28). For CS's role in this convention see DD, 1:243–47.

5. Samuel Gray Ward (1817–1907), Boston banker, agent for Barings.

6. William's uncle, Thomas Wetmore (1795–1860), Boston lawyer.

7. Hillard's *Six Months in Italy* (1853).

8. Harriet Elizabeth Leveson-Gower (1806–68), antislavery activist.

9. In his speech "The Representative System, and its Proper Basis," delivered at the convention on 7 July, CS laid out his argument that absolutely equal representation for all citizens, "the District System," was preferable, but that he would bow to pressure for compromise if necessary and give more proportional representation to rural towns, the "Town System" (Wks, 4:33–61). The *Boston Courier* (28 July 1853:2) attacked those favoring the "Town System," which the *Courier* labeled a "trick" brought about by "the political quacks of the convention."

10. Crowninshield is probably Francis Boardman Crowninshield (1809–77), Boston businessman. George Ticknor Curtis wrote Webster's will, which the latter signed three days before he died. In a letter to Bigelow, 17 January, CS scoffed at the "Walter Scott mania" of Webster's will, which asked friends to support his household and which freed servants who by Massachusetts law were already free (ALS, Bigelow Papers, Union College; PL, 70/650, PCS).

11. Crawford had won a commission to sculpt marble pediments for the U.S. Capitol's Senate wing.

12. William L. Marcy (1786–1857), Pierce's secretary of state, 1853–57, issued on 1 June the "Dress Circular," instructing diplomats abroad to wear only simple evening dress at court functions (H. Barrett Learned, "William Learned Marcy," in *American Secretaries of State*, ed. Samuel F. Bemis, 6 [1928]: 263–65).

13. Caleb Cushing served as U.S. attorney general, 1853–57; James Guthrie (1792–1869) was later U.S. senator (Dem., Tenn.), 1865–68.

14. Lewis Cass, Jr. (c. 1810–78), chargé d'affaires for the Papal States; minister to Rome, 1854–58.

To Salmon P. Chase

Newport R.I. Aug. 21st '53

My dear Chase,

I have just read under the telegraphic head a brief abstract of Judge McLean's decision.[1] My soul is sad & sick. I feel as I did when we came away from Pierce's Inaugural.

You know the sincere interest I have always felt in the fame of Judge McLean. Why could he not have risen to the occasion? A brief analysis of the noon-day unconstitutionality of that law would have given him a place not only in the hearts of men, but in the history of jurisprudence. It will be hereafter the shame of our judges that they sustained that enactment. I wish from my heart that McLean was relieved from it.

I observe that he declares the constitutionality of the law of '93. But it appears from the life of Judge Story,[2] that he said that the objection founded on the denial of Trial by Jury was never argued before the Sup. Ct. & that it was still an "open question." Why did not McLean seize this valid objection & quash the whole wretched abortive abomination! Alas! alas! This teaches us that we must rely upon the coming generation. They will rejudge the justice of our courts.

My brother George is here now, with grand ideas of the West, & pleasant recollections of his drive with you at Cincinnati.

I was glad to see Ball here. I shall be sorry to lose Pierce from Massachusetts.[3] But I shall happy to know that he is under good auspices. With his great application, his clear intellect, & his well-trained powers, I cannot doubt that he would be soon among the foremost of yr bar, & at once a great help to yr business.

"Watchmen, what of the night"![4]

Ever Yrs, Charles Sumner

ALS DLC (71/112, PCS)

1. John McLean ruled in the federal circuit court for Ohio that an escaped slave, Washington McQuerry, should be returned to his master. McLean's opinion recog-

nized Congress's authority to enforce the fugitive slave laws of 1793 and 1850, stating the laws were justly based on article 4, section 3, of the U.S. Constitution (*New York Tribune*, 22 August 1853:6; Francis P. Weisenburger, *The Life of John McLean* [1971], 194).

2. See CS to Charles Francis Adams, 1 March 1843, and to John Jay, 23 November 1852.

3. Edward L. Pierce was moving soon to Cincinnati to work for Flamen Ball, Chase's law partner.

4. Isaiah, 21.11.

To Theodore Parker

Newport R.I.
August 21st 1853.

My dear Parker

Each member of Congress has a single copy of the archives and of many other Public Documents. Mine is at Washington, and forms part of my little collection there.[1] If here it would be at your service.

Mr [*Ellis Gray*] Loring and myself pressed J. Q. Adams at Quincy to sign the Interrogatives, and address them to the Governors of the British West Indies and he declined.[2] This was just before his death. Since then I have often thought of them, and now more than ever desire the answers. I anticipate discussions next session which may be helped by such responses as we should have. These interrogatives are pointed and searching.

I am at a loss what to do with them. Lord Carlisle is not in England. He has gone to the East. Lord Brougham is aged and uncertain. I have thought of addressing the interrogatives in my own name to the Governors: but on some grounds I shrink from this. I should still be glad of your councils.

I am anxious to have you exhibit in speech or tract of the operation of Emancipation: that which you forbore at Framingham. For your kind interpretation of me believe me grateful. Let me say, however, that, while I feel that at Plymouth, I did no justice to myself or my own thoughts, I do not think I could have more strictly spoken without violation of the implied compact under which I accepted the invitation.[3] It is my delight always to take advantage of opportunities to vindicate the good cause, and I believe I have used them as often as any body in New England. I refer of course to general occasions, not to special Anti-Slavery gatherings. Pardon this egotism.

Here is a note from Mr Hodgson, who married one of the largest slave properties of Georgia, which may interest you.[4]

Ever yours, Charles Sumner

C MHi (71/114, PCS)
Enc: William B. Hodgson to CS, Newport, 13 August 1853, C

1. Parker asked CS for an additional volume of the archives, as well as census data of 1840 and 1850, for a forthcoming speech showing the effect of slavery on population increase and production, 1800–50 (18 August [1853], misdated 1854, 11/590, PCS; see Parker's "An Anti-Slavery Address," *Works of Theodore Parker*, ed. Frank Sanborn [1911], 12:153–95).

2. Parker also sought advice from CS on asking British authorities for information on slavery and emancipation in the West Indies. He hoped Harriet Beecher Stowe, soon to leave for Europe, could pass on the questions to the proper person, and suggested Lord Brougham or the earl of Carlisle. In "The Progress of America" (1854), Parker compared British West Indian treatment of slaves with that in the U.S. (ibid., 230–33).

3. Although CS ostensibly honored the English Separatists in his speech 1 August 1853, "Finger-Point from Plymouth Rock," his tribute could be seen—and was, by Edward Everett, for example—as directed toward antislavery leaders: "Better be the despised Pilgrim, a fugitive for freedom, than the halting politician, forgetful of principle, 'with a Senate at his heels'" (1853, 10–11; Everett to CS, 15 October, 10/262).

4. William B. Hodgson's letter to CS (71/115) expressed the wish that Parker's "Discourse on Webster," a "glorious composition," had been printed with the other obituary notices CS had sent him.

To William H. Seward

Boston Sept. 21st '53

My dear Governor,

I have read with gratitude & admiration yr recent plea for the true idea of the Republic.[1] Truth is here quietly commended, & I felt the beginning of the new order of things.

I could not but compare your tone with the wretched gilded (*gilt?*) flybusterism of my colleague.[2]

How amazing in audacity the Democrats have been in their recent conventions![3]

It is long since I have heard of Mrs Seward. How is she? Write me a word of her.

Ever Yours, Charles Sumner

P.S. Henry Wilson will be our next Governor *sans faute*.[4]

ALS NRU (71/117, PCS)

1. "The Destiny of the Republic," delivered at dedication ceremonies at Capital University, Columbus, Ohio, 14 September 1853.

2. CS refers to Edward Everett, noted for his oratory.

3. At their convention of 22 September, Massachusetts Democrats split into anti-administration, coalition, and "pure" factions (Roy F. Nichols, *The Democratic Machine 1850–54* [1923], 215–16). Meanwhile, at their Syracuse, New York, conven-

tion, 14 September, pro-Pierce and antislavery Democrats, the old Hunkers and Barnburners, split into two factions (*New York Times*, 15 September 1853:1, 3; 16 September 1853:1, 3).

4. Henry Wilson secured the Free Soil (or Free Democrat) nomination for governor, but lost the election. *Sans faute*, "without fail."

To William H. Seward

Boston Nov. 15th '53

My dear Governor,

I was glad to hear from you;[1] but should have been better pleased, had you told me something of yr wife.

The new Constitution is defeated. This is a calamity to the Liberal Cause. Of this I do not doubt.[2]

[*William*] Schouler, who was a working member of the Convention, sustained the new Constitution. Edward Everett, who was not a member of the Convention, opposed it. On the adjournment of the Convention, the country Whigs were in favor of it; the leading Whig paper out of Boston openly declared that it was "better than the old." But the Boston cabal, whose home is State St, & whose breath is Silver Grey Websterism, rallied the Whig party against it, & they have triumphed. This triumph will continue the domination of Mass. in the hands of the Boston financiers & politicians.

The ostensible ground has been the alleged inequality in the representative system; but here the new is an improvement on the old.[3]

I have spoken some 18 times—almost invariably to very large audiences. I think I have addressed more persons than any have ever before been addressed in the same space of time by one man in Mass.[4] The meeting at Faneuil Hall was larger than any there for years.

I am weary, & hope to leave to-day for New York, partly for rest, & partly to see the Crystal Palace,[5] which I have not yet seen. I shall be gone only 2 or 3 days, & expect to be in Washington on Saturday before Congress. Regards to Mrs Seward

Ever & ever Yrs, Charles Sumner

ALS NRU (71/129, PCS)

1. Seward wrote 12 November 1853 from Auburn (10/277, PCS), "I do not understand your new constitution further than to have a vague idea that it is neither altogether right nor altogether wrong. Massachusetts politics are becoming as intricate as those of New York are said to be."

2. The revised version of the Massachusetts Constitution, a product of the summer convention, had been looked upon by many Free Soilers and some Democrats as a

means of permanently defeating the Whigs, and its adoption had taken on this partisan political tone. It was defeated on 14 November by five thousand votes (Frederick J. Blue, *The Free Soilers* [1973], 276–78).

3. The new constitution had proposed generally to reduce the number of representatives from cities and increase the number from small towns (Prc, 3:330–31).

4. Pierce enumerates (Prc, 3:336–37) CS's speeches supporting the new constitution.

5. A World's Fair exhibit had opened in New York City in the summer.

To Charles Francis Adams

Hancock St.—Nov. 21st '53
Tuesday evng.
[*22 November 1853*]

My dear Adams,

It is true, that I was pained by the manner in which I was mentioned in yr speech.[1] I felt, with my whole heart, that I did not deserve it.

I never turned at the suggestion of any friends from the support of the right to the expedient. In taking the course that I did in the convention I was advised by nobody. My convictions were in favor of the District System, & I resolved to maintain them. Accordingly, I voted for it always & spoke for it as well as I could. At the same time I recognized the difficulties in the way of introducing such a system, & avowed in conclusion, that, while anxious for this system & determined to vote for it at all times, I should vote for the proposed Town System as a palpable improvement on the old. At the last stage of this question, after my speech, the District System was moved, & I recorded my vote for it. The question then recurred between the proposed Town System & the old, & there I recorded my vote for the new. In this course I see no abandonment of any principle.

It is also a mistake to say that I bent to the rod of party.[2] You know well that I have little liking for the contests of party. Gladly would I have been excused from the labor which I have encountered; but I have never at any time any where sustained any measure with a more entire conviction that I was in the right. To me the whole question was as plain as a diagram.

The new Constitution seemed to me to commend itself to every supporter of a Town System as an unquestionable improvement on the old; also to every supporter of a District System, like myself, as affording the surest means of securing that system, if acceptable to the popular will.

In other respects the Constitution seemed to me most beneficent; but I regarded its adoption as of incalculable importance to Anti-Slavery, inasmuch as it would break the back-bone of the Boston oligarchy. Its defeat, I thought, would be a calamity to our great cause.

With these views I went into the contest earnestly, bending to no rod of party, but to my own convictions. You can now understand the pain which I experienced in finding myself misinterpreted in a quarter from which I expected no such thing.

It is not in my nature to treasure offence where none was intended. Let this pass.

Pardon me if I say that I have no pleasure in any popularity acquired at yr expense;[3] & it adds to my pain that we should be placed in antagonism. But the Future, I trust, will make all right.

As ever Sincerely Yours, Charles Sumner

Hon. C. F. Adams

ALS MBApm (71/136, PCS)

1. On 5 November 1853 Adams had delivered a speech at Quincy opposing the revised constitution, with its representation system favoring smaller towns. Adams specifically singled out CS's support of the constitution (*Boston Daily Atlas*, 7 November 1853:2). Upon hearing from Dana that CS was upset by the attack, Adams wrote CS 21 November (Boston, 71/131, PCS). He regretted that CS found his speech "personally unkind" but maintained that he could not "view a question of representation as one of compromise" as CS could. He closed his letter with best wishes to CS for his political success.

2. Adams declared in his Quincy speech that CS had "bowed his neck to the iron rod of party."

3. In his letter, Adams stated that one "compensation" of Adams's criticism had been that it had succeeded "in drawing to you still more our old political friends" who considered CS "unjustly attacked."

To Edward L. Pierce

Washington Dec. 18th. '53

My dear Pierce,

I send you one word of greeting!—

I heard nothing of you before I left home. Perhaps, I should have written to you. Indeed, I was guilty of *latches*[1] with regard to that letter for Judge McLean.[2]

Do you know Judge Walker?[3] If not, *salute him from me*.

I hope to hear of yr prosperity. Indeed I cannot doubt it. The first thing, however, is to deserve success; & that you do.

Here is a letter which I have tardily answered by enclosing that copy you kindly gave me of Mr Palfrey's sketch of me,—with the request that it be returned to me. I do not precisely understand the object of the writer.

I deplore the loss of our Constitution. It is a catastrophe for our state & the country. It is due to *three things*. I mention those which were unexpected, as they were eccentric. I say nothing, of course of the Whigs or Hunkers; but attribute our defeat—(1) to Mr P's defection, which inspired the Whigs, (2) to Cushing's letter which paralysed the Dem. leaders; & (3) to the Catholic Bishop.[4] Had either of these influences been removed the Constitution would have been adopted. Eheu! Eheu! For a while we must eat our political bread in great humility.

Let me hear of yr success.

Ever Yrs, Charles Sumner

Chase is well & noble in resolve & faculties.

ALS MH-H (63/622, PCS)

1. Misspelling for *laches*, Latin for "negligence."

2. Apparently a letter of introduction to John McLean. Pierce wrote from Cincinnati that "the letter to Judge McLean would be welcome" (28 December 1853, 10/365, PCS).

3. Timothy Walker (1802–56), Cincinnati lawyer and legal writer.

4. John Gorham Palfrey circulated a pamphlet published 28 October 1853, *Remarks on the Proposed State Constitution by a Free Soiler from the Start*, opposing the revised constitution. In addition, Caleb Cushing wrote a public letter, 9 October, to the editor of the *Boston Post* which stated that the Pierce administration opposed any Democratic cooperation with a third party, i.e., Free Soilers. Catholics, led by Bishop John B. Fitzpatrick (1812–66), opposed the new constitution because it prohibited using public funds for parochial schools (Frederick J. Blue, *The Free Soilers* [1973], 278–79).

To James M. Stone

Washington Dec. 23d '53

My dear Sir,

I was glad to hear from you & to know that our friends are in good heart.

The Whigs seem mad with exultation & animosity. I trust their rage will have a fall. Mr. Walker's article is strong & effective.[1]

I have neither time nor will to write out that old speech. It is a "dead horse."[2]

Chase & myself voted for Tucker.[3] Had we been sure of the defeat of Armstrong without our votes, we should probably have cast them for a third candidate. On counting the votes the opposition—"coalition" they call it—found itself stronger than it expected. But we felt that the defeat of the *Union* would be a blow to the Administration & especially to that policy of intervention in State affairs which we desired to condemn.

The fate of the nominees of the President is doubtful. The *real Hunkers* in Mass. seem to be safe; but the Coalitionists are less secure. Redfield's case is very doubtful.[4]

I am glad that you are to stir the people. This is right. Were I at home, I should deem it a pleasure & a duty to distribute the circulars under my frank.[5] But I cannot frank blank envelopes here to be [sent?] in Boston without violating a regulation of the post-office; &, though I doubt the correctness of the regulation, yet, in my position, I am unwilling to set it at defiance. Chase agrees with me in this, &, indeed, counsels it strongly.

I shall always be glad to hear from you. Believe me, dear Sir,

Faithfully Yours, Charles Sumner

P.S. Let me ask your attention to a criticism on yr circular which I have made as a *memorandum* upon it.

ALS DLC (71/154, PCS)

1. With his letter of 20 December 1853 from Boston (10/341, PCS) James M. Stone, an editor of the Boston *Commonwealth*, had enclosed an article on constitutional reform, probably written by William Walker of Pittsfield.

2. Stone wished CS would publish his speech, delivered throughout Massachusetts in the fall, endorsing the revised constitution.

3. An election for printer of the Senate was held 12 December; contestants were Beverly Tucker, editor of the Washington *Sentinel,* and Robert J. Armstrong (1792–1854), editor of the Washington *Daily Union*, a pro-Pierce newspaper. Tucker received twenty-six votes to Armstrong's seventeen (*Globe*, 33rd Cong., 1st sess., 1, 28).

4. Probably Heman J. Redfield, a moderate Democrat, whom President Pierce had nominated as collector of the port of New York (Roy F. Nichols, *The Democratic Machine 1850–54* [1923], 212). Stone wrote that he hoped Redfield would be rejected along with Caleb Cushing's nominees, thus effecting an "interchange of civilities between our friends & Redfield's opponents." The Senate confirmed Redfield 26 January 1854, with CS voting for confirmation (*Executive Proceedings*, 9:217).

5. Stone had written he was promoting antislavery lectures and asked CS if five hundred circulars announcing the lectures could be mailed under CS's senatorial frank.

To Julia Kean Fish[1]

Senate Chamber
9th Jan. '54

My dear Mrs Fish,

Mr Everett kindly came to see me this morning at my room. Together we committed to the flames every written trace of our unhappy difference.[2] On my heart there shall be no record of it.

Meanwhile I mourn the embittered tone of the newspapers, which seems to deepen in the distance, as it echoes from small towns & villages. But this, I trust, will die away.

You are the author of a Treaty of Peace, which you must remember with joy, as a Good Work. For me there is joy also & gratitude. If in any respect I have seemed exacting or ungentle, I trust to yr charitable judgment, & remain,

Ever sincerely Yours, Charles Sumner

ALS ICbs (71/178, PCS)

1. Julia Kean Fish (1816–87), married Hamilton Fish, 1837.
2. According to newspaper accounts, Edward Everett opposed Seward's proposal that CS be placed on a Senate standing committee. Everett thought that, since CS was not a Whig, he was not deserving of a committee appointment (Prc, 3:345; *National Era*, 5 January 1854:2).

To John Jay

Senate Chamber
12th Jan. '54

My dear Jay,

I have read yr lecture in the *Evng Post—Tribune* & *Herald*, that I might get as much of it as possible.[1] You have struck a good blow. Pray publish the lecture at once. Like all that you do it seems to be admirably complete in form, as it is true & lofty in sentiment.

Seward gave his petition to Chase. He thinks it better for him to cultivate silence for the present. Chase presents the petition to-day. I have reserved mine till the next day of meeting, so that the voices may be renewed, in succession.[2] It will be for the people to enable us to present a petition each day.

For the present, it is important that the petitions should be pointed at Nebraska—& against the violation of the Missouri Compromise. Let petitions against the enormity be circulated. If you would prepare such a petition, & confer with Mr Tappan, I think a public opinion might be accumulated which would be felt.[3]

The Census is not yet printed for distribution.

I note yr suggestions about the *Era*.[4]

A petition when presented in either body cannot be withdrawn from the file without consent or formal motion. Petitions on Slavery must, therefore, be prepared in duplicate, to be presented contemporaneously in each body. But, the petition may be more effective on public opinion in the Senate, than in the House; for, in the former body, it may be openly presented, whereas in the House it is simply filed under the rule.

I agree with you in yr response to Mr Ingraham's criticism on yr Bill.[5] The subject is now before the Judiciary Committee, who have not yet come to any conclusion.

Ever Yours, Charles Sumner

ALS NNCB (71/180, PCS)

1. Extracts from Jay's lecture on the "First Abolitionist Society of New York," emphasizing the fervor and dedication of the early abolitionists, were published in the New York *Evening Post*, 11 January 1854:1.

2. In his letter of 10 January 1854 (misdated 16 January, 10/411, PCS) Jay had enclosed a petition from New York City citizens asking for separation of the federal government from "all connection whatever with slavery and the slave trade." CS presented it 17 January. Chase's petition from citizens of New York City asked for prohibition of slavery in the territories (*Globe*, 33rd Cong., 1st sess., 184, 158).

3. On 4 January, Stephen A. Douglas had asked that the Committee on Territories Report be printed for Senate consideration (ibid., 115). The report proposed to allow settlers of the Kansas-Nebraska territories to determine themselves whether or not slavery would be established there. It thus abrogated the Missouri Compromise, which forbade slavery above 36° 30′. Lewis Tappan (1788–1873), a New York merchant and abolitionist, was a founder of the New York Antislavery Society and the American Antislavery Society.

4. In his letter of 9 January (10/390) Jay suggested that the *National Era* initiate daily coverage of the congressional debate on the Nebraska territories and that CS, Chase, and Giddings write "first rate Editorials" on the issues.

5. Apparently a reference to a congressional resolution of thanks to Duncan N. Ingraham (1802–91), a naval officer. Ingraham had freed a Hungarian refugee, Martin Koszta, from Austrian rule and brought him to the U.S. (*Globe*, 33rd Cong., 1st sess., 16 January, 15 July, 176, 1760).

To Samuel Gridley Howe

Senate Chamber
18th Jan. '54

Dearest Howe,

With yr note came one from my dear sister, giving me the first tidings of her engagement & of her illness.[1] Tears of emotion & anxiety fill my eyes, as I think of her. More than ever I feel the eminent excellence of her nature, & long for her happiness.

I have written to her my sympathy; but I feel how poorly I have done it. I have also sent a welcome to Dr Hastings.

Do tell me of them both. Have you learned to know him? And what is her health? I write to you freely. To my mother I cannot write without Julia's knowledge; & George is much absorbed in his own plans.

The book of Poems is a work of genius, which reminds me of Elizabeth Barrett.[2] The genius is rare.

You observe that the Nebraska Bill opens anew the whole Slavery Question. Cannot something be done to arouse our Legislature to resolutions affirming their original position in 1819?[3] Here all is uncertain. I have a hope that it may be tabled at once. The threat is to push it to a vote without delay.

Ever & ever Yrs, Charles Sumner

ALS MH-H (63/631, PCS)

1. Howe wrote CS 16 January 1854 from Boston (71/185, PCS) about Julia Sumner's engagement to John Hastings (1814–91), a physician. He also described Julia's tuberculosis as "alarming" and advised that she travel to the South.

2. Howe's wife, Julia Ward Howe, had published anonymously her first book of lyrics, *Passion Flowers*. Howe had asked CS for his frank opinion of her work.

3. In 1819 the Massachusetts legislature had voted to support the Missouri Compromise. Howe wrote CS about plans for a convention of Free Soilers in Boston and informed him that petitions protesting the Kansas-Nebraska Bill were being prepared. He urged CS to speak soon: "For God's sake & man's sake . . . strike for freedom while it is yet time" (25 January, 71/206).

To John Jay

Washington 21st Jan. '54

My dear Jay,

Yr meeting will do great good.[1]

In yr proceedings recite & state precisely the Missouri Compromise,

& then *resolve* that any legislation of Congress, which shall abrogate or in any way contravene this Compromise, must be opposed.

Refer also to the public meetings in New York in 1819–20. See Niles's Register vol. 17 Index—*Slave Question*. There you will find the proceedings in most of the states. All these should be published in a broad-side of the Tribune. They would fix Northern sentiment now.

You might also *resolve*, that ye alleged Compromise Acts of 1850, so far from repealing the earlier Compromise expressly recognise the prohibition of Slavery North of 36° 30′.

Genl. Tallmadge's speech ought to be republished now. See [*Richard*] Hildreth's 3d vol. 2 series—Hist of U.S.[2]

If Douglas succeeds in taking the bill up on Monday, I think the discussion will be postponed.[3] Houston & John Bell are warmly against it on Indian grounds, & our desire is to draw their fire first, that they may be committed before the country.

Ever Yours, Charles Sumner

The petitions vs. Fug. Sl. Bill & Slave Trade I have not yet presented. *My* desire is to move their referral to one of the standing Committees & have a vote. Chase does not incline to this course. At all events I await Seward's return.

ALS NNCB (71/202, PCS)

1. Jay wrote CS from New York 19 January 1854 (10/419, PCS) describing plans for a meeting of New York merchants and bankers to protest the "violation" of the Missouri Compromise.

2. James Tallmadge (1778–1853; U.S. congressman [Dem., N.Y.], 1817–19), had on 15 February 1819 introduced an amendment to the bill admitting Missouri to the Union. He proposed that no more slaves be brought into Missouri and that those in Missouri be eventually emancipated (*Annals of Congress*, 15th Cong., 2nd sess., 1203–14). Hildreth's six-volume *History of the United States of America* was published between 1849 and 1852.

3. Douglas introduced the Kansas-Nebraska Bill on Monday, 23 January, but debates did not begin until 30 January. He had amended the bill, proposing that two separate territorial governments be organized (*Globe*, 33rd Cong., 1st sess., 221–22, 273–82).

To John Jay

Washington 22nd Jan. '54
Sunday

My dear Jay,

Yr letter of the 20th did not reach me till to-day. I have lost no time in seeing Col. Benton.[1] He is much in earnest, but does not wish to be quoted until at his own time & in his own way he gives his views to the country. He does not think it advisable for him to connect himself with the New York meeting.

I rejoice in the success which you are now "organizing." It will tell strongly here & throughout the country. Politicians here are indifferent to every thing except the popular voice. If that thunders they will give heed.

Benton says that every Northern man who sustains Douglas's bill is irretrievably ruined. As for Douglas, if he does not succeed in his plot, he will be kicked by the South; if he does, his brains will be dashed out at the North.

The "Friend's Journal" of Philadelphia shews how the Quakers are moving. Good!—

Ever Yours, Charles Sumner

ALS NNCB (71/204, PCS)

1. Jay wrote CS from New York 20 January 1854 (10/421, PCS) with further information about the protest meeting in New York City. He asked if CS would ask Thomas Hart Benton to speak at their meeting, believing that his presence, as a congressman from Missouri, would be highly significant.

To John Jay

Senate Chamber
Jan. 26 [*1854*]

Dear Jay,

As yet we have no copies of our Address.[1]

You will perceive that the Privilege Question on Phelps's seat has been started.[2] This promises to occupy several days & will take the lead of Nebraska—so we hope. We seek delay, that public opinion may be felt. But the effort will be to press the measure.

Ever Yrs, Charles Sumner

ALS NNCB (70/066, misdated [1853], PCS)

1. On 19 January 1854 an "Appeal of the Independent Democrats in Congress to the People of the United States," written largely by Chase, was issued and signed by six congressmen, including CS, Giddings, and Gerrit Smith (1797–1874; philanthropist; U.S. congressman [Independent, N.Y.], 1853–54). It protested the Kansas-Nebraska Bill, concluding: "Whatever apologies may be offered for the toleration of slavery in the States, none can be urged for its extension into Territories where it does not exist. . . . Let all protest earnestly and emphatically, by correspon-

dence, through the press, by memorials, by resolutions of public meetings and legislative bodies, and in whatever other mode may seem expedient, against this enormous crime." Chase introduced the "Appeal" in the Senate 30 January (*Globe*, 33rd Cong., 1st sess., 281–82). Jay had asked CS for 250 copies of the "Appeal" to distribute to clergymen in New York City and Brooklyn (25 January, 10/435, PCS).

2. On 18 January the Senate postponed until 25 January consideration of the right of Samuel S. Phelps (1793–1855; U.S. senator [Whig, Vt.], 1839–51, 1853–54) to a Senate seat. Both Chase and CS argued that debate on the Kansas-Nebraska Bill be taken up after the Phelps issue (*Globe*, 33rd Cong., 1st sess., 196–97).

To Richard Henry Dana, Jr.

Senate Chamber
March 1st '54

My dear Dana,

Read me in the pamphlet.[1]

Thanks for all that you write. I mourn the discord among Anti-Slavery brothers; but we shall soon close up in close ranks again.[2]

I have reason to be satisfied with the impression my speech has produced, even on Southern men. I hear that they are loud in its praise.

Mr F. P. Blair, the old editor under Jackson but now a good Free Soiler, thanked me gushingly for it, & said it was the best speech in Congress for 25 years. I hear also that Seaton[3] of the Intelligencer pronounces it the best he has ever read, always excepting Webster's reply to Hayne. With these a modest man may be content; & I communicate them to you in the fullness of our friendship.

Regards to Mrs Dana,[4] & *imperial* kisses to the children.

Ever Yrs, Charles Sumner

P.S. I am happy that I have done no discredit to Massachusetts.

ALS MHi (71/235, PCS)

1. Dana wrote CS (26 February 1854, 10/522, PCS) of Boston's approval of CS's speech "Landmark of Freedom," opposing the Kansas-Nebraska Bill (see *Globe*, 33rd Cong., 1st sess., appendix, 262–70).

2. Dana described a recent Boston meeting of the Free Soilers to protest the Kansas-Nebraska Bill, and stated that he, along with Charles Francis Adams, Charles Allen, John Gorham Palfrey, and Wendell Phillips, had refused to attend. He berated the "Littleness of [*Francis W.*] Bird" and the "spite of Wilson," the meeting's organizers, who, he wrote, excluded both conservatives and those "who will not follow a certain lead."

3. William W. Seaton (1785–1866), journalist and editor; publisher of Senate debates, 1834–56.

4. Sarah Watson Dana (1814–1907).

To Theodore Parker

Senate Chamber
9th March 1854

My dear Parker,

Thanks for your words of cheer.[1] Freedom is for a while defeated: but I turn to the country and to God, and do not despair.

Benton says that the North will never be on its legs. He speaks with infinite derision of the Senate, and says that it will be a bye-word of shame, to be repudiated by the country.

This wickedness has tried me much. It has taken from me sleep and appetite. Upon Chase and myself has fallen the [full?] brunt.

At midnight on the last day, I took the floor to speak for an hour or more again: but Douglass held it against me, and afterwards I was dissuaded by friends not to speak again.[2]

I hear nothing from Howe. Is he ill? I trust not.

Ever yrs Charles Sumner

P.S. In my course, you will observe, that I have been governed by my own individuality—not following others but myself.

P.S. Send me a *list of references* on the character and condition of the negro-race in every aspect.[3]—*soon*

C MHi (71/247, PCS)

1. The Kansas-Nebraska Bill passed the Senate on 3 March 1854, 37–14 (*Globe*, 33rd Cong., 1st sess., 532). Parker wrote from Boston 5 March (10/581, PCS) thanking CS for his "noble speech. . . . I hope you will always keep the Integrity of your own consciousness. We shall be beaten—*beaten*—*beaten*—I take it. But must fight still."

2. See *Globe*, 3 March, 33rd Cong., 1st sess., appendix, 325.

3. Parker sent two unidentified books on the "Negro Character" (14 March, 10/635) and recommended two others.

To Frances A. Seward

Senate Chamber—
30th March '54

Dear Mrs Seward,

Gladly I send the speech, according to yr suggestion, & am proud of the opportunity.[1]

I trust yr husband will be here next week to vote against the Gadsden Treaty.[2]

We have had a desperate battle here, which is now transferred to the House. Had Chase & myself shewn the sensibility of Cutting we should have fought half a dozen duels.[3]

Auburn has happily been saved the shame & pain of surrendering a fellowman to bondage.[4] God be praised!—

I trust to hear that you are gaining health & strength. Mrs Fish has with her a young friend of peculiar refinement & culture, a type of American beauty, fair & fragile—almost too much so "for human nature's daily food."[5]

Ever sincerely Yours, Charles Sumner

P.S. I have never told you that my sister—my only sister—became engaged to be married this winter, & shortly afterwards was taken ill with a hemorrage of the lungs, & went, with my mother & one of my brothers to Cuba, where she is now. I shall soon be more alone in the world than ever.

ALS NRU (71/284, PCS)

1. Frances Seward had asked CS to send a copy of "Landmark of Freedom" to her sister (Auburn, New York, 25 February 1854, 10/518, PCS).

2. The Senate debated the treaty 15–27 March in executive session. U.S. minister to Mexico James Gadsden had negotiated the U.S. purchase for $10 million of a strip of land along the northern border of Mexico. Antislavery senators opposed the purchase not only because it brought more slave territory to the U.S., but also because it provided railroad access to the Pacific for Southerners (Paul Neff Garber, *The Gadsden Treaty* [1924], 118).

3. During the House debates on the Kansas-Nebraska Bill, Francis B. Cutting (1804–70; U.S. congressman [Dem., N.Y.], 1853–55) argued that the Kansas-Nebraska Bill was good for the North because it prohibited congressional intervention in the territories. He engaged in sharp verbal altercation with John C. Breckinridge of Kentucky, who charged Cutting with being secretly against the bill (ibid., 27 March, 759–64). Rumors then circulated that Cutting challenged Breckinridge to a duel (New York *Evening Post*, 29 March 1854:2).

4. Frances Seward described a fugitive slave rescue in Auburn that had encountered no resistance.

5. Wordsworth, "She Was a Phantom of Delight," 1.18.

To Amasa Walker

Senate Chamber
26th April '54

My dear Walker,

I am glad that yr knowledge & talents are to be employed congenially at Amherst & for the benefit of the young.[1] If I were not in my present place, I would be a professor—if I could. I have always had a taste for the academy.

I trust, in yr personal commingling with men, you will not fail to expose the incompetency of the two old parties, in the present exigencies. My soul sickens at the names Whig & Democrat. The North must be united, & take the control of the Govt., or we shall sink under the despotism of the Slave-Power.

I say to you *confidentially*, that I have tried to bring the President to tender the mediation of the United States to the great belligerents of Europe, & I have dwelt on the grandeur of our position in thus entering upon the European scene.[2] The President has parried the whole matter by alluding to "complications." Bah! It is *Slavery*!! Slavery stops every thing that is good.

If we offered mediation, we should be constrained to accept a proffered mediation, in the event of a war between us & Spain. Besides Slavery desires the success of Russia, & the humbling of England & France, so that the latter may be disabled from watching us.

All this I trust sometime to expose.

Ever Yours, Charles Sumner

P.S. I acknowledge yr $10, which I shall apply at once to a new edition of my speech.

ALS MHi (71/305, PCS)

1. Walker wrote from North Brookfield (25 April 1854, 11/017, PCS) that he was to give a series of lectures to the Amherst College senior class on political economy.

2. In March 1854 Great Britain and France had become allies against Russia in the Crimean War, and Marcy had sent instructions on American neutrality to U.S. ambassadors in London, Paris, and St. Petersburg (H. Barrett Learned, "William Learned Marcy," in *American Secretaries of State*, ed. Samuel F. Bemis, 6 [1928]: 237–39). In a letter (4 April, 63/638) to the liberal M.P. and peace activist Henry Richard (1812–88), CS wrote that he had recently seen Pierce regarding mediation: "I am not at liberty to disclose the details of our conversation; but I cannot forbear saying for yr *private* satisfaction, that he welcomed cordially the suggestion & promised to it a most careful consideration."

To Henry W. Longfellow

Senate Chamber
9th May '54

Dearly-beloved Longfellow,

I am yr debtor & Fanny's too for kind letterets, which I shall not forget.

Here is a letter from Sam. Ward which has come to me unexpectedly this morning. You will be interested in reading it. Let me have it again.

Medora Ward has been passing the winter here—more brilliant in person & conversation than ever. She makes no allusion to her husband, & I have not ventured to mention his name. On inquiry, I hear unpleasant things of his habits & position. But his letter has not only the breath of friendship but the odor of good things.[1]

The Nebraska-ites are pressing their purpose, & will, probably, triumph;[2] it will be an evil day for them, unless the North is again lulled. Can this be so? Oh! for union among good men, forgetting whether they are Whigs or Democrats! This must be done or the Republic will become a great pirate. It now watches its chance,—when England & France have their backs turned—to make a quarrel with Spain.[3] Great, magnanimous people!—

For myself, I rejoice in the strength of England, that she may watch our piratical designs & keep them in check.

If you knew how pleasant yr notes were you would let me have the comfort of them oftener.

To-day is pleasantly warm, & I am in nankeen trousers. My mother & sister are at Aiken—a [retired?] place among the pine woods of S.C.

Ever & ever Yrs, C. S.

ALS MH-H (71/317, PCS)

1. Medora Grymes Ward was then estranged from her husband, Sam Ward, who had recently written CS from San Francisco (25 March 1854, 10/685, PCS), mentioning among other topics the friendship between his sister and Longfellow.

2. The House approved the Kansas-Nebraska Bill, 113–100, on 22 May (*Globe*, 33rd Cong., 1st sess., 1854).

3. On 8 April the American minister to Spain, Pierre Soulé, had presented Spain with a claim for damages when a U.S. ship, the *Black Warrior*, had been seized in Havana by Spanish authorities. Soulé's demand for immediate compliance exacerbated U.S. relations with Spain.

To Richard Henry Dana, Jr.

Washington
4th June '54 Sunday

My dear Dana,

The *Evening Post* of last evng, under its telegraphic head, announces an outrage to you, which fills me with grief & indignation. I trust you are not much hurt. But that very blow will tell on Slavery more than on you.[1]

The same paper has your beautiful, complete & high-toned argt.[2]—a model professional effort—so clear & just in its distinctions, so firm & loyal, with all that elegant simplicity which is a part of yourself; & I was filled with gratitude as I read it.

The evidence seems to have been of that precise character to allow a conclusion either way, for Freedom or Slavery, according to the general biases of the magistrate or the presumptions which he recognized. It will be an evil event for Loring[3] & his name, that he leaned to Slavery.

Should I not, at an early day, give notice of a Bill to repeal the Fug. Sl. Act? or should I allow Mass. to ferment still more before I move?

Can a pension to Batchelder's widow be opposed on grounds which will be sustained by public sentiment in Mass?[4] Regarding the act as unconstitutional & odious, I would cut off even the fees of the magistrate & marshall, much more than of a volunteer; but I would not, at this moment, when it is important to present an unbroken front, raise a question which may create a division. Let me have yr views on these things.

Ever & ever Yours, Charles Sumner

P.S. Do not forget an abstract of the statute which we desired.[5]

ALS MHi (71/340, PCS)

1. The arrest in Boston, 25 May 1854, of Anthony Burns, a runaway slave from Virginia, had created much excitement in both Boston and Washington. Dana had been engaged to defend Burns, whose trial took place 29–31 May; on 2 June the court ordered that he be returned to his master. That evening, as crowds gathered and the militia was ordered to put down any violence, Dana was assaulted on the streets of Boston, apparently by two men who had been guards for Burns (*Journal of Richard Henry Dana, Jr.*, ed. Robert F. Lucid [1968], 2:625–38; New York *Evening Post*, 5 June 1854:1)

2. "The Boston Slave Case," argument in defense of Anthony Burns.

3. Edward G. Loring (1802–90), U.S. commissioner presiding over the Burns trial.

4. When a group tried to rescue Burns on 26 May, James C. Batchelder, a truckman who had volunteered to guard Burns, was killed. Dana advised CS not to become involved in congressional efforts to provide a pension for Batchelder's widow (Boston, 5 June, 11/122, PCS).

5. Dana sent CS a draft of Massachusetts State Senator Samuel E. Sewall's bill (unidentified), which had passed both houses of the Massachusetts legislature, but was later reconsidered and defeated, according to Dana, through the efforts of former governor Boutwell.

To John Gorham Palfrey

Washington 6th June '54

My dear Dr,

I am obliged by yr sympathy; but I would not gain credit for danger not incurred.[1] It is true that the press here has done all it could to excite personal hostility towards me, & evil-minded persons, at the corners of streets, in drinking rooms, & gambling saloons, have belched forth their menaces; but I have never for a moment been disturbed. But enough of this.

You know well that I have always most truly honored yr character. In the same proportion, have I been troubled by yr course last autumn,[2] so strange towards myself & directly affecting friends with whom you had been associated & the great cause to which we were all devoted. But at this moment, when union among all good men is so needed to stem the slave-torrent, I am unwilling to discuss those events, so painful to myself & disastrous, beyond repair, to Freedom.

You have already done much for the good cause, & my soul swells with gratitude at the thought of it. But I have often thought & now frankly say, that, it seems to me Freedom in Massachusetts has recd. from you a more deadly blow than from any other living citizen of our Cwelth. But I turn from the Past, & welcome gladly your co-operation in the Future.

Full well I know the integrity of yr life, & I now make no suggestion against it; nor should I have said a word on the subject of our differences except in response to the allusions of yr letter.[3]

Let us forget, then, that unpleasant passage, & believe me, my dear Dr, with much regard,

Ever sincerely Yours, Charles Sumner

Hon. J. G. Palfrey

ALS MH-H (71/343, PCS)

1. CS had been blamed by some pro-Southern newspapers for indirectly causing the murder of Batchelder. The Washington *Star* wrote, "Why does he not expose himself to danger alongside of the deluded men whom he has designedly led astray?" (quoted in New York *Evening Post*, 31 May 1854:1). Palfrey wrote CS from Cambridge 1 June 1854 (11/094, PCS) of his alarm at threats posed to CS.

2. See CS to Edward L. Pierce, 18 December 1853.

3. Palfrey began his letter, "If you have turned your back on me, my heart still warms to you." Although Palfrey had written CS two letters trying to explain his opposition to the new constitution and to mend the breach between them (29 No-

vember 1853 and 3 January 1854, 71/139, 170), CS apparently had not answered. They now resumed correspondence on a fairly regular basis.

To Theodore Parker

Washington 7th June 1854

My dear Parker,

I had just read and admired your great New York effort, as reported in the Anti-Slavery Standard, when the *Commonwealth* came this morning with that other fulmination from Boston.[1] Such efforts will deeply plough the public heart. Other ages will bless you, even if we do not all live down the clamor which now besets us.

At last I see daylight. Slavery will be discussed with us *as never before*, and that Fugitive Bill must be nullified in the house. Peaceful legislation by our Commonwealth will do it all. *At once* should be commenced an organization to secure petitions. (1) to Congress. (2) to our own Legislature. Get people committed at once to the absolute refusal of the whole wickedness.[2]

Income from Boston—is sack cloth and ashes. Alas! for the poor Commissioner [*Edward Loring*]. I think now of my own words in the Senate—"Better be the Slave returned to bondage, than the unhappy commissioner."

The curtain will soon lift up here—Cuba—Hayti—Mexico. You know the plot. And yet the people sleep. The Spanish plot does not work well.[3] It is difficult to bring the machinery to bear.

Ever yrs, Charles Sumner

C MHi (71/346, PCS)

1. Parker had spoken 12 May 1854 before the New York Antislavery Society, attacking slavery and Southern expansionist designs on the Southwest and Cuba ("An Anti-Slavery Address," *Works of Theodore Parker*, ed. Frank B. Sanborn [1911], 12:153–95). The Boston *Commonwealth*, in editorials and news articles 3–7 June 1854, defended those opposing the capture of Burns.

2. A petition from 2,900 citizens of Massachusetts, introduced in the Senate on 22 June, proposed to repeal the Fugitive Slave Law. After debate on 28 June, the petition was referred to the Committee on the Judiciary (*Globe*, 33rd Cong., 1st sess., 1472, 1552–59).

3. The State Department was then engaged in plans to purchase or "detach" Cuba from Spain (see H. Barrett Learned, "William Learned Marcy," in *American Secretaries of State*, ed. Samuel F. Bemis, 6 [1928]:192–98).

To James Freeman Clarke[1]

Washington 10th June '54

My dear Clark,

I have just read yr discourse, with a grateful heart.[2] I am happy that such true words have found welcome in Boston, & I am happy too at the new vows to Freedom which you assume.

The Future will need all our energies. And unless the North arises, & without distinction of party, forgetting the effete differences of Whig & Democrat, takes possession of the National Govt., we shall be degraded to a serfdom worse than that of Russia.

I am humbled in dust, that the Fug. Slave Bill has been again enforced in Boston. In my speech at Faneuil Hall in 1850 [*"Our Immediate Antislavery Duties"*]—in the 2nd vol. of my speeches—I endeavored to mark out the course which should be pursued. Had that been followed, there would have been a moral atmosphere, deadly to the Slave Bill. I think the time has now come for that Public Opinion which shall render the Bill (I never call it a law) ineffective in Mass. Let us make Mass. at [least?] holy ground where the Slave-Hunter shall not come, & then, let us unite to put the National Govt on the side of Freedom.

Ever Yours, Charles Sumner

ALS MH-H (71/352, PCS)

1. James Freeman Clarke (1810–88), Boston minister, the Church of the Disciples, 1854–88; abolitionist and writer.

2. "The Rendition of Anthony Burns. Its Causes and Consequences. A Discourse on Christian Politics, Delivered in Williams Hall, Boston, on Whitsunday, June 4, 1854" (1854).

To Ralph Waldo Emerson

Senate Chamber
12th June '54

My dear Emerson,

Amidst hardships & conflicts here I have looked towards Massachusetts & felt strong in the sympathy of true hearts, beating I know in tune with mine. Yours I have often felt, though I had no written word from you till now.[1]

I am proud of my cause; proud also of the friends who cheer me. A goodly company. I would not exchange them for all the supporters of this Nebraska shame.

But new outrages are at hand, in the concatenation by which the Despotism of Slavery is to be fastened upon the National Govt. These can be wrestled with successfully by no individual; but by nothing short of a united people. At all times without any flinching, I shall oppose them to the end; but I cry for "help" from the North.

Gratefully & sincerely Ever Yours, Charles Sumner

ALS MH-H (71/354, PCS)

1. Emerson wrote CS 9 June 1854 from Concord (71/349, PCS) thanking CS for his speeches and encouraging him: "Stand fast to the end: making all of us your honorers & debtors."

To Theodore Parker

Senate Chamber
12th June 1854

My dear Parker,

Let the *dementia* work, even to the indictment of yourself and Phillips.[1] Good will come of it.

The great petition for repeal of Fugitive Slave Bill ought to be presented in the Senate, where its character and history can be recorded, and a debate upon it provoked. In the house it must be presented under the rule, without opportunity for even a word.

Bear these things in mind: but *without mentioning my name*. To present it would be a grateful service for me: but I would not seek the opportunity. I should follow it *at once* by notice of a Bill to repeal the Fugitive Slave Bill. My first impression was to give this notice to day: but I have concluded to wait the movement of the Boston petitioners; and to put myself in the position of carrying out their desires.[2]

I am glad you liked those few words of mine.[3] I had intended to make an elaborate speech of a different kind, but the determination to close the debate that night induced me to change my purpose.

The rulers of the country are the President, with [*Caleb*] Cushing, [*Jefferson*] Davis, and Forney.[4] Nobody else has influence. These are hot for Cuba and war. The howl of the press here against me has been the best homage I ever received. My opposition to all that iniquity is not merely by speech, but in every available way, and they know it.

Ever yours Charles Sumner

P.S. The threats to put a bullet through my head and hang me—and mob me—have been frequent. I have always said: "let them come: they will find me at my post."

C MHi (71/356, PCS)

1. On 10 June 1854 (11/155, PCS) Parker wrote CS from Boston that CS's next note "may find Phillips and myself in jail" for trying to rescue Anthony Burns from the courthouse 26 May. Neither, however, was immediately indicted by the grand jury.

2. CS spoke 26 June supporting the Boston petition for repeal of the Fugitive Slave Law (*Globe*, 33rd Cong., 1st sess., 1515–16).

3. Parker had congratulated CS on his final speech against the Kansas-Nebraska Act, 25 May (*Globe*, 33rd Cong., 1st sess., appendix, 784–786).

4. John Wien Forney (1817–81), a Philadelphia journalist, was clerk of the U.S. House of Representatives, 1851–56.

To Theodore Parker

Senate Chamber
13th June 1854

My dear Parker,

The review containing the article to which you refer, I have not. I think that I sent it to the *Commonwealth*. But it did not compare in atrocity with previous articles in the *Union* and *Bee* on me—in most of which you and Phillips also are introduced.[1]

Here in Washington I am attacked as chief firebrand, associate and even leader of Phillips and Parker. In Boston I am arraigned by Phillips himself for short-comings. Each man has his own way. None has been pursued with sure consistency for a longer time than even Phillips has been in the warfare with slavery.

The war plots of the administration are not succeeding. The Beach Morgan case is nearly settled.[2] Nothing remains but the charge of Africanization and here the evidence is strong, that Spain has no such purpose, except in self-defence. What can the *3 Brigadiers* who now rule the land, do?[3]

Ever yrs Charles Sumner

C MHi (71/358, PCS)

1. In his letter of 10 June 1854 (11/155, PCS) Parker asked CS for the copy of the Washington *Daily Union* article on CS. The *Union* (7 June 1854:2) described Wendell Phillips as "one of the most violent inciters to murder" and CS as a hypocrite, for,

although he professed belief in God, "he invokes in the next breath, boldly to bloodshed." Again on 13 June 1854:2, the *Union* referred to Boston's "damp and noxious atmosphere which ever surrounds the pestilent and treasonable heresies of such men as Parker, Phillips, Sumner, Banks and Hudson."

2. Theodore Parker's wife, Lydia, may have mistakenly transcribed "Black Warrior" as "Beach Morgan." On the *Black Warrior* see CS to Longfellow, 9 May 1854. After Spain refused the U.S. claim for indemnity, Marcy prepared a lengthy paper elaborating the U.S. case and instructing Soulé to wait for further guidance from the administration (H. Barrett Learned, "William Learned Marcy," in *American Secretaries of State and Their Diplomacy*, ed. Samuel F. Bemis, 6 [1928]:197–98).

3. See CS to Parker, 12 June 1854.

To Charles H. Branscomb[1]

Senate Chamber
15th June '54

My dear Sir,

No documents have been published by Congress touching the condition of the Nebraska Territory, nor have I any information with regard to it, which is not accessible to all. From time to time, articles have appeared in the *Tribune* of NY, also in various papers of Mass. calculated to throw light upon it, & which I have read with interest.

I presume that Dr Webb,[2] the Secretary of the Emigrt. Co. must have more information on the subject than could easily be obtained elsewhere.

The laws with regard to the public lands will be found in Little & Brown's edition of the Statutes at Large.

I am not aware that the Govt. has ordered its offices to prevent persons from settling in Nebraska, nor do I see how it can interfere with free emigration. I do not doubt that Slavery will have every possible advantage, that can be secured by friendly Governors & judges; but these can be counterbalanced by the votes of people who love Freedom.

I am obliged by yr sympathy & beg you to let me serve you where I can.

Very faithfully Yours, Charles Sumner

Charles H. Branscomb Esq.

ALS KUS (71/361, PCS)

1. Branscomb, then a lawyer in his thirties, had been delegated as an agent for the New England Emigrant Aid Company to travel to the Nebraska Territory and prepare a report on suitable settlements there. He left Boston in late June (Samuel

A. Johnson, *The Battle Cry of Freedom: The New England Emigrant Aid Company in the Kansas Crusade* [1954], 51, 58).
2. Thomas H. Webb (1801–66), Boston physician.

To John Bigelow

Washington—17th June '54

Dear Bigelow,

You seem to forget that Douglas's resolution, directing our Committee of F. Affairs, to consider the expediency of acknowledging the independence of Dominica, lies on our table—not yet acted upon & ready to be called up any morning.[1] For a fortnight I have not been out of my seat for a moment, during the morning hour, fearing that the resolution might be sprung upon us. Should it come up I propose to move an amendment by adding "and Hayti."

Where are yr letters on Hayti?[2] They move slowly.

I said nothing at the time to which you refer[3] for several good reasons, one of which was Houston's earnest request to me to say nothing but to leave Douglas to him.

I learn that Houston will probably be in New York on July 5th. He would like to speak in the Park.

Ever Yrs, Charles Sumner

P.S. Should you not publish Smith's judgt. vs. the Fug. Sl. Bill?[4] It is able grave & powerful. If well sustained by the press, it may influence public opinion, also other courts.

ALS NSchU (PL, 71/375, PCS)

1. Bigelow wrote CS 15 June 1854 (New York, 11/166, PCS) that he would not write more for the New York *Evening Post* protesting the recognition of the neighboring Dominican Republic (which CS mistakenly called "Dominica") until there was "some motion in Congress." Douglas introduced his resolution on 23 May; Chase objected and it was tabled (*Globe*, 33rd Cong., 1st sess., 1280). Antislavery leaders feared proslavery elements in Congress would try to annex the Dominican Republic (Charles Tansill, *The United States and Santo Domingo* [1938], 178).

2. Bigelow had visited Haiti December 1853–January 1854 to assess the "most successful experiment in self-government" by blacks. In a footnote to the printed version of CS's letter, Bigelow wrote that mounting conflict in the South over slavery made his letters about Haiti now seem "like fiddling while the country was burning" (*Retrospections of an Active Life* [1909], 1:146–53, 160).

3. In his letter to CS, Bigelow praised CS's "Final Protest Against the Kansas-Nebraska Act" but said he wished CS had made the speech "when poor Everett's back gave way."

4. Sherman M. Booth (1812–1904), a Racine, Wisconsin, journalist and Free Democrat, had been arrested 16 May for "obstructing execution" of the Fugutive

Slave Law when he helped rescue an escaped slave, Julian Glover, who then fled to Canada. Ruling in the Booth case on 29 May, Judge Abram D. Smith (1811–65) stated that Congress had no power to legislate for the return of fugitive slaves; individual states should provide this legislation. Further, Smith declared the Fugitive Slave Law unconstitutional since it "violates" the constitutional principle entitling all persons to "due process of law" (*New York Times*, 14 June 1855:1; letter of Sherman Booth to CS, 25 February 1856, 13/013; Wilson, 2:444–45).

To Horace Greeley

Senate Chamber
21st July '54

My dear Greeley,

I am always ready for any forlorn hope to establish justice, &, I believe an International Copyright to be one part of justice.[1]

The treaty was reported months ago[2]—without any recommendation of the Committee (oh! the dodge!). If it had contained a clause for hunting negros, it would have had a strenuous recommendation, & the chairman would have pressed it with sublime pertinacity. But what does Mason know or care about books or authors & their rights? Virginia has no authors.

At present it is on our calendar—with other things untouched—the Slidell proposition to recall the African Squadron (stopped I think by a proposition of mine)—the reciprocity Treaty,[3] & I know not what else.

Now the practical question is this? Is any thing gained by calling up the Treaty, & pressing a vote, pretty sure to be adverse?—Or is any thing gained by *trying* to call it up, when it is pretty certain that the Senate will not take it up?

Let me have your counsel.[4] I will take any course which its friends desire.

Horne Tooke,[5] before bending to receive the admonition of the House of Commons, brushed the floor with his handkerchief saying—"This is a *dirty* house." Is not the Senate "a *dirty* house." Pah! the vulgarity, the swagger, the vileness—nobody knows who has not sat in it. *You* don't know it. You think you do.

Ever Yours, Charles Sumner

ALS PCarlD (71/405, PCS)

1. Greeley expressed his concern that the treaty between Great Britain and the U.S. for establishment of an international copyright was not properly understood in the Senate, and feared that it would not receive its wholly deserved consideration (New York, 20 July 1854, 11/487, PCS).

2. On 24 January (*Executive Proceedings*, 9:216).

3. Slidell had argued against a Senate resolution to prohibit American protection of ships engaged in African slave trade (*Globe*, 33rd Cong., 1st sess., 22 May, 1258–61). The Reciprocity Treaty between Great Britain and the U.S., permitting duty-free trade between the U.S. and Canada, was approved by the Senate 4 August (ibid., 2212).

4. Greeley answered (23 July, 11/504) that if the treaty had a chance of eventually passing, postponement now would be wise. However, if it would definitely fail, "I think it decidedly advisable that it be called up and slaughtered *now*. . . . For you see, its non-ratification is precisely equal to its rejection." The treaty was not considered again in the 33rd Congress.

5. John Horne Tooke (1736–1812), radical British politician and philologist.

To Heman Lincoln

Private

Senate Chamber
24th July '54

My dear Sir,

I remember you well as a friend of my father, & I have also myself more than once had the pleasure of meeting you.[1]

It gives me great gratification to know that I have so much of yr sympathy. Let me assure you that I have not hastily adopted my views with regard to the obligations of the oath to support the Constitution.[2] One of the most solemn counsels I received from John Quincy Adams, constituting a sort of legacy, given to me as he lay in his bed between the white sheets related to this subject. He then said, with an earnestness, which now thrills through me, that the best & truest thing ever said by Andrew Jackson was that in swearing to support the constitution he *swore to support it as he understood it*. Mr Adams, who had so often opposed Genl. Jackson & particularly with regard to the Bank[3] on which he made this very declaration, yet concurred with him in this rule of interpretation.

You will observe that in common matters, there would be a cheerful deference to the opinion of the Sup. Ct.; it is only in an *exceptional case*, of transcendent importance or touching the conscience, that any question would arise.

Mr Rockwell[4] was gratified by yr kind remembrance.

Believe me, dear Sir,

very faithfully Yours, Charles Sumner

ALS MeWC (71/408, PCS)

1. Heman Lincoln, Boston businessman, wrote 22 July 1854 urging CS to "Agitate! Agitate! Agitate! till the work is done" (11/501, PCS).

2. CS had been under attack from Southern senators for his apparent inconsistent attitude in both swearing to uphold the Constitution and asserting he could not obey the Fugitive Slave Law (*Globe*, 33rd Cong., 1st sess., 26 June and 28 June, 1517, 1558–59; DD, 1:263–65). Lincoln wrote that he disagreed with CS "in some of your views of the Constitution. Must there not be some standard for *final* appeal?"

3. In vetoing the bill to recharter the Second Bank of the U.S., Andrew Jackson had said, "Each public officer who takes an oath to support the constitution, swears that he will support it as he understands it, and not as it is understood by others" (10 July 1832, *Gales & Seaton's Register of Debates in Congress*, 22nd Cong., 1st sess., appendix, 76). CS used this example in his 7 September speech, "Duties of Massachusetts at the Present Crisis. Formation of the Republican Party in Worcester" (Wks, 4:269–70).

4. Julius Rockwell (1805–88, U.S. congressman [Whig, Mass.], 1845–51; U.S. senator, 1854–55) had been appointed to the Senate 3 June when Everett resigned.

To Dorothea Dix

Senate Chamber
28th July '54

My dear Miss Dix,

I send you two lists, the first of the vote in March on the final passage of the Bill, & the other of the vote after the Veto.[1]

The 2nd part of the Patent Report is not yet printed.

Lieber's course is incomprehensible to me.[2] I have toiled for him, & always sought occasions to speak for him. Of late I have been almost inclined to hearken to reports with regard to him from his brother Germans. I do not know to what he refers in our intercourse. I am not the only one of his Northern friends who has keenly felt his course, though, perhaps, I am the only one who has been so placed as to feel it personally. But I am unwilling to dwell on these things.

Yours ever, Charles Sumner

P.S. You observe that Livermore—one of the purest & most single-minded of men—sides warmly with Jewett in this sad Smithsonian controversy.[3]

ALS MH-H (71/410, PCS)

1. In her letter of 27 July 1854 from Trenton (11/530, PCS) Dix had asked for an "exact list" of votes on a bill granting land to states and territories to provide for the poor and the insane. The Senate passed the bill, 25–12, 8 March, but on 6 July failed (21–26) to override Pierce's veto (*Globe*, 34th Cong., 1st sess., 572, 1621).

2. Francis Lieber and CS had gradually grown apart over the slavery issue. Lieber opposed CS's election to the Senate and what he regarded as CS's radical politics, although the two rarely discussed this divisive issue. Apparently they had not corresponded in over a year. Dix wrote that CS had "*sharply* and deeply wounded Lieber by some strong phrase in one of *yr* letters and which was connected with some Abo-

lition questions." See CS to Lieber, 25 June 1851, Lieber to CS, 4 February 1853, 2 May 1853, 63/437, 71/007, 070; DD, 1:242–43; Frank Freidel, *Francis Lieber* (1947), 265–66.

3. Charles Coffin Jewett (1816–68), librarian at the Smithsonian Institution, was recently dismissed from his post because he believed the Smithsonian should be a reference library, not a resource center for scientific investigation. From Boston George Livermore (1809–65), Cambridge merchant and rare book collector, wrote that he was sorry Smithsonian secretary Joseph Henry had prejudiced Dix against Jewett; he believed Jewett's forthcoming publication on the Smithsonian would expose Henry's mismanagement (23 July, 11/506).

To Wendell Phillips

Senate Chamber
5th Aug. '54

My dear Wendell,

I cannot close my affairs here without letting you know, by this hasty scrawl, that I have not been insensible to yr kind appreciation of my course.[1]

I have often thought of you. Indeed, our names have been much coupled by an abusive press. And it has sometimes occured to me that the various assaults & menances, in newspapers & debates, which I have encountered, would have done honor even to your known & unquestioned fidelity to our cause.

Ever Yours, Charles Sumner

ALS MH-H (71/419, PCS)

1. Phillips wrote CS 11 July 1854 (11/439, PCS) that the "whole state is very proud of you just now."

To Byron Paine[1]

Washington 8th Aug. '54

My dear Sir,

I was about to suggest to you to have the opinions of the court, & the argts. of counsel in Mr Booth's case collected & published in a pamphlet, when I observed that there was a pamphlet containing the most valuable portion of them.[2] Let me ask you to do me the favor of sending me a copy of this pamphlet to my address at Boston.

I congratulate you, my dear Sir, upon yr magnificent effort, which does honor not only to yr state but to the country. That argt. will live in the history of this controversy.

God grant that Wisconsin may not fail to protect her own rights & the rights of her citizens, in the exigency now before her! To her belongs now the lead which Massachusetts should have taken. Of the final result I have no doubt.

Believe me, my dear Sir, with high esteem,

Faithfully Yours, Charles Sumner

P.S. Judge Smith's opinion shewed the true metal.[3] That too will live. Indeed, you & he have been making history.

Byron Paine Esq.

ALS WHi (71/422, PCS)

1. Byron Paine (1827–71), associate justice, Wisconsin Supreme Court, 1859–61, 1867–71; then a Wisconsin attorney.

2. "Unconstitutionality of the Fugitive Act. Argument of Byron Paine, Esq. and Opinion of Hon. A. D. Smith, Associate Justice of the Supreme Court of the State of Wisconsin" (1854?).

3. See CS to Bigelow, 17 June 1854. Paine replied from Milwaukee on 14 August (11/583, PCS) that "Either judicial power or revolution must overthrow the accursed Fugitive Act."

To Henry D. Thoreau

Boston 31st Oct. '54

My dear Sir,

I am glad to send books where they are so well appreciated as in your chamber.[1]

Permit me to say that the courtesy of yr letter admonishes me of my short-coming in not sooner acknowledging the gift of yr book.[2] Believe me I had not forgotten it; but I proposed to write you, when I had fully read & enjoyed it. At present I have been able to peruse only the early chapters, & some detached parts,—enough, however, to satisfy me that you have made a contribution to the permanent literature of our mother tongue, & to make me happy in your success.

Believe me, dear Sir,

Sincerely Yours, Charles Sumner

Henry D. Thoreau Esq.

ALS TxU (71/469, PCS)

1. In his letter of 30 October 1854 from Concord (71/468, PCS), Thoreau thanked CS for his speeches, the 1852 coastal survey report, and a second report about the Amazon.

2. *Walden* had been published earlier in 1854.

To Julia Kean Fish

Boston 15th Nov. '54

My dear Mrs Fish,

It was very kind in you to write me that generous letter. I knew of yr husband's great loss & had been often on the point of sending to him my sympathy, which he had most sincerely.[1]

I send you my doings, in the assurance that you will receive them with candor, & will appreciate their aim. That is all.

You will observe the curious course of things in Mass.[2] The explanation is simply this. The people were tired of the old parties & they have made a new channel. Had the Whig leaders been disposed to "Fusion" here we could have formed a party which would have controlled the state.

It is evident that George Curtis will marry that graceful damsel.[3] He loves her; she knows it, & receives his addresses. That is enough. His friends here, I find, consider it beyond recall *une affaire accomplié.*

I feel humbled by the public proceedings of our Govt. every where. When shall we become respectable?

With best regards to yr husband & those ["neighbor?] ladies"

Ever Yours, Charles Sumner

ALS DLC (71/473, PCS)

1. Julia Fish wrote from New York (12 November 1854, 11/692, PCS) to thank CS for his 7 September speech, "Duties of Massachusetts at the Present Crisis. The Formation of the Republican Party," at the Republican State Convention. She also noted that Hamilton Fish's mother died 6 September.

2. In February 1854 antislavery men from the Democrat, Free Soil, and Whig parties had met in Ripon, Wisconsin, to form the Republican party. CS had argued at the September state convention that the Republican party provided the means to oppose slavery. Many Free Democrats, including Henry Wilson, had, however, joined the American or "Know-Nothing" Party, an anti-Catholic, anti-immigrant political group that had recently gained a national following. The party's nominee, Henry J. Gardner (1818–92), had recently been elected governor of Massachusetts.

3. According to Julia Fish, George William Curtis (1824–92; associate editor, *New York Tribune*, 1852–72; editor, *Harper's Weekly*, 1863–92) was courting Eliza Winthrop. But he did not marry her.

To Julius Rockwell

Boston 26th Nov. '54

My dear Rockwell,

Your letter was the best plaster for my pain. It was very kind in you to write me.[1]

My disability is passing away, so that I count upon starting for Washington on Wednesday. Had it not interfered with public engagements, I should have stuck to my bed for a few days & nothing would have been known of it out of my mother's house. I do not like being gazetted as a sick man.

Should you differ from me seriously on any of the important questions, which promise to agitate the country, I should certainly reconsider my own course; for I am satisfied that we are both aiming at the same results.[2] For the present, each seems without a party in the Commonwealth. I am ignorant enough; but I am not a Know Nothing.

More than three quarters of the people of Massachusetts substantially agree with us in sentiment, & I cannot but think that they will yet get together in a solid, compact & healthy organization. I hope soon to discuss these things with you face to face. I trust you will be at Washington at the beginning of the session. I am curious to see how our committees will be marshalled, &, by what caucuses. Will Hamlin[3] caucus with the Dems? Will you & Fessenden & Wade caucus with the Southern Whigs? There's the point.

Ever Yours, Charles Sumner

P.S. I especially regret the defeat of Eliot, Upham & Goodrich[4]—all good & faithful men, with experience needful among pirates.

ALS NNHi (71/482, PCS)

1. Rockwell hoped the news was untrue that CS was ill with rheumatism (Pittsfield, 24 November 1854, 11/731, PCS).

2. Rockwell wrote that although he disagreed with parts of CS's speeches, these areas were but "parentheses" in their general accord.

3. Hannibal Hamlin (1809–91), U.S. senator (Dem., Maine), 1848–56, (Rep.), 1857–61, 1869–81; U.S. vice president, 1861–65.

4. Thomas Dawes Eliot (1808–70), U.S. congressman (Whig, Rep., Mass.), 1854–55, 1859–69. Charles Wentworth Upham (1802–75), U.S. congressman (Whig, Mass.), 1853–55. John Z. Goodrich (1804–85), U.S. congressman (Whig, Mass.), 1851–55; collector, Boston Custom House, 1861–65.

To Theodore Parker

Senate Chamber
9th Jany 1855

Dear Parker

I have not been able to consult books on the points to which you call my attention. I can answer only by giving *impressions* rather than *opinions*.[1]

The oath of the Grand Juror binds to secrecy: but it seems to me that you must refer to the statutes and common law in order to find the *precise character* of this obligation. There you will learn whether it is applicable to the severe cases which you propose. To some of them it seems to me that it cannot be applicable. Besides fraud or corruption may always be exposed; nor can any oath stop the exposure. Under this head it seems to me might come an appeal to motives clearly inconsistent with the upright discharge of duty.

I am sorry that I cannot answer you more definitely. I spoke with Chase on the subject, who agrees substantially with me: but would not give a positive opinion without study.[2]

Of course, *you must* speak for yourself before Pontius Pilate.[3] I think you should make the closing speech, and review the whole movement in Boston, which culminated in your indictment, and arraign its intent and action—of course touching upon the courts. The opening counsel might argue the constitutionality of the Act, though I hesitate to give the Judges another opportunity to drive a nail into our coffin. Whoever you have to speak at any stage should be able to do something *historical*; for the time will belong to history—God send you a good deliverance!

Ever yrs, Charles Sumner

P.S. I read an admirable summary in the *Tribune* of the Curtis movement.[4] There was one statement that gave me a momentary twinge. It is that Curtis convened a meeting of the Commisioners to consider what should be done in slave-cases. I believe this is true: but I was never bidden to that feast. Had I been I should have gone, and without hesitation, denounced the Act at the time. I longed to do this officially—from the tripod of the court. As my name was on the list of Commissioners, it might be supposed that I had participated in that conference, or at least had allowed it to proceed without any expression of dissent: a position which I should be pained to occupy.

C MHi (71/513, PCS)

1. On 29 November 1854 Parker had been arrested, as he had expected, for resisting arrest in the Burns case, and was scheduled to appear in court 5 March 1855. He posed a number of questions to CS in his letter of 4 January from Boston (12/038, PCS) regarding grand jurors' obligations to secrecy. He also sought advice on the best counsel.

2. Parker asked CS to show his letter to Chase and Seward, for "the Rights of America are as much concerned in the matter as mine."

3. Benjamin R. Curtis (1809–74), U.S. Supreme Court justice from Massachusetts, was to be the presiding judge in Parker's trial.

4. A letter on the Phillips and Parker indictment from "A Citizen of Boston," dated 2 January (*New York Tribune*, 5 January 1855:6), devoted several paragraphs to the Curtis family of Boston. The writer stated that in November 1850 George Ticknor Curtis had convened a meeting of four U.S. commissioners and persuaded them to require the U.S. Circuit Court to arrest the fugitive slaves William and Ellen Craft. CS had been appointed a commissioner in 1842 (DD, 1:83).

To Samuel Gridley Howe

Confidential

Senate Chamber
24th Jan. '55

Dear Howe,

Houston told me to-day that he wished to give me his platform. "I have but two planks" said he.—"The Constitution & the Union." To which I replied—"Those are mine *precisely*; but we differ on the meaning of the Constitution." He says that his whole lecture will be contained in those two points.[1]

I think the General shews some sensitiveness, with regard to his address. Many here regard the whole thing as an important political step, calculated to affect his Presidential prospects.

I have promised the General a kind & cordial reception. This he will have surely. But I think that some person in the audience might properly address him, in the course of his remarks, some pertinent inquiries. You know that he is accustomed to such interruptions. For instance, ask him—Does *he* recognise ppty in man? Where *does* the Constitution recognise ppty in man? Has not the South been the aggressor? In what has the North been the aggressor? Such questions as these would bring him to precise points. Think of them; but say nothing of me.

Ever Yrs, C. S.

ALS MH-H (63/654, PCS)

1. Howe had been helping to arrange a series of lectures in Tremont Temple, and U.S. Senator Sam Houston was invited to speak. In an earlier letter (15 January 1855, 63/650, PCS) CS had told Howe that Houston would essentially plead that the South be left alone. "I feel a personal regard for the General & would not suggest anything inconsistent with complete loyalty to him. Let him be heard kindly; but let his erroneous views be answered by the press, &, if possible—also by some lecturer who is to follow him." Houston gave his lecture 22 February.

To Samuel Gridley Howe

Washington
28th Jan. '55

Dear Howe,

I enjoyed very much the report of Emerson. His lecture must have made an impression.[1]

Is it not strange that Harvard College nominates a Slave-Hunter as a lecturer?—I am humbled for poor Massachusetts now. Compare her position with that of Maine & Michigan. The governors of these states have satisfied me completely in their messages,—covering our whole doctrine.[2] Alas! alas! Massachusetts!

Ever Yours, Charles Sumner

P.S. What is the matter with the *Telegraph*.[3] It seems to have lost its vitality. Is it going the way of its predecessors, & drooping into imbecility?

2nd P.S. How is Mr Rothwell?

ALS MH-H (63/656, PCS)

1. "Lecture on Slavery" before the Massachusetts Anti-Slavery Society, 25 January 1855.

2. The appointment of Edward Loring as law lecturer was eventually rejected by the Harvard overseers, 20–10 (Ronald Story, *Harvard and the Boston Upper Class* [1980], 143). The two recently elected governors of Maine and Michigan, Lot M. Morrill (1813–83) and Kinsley S. Bingham (1808–61), had both run on coalition tickets protesting the extension of slavery (William Gienapp, *The Origins of the Republican Party* [1987], 104–6, 130–33).

3. Both CS and Howe feared the nativist leanings of Henry Wilson, who was then a candidate for the U.S. Senate with a backing of Know-Nothings, Free Democrats, and Democrats. As the legislature prepared to vote on Massachusetts' next senator, the Boston *Evening Telegraph* supported Wilson (Howe to CS, 9 February, 71/542; Richard H. Abbott, *Cobbler in Congress: Life of Henry Wilson, 1812–75* [1972], 62–63).

To Julius Rockwell

Senate Chamber
6th Feb. '55

My dear Rockwell,

This is the second day on which I have missed you from yr accustomed seat. I look in vain for yr steady presence over there on the opposite side of the chamber. Yesterday you were specially needed, for suddenly the Bounty Bill was taken up & suddenly an amendment was moved striking at our Masachusetts troops. Cass pushed his prejudices into legislation.[1] I wonder that the father of his daughter could make such a speech!—

On Saturday in the morning I went to yr Hotel & penetrated even to yr chamber-door; but I found no response when I knocked. I wished a farewell talk.[2]

As I am to stay here a little while longer I wish you would remember that I am always at yr command in any thing which I can do.

Believe me, with much regard,

Sincerely Yours, Charles Sumner

ALS NNHi (71/538, PCS)

1. On 5 February 1855 a bill granting land to soldiers and officers of the U.S. military was proposed. Senator Henry Dodge offered an amendment that would exclude those soldiers in state militias whom the state had refused to place "in the service of the United States." In the ensuing debate, senators referred to Massachusetts' refusal in the War of 1812 to allow its militia to serve in the United States armed forces (*Globe*, 33rd Cong., 2nd sess., 563–66).

2. Rockwell's successor, Henry Wilson, had actually become U.S. senator on 31 January.

To Theodore Parker

Senate Chamber
14th Feby 1855

Dear Parker,

I need not bring back with me the life of Shakespeare: for I have received at Boston from London the 2nd. Edition of the work—and it is much at your service. I will look after the life of Horne Tooke.[1]

I fear that you and Phillips will never be tried. Your recent studies must have enlightened even you on courts. In all ages and countries they have been the grave instruments of prevailing error and wrong.[2]

I note what appears in the *Advertiser*, which I take now.[3]

Ever yrs C. S.

C MHi (71/547, PCS)

1. Parker had asked CS for several volumes. CS refers to Alexander Stephens's *Memoirs of John Horne Tooke* (1813) and James Orchard Halliwell Phillips's *Life of Shakespeare* (1853).

2. Parker replied that he anticipated "no fairness" in his trial for the attempted rescue of Burns but "we will fight them inch by inch." He asked CS for examples of "*bad* Judges, of *tyrannus courts* & of perversions of Law" (Boston, [February 1855], 12/150, PCS). Parker's trial took place 3 April, but the indictment was quashed before Parker could testify. His defense was privately published as "The Trial of Theodore Parker" (1855); see *Works of Theodore Parker*, 14, ed. Charles W. Wendte (1911):348–90.

3. In a series of editorials 9–14 February, the *Boston Daily Advertiser* critized the recent movement in the Massachusetts legislature to have Edward Loring removed as judge of probate.

To Frances A. Seward

Boston 21st May '55

My dear Mrs Seward,

This is my first day of rest, after my various pilgrimages, & this is the first note of friendship which I write. It was kind in you to remember me, as you did, after I left Auburn, & I should have sooner responded; but you will accept even these tardy words.[1]

Since leaving Auburn I have been constantly occupied—as you may have seen from the papers; but I have now closed these labors for the present. In the city of New York I was honored by large audiences who listened faithfully even to the end of my long address.[2]

I dined once with the Fishes & found them pleasant & kind as always. She must be happy in her daughters, who are ripening into beautiful women. With such a home & family I am astonished that he can be tempted by Washington or any thing there—senatorial or Presidential. It seems to me that nothing but my interest in the Slavery Questions would keep me there another session.

I start very soon on my journey to the West—passing through Penn. Ohio, Indiana to St Louis, then round by Iowa, Wisconsin & the Lakes home. The weather is now very agreeable, but I expect soon to find hot days.

The *Herald* announces a grand conspiracy[3] between yr husband, Wilson, Chase, Sumner &c, all of whom are represented in conclave at the Astor House. For myself I have not had the good fortune to see yr husband since I parted from him at Auburn, nor even to hear of his whereabouts. I trust he is well. Remember me to him kindly, & believe me,

Ever sincerely Yours, Charles Sumner

ALS NRU (71/576, PCS)

1. CS had toured Massachusetts and New York, delivering his "The Anti-Slavery Enterprise: Its Necessity, Practicability and Dignity" (Wks, 5:7–51; Prc, 3:415). Frances Seward wrote CS a note of thanks "for his philanthropic efforts" (29 April 1855, 12/260, PCS).

2. Delivered at the Metropolitan Theatre, 9 May.

3. The *New York Herald* (18 May 1855:4) reported that Sewardites hoped to attract the New York Know-Nothings into an antislavery alliance in New York and to split the national Know-Nothing party over the slavery issue. The *Herald* described a meeting attended by Chase, Wilson, Corwin, CS, and Seward to plan this maneuver.

To William Schouler

Louisville Ky—[1]
Thursday night
[*14 June 1855*]

My dear Sir,

I left Cincinnati without calling on Judge Storer,[2] as I had intended to do. As you kindly accompanied him will you kindly let him know of my purpose unperformed & of my regret.

I leave in a few hours for the Mammoth cave, & for Nashville, whence I go by the Cumberland River, if navigable, to St Louis. We have not yet learned here the result of the doings at Phila; but they are watched with prodigious interest.[3] Oh! I do hope the time will come for the rally of the North! In this work you can do much.

I have to thank you for the councils which sent me to Lexington, Paris, & Frankfort where I have seen much to admire, & much which I can never forget—the magnificent woodland pastures & the cattle—& the slaves. I was present at the sale of a slave on the court-house steps!

Yours faithfully, Charles Sumner

Wm. Schouler Esq.

ALS NcD (71/583, PCS)

1. CS had already visited Horace Mann in Yellow Springs and Chase in Cincinnati on his tour of the Midwest. In Louisville, he stayed with the Whig Congressman William Preston (Prc, 3:417–19).

2. Bellamy Storer (1796–1875), judge, Superior Court of Cincinnati, 1854–72.

3. The Know-Nothing National Convention met in Philadelphia 5–14 June 1855. The majority report, adopted by the group as its platform 13 June, was pro-Union and procompromise. It stated that to ensure domestic peace, all citizens should "abide by and maintain the existing laws upon the subject of slavery" (*New York Tribune*, 14 June 1855:5; W. Darrell Overdyke, *The Know-Nothing Party in the South* [1950], 128–32).

To Julius Rockwell

Boston 22nd Sept. '55

My dear Governor—that shall be!

At last there is promise of a party that shall truly represent the heart & head of Massachusetts. I rejoice in what has been done.[1]

It seems to me the Address & resolutions of our Convention are admirably suited to the times. Great solicitude is expressed that in accepting the nomination you should put yourself distinctly upon them. It is supposed that this may prevent embarassment from the Convention calling itself Whig which will soon meet.[2]

I desire for you votes from all quarters; but I should be unwilling to see your position as adopted chief of the Republican Party compromised by any relations with another convention, which were not shared also by yr associates on the ticket. I venture on these hints, as it has been suggested that the Whig convention might nominate you, & drop your associates.

If the Hunker *Courier* Whigs will go about their business, & nominate one of themselves, we shall all be glad.[3] They cannot act with us, & I do not wish to be responsible for their pro-slavery fanaticism.

Ever sincerely Yours, Charles Sumner

ALS NNHi (71/592, PCS)

1. Rockwell, who endorsed fusion with other antislavery elements, had been nominated for governor of Massachusetts by its Republican party, 20 September 1855, over Henry J. Gardner, the Know-Nothings' candidate. According to Donald, CS did not attend because he feared that involvement in fusion politics might threaten his reelection in 1856 (DD, 1:273–74; see also William Gienapp, *The Origins of the Republican Party* [1987], 217–20).

2. Nathaniel P. Banks presided over the Massachusetts Republican Convention, which adopted resolutions stating that opposition to slavery was not a sectional issue. The party's motto was "No North, No South; Freedom for all Territories; No New States but Free States, North or South" (*New York Tribune*, 21 September 1855:4).

3. The Whigs met in Worcester 2 October, nominated Samuel H. Walley for governor, and adopted a platform opposing any alliances with other parties (*New York Tribune*, 3 October 1855:4).

To William H. Seward

Boston 15th Oct. '55

My dear Seward,

I have devoured yr speech with admiration & delight.[1] The latter half I read aloud to the Longfellows who enjoyed it with me. It is very finely thought & composed.

I am so happy that you & I are at last on the same platform & in the same political pew. I feel stronger for it.

I am to say something soon; but I know not what argument to build.[2]

Remember me most kindly to Mrs Seward, who, I trust, is well at last.

Ever sincerely Yours, Charles Sumner

ALS NRU (71/613, PCS)

1. Of his Albany speech 12 October 1855 for the New York Republican ticket, "The Advent of the Republican Party," Seward wrote CS that he hoped "it may do no harm. This transition to a new organization has become necessary, but it is not an easy thing" (Auburn, New York, 22 October 12/512, PCS).

2. CS spoke at a Republican rally in Faneuil Hall, 2 November, on "Political Parties and Our Foreign-Born Population" (Wks, 5:63–82), dismissing the Democrats as slavemongers, the Whigs as dead, and the Know-Nothings as "an isolated combination." The "practical purpose" of the Republican party, said CS, was to destroy the "Slave Oligarchy."

To Gerrit Smith

Boston 16th Oct. '55

My dear Gerritt Smith,

Pardon me; but I do not see on what ground you can be excused from a public lecture here in Boston & also in New York.[1] Here is an opportunity to do much good. Yr presence would give character & weight to our cause. It cannot afford to miss you.

You excuse yourself on account of yr many engagements at home. I understand these; but we have a right to expect you to make the necessary sacrifice. *You are rich, & can afford it.* Let yr great fortune miss for a short time yr watchful eye, & come to us in Boston & New York. One lecture will do for both places.

Here also is an opportunity to commend yr views by argt. & personal presence, which you should not abandon.

I do long to have our great controversy, which is so much discredited in the large cities, upheld by yr voice. Come among us. Let us have those rich tones, & that generous heart, & that immitigable hatred of Slavery to leaven our masses. Come. Do.[2]

Ever sincerely Yours, Charles Sumner

Honble. Gerritt Smith

ALS NSyU (71/615, PCS)

1. Smith had written from Peterboro, New York, 31 August 1855 (12/420, PCS), that he could "do anything better than write a speech. I have not time for it—and I must not extemporize before a Boston or New York audience."

2. Smith replied 28 October (12/516) that although he was "more than half ashamed of myself for refusing," he had private business to attend to and no time to prepare or deliver a series of lectures.

To John Jay

Boston 18th Oct. '55

My dear Jay,

Nothing that you can do in the P. W. case can be wrong.[1] It is an outrage which cannot be kept too much before the public. But I should not move unless sure of a strong meeting.

The petition to the Presdt. should set forth that this is done as the only practicable expedient for rescuing Williamson from an unjust judgment. That last opinion of Kane was feeble as it was audacious.

This month of October is superb; & I envy yr house in the country & all its happiness—*domus et placens uxor*.[2] If I were not enlisted politically here in Massachusetts I should be tempted to run to you at once.

The K.N's here behave badly. Our contest seems to be with them.[3] Still I think the Republicans will prevail. They *must* prevail. They *shall* prevail.

I am curious to see the letter of yr father to the Jerry meeting,[4] which was read with one from me;—since our friend Gerritt Smith has so politely animadverted upon us.

What a fall is that of John Van Buren![5] The ghost of '48 must rise before him sometimes!

Ever Yours, Charles Sumner

ALS NNCB (71/618, PCS)

1. Philadelphia abolitionist Passmore Williamson and five blacks were tried 20 July 1855 on charges of carrying off a black female servant and her two children, the alleged property of John Wheeler, minister to Central America. Judge John K. Kane (1795–1858) ruled that Williamson had interfered with Wheeler's rights. Recently, on 12 October, Kane had stipulated that a slaveholder could hold slaves in a free state as slaves, and continued to hold Williamson a prisoner (Wilson, 2:448–51; *New York Times*, 21 July 1855:1, 6; 13 October 1855:4). Jay asked CS, in his letter of 13 October (Katonah, New York, 12/500, PCS), what kind of protest against Williamson's imprisonment could be organized, and suggested submitting a petition to President Pierce (Williamson was finally released on a legal technicality in November [Wilson, 2:451]).

2. "House and pleasing wife."

3. The Massachusetts Know-Nothings had nominated Henry J. Gardner in the four-way contest for governor.

4. The rescue of an escaped slave, Jerry McHenry, on 1 October 1851 (called the "Jerry rescue") was celebrated annually by antislavery organizations.

5. John Van Buren fully endorsed the New York Democratic party's principles at its Syracuse convention, 31 August, including Democrats' approval of the Kansas-Nebraska Act (*New York Times*, 1 September 1855:4; letter of John Van Buren, 2 November, *New York Times*, 3 November 1855:1).

To William H. Seward

Boston 11th Nov. '55

My dear Seward,

At this moment we have in Mass. the best party, composed of the best men, with the best characters & best talents, that has ever been in Massachusetts—& devoted to the best cause. It is humiliating that this American faction should have thus triumphed;[1] but here in Mass it was done only through professions of Freedom. Large numbers of true men were thus carried off into this false coup.

I first met yr Buffalo speech in an Iowa paper—next in the Era.[2] It is worthy of the cause & of yourself.

Ever Yours, Charles Sumner

Hon Wm H Seward.

ALS NRU (71/628, PCS)

1. Gardner was reelected governor on the Know-Nothing (American) ticket, over the Republican, Whig, and Democratic nominees.

2. Seward's speech of 19 October 1855, "The Contest and the Crisis," was published in the *National Era* 8 November 1855:180.

To the Editors of the Boston Post

HANCOCK STREET
Nov. 16, 1855.

Sirs—

In your paper of yesterday, you are pleased to say, 'When Charles Sumner was at the South, he was silky as possible upon the subject of slavery,'[1] and you then proceed in confirmation of your own words, to quote an article from a Louisville paper, to this effect:—

'At Lexington he first became acquainted with slavery, and such an effect did its "horrors" have upon him, that he could not resist acknowledging to gentlemen of our acquaintance how egregiously he had heretofore been mistaken. It happened, fortunately, that he passed the Sabbath in Lexington, and attended the African Baptist Church. The sight of so many well-dressed and well-behaved slaves opened his eyes.—When he saw that they worshipped without molestation or surveillance, he was further astonished, and, when he studied their demeanor and countenances, all indicative of perfect happiness and contentment, he could but confess that his previous belief concerning slavery had been based upon information wholly incorrect. * * * In our city (Louisville) Mr. Sumner received the hospitable attention of several of our citizens. * * * While here, his expressions concerning slavery were in terms of agreeable surprise at the state of affairs.'

Now, Sirs, to this detailed statement I desire to make a denial, both general and particular. I deny it as a whole, and I deny it in all its details.

Never any where in the slave States, or out of them, in public or in private, have I expressed opinions on slavery inconsistent with those I have uttered from my seat in the Senate or at home in Massachusetts.

I did not pass the Sabbath in Lexington; I never attended the African Baptist church there; I never saw its 'well-dressed and well-behaved slaves'—I never 'studied their demeanor and countenances, all indicative of perfect happiness and content;' and I never made any confession that my 'previous belief concerning slavery had been based upon information wholly incorrect.' This whole story is baseless as a dream.

It is true that I was at Lexington; but I saw nothing there calculated to mitigate my previous aversion to slavery; nor did I ever acknowledge to anybody that I had been mistaken 'egregiously,' or otherwise.

It is true also that I was at Louisville for a single day, cheered by pleasant hospitality; but I had no occasion to express any opinions on slavery. If I manifested an 'agreeable surprise' at anything, it was at the thorough-bred cattle, the woodlawn pastures and the blue grass, which are the pride of Kentucky. There was a 'surprise' of a different character which I could not fail to manifest, at another place, when I witnessed the disgusting sale of human beings on the steps of a court-house; and the honorable Kentuckian who was with me cannot have forgotten the pain and indignation which I was unable to repress.[2]

It is not my habit to notice assaults on my opinions or public course, but I am unwilling that gross misstatements of fact, like those you have circulated, should pass without a point-blank contradiction. I am, Sirs,

your obedient servant, CHARLES SUMNER.

PL *Liberator*, 23 November 1855:186

1. *Boston Post*, 15 November 1855:4. The article continued, "but the moment he reached home the abolition chills seized him, and he shook with all the horrors of negrophobia."

2. See CS to William Schouler, 14 June 1855. Cassius M. Clay (1810–1903), a Kentucky antislavery activist, described years later CS's reaction to slavery when Clay took CS to visit Clay's brother's plantation near Paris, Kentucky. CS said little, wrote Clay, but showed great sympathy for a small boy who, though enjoying physical comfort, was still a slave (Prc, 3:418).

To Samuel Gridley Howe

Washington 14th Dec. '55

Dear Howe,

Have you learned from Mr May any thing of the picture of Dr Holly?[1] Do let me know.

You will note the complete supremacy of Slavery in the Senate. Study those Committees.

I have sent to Theodore Parker a marked list.[2] If the people of Massachusetts are not absolutely hunkerized they will be stirred by this outrage.

Ever yrs, C. S.

P.S. Seward will be at the Tremont House next Wednesday forenoon on his way to Plymouth.[3] Call on him.

ALS MH-H (63/667, PCS)

1. Myron Holly (1779–1841), New York lawyer, abolitionist, and a founder of the Liberty party. Apparently CS wanted to purchase the portrait either for himself or another. Samuel May, Jr. (1810–99), Boston Unitarian clergyman and abolitionist, may have been acting as an intermediary.

2. On 13 December 1855 the list of standing Senate committees was announced. Southerners Andrew P. Butler, Judah P. Benjamin, and John Slidell chaired the Ju-

diciary, Private Land Claims, and Roads and Canals Committees respectively. Mason and Douglas retained their chairmanships of the Foreign Relations and Territory Committees. Meanwhile the antislavery senators, Wade, Wilson, Seward, CS, and Hale, were placed on the Private Land Claims, Pensions, Enrolled Bills, and Engrossed Bills Committees (*Globe*, 34th Cong., 1st sess., 13 December, 22–23). In sending the list to Parker, CS admonished him to "learn the power of Slavery, first in grasping the places of power, and secondly in excluding from those places the special and obnoxious friends of Freedom" (14 December, 71/646).

3. Seward delivered an oration at Plymouth before the Pilgrim Society 21 December.

To Henry W. Longfellow

Washington 15th Dec. '55

Dear Longfellow,

It is even as I said it would be. You are vanquishing all the critics. Indeed yr success is becoming more & more complete.[1] You speak of the English papers. Have you not letters also which give assurance of the triumph?

I dislike Hurlburt's subtle assault as much as Mr P's of Pennsylvania.[2] Both were thoughtless, presumptuous & sciolistic.

Mrs Fish has enjoyed Hiewatha much

I was pleased by yr report of George's lecture.[3]

Please look at the two mottoes I enclose. Which shall I take? The first or second? or *both?* or none? Let me know at once, as I expect the proof daily.[4]

Ever Yours, C. S.

P.S. I think Banks will be elected—a prodigious triumph![5]

You will note how Slavery has absorbed every thing in the Senate! The feeling is intense towards Seward & myself. I accept this as a tribute to our position.

ALS MH-H (71/647, PCS)

1. *The Song of Hiawatha* was published in November 1855.

2. William Henry Hurlbert (1827–95), a New York journalist, concluded his review by ranking Longfellow as an accomplished but not great poet (*Putnam's Monthly* 6 [December 1855]: 587). "Mr P of Pennsylvania" is probably Thomas Conrad Potter (1822–1901) of Franklin and Marshall College, who in the *National Intelligencer* of 27 November 1855 accused Longfellow of plagiarizing from the Finnish epic *Kalevala* (HWL, 3:503).

3. Longfellow wrote 13 December that George Sumner had given an "excellent Lecture" at the Lyceum 12 December (Cambridge, 71/644, PCS).

4. CS had enclosed two mottoes, one from *Faust*, 2.5.6, and another from John of Salisbury's *Polycraticus*, book 7, chapter 25, for his forthcoming volume, *Recent Speeches and Addresses*. Longfellow recommended the Latin one, which translated reads, "Nothing is more glorious than liberty, except virtue, that is, if liberty can rightly be distinguished from virtue" (1 January 1856, 72/001).

5. In the election for Speaker of the House, Nathaniel Banks had received the highest number of votes, but not the necessary majority (*Globe*, 34th Cong., 1st sess., 10–13 December 1855, 14–26).

To Samuel Gridley Howe

Washington 20th Dec. '55

Dear Howe,

The *Courier* of yesterday contained a *very* bitter article on me, in which among other things it charged me with having abused the Sup. Ct., & it quotes epithets which it says I have applied to them—*all absolutely false*.[1] I have never spoken of the Sup. Ct. except with respect.

I have in my *Worcester* speech last year shewn that judges have sanctioned bad things; & in my late Faneuil Hall speech, I have made an allusion to Kane as a "tool."[2] That is all. Kane is not a judge of Sup. Ct.

It is a little hard that, when attacked in papers like the *Advertiser* & the *Courier*, there is no paper in Boston, to reply.

I send you these two speeches marked; & there is all my criticism of the Sup. Ct; not a word more

Ever Yrs, C. S.

ALS MH-H (63/669, PCS)

1. The *Boston Daily Courier* responded to the *Boston Daily Advertiser*'s criticism of Senate committee appointments, which the *Advertiser* said slighted Massachusetts. CS's relegation to a minor Senate committee instead of a major one such as the Judiciary Committee was not unwarranted, stated the *Courier*: "Mr. Sumner's whole course as a politician has been marked with bitter hostility to the national Judiciary. He has done his utmost to excite against it the popular hatred in his own section. . . . Does this qualify him for a place on the Judiciary Committee?" (19 December 1855:2).

2. In "Formation of the Republican Party," 7 September 1854, CS stated that judges "in all ages have shown a full share of human frailty" and compared the judges at the Salem witch trials to those presiding over recent fugitive slave cases (Wks, 4:272–76). In his 2 November 1855 speech, referring to Kane's jailing of Passmore Williamson, CS stated: "Alas! the needful tool for such work is too easily found in places low and high—in the alleys and cellars of Boston—on the bench of the judge—in the chair of the President" (*Recent Speeches and Addresses* [1856], 544).

To Samuel Gridley Howe

Washington 28th Dec. '55

My dear Howe,

I note the *Advertiser*'s response to the *Courier*; but of course Hunker No 1 will not throttle Hunker No. 2,—as might be done.[1] A proper article would at once vindicate me against the vilipending of the *Courier*, shewing—*first*, the absolute falsehood of what the *Courier* alleged, & *secondly*, something of the service I had done to the State.

Wilson says it was understood in Boston that Hillard wrote the article in the *Courier*. I do not believe it. He could not have done it.

Do not believe me too sensitive. I am the representative of a great cause & a powerful party, both of which suffer when I suffer. Besides my good name is now inwoven with these, & the political struggle of next autumn will be affected by any thing in my disparagement. This early effort to traduce me is the beginning of the campaign.

Write me of things in Boston. How was Raymond's lecture? & what impression did Seward make?

I believe that the best thing our friends can do in Congress is to keep on voting for weeks longer. The example of unity & organization set by the 105 will affect the country more than any speech.[2] It is an *act*, which you know is better than *words*.

Ever Yrs, C. S.

ALS MH-H (63/671, PCS)

1. The *Boston Daily Advertiser* (24 December 1855:2) backed its earlier criticism of Senate committee appointments although the paper would not unreservedly support either CS or Wilson. The *Advertiser* stated that it was not "inoculated with the rabid virus of free-soilism," but still believed Massachusetts deserved adequate representation on the Senate committees.

2. Balloting to elect a Speaker of the House continued, with Banks receiving the most votes, but never the required majority. On most occasions, Banks received 105 or 106 votes, representing the "unity & organization" to which CS refers (*Globe*, 34th Cong., 1st sess., 16–89, passim).

To Charles Francis Adams

Washington
9th Jan. '56

Dear Adams,

I note that yr father in his Message on the Panama Mission expounds the *Monroe doctrine* in a way entirely inconsistent with the uses to which it is now put.[1]

I should be glad to set this matter right, & to exhibit this doctrine as a determined expression of the great right of self-defence without the Quixotism of setting a lance in rest against every distant colonizer.

This Administration is bent on mischief in our foreign relations, particularly with England. *Cushing thinks there must be war!* This you know is his cure for domestic-disorders.

A peremptory demand has been made for the recall of Crampton.[2]

Ever Yours sincerely, Charles Sumner

ALS MBApm (72/005, PCS)

1. CS had written Adams 3 January 1856 (72/002, PCS) asking him for references from his father's diary on the origin and extent of the Monroe Doctrine. On 15 March 1826 John Qunicy Adams had sent a special message to the Senate stating that the U.S. should countenance no interference from Europe in the Western Hemisphere and that any treaty between the U.S. and a European power should contain such a provision (Samuel F. Bemis, *John Quincy Adams and the Foundations of American Foreign Policy* [1949], 554–55).

2. Secretary of State Marcy had instructed James Buchanan, American minister to Great Britain, to try to persuade that country to "withdraw from all control" over Central America, and to negotiate a treaty to that effect (H. Barrett Learned, "William Learned Marcy," in *American Secretaries of State*, ed. Samuel F. Bemis 6 [1928]: 220–21). In addition, John F. T. Crampton (1805–86; British minister to the U.S., 1852–56) had been active in surreptitious and illegal recruitment of Americans as soldiers in the Crimean War. On 28 December 1855 Marcy instructed Buchanan to inform George William Frederick Villiers, Lord Clarendon (1800–70; British foreign secretary, 1853–58) that Crampton's behavior "rendered him an unacceptable representative of Her majesty" (ibid., 257).

To Frances A. Longfellow

Senate Chamber
16 Jan. '56

My dear Fanny,

I am obliged to yr kindness for the privilege of reading the letter of yr sister, whom I bear in constant memory. I did not know before that Mackintosh had returned to his fast-anchored English home.[1]

When you write to yr sister let her know that I am grateful for her kind regard, & tell Mackintosh that I wish I could see him for a little while to talk of many things. Has he finally abdicated his Govt.—like James 2nd—never to return?

Our affairs with England are at this moment in as critical a condition as this Administration can bring about. It would not be sorry for foreign strife, even war, in order to distract attention from Kansas & our domestic affairs. Besides, it is governed by a vulgar jealousy & hatred of England, & thinks it behaves grandly when it sends a menace at this Power. The diplomatic *corps* here are all anxious for the result.

Cushing, who is the special marplot, does not see how the pending questions can be settled without war! And he talks about this contingency as he would about his dinner.

I was under epistolary debt to yr family, beginning with dear little Erny, which I shall repay.[2]

How bravely Hiewatha's boat is sailing into the sky!—

Ever Sincerely Yrs, Charles Sumner

ALS MLNHS (72/020, PCS)

1. In his letter to CS on 14 January 1856, Henry Longfellow sent a note from Mary Appleton Mackintosh to her father Nathan Appleton. Fanny Longfellow thought CS would find Mrs. Mackintosh's remarks on "the slave at Antigua" of interest (Cambridge, 72/010, PCS). Her husband, Robert, governor general of the Leeward Islands in the West Indies, had apparently returned to England.

2. The Longfellows' son, Ernest Wadsworth, 1845–1921.

To Byron Paine

Washington 18th Jan. '56

My dear Sir,

You touch the question to the quick. For a long time I have seen it as you do.[1]

If the Sup. Ct. has the power which it claims, then are all the rights of the States subordinated to this central Power. I am disposed to believe that the authors of the Constitution did not foresee the dilemma presented.

If the North were really aroused, the question would be settled, or avoided, while State Rights would be secured. It were well that the *self-defensive* power of the states should be recognized—like that *senatus consultum* of Cicero, *tanquam gladius in vagina*[2] —; but that the occasion for its exercise might be avoided. But surely we have as great cause for complaint now, as can ever be anticipated. What usurpation more intolerable than the Fug. Bill can be hatched?

I have read Judge Smith's opinions. He has placed the lovers of Constitutional Freedom under renewed obligations.[3]

It will give me pleasure always to hear from you & to have yr suggestions.

Believe me, dear Sir, with much regard,

very faithfully Yours, Charles Sumner

Byron Paine Esq

ALS WHi (72/028, PCS)

1. CS had recently read the judicial opinions on the Sherman Booth case in both the Wisconsin State Court and the District Court of the U.S. (on Booth, see CS to Bigelow, 17 June 1854). Since his discharge from the Wisconsin State Supreme Court on 28 June 1854, Booth had been rearrested by U.S. District Court officials. When a mistrial in the U.S. District Court case was declared on 29 January 1855, the court appealed Booth's case to the U.S. Supreme Court, where it was now pending (Sherman Booth to CS, Milwaukee, 25 February 1856, 13/013, PCS). Paine wrote CS that he thought the final decision regarding Booth and the constitutionality of the Fugitive Slave Law would be made on the appellate jurisdiction of the U.S. Supreme Court over state courts: "If that jurisdiction exists, the efforts of the State Courts, will be of little avail. If it is denied, then there is the danger of conflict & collision." Paine believed that appellate jurisdiction did not exist, for it was "inconsistent with the nature of relations between the State & Federal Governments, & with the preservation of the reserved rights of the States, which is one of the leading ideas in the history of the Constitution" (Madison, 12 January, 12/656).

2. "A decree of the Senate against which no protest has been made"; "just as a sword in the sheath."

3. Paine had written of the rulings of Abram D. Smith, "I think we can rely on him on the question of States Rights & man's rights, in every emergency."

To Theodore Parker

Washington 20th Jany. 1856

Dear Parker,

10, 15, and 20 years ago, when the Anti-Slavery sentiment was feeble, petitions were organized into a battering-ram under which Congress itself reeled. Now when we are powerful, nothing is done. This is wrong.[1]

There is a judge in Wisconsin who ought to be made to shake. If you give [*Sherman*] Booth a hint, he will do the rest.

A few petitions setting forth what these judges have done and said will teach them their accountability. I am astonished that you do not feel its importance.

The House is at a dead-lock. The Slave Oligarchy now says, "anybody but Banks." If the Republicans would seriously unite on another man the enemy would allow the Plurality vote, and a consequent election:

but this would give victory to (1) The Slave Oligarchy. (2) The petty squad of dissentients and (3) the American organization in contradistinction to the Republican. My counsel has been to stick to Banks, and leave the future to take care of itself. Among possibilities—probabilities—is *that the House will not be organized.* Inter nos Giddings thinks it never will be organized. You see the consequences!

Meanwhile the Administration will try a war with England. Forney said yesterday to one of our men, as a reason for organization, that we "are on the eve of war."

Ever yrs C. S.

C MHi (72/036, PCS)

1. In his letter to CS from Boston (14 January 1856, 12/663, PCS) Parker had devoted one paragraph to antislavery petitions, saying, "I think we had better limit our efforts to *Kansas* at first—but yet I would have the Petition so general as to cover every case of attack upon the Rights of Man." He added that one petition was being prepared and, according to Wendell Phillips, others were in progress. Parker also urged CS that the time had come "to strike a great blow. The North is ready—if you err at all *let it be on the side of going too fast & too far*, not the other."

To Charles Francis Adams

Senate Chamber
5th Feb. '56

My dear Adams,

I have too long delayed my acknowledgment of yr letter. I was prepared for yr conclusion, which I accept as entirely reasonable.[1]

There are circumstances at this moment which draw special attention to the Monroe doctrine, & which would give strong interest to any revelations from yr Father's Diary; but, of course, this could not be done without associating his name with present controversies. I doubt not you have judged well; & yet I part with regret from the opportunity of introducing to the country such interesting testimony.

While I write, Mr Foot is speaking on Seward's lead, saying some things of England, which if said in Parliament about us would set the Republic in flames; but England pardons such outbursts, as we pardon what we are obliged to hear from some country bumpkin. Cass has done the same thing. Seward's speech is felt to have killed all idea of war. By invoking war he has made it impossible for this Administration to press it.[2] I have been on the point of speaking upon the question fully, but I cannot now regard it as a reality. It seemed to be like a question before a Debating Club. I first learned from the New York papers that my colleague is to take the floor on it.[3]

At last Banks is elected.[4] I was present when he was conducted to his chair. It was a proud historic moment. For the first time during years there seemed to be a North. I fancied I saw the star glittering over his head. His appearance, voice & manner were in admirable harmony with the occasion.

Cannot you go to Pittsburgh on the 22nd?[5] I hope so.

The article on the "Monroe Doc." in the Intelligencer is from a pen *outside* of the paper.[6]

Remember me kindly to yr family, & believe me,

as ever yours, Charles Sumner

Hon. C. F. Adams

ALS MBApm (72/059, PCS)

1. Adams wrote on 16 January 1856 from Boston (72/019, PCS) that he did not wish to have excerpts from his father's diary publicized; he preferred to withhold mixing his father's name with the "miserable contentions of these factions now on the stage."

2. On 31 January Seward attacked Lord Clarendon for trying to interpret the Clayton-Bulwer Treaty so as to allow Great Britain to remain in Central America. In his speech Seward treated war with Britain as a distinct possibility. Solomon Foot (1802–66; U.S. senator [Whig, Rep., Vt.], 1851–66) generally agreed with Seward in language that was not remarkably inflammatory. Cass on 28 January also remonstrated against British incursions in Central America (*Globe*, 34th Cong., 1st sess., appendix, 75–80, 81–84, 67–73).

3. On 12 February Henry Wilson argued that the U.S. should abrogate the Clayton-Bulwer Treaty, negotiate a new one and send diplomats to Central America to negotiate transit routes. He specifically quoted portions from John Quincy Adams's March 1826 message to the Senate on the Monroe Doctrine (ibid., 84–87).

4. Banks was elected Speaker of the House on 2 February (*Globe*, 34th Cong., 1st sess., 342).

5. An informal convention of Republicans was scheduled on 22 February.

6. The unidentified writer of the "History of the Monroe Doctrine" in the Washington *Daily National Intelligencer* (5 February 1856:3) stated that the doctrine could now be considered "a dead letter alike in our parliamentary and diplomatic history." He criticized the doctrine's supporters who would apply it too generally, "to guard all the territory of the New World from such occupation by European States."

To Nathaniel Banks

Memdum—

[*c. 10 February 1856*]

1st. As Mr G. was in former days Chairman of a Committee he ought to be so now.[1]

2nd. He should be chairman of a committee where his peculiar knowledge & experience can be of most use.—I think this would be one of the committees of political influence.
3d. It would be of doubtful expediency to place him at the head of the Judiciary or District of Columbia, because his views on the questions before those committees might be in advance of the majority of the House.
4th. On all questions before the *Committee on Territories* his views would be in substantive harmony with a majority of the House; & on that committee all his Anti-Slavery zeal & knowledge would have free course in channels where the majority of the House would follow.
5th. His nomination as chairman of the Committee on Territories would be notice to the country of *the fixed policy of the House with regard to Slavery in the Territories*.[2]

C. S.

ALS DLC (72/087, PCS)

1. Joshua Giddings had been chairman of the Claims Committee (*Globe*, 27th Cong., 1st sess., 36).

2. Banks named Giddings chairman of the Claims Committee and second ranking Republican on the Committee on Territories (*Globe*, 34th Cong., 1st sess., 13 February 1856, 411–12).

To Charles Francis Adams

Senate Chamber
16th Feb. '56

Dear Adams,

Surely there is no faith in man! Long ago I spoke to Mr Forney, & he promptly replied that the continuation of Gales & Seaton's debates belonged to you, & he said that he would order them sent without delay. I will now speak to his successor.[1]

I think Seward has made a grievous mistake by his Central American speech.[2] He has given a new argt. to those who say that he leaps upon every hobby, without regard to principle.

I have felt very sore towards Banks for not putting Giddings at the head of the Territorial Committee. His name there would have been a proclamation to the whole country, North & South, that, on Slavery in the Territories, we are in earnest. There is much private & public gnashing of teeth over the committees, & I have heard it said that Banks could not now command 40 votes for Speaker. But all this was doubtless anticipated by those who have had experience.

The author of the article in the Intelligencer on the Monroe doctrine has confided his secret to *me alone*, outside of the paper. Of course it is not Everett.

Alas! for our delegation. Its imbecility is greater than I had supposed. I do hope that Joseph Hiss will not be found in it under the *alias* of ______[3]

I am glad that you are doing so well with the Life of yr grand-father,[4] which will be an important contribution to our history.

I was with yr family here a few evngs ago. Mr Johnson has gone to Iowa, & his wife was quite cheerful at the idea of him sitting all night snowed up in a rail car.

Ever Yrs C. S.

ALS MBApm (72/071, PCS)

1. In his letter of 10 February 1856 from Boston (12/728, PCS), Adams had asked about continuing to receive the debates of Congress. William Cullom of Tennessee succeeded Forney as clerk of the House of Representatives.

2. Regarding Seward's 31 January speech, Adams advised CS not "to follow in such a track. The material points in dispute may be gained by a different style of reasoning with the British and by a less offensive manner."

3. Joseph Hiss, a Know-Nothing member of the Massachusetts legislature, had been expelled for excessive and suspicious expenses incurred when his committee investigated Roman Catholic institutions in the commonwealth. Richard Henry Dana, Jr., believed Hiss had been made a "scapegoat" (*The Journal of Richard Henry Dana, Jr.*, ed. Robert F. Lucid [1968], 674; Carleton Beals, *Brass-Knuckle Crusade* [1960], 228–29).

4. *The Life of John Adams* was published in November 1856.

To Theodore Parker

Senate Chamber
25th. Feby 1856

Dear Parker,

I am glad of the *Petitions*.[1] It is curious how the circle is complete. I prompted you and now the Chairman of the Judiciary in the House[2] comes to consult me *confidentially* on points of law involved in them.

Weeks ago I brought forward the Library proposition and it is now before the Committee on Military Affairs. I think Buchanan stands the best chance for the Democratic nomination.[3] Nobody can predict our Republican nomination. The pettiness of personal ambition may interfere with our plans. I am disgusted particularly with Know Nothings.[4]

Alas! for poor Massachusetts. Had Julius Rockwell been elected governor, the Know Nothings then would have been scattered, and the whole obscene brood all over the country would have felt the defeat and Kansas might have been saved.[5] It is not too much to say, that in our defeat last autumn, we involved all these late reverses, and our present solicitude for the future. The Advertiser, which helped defeat Rockwell, has struck a blow at Kansas, which all its plausible writing cannot cure.[6]

Wilson has earned his senatorship. He struck a hard blow, and made them all very angry, almost as much as with me: not quite. It was the great event of his life. Circumstances cast upon him the office of answering Yancy [*Toucey*], and he did it with effect.[7] We shall all follow. The debate has begun, and you will hear nothing but Kansas from this time forever——There ought to be public meetings, resolutions, and petitions.

Ever yrs C. S.

C MHi (72/081, PCS)

1. Parker's letter to CS of 16 February 1856 from St. Alban's, Vermont (12/747, PCS), mentioned that petitions against the administration's Kansas policy "are all going very well."

2. George A. Simmons (1791–1857), U.S. congressman (Whig, N.Y.), 1853–57.

3. Parker reminded CS to introduce a bill "providing Books in all *Military* Posts." CS had done so 28 January (*Globe*, 34th Cong., 1st sess., 303). Parker also asked who CS thought the presidential nominees would be.

4. Besides his political differences with the nativists, CS felt personally threatened. Henry Gardner, the recently elected Know-Nothing governor, and his allies talked of CS's resigning, and Gardner had his eye on CS's seat (DD, 1:275).

5. The Kansas-Nebraska Act of 1854 stipulated that settlers in a territory were "perfectly free to form and regulate their domestic institutions." Since 1855 two governments in Kansas had been vying for recognition as the true representative body of that territory. A proslavery legislature was established in Shawnee Mission, elected partly by Missourians crossing the Kansas border to vote illegally. Antislavery forces formed their own antislavery government in the Topeka-Lawrence area. In a special message to Congress, 24 January 1856, President Pierce denounced the antislavery legislature and his proslavery predilections were further evidenced by his appointment of Wilson Shannon (1802–77; U.S. congressman [Dem., Ohio], 1853–55) as governor of the territory.

6. The *Boston Daily Advertiser* (22 February 1856:2) expressed confidence that Pierce had changed policies, in that he might now intervene in Kansas to prevent a civil war.

7. In response to documents submitted to the Senate by proslavery officials in Kansas, Henry Wilson addressed the Senate 18 and 19 February. Wilson declared the antislavery settlers in Kansas law-abiding and the elections sending proslavery men to the territorial legislature fraudulent. Governor Shannon, stated Wilson, was incompetent and should be removed. Isaac Toucey (1796–1869; U.S. senator [Dem.,

Conn.], 1852–57) defended Pierce's Kansas policy and stated that "there is no other government in Kansas" besides the one submitting the documents (*Globe*, 34th Cong., 1st sess., 439–40, appendix, 89–95).

To Salmon P. Chase

Senate Chamber
26th Feb. '56

Dear Chase,

John Bell[1] is now speaking on Central America, & I send you a short word of friendship.

We all miss you—yr steady councils, & yr ready voice & the strength of yr presence. Come back. Do.[2]

Wilson's speech opening our Kansas debate is the grand effort & culmination of his life, & is worth a senatorship. It is a conglomerate & pudding-stone of *facts*, & these, at this stage of the discussion are particularly important. He has drawn down much bitterness upon himself. This shewed itself in the Exec. Session, on the same day, when Shannon was pushed through.[3] Several senators there directly insulted him. Yr successor[4] spoke then for the first time, briefly but effectively, with positive richness of voice & freedom of language.

The course of the Administration towards Kansas seems diabolic. I have not been able to go near the Presdt. during this whole session.

What say you of affairs?[5]

Ever Yrs, C. S.

ALS DLC (72/083, PCS)

1. "Our Relations with Great Britain," *Globe*, 34th Cong., 1st sess., appendix, 109–15.

2. Chase had been elected governor of Ohio in November 1855 as a Free Soil Democrat.

3. Wilson Shannon was confirmed as governor of the Kansas Territory 19 February 1856 (*Executive Proceedings*, 10:49–50).

4. George E. Pugh (1822–76), U.S. senator (Dem., Ohio), 1855–61.

5. Chase replied from Columbus 18 March (13/076, PCS) that he wished CS would "take off your coat & go into the every day fight. You would easily gain for yourself a reputation in this necessary [feat?] of Senatorial duty as great as you have gained by your elaborate efforts as an orator & logician."

To Edward Everett Hale

Private

Washington 1st March '56

My dear Hale,

I wish I could have the advantage of direct conversation with you for a brief hour on Kansas.[1]

It is clear that *this Congress* will do nothing for the benefit of Kansas. In the House we are weak; in the Senate powerless. This Know Nothing madness has demoralized Northern representatives. In the Senate, the small squad of Republicans constitute the only reliable friends. Nothing can be expected from Cass or Douglas. The latter in Executive session on Shannon's case, expressed great indignation with him for condescending to make a Treaty with rebels at Lawrence.

To what point, then, should we address ourselves? The first question will be on Reeder's case. This belongs exclusively to the House; but the facts evolved there will throw light on the whole subject.[2]

Then comes the application for admission into the Union. Here is a difficulty arising (1) from the small population at the time the Constitution was adopted, & (2) from the slender support it recd. at the polls, owing doubtless to the invasion then proceeding.

How shall these matters be dealt with? Pray let me have yr counsels.[3]

Of course the pretended Legislature & its acts must be exposed as invalid. But what next? Clearly there must be a Govt. there; [&?] the promptest way of getting it is by the recognition of the new Constitution.[4] But this will be opposed as lacking what will be called essentials.

I know yr interest in the question, & therefore, make no apology for this hasty note.

Ever sincerely Yours, Charles Sumner

ALS NcD (72/089, PCS)

1. Edward Everett Hale (1822–1909), Unitarian clergyman, was then vice president of the New England Emigrant Aid Company, an organization formed in 1854 to promote settlement of free state proponents in Kansas. Recently CS had received a number of letters from antislavery settlers in Kansas asking his help in recognizing the free state government. For example, Hannah Anderson Ropes wrote 22 January 1856 from Lawrence, Kansas: "Where should the weak flee if not to strong heads and hands like yours?" Henry P. Waters wrote on 21 January from Topeka, "We place but little reliance upon the protection of *Gov* —but we do hope that Congress will take some measure to defend us from such enemies as we have thus far had to encounter" (72/042, 037, PCS). See also Samuel Tappan, Lydia Hall, and Charles Stearns to CS, letters of 18 January and 19 March, 27 January, 10 February, 72/031, 109, 055, 065.

2. Andrew H. Reeder (1807–64) had been appointed by Pierce in 1854 as governor of the Kansas Territory, then removed 31 July 1855 because he opposed the proslavery Kansas legislature. On 9 October 1855, Reeder had been elected by the antislavery legislature as territorial delegate to the House of Representatives, while John W. Whitfield was chosen by the proslavery faction in Kansas. Thus the House was to determine which man would represent Kansas.

3. Hale replied 5 March from Hartford (13/037) that he believed the question of legitimate representation would be "settled in the valley of Kansas & not in Washington." He expected antislavery emigration to continue and was not upset at the delay in securing a government for Kansas: "For no man carries any negroes there. And you cannot make a Slave State without slaves." He urged CS to "Keep up a bold face, and treat the question as what it is, the mere question of a few months."

4. The Topeka Constitution, prepared by antislavery delegates 23 October 1855.

Henry J. Raymond[1]

Washington 2nd March '56

My dear Sir,

Public report attributes to yr pen the authorship of the Address adopted by the Pittsburg Convention.[2] Therefore, I express to you the pleasure, sympathy & gratitude with which I have read it. From beginning to end I adopt it as a practical exposition of the true aims of the Republican Party.

For a time my desire has been to make an issue with the Slave oligarchy; & provided this can be had, I am indifferent to the special point selected. Of course, at this moment Kansas is the inevitable point. In protecting this territory against tyranny we are driven to battle with the tyrants, who are the Oligarchs of Slavery.

Your Address carries the reader along satisfied to the end. It is strong & yet moderate, conservative & yet progressive, with clearness & eloquence, & the great force which comes from completeness of arrangement, applied to ample knowledge, while the argument seems to move with a firmness of tread, which has the promise of victory.

Believe me, my dear Sir, with much regard,

Faithfully Yours, Charles Sumner

P.S. Allow me to call attention to two slight errors, one of which at least is against us.

(1) The Bill embodying the admission of Missouri as a Slave State & the Prohibition of Slavery in the Territory North of 36° 30′, passed the Senate by the vote of *every Southern Senator*, except *two*; Macon of N.C. & Smith of S.C., & against *the vote of every Northern senator*, except the two from Ill., one from R.I. & one from N.H. These facts are given in my speech of 21st Feb. 54 on the Nebraska Bill, & I then [held] the record in my hand.[3]

(2) I am not aware that any Southern Senator has directly proposed to

open the African slave-trade.[4] It was proposed to annull our Treaty with Great Britain & to withdraw our African squadron. This was pressed by Slidell, on the avowed object that the ships would do more good on the coast of Cuba!—And I am happy to think that I stopped his plot.[5]

Honble. Henry J. Raymond

ALS NN (72/096, PCS)

1. Henry J. Raymond (1820–69), founder of the *New York Times*, 1851; lieutenant governor of New York, 1854; U.S. congressman (Rep., N.Y.), 1865–67.

2. The Republican convention, meeting 22 February 1856, adopted three resolutions: 1) the repeal of any laws permitting slavery in territories "once consecrated to Freedom," 2) the admission of Kansas as a free state, and 3) a call "to resist and overthrow the present National Administration" (*New York Tribune*, 25 February 1856:4). In his address, "The Aggressions and Usurpations of the Slave Power" (*New York Tribune*, 1 March 1856:5), Raymond denounced the Pierce administration for repealing the Missouri Compromise and supporting the proslavery government in Kansas. He ended with a call for delegates to the first national Republican convention in Philadelphia, 17 June.

3. See *Globe*, 33rd Cong., 1st sess., appendix, 265; the senators were Nathaniel Macon (1757–1837) and William Smith (1762–1840). In his speech, Raymond said eight senators from slaveholding states opposed the Missouri Compromise.

4. See CS to Horace Greeley, 21 July 1854. Raymond stated in his speech that a senator on the floor of Congress demanded the restoration of the African slave trade.

5. Replying to CS from Albany on 6 March (13/046, PCS), Raymond promised to make the corrections CS suggested. He thought the Know-Nothing party's nomination of Fillmore for president would help the Republican party's election prospects; the Know-Nothings "like all other 'National' parties have fallen under the domination of the Slave Oligarchy."

To John Jay

Senate Chamber 4th March '56

My dear Jay,

I have watched closely the questions between us & England & never at any moment have they seemed to me to have any vitality. I have thought it a mistake on the part of Seward to take part in them.[1] & thus help magnify them, or at least draw to them public attention, which is precisely what the Administration desires.

There is no honesty in the way in which these questions have been pressed. The old trick of Alcibiades is repeated, who cut off his dog's tail in order to give the people of Athens something to talk about. Every thing is now attempted to divert attention from Kansas.

I have the cause of Arbitration, & of Peace so much at heart, that I should be glad in any demonstration for them, which did not tend to magnify our foreign dangers & preoccupy the public mind. Feeling that I could not touch these questions at this moment without giving the enemy an opportunity for a new cry, & that, in point of fact, there has not yet been any real exigency, I have thus far been silent. Should the danger threaten you will hear from me.

What say you to the objection to the admission of Kansas with her present Constitn, founded (1) on the small population & (2) on the imperfect returns of votes on the Constn, caused by the invasion.[2] Think of these things & let me know yr views. I also presented them to yr father; but, as I have not heard from him, I fear he did not take note of them in my letter.[3]

Why not at once stir the public on Kansas & its wrongs, by public meetings & memorials, precisely as you stirred the North when the Nebraska Bill was pending? This is needed. I wish I had memorials, & the resolutions of public meetings to present daily.

Ever Yrs, Charles Sumner

ALS NNCB (72/101, PCS)

1. See CS to Adams, 5 February 1856. Jay suggested organizing petitions supporting Great Britain's proposal to refer the Central America issue to arbitration (3 March, 13/030, PCS).

2. Jay replied that he thought that "there was sufficient evidence of the maladministration of the Territory under Federal Authority & of pain & violence at the polls to overbear an objection to her [*Kansas's*] organization in a state based either upon her small population—or the unperfect record of votes in the Constitution" (New York, 20 March, 13/082).

3. In his unrecovered letter of 22 February (printed in Prc, 3:432) CS asked William Jay if he had any suggestions or arguments for CS's forthcoming speech.

To Samuel Gridley Howe

Washington
7th March [*1856*]
dies iras, dies illa[1]

Dear Howe,

Wilson tells me that he learns by letters that a proposition will be made to elect a senator.[2] He thinks that a stiff article should appear in the *Atlas*, introducing the letters. Talk with Andrew on this matter.[3]

Ever Yrs, C. S.

ALS MH-H (63/677, PCS)

1. "Day of wrath, that awful day."

2. The *Boston Daily Advertiser* (10 March 1856:2) criticized as "unprecedented" a

Know-Nothing plan for the current state legislature, instead of the one to be elected in November 1856, to choose a senator. Know-Nothings hoped that a strong nativist would replace CS.

3. Howe replied 15 March 1856 that his article would be printed in the *Boston Daily Atlas* that day (Boston, 72/122, PCS). The *Atlas* article called plans for an immediate election of a senator a "virtual fraud upon the people" and quoted a letter from the Senate secretary, Asbury Dickens, setting forth historical precedents for the current policy (15 March 1856:2).

To Edward Everett Hale

Senate Chamber
13th March '56

My dear Hale,

I am obliged by yr instructive letter, which contains important hints.

You will read Douglas's elaborate assault on the Em. Aid Co.[1] Allow me to suggest to you to have the Company present a Memorial to the Senate directly responsive to this assault, point by point, & vindicating its simple rights. On this head I need not give you any hints.

The Memorial should be as short as is consistent with a complete statement of the case; but it should be a document that will make the position of the Co. understood by the country.[2]

The whole atrocity in Kansas is now vindicated as a natural counter-movement to the Em. Aid Co.; & your Co. is gibbeted before the country as a criminal.

I venture to suggest that this be attended to at once. But I leave it all to your discretion.

Ever faithfully Yours, Charles Sumner

P.S. To me this assault is quite natural; for I have long observed that the Slave Power sticks at nothing!

Revd. E. E. Hale

ALS MBU (72/118, PCS)

1. The Committee on Territories' report (U.S. Senate, Committee on Territories, *Affairs of Kansas*, Senate Report no. 34, 1856, serial set 836) devoted six pages to criticism of the Emigrant Aid Company for interfering in the internal affairs of a territory and raising the level of violence in Kansas. It condemned "the violence of their language, and the unmistakable indications of their determined hostility to the domestic institutions of that State" (5–10). During discussion on 12 March 1856 of the order for printing the report, CS declared that, although he sought no debate on the report that day, he must protest the assault on the Emigrant Aid Company (*Globe*, 34th Cong., 1st sess., 638–40).

2. The memorial was not presented until 25 June when Wilson introduced a claim

on behalf of the Emigrant Aid Company for recompense for "losses and injuries sustained by the recent disturbances" in Kansas (*Globe*, 34th Cong., 1st sess., 1463–64).

To Gerrit Smith

Washington—
18th March '56

My dear Gerritt Smith,

I have yr vol. & am glad to possess it.[1]

I am happy also that it owes its origin in any degree to a hint from me.

Of this I am sure. It will remain a monument of yr constant, able & devoted labors during a brief term in Congress, & will be recognized as an arsenal of truth, whence others will draw bright weapons.

Douglas has appeared at last on the scene, & with him that vulgar swagger which ushered in the Nebraska debate. Truly—truly—this is a godless place. Read that report, also the Presdt's messages, & see how completely the plainest rights of the people of Kansas are ignored. My heart is sick.

And yet I am confident that Kansas will be a free state.[2] But we have before us a long season of excitement, & ribald debate, in which Truth will be mocked & reviled.

Remember me kindly to yr family, & believe me, my dear friend,

Sincerely Yours, Charles Sumner

ALS NSyU (72/129, PCS)

1. Smith had sent copies of his book, *Speeches in Congress, 1853–54*, to CS and Chase. He lamented, "How long, my dear friend, shall we delay having an *Abolition* party? Nothing short of that can meet our wants" (Peterboro, New York, 2 March 1856, 13/023, PCS).

2. Smith agreed that Kansas would be free, and noted CS's public work toward that end, to which Smith had contributed funds and given speeches (20 March, 13/084).

To Theodore Parker

Senate Chamber
26th March 1856

My dear Parker

I am full of hope now. The Committee is the thing to catch the conscience of the King.[1]

I am glad you are to open on Kansas. Let me suggest to press the admission of Kansas *at once* with her present constitution. *This is the policy we have adopted*, and it will crowd Douglass and Cass infinitely. This proposition is something practical; and on this we must fight the Presidential election.

Let public meetings and petitions now call *at once* for the admission of Kansas as a state. Cannot our Legislature be induced to pass resolutions making this demand.

Seward will make a grand speech. I shall follow as soon as possible, and use plain words.[2] Oh! this enormity is not really understood! The more I think of it the more its wickedness glares.

Ever yours Charles Sumner

Revd. Theodore Parker

C MHi (72/138, PCS)

1. With his allusion to *Hamlet* (2.2.633–34), CS apparently refers to the Committee on Territories' report, *Affairs of Kansas.* The report stated that the "Kansas difficulties" stemmed from "an attempt to violate or circumvent" the Kansas-Nebraska Act. The committee recommended that a "duly elected" convention prepare a constitution for Kansas as part of the territory's application for admission as a state (U.S. Senate, Committee on Territories, *Affairs of Kansas*, Senate Report no. 34, 1856, serial set 836, 40–41). Senate debate on the recommendations began 20 March 1856.

2. Seward spoke on 9 April (*Globe*, 34th Cong., 1st sess., appendix, 399–405), in favor of immediate admission of Kansas. Pointing out Pierce's contradictions in his support of the proslavery government in Kansas, Seward asked, "why, without reason, or authority of public or of national law, does he denounce Massachusetts, her emigrant aid society, and her emigrants? If 'propagandist' emigrations must be denounced, why does he spare the [*proslavery*] Platte County Self-Defense Association?" (13/020, PCS). For CS's elaborate preparation for his "Crime Against Kansas" speech, see DD, 1:280–82.

To Samuel Gridley Howe

Senate Chamber
31st March '56

My dear Howe,

Let matters at the State House go. I have no solicitude on that matter. I am sure that there can be no *snap* election, & I am also sure that a person chosen under such a proceeding would not be allowed to take his seat in the Senate. Since I wrote you I have learned that in 1817 Mr Burrill of R. Island was chosen in this way—came to the Senate for his seat, but was dissuaded by Rufus King & others from presenting himself, & actually went home & was elected again![1]

But this whole plot ought to be used as a wedge to split open the K.N.'s.

As to my book, I have already told you to do with it as for yourself.[2] But I never told you to assume any personal liability. No. This is my affair, & I must insist upon paying for the plates. You have some funds of mine, & I can also save some more out of my *per diem*.

My expenses this session have already been considerable for docts. which I have circulated, & will be much more. These, I should not object to others at home sharing; for they are strictly on general account. But my book is a private affair.

What is the price of the plates?—

I have no engraving for the book. The best head is that in the "Champion of Freedom," which might be copied; but it should be done well.

Neither you nor Longfellow shall take any risk on my account. That I cannot allow.

I shall speak on Kansas just so soon as I can fairly get the floor; & I believe you will be content with what I shall say. But I doubt if the vol. ought to contain this speech.[3] It is already quite large—Fields thought too large —, & closes with a political speech which sums up our duties at this moment.

When shall we see you here?

Ever Yrs, C. S.

ALS MH-H (63/682, PCS)

1. Howe wrote CS from Boston 15 March 1856 (72/122, PCS) regarding CS's reelection prospects and competition from the Know-Nothing governor, Gardner. Howe believed that the Massachusetts House "would not go barefacedly into an election" for U.S. senator; Howe's Republican colleagues thought any attempt to elect Gardner at this time would not succeed. James Burrill (1772–1820) served as U.S. senator from 1817–20. Rufus King (1755–1827) was a Federalist U.S. senator from New York, 1780–96, 1813–25.

2. Howe wrote he was seeing to "arrangements" with Ticknor and Fields, the publishers of CS's *Orations and Speeches* (1850). Howe ultimately secured Higgins, Bradley, and Dayton of Boston as publishers for the new volume, *Recent Speeches and Addresses*, although Ticknor and Fields's name remained on the title page.

3. Howe replied (2 April, 72/147) that the new publishers Higgins, Bradley, and Dayton, wanted a recent speech which would "half sell the book." The first edition ended with CS's 2 November 1855 speech, "Political Parties and Our Foreign-Born Population"; later editions of the book included "The Crime Against Kansas."

To Salmon P. Chase

Senate Chamber 15th May '56

My dear Chase,

I was glad to hear from you[1] & chide myself for my much silence. But this has been with me a very busy winter. My engagements of business have grown, & I have also occupied myself with [several?] public questions.

I have the floor for next Monday on Kansas, when I shall make the most thorough & complete speech of my life.[2] My soul is wrung by this outrage, & I shall pour it forth. How small was all that our fathers endured compared with the wrongs of Kansas!

From Presidential talk I have kept entirely aloof, except to say, on every proper opportunity, that my preference is for the old guard, in which I recognised you & Seward as foremost. The latter has behaved magnanimously this winter, & striven well to keep the standard of our principles at their just height. In the caucuses he has developed unexpected power of fervid extemporaneous speech. His friends do not allow him to be considered a candidate. The talk seems now to fasten upon [*John*] McLean & Fremont.[3]

Surely we can succeed—*we must succeed* in the coming election. If we do not, well may we despair!

Report says that my fair neighbor is soon to be married; but I learn nothing from the family, & some weeks ago she volunteered to tell me that there was no truth in it.

Ever Yrs, Charles Sumner

P.S. I miss you much. *Ducite ab urbe dominum!*[4]

ALS DLC (72/174, PCS)

1. Chase wrote CS 3 May 1856 from Columbus (13/165, PCS) about Ohio antislavery protests and the forthcoming presidential election.

2. CS delivered "The Crime Against Kansas" on 19 and 20 May. In it CS excoriated the South for introducing slavery into the Kansas Territory and attempting to secure its admission as a slave state. He especially singled out senators Stephen A. Douglas of Illinois and Andrew Butler of South Carolina, chastising the latter for having as his mistress the "harlot slavery" and asserting that South Carolina had contributed much less than Kansas to human progress (*Globe*, 34th Cong., 1st sess., appendix, 529–44; see especially 530 and 543).

3. John C. Frémont (1813–90), explorer and military leader; U.S. senator (Free Soil, Calif.), 1850–51.

4. "Take the master from the city!"

IV

RECOVERY FROM ASSAULT

June 1856 – August 1859

After Sumner's beating, many sceptics noted, and accurately, that his physical condition improved whenever he left Washington. Sumner himself wrote the duchess of Argyll about returning to the Senate, "I cannot work with the mind, except in very narrow limits" (22 December 1857). His pain, whether caused by the actual beating or a neurotic dwelling on it, was real. As these letters (and hundreds more) indicate, Sumner was fixated on his recuperation. And given the national uproar over his beating, Sumner understandably, if excessively, reported health details to his concerned correspondents.

Sumner's letters from 1856 to 1859 also indicate his lively interest in politics on both sides of the Atlantic. From the United States and abroad, Sumner exhorted the British to lead the way in outlawing the slave trade and to publicize widely the results of their act of 1833 emancipating slaves in the West Indies. So earnest was Sumner that, because a wrong had been righted, he typically overlooked or belittled the economic difficulties associated with British emancipation: blacks' "moral elevation" was "enough," he wrote Lord Brougham, "even if coffee & sugar did fail. The crops may go down, if man can go up." Of course, Sumner liked to believe that "both have gone up" (21 April 1858). In Italy in 1859, analyzing events leading toward its unification, Sumner asserted that the country showed as much promise for developing truly liberal institutions as the United States.

From Stuttgart or Montpellier, or even from a bed in Longfellow's house, Sumner could have ignored the struggle in Kansas. But weak or wily leaders such as Governor Banks, President Buchanan, and Senator Douglas needed Sumner's surveillance. Slavery, he wrote to Salmon P. Chase, "degrades us in the family of nations & prevents our example from acting as it should be in Europe" (Ostend, 18 September 1857). Sumner blamed the U.S. minister to France, John Y. Mason of Virginia, for American support of the "great imposter," Napoleon III. Such Americans abroad were to Sumner a source of chagrin. As always,

Americans' stand on slavery was the touchstone by which he judged their character. "How long will this shame continue?" he wrote Longfellow from Paris (2 June 1859).

Throughout his convalescence Sumner repeatedly expressed his intention to return to the Senate. After months of progress, then relapse, Sumner finally affirmed to Howe from Paris on 24 November 1858, "I am to be a well man" (no doubt to forestall Banks's plan to replace Sumner he wished Howe to spread this affirmation to impatient Massachusetts constituents). By July 1859 Dr. Brown-Séquard's cure had worked as effectively on Sumner's emotional as on his physical condition. Resolved and eager to resume his Senate duties, Sumner wrote John Jay from France (23 August 1859), "There is work to be done, & I mean to do it."

To Richard Henry Dana, Jr.

Silver Spring near Washington[1]
23d June [*1856*]—

My dear Dana,

I have longed to write to yr little girl, who wrote to me so kindly, & also to write to you, particularly in acknowledgment of that beautiful speech, which touched me much;[2] but as often as I turned to do it, my strength seemed to fail. It is now nearly five weeks,—during which I have written only *five* letters, two of which were on public matters. My whole system has been overthrown, & I am now obliged to keep on my bed much of the day. When this will end I know not.

I do not like that you should go to England & stay so short a time.[3] But you will enjoy all that you see & quaff it as nectar. Do not forget the cathedrals—or English country scenery, in yr addiction to courts & parliament.

I shall send you letters in a day or two.

Ever affectnly Yrs, Charles Sumner

ALS MHi (72/213, PCS)

1. On 22 May 1856, as CS was seated at his Senate desk, he was severely beaten by Preston Brooks (1819–57; U.S. congressman [States Rights Dem., S.C.], 1853–56, 1856–57). Brooks sought to avenge CS's insulting remarks about Brooks's cousin, Senator Andrew P. Butler, in his "Crime Against Kansas" speech. CS retired to the home of Francis P. Blair in Silver Spring to recuperate from his injuries.

"My passion has been to make at least one speech more from the seat where I was struck down" (to Salmon P. Chase, 26 August 1856). From the collections of the New York Public Library.

2. Letters flooded CS's mail, including one from the citizens of Bullock County, Georgia, supporting Brooks (2 June, 13/548, PCS) and another from the citizens of Millbury, Massachusetts, requesting that Brooks be punished as an assassin (28 May, 13/451). Dana's daughter, Mary Rosamund Dana (b. 1848) wrote CS describing an effigy of Brooks made by the schoolboys of Cambridge; they "laid it down on the ground and let the dogs and carriages run over him, and whipped him and beat him" (21 June, 13/621). Dana was one of a number of speakers at the Cambridge meeting held 2 June protesting the Brooks assault. See DD, 1:298–301.

3. Dana left for England 2 July and returned 3 September (*Journal of Richard Henry Dana, Jr.*, ed. Robert F. Lucid [1968], 2:692, 819). He had asked CS for letters of introduction in England, "if your account is not over-drawn" (Cambridge, 18 June, 14/033).

To Phillip Barton Key

Silver Spring, 4th July '56

Dear Sir,

Late last evng I recd yr communication of 2nd July.[1]

It is not probable that I shall be able to be present in court at the time you mention. But I repeat now what I expressed to the Grand Jury, that I have no desire to take any part in this proceeding. In mentioning the name of a witness, to whom you refer in your letter, it will be remembered,[2] that I did it in the Grand Jury room, in direct response to a question from the Foreman of the Grand Jury, & afterwards in response to your perso[*end of MS letter; rest from printed copy*]nal inquiries. At no stage of the proceedings and in no respect have I been a volunteer.[3]

I am, dear sir,

your obedient servant, Charles Sumner

P. Barton Key Esq.
Attorney of U-S

AL and PL DLC (72/231, PCS)

1. Phillip Barton Key (1818–59), attorney for the District of Columbia, had written CS twice about arranging CS's appearance at the trial of Preston Brooks in the U.S. Circuit Court. He thought there was no "impropriety" in seeking CS's appearance and stated that 8 July 1856 had been set as the date for witnesses' appearance (30 June, 2 July, 14/168, 199, PCS).

2. William Y. Leader, a Philadelphia journalist, was serving as a witness for the U.S. His account is given in Wks, 5:268–70. CS had already departed for Philadelphia when the trial took place.

3. Brooks was fined $300 and released (Prc, 3:487).

To Joshua R. Giddings

Private

Cape Island—
Cape May—N.J.
22nd July '56

My dear Giddings

I see that Burlingame has deliberately opened the door to the duel.[1] Perhaps while I write the duel has taken place. If not too late it must be prevented. Surely the House is not powerless. The British House of Commons would not tolerate the scandal. It would impose an obligation *at once* upon the party or parties not to receive or give a challenge. If such a proposition should be offered in our House, it surely would pass. Do think of this.

Alas! for Burlingame he has deliberately discarded the standard of Northern civilization to adopt the standard of Southern barbarism; he turns his back upon the Public Opinion of Mass. to bow before that of S. Carolina![2]

Tell yr neighbor Mr Bingham with what pleasure & pride I read so much of his admirable speech as I found in the *Times*.[3]

My earnest hope is to take my seat in the Senate this session; & I do not think I shall resign this hope until the session is closed; but I am at times much discouraged. For a week I prospered here; but I have just had two wretched days, which have put me back about where I was when I came here. I would give much to be again in the Senate with strength restored, that I might expose anew the Crime.

Ever sincerely Yours, Charles Sumner

ALS MH-H (63/688, PCS)

1. In his House speech of 21 June 1856, "Defense of Massachusetts" (*Globe*, 34th Cong., 1st sess., appendix, 653–56), Burlingame compared Preston Brooks's assault to Cain's killing his brother. He also stated, "There are men from the old commonwealth of Massachusetts who will not shrink from a defense of freedom of speech, and the honored State they represent, on any field, where they may be assailed." Although colleagues tried to arrange a nonviolent settlement, Burlingame stood by his speech and Brooks challenged him to a duel. Intermediaries arranged that the duel take place in Canada, but, when Brooks refused to travel through the North, the duel was canceled (Wilson, 2:491–93; DD, 1:308, *New York Times*, 22 July 1856:1).

2. Giddings replied from Washington, 24 July (14/321, PCS), that he also lamented the duel: "I endeavoured to express my views of this different State of Civilization in the free States from that of the Slave States in my house speech on Brooks's trial."

3. John A. Bingham (1815–1900; U.S. congressman [Dem., Mich.], 1847–51; U.S. senator [Rep., Mich.], 1859–61) had denounced the Brooks assault in a 9 July speech in the House (*Globe*, 34th Cong., 1st sess., 1577–81).

To William H. Seward

Baltimore Tuesday—
[*29 July 1856*]

My dear Seward,

Should Wilson be absent, & the Senate proceed with the R & Harbor bills, I wish you would see that my first bill on the improvement of the Public Works in Mass is amended by inserting the words, "under the direction of the Secretary of War." These words are not in General Cass's bill, which has already passed; but I desire them in mine, so as to put it beyond cavil.[1]

I stood my journey here very well, & shall leave for Philadelphia tomorrow morning. I am still feeble; but I am less disturbed in my head. I hope to be with you in a fortnight.[2]

Ever Yours, Charles Sumner

ALS NRU (72/247, PCS)

1. Cass's bill funding harbor improvements in the Kalamazoo River passed the Senate 24 July 1856 (*Globe*, 34th Cong., 1st sess., 1743).

2. On 31 July Seward requested that consideration of the Massachusetts river and harbor bill be delayed because CS was absent (ibid., 1855). Seward wrote CS from Washington on 2 August telling him not to hurry back to the Senate but to save his strength for the presidential campaign (14/353, PCS).

To Ralph Waldo Emerson

Cresson—Alleghany Mts—
Penn. 16th Aug. '56—

My dear Emerson,

I write now in a library where every printed word of yours is treasured & under a roof where yr name is daily mentioned with admiration & delight. I had not been here 15 minutes before my physician host, Dr Jackson,[1] shewed his partialities, establishing with me a spiritual & kindly communion at once. Since then you have been our great resource. In the woods especially we have quoted you, while the excellent [*William Henry*] Furness, who has been here as my friendly guardian, has joined us in sweetest concord.

Often since that most beautiful speech of yours have I thought of your sympathy[2]—as I lay weak & shattered on my bed—& my eyes have moistened, while my soul gathered strength. Thanks for the succor you have given.

At last I am physically convalescent. Three times, in this mountain air, have I ridden on horse-back, & I begin to feel returning strength. How long I shall be obliged to forego mental exertion & especially the excitement of public speaking; I know not. Never did I renounce any thing with deeper regret than I renounced the opportunity of speaking again this session from that seat where I was struck down. This has been hard to bear.

I rejoice in the passages from yr new book {*English Traits*} which I have seen in the papers & long for the whole. Believe me, my dear Emerson, with much regard,[3]

Ever sincerely Yours, Charles Sumner

ALS MH-H (72/265, PCS)

1. Robert M. S. Jackson (1815–65), Cresson physician.

2. Emerson spoke at a Concord meeting 26 May 1856, protesting the assault (*Works of Ralph Waldo Emerson*, 11 [1911]:247–52): "Let him hear that every man of worth in New England loves his virtues."

3. Emerson replied from Concord 26 August (72/281, PCS) that the attack was a "strange manifest benefit" to the U.S.; "the approach & fusion of sensible & forcible people of all shades of party was never so swift as now."

To Salmon P. Chase

Cresson—Alleghany Mts—
Penn. 26th Aug. '56

My dear Chase,

My physician still postpones my recovery for another month, though I am daily becoming stronger. For the last ten days I have been on horseback. But it is still uncertain when it will be safe for me to make any mental effort. I have felt this divorce from my public duties at this time keenly. Never before could I have spoken with so much effect; & I have longed to be heard. Never before have been so well prepared on various topics before the Senate. But my passion has been to make at least one speech more from the seat where I was struck down; & I have often said & felt for three weeks of strength at the close of this session I would barter as many years of any future political life in store for me. But I must submit.

There are many things on which I should be glad to commune with you—both public & personal. As to the governorship,[1] I have no question on its comparative honor by the side of the post I now hold. I remember that J. Q. Adams kept himself aloof from local politics, & thought that a person, who wished to be useful on the national field, should do this. It is said that no man can be governor of Mass. without entanglements. These I wish to avoid. My aim is to serve *our cause*, & I am unwilling to enmesh myself in the questions, & controversies, both personal & public, which are peculiar to our State. I dare say Ohio is different. But I write of this, according to my first impressions—away here in the forest without an opportunity of conferring with any body.

There is another consideration of some importance. I observe that the S.C. papers have nominated my assailant for Govr of his State. Would you have me put in any such competition with him?—

It does seem to me that we are about to succeed. Pennsylvania is now [quivering] to its centre, & must finally declare for Fremont.[2] God bless you! dear Chase,

Ever sincerely Yours, Charles Sumner

Remember me to yr intelligent daughter,[3] who must be now a great comfort to you.—How well Wilson has done![4] He is now a power in the land.—

ALS DLC (72/278, PCS)

1. Regarding the talk that CS be a candidate for governor of Massachusetts, Chase wrote CS to consider such action seriously. A governor was, according to Governor Chase, "on a higher position than Senator" (New York, 22 August 1856, 14/448, PCS).

2. The Republican party had unanimously nominated Frémont for president 17 June.

3. Either Katherine Chase Sprague (1840–99) or Janet Chase Hoyt (b. 1847).

4. Besides delivering an address at the Republican National Convention in June calling for cooperation among Whigs, Democrats, and Know-Nothings behind the antislavery, now Republican, cause, Wilson also worked diligently in Massachusetts to unify those factions behind Frémont (Ernest McKay, *Henry Wilson, Practical Radical* [1971], 113–14).

To Richard Cobden

Philadelphia—20th Sept. '56

My dear Mr Cobden,

I was happy in yr letter,[1] long ago, & should have replied to it at once, had I been strong. But since then I have done little more than toil & pray for health, which comes slowly, very slowly. My nervous system, naturally tough & elastic as steel, has suffered sadly, & it is now all jangled. It is hard for me to be constrained to silence at this time.

But never was I so little needed. The cause speaks, & the country is aroused. We are on the eve of our first great triumph. Fremont will be elected President. This will begin a new era. Good ideas will then commence. The Satanic spirit, inspired by Slavery, will be driven back.

I rejoice in the course of England with regard to our difficulties;[2] for though I have no sympathy with the spirit in which our Govt. has conducted its negotiations, yet I am happy that England did not jeopard international peace on any point of honor or pride. This in itself is a triumph of the Peace cause.

The conferences at Paris are a testimony to our cause. These should be followed up. If Mr Marcy's proposition should be adopted, & private ppty on the ocean be exempted from seizure, a great step will be gained.[3] Soon the rest will come—leading the way to the disarmament of the nations & their approximation in judicial tribunals. Surely this is a cause worthy of all effort. I know well how much of trial it has cost you, but I know also that it has given you a position of true honor better than any office.

I was cheered by the sympathy of yr letter, & by its friendly hint. I know too well what belongs to myself, & the cause I have at heart, involving civilization every where, to make the mistake which you feared, even if all my instincts & maturest convictions did not recoil from it.[4]

I write now away from my home, which I have not yet reached.

Believe me, with much regard,

Ever Sincerely Yours, Charles Sumner

Richard Cobden Esq. M.P.

ALS GBWSR (72/315, PCS)

1. Midhurst, England, 16 June 1856, 14/010, PCS.

2. CS probably refers to the threat Crampton's dismissal posed to Anglo-American relations in the spring of 1856 (see CS to Adams, 9 January 1856). After several diplomatic exchanges and discussion of the Crampton affair in Parliament in June, Lord Clarendon formally accepted the dismissal 26 June and declared that relations between the two countries would remain friendly (H. Barrett Learned, "William Learned Marcy," in *American Secretaries of State and Their Diplomacy*, ed. Samuel F. Bemis, 6 [1928]: 258–62).

3. An international agreement on maritime rules of warfare, "The Declaration of Paris," was issued 16 April by the European powers. It abolished privateering and declared that all neutral goods, except for contraband, could not be taken from an

enemy's ship. Marcy, on behalf of the U.S., stipulated that, unless an amendment was included stating that private property on a belligerent ship also be exempted from seizure, the U.S. would not become a party to the agreement (ibid., 283–84).

4. Cobden had admonished CS "not under any amount of provocation to so far forget your self-respect as to descend to the use of the weapons of your assailants. . . . [Y]our political opponents (they who identify themselves with your assailants) have by this act done more than you could have ever accomplished to convince the world of the hopelessness of their cause."

To Julia Kean Fish

Philadelphia 27th Sept. '56
at Mr Furness's

My dear Mrs Fish,

I am so happy in yr husband's truly able & effective letter that I cannot forbear writing to say it.[1] That letter is a document & must have a great effect. I have rarely read any thing which seemed more firm & at the same time so guarded.

All things foretell the result. I do not doubt that Fremont will be elected. Meanwhile I am still detained in seclusion. My physician is unwilling that I should leave here, though I am confident that I shall be shortly *almost as well as ever*. Indeed I have never had the look of health which I now have, owing to the life in the open air which I have latterly led. But it is hard—very hard to be thus shut out not only from the duties of life, but also from the world & its society.

It was only yesterday that Dr Wister[2] revealed to me the solicitude my case had given him. For sometime, it seems he was in great doubt as to the condition of my brain—whether it was laboring under organic or only functional derangement. Had it been the former death would have been my prayer. At present, however, all this is passed, & I have now nothing but a lack of strength, & a morbid sensibility of the nervous system, which requires the greatest caution in all exertion, physical or mental.

And while thus suffering for more than four months, I have been charged with the ignoble deed of *shamming illness*![3] It seems to me, if any thing could add to the character of the original act it is this supplementary assault on my character. Pardon this allusion. It is the first time I have expressed it to a human being, although it has often risen to my mind. Remember me kindly to yr husband & family, & believe me, with much regard

Sincerely yours, Charles Sumner

P.S. I know not where you are, but send this to New York.

ALS DLC (72/326, PCS)

1. Hamilton Fish's letter of 12 September 1856 endorsing Frémont was published in the *New York Times*, 26 September 1856:2. Writing to James A. Hamilton from Newport, Fish declared that, although still decidedly a Whig, he believed candidate Fillmore had no stronger claims on him than Frémont.

2. Caspar Wister (1817–88), the Philadelphia physician who treated CS in 1856, was a son-in-law of William Henry Furness.

3. The *New York Times* (27 September 1856:3) printed at length a description of CS's prolonged recuperation written by Dr. Robert M. S. Jackson. Jackson addressed accusations against CS: "Again his enemies mockingly assert that he 'looks well', 'has a good appetite', 'rides on horseback & walks', 'altogether seems well, why is he not in his seat in the Senate?' . . . It seems bitter then, illustrious Senator, to be so sadly misunderstood, to be so wickedly misrepresented."

To W. M. Whitehead, A. G. Rowland, and Sidney Denning

Philadelphia
10th Oct. '56

Gentlemen,

With sincere sorrow I resign the opportunity with which you have honored me.[1] Were I to take counsel only of my desires I should be with you; but my excellent physician,—who insists upon my careful avoidance of all such scenes, as essential to my recovery, does not leave me free to choose.

Most confidently did I hope to be able to address my fellow-citizens of Philadelphia & to unfold something of their high duties at the present hour—so far as a stranger, grateful for hospitality & kindness, might thus presume. I hoped to shew that in the conflict now pending, there is but one side which they can take;—unless they are willing to forget all the examples of the Past, & all the suggestions of the Present, & all the demands of the Future;—unless they are willing to join in heaping dishonor on the Declaration of Independence first proclaimed in their public square;—unless they are willing to trample on the words of her great citizens, *Benjamin Franklin* & *Benjamin Rush*, uttered in the earliest days, & also on the words of her other great citizens, *John Sergeant* & *Horace Binney*,[2] uttered at a later period, each of whom has borne a testimony against Slavery, which is better for his fame than any professional renown;—unless they are willing to behold the legislation of Pennsylvania & the recorded sentiments of this honored Commonwealth all falsified;—[*inserted in margin*] unless they are willing to exalt slave labor to destruction of free labor & to avow the principle that capital should own labor, rather than the principle that labor should own capital;—[*end insert*] —unless they are willing to sanction, not merely the extension of Slavery, but its extension *by force*; —unless they are willing to make the violence & brutality, which now prevail in Kansas, iniquitously legal throughout that territory;—unless they are willing to help erect the 347,000 slave-masters into a dominant Oligarchy, with the complete control of the National Government—determining now its offices & now its policy, and directing all its powers according to their will, whether to seize Cuba or to carve another slice of Mexico, or, it may be, to open the slave-trade; & finally, unless they are willing to renounce those great interests, commercial, manufacturing & productive, the sources of wealth, prosperity & power, which, depending on peace at home & peace abroad, will be surely disturbed if not destroyed by the election of James Buchanan.[3] But I am not permitted to present these things to you by speech or to dwell on them by letter.

In these few words I have presented faithfully, in its various forms, the issue on which the citizens of Philadelphia are to pass by their votes.

Accept my thanks for the good wishes which you kindly offer for my speedy restoration to health, & believe me, gentlemen, with much respect,

Faithfully Yours, Charles Sumner

W. M. Whitehead Esq
A. G. Rowland Esq
Sidney Denning Esq Committee &c

Dft PHi (72/343, PCS)

1. Elections for Pennsylvania state, county, and local officials would take place 14 October 1856. CS may have intended to have this letter read at a Frémont rally held 9 October in Independence Square, Philadelphia, and perhaps was unaware of the date of the rally or misdated the letter (Philadelphia *North American and United States Gazette*, 10 October 1856:2).

2. Besides Franklin and Binney, the other Philadelphians are Benjamin Rush (1745–1813), physician and signer of the Declaration of Independence, and John Sergeant (1779–1852), U.S. congressman (Fed., Nat. Rep., Pa.), 1815–23, 1827–29, 1837–41.

3. Buchanan had been nominated by the Democrats 2 June.

To John Jay

Cambridge—15th Nov. '56
at Longfellow's—

My dear Jay,

My physician shortly after my return insisted upon my leaving the streets of Boston, & here I have been since.[1] Seclusion, exercise, the cool air & time seem to be doing their work. I have felt much better during the last 3 or 4 days; & yet I am still an invalid. But for the coming Congress I should go at once to Europe, & forget myself in the sight of pictures, monuments & the Alps & the enjoyment of society, & thus pass unconsciously out of my present condition. But I cannot give up the idea of taking my seat—if not at the beginning of the session—very soon.

I enjoyed yr speech,[2] which, like all that you do, makes me regret that you have not a broader scene on which to speak. It was most able & excellent.

Our defeat is Bunker Hill again, full of great auguries.[3]

I was feeble, & saw not a human being that I knew, as I passed through New York,—going directly from the Phila. station to my state-room in the Fall River boat.

Longfellow sends kind regards & thanks also for yr speech which he thinks very highly of. Remember me to all yr family, & believe me, dear Jay,

Always Yours, Charles Sumner

ALS NNCB (72/376, PCS)

1. Dr. Marshall S. Perry of Boston (d. 1859) had also treated CS in Washington. On 2 November 1856 CS returned to Boston to vote and then retired to Cambridge.

2. Jay's speech, "America Free, or America Slave," was delivered 8 October in Bedford, New York.

3. The election, 4 November, gave Buchanan the presidency (1,838,169 votes), with Frémont second (1,341,264 votes) and Fillmore third (874,534 votes). Jay had written CS from New York (7 November, 14/681, PCS): "The news from Michigan & Illinois is glorious—& I cannot but hope that many of the democratic members of Congress from the North & West who have been voted for under assurances of opposition to Slavery extension, will yet [range?] themselves in opposition to their party & on the side of Free Kansas."

To Obadiah W. Albee

Boston 9th Dec. '56

My dear Sir,

Your agreeable letter of 28th Nov. should have been sooner answered.[1] My only excuse is found in my present condition & the counsels of my physician.

I trust Massachusetts will do something for Kansas not unworthy of the lead she now enjoys through her generous civilization & her overflowing majority for Fremont. But I have not applied my mind to the matter so far as to digest any form of proposition. I understand that this has been carefully done by Judge [*Richard*?] Fletcher of Boston, & also by Professor Parker of the Law School at Cambridge.[2] Their views, I presume, are well-known at the office of the Emigrant Aid Co. in Boston, where I think you had better apply.

I enclose a report to the Legislature of Vermont, which will interest you. Mr Marsh,[3] of Brandon, made a couple of speeches on the subject, while it was before the legislature, in which he answered objections & reviewed the precedents. I doubt not you could obtain these by writing to him.

I am sorry that I can make no better return for the felicitous image in yr letter.

Believe me, my dear Sir, with much regard

Faithfully Yours, Charles Sumner

Hon. Mr Albee

ALS MBU (72/393, PCS)

1. Obadiah W. Albee, a former state senator from Marlborough, wrote on 28 November 1856 (14/739, PCS) to ask CS's advice about introducing in the Massachusetts legislature "some proposition in aid of Kansas." He wanted to know "what course would be constitutional and practicable."

2. Joel Parker (1795–1875), professor of law at Harvard, 1847–68.

3. R. V. Marsh, chairman of the Vermont legislature's Select Committee on Slavery and Kansas, had sent CS a copy of his committee's report. He wrote CS that a bill for relief of antislavery settlers in Kansas had recently been passed by the Vermont legislature (Brandon, Vermont, 13 December, 15/052).

To William Henry Herndon

Boston 12th. Jan. '57

My dear Sir,

With a pang I have seen time pass, & found myself constrained to silence; especially during the Presidential canvass. My prostration has been great; but at last I see my recovery sure. Sometimes I think it has almost come; but I am still obliged to take to my bed at the beginning of the evening.

My hope is to reach Washington before the session closes.

I rejoice in all the good news from Illinois.[1] With Bissell for Governor[2] surely this mighty prairie State can be put actively on the side of Freedom. I had expected to take part in the late canvass there; but this is among the satisfactions which I lost.

But the Future is safe. I am sure of it. The ruffians & their allies will be defeated, in serious, solemn battle. Meanwhile all of us must work; & I am glad the cause has a friend so faithful as yourself.

Accept my thanks for the kindness of yr letter & believe me, my dear Sir,

Faithfully Yours, Charles Sumner

W. H. Herndon Esq

ALS DLC (72/433, PCS)

1. William Henry Herndon (1818–91), then a law partner of Abraham Lincoln's, had written CS of the Republican party's status in Illinois (Springfield, 8 January [1857], 15/146, PCS). He noted that the Democrats were "a decaying party in Illinois" and that even if Frémont had not carried Illinois, he had come very close. Herndon looked forward to a Republican success in 1860.

2. William H. Bissell (1811–60), U.S. congressman (Dem., Ill.), 1849–55; Republican governor of Illinois, 1857–60.

To John Jay

Washington 2nd March '57

My dear Jay,

Perhaps my letter from Boston to you miscarried. At all events I venture to enclose to you a check. I do not know precisely my passage-money; but I presume this will cover it.[1]

I hope to leave here on the afternoon of Wednesday, reaching Phila. that night, & New York Friday forenoon, when I shall be happy to be yr guest.

I have sat in the Senate but a short time. My vote turned the scale on the Tariff three times.[2] Part of the time I was in torment; but I am now quite comfortable.

Ever Yours, Charles Sumner

The check is of Chubb Brothers on E. W. Clark Dodge & Co. N.Y. for $150 & is numbered 225.

ALS NNCB (72/468, PCS)

1. In early January, CS wrote Jay that he had decided to go to Europe in hopes of recovering his health. CS had written Jay earlier asking him to arrange for his passage on a steamer (6 January, 18, 22 February 1857, 72/425, 447, 455, PCS).

2. The *Globe* noted on 26 February that CS appeared in his seat (34th Cong., 3rd sess., 907). He voted at least seven times during the debate that day on amendments and for a tariff that reduced the duty on manufactured woolens and admitted wool almost duty-free, the latter favored by New England manufacturers (ibid., appendix, 351–58; Frank W. Taussig, *The Tariff History of the United States* [1923], 149–51).

To Theodore Parker

New York at Mr. Jay's
6th March 1857

My dear Parker,

I fear that you are too harsh upon Wilson;[1] and I fear that you and others will help undermine him, by furnishing arguments to the luke-warm and to the Hunkers. Bear this in mind and be gentle.

My address is for two months care of *I. Munroe & Co Paris* and afterwards, care of *Baring Brothers, London* who will forward any thing to me, wherever I may be. Those are my two pivots.

Let me know how things move

Ever yrs, C. S.

P.S. I wish that I could make Howe happy.[2]

C MHi (72/480, PCS)

1. Parker wrote CS from Boston (5 March 1857, 15/363, PCS) that Henry Wilson "is a little jealous of you & your influence so his advice must be taken *cum modis solis* [on its own terms]."

2. Although the reference is not clear, Howe had expressed great concern for CS's health in a recent letter ([February 1857], 72/466).

To Michel Chevalier[1]

Hotel de la Paix
31st March '57

My dear Sir,

I was sorry not to find you at home when I called at yr house; I was more sorry to miss you again when you did me the honor to call upon me.[2]

Your public labors & writings have for a long time interested me in your career, & I look with pleasure to the opportunity of making your personal acquaintance.

Allow me through you to accept the invitation with which I have been honored to dine on Saturday next with the distinguished *Societé d'Economie Politique.*[3]

Believe me, dear Sir, with much regard,

very faithfully Yours, Charles Sumner

Monsieur Michel Chevalier

ALS MH-H (63/720, PCS)

1. Michel Chevalier was then writing *Cours d'économie politique* (1855–66).
2. Sailing from New York on 7 March 1857, CS arrived in Paris 23 March. He recorded his 1857 European activities in a journal, portions of which are published in Prc, 3:529–55.
3. CS's description of the dinner is printed in Prc, 3:532. He found Chevalier's appearance "not prepossessing" at first, but grew to like the political scientist better as he spent more time with him.

To Samuel Gridley Howe

Paris—23d April '57

My dear Howe,

It is now a month since I wrote you from the British Channel. In this interval I have had many experiences, mostly pleasant. My time is intensely occupied. Besides making acquaintances here & seeing the world more than any other American at this time, I am visiting the museums & other objects of interest most systematically. But I am sometimes troubled to find how little I can bear now compared with that insensibility to fatigue which I had once—even a year ago. My whole system is still morbidly sensitive &, after a walk which would have been pastime once, I drag my legs along with difficulty. Add to this a terrific cold—they call it a *grippe* here—which I have had for three weeks & which has compelled me to keep the house several days—& you will see some of my draw-backs. My present purpose is after to-day to shut myself up until I have conquered this malady. I must be well.

Paris is very gay & beautiful & abounds in interesting people. Of those I have seen Tocqueville & Guizot have impressed me the most. They are very superior men; I am disposed to believe them the first men in France. I have also seen Berryer, & only two days ago had a long interview with Drohyn de l'Huys,[1] who was for three years the chief Minister of Louis Nap., in which he recounted to me the whole history of his relations with the Emperor. The feeling on the subject of Slavery is very strong. All consider it inexcusable Barbarism, except an old Admiral that I met in society one evening, who had commanded the French squadron in the West Indies, & who considered himself on this account perfect master of the subject. Last evening I dined with Count de Kergorlay & met a large number of persons attached to the present Govt, chiefly counsellors of State, & tonight I dine with Count de Montalembert, who, aristocrat as he is, welcomes any govt. in preference to the present.[2]

The intelligence & education, constituting the brains of France, are all against the Emperor, who has the *ateliers* & his own immediate adherents. All admit that this baby who was born with such parade & who is now escorted by cavalry when he takes an airing, can never succeed to the power;[3] but I have not yet seen a human being, who undertakes to say what will take place in the event of the death of the Emperor. *Il y aura une lutte; voila tout.*[4] My own impression is that the Emperor's superiority is found in his *fixed will*. His purpose is clear; & he is almost the only man in this condition. I have not seen him & I doubt if I shall. I have not seen Mr Mason, our Minister,[5] yet; & it is only through him that I could see the Emperor naturally. I am entirely willing that my experiences here should be independent of this tobacco-chewing slave-driver who where he is known here, is a cypher.

I learn from George that the recent murders in the State Prison have opened some eyes to the true condition of things there. Is not this a good time for you to strike? I inquired the other day of de Tocqueville with regard to the present condition of the question in France. He confessed that for some time he had withdrawn from this discussion; but, while he admitted that there might be doubts as to the application of the Sep. System to long-termers he was thoroughly convinced that it ought to be applied to short-termers & also to all Houses of Detention. I wish a copy of yr pamphlet[6] could be put in the hands of every member of the Legislature. That document is the best thing on Prison Discipl. ever written.

I tremble for Kansas, which seems to me a doomed territory.[7] How disgusting seems the conduct of those miserable men who thus trifle with the welfare of this region. My blood boils at this outrage & I long to denounce it again from my place. *Le jour viendra.*[8] —Vattemare[9] has just left me & sends his regards to you. I have seen much of him, & have been truly impressed by his character. In America I always distrusted him, though I felt a sympathy with his idea. My distrust has all gone. He loves our country & seeks to do us good with as little regard to common selfish considerations as I have ever seen.—I expect a letter from you soon.

Always Yrs, C. S.

A friend who is now with me tells me that he lately picked up at a stall on one of the quais a report on the Blind by Dr Howe,[10] translated into French.

ALS MH-H (63/724, PCS)

1. Edmond Drouyhn de l'Huys (1805–81; minister of foreign affairs in the Second Republic, 1848–49; minister to London, 1849–51) served as minister of foreign affairs in the Second Empire, 1852–66.

2. Florian Henri Kergorlay (1801–73), member of the French legislature, 1857. Charles F. Montalembert, Comte de Tryon (1810–70), French historian; publicist; member of the opposition in the French legislature, 1852–57.

3. Napoléon Eugène Louis Bonaparte (1856–79).

4. "There will be a struggle; that is all."

5. John Y. Mason (1799–1859), U.S. congressman (Dem., Va.), 1831–37; U.S. minister to France, 1854–59.

6. *An Essay on Separate and Congregate Systems of Prison Discipline* (1846).

7. On 4 March 1857 John W. Geary, Shannon's successor as governor of the Kansas Territory, resigned. After vetoing the proslavery legislature's recommendations for a constitutional convention, Geary lost President Pierce's support. Both pro- and antislavery forces in Kansas continued to insist they represented Kansas settlers.

8. "The day will come."

9. Nicholas M. Alexandre Vattemare (1796–1864), French art and book dealer who helped establish libraries in the U.S.

10. Possibly *Dr. Howe's Report on the Case of Laura Bridgman*, 1843.

To Charles Francis Adams

Athenaeum Club [*London*]
17th July '57

My dear Adams,

I make you but a poor return for yr good letters. That of June was recently recd. I wish you could write more cheerfully of our party as a *consolidated unit*.[1] But I am sure that day is to come.

I should think the scene on Bunker H. on 17th June must shock our people. Does it not?[2]

Since last I wrote you my health has steadily improved; but I am entirely satisfied that Dr Bigelow[3] understood my case when he postponed my complete recovery till next winter. If I am thoroughly well then I shall be happy. I learn constantly that others, who have been wounded on the head, have gone through stages slower even than mine, while, as in my case, the spinal column has been the last to get well. I came to London with hesitation, fearing the effect of social life upon me; but thus far I have continued to gain. Sometimes I am obliged to seek my sofa & lie down; but I continue to see a good deal of life, avoiding rigidly every place where I might be forced to public speaking or receive any expression of public sympathy. The dinner of the Temple Benchers was purely professional & not public. The honor was so peculiar that I could not resist it. Brougham pressed me to a public dinner where he was to propose my health.[4] I positively refused; & I mean to go on. My health is an all-sufficient reason; & I see well that I could not receive any such sympathy without furnishing weapons to my enemies at home.

The late course of our Govt.—particularly its pro-Sl. character, has degraded us in the eyes of Europe more even than you are aware. I see no chance of any change in feeling to us except by our taking the Govt. & putting it on another tack. I do not detect much sensibility with regard to our dismissal of Crampton. That affair has produced no permanent impression.

I hear constant inquiries with regard to Palfrey & Dana, & the kindest language of interest & admiration. Pray tell them of this. Let the good Dr know if you see him, that sometime in September I shall be with his friends in Scotland & they will be glad to hear of him through me.

There is another Bostonian [*George Ticknor*] who has been busy here, whose name is sometimes mentioned, but who knows more of Spanish literature than American politics. I could amuse you by recounting certain incidents with him; but these I reserve for my return. On two occasions I was compelled to announce him as "the most bitter supporter of the Fug. Sl. Bill in my part of the country." An exclamation ensued—"why, that is the worst thing he could do"! It is very evident that his true character was not known here. Had it been, many doors which he entered would have been closed.

I passed last Sunday at Ockham Park, the seat of old Ld Chancellor King, & now the home of Dr Lushington,[5] the head of the Admiralty Court & a life-long abolitionist. He entered Palt. in 1806, & in 1807 made an Anti-Slavery Speech. We sat together for hours under the venerable trees in the garden & Anti-Sl. past & future. It was a pleasant day with a good man.

The case of the Mormons excites considerable interest here;[6] but some derision that we are so shocked by polygamy when we swallow Slavery. When will our people see Slavery as other people see it?—

I am sorry that you are not strong & well; but I trust that this summer will set you right. Where is that letter Mrs A. was to write me?

Ever Yrs, C. S.

ALS MBApm (72/534, PCS)

1. Adams wrote CS from Quincy 26 June 1857 (15/539, PCS), disturbed that the influence of moderates like Nathaniel Banks on the Massachusetts Republican party weakened its antislavery policy.

2. Adams described the anniversary celebration of the Battle of Bunker Hill, with its speeches by Everett, Winthrop, and Virginia Senator James M. Mason: "How they all saved the Union—. . . Is there any end to the servility of the public men of the last generation?"

3. Henry Jacob Bigelow (1818–90), Boston surgeon.

4. On 1 July, CS responded to a toast given in his honor at a dinner given by the Benchers of the Inner Temple. On 4 July he refused a dinner invitation from the Law Amendment Society (CS Journal, Prc, 3:544–45; CS to Lord Brougham, [July 1857], 72/555).

5. Peter King, first baron King of Ockham (1669–1734). Stephen Lushington (1782–1873).

6. U.S. troops had been sent to Utah in the spring of 1857 because both the territorial government and Mormon courts were disregarding U.S. legal procedures. The American correspondent of the London *Times* noted with amusement that Mormon leader Brigham Young had denied the U.S. government's right to interfere with the "domestic institution of the territory" (19 May 1857:5; see also 17 June 1857:5).

To Henry W. Longfellow

Athenaeum Club—
[*London*]
24th July '57

My dear Longfellow,

I hope you have not abused me much because of my silence. For a time I had no heart to write, & now I have no time. Meanwhile my strength steadily increases, though I must confess that I am not yet returned to my normal condition.

I have seen almost every body in the great world, & have made already engagements in the country. Next week I pass two days with Ld Stanhope to meet Mr Macaulay, & then I visit the Archbishop of Canterbury; then Mr Labouchere at Stoke[1] ([*Thomas*] Gray's burial place) then Mr Cobden; & then at the beginning of August go over to de Tocqueville in France & then to Switzerland. Afterwards I count upon two solid months in which to travel about the 3 kingdoms.

Tennyson & his wife were in town for a single day & called upon the Duchess of Argyll; but hurried back to the Isle of Wight. He has a poem already printed, & read by several persons, among others by [*Richard Monckton*] Milnes, who advises against its publication.[2]

Yr fame is great here. Every body is glad to hear about you, & when I say that you are my friend I feel new amenities of courtesy. Two evngs ago I sat at dinner next to the young Lady Annabella King, the granddaughter of Byron,[3] who had been much interested by Hyperion. How honest & warm she is against Slavery! But this is the tone here. A certain Bostonian here, seems to have adopted a tone, which he had not at home. I have been asked if it was true that "he supported the Fug. Sl. Bill & was in favor of the surrender of fug. slaves." My catechist said that "he talked so liberally" that it seemed impossible he could do any thing so bad.

The [*Robert J. and Mary Appleton*] Mackintoshes whom I saw constantly for a while have left town, & I know not where you are; but suppose you are at Nahant, with a sea-breeze fanning you.

If you see Mr [*John Ellerton*] Lodge give him my regards, & remember me to Prescott. With love to Fanny & the children,

Ever affectionately Yrs, C. S.

P.S. I have been disappointed & almost unhappy in not hearing from you by the last Steamer. But I recd. on my arrival a note through Mrs M.

Mackintosh has kindly invited me to stay with him; but my stay in London will be so brief that I stick to my Hotel—near the clubs.

I meet constantly some of yr admirers—among many Lady Theodora Grosvenor.[4]

Good bye!

ALS MH-H (72/544, PCS)

1. Philip Henry Stanhope, fifth earl (1805–75), M.P. (Tory), historian, and patron of the arts. John Bird Sumner (1780–1862), archbishop of Canterbury, 1848–62. Henry Labouchère (1798–1869), M.P.; member, Privy Council; president, Board of Trade.

2. The poet laureate, Alfred, Lord Tennyson (1809–92), and his wife, Emily Sellwood Tennyson (d. 1896), lived on the Isle of Wight. He had recently completed "The Marriage of Geraint," one of the poems that would later make up *Idylls of the King*. It was printed in 1857 as "Enid and Nimue: The True and the False" (*Letters of Emily Lady Tennyson*, ed. James O. Hoge [1974], 101, 119). CS met Elizabeth Georgiana Campbell, duchess of Argyll (1824–78), in late June, soon after he arrived in London (CS Journal, Prc, 3:544).

3. Anne Isabella King Blunt (b. 1838), daughter of Ada Byron and William King

(Ethel Colburn Mayne, *The Life and Letters of Anne Isabella, Lady Noel Byron* [1929], 396, 429).

4. Lady Theodora Grosvenor, British writer; daughter of Richard Grosvenor, third marquess of Westminster (1795–1869), British M.P.

To Salmon P. Chase

Ostend—18th Sept. '57—

My dear Chase,

No *Ostend* letter[1] shall I write, though I write from Ostend. Here I am—detained by one of the disagreeable incidents of travel, & I turn to you for solace.

As I lay on my bed at Cologne I read in an American newspaper, which a friend put into my hands, a brief account of yr speech at Cincinnati. I always read you with more than pleasure, & my heart beat as it felt yr strong words. I am glad you are again a candidate. You must be elected, & persist in keeping Ohio on the side of Freedom.[2]

Looking at our cause from this distance I see its grandeur more than ever. I also see more clearly than ever its certain success. It may be interrupted for a moment, but it cannot be stopped. The men in power, whether President or Senators, are not strong enough to do what they want to do.

Slavery seems more hateful; for I see now better than before how it degrades us in the family of nations & prevents our example from acting as it should in Europe. Liberty every where suffers through us.

Poor Kansas![3] I am pained by the trials & sorrows of this territory; & my indignation overflows when I see the President & Cabinet lending themselves to the cruel work. I envy you the opportunity & the ability of speaking for our cause thus imperilled.

As for my myself, I am *almost* well. My disease spins out slowly, but surely. Latterly I have been ranging through Switzerland, visiting mountains & lakes. I crossed the St Gotherd into Italy, sailed down the Lago Maggiore, then turning up the Val d'Aosta, returned by the Grand St. Bernard, resting a night with the monks. Afterwards I went to the foot of Mont Blanc, then to Geneva & the beautiful Lake Leman. This whole tour, though at times fatiguing, has been most agreeable, & also advantageous to my health. The Alps, & also the Pyrenees I have seen. You will next hear of me in the Highlands of Scotland.

Returning from Switzerland by the Rhine, I have been tempted into Holland, where my curiosity was much gratified, but where I had the mortification of not understanding a word that was said. In other languages I can do something more than beg my bread & butter, but in Dutch I can say nothing. I shall have time to hear from you before my return. God bless you!

Ever sincerely Yours, Charles Sumner.

ALS DLC (72/585, PCS)

1. A reference to the Ostend Manifesto, 15 October 1854, in which the United States ministers to Spain (Pierre Soulé), France (John Y. Mason), and Great Britain (James Buchanan) urged the U.S. to purchase Cuba from Spain, or possibly even attempt to seize the island.

2. Chase was campaigning for a second term as governor of Ohio. His Cincinnati speech, 20 August 1857, was printed in the *New York Times*, 29 August 1857:3. In it Chase deplored the slave power's dominance in the federal government, including President Buchanan's administration.

3. In the summer of 1857 Robert J. Walker (1801–69), the new governor of the Kansas Territory, convinced the antislavery leaders there to participate in forthcoming elections for the territorial legislature. Southern leaders then demanded that any constitution adopted by the proslavery (Lecompton) legislature should go into effect without ratification by the residents of the territory. President Buchanan supported the Lecompton Constitution, thereby favoring the admission of Kansas as a slave state.

To Edward L. Pierce

Sunday—11th [*and 15th*] Oct '57
Glenquoich—Scotland

My dear Peirce,

I am here further North than Iona & Staffa—beyond Morven—& near the Isle of Skye, where Flora Macdonald sheltered Charles Edward.[1] There is no family living within 40 or 50 miles of the friend whose guest I now am,[2] & whose estate stretches for miles & miles. In front of the window at which I write are the hills of the immense possessions of Lochiel.

I am away from American papers & without letters. By chance some days ago I had a newspaper which contained Wilson's speech at Worcester[3]—His best effort. Indeed, I always think his last is his best. Never have I known any person whose improvement was so palpable.

I am pained to hear of dissension in Mass. which, at this distance, & without papers, I cannot comprehend.[4] I long to see our noble State a *unit* at the head of our great battle for civilization.

Before leaving the continent I addressed you a brief line at Chicago. On passing through London I found yr most excellent work on Rail-Roads[5] by which I learned yr change of domicile. After glancing at the book, which I liked much, I gave it to a friend, a veteran lawyer, who promised to notice it in the *Times*. I also mentioned it to the Chancellor.[6]

This note beginning in a glen, I finish at an Inn in Elgin 15th Oct.—I wish I could hear from you again before I return; but I cannot.

Ever Yrs, C. S.

P.S. I have lived with reference to my health—keeping in the open air—taking as much exercise as I can bear—enjoying society—seeing mountains & Lakes—in Pyrenees, Alps, & now the Scotch Highlands, but I have not yet exterminated all of my malady. Slowly, slowly it yields.

ALS MH-H (63/731, PCS)

1. After his defeat at the Battle of Culloden in 1746, Prince Charles Edward (1720–88), pretender to the British throne, escaped to France with the help of Flora Macdonald (1722–90).

2. CS visited Edward Ellice here (Prc, 3:551).

3. Henry Wilson spoke 8 September 1857 at the Young Men's Ratification Convention, endorsing Nathaniel P. Banks for governor of Massachusetts. Wilson stated that Banks supported CS, and voters should rally behind Banks as they had Frémont (*Boston Daily Advertiser*, 9 September 1857:1).

4. Know-Nothings and Republicans still disagreed over antislavery principles and candidates. Although Banks had won the gubernatorial nomination of Know-Nothings and Republicans, some of the latter, led by Francis W. Bird, nominated their own candidate. Pierce wrote CS from Milton ([September], 16/071, PCS) about these maneuvers, and Banks's recent speech "approving the warfare on foreigners." Pierce thought CS's absence was beneficial since CS could not divorce himself "from the mass of party, & yet you would not wish to commit yourself to Mr Banks' position."

5. *A Treatise on American Railroad Law* (1857).

6. Robert Monsey Rolfe, Baron Cranworth (1790–1868), lord chancellor, 1852–58.

To Lord Hatherton[1]

Eaton Hall—Thursday—
[*5 November 1857*]

Dear Lord Hatherton,

On Tuesday about 5 o'clk I reached John Bright at Llandudno.[2] I had never seen him before, & was astonished at his look of strength & soundness. We talked throughout the evng & the next forenoon till I left at 1 o'clk. & his mind seemed to sustain itself without any flagging.

And yet his physicians & friends insist upon his giving himself more rest.

His purpose is to keep quiet till Parlt. meets & then determine whether it will be safe to venture. But he wishes for eight months or a year longer, & says that if he were in America he would keep there & not return to England until time had confirmed his health.

All this is applicable to my case; for I fear that in some respects we may be alike.

But I cannot be contented to stay, & I am not happy in going. Lord Bacon's words come to me often—"the duties of life are more than life," &, taking all things into consideration I feel that it is my *duty* to go. Therefore I sail on Saturday, & my address till then will be care of *Messrs MacIver & Co. Agents of the Cunard Steamers*, Water St. Liverpool.

I cannot forget Lady Hatherton & yourself, who have been so kind to me.

Ever sincerely Yrs, Charles Sumner

P.S. Yesterday I reached Hawarden, where was Ld Lyttleton. Gladstone has an angelic nature.[3]—Today at lunch I reached this magnificent house & was most kindly welcomed.[4]

2nd P.S. I was sorry to leave Mrs Gaskell[5] without having seen more of her.

ALS GBStR (72/626, PCS)

1. CS stayed with Edward John Littleton, first baron Hatherton (1791–1863), British M.P. (Whig), and his wife, Caroline (1809–97), at Teddesley Park near Stafford, 31 October to 3 November 1857 (CS journal, Prc, 3:554).
2. John Bright (1811–89), British Radical and M.P., 1843–89.
3. CS's description of his visit with the British Liberal leader William E. Gladstone (1809–98) and George William Lyttelton (1817–76), British M.P., appears in his journal (ibid.).
4. Home of Richard Grosvenor, marquess of Westminster.
5. At the Hathertons' CS had met the novelist Elizabeth Gaskell (1810–65) (ibid.).

To Lord Brougham

[Washing]ton—
U. States of America—
14th Dec. '57

My dear Lord Brougham,

The letter to Nashville has been promptly forwarded to the proper address; the book on Newton given to the Library of Harvard University

& the numbers of the Law Magazine, after being read by myself, have been distributed among members of the bar.[1]

Be assured of the pleasure I find in executing these little commissions. Do not fail at any time to command me.

I deplore the lead which the French Govt. seems to be giving in a bad direction;[2] but I trust that your energetic efforts will yet prevail. Surely here is the old Slave-trade under a new *alias*.

I find that the commercial convulsion has impoverished families & overturned firms, that seemed rich & permanent.[3] But the country is already beginning to right itself, & I am inclined to believe that the reaction will come as rapidly as the reverse. Two interests particularly will suffer; *first*, the *rail-ways*, which have been in the hands of speculators & jobbers & which have been built poorly but improvidently; & secondly, the *manufacturing interest*, which has been managed loosely & with an expenditure of salaries which would bankrupt yr Lancashire mills. Besides these two interests, the East India Trade is also beginning to suffer.

Meanwhile Mr Buchanan pursues his dishonest pro-Slavery policy. His message is plausible & velvet-pawed; but he is in the hands of the *ultras* of Slavery, & is now cooperating with them to plant Slavery in Kansas. The unfriendly paragraph in the message about Spain is simply to keep something open which, at an opportune moment, may be laid hold of for the sake of Cuba. The acquisition of this Island is his darling idea.[4]

Every where among my countrymen there is a strong interest in yr character & fame. I am constantly asked about you.

There are many things which I wish I could talk about with you; but I cannot forget the opportunities I have enjoyed. If your family has gone with you to Cannes, pray remember me to them most kindly & believe me, dear Lord Brougham,

Ever sincerely yours, Charles Sumner

ALS GBUCL (72/670, PCS)
Enc: Unidentified newsclipping, "The French and the Slave Trade," no date.

1. In his letter from London 11 November 1857 (16/193, PCS), Brougham asked several favors of CS: to forward a letter to the Nashville Historical Society which had made him an honorary member; to donate the book *Newton* to Harvard College; and to pass the law reviews along to any interested party.

2. The clipping CS enclosed stated that the French were rumored to have a contract to buy 20,000 blacks from the Congo.

3. On 24 August, a life insurance company failure set off an international depression known as the Panic of 1857.

4. In his presidential message of 8 December, Buchanan called the free state sup-

porters in Kansas "revolutionaries" and affirmed his support for the upcoming referendum on the Lecompton Constitution, which contained a clause allowing slavery. On Spain, Buchanan noted the lack of progress on American citizens' claims against the Spanish government: "the general tone and temper of the Spanish Government toward that of the U.S. are much to be regretted" (*Globe*, 35th Cong., 1st sess., appendix, 3).

To the Duchess of Argyll

New York 22nd Dec. '57

My dear Duchess,

After 10 days at Washington I take advantage of the earliest Steamer to comply with yr kind injunction. I wish that I could make a better report than I can. Unhappily those medical authorities were too nearly right. They understood the subtle character of my injuries & the necessity of protracted repose better than their patient.

Though in most respects *entirely well* I am constrained to confess that in other important particulars I am still an invalid. While in Europe without care or responsibility & in constant recreation of body & mind, happy in all my experiences, I was not conscious of the extent of my disability. But here it is presented to me most painfully. I cannot work with the mind, except in very narrow limits. To sit in the Senate is exhausting, even although I renounce all special interest in the debates & leave every thing to others. This is hard—very hard. It is hard to be so near complete recovery, & still to be kept back.

The trial I made at Washington was not satisfactory, & I have now left for some weeks to enjoy myself—if that be possible, where I cannot escape from the thoughts of my disappointment. Pardon this long story, which I tell, because you bade me, & because yr kindness inspires the freedom of friendship.

At Washington I saw Ld Napier several times. His desire to please leads him to strange sympathies, personnal & political. He accepts the whole democratic dogma or "dodge" on Kansas, & talks as glibly as the Presdt on "popular sovereignty" & the right of the settlers to establish Slavery if they see fit. Sir Wm. Ousley is clearly in a different mood.[1] Before leaving I had talked plainly with Ld Napier. I respect entirely all the *convenances* of his position as Minister & am glad to have him keep on good terms with the Administration; but I do not like to see him giving them his head & heart. Indeed, it is not pleasant to find the influence of his *talk* against us. Imprimus, he needs light on yr West India Emancipation.

Lady N. is much liked.[2] I found her gentle & agreeable. He told me what he had written to Ld Clarendon about the Presdt's Message. Never was there greater misapprehension. The Northern leaders of the Democracy refuse to follow the Presdt. & there are signs that his party will be split, & his Administration left in a minority. His course towards Kansas is unfeeling & base. I use this language because it is applicable. What he said in his message was calculated to mystify people at a distance. In plain terms, it meant—"I am the tool of the South for the establishment of Sl. in Kansas."

The passage in the Message on Spain was calculated to keep open differences with that nation, in the hope that something might "turn up" by which we may acquire Cuba. At the same time Russia & France were kindly noticed, in order to have their good will or connivance in the piratical plans.[3]

Our financial troubles are already passing away, leaving many persons poor who were once rich & others with diminished fortunes. The estate of the late Abbott Lawrence is said to have shrunk one million of dollars—say £200,000.

Enough of these things, my dear Duchess. How are you & those children & the Duke?[4] You did make me happy, & I am happy still when I think of all that I enjoyed through the friendship of yr family. On reaching home, I had a disappointment. I expected to find in a roll from Stafford House you & the Duke, to say nothing of yr sisters. But they were missing. I thought that yr mother promised them. How good to me was the Duchess of Sutherland!—Tell her that I think often of her with gratitude & friendship.

I found my friends well. Prescott since I left had taken a new start, & enjoyed keenly my experiences, while his wife listened.[5] So also did Palfrey, who remembers Inverary almost as freshly as I do.

It is understood here that Mr Dallas desires to remain in London, but that the Presdt. is not friendly to him, & will probably give his place to some more faithful follower.

If you write to me—& you will, surely—address me at Washington. Tell me every thing about yourself, family, friends & England, & with best regards to my dear Duke, believe me,

Always sincerely Yours, Charles Sumner

ALS CSmH (72/685, PCS)

1. CS apparently dined on 11 December 1857 with Francis Napier (1819–98), British minister to the U.S., 1857–58, and William Ouseley (1797–1866), British diplomat then on a mission to look into British interests in Central America (Napier to CS, Washington, 8 December 1857, 16/243, PCS). In Kansas, an election was held 21 December to ratify a clause in the Lecompton Constitution guaranteeing the right to own slaves. Most free state proponents refused to vote on this clause and it was overwhelmingly adopted.

2. Anne Lockwood Napier (1824–1911).

3. Buchanan characterized relations with all European nations but Spain as being "as peaceful as we could desire" (*Globe*, 35th Cong., 1st sess., appendix, 3).

4. George Douglas Campbell, duke of Argyll (1823–1900), lord privy seal, 1853–55, 1859–66, 1880–88; secretary of state for India, 1868–74.

5. Susan Amory Prescott (1802–69).

To Salmon P. Chase

Boston—10th Jan. '58—

I have this moment, my dear Chase, finished yr message, as it appears in the *Tribune*.[1] I am with you on the question of jurisdiction, & nothing could be better than yr statement of the Kansas case. I shall send it to Lord Napier, who unhappily is in much need of light.

You have sculptured the whole Case, so that it stands forth with the distinctness & simplicity of a *bas-relief*.

I wish that we could talk together for an evng. Our experience of Douglas, I think, would prevent any strong confidence in his labors for the good cause. His essential baseness has been too often manifest. Besides, the personal motive of his present movement is too obvious.[2] I cannot at this point of time undertake to say whether he will be successful or not. This, however, seems certain to me, that if he had not taken his present course, he would have been defeated in Illinois. He let the office-holders in New York know that he would not be "in Walker's way in 1860."[3] Indeed, he is obviously struggling now, not for the Presidency, but for a re-election. It is a little strange that some of our friends & papers should play into his hands.

I envy you many things, but now chiefly the capacity to work,—which unhappily I cannot. But all is surely coming back, &, some hours during this last week, I have been disposed to believe that it had come. But I must wait yet a little longer. Oh! I do long to speak.

You are happy with yr daughters about you. God bless them & remember me most kindly to them. If you have not struck me from yr lists as an unresponding correspondent, let me hear from you soon, & believe me, dear Chase,

Ever sincerely Yours, Charles Sumner

ALS DLC (73/008, PCS)

1. Extracts from Chase's gubernatorial message were printed in the *New York Tribune*, 8 January 1858:6. In it Chase criticized the "disposition to extend the range of Federal Power" over the rights of states: "the whole power of the National Government has been exerted to force Slavery upon the reluctant people of Kansas."

2. Douglas denounced the Lecompton Constitution 9 December 1857, openly opposing President Buchanan. Douglas criticized the constitution not for its proslavery bias, but rather for the fact that the entire constitution would not be submitted to a popular vote (*Globe*, 35th Cong., 1st sess., 14–18).

3. Douglas had recommended his friend Robert J. Walker to be governor of Kansas in 1857. Walker agreed with Douglas on the inadequacy of the ratification process of the Lecompton Constitution and resigned 15 December. Apparently, Walker, like Douglas, had presidential ambitions (Robert W. Johanssen, *Stephen A. Douglas* [1973], 563–64, 594, 701).

To the Duchess of Argyll

Boston—U.S. of America
12th Jan. '58

My dear Duchess,

This evng has brought me yr little letter from Trentham with its pleasant Xmas wishes, & the assurance that I am not yet forgotten where I am so happy in being remembered.[1] I write now at once in order to take advantage of the Steamer that sails tomorrow.

I wish that I were well; but I am not. Since leaving Washington I have led a quiet life, among a few friends, & amusing myself chiefly with engravings—by this substitute consoling myself for the grand Art Treasures of Europe. I have been deep in Durer, Rembrandt & Marc. Antonio Müller, Longhi, & Toschi.[2] In this way I have occupied myself & for a while forgotten public life.

Many still insist that I should return to Europe & there allow this slow convalescence to run its course. I have been tempted, & have even had visions of Italy & Egypt. The newspapers have announced me as on the way. But my fixed purpose is to linger here during the session of Congress, &, if my vote is needed at any time to appear in my seat.

All this is very unsatisfactory, & at times makes me unhappy. But I try to bear it. For several days I have been with only very slight indications of my disability; but to-day I am feeble & am obliged to confess it. Tomorrow I hope to be better.

The news from Kansas is not yet definitive, but it is cheerful.[3] All things indicate that Slavery will be defeated there; but I am not sure that it will be without bloodshed.

In close fellowship with the Crime against Kansas is the Crime of the Filibuster Walker—both having the same origin—the desire to spread Slavery.[4] Oh! how I do loathe the authors of this two-fold iniquity.

Mr Buchanan has not dared to sacrifice Commd. Paulding—although he has hearkened to the friends of the Filibuster & pretended sensibility for the Law of Nations said to be wounded by the seizure of

Walker on the soil of Nicaragua. Paulding's act & letter[5] are the most creditable things that have yet occurred under this Administration.

Poor Napier! He has allowed himself to be crammed with all the subtleties & apologies by which the Administration has surrounded its course in Kansas. This is painfully apparent in a long letter which I have recently had from him.[6] I trust, however, that, as the discussion proceeds, he will change some of his views, while he does not lose the good-will of the Administration.

Constantly I think of yr kindness to me; & all yr family, parents, sisters, husband & children, seem almost to belong to me. I hope to hear always of their happiness.

By accident I met Mrs Stow & her husband. They were very earnest in their inquiries about yr whole castle-full.[7] She was amused at my account of the travels of that newspaper with her letter on communication with spirits. I was sorry to learn that she also is suffering in the head.

Where is Lady Emma?[8] Had I stayed another day at Inverary she would have told me all about Tennyson. Remember me to her & to yr Duke, whose health I am glad to know is better, & to yr quiver of golden arrows.

Ever sincerely Yrs, Charles Sumner

To the Duchess of S. give my gratitude & affection, & remind Lady Mary[9] of her American friend.—Prescott is pretty well; Palfrey very well.

ALS CSmH (73/017, PCS)

1. 24 December 1857, 16/289, PCS.

2. Besides the artists Albrecht Dürer and Rembrandt, CS refers to lesser-known artists, Pier Francesco Toschi (d. 1567) of Florence, and possibly Marcus Müller (fl. 1712–43). Longhi is possibly Luca Longhi (1507–80) of Ravenna.

3. On 29 December 1857 the *New York Times* correspondent reported from Tecumseh, Kansas Territory, that free state voters there would turn out solidly for the election of members to the territorial legislature on 4 January 1858 despite their objections to the Lecompton Constitution (12 January 1858:5).

4. The American adventurer William Walker (1824–60) invaded Nicaragua in 1855 and, backed by certain U.S. commercial interests, established a government in July 1856. He resigned in May 1857, but during a second invasion in November 1857 was arrested by U.S. Navy Commodore Hiram Paulding (1797–1878). In a presidential message to Congress 7 January 1858 (*Globe*, 35th Cong., 1st sess., 216–17), Buchanan criticized Paulding for arresting Walker but commended Paulding's patriotic motives.

5. In a letter dated 18 December 1857 to Secretary of the Navy Isaac Toucey, Paulding described the capture of Walker without bloodshed and praised the "excel-

lent discipline and fine bearing" of his men as they carried out "this most unpleasant service" (*New York Times*, 1 January 1858:3).

6. Writing CS from Washington on 31 December 1857 (16/298), Napier expressed regret that Kansas voters had not rejected the slavery clause in the Lecompton Constitution, but also lamented that there was in Washington "no spirit of compromise for the general good, no persistency of patience in the pursuit of a laudable object by moderate means." The duchess agreed with CS about Napier in her letter of 4 February (16/372).

7. Harriet Beecher Stowe and her children had visited the Argylls at Inverary in September 1856 (Robert Forrest Wilson, *Crusader in Crinoline* [1941], 424).

8. Emma Campbell (d. 1893), sister of the duke of Argyll.

9. Probably Mary Howard, sister of the duchess of Sutherland.

To Samuel Gridley Howe

Washington
26th—[*February*] '58—

Dear Howe,

At last I leave W. to-day—having voted against the Army Bill, & helped its defeat.[1] Thus far I have kept aloof from the debates, employing myself on books away from politics.

I shall be for a few days at the Brevoort House, N.Y. ready to give my vote whenever it is needed.

The Kansas debate will probably stretch on for weeks.[2]

I long to see you or at least hear from you.

Ever & ever Yrs, C. S.

ALS MH-H (63/744, PCS)

1. The Senate voted down a bill "to increase the military establishment of the U.S." on 25 February 1858 (*Globe*, 35th Cong., 1st sess., 876).

2. Senate debate on President Buchanan's recommendation that Kansas be admitted under the Lecompton Constitution began 1 March (ibid., 901).

To William Pitt Fessenden

New York—Brevoort House—
28th Feb. '58.

My dear Fessenden,

You first made the point, that the Presdt. had no authority under the laws of the U.S. to fill Kansas with Federal troops as a *posse comitatus*.[1] It has never been answered. I do not think it can be.

The wolf must be held by the ears, & kept in that condition. In other words, the Administration must be held before the country, as violating the laws for a *tyrannical & sectional* purpose, & kept so completely in the wrong, that the troops will be innoxious. At all events, try; & it belongs to you to make the effort.

Let it be by resolution, calling upon the Presdt. for reasons why he undertakes to keep troops in K. as a *posse comitatus*? Or, introduce a bill, ordering the withdrawal of the troops. At all events make the point, & do it constantly. Challenge an answer.

I wish that I could help you. I should enjoy following you in the attack. But my time will come—pretty soon, I think.

Ever Yours, Charles Sumner

ALS MH-H (73/053, PCS)

1. When Buchanan sent the Lecompton Constitution to the Senate to approve and admit Kansas, Senator Fessenden objected to Buchanan's intention to station troops in Kansas in order to protect the new government there (*Globe*, 35th Cong., 1st sess., 8 February 1858, 608–9).

To the Duchess of Argyll

New York—2nd March '58

My dear Duchess,

I write especially to send you the late good news of Prescott. I hear constantly of his improvement, & enclose a note which is most cheering.[1]

I must thank you at once for that most pleasant letter which gave me a glimpse at scenes & persons so dear to me.[2]

Since I last wrote I have passed a few weeks in Washington, which I have again left—not because of any relapse, but simply that I might be further away from all the temptations to hard work. I shall be here for a short time & then try the Senate again.

Last evng I heard for the first time Rossini's Otello, which interested me more than I had expected. Do you remember that in the first scene Otello, addressing the Doge says—*D'Affrican figlio, Qui straniero son io.*![3]—These words were omitted by the politic singer!

There is one service which can be done in England, which will help us in our contest with Slavery. Let your grand act of Emancipation be vindicated[4]—in all the reviews—*Edinburgh, Quarterly*, & even in the *Times*. Shew how much has been gained. The figures are very telling with regard to every island, except Jamaica, & here are anomalies which account for any seeming failure. Even if sugar had diminished, you & I would not admit that the good cause was discredited, but the sugar argt. is on our side.

Why will not Mr Helps set this forth? or Sir James Stephen? or better still, both?[5] In displaying the results of Emancipation, the argt. against Slavery can be presented in its strongest form, & one of England's greatest victories be kept prominent for example & generous envy. If Mr Macaulay would do it, he might by one article do as much against Slavery as his father did in his whole life. When at Westminister Abbey I sought out the monument to the late Mr Macaulay,[6] & stood before it with reverence. It is on the left of the great door as you enter. I wish the great historian could add similar titles to the many he has upon our admiration & gratitude.

At last Bancroft is moved.[7] He has borne all previous outrages; but he denounces this effort to force the Lecompton constitution with Slavery upon Kansas. Best regards to the Duke & all the little ones,

Ever sincerely yours, Charles Sumner

I am sorry to hear that the Duchess yr mother has not been well. The request I made to you sometime ago I shall make directly to her.

ALS CSmH (73/058, PCS)

1. William Hickling Prescott suffered a stroke 4 February 1858. Longfellow wrote CS on 24 February that Prescott's recovery was remarkable for a man over fifty (Cambridge, 73/048, PCS).
2. Kensington, 4 February, 16/372.
3. "Son of an African, here I am a stranger."
4. Great Britain's law gradually emancipating all slaves in her West Indian possessions.
5. Arthur Helps (1813–75), British historian, author of *The Spanish Conquest in America and its Relation to the History of Slavery and to the Government of the Colonies* (1855–61). James Stephen (1789–1859), British colonial undersecretary who had prepared the 1833 emancipation bill.
6. Zachary Macaulay (1768–1838), philanthropist and editor of the *Christian Observer*, an antislave-trade periodical, and father of Thomas Babington Macaulay.
7. In February Bancroft presided over a meeting of New York Democrats supporting Douglas's anti-Lecompton policy (Lilian Handlin, *George Bancroft* [1984], 265).

To Samuel Gridley Howe

New York—Brevoort Hotel
4th March '58

Dear Howe,

I pass hours at the Astor Library—ranging at will in its pleasant alcoves.

Poor Cogswell! he has been obliged to leave for the present. The hand of death seems to be upon him. It is *he* who is really the *fundator perficiens*[1] of this beautiful Library.

How grand that speech of Parker was! But why did he end it with that tasteless story?[2]

Mass. seems stifled. Not a voice against {*Edward*} Loring—not a voice against the Kansas Usurpation—not a voice against the Dred Scott diabolism[3]—not a voice against entertaining & feasting the chief Slave-Hunter {*James M. Mason*} at B. Hill—not a voice against the wickedness which rules the land. Where is the Republican Party? I am for a new one. Where is {*John*} Andrew?

The Cwlth needs a voice.

Here is a letter from Wm. Story. Read it & ponder the part about Crawford, & send it back to me.[4]

Send me Combe's letter. I should be happy to renew my recollections of this sincere cordial good man. Thanks for yr note which came today.[5]

Ever Yrs, C. S.

P.S. What are those publishers doing with my book?

ALS MH-H (63/746, PCS)

1. Joseph Green Cogswell (1786–1871), superintendent of the Astor Library, 1848–61; "excellent founder."

2. On 29 January 1858 Parker delivered a speech, "The Present Aspect of Slavery in America and the Immediate Duty of the North," before the Massachusetts Anti-slavery Convention in Boston. In it he warned his audience not to be influenced by Southern threats to secede; the South could not survive alone. Parker ended by comparing the South to a spoiled boy who asks, not for just a piece, but the *whole* "pickled elephant," and threatens to run away if he doesn't get it (44). On 18 March Parker wrote CS defending the close of his speech as being an intentional "*desinet in piscem*" (tail of a fish). He had wanted to show "utter contempt for this threat of disunion" (Boston, 16/474, PCS).

3. CS was embarking for Europe 6 March 1857 when the Supreme Court decided that Dred Scott, a slave who had been moved to a free state, was not a U.S. citizen and that the Missouri Compromise was unconstitutional.

4. Story had written CS from Rome 27 January (16/351). He mourned the death of Crawford but tempered his praise of Crawford's work; the sculptor had "more Fancy than imagination."

5. In his letter to CS of 1 March from Boston (73/055), Howe wrote he had recently received a "warm letter" from George Combe (1788–1858), a British phrenologist.

To Theodore Parker

Philadelphia at the Furness'
22d. March [*1858*]

Dear Parker,

I have great joy in the removal of the Slave-Hunter. This is much.[1]

But I deplore the recommendations of the Governor—especially those which propose to allow Massachusetts justices of the peace, and attorney's of law, to hunt slaves. Shades of Adams and Quincy!

How strangely the Governor confuses duties! Every criminal, even a Slave-Hunter when his life or liberty are in jeopardy, should have counsel. This is Just. But no Slave-Hunter or other criminal should have *official assistance* in carrying out his crime. To hunt Slaves is a crime.

I leave to-day for Washington.

Thanks for your letter

Ever yrs C. S.

C MHi (73/077, PCS)

1. On 22 March 1858 Governor Nathaniel Banks approved the recommendation of the Massachusetts legislature that Edward Loring be dismissed as probate judge of Suffolk County (*New York Times*, 19 March, 24 March 1858:2). Banks's message on the removal also, however, criticized sections of the 1855 statute that had provided the grounds for Loring's removal. Provisions that enforcers of the Fugitive Slave Law be fined or penalized in some way, said Banks, were "inconsistent . . . with the professional traditions" of Massachusetts, traditions linked indissolubly with Adams and Quincy (*New York Times*, 25 March 1858:2).

To John Andrew

Washington
24th March '58.

Dear Andrew,

Till I reached Washington I did not know the half you had done. Here I found the *Bee* with your complete & admirable speech on the Dred Scott case, & yr first speech on the removal of Loring—both of which filled me with delight.[1]

I do enjoy a good speech—on the right side.

The good cause must not suffer through what seem the indiscreet recommendations of the Governor. How much better—had he simply & quietly removed Loring!

The vote in the Senate has been taken,[2] & I again run away to New York, where I shall be for a short time at the Brevoort House.

Our friends are now in good spirits, & hope to defeat the Villainy.

The good time is coming! Let us all help it.

Ever yours, Charles Sumner

ALS MHi (73/078, PCS)

1. In the Massachusetts House of Representatives, 5 March 1858, Andrew denounced the Dred Scott decision, stating it was not law but merely a judicial verdict that did not reflect the Constitution framers' intentions (*Boston Daily Advertiser*, 6 March 1858:1). In another speech 16 March, Andrew defended the House's removal of Loring (ibid., 17 March 1858:4).

2. On 23 March, CS voted twice opposing amendments to the bill to admit Kansas under the Lecompton Constitution and once supporting Crittenden's substitute that the Lecompton Constitution be first submitted to Kansas voters. CS was against the majority on these votes and on the final vote on the bill, which passed the Senate, 33–25 (*Globe*, 35th Cong., 1st sess., 1258–64).

To Samuel Gridley Howe

Brevoort House Friday—
[*26 March 1858*]

Dear Howe,

Again I am here—conscious of being better but still unhappily conscious that I am not yet entirely well. *But I am resolved to be well*, & I trust that this may be before this session is passed.

All that I did against the great Villainy was to cry out with a loud voice "No."—

I have returned to my amusement in the Astor alcoves.

I deplore Banks's course. His message is poorly written—poorly conceived & has no particle of Anti-Slavery. I trust that our friends will resist his suggestions. Andrew has done grandly. He must fight his last battle & if need be, "hold the bridge" alone against the conservative forces headed by a Republican governor.

No speech has pleased me more than Pitmans which I read in the Advertiser.[1] It was well put & contained the argt. & the sentiment of the case.

Unless summoned to Washington I shall linger here a week.

On my way from Washington my pocket was picked—damage $50.

Ever yrs, C. S.

ALS MH-H (64/005, PCS)

1. Robert C. Pitman, a Massachusetts legislator from New Bedford, defended the removal of Judge Loring (*Boston Daily Advertiser*, 12 March 1858:4).

To the Duchess of Argyll

New York—
30th March '58

My dear Duchess,

Here I am again—away from Washington—doing very well, except so far as I chafe at the political inactivity which friends & physicians impose upon me yet a little while longer. And this morning I have been cheered by yours of 7th March.

I think that shortly after yours was written one or two notes of mine must have been received chiefly about Prescott. He has written me since gayly & hopefully, but with a slight complaint of the discipline to which he is subjected.[1] I hear through a friend who has seen Mrs Prescott that she is still very anxious about him. Indeed, after such an experience who would not be anxious?

I anticipated the equanimity of the Duke at the change of ministry.[2] And I also expect very soon to see him in another ministry, which will not be merely a transition govt. Perhaps it is well for his health that he should be relieved for a while of these cares.

The Kansas question is still unsettled; but at each stage the Administration, which is entirely in the hands of the South, shews still more the cloven foot. I have no patience in thinking of it; for it seems to me unutterably wicked.

It is supposed that in a few days the question will be removed from Congress, either by the adoption or the defeat of the Lecompton fraud. Then the President will open his next chapter. This concerns Cuba. An endeavor will be made to press Spain to sell the island; & if she will not sell it then a quarrel will be made & the Ostend Manifesto carried out. But Cuba is to be sought—as I once said in a speech—"by violent war or hardly less violent purchase."[3] It remains to be seen if this plot can succeed.

Meanwhile the South is on the point of opening the Slave-trade itself. Public opinion there has been tending in this direction for sometime; but I think that it has been mightily stimulated by the course of France in opening slave-trade under a new name. I send by this post a paper containing a brief discussion in the Senate on this point, in which Mr Mason of Virginia, the author of the Fugitive Slave Bill, undertook again to attribute a pro-slavery policy to the British Govt. & to take issue directly with the Duke of Argyll. I am glad the latter contradicted the statement in his speech at the Livingstone dinner.[4] Give him my thanks.

Since my last letter I have thought more than ever that the time has come when the British Act of Emancipation ought to be vindicated, & in the most authoritative manner. At first I only thought of reviews & papers. But why not in Parlt? Why will not your Duke do it? Ld Brougham, of course, would be ready, & if Ld Macaulay would join in the discussion, even if briefly only, such an impression would be produced as to prevent slave-masters from calling that beautiful act a failure & invoking it for slavery, while British ministers abroad would be prompted into a proper regard for one of the truest glories of their country. Pray think of this.

I enclose a couple of notes from a young colored person, whom I have never seen, but which shew a sensibility at the condition of her race which will touch you. The autographs of the Duchess of S.[*utherland*], & yourself to which she refers were envelopes.—On reading one of the letters I find that it refers to myself more than I had at first supposed. But I send it nevertheless.

Ever Yrs, Charles Sumner

I shall be glad to have those prints; & also the Duke & Duchess.[5] Anything will reach me easily sent, to the care of *Messrs Ticknor & Fields*, booksellers, *Boston*, & left at *Messrs Tribiner & Co., Paternoster Row, London*.

P.S. I am glad the children are well & wish you joy in a complete *decade*.

ALS CSmH (73/084, PCS)

1. In her letter of 7 March 1858 (16/445, PCS) from Kensington, the duchess, recuperating from the birth of her tenth child, inquired about Prescott's health. Prescott wrote CS from Boston 26 February (16/425) that his health was improving but he disliked his vegetarian diet.

2. In February 1858 Palmerston's government was replaced by a Conservative one under Edward G. S. Stanley, fourteenth earl of Derby (1799–1869). The duchess wrote that the duke "does not take to heart being out of office."

3. CS's speech was probably made in executive session in 1852 or early 1853 (DD, 2:241).

4. At the London dinner honoring British explorer David Livingstone (1818–73) on 13 February, Argyll said that he was "astonished" to see an allegation in a U.S. paper that the British government supported slavery and he wanted "to give it a most emphatic denial" (London *Times*, 15 February 1858:3). Seward read Argyll's denial in the Senate 24 March and Mason responded that he still believed that the British

government would "follow" France in legalizing the slave trade, "the Duke of Argyll to the contrary notwithstanding" (*Globe*, 35th Cong., 1st sess., 1295).

5. The duchess wrote she would soon send CS a print of some of her children.

To Henry W. Longfellow

Washington
12th April '58

Dear Longfellow,

I am pained to hear of Felton's ill health.[1] It is hard—very hard—to carry about the character of an invalid. Give him my love, & best hopes that he may soon be well again.

During the last few days I have had a pull back, which makes me very unhappy—especially because it shews me that my infirmity has not yet left me. I had flattered myself that I was near the end of my case. Perhaps, those English medical authorities were right; & I must wait till next year.

Wait! When will this waiting end?

Helps's book is original, thoughtful & conscientious. It opens some new veins. He has a genuine hatred of Slavery. Witness the last edition of his "Friends in Council."

Livingstone's book[2] puts a new gloss on the African character, & gives new scorn to the slave-holder.

I send a couple of late letters from the Duchess of A[*rgyll*].

I was glad to have a gay letter yesterday from Prescott,[3] who surely must be mending.

Everybody will be well—while I linger still an invalid!

Think of Everett,—while the country is on the verge of civil war, aroused by an attempt to perpetrate an infamous wrong,—travelling to Savannah & Mobile to hawk his rhetorical wares! & to exhibit Washington without his Anti-Slavery![4]

What are you doing now?

Ever & ever Yrs, C. S.

ALS MH-H (73/098, PCS)

1. Longfellow wrote CS on 7 April 1858 that Cornelius Felton was "quite ill" and might go to Europe for his health (73/096, PCS). The two had become reconciled since CS's beating (Prc, 3:499; see Felton to CS, 24 April, 17/071).

2. In his letter to CS, Longfellow recommended David Livingstone's book, *Missionary Travels and Researches in South Africa* (1857), along with Helps's *The Spanish Conquest in America*.

3. Boston, 9 April, 17/019.
4. Everett had embarked on a lecture tour of the South to raise money for Mount Vernon; his main presentation was "The Character of Washington" (Paul R. Frothingham, *Edward Everett* [1925], 385).

To Wendell Phillips
Private

Phila—at Mr F's—
20th April '58

My dear Phillips,

I ought to have answered yr letter at once; but I have not been well. Of course my first strength must be given to my public duties, & I know not when this will be.[1] It is now about a fortnight since I had a "pull-back" without any adequate cause, which has left me very feeble, so that I do not walk without pain nor am I a single moment without the consciousness of being an invalid. The Englishmen were right, when they said I should not be well till next year. Sometimes I think it will never be. But generally I am hopeful.

Two years in May gone—cut out of my active life—& no man can now tell when I shall regain my powers! This is hard. But it is not so much as is in the lot every slave.

In my visits to Washington I marvel that our reps. can fraternize with men who to me seem so inhuman. But perhaps, my experience renders me too sensitive. I think, however, if one of my associates had been brutally felled to the floor—almost murdered—& then, after a lapse of nearly two years, was still halting about, constrained in his efforts, & even at each step reviving his pains,—that I should have small truce with any of the accomplices before or *after* the act.—For myself, I rejoice to have nothing to do with any of them, & the happiest day in store for me will be when I can tell them what I think of them.

I wish that I could do something for Dr Black. If I were in Boston & could confer with him I might—perhaps. But I see difficulties in the way. Ld B.[*rougham*] is 79 years old—much occupied. Do you know Dr B? Is it necessary that he should go to Europe? A person introduced by me once got £10. out of a friend. I owe it to persons on the other side to ascertain the true character of any body introduced by me. All that I know of the Dr. is excellent.

The chance of Emancipation in Cuba is great news.[2] Should it be verified, our struggle would draw towards its close. That act would be the most important for this continent since the Dectn. of Indep.

I rejoice in the removal of Loring; but mourn the price paid for it. Indeed, I should prefer to see that Law on the Statute-book. We lost more than we gained. So it is. Mass. now on the recommendation of a Republ. Govr. voluntarily removes an impediment to Sl.-Hunting, which no martinet of Slavery had ever ventured to call unconstitutional. She now says to her children; "Help, if you please, the hunt of Slaves; & do it in the name of Quincy & Adams."

While in N. York I amused myself at the Astor Libry, & met many things which recalled you; particularly with regard to Toussaint L'Ouverture.[3] Pray when there ransack what they have on St Domingo & the great chief. Do you know these books?

> "The History of Things Lost which were in use among the Ancients &c written originally in Latin by Guido Pancirollus—2 vols. London, 1785."

> "Recherches sur l'Origine des Decouvertes attribuées aux Modernes, ou l'on demontre que nos plus celebres Philosophes ont puisé la plupart de leurs connaissances dans les Ouvrages des Anciens {[By Dutens]} Paris, 1766."[4]

Both these are in the Astor.

Pray do what you can to make our public men shew themselves in earnest against Slavery. No truce—no parley! And the men who sustain a brutal act must be made to feel the reprobation of their associates.

I am here for a few days—sometimes very unhappy. Opportunity—which is what we live for—comes daily in my public duties, & I am silent! Where I shall go next I know not;—perhaps, back again to Washington; perhaps, to Europe; perhaps, to a Water-Cure. I must regain my health, or cease to cumber the earth. That vacant chair must be filled. Emerson's *mot* has run out.[5]

God bless you!

Ever, dear Phillips,

affectionately Yrs, Charles Sumner

ALS MH-H (73/112, PCS)

1. Phillips's letter of 5 April 1858 invited CS to address the American Antislavery Society in New York 11–12 May (17/010, PCS).

2. The *New York Times*, 19 April 1858:1, reported what it called a "rumor" that a Spanish proposal to abolish slavery in Cuba would be submitted to the Spanish legislature.

3. François-Dominique Toussaint-Louverture (c. 1743–1803), black Haitian leader, had established a republic in Haiti and Santo Domingo that was subjugated by France in 1802.

4. Guido Panciroli (1523–99). Louis Dutens (1730–1812), "Inquiry into the Discoveries Attributed to the Moderns."

5. Possibly a reference to the close of Emerson's speech, "Assault Upon Mr. Sumner": "And if our arms at this distance cannot defend him from assassins, we confide the defence of a life so precious to all honorable men and true patriots, and to the Almighty Maker of men" (*Works of Ralph Waldo Emerson*, 11 [1878]:252).

To Lord Brougham

Private

Washington—21st April '58

My dear Lord Brougham,

I follow with constant interest & gratitude yr efforts for the poor Africans. It is painful that, after yr long struggles in Europe, the battle should be again revived. But since it must be so, I am happy that you still live to conduct it.

You will observe the recent suggestion from General Cass that the naval forces should be withdrawn from the coast of Africa & kept about Cuba, so as to prevent the landing of slaves there.[1] A better suggestion still, & entirely free from [the?] filibustering *arriere pensée*[2] of Genl. Cass, would be that Spain should follow other European Powers & establish Freedom in her colonies. A recent report that this was to be done struck consternation into the slave-holding chiefs here. Cannot this be pressed upon Spain? The violation of existing treaties with England with regard to the *Emancipados* would authorize the English Govt. to open the subject diplomatically. And Spain might be pressed by several considerations. (1) The Public Opinion of Europe, as shewn in the example of England, France, Sweden, Holland & Denmark. (2) The great example of Russia.[3] (3) The importance of destroying the appetite for Cuba of the slave-holders of the U.S.—which will be done at once by Emancipation there, & thus Peace be secured.

There are other considerations to which, however, Spain would be insensible. In no way practicable could such a blow be struck at Slavery. Indeed, Emancipation in Cuba would do more for the downfall of Slavery than all other acts in the long history of our struggle. It would take from the Slave-interest the great *point d'appui*[4] to which it is perpetually looking, & would precipitate the settlement of our own domestic question.

I do not know how these views may strike you or to what extent you will regard them as practicable; but I venture to commend them to yr consideration.

There is another service, which we in America may claim. The English Emancipation Act is constantly assailed as a failure; & this assault has latterly taken an official form. Mr Mason, our Minister at Paris, a diplomatic ignoramus from Virginia besotted by Slavery, in a recent despatch just communicated to Congress, characterises it as a "grave political error"; & a recent speaker from South Carolina in our House of Reps. has made the same accusation.[5] I enclose slips containing what they have said. Now, in view of these things, I ask if the time has not come when this grand & beneficent Act should be vindicated openly in the British Parliament? The productive powers of the smaller islands can be shewn to have increased, while in all the moral elevation of the African race through the influence of Freedom, can be displayed beyond all doubt; & this alone would be enough, even if coffee & sugar did fail. The crops may go down, if man can go up. But in this case every where except in anomalous Jamaica, & perhaps even there, both have gone up.

Permit me to say that this occasion seems every where worthy of your fame. It is fit that one who did so much to establish Emancipation should vindicate it before the civilized world when it is assailed; especially when the effort will help the cause every where. Such a speech would tell powerfully on the public sentiment of the civilized world, & particularly in America. Lord Derby surely would not allow it to be made without taking the occasion to place himself anew on the Act which he promoted originally.

Pardon my freedom, for the sake of the cause we both have at heart, & believe me, dear Lord Brougham,

Ever sincerely Yours, Charles Sumner

ALS GBUCL (73/116, PCS)

1. The *New York Times* (20 April 1858:4) carried a report that eighteen British gunboats were stationed around Cuba to prevent slave-trade ships' landing. In an editorial (27 May 1858:4), the *New York Times* stated that Secretary of State Cass had "advised Lord Napier to send English men-of-war to blockade the coast of Cuba, and prevent the landing of slave-cargoes there."

2. "Mental reservation."

3. The press had been filled recently with news of Alexander II's proposal to plan for the emancipation of Russian serfs. See, e.g., *New York Times*, 7 January 1858:1, 17 April 1858:1.

4. "Point of support."

5. On 25 March William W. Boyce (1818–90; U.S. congressman [Dem., S.C.], 1853–60) stated that in the British West Indies, "the enfranchised blacks are worse off now than in a state of slavery" (*Globe*, 35th Cong., 1st sess., 1361).

To George William Curtis

Philadelphia at Mr Furness's
24th April '58

My dear Curtis,

Yr pleasant letter followed me from Washington here. Thanks. It made be better & stronger.

Truly my case is hard, & yet I try not to be impatient. When in New York I thought myself so nearly well that I talked of speeches & all my old activity. But this "pull down" fills me with despondency. For more than two weeks I have not walked without pain. But enough of this.

I long to be at my post, & try to help our public sentiment. I would teach our friends to hate baseness more than they do. On my visits to Washington, I observe that republicans fraternize most amiably with men who sustain every enormity, even with those who were accomplices *after* if not before the act under which I am still suffering. Perhaps I am too sensitive; but were the case reversed & one of my associates in my place, I know well that I should never tire in heaping scorn upon the whole set of accomplices. There seems to be little spirit or even self-respect among the Anti-Sl. Senators. This must be put into them.

From this lack of true feelings comes the insensibility to the true character of Douglas.[1] For myself, I seek no personal vengeance. But I am jealous of the course which I have at heart, & do not like to see my associates embrace so warmly a man who has never uttered an Anti-Sl. sentiment, & whose baseness on repeated occasions I have known down to the moment when I fell senseless on the floor of the Senate. Read the discussions on the old Nebraska Bill, & there you will see & understand this selfish demagogue. And yet I do not begrudge any credit precisely given for what he has lately done.

As for Presidential calculations, nothing shld be said or done for a year or more. Nobody can tell how the field will lie, & who will then be the conspicuous man. We are on the eve of great events, where the ever-living Sl. Qu. will have new forms.

I always watch you with special interest & hope, & read what you say with admiration & delight. Remember me to yr beautiful wife & her beautiful mother[2]

Ever yours, Charles Sumner

ALS MH-H (73/124, PCS)

1. In his letter of 21 April 1858 (Staten Island, 17/052, PCS), Curtis wrote CS that "Douglas stands baldly separate among the rest by his conduct to you. Events

have made you the representative young man of the North." In a letter 11 April to E. L. Pierce, CS elaborated further on Douglas: "He is esentially a partizan. Therefore, in quitting Democracy, he must ultimately come into our camp. But he must come there at least before he can rank with Republicans. *He has not yet arrived*" (64/009).

2. Anna Shaw Curtis (1836–1923) and Sarah Blake Sturgis Shaw (1815–1902).

To Theodore Parker

Philadelphia at Mr Furness'
28th. April [*1858*]

Dear Parker,

I am cheered by your letter which came this morning—As I sit in my chair or recline on a couch, I am comfortable: but at each step I am in pain, and feel bereft of strength. Perhaps this will pass over. It was such an attack that I had in Paris just a year ago—precisely. But this shows the morbid condition of my system. How I envy people that I see in the street stepping off with alacrity.

Banks' course pains me. There is much in him to like. But he is a politician; and against Slavery only *qua* politician. Could you not talk with him? I can think of nothing better.

Oh! I wish I could breathe into every public servant, whether at Washington or in Massachusetts something of my own hatred of Slavery and of my own gulf-wide separation from its supporters. I do not believe in friendly courtesies with men engaged in murdering my colleague!

What grandeur of news seems to impend from Spain. If she is not frightened so as to back down. Emancipation in Cuba will be the greatest event for this Continent since the Declaration of Independence. Several things lend to it. (1) The desire to keep Cuba in peace, without vexation from our Republic whether fillibustering or in war. (2) The urgency of England. (3) The concurring sentiment of the European World, as shown in all acts of Emancipation by England, France, Sweden, Denmark and Holland. (4) and most important perhaps now, the example of Russia and the western stroke of the Emperor for Pan-Slavism and Harmony.

That telegram to the *Nord*[1] (the Russians paper at Brussels) probably came from the Russian embassy—so I like to think. *Inter nos*. I never forgot this point while I was abroad.

Ever yrs C. S.

P.S. Nobody at Washington on *our side* seemed to feel the importance of this news. Even Seward was frigid and my colleague more so. The South caucused at once: so did the Cabinet.

C MHi (73/131, PCS)

1. Reporting on the rumored emancipation of Cuban slaves, the *New York Times* (19 April 1858:1) said the story stemmed from a dispatch to *Le Nord*.

To Lord Brougham

Paris—20th June '58—
Hotel & Rue de la Paix

My dear Lord Brougham,

Again I find myself in Europe, at the command of my physicians & here in Paris under what is called active treatment by fire in order to exterminate the remains of my infirmity caused by the assault more than two years ago.[1] On my arrival in the Channel I found a newspaper which contained yr speech before the Anti-Slavery Society. Be assured that I read it with delight & gratitude. I have also read this morning the remarks you have lately made in the House of Lords.[2]

Allow me to ask if the British Emancipation Act is not worthy of a more formal effort in Parliament? The audacity of the slave-masters, in utterly denying its beneficent character, invites, if it does not positively require a renewal of the battle. And, while vindicating this sublime historic act, you will be able without one word of interference with American Slavery, to furnish the strongest possible arguments against it.

Of course, it is all-sufficient to every civilized man, if it be shewn that men have been elevated in the scale of humanity—even if sugar has gone down. The old Roman Ulpian has given us the true rule when he said—*neque humanum fuerit ob rei pecuniariae quaestionem libertati moram fieri*.[3] But it can be fully shewn that by this Act Man & Sugar have both gone up.

This recent imbroglio from the slave-trade with Cuba brings me again to the importance of putting an end to Slavery there.[4] If this were done cruisers, British & American would no longer be sent upon this dismal work; the slave-trade would cease, & Slavery itself would receive its death blow. The Slave-Power of the U.S. must then prepare to die. England, by simply insisting upon the performance of the treaties of

1817 & 1835,[5] would emancipate half the existing slaves of Cuba, & Spain might be pressed to complete the good work. But this is an affair of diplomacy, which Ld Derby might well have at heart.

I write to you freely encouraged by yr constant kindness to me & by yr well-known devotion to the cause.[6]

Ever sincerely Yours, Charles Sumner

ALS GBUCL (73/187, PCS)

1. CS had sailed from the U.S. on 22 May 1858.

2. On 17 June Brougham stated it was the duty of Great Britain, Spain, and France to stop the slave trade to Cuba (*Hansard's Parliamentary Debates*, 3rd series, 150:2202–5).

3. Ulpianus, the Roman jurist (d. 223); "nor would it be human for there to be a delay to liberty on account of an inquiry concerning a financial matter."

4. The British navy had recently stopped and seized several American vessels off Cuba on the grounds the latter were illegal slave traders, and Secretary of State Cass issued a protest to Britain (Lewis Einstein, "Lewis Cass," in *The American Secretaries of State and Their Diplomacy*, ed. Samuel F. Bemis, 6 [1928]:318–21).

5. In their treaties of 1817 and 1835, Great Britain and Spain declared the slave trade a piracy and agreed to suppress it.

6. Brougham replied from London 27 June (17/196, PCS) that his recent remarks had received "a most general approval" in Britain. He looked forward to CS's "further suggestions."

To Nassau Senior

Paris—22nd June '58
Hotel & Rue de la Paix.

My dear Senior,

I cannot be so near you without at least reporting myself.[1] I am here at the command of my physicians & am undergoing medical treatment.

The English physicians last autumn said that I could not expect at once to be equal to the excitements of public life & advised against my return. I did not believe them. But it has turned out that they were right. My winter & spring were passed without for a day escaping the condition of an invalid. At last, without any sufficient cause, I had a relapse which left me feeble & entirely *hors de combat*. Then I was told to come abroad again.

Here I have learned precisely my present condition. The physician finds me suffering still from an effusion in the membranes of the brain, & from *contre-coups* in the spine,—the latter infirmity caused by the blows on the head *while I was seated*.[2] He thinks that without active treatment this diseased condition would sometimes make itself felt in a sudden, & serious pull-down, & that it can only be reached by a system of counter-irritants. Accordingly he applies *fire* to my neck & spine. Fire is fire; coals are coals;—as I have ample occasion now to know. But I hope some good will come out of it.

If I can get through this fiery treatment I hope to take another look at Switzerland & also at Germany—perhaps to go as far as Russia.

I trust that England will not abandon her Anti-Slavery policy, or allow her animosity against Slavery to be in any respect mitigated. It will be her pride & glory in history. She must hold fast to it. But I understand that there may be differences of opinion as to the way in which this policy shall be manifested. If any change in manner takes place especial care should be taken that the cause does not suffer.

We are now approaching a crisis in the Slavery Question,—depending on Cuba. All that Mr Buchanan is doing, & this whole imbroglio about the slave-trade, really mean Cuba. The only *idea* of the present American Govt. is Cuba,—& in order to fortify Slavery. If this plot is successful, several things may occur; (1) The mischievous & vulgar Slave-Power will have a new lease of life in my country, through its predominance in the Senate, & there will be new schemes of Slavery-extension. (2) The Slave-trade *may* be opened then openly under the American flag; or (3) finding that this cannot be done, the "fire-eaters" will at once separate, constitute a slave-holding Govt. & commence this traffic. These I mention as possibilities. And, surely, with the acquisition of Cuba the slave-interest of the U.S. will be immensely fortified & the Anti-Slavery cause receive a check.

Now there is one way in which all this can be counteracted. *Prevail upon Spain to emancipate her slaves*, & you will then see the beginning of the end. Our Slave-Power will be checked; the Slave-trade will have no demand; cruisers may come home; & the Anti-Slavery cause will be without impediment.

If England & France were of accord, I think this subject could be presented to Spain in such a way that she might adopt the policy of Emancipation, & thus, by an historic act, save herself from an inglorious surrender to the money or the filibusters of our slave-holding Oligarchy.

At this moment the longer continuance of the Slave-trade, & the expansion of Slavery all depend upon the *policy of Spain in Cuba*. It is to that point that our efforts should be directed.

By the existing unperformed treaties of 1817 & 1835 between Spain & England, at least *one half* of the slaves in Cuba are entitled to Freedom. Let these be enforced; & Spain be induced to act generously—no justly—by the rest.—Pardon this homily.[3] Present my complts to yr family, & believe me,

Ever sincerely Yours, Charles Sumner

ALS CSmH (73/190, PCS)

1. CS had met Nassau Senior (1790–1864), Oxford professor of political economy, in June 1838, during his first trip to Europe (Prc, 1:322).

2. The French doctor Charles E. Brown-Séquard (1817?–94) began a series of treatments in Paris 10 June 1858. For a full discussion of them see DD, 1:337–41.

3. Senior replied from Kensington 24 June (17/192, PCS) that prospects of an agreement between Britain and France on antislavery policies were highly unlikely. As for Spain, she "would restore slave & the slave trade in [the?] largest expansion tomorrow, if she dared." Senior believed Britain to be halfhearted about abolishing the slave trade; she might eventually do so unilaterally.

To Samuel Gridley Howe

Paris—
Hotel & Rue de la Paix
1st July, '58

My dear Howe,

Since yr brief missive from Newport I have heard nothing of you. That was once a pleasant place to me; but I doubt if I should be content there now. Although with *health complete* it seems to me I could be content almost any where.

To you & George I have made reports of my case & the treatment of Dr Séquard. He shews much interest in me & has analysed my condition with great skill. Fire is a torment when it is on your bare skin, & also still more, if possible, in its consequences. During these unparalelled heats, with the thermometer at 90, I have been tormented by blisters at every gradation of inflammation & suppuration. What is life on such terms? The Dr. is confident that without this treatment I should have been permanent invalid. It remains to be seen if this will make it otherwise. He has made some ingenious examination with an instrument *à deux points*, in order to determine where I felt the two points, & where the two, though actually apart, produced but one sensation. By this experiment he has been able again to ascertain the precise range of the disease in the spine & the neck.

Besides fire externally, which has been applied six times, I take terabanthene pills, & am to close with strychnine. You will see that my weapons are deadly. Indeed, I am now at close quarters with the enemy.

The Dr has never before applied the fire without chloroform, & he kept it upon me some 5 or 7 minutes. During this time, as I constrained all expression of pain, I thought sometimes of St. Lawrence on the gridiron—sometimes of Amor wounded by burning oil dropped accidentally by Psyche—sometimes of Prometheus with the vulture at his liver, & also of many others in the list of fire-suffering ending with John Rogers[1] & with "the 9 small children & one at the breast."

I see that at last Congress has adjourned. That wretched game of brag has been played out.[2] I cannot express to you the shame which their proceedings have brought upon our country. I was happy that I had left the country; for had I remained, the temptation to embark in the strife would have been irresistible.

My plans are all disordered. This evening—in an hour—my doctor comes again—perhaps to burn me. But it is still unsettled how long this treatment will continue.

Meanwhile at home people already dispute about my resignation.[3] Perhaps, I am mistaken; but it seems to me that few have had an experience equal to mine of the heartlessness, not to say the baseness of men. The accessories (*after* if not *before* the fact) to my assassination are welcomed in the state which I represent, & my own colleague fraternises with them at Washington. But, only give me my ancient health, & others may do as they list. I will then take care of myself, &, God willing, do something for the cause.—God bless you!

Ever Yrs, Charles Sumner

ALS MH-H (73/205, PCS)

1. Along with the mythical martyrs are John Rogers (1500–55), British protestant burned at the stake, and St. Lawrence (d. 258), said to have been broiled alive.

2. A compromise bill on the Kansas admission issue passed both houses in April. When the Senate voted 30 April, the *Globe* reported that CS was "detained in Philadelphia by a relapse in his case" (*Globe*, 35th Cong., 1st sess., 1899). The bill stipulated that the complete Lecompton Constitution be submitted to voters for ratification before the territory sought admission as a state. Congress adjourned 16 June.

3. In an earlier letter to CS from Boston (18 May, 73/161, PCS), Howe had advised CS to consider the possibility that he might have to resign as senator and accept life as an invalid. Howe wrote CS from Boston on 11 July (73/212) that much effort had been made to "correct the impression that you are *shamming*," and that he believed the public was gradually accepting the seriousness of CS's condition.

To Charles Francis Adams

Aix-les-Bains. en Savoie
8th Sept. '58.

My dear Adams,

Yr letter came to cheer me just as I was leaving Paris. At the same time I had the good fortune to see the Kuhns,[1] who had just arrived. I regretted much that they had not come earlier; for it would have been a great pleasure to shew them Paris.

The quiet of my present retreat & my *incognito* is a luxury, while the treatment which I pursue is in entire contrast with those dismal experiences at Paris. Here it is water; there fire. I have water now in every form, & at every temperature, but chiefly by *douches*. After my morning bath I am carried in a *chaise à porteur* & laid upon my bed. After breakfast comes a ramble in this beautiful country; then again 2 or 3 hours on my bed; then dinner; another ramble; a short time at the Casino for newspapers & music; & then to bed. Not a very profitable day; but not uncomfortable, except when I am overtaken by my tortures on the breast, &, during a walk by my weakness in the spine.

I do not understand how any person, who is not indifferent on the question of slavery, can hesitate to support you for Congress & with all his might.[2] But I see no American papers, & am entirely ignorant of the schemes of politicians. You must be elected. I shall regard your entry into the House as an epoch. Our friends need somebody who, by his example at least, can teach them to respect their cause & to respect themselves.

It is an important step which Henry proposes to take, calculated, of course, to influence his whole life.[3] It may be of immense good; but I know well the dangers. If he learns German & French well, that will be much. But he must not lose his early habits of industry. Wherever he is,—although for a day—he must work. That was the rule I followed when I first went abroad; & I wish that I were able to follow it now.—I shall probably, be in Paris at the end of October, for I have promised to report myself to my physician there. If he passes through, he must let me see him, & we will discuss studies.

It was very kind in Mrs Adams to write me that second generous letter.[4]

France where I have been a prisoner so long seems to enjoy unexampled prosperity. Every where are the signs of wealth & luxury, & the Emperor seems again firm in his seat. It is supposed that there can be no change as long as he lives; for, should a revolution shew its head, he would not hesitate to crush it at the cost of any amount of lives, or if unable to do this, he would sacrifice himself. Had Louis P.[*hilippe*] or Charles X[5] had this fixed *will* two revolutions might have been averted.—But just so long as Louis N. reigns our cause can expect no support in France. His Govt. is naturally heartless, & he is too happy in the good will of the ruling interest of our country to disturb it. The Emperor of Russia is a philanthropist; but L. N. is a selfish despot.—All our representatives in Europe are slave-drivers—except my friend [*Theodore Sedgwick*] Fay at Berne, who enjoys an enviable reputation among Europeans both for character & intelligence. I have heard him discussed at the *table d'hote* here with great praise. As for our Minister at Paris [*John Y. Mason*]—he is disgusting.

I am glad that you are occupied with yr father's papers.[6] That is a filial labor which must give you pleasure & pride. Remember me to Mrs A. & to the children,

Ever Sincerely Yrs, Charles Sumner

ALS MBApm (73/253, PCS)

1. Adams's daughter, Louisa (1831–70), married Charles Kuhn (1821–99), a wealthy Philadelphian, in 1854.
2. The Massachusetts Republican party was considering nominating Adams for a U.S. congressional seat. Adams had written 1 August 1858 from Quincy that his "*uncompromising*" stand might damage his election prospects, "yet it is barely possible they may have to swallow the dose" (73/230, PCS). Adams was officially chosen as a candidate in early October (Adams to CS, 8 October, 73/268).
3. Adams's son Henry (1838–1918) proposed to spend at least a year studying law in Berlin; he sailed from the U.S. 29 September (ibid.).
4. Quincy, 26 July, 17/250.
5. Charles X (1757–1836), king of France, 1824–30.
6. Adams wrote he was "slowly gathering up my material" for an edition of his father's diary; however, the work was not published until 1874–77.

To Alexander von Humboldt

[*Berlin c. 25 October 1858*]

Monsieur Sumner, Sénateur des États Unis d'Amerique, se trouvant à Berlin, pour le moment, s'empresse d'offrir ses hommages à Monsieur le Baron de Humboldt.

Dans le *shatzkammer*[1] de sa vie il a toujours placé le souvenir du bon acceuil que Monsieur le Baron a daigné lui accorder, tout jeune qu'il était, pendant les quelques semaines qu'il avait le bonheur de passer à

Berlin, il y a 19 ans. À sa reconnaissance personelle se méle non seulment l'admiration qu'il partage avec le monde civilizé des services grandioses rendit à notre siècle—à tous l[es] siècles—par les travaux scientifiques du Monsieur le Baron et par l'exemple de sa vie servile et laborieuse vouée à la Verité, mais aussi une sensibili[té] toute particulière à cause des paroles hautes et fletrissants qu'il a laissé tomber sur l'Esclavage aux États Unis—cette honte, ce fleau & crime d'une patrie bien aimée.[2]

Dft MH-H (63/735, PCS)

Translation:

Mr Sumner, Senator of the United States of America, finding himself momentarily in Berlin, wishes to pay his respects to Baron Humboldt.

In the *shatzkammer* of his life he has retained the memory of the kind welcome that the Baron was good enough to accord him, when he was quite young, during the weeks he was fortunate enough to spend in Berlin, 19 years ago. To his personal gratitude is mingled not only the admiration that he shares with the civilized world for the great service rendered to our century—to all centuries—by his scientific work and by the example of his life of service and labor dedicated to Truth, but also a most particular sensitivity on account of the lofty and incriminating words with which he stigmatized Slavery in the United States—this shame, this scourge and crime of a beloved country.

1. "Treasure room."

2. In his study on Mexico, *Political Essay on the Kingdom of New Spain*, the explorer and scientist Humboldt included a strong protest against slavery. In issuing an invitation to visit him on 28 October 1858, Humboldt said he was touched by CS's praise (Berlin, 26 October, 17/322, PCS).

To Abigail Brooks Adams

Stuttgart—7th Nov. '58

Dear Mrs Adams,

For one week it has snowed wherever I have been—with the exception of a single day. At Munich the snow was six inches deep in the streets. Here I see children with sleds. All this is beyond my Boston experience at this season. The storm began in October. But just before the storm was sunshine—to me. I saw two of yr children.

It was at Berlin. I was driving in an open carriage from Baron Humboldt's, when I heard my name, & soon saw Henry, who had leaped on the steps & at once clambered in.[1] He was well, but, perhaps, a little disheartened by a sense of loneliness & his isolation from present inability to understand what is said about him. But I was rejoiced to find the firmness of his purposes. Be assured that I did all that I could by conversation & counsels to put him in the right direction. He was with me much of the time that I was at Berlin. We visited the galleries together, & I had the pleasure of his initiation in the great European world of art. He was with me when I recd. his father's letter.[2] After reading it I handed it to him—saying—"You will see that yr father is concerned with regard to yr course"—"That is very natural" he replied. I then said to him pleasantly that I held a mortgage on him which he must redeem. I have promised to write him from Paris as soon as my course is determined.

Being at the Opera, with Baron Gerolt,[3] the Prussian Minister at Washington, listening to Wm. Tell, I was astonished to hear my name & see before me Mr Kuhn, who, after the first moments of greeting, began to vent some of his pent up feelings with regard to Germans, until I quieted him by letting him know who was by my side. The language he was beginning was not complimentary. The Opera was over at 9 o'clk—good honest hours these Germans keep—& I went to his hotel where I saw his wife, who seemed to have enjoyed herself very much. Afterwards in Munich, being at the great Art-shop—*Kunst-Handling*—& conversing about purchases I was shewn a list of American names & at once lighted upon Charles Kuhn. I spoke of him as a friend of mine, & the salesman described him & his wife—saying that both spoke French well, but particularly his wife, who spoke it *avec tout de facilité et de vivacité* that he took her for French.

At Berlin the venerable Humboldt expressed his regret at Mr E[*verett*]'s course on Slavery, & then referred to Mr [*George*] Ticknor as being quite right. He was astonished when I assured him that he was not known at home as an Abolitionist—nor in any way as an Anti-Slavery man. The Baron was astonished to know that he was a follower of Mr Webster, said that in conversation with him, he was "full of noble sentiments," &, that he made no defence of Mr Webster when the Baron condemned him. He was pained to learn that he could be so double.

The election has taken place & yr husband has at last the first installment on what is due to his ability, integrity & loyalty to our cause. Of course, I can know nothing as yet; but I assume that this must be so.[4] I hope that he will not be prevented from working still at the edition of his father's writings. This must be done. As for myself, I wish that I could say that I am well. During the last month & even fortnight I have been conscious of a positive gain. I can now endure a certain amount of fatigue without provoking the bad symptoms, but they are not yet entirely cast out. In a few days I shall be in Paris where I shall review my case with my physician & determine what to do. Best regards to all.

Ever sincerely Yrs, Charles Sumner

I have seen but one Boston paper for 3 mos. I cannot express my disappointment & mortification that I find myself still halting about with a broken back.

ALS MBApm (73/280, PCS)

1. Henry Adams describes his meeting with CS in *The Education of Henry Adams*, chapter 5.

2. In his letter from Quincy, Adams had written CS that, although Henry's goals were worthy, "the best resolutions of young men often melt like wax before the attractive warmth of sensual enjoyments." He asked CS to "encourage him . . . to continue his exertions" (3 October 1858, 73/268, PCS).

3. L. M. Gerolt, Prussian minister to the U.S., 1854–68; North German Union minister to the U.S., 1868–71.

4. Abigail Adams's husband was overwhelmingly elected to Congress (Charles Francis Adams to CS, 21 November, 73/283).

To Samuel Gridley Howe

Steamer on the Rhine
10th Nov. '58

My dear Howe,

Cold & fog have driven me below & I take to my pen. I am now near the Druckenfels. Tonight shall sleep at Cologne—tomorrow night at St. Quentin & the next day be in Paris, where I shall at once seek my physician & hear what he has to say on my case. He has talked of more fire; but I believe—I trust—that I am already beyond that. The last 6 weeks have witnessed a constant—almost daily improvt. Perhaps this may be attributed to the life of travel I have led—in the open air—taking as much exercise as I could bear; perhaps to the operation of the fire & water. I know not. But I am positively better. At last I am sure of the result; but know not if it will be consummate in 1 month or 1 year.

I can now bear fatigue which two months ago would have left me in a wretched condition. But I feel daily that my disease is not yet entirely exorcised.

Except a solitary *Liberator*, I have not seen a Mass. paper for more than 3 months, & I have recd. very few letters. Since those *protestant* letters from you—nothing. I trust that you are well. If so I know that you must have the happiness of doing good. Perhaps you are in Congress! The very thought of it makes me jump. I fear, however, nothing so good as this can come to our cause—except, perhaps, the election of Adams, which surely must have taken place. But I shall learn all at Paris.

From German & French papers I learn that late elections have gone against the Democrats. I trust that Douglas's fate is fixed.[1] Before I get back to the Senate death & the people will have thinned out my enemies. I correct myself; it will have removed many; but a host will remain; for every slave-master is my enemy. I am content; & with assured health I shall welcome them all. Oh! I do long for that day. But I must have all my force for the shock.

In my rapid rambles I have enjoyed much of nature & art. Switzerland every moment—in every mountain, hill, lake, river, valley & field, filled me with delight. The north of Italy left a painful impression, for every where were white-coated Austrians.[2] Germany more than satisfied me by its prevailing intelligence & civilization. I have made many little pilgrimages;—to Brescia, because there was the original of Thorwaldsen's Day & Night; to Verona, because it sheltered Dante in his exile; to Vicenza, because it was home of the architect Palladio, & to Worms, because of Luther. These days have been sweet & happy.

No building or institution has impressed me so much as the Emperor's[3] stalls at Vienna—with 700 horses stalled in a palace. I left it with admiration of the palatial structure, vast in extent & of the horses, which were most beautiful in every respect; but with a poignant conviction of the injustice on which it was founded. I saw how this was all for the luxury of one man; & in this seemed to be typified the Austrian empire. Surely it cannot last. At least it has my malediction. With the downfall of Napoleon it will crumble in pieces.

In Venice & Milan I was disturbed by the visible signs of military domination. A foreign army, speaking a foreign language, quartered in those beautiful cities, held there in subjection. The Italian levies, on the other hand, are ingeniously used to keep in subjection Hungary & Bohemia. In Prague, which is far away from Italy, I noticed public guide boards in Italian.[4] Tyranny is cunning.

Every where I have taken to the pictures & also to the Engravings. The gallery at Dresden is most charming. But you remember well all these things.

Goodbye! God bless you! But for Congress I should hurry at once to the Nile & float there during the winter, or go to a water-cure in Belgium for 3 months; I think the latter.

Ever & ever Yrs, Charles Sumner

Such weather I have never known any where at this season. I left Berlin in a snow-storm & travelled with it 6 days. Between Munich & Ulm the snow was 6 or 8 inches deep. I saw children with sleds.

ALS MH-H (64/041, PCS)

1. In congressional elections Republicans gained eighteen seats and won state elections in every northern state but Illinois and Indiana. In the Illinois senatorial contest, however, Douglas defeated the Republican candidate, Abraham Lincoln.

2. Venice and Lombardy had been occupied by the Austrians since 1814.

3. Francis Joseph I (1830–1916), emperor of Austria, 1848–1916.

4. Italian troops had been drafted by the Austrians and sent to Hungary and Bohemia.

To Samuel Gridley Howe

Paris—24th Nov. '58

Dear Howe,

If I send any letters of resignation *you* will know it as soon as any body.[1]

But I am to be a well man. This is the solemn judgt. of the drs—after consultation—Trousseau—Brown-Séquard—& Hayward;[2] but they all insist that I shall not return to my duties this winter. *For the present* I consent, & tomorrow start for Montpelier in the South of France, where I am to devote myself to a Systematic treatment—capsules de terebenthine—*pilules* de bella donna—& dry cupping the length of the spine—to be followed by *douches*.

If my position were merely political I should resign at once; but I am unwilling to renounce the opportunity of again meeting the enemies of Freedom in the Senate. My resignation would delight the slave-drivers, & I have some reason to believe, it would pain, the true A-Sl. men of the country. Unless something occurs which I do not anticipate that delight & that pain shall not come from me.

You have my money affairs in hand, & will, doubtless see that my credit with the Barings is sustained. There were $2000 in L[*ongfellow*]'s hands. Besides more than this sum, which will be due at Washington 4th March. Should I not return, I shall write to Wilson, &, through him hope to touch it.

When I arrived in Paris among the menacing [incidents?] of my case was a derangement of the kidneys. From this quarter there was danger, which seems now to be passed, though I am not beyond treatment. The head—spine—& chest all still shew that they are not in their normal state; but they shew this very much less than last summer.—Let me hear from you.—care of *Barings*.

Ever Thine, C. S.

P.S. There may be something from $10—to 100—to be paid at Washington—on account of my rooms. Will you honor the draft of my clerk to this amount—A. B. Johnson?[3]

ALS MH-H (64/043, PCS)

1. In his letter to CS of 6 November 1858 (Boston, 73/278, PCS), Howe described a rumor that CS had sent Governor Banks a letter of resignation, which Banks was to "use at his discretion." Howe wrote that he had denied the rumor but had not mentioned CS's distrust of Banks.

2. Armand Trousseau (1801–67), French physician. George Hayward (1791–1863), professor of surgery, Harvard Medical School, 1835–49.

3. Arnold B. Johnson (1834–1915), journalist; secretary to CS, 1855–61.

To Frances A. Seward

Montpellier—France
25th Jan. '59

Dear Mrs Seward,

Yrs of 4th Jan. gladdened me this morning just as I had recovered from the exhaustion of my daily torments. Nobody but you writes me from Washington. [*inserted in margin*] I must except my clerk, who has written once.[1] [*end insert*] "The absent are always wrong," says the French proverb. Perhaps this is applicable to my case.

The [*Hamilton*] Fishes are in Paris. I have heard from them once since I have been here. I think that they are living very discreetly.

Did I not recount to you my experience with the Wises?[2] They were on board the Steamer in which I came out. On the 2nd day he crossed the deck & coming up to me, put out his hand & said "How do you do, Mr S.?"—I looked him steadily in the face & then turned away. Of course I took no notice of his wife. With the accession *after* the fact to an act of assassination or at least its compurgators I hold no parley. Do not think me harsh or austere. After all my suffering I have kept my temper pretty well.

How small is Mr E's career! While a great wrong is overshadowing the land he goes about with a holiday speech begging money for a tomb.[3]

I have not seen yr husband's Rochester speech;[4] but from the way in which it has been abused I think it must be admirable.

I often wonder at myself, so retired & tranquil here—seeing only a few people, chiefly professors—enjoying books—lying on my back some 16 hours a day—& in my walks looking out upon the Cevennes the seat of that terrible Protestant convulsion which for a while shook France.[5]

Remember me to yr husband—sister & daughter.

Ever sincerely Yrs, Charles Sumner

P.S. Yr husband will kindly frank the enclosed.—

I wonder if good Mr Morgan recd. a little letter from me at Aix.[6]

ALS NRU (73/334, PCS)

1. Arnold B. Johnson wrote CS a long letter full of political news on 15 October 1858 from Boston (17/316, PCS).

2. In her letter to CS from Washington, Mrs. Seward asked, "When did you part with *your friend* Mrs Wise?" (4 January 1859, 17/373). CS probably refers to Charlotte Everett Wise, Edward Everett's daughter, and her husband, Henry A. Wise, naval officer and cousin of Virginia governor Henry A. Wise (Paul R. Frothingham, *Edward Everett: Orator and Statesman* [1925], 312–13).

3. On Everett's lecture tour see CS to Longfellow 12 April 1858.

4. Seward stated in his 25 October speech that slave and free labor systems could not coexist in the U.S. and would produce an "irrepressible conflict" in which one system would eventually prevail. Seward also declared that Republicans were duty bound to defeat the Democratic party, which represented the slave interest.

5. The War of the Camisards (1702–10), in which the Huguenots rose against Louis XIV (Geoffrey Treasure, *Seventeenth Century France* [1966], 392–95).

6. CS wrote Edwin B. Morgan (1806–81; U.S. congressman [Rep., N.Y.], 1853–59) on 15 September (73/264).

To Charles Francis Adams

Montpellier, France
5th Feb. '59

My dear Adams,

I have too long delayed my answer to yr last letter, & now my debt to yr family is increased by a most pleasant epistle from yr wife;[1]—but I shall keep these accounts separate.

I am inclined to believe that, had you been in my condition—after more than two years of *ups & downs*, still a serious sufferer—unable to do what you had most at heart & with chances most menacing worse than death—you would have intrusted yourself unreservedly to medical skill which had already inspired yr confidence by a most careful & intelligent diagnosis.[2] I will not now undertake to say that the painful treatment which I have endured was necessary, nor, indeed, that it has brought me to my present condition of convalescence & confident hope; but the careful examination at Paris made me precisely aware of my case in its details. With this knowledge I am able to tell to what extent I have succeeded in exterminating the remains of my original injuries.

While I recognise still some symptoms, mischievous in character, I feel a sense of health & capacity for work to which I have been for a long time a stranger. But I do not in the least intermit my treatment. I begin the day with my prescribed torment—I feed on my poisons—&, while keeping in the open air for some time daily, I avoid all fatigue, & seek repose on my bed or sofa.—I have determined that no care or efforts on my part should be wanting to carry forward this care.

Of course, I am often pained by the thought of my public duties neglected; &, you can well imagine that, were I in health, some other place than Montpellier would attract me. But let me confess that I have not been *ennuyé*. My love of books has been to me here solace & society. I have access to several libraries public & private, & I have used them all to the full measure of my strength. [Being?] here, my chief companions are the professors, & I find positive pleasure in the courses of several.

But I have said too much of myself; & yet I must add one word more. The meeting of Congress this winter presented a question of painful embarassment. There were several courses to take. To go home in the face of the positive counsels of eminent medical authorities, &, with a consciousness that I was still an invalid, seemed rash, & hardly to be vindicated. But to leave my seat vacant throughout a whole session seemed inexcusable. It only remained, that I should resign. Had I not felt that my case was exceptional, & not that of ordinary political life, of course I should have yielded to the irresistible necessity of this step. But I could not abandon a position, dearer to me now than ever, because more than ever—with returning health—I can hope to serve our cause, & because I have at heart to be heard again from the seat where my assassination was attempted. Pardon me also if I deceived myself by the belief that my resignation would have caused pain to many all over the country who are in earnest against Slavery.

But the present session of Congress will soon be over,[3] & a legitimate vacation of months will then be before me in the course of which I have every reason to expect to confirm & anneal my convalescence so as to be beyond relapse. How I do long for this hour!

You know well the satisfaction I have had in yr election.[4] "Returning justice lifts aloft her scales." But I foresee responsibilities—not inviting—kindred to my own. Our friends must be taught to be in earnest, & to shew faith in their cause. They must be proud of it. Of couse, such an austerity of principle will not make public life a path of roses. Among new accessions to our forces will be Mr [*Thomas Dawes*] Eliot, &, I trust also Mr [*John B.*] Alley.

I hear nothing from Washington—nothing from my colleague, who I suppose is already occupied in making the next Presdt.—I mention I am inclined to think that were our cases reversed, I should on some occasions have acted differently from him.

I am disgusted at what I read of the reception of Mr Douglas at N.Y. & Phila.[5] This man, as I see him through my telescope, is one mass of spots. His speeches shock me by their bare-faced inhumanity. The reports of Congress. speeches pain me by their vulgarity. It is frightful. And the whole tone of our Govt, particularly as it is reported in the European papers, is ineffably disgusting. Of course I see in this the slave-holding influence, which has year-by-year degraded the Administration to its own vulgar level.

Europe at this moment seems on the eve of a convulsion coming from Italy. Two French letters which I have to-day from Paris regard it as imminent—& it is thought that in a few [weeks?] the issue will be made. It may pass over for the moment; but the position of Austria in Italy is too thoroughly unnatural *contra naturum* to continue. *On ne peut s'asseoir sur les baieonettes*[6] said the first Nap. Let me hear from you soon.

Ever sincerely Yours, Charles Sumner

I have a letter from Henry which charms me. He is taking the right course.—Remember most kindly to Dr Palfrey whose new success I enjoy greatly.[7]

ALS MBApm (73/342, PCS)

1. Boston, 10 January 1859, 17/380, PCS.

2. In his letter from Boston, 21 November 1858, Adams wrote CS he agreed with Howe that the Brown-Séquard treatment would not be beneficial: "This beautiful and delicate tissue was never made to undergo the application of such coarse and violent agents" (73/283).

3. The second session of the 35th Congress ended 3 March 1859.

4. Adams had written CS on 21 November 1858 that "we now have *for the first time*, a delegation to Congress throughout exclusively republican." In responding to CS's congratulations, Adams wrote 2 March 1859 that he had not the zeal he had ten years ago to carry on the battle against slavery, but, as the "representation of a principle, pure and simple" he hoped "to maintain the integrity of the party policy among us" (17/435).

5. The *New York Times* (1 January 1859:1) reported New York City officials' rousing welcome to Douglas, and, in Philadelphia, a "great crowd" at Independence Hall (5 January 1859:8).

6. "One can not sit on top of the bayonets"; i.e., one must stay on the march. Camillo Cavour (1810–61), prime minister of Sardinia (sometimes called Piedmont), had been negotiating with Napoleon III for French assistance in driving the Austrians from Italy; a formal treaty of alliance was signed 26 January.

7. Henry Adams, then a student in a Berlin gymnasium, wrote CS from Berlin 28 January (17/388). Palfrey's *History of New England*, vol. 1, had been published in 1858.

To Byron Paine

Rome 12th May—'59.

My dear Sir,

Of late I have recd. very little political intelligence from home, & in the depression of a protracted disability, I have hardly missed it; but today I have been gladdened & strengthened by the news that the people of Wisconsin have elected you a Judge of the Sup. Ct. on the issue distinctly presented, that it is the duty of the State to throw the protection of its process around all within its borders.[1] Better news for Freedom never in the long line of history, reached this ancient capital. Wherever I go I feel the new influence, & the venerable monuments about me flash for the moment with the brightness of youth.

God bless the people of Wisconsin who know their rights & knowing dare maintain! God bless the champion they have chosen! God bless the cause! To the people—to the champion & to the cause an American citizen far away in a foreign land sends the best wishes of his heart.

In this event I have the certain beginning of a new order of things in our country. Trial by Jury, *habeas corpus* & the other safeguards of the rights of all,—struck down by the preposterous & tyrannical pretensions of Slavery under the National Constitution,—will again become realities! The occupation of the Slave-Hunter will cease! A happy day it will be for the peace & good name of the Republic when this is achieved. Meanwhile Wisconsin has nobly set the example, which older states must follow. The end cannot be doubtful.

I congratulate you, my dear Sir, upon the distinguished position you have been called to occupy; but permit me to add that honorable as it is to be a judge, the cause you represent gives to you a better glory.

Believe me, my dear Sir, with much regard,

very faithfully Yours, Charles Sumner

The Honble. Byron Paine &c &c &c

ALS WHi (73/383, PCS)

1. Paine was elected associate justice of the Wisconsin Supreme Court in April 1859 on a campaign emphasizing "States Rights and Byron Paine" and Paine's defense of Sherman Booth (Richard N. Current, *The History of Wisconsin* [1976], 2:270–71).

To William Wetmore Story

Turin—18th May '59—

I hope, dear Wm, that you have already recd. my *petit mot* from Genoa.[1] As for the papers I suppose they have been seized! The journey from Genoa to this place was uncomfortable from the rain—much such as on the day I left Rome—& from the delays to accommodate the French troops. And yet it was full of interest. At every point where the common road was visible, there were French soldiers without number all daubed with mud & draggling in the rain. Several thousand were sheltered in the station of Rail Road at Alexandria. The train, as it entered, seemed to penetrate this living mass; & yet all was order & tranquility.

Nobody knows the counsels of the Emperor [*Napoleon III*] —I mean, of course, outside those about him. I heard a French officer of rank, who got into the carriage when I was at Alexandria say to his [companion?]—l'Empereur est arrivé avec un plan tout-à-fait arrété.[2] It is understood that Sardinians wished to commence the attack, but have been restrained by the Emperor, whose policy for the moment is delay —qui nobis cunctando restituit rem[3]—until he marshals all his forces. I should think the rain which has lasted 3 days must have damaged the enemy much. Their course is one of pillage & robbery. They live upon the people. But little of detail is known here, as all communication with the country is arrested.

Yesterday I passed half an hour with the Ct. de Cavour. He recd. me in his bedroom, where he was writing. Let me say, that a note which he kindly wrote me in French was in the clear round hand of his country, so different from the French, which is small & flowing, like their language.[4] This national pecularity of hand-writing is curious to observe particularly in its relation to languages.—He was calm as if he felt himself "master of the situation," & asked me to observe the tranquility of Turin with not a soldier to be seen. To my inquiry if he thought the Austrians would be driven from Italy this summer he quietly said—*Je l'espere*. And when I dwelt upon the strength of the fortifications at Verona he said that he thought they could be taken. He seemed to understand the condition of things at Rome—that Lady Wm Russell[5] is *tres-Autrichienne*—that the people there are right; but as he spoke of the *Saint Pere* I thought the *subrisus*[6] of his face seemed to expand. It is evident that he does not doubt the result.

I have also passed several hours at the house of the Countess de Coligno & also Mdme. Arconati. This I owe to Miss Weston.[7] Pray let her know how completely her introduction has been honored. There I learn that every body is full of confidence & anticipating victory. They say that this is to be their last war, & great armies will no longer be needed. But nobody seems to understand the plan of campaign. All, however, are sure that the Austrians are to be beaten. Madme. de Coligno seemed much moved at the thought of the blood that must be shed to dispossess the enemy of those immense fortifications.—It seems that in the Hospitals of Turin is a solitary Austrian soldier wounded & taken prisoner in a recent skirmish. These humane ladies, who speak German, had visited him; but he could not understand them. He turns out to be a Hungarian.—The ppty of Mdme. A. is near the Ticino, &, of course, is now in the possession of the Austrians. She describes their conduct as barbarous.—But in the present deplorable condition of their finances they can only live by turning highwaymen.

My Simplon plan, including Mrs Field & a parting view of the Leman Lake, must be abandoned—as the rail-road between here is partly destroyed & that whole country in the hands of the enemy. It only remains to take the route of Mt Cenis, which is open. Tell our friends that the journey here by Genoa is not only practicable but easy. Turin they will find more tranquil than a Washington hotel. The Savoyards are shewing their monkeys in the streets—the boys playing marbles—the theatres thronged—the tables at the Hotel served with abundance—although the Austrians are within a few hours of the capitol. —— I have been charmed to learn that Manzoni, who is in his house at Milan, under the roof of the enemy, is Italianissimo. From one of his grand-children here [Cnt?] Bentivoglio, who has called on me, I have learned the sentiments of the distinguished author.—The weather is execreble; but I trust that it will make the Austrians suffer. Thus far it has prevented me from going to the Superga, where Ld. Aberdeen told me he enjoyed the view of the Alps more than from any other place.—To-night I am to meet a party invited expressly to put me *au courant* of affairs here. God bless you!

Ever Yrs, C. S.

As for my health—I am satisfied that I have completely turned the corner. I can walk & do many things which I could not do 6 weeks ago.

The Photographs—my *pezzo di Roma* —I think of constantly. I hope they are on their way. When you receive this, I shall be at Paris at my old quarters—Hotel de la Paix Rue de la Paix.

Let me know how you all are in the B. hive.

I have sent you daily a parcel of 4 newspapers—twice with yr address in English—once in Italian—& once in French. Have they all been seized?—

ALS CSmH (73/391, PCS)

1. CS had visited Story and his family in Rome from 20 April to 13 May 1859. His first letter after leaving Rome was written 14–15 May (73/385, PCS).

2. "The Emperor has arrived with a plan entirely concluded." Austria had gone to war against Sardinia over Austrian possessions in northern Italy, and the French had entered the war on behalf of Sardinia.

3. "Who gives us time by delaying the thing."

4. Cavour wrote CS arranging the midday meeting for 17 May (Turin, 16 May, 17/507).

5. *Je l'espère:* "I hope for it." Elizabeth Anne Rawdon Russell married General Lord George William Russell in 1817; Henry James describes her character but not her politics in *William Wetmore Story and His Friends* (1903), 2:188–95.

6. "Smile."

7. The Countess Collegno (d. 1868) was the widow of Giacinto Provana di Collegno, who had been minister to Paris from Sardinia (Prc, 3:585); her sister, Costanza Trotti Arconati Visconti (1800–71), from Milan, was an ardent supporter of Italian independence from Austria. Emma Forbes Weston was a friend of James Russell and Maria Lowell as well as the Storys.

To William Wetmore Story

Susa—20th May '59

Thus far I have come, dear Wm, & tomorrow morning I shall quit Italy. I am unhappy at the thought, for I shall never see it again. My travels will soon end—only to be renewed in memory & photographs. I shall take my last look of this land—

Oh forte tu sei bella o almen piu forte[1] as of a face that one loves.

Rome haunts me perpetually. I wish that I were there again—at least to ask you a hundred questions which I forgot.

I believe this is my 4th despatch. Since my last I have been in the way of hearing something more of opinion in Turin—particularly from a leading deputy of the *gauche*. He looks for sympathy from the King-that-will-be of Naples[2] & counts upon at least [??] a great Northern Italian kingdom. I am astonished at the warmth with which the king is spoken of. He is said to be not only *bien-aimé* but *adoré*. He mingles with his people without state or ceremony. Only the other day when Cavour returned from Paris & a crowd assembled under his windows to cheer him it is said the King was among them, crying *Vive Cavour*. But the representatives of the *gauche* are not strongly attached to Cavour. They say that he has adopted his present opinion as the means of advancing himself & that he allows no first-rate talent to be associated with him in the cabinet, which might impair his pre-eminence.

The news has continued to arrive of the barbarous conduct of the Austrians in subsisting their troops at the expense of the provinces where they are. To-day came the further news that they had blown up the magnificent double bridge for rail-way & common road which had cost 5 millions at Vercelli. And on top of this is the forced loan of 45 millions imposed on Lombardy & 30 millions on Venice. But this cannot save their finances.

The Ct. de Cavour asked me to observe that, though now invested with absolute power the Govt had put but one restriction on the press, which was not to publish news about the war except sanctioned by the regular bulletins.

At last the weather is dry & warm. The two armies are now near each other. Can a battle be long postponed?[3] It is evident that the first move of the Tedeschi[4] has signally failed. They had expected even to capture Turin, &, to guard against chances some portion of the archives have been removed to a place of security.—Some talk has been caused to-day by shooting a spy who was captured at some distance from Turin. The principal evidence against him was that he did not give a clear account of himself & spoke bad Italian (God save the mark!). But why do I trouble you with this illegible scrawl? Better for us both that I go to bed at once.

Three cheers for Italy! And may the Austrian empire cease to exist!

Very soon I shall be in Paris again, which interests me next to Rome.

Good night! I ought to have preached to you a little patriotism which you sadly need.

Ever thine, C. S.

ALS CSmH (73/395, PCS)

1. "Strong and beautiful you are or at least stronger."
2. Victor Emmanuel II (1820–78), then king of Sardinia, later king of Italy.

3. In the Battle of Magenta, fought 4 June 1859, the Austrians were defeated.
4. Italian for "Germans."

To Henry W. Longfellow

Paris—
Hotel & Rue de la Paix—
2nd June—'59

Dear Longfellow,

On reaching here I found 3 letters from you of dates Feb 18—April 25—& April 27.[1] These former had been kept back by some negligence of the bankers.

The great hours of history seem to be tolling now. Nothing so solemn has been heard since 1815. Perhaps, you have heard something of my visit to Turin, & of the noble hearts I found there. A week in Paris has revealed to me something of French opinion. The *bourgeoisie* & the people generally sympathize with the War, but the *salons* are bitterly against it. They distrust L.N. {*Napoleon III*} & think that no good can come from him, while his success in Italy was confirm[ing] his power in France. Last Monday I dined at the Princess Belgiojoso, where were {*François*} Mignet, {*Victor*} Cousin, Henri Martin,[2] & others. At dinner the conversation was literary & academic. I said to the Princess,—by whose side I sat, that I trusted M. Mignet was right on the Italian question—"Malheureusement—no" was her reply. "Il deteste l'*Empereur* tellement qu'il oublie l'Italie."[3] Of course she is charmed with the contest. But Henri Martin, in a tete-à-tete in the drawing room, avowed to me his perfect sympathy with the Emperor in his present movement. Indeed, he said that the Emperor had put himself at the head of the Revolution. The Ct. de Montalambert, whom I met first at the Duchesse de {Ronzon's?} with the vieille {roche?}[4] of Legitimacy, amidst a mob of duchesses, sees in the war only a new tyrant for Italy, & new chains for France.

M. de M. complained that Americans were all worshippers of L.N. I questioned the fact, but added that, in the first place, many who came here knew little of French politics & were dazzled by his success; &, in the second place, they took their ideas from the American Minister here, who constantly sounded the praises of the Emperor. Qui est-il comment s'appelle il—votre Ministre—said the Count—"Mr Mason," said I. "De quel état est-il?"—"De Virginie."—"Peut être il est maitre d'esclaves"—"Vous avez raison; non seulement maitre d'esclaves, mais rempli—même petri d'esclavage," said I. "O! cela s'explique; tout maitre d'eslave doit être pour l'Empereur parce que[5] (& here he changed into English) he makes *niggers* of us all!"

I think I never heard more summary execution done than the other evng at poor Alexandre Dumas[6] & particularly by Cousin, who was asked when Dumas would be admitted into the Academy,—"Never" said here ["]while I live if I can help it."—And he added that no man should come into the Academy that he would not meet in a *salon*, & surely he would never meet that *drole* that *farceur*; & then came from the company a variety of stories to illustrate the theme. The Princess was moderate in her judgt; but she said that she did not like—"parce qu'il m'ennuyé toujours."[7]—Cousin seems to have forsaken philosophy to play "Old Mortality" to the fine ladies of the 17th century. For half an hour he talked about Madme. de Sévigné, whose letters, it seems, are known only through garbled & altered copies very unlike the originals, which are supposed to have been assez scabreuse.[8]

No American reputation has latterly shot up in Europe like Channing's; & this has been caused a good deal by what he wrote on Slavery & Self-Culture. M. Laboulaye[9] came to see me yesterday, & inquired at once if I had known Channing. He said what I have already observed, that nobody can now venture to cite American example in Europe; for the single all-sufficient answer is *Esclavage!* How long will this shame continue?

I should like to tell you of my day across the Alps—an open carriage *en poste*—where I met the French lancers descending. Nothing could be more picturesque; I seemed to be travelling through an immense scene of the Grand Opera.—Where do you pass the Summer, & what has become of Uncle Tom [*Appleton*]?—I imagine you at Nahant. In the autumn expect me back well—my long suffering ended—& ready for action. God bless you! Love to all!

Ever & ever Yrs, C. S.

ALS MH-H (73/406, PCS)

1. Cambridge, 73/375, 379, PCS. For 18 February 1859 CS may mean Longfellow's letter of 13 February, unrecovered; a printed version appears in HWL, 4:120–21.

2. Christina Belgiojoso-Trivulzio (1808–71), writer and author, disciple of Mazzini. Henri Martin (1810–83), French writer and historian.

3. "Unfortunately, no. . . . He detests the Emperor so much that he forgets Italy."

4. "Old rock." *Roche* could be *vache*: "cow."

5. "What is the name of your minister—"

"From what state is he?"
"From Virginia."—
"Perhaps he is a slaveholder—"
"You are right; not only a slaveholder but filled—even consumed with slavery," said I.
"Oh! That explains it; all slaveholders must support the Emperor, because . . . "
6. Alexandre Dumas (1802–70), French novelist and dramatist.
7. "Because he bores me."
8. Marie de Rabutin-Chantal Sévigné (1626–96), French writer; "rather rough."
9. Edouard Laboulaye (1811–83), French jurist.

To Charles Francis Adams

London 13th July '59

My dear Adams,

I have been long yr debtor; but I felt sure that you kept no strict account with me. And latterly I have seen so much of Louisa [*Adams Kuhn*], that I have seemed to be in communication with you. Few persons have observed more in their travels than she has.

I am glad to assure you that I am to return a well man. Even at Rome I was obliged to seek repose during the day & to avoid all walking; but I have got beyond this now. Imagine my happiness at being able again to move about without pain or any considerable fatigue. But there is still a something lurking in the system which must be eradicated, & my physician prescribes a course of baths & medicines. For this purpose I went to Dieppe, but soon became dissatisfied. There was water enough, but no libraries or books; & I at once left for London.

Yesterday everybody was surprized by the news of *peace*;[1] but so far as the terms are known, it is regarded as most unsatisfactory, affording no assurance for the future, & really settling nothing. It is said that the intolerable heats, under which his troops were fast becoming *hors de combat*, brought L.N. to this step. But what becomes of his solemn programme—que toute l'Italie soit libre jusqu'à l'Adriatique[2]—if the famous quadrilateral is left in the hands of Austria? The whole will have to be done over again. Those who have put confidence in the Emperor complain that they have been *joué* or in plain English "sold."

I have never believed him as bad or as good as he is painted by different persons; but I have never had confidence in him, except so far as his self-interest harmonized with the public interest. There are many French whom I know & most intelligent English also, who do not hesitate to declare that his plan is first to disable Austria—then to take a slice from Prussia—then Belgium—& then to attack England.

People here are in a panic with regard to their defences, & fear that he may land in the "fast-anchored isle." Of course, all this seems to me absurd.

It is generally supposed in Paris that it was the fear of other Orsini's which impelled him to this Expedition, & Count Zamorski, the eminent Pole, told me only two days ago, that, if he adopted the line of the Mincio,[3] he would live with a stiletto at the back of his neck. His old associates the *carbonari* are unrelenting. It remains to be seen how they will treat the recent Peace.

Some think that Italy is not fit for liberal institutions; but in this opinion I do not concur. Count Cavour, when I saw him at the end of May, anticipated no such result as the present Peace. He expected to take the fortifications & drive the Austrians out of Italy.

At Paris I found Palfrey's book which I read at once with great interest. It is admirable in all respects. Dana's book I hear of in the hands of his London friends. I found Lady Cranworth much pleased with it.—Ld Stanhope finds his "old friend W. Irving's" life of Washington very poor, entirely unworthy of the subject & of the author.[4] The life of John Adams he recognises as a very different work & of positive merit.

I hear of Seward's visit, but have not yet seen him. Since I have been in London he has been in the provinces,—where he went partly to escape the 4th July dinner. Is he to be our candidate?[5]

I hope you have good news from Henry. I owe him a letter.

Ever yours & Mrs Adams's Charles Sumner

ALS MBApm (73/421, PCS)

1. At Villafranca on 11 July 1859, Napoleon III negotiated his own peace with the Austrians without consulting his ally, Sardinia. The peace treaty called for a confederation of northern Italian states headed by Pope Pius IX; Venice would remain in the Austrian empire, as well as the quadrilateral of Lombard fortresses.

2. "That all Italy is to be free to the Adriatic."

3. The Italian republican Felice Orsini (1819–58) had attempted to assassinate Napoleon III in January 1858. Wladyslaw Zamoyski (1803–68) had fought for Poland in the 1830–31 insurrection and later emigrated to England. The Mincio River in northern Italy separated the regions controlled by Austria and Italy in 1859.

4. *To Cuba and Back: A Vacation Voyage* (1859); Irving's *Life of George Washington* (1855). Laura Carr Cranworth (d. 1868), married Robert Monsey Rolfe, Baron Cranworth, 1845.

5. No reply from Adams has been recovered. In his letter of 2 March, Adams expressed the hope that the Republican presidential nominee would be a man of integrity; a proper candidate was "yet to be found" (17/435, PCS).

To Samuel Gridley Howe

Bains Frascati près du Havre
26 July '59

My dear Howe,

Here I am—as it seems to me, established for weeks. Of course, the object & pivot of the day is my bath; but beyond this I find resources in the Public Library—in the Cercle to which I am introduced—in my walks & in books at home. I trust this will be my last discipline, & that I shall leave here *as well as ever*. At all events I feel sure of being again a *working man*.

The skies brighten. Oh! how many dark days I have had & nobody near to comfort me! But these are passed.

In London I met [*George*] Hillard; but his course to me, I think was unfeeling—perhaps it was all that I should have expected from the editor of the *Courier*.

The peace [*of Villafranca*] shocked me—if peace can ever be otherwise than agreeable. It was unexpected & seemed to sacrifice avowed objects of the war. But the more I reflect upon it, the more of good I find it (1) First & foremost, there is peace, & bloodshed & devastation are stayed. (2) Lombardy is taken from Austria—(3) Piedmont, which represents the liberal interest in Italy is strengthened. (4) Austria is weakened. (5) The duchies, Parma certainly & probably Modena & Florence, are taken from Austrian influence. (6) The idea of Italian Independence has acquired a footing before Europe & (7) Italy itself is aroused to a consciousness of its power.

These things, of course, are far from what was promised, but in this world of slow stages, they are much. But I do not like L.N. & I cannot regard him otherwise than as a great imposter. I trust some day to see him tumble.

Seward whom I saw in London seemed in good cheer.[1] Indeed, he went so far as to say that the victory was already won!

Today I have been on board an American Steamer—the Fulton—& was tempted to start for home; but I will not go till I have the consciousness of being well.

I trust you have recd. my two last letters on *business*.[2] Do not fail to look after my account.

God bless you!

Ever Yrs, Charles Sumner

ALS MH-H (73/444, PCS)

1. For Seward's trip to Europe, May–December 1859, see Glyndon Van Deusen, *William Henry Seward* (1967), 211–13.

2. In his letters of 12 and 22 July (64/062, 066, PCS) CS asked Howe to deposit more money in his Baring's account. (He may not have yet received Howe's letter of 19 June from Boston informing him that the Baring's account now had $5,000 in it.) Howe added that George Sumner was concerned that CS was spending too much money abroad and that George considered CS "a mere babe as to worldly matters" (73/414). Invoices on reels 17 and 18 indicate CS's expenditures on rare books, manuscripts, and engravings, estimated by Pierce at over $2,500 (Prc 3:594).

To William Wetmore Story

Bains Frascati près du Havre—
15th August '59

My dear Wm,

It was a wretched letter which I wrote you in reply to yours so excellent & abundant & now I write another wretched one to confess my consciousness of the character of the other.[1]

Today the wind is strong & the sea is heavy, & I lose my bath. But this seclusion here is profitable & not unpleasant. Yesterday, however, I broke away from it to see the entry of the troops, with the Emperor & his marshals—the most remarkable triumph since Paulus Emilius mounted the capitol on his return from Greece,[2] & I doubt not the most imposing spectacle ever seen in Paris. Why not say in the world? The arrangements & appointments were perfect. I was in a balcon au premier near the corner of the rue de la Paix & the Boulevards—a most excellent place to see—price of my chair 50 francs—& I looked closely at all that passed. The Emperor was for some time at the corner near me. He was superbly mounted & sat his horse well; looked in good health, & bronzed by sun. More than any Marshall or general, he held his head down, bowed only occasionally & seemed to crawl along. While near where I was he was occupied in twirling & smoothing his moustache. As he passed there was a hush of silence & intense curiosity *but no enthusiasm*. Of course with the national guard on both sides, & the sidewalks covered with people, there were voices enough, if they could have been commanded.

MacMahon looked more like an American than an Irishman. Canrobert[3] had a joyous look, as he turned to the right & left to receive the applause.

The news from Tuscany is inspiring. Pray help them to be firm. The Brownings must work. The ducal family has ceased to reign; let this be the decree. If they consent to take back the son,[4] the battle is postponed to another day.

In London I met one evng at Lady Granville's the run-a-way Prince Corsini,[5] & heard him say that he was going to join his Grand Duke. I understand that he announced the ministry that would be formed on the Grand Duke's return to Florence. An amusement of exile! Lady G. asked me if I noticed his most excellent Tuscan.

I see by the late papers that Roba di Roma[6] again appears in the Atlantic. Oh! I do love Italy, & wish that I were there, to lap myself in its Elysium. But I shall be in another place, in scenes very different, amidst tobacco-spitting, swearing slave-drivers—abused by the press—insulted so far as is possible—pained & racked by the insensibility about me to human rights & the claims of human nature—finding little true sympathy—; but cheered, let me confess, by the dignity of the cause I serve.

In a letter which I recd this morng from an English friend at Montpellier, who is "a sort of Papa" to Madame de Schwartz,[7] I learn that she has been to see him. He says of her "as far as anecdote, general information, & easy graceful manners go I scarcely ever met with her equal." Garibaldi has confided to her all his docts. & papers—in short every thing that can contribute to the history of his life which she is about to write—"She expresses herself in terms of much admiration of yr friends of the Barberini Palace—of the beauty of Madame & of the artistic talent of Monsieur."—Did I tell you that I saw Hillard in London—once in society trying to be eloquent as if with Mrs T.[*icknor*]—He seemed so little at ease—so like a *manant*[8] that I asked if it could be he. Good bye! Love to the two "E's" [*Emelyn and Edith Story*].

Ever Yrs, C. S.

ALS CSmH (73/467, PCS)

1. Story's letter from Siena, 22 July 1859 (17/626, PCS), was answered by CS from Bains Frascati 11 August (73/464), in which he analyzed the dubious achievements of Napoleon III.

2. Lucius Aemilius Paulus (c. 229–160 B.C.) was honored in Rome in 167 B.C. after his conquest of the Macedonian kingdom.

3. Marie Edmé MacMahon, duc de Magenta (1808–93), and François Canrobert (1809–95) had both commanded French troops in Italy.

4. Italian republicans, dissatisfied with the Franco-Austrian peace treaty, drove out Leopold II, grand duke of Tuscany, who fled to Vienna. The Tuscans then held a plebiscite for annexation to Sardinia (Harry Hearder, *Italy in the Age of the Risorgimento* [1983], 225–27). Leopold's son, Ferrante IV (1835–1908).

5. Maria Louisa Granville (d. 1860), wife of British statesman George Leveson-Gower, second earl of Granville (1815–91). Nero Corsini, former minister in Leopold II's government (ibid., 80).

6. Story's essay on Italy was published in the *Atlantic Monthly*, April 1859: 454–65; July 1859:207–19.

7. In a letter from Montpellier, 12 August (17/673), J. Richard Gordon (d. 1863) described how the Italian patriot Giuseppe Garibaldi (1807–82) had stayed with Marie Espérance Brandt von Schwartz (1818–99; German writer and editor of Garibaldi's letters) during the siege of Rome.

8. "Peasant."

To Theodore Parker

Bains Frascati au Havre—
22d August 1859

Dear Parker,

Your letter cheered me by its good news of your health: but the cough must stop. Rest, good nourishment and a happy life will be your best medicines. Will not Rome be apt to try you by its cold? Of course it is infinite in resources—perhaps even too stimulating. It must be hard to renounce seeing Egyptian architecture and the long course of the Nile. If you can carry the Apthorps with you it will be next to a good climate.[1] You are happy in friendship. This is indeed my only possession: but I sometime think it is diminishing and becoming dismally less. Of course death helps this, but changes of heart and mind, do more.

You will mourn Horace Mann.[2] He has done much. But I wish he had lived to enjoy the fruits of his noble toils. He never should have left Massachusetts. His last years would have been happier and more influential had he stayed at home. His portrait ought to be in every public school of the State, and his statue in the State House. The aesthetic development of the people, in pictures and statues, he never appreciated: but these ought to do him honor for the impulse he has given to that civilization in which they will be sure to thrive at last.

I have a tender feeling for Choate.[3] For years he was my neighbor in Court Street, and I never had from him anything but kindness. The last time I saw him was in Winter Street. He asked me what my physicians in Europe said of my case—I reported the opinion of Sir James Clarke[4] and George C.[*ombe*]—"The voice of science itself" said he: "you will be mad not to follow it"—His best powers were given to his profession: but I ask myself what single forensic effort he has left, which will be remembered? Not one. Seward's defence of the negro Freeman[5] is worth for fame more than the whole forensic live of Choate.

I heard Gladstone say lately in London, that it was the "finest *forensic* effort in the English language."

How beautifully things move in Tuscany. Who says a people thus composed, amidst the grandest trials, is not fit for Freedom. Who is fit for it I pray? The Americans with 4 millions of slaves, and with a leaven of slave-holding tyrants, and foreign immigrants who cannot speak our language! Why these more than the Italians full of genius invention, and all knowledge? Against the proletarianism of Italy, I put the slavery of our country, and hold that Italy is full as apt for free institutions as the United States. You doubt. I must borrow a phrase from Charles Fox,[6] addressed to Bonaparte, 1st consul [*Napoleon I*]—"clear your head of that nonsense." Of course I am for freedom every where. If I heard of a revolt in the Seraglio I should be for it.

Think of old Gino Capponi blind, led to the urn and voting for the Emancipation of his country. Well-done gallant veteran! It was his ancestor who went forth from Florence to meet Charles 8th of France and when the King threatened if his terms were not accepted "to sound his trumpets," the ambassador of the Republic replied—"If you sound your trumpets, we will ring our bells."[7] Three cheers for the bells of Florence!—May they ring, so as to be heard throughout Italy!

I have heard of you *via* Montpellier, in terms of warmest admiration and regard.[8] I am glad that you have seen my friends.—As I write now, from my window, I look out upon the sea in which I shall soon be swimming. My life is secluded. At 9 o'clock, I am a-bed. Here I stay through the first week of September. Let me hear from you again. Best regards to all your circle.

God bless you!

Ever yrs, Charles Sumner

—I know not what you hear about me. I have no secrets. Is it what Howe wrote about? that I was engaged to a person with whom I have not spoken for years, and whose whereabouts is to me unknown? A fabrication, pure and simple!—Have you heard of the fall of T—— ——?—claiming *les petites* [*vies*?][9] of a beautiful damsel at the Public Library?—

Your printed letter has not reached me:[10] but I shall find it in London.

C MHi (73/476, PCS)

1. Parker had recently come to Europe to battle the tuberculosis that had forced him to leave his ministry. He and CS met frequently in Paris in June 1859 (Prc, 3:587–88). On 13 August, Parker wrote CS from Neuchâtel, Switzerland (17/677,

PCS), that he had gained strength but "still *cough, cough, cough*." He planned to pass the winter in Rome and hoped Eliza Hunt Apthorp (b. 1817) and Robert East Apthorp (1811–82), Bostonians traveling with Parker in Switzerland, would accompany him.

2. Horace Mann died 2 August, in Yellow Springs, Ohio, where he had been president of Antioch College since 1852.

3. Rufus Choate died in Halifax, Nova Scotia, 13 July.

4. Sir James Clark (1788–1870), physician to Queen Victoria.

5. In 1846 Seward had unsuccessfully defended William Freeman (1824–47), a black accused of murder, asking the jury not to consider Freeman's color (Glyndon Van Deusen, *William Henry Seward* [1967], 93–96).

6. Charles Fox (1749–1806), British liberal leader.

7. Gino Capponi (1792–1876) was a historian who served as prime minister of Tuscany in 1848. When Charles VIII (1470–98) invaded Italy in 1494, he met resistance in Florence from Pietro Capponi, a resistance that dissuaded Charles from retaining possession of key Tuscan fortresses. The bells incident is described in J. S. L. Simonde de Sismondi, *A History of the Italian Republics* (1803–18), ed. Ernest Rhys (1907), 261–63.

8. J. Richard Gordon wrote CS 12 August (17/673) that his son and family were enjoying Parker's company in Switzerland.

9. CS's French (as transcribed by Lydia Parker), as well as his personal references, is obscure.

10. "Theodore Parker's Experience as a Minister, with Some Account of His Early Life, and Education for the Ministry," 1859. In his 13 August letter Parker wrote that CS should read his recent public letter "as the work of a *sick man*, writing under many difficulties" and to consider the little book as "Parker's Apology for himself." Parker's struggle to regain his health was unsuccessful; he died in Florence, 10 May 1860.

To John Jay

Bains Frascati près du Havre
23 August '59—

My dear Jay,

Why have I not heard from you? It is long—long since I have had an opportunity of welcoming yr friendly autograph. What have I done? or failed to do?

While in London I tried to see yr daughter,[1] but missed her. I hope to have better luck in Paris, where I shall pass a few days at the end of Sept, & bid Good bye to that beautiful metropolis.

Already for a month I have enjoyed the sea-bathing & seclusion of this place, but am not yet ready to leave. Of course, I stay only because it seems to be best for my health. But this is the last prescription of my Dr. In Novbr I shall return—a working man, I trust.

If Mr Gibbs[2] presents you a letter of introduction from me, you will be glad to know in advance, that he was for a long time the Tutor of the Prince of Wales, of course, therefore, a beautiful scholar & most finished man—much regarded & admired wherever he is known—still young. He was to sail with Sir Henry Holland by the way of Canada, & probably, reach New York in the autumn. I think you will enjoy his society much.

During last winter I saw no Massachusetts papers; & only an occasional journal from New York. Since then I have seen more, but I have no accurate knowledge of the political field. Seward tells me the battle is already won.[3] What a mistake! If it were, then would I withdraw & leave to others the easy honors. But there is work to be done, & I mean to do it.—God bless you & Mrs Jay & the children!

Ever Yrs, Charles Sumner

ALS NNCB (73/480, PCS)

1. In his letter to Longfellow, 29 September 1859 (Paris, 73/500, PCS), CS described meeting Eleanor Jay Chapman (d. 1921), wife of the stockbroker Henry Grafton Chapman.

2. Frederick Waymouth Gibbs (1821–98).

3. After meeting Seward in London in July, CS also wrote Frances A. Seward that her husband believed "our glorious cause is already won. Would to God this were true!" (Paris, 2 August, 73/448).

To Richard Cobden

Bains Frascati près du Havre
31 Aug. '59

My dear Cobden,

I am sorry not to have you here listening to the sound of the sea & talking on the great Future of a true civilization. But verily I rejoice in the power with which you have stepped anew upon the old scene. Both yr speeches have told in France, & have been much noticed.[1]

M. de Morny has thrown down the gage of Peace.—Yes—war with England! to see which can excell in the works of civilization.[2] Why should not that idea be *exploitée?*

It pains me to see the enormous sums now diverted in France & *England* from *productive* industry. It is sad to think that 4 millions more are about to take the same course in England. Can not this be arrested, & the money saved for some good purpose? It is vacation now. So much the better. The attention is not absorbed by Parlt. Why not constitute a strong Committee,—to be introduced by you—to wait on Ld P. & Mr G.;[3]—to represent the case against this waste; to shew (1) how useless it is with its proposed destination & (2) how beneficent it might be in other ways; &, as a *practical* way of rendering it unnecessary, to call upon the Govt, earnestly, simply & in good faith, to propose to the French Govt. a reciprocal reduction of armaments? This is all your "thunder." Why not use it again? If it were really pressed upon the French Emp.—would he not hearken to it? At all events the idea would make a lodgment in the mind of Europe.

After another week I go to St Malo & at the end of the month reach London.

Ever Yours, Charles Sumner

ALS GBWSR (73/482, PCS)

1. Cobden had written from London 15 August 1859 (17/684, PCS) that other engagements prevented him from joining CS at Bains Frascati. He had recently been returned to the House of Commons and spoke about parliamentary reform 17 and 18 August to his constituents at Rochdale (speeches in the London *Times*, 18 August 1859:8; 19 August 1859:7).

2. Charles Auguste de Morny (1811–65), Napoleon III's half brother and president of the Legislative Chamber, gave an inaugural lecture 26 August to that body. In it he stated that France had no intentions of waging war with England and asked the British to trust Napoleon III's pledges for peace (London *Times*, 29 August 1859:8).

3. Palmerston was then prime minister and Gladstone chancellor of the exchequer.